Convergence and Hybrid Information Technologies

Convergence and Hybrid Information Technologies

Edited by

Marius Crisan

Convergence and Hybrid Information Technologies
Edited by Marius Crisan

CBS, Edition **2016**

Published by InTech

Janeza Trdine 9, 51000 Rijeka, Croatia

Technical Editor Teodora Smiljanic

Cover Designer Dino Smrekar

Additional hard copies can be obtained from orders@intechopen.com

Convergence and Hybrid Information Technologies, Edited by Marius Crisan
p. cm.
ISBN 978-953-307-068-1

Preface

Technology is a product of science and reflects our ability to interact with the environment. As science developed in time and became too vast for any one person to master, different technologies emerged, consequently, in their attempt to reach excellence. Although originally meant to work together, for a long time technological sectors developed independently pursuing their own goals. In the recent times, since the value of information became predominant in all spheres of human activity inevitably the scope of one technology overlapped with another one. This was the impetus for convergence of various technologies towards a higher level of interdisciplinary interaction.

Starting a journey on this new path of converging information technologies is the aim of the present book. Extended on 27 chapters, the book provides to the reader some of the leadingedge research results regarding algorithms and information models, software frameworks, multimedia, information security, communication networks, and applications. The first two chapters are dedicated to algorithms for multiclass classification and optimization problems. The next two chapters present dynamic models with applications in linguistics and semantics, and traffic assignment. They are followed by a group of four chapters concerning software frameworks for information extraction, semantic integrity checking, building automation systems, and educational virtual environment. Multicriteria decision making and a cost-based decision making application are the subjects of the other two chapters that follow. A next series of five chapters provides solutions to multimedia problems such as the quality of multimedia streaming services, secure and mobile multimedia convergence, resource scheduling, animation based edutainment platform, and an application related to auto-exposure in image processing. Information security and cryptography is another main topic of this book that is extended on seven chapters. In three chapters, the reader may learn about security architecture for sensitive information systems, security protocol for ubiquitous sensor networks, and program obfuscation. The other four chapters provide cryptographic solutions for generation of an irreducible polynomial, and pairing-based applications. Another group of three chapters deals with wireless networking applications. This is followed by a new approach to the design of weighting functions for linear frequency-modulated signals. The last chapter completes the book by an interdisciplinary applied study on chronic stress factors.

Information technologies are only at the dawn of a massive transformation and adaptation to the complex demands of the new upcoming information society. It is not possible in one book to achieve a thorough view of the field. Nonetheless, we have the hope that at least the book can offer the first step into the convergence domain of information technologies, and the reader will find it instructive and stimulating.

February 24, 2010

Editor

Marius Crisan
University "Politehnica" of Timisoara
Romania

Contents

1

A New Divide and Conquer Based Classification for OCR

Hamid Parvin, Hosein Alizadeh and Behrouz Minaei-Bidgoli
Iran University of Science and Technology, Tehran, Iran

1. Introduction

Recognition systems have found many applications in almost all fields these years (Parvin et al., 2008a,c). Improving the recognition performance is one of the most challenging tasks in pattern classification (Parvin et al., 2009a). However, Most of classification algorithms have obtained good performance for specific problems; they have not enough robustness for other problems. Therefore, recent researches are directed to the combinational methods which have more power, robustness, resistance, accuracy and generality (Kuncheva, 2005). Ensemble learning algorithms train multiple base classifiers and then combine their predictions. Since the generalization ability of an ensemble could be significantly better than a single classifier, ensemble learning has been a hot topic during the past years (Dietterich, 2002). It has been established firmly as a practical and effective solution for difficult classification problems. It appeared under numerous names: hybrid methods, decision combination, multiple experts, mixture of experts, classifier ensembles, cooperative agents, opinion pool, decision forest, classifier fusion, combinational systems and so on. For a good coverage on ensemble learning the reader is referred to (Dietterich, 1997; Minaei et al., 2004; Jain et al., 2000).

A large number of researches for improving the performance of classification methods have been done. Most of the late researches are about ensemble methods of classification. Although they improve significantly the performance, they cannot reach an effective way in the case that the number of classes are fairly large. This paper suggests a new method which transforms a multiclass problem to pairwises classes ones. To do this operation it uses confusion matrix to determine which of pairwise classes can be better distinguished. The confusion matrix determines the error distribution on different classes (Parvin et al., 2008d). The entry a_{ij} from confusion matrix determines that how many samples of class c_j are classified as class c_i. In order to achieve this matrix, we have to examine the classifier on validation set.

To optimize the division of classes, the proposed method employs genetic algorithm. This optimization phase is applied each time for dividing a metaclass (a set of classes) into two smaller metaclasses optimally. This method is similar to creation of a binary tree. Each node is equal to one classifier that distinguishes the classes of the left and right nodes. This process continues until each group of classes contains just one class in leafs. This new method is applied on a very large OCR dataset (Khosravi et al., 2007) which is a challenging problem in Farsi languages.

To better understand the proposed method one should take an overview on the following subsections 1.1 to 1.4. These subsections include a brief coverage of the related methods.

1.1 Decision tree

A common and obvious way for classifying an instance is from a sequence of questions, so that next question is asked with regard to this current question. Using trees are the most common representation way for theses question-answers. Decision tree is used to create a classifier ensemble, expansively. Also, they are used for the application of data mining and clustering. Their functionality is understandable for human. Besides, unlike other methods such as ANN, they are very quick. It means their learning phase is quicker than other methods (Duda, 2001). Different structures of decision trees are described in (Breiman, 1984; Duda, 2001). One of the most important specifics of them is that each node asks a question only on one feature. In this paper, a new classification method is proposed which operates like decision trees, however it makes decision over all features.

1.2 K-Nearest Neighbor

Nearest Neighbor techniques are simple but powerful non-parametric classification systems (Darasay, 1991). The simplest version of them is Single Nearest Neighbor. It bypasses the problem of probability densities completely and simply classifies an unknown sample as belonging to the same class as the most similar or nearest sample point in the training set of data. Nearest can be taken to mean of the smallest Euclidian distances in n-dimensional feature space. Although Euclidian distance is probably the most commonly used distance function or measure of dissimilarity between feature vectors, it can be used from other metrics like: Manhattan or Maximum distances.

A more general version of the Single Nearest Neighbor technique bases the classification of an unknown sample on the "votes" of K of its nearest neighbor rather than on only its Single Nearest Neighbor. The K-Nearest Neighbor classification procedure is denoted by KNN. If the costs of error are equal for each class, the estimated class of an unknown sample is chosen to be the class that is most commonly represented in the collection of K nearest neighbor (Gose et al., 1996). In this paper, the KNN with the Euclidian distance is used as a base classifier.

1.3 Neural Network

The Artificial Neural Network or ANN algorithms are the commonly used as base classifiers in classification problems (Roli et al., 2001). The first wave of interest in neural networks emerged after the introduction of simplified neurons by McCulloch and Pitts in 1943. These neurons were presented as models of biological neurons and as conceptual components for circuits that could perform computational tasks.

The elements of the ANNs are input vectors, output vectors, target vectors, weight, transfer function and bias. There are different forms to connect the neurons, and then the result is different network topologies (Sanchez et al., 2006).

Each unit of neural network performs a relatively simple job: receive input from neighbors or external sources and use this to compute an output signal which is propagated to other units. Apart from this processing, a second task is the adjustment of the weights. The system is inherently parallel in the sense that many units can carry out their computations at the same time. Within neural systems it is useful to distinguish three types of units: input units

which receive data from outside the neural network, output units which send data out of the neural network, and hidden units whose input and output signals remain within the neural network. During operation, units can be updated either synchronously or asynchronously. With synchronous updating, all units update their activation simultaneously; with asynchronous updating, each unit has a probability of updating its activation at a time t, and usually only one unit will be able to do this at a time. In some cases the latter model has some advantages.
In most cases we assume that each unit provides an additive contribution to the input of the unit with which it is connected. The total input to unit k is simply the weighted sum of the separate outputs from each of the connected units plus a bias or offset term θ_k as equation 1:

$$s_k(t) = \sum_j w_{jk}(t)y_j(t) + \theta_k(t) \quad (1)$$

The contribution for positive w_{jk} is considered as an excitation and for negative w_{jk} as inhibition. In some cases more complex rules for combining inputs are used, in which a distinction is made between excitatory and inhibitory inputs. We call units with a propagation rule sigma units. Generally, some sort of threshold function is used: a hard limiting threshold function, a linear or semi-linear function or a smoothly limiting threshold. A neural network has to be configured such that the application of a set of inputs produces the desired set of outputs. Various methods to set the strengths of the connections exist. One way is to set the weights explicitly, using a priori knowledge. Another way is to train the neural network by feeding its teaching patterns and letting it to change its weights according to some learning rule like Gradient Descent (Haykin, 1999). In this paper, the Multi Layer Perceptron is used as a base classifier. As mentioned, the KNN and MLP are two base classifiers used in this paper and we compare our proposed method with them, too.

1.4 Genetic Algorithm

Genetic Algorithm is a random search technique based on natural genetic. It has been shown to be an effective tool to use in data mining and pattern recognition (De Jong et al., 1993). There are two different approaches to applying GA in pattern recognition: apply a GA directly as a classifier and use a GA as an optimization tool. In this paper we will focus on the second approach and use a GA to minimize the classification error.
A Genetic Algorithm can be considered as a composition of three essential elements: first, a set of potential solutions called individuals or chromosomes that will evolve during a number of Generations. A chromosome contains a sequence of genes. The number and type of genes of each chromosome depend on the problem. This set of solutions is also called population. Second, an evaluation mechanism that allows assessing the quality or fitness of each individual of the population. And third, an evolution procedure that is based on some genetic operators such as selection, crossover and mutation. The crossover takes two individuals to produce two new individuals. The mutation consists in modifying randomly a gene of an individual. The basic steps of GAs, which are also followed in the proposed classification method, are shown in Fig. 1.
In the rest of this paper, in section 2, the proposed approach will be described. Section 3 says that how Genetic algorithm optimizes the ensemble tree construction. Section 4 contains its

results on Farsi OCR dataset. It also compares them with previous methods. Section 5 concludes the study.

```
Begin
        1. t=0
        2. Initialize population P(t)
        3. Compute fitness of P(t)
        4. t=t+1
        5. If termination criterion achieved go to step 10
        6. Select P(t) from P(t-1)
        7. Crossover P(t)
        8. Mutate P(t)
        9. Go to step 3
        10. Output best and stop
End.
```

Fig. 1. The original GA which is used in the proposed method

2. Proposed method

The main idea of the presented method is dividing the classification problem into smaller problems. Suppose that a metaclass is a subset of classes (minus null). Also, suppose that all classes are in a one large metaclass. So, in each level, there is a classifier to divide a metaclass into two smaller metaclasses. Indeed, this method is like divide-and-conquer method.

For this method, the dataset is partitioned into three sets: training, evaluation and test sets. Our approach contains several steps. In the first step, by using a base classifier, we do a primary classification and extract the confusion matrix from the evaluation data set. Table 1 shows this confusion matrix on evaluation data. In this step a multiclass classifier is trained on training dataset. Then, the confusion matrix is made by using the results of this classifier on evaluation data.

	0	1	2	3	4	5	6	7	8	9
0	1943	0	0	6	1	30	2	0	0	2
1	6	1985	4	0	4	10	7	3	1	25
2	2	1	1957	38	17	2	8	7	0	2
3	0	0	18	1918	23	1	4	4	0	3
4	6	2	6	32	1945	5	6	2	0	4
5	29	1	0	0	2	1948	5	0	0	1
6	3	9	7	1	5	0	1942	9	2	9
7	8	0	3	2	2	1	1	1975	0	0
8	2	1	0	1	0	3	2	0	1991	1
9	1	1	5	2	1	0	23	0	6	1953

Table 1. The confusion matrix corresponding to Farsi OCR dataset

This matrix contained important information about functionality of classifiers. Also, close and error prone classes are recognized using this matrix. In fact, the confusion matrix determines error distribution on different classes. Item a_{ij} from confusion matrix determines how many instances from class c_j are recognized as class c_i. In the second step, we use a classifier ensemble more or less like decision tree. We train one classifier correspond to each node that divides the data into two metaclasses. Each of metaclasses can contain several classes. This categorization is done based on error rate of confusion matrix. For example, suppose that the first level classifier divides data in two metaclasses. One is contained classes 0-4 and the other classes are in metaclass two. We will have 214 error based on the confusion matrix. Also, if the metaclass 1 contains classes 0,1,2,4 and 5 and metaclass 2 contains the other classes, we will have 245 errors. As shown in the table 1, metaclasses 1 and 2 are highlighted by gray levels such that the metaclass 1 is lighter than 2. Thus, all white cells are counted as errors between metaclasses. Also, in this step, each of these metaclasses is divided in two new smaller metaclasses. This procedure continues, until there is one class in each node. The optimal selection of these metaclasses is executable by different methods, such as recursive methods and GAs.

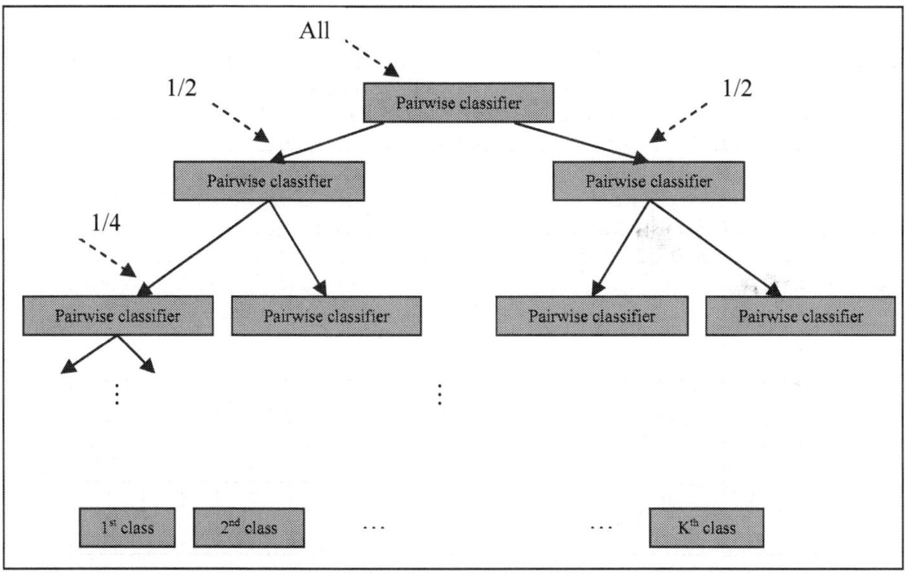

Fig. 2. The structure of proposed method for multiclass

There is a question that does this method like decision trees? Decision tree does comparison on only one feature in each node. This is implemented with only a simple thresholding or comparison, whereas, the classification in new method is done on the total feature space by MLPs or KNNs. As Deviparikh's definition of classifier fusion in (Parikh et al., 2007), the new proposed method cannot be a classifier fusion, too. In fact, it is a new kind of classifier ensemble.

3. Tree construction

Bandyopadhyay and Muthy in (Bandyopadhyay et al., 1995) have used GA as an effective tool in pattern recognition. Most applications of GAs in pattern recognition optimize some parameters in the classification process. The searching capability of genetic algorithms is used in this paper for the purpose of appropriately deriving the optimal tree. In fact, GA is used to optimize the selection of classifiers. The fitness function for GA is the total error of all nodes and the main problem of GA is the total error minimization. The total error is the sum of errors in all levels. So, it seems that when the constructed tree is balanced, the error is less. Fig. 2 depicts our proposed approach. As shown in this figure, for each node there is an MLP or a KNN as base classifier.

Each chromosome in GA contains 26 genes. The value 1 for each gene means that the corresponding class is on the right side of the tree; otherwise, it is on the left side of the tree. Genes 1-10 are used for first level. They determine the left and right sub trees. In the next level, genes 11-15 are used for left side. Similarly, genes 16-20 are used for right side and so on.

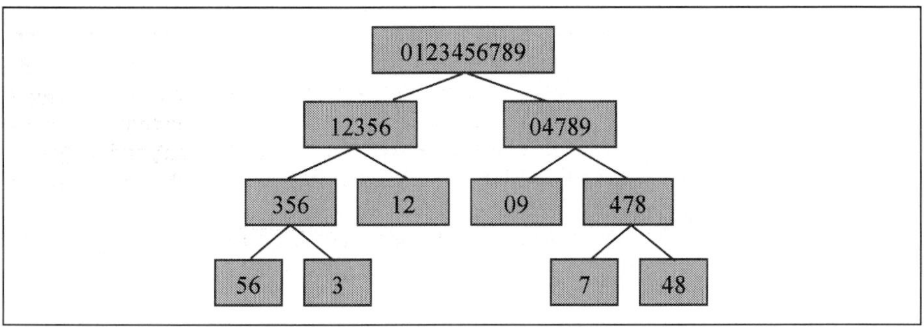

Fig. 3. The Corresponding tree of chromosome 1000100111,11000,01110,100,101.

For example, suppose that there is a chromosome like 1000100111,11000,01110,100,101. The first ten genes means that the metaclass in the first level is divided into classes 0,4,7,8 and 9 in the right node and other classes in the left node at next level. See the corresponding tree of this chromosome which is shown in Fig. 3.

4. Experimental results

In this section, experimental results of the study are shown. After introducing dataset, the used parameters and results are explained.

4.1 Dataset

There is a long time that offline handwritten OCR recognition system is known as an important topic. Recently, a large part of researches have been focused on improving accuracy of character recognition system. We evaluate our method on Farsi digits OCR. We use a large handwritten dataset of Farsi digits, named "Hoda" (Khosravi et al., 2007). We divide the data into 3 parts: training, evaluation and test sets which contain 40,000, 20,000 and 20,000 instances, respectively. The validation data set acts as pseudo-testing for obtaining fitness of each chromosome as it was explained above. In this study, the 106 extracted features from this data are utilized which are described in (Khosravi et al., 2007). Some examples of instances of this dataset are depicted in Fig. 4.

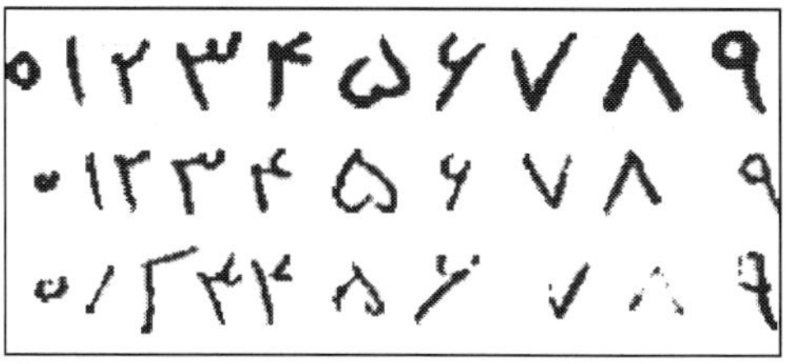

Fig. 4. Some instances of Farsi digits OCR dataset

4.2 Used parameters

In this empirical study, a two hidden layer Perceptron is used as a base classifier. Also, the KNN with K=3 is another base classifier. The confusion matrix is obtained from these classifiers. After that, GA is used to determine the optimal tree. We use Gaussian and Scattered operators respectively for mutation and crossover. The Scattered crossover function creates a random binary vector and selects the genes where the vector is a 1 from the first parent, and the genes where the vector is a 0 from the second parent, and combines the genes to form the child. The Gaussian mutation on each entry of the parent vector follows a Gaussian distribution. For GA optimization, we use 200 individuals in our population, running the GA over 500 generations. Fitness function for GA is the error ratio obtained from confusion matrix.

4.3 Experiments

Table 2 shows the results of classification performance by previous and proposed method. We ran the program ten times and got the averages. As shown in Table 2, the recognition

	Obtained Accuracy by Base Classifier	
	MLP	KNN
Simple Classifier	95.7	96.66
Full Ensemble	96.01	-
Unweighted Static Classifier Selection	97.11	-
Weighted Static Classifier Selection	97.15	-
Proposed method	97.20	96.86

Table 2. The results of proposed ensemble method

ratio has improved approximately 1.42%, by applying the proposed method by MLP. Also, we arrived to 0.2% improvement by KNN.

5. Conclusion and future works

We proposed a new method for improving the performance of multiclass recognition system. This method uses population based approaches, in special GA, to obtain best way to conquer classification the classes from each other. Also the method is based minimizing error on evaluation set without learning the evaluation. This is because of necessitated speed in evaluating the chromosome. Applying the proposed approach leads to more accurate logical results than the simple classification, on handwritten digits dataset. We used this method on two classifier ensemble systems. Also, we used one kind of base classifier per experiment. It yields to a better result in both cases. We divided the classes as balanced as possible, in each level. As future work, it can be worked on as unbalanced division. However, hereby, our optimization has been done globally; we can further, focus on the level based optimization as well on future.

6. References

Alizadeh H., Minaei-Bidgoli B., & Amirgholipour S.K. (2009). A New Method for Improving the Performance of K Nearest Neighbor using Clustering Technique, *International Journal of Convergence Information Technology, JCIT, (DBLP Indexed)*, ISSN: 1975-9320.

Bandyopadhyay S. & Muthy C. A. (1995). "Pattern Classification Using Genetic Algorithms", Pattern Recognition Letters, (1995).Vol. 16, pp. 801-808.

Breiman L., Friedman J., Olshen R & C. Stone (1984) Classification and Regression Trees, *Wadsworth International*, Belmont, California.

Darasay B.V. (1991). *Nearest Neighbor pattern classification techniques*, Las Alamitos, LA: IEEE Computer Society Press.

De Jong K.A., Spears W.M. and Gordon D.F. (1993). Using genetic algorithms for concept learning. *Machine Learning* 13, pp. 161-188.

Dietterich T.G. (1997). "Machine-learning research: four current direction," *AI Magazine*, 18, 4, pp. 97-135.

Dietterich T.G. (2002). *"Ensemble learning," in The Handbook of Brain Theory and Neural Networks, 2nd edition*, M.A. Arbib, Ed. Cambridge, MA: MIT Press.

Duda R. O., Hart P. E., and Stork D. G.(2001). Pattern Classification, 2nd ed. John Wiley & Sons, NY.

Gose E., Johnsonbaugh R. & Jost S. (1996) *Pattern Recognition and Image Analysis*, Prentice Hall, Inc., Upper Saddle River, NJ 07458.

Haykin S. (1999). *"Neural Networks, a comprehensive foundation", second edition*, Prentice Hall International, Inc. ISBN: 0-13-908385-5.

Jain A.K., Duin R.P.W. & Mao J. (2000). "Satanical pattern recognition: a review," *IEEE Transaction on Pattern Analysis and Machine Intelligence, PAMI-22*, 1, pp. 4-37.

Khosravi H., Kabir E.(2007). "Introducing a very large dataset of handwritten Farsi digits and a study on the variety of handwriting styles", *Pattern Recognition Letters*, vol 28 issue 10 pp:1133-1141.

Kuncheva L. I. (2005) "*Combining Pattern Classifiers,*" *Methods and Algorithms*. New York: Wiley.

Minaei-Bidgoli B., Kortemeyer G. & Punch W.F. (2004) "Optimizing Classification Ensembles via a Genetic Algorithm for a Web-based Educational System", (*SSPR /SPR 2004), Lecture Notes in Computer Science (LNCS)*, Volume 3138, Springer-Verlag, ISBN: 3-540-22570-6, pp. 397-406.

Parikh D. and Polikar R. (2007). "An Ensemble-Based Incremental Learning Approach to Data Fusion," IEEE Trans. Syst., Man, Cybern. C, Appl. Rev., vol. 37, no. 2.

Parvin H., Alizadeh H., Minaei-Bidgoli B. & Analoui M. (2008a). "CCHR: Combination of Classifiers using Heuristic Retraining", 4th *Int. Conf. on Networked Computing and advanced Information Management, NCM08*, Korea, pp.302-305, by IEEE CS, ISBN: 978-0-7695-3322-3.

Parvin H., Alizadeh H. & Minaei-Bidgoli B. (2008b). "A New Approach to Improve the Vote-Based Classifier Selection", 4th *Int. Conf. on Networked Computing and advanced Information Management, NCM08*, Korea, pp.302-305, by IEEE CS, ISBN: 978-0-7695-3322-3.

Parvin H., Alizadeh H., Moshki M., Minaei-Bidgoli B. & Mozayani N. (2008c). "Divide & Conquer Classification and Optimization by Genetic Algorithm", *3rd Int. Conf. on Convergence and hybrid Information Technology, ICCIT08*, pp.858-863, ISBN: 978-0-7695-3407-7, by IEEE CS, Korea.

Parvin H., Alizadeh H. & Minaei-Bidgoli B. (2009a). Using Clustering for Generating Diversity in Classifier Ensemble, *International Journal of Digital Content: Technology and its Application, JDCTA*, (*DBLP Indexed*), ISSN: 1975-9339, Vol. 3, Num. 1, pp. 51-57.

Parvin H., Alizadeh H. & Minaei-Bidgoli B. (2009b). A New Method for Constructing Classifier Ensembles, *International Journal of Digital Content: Technology and its Application, JDCTA*, (*DBLP Indexed*), ISSN: 1975-9339.

Parvin H., Alizadeh H. & Minaei-Bidgoli B. (2009c). "Validation Based Modified K-Nearest Neighbor", *Book Chapter in IAENG Transactions on Engineering Technologies, Vol. II– Special Edition of the World Congress on Engineering and Computer Science, AIP Conference Proceedings, Volume 1127, pp. 153-161.*

Parvin H., Alizadeh H., Minaei-Bidgoli B. & Analoui M.(2008d) "A Scalable Method for Improving the Performance of Classifiers in Multiclass Applications by Pairwise Classifiers and GA", 4th Int. Conf. on Networked Computing and advanced Information Management *(NCM 2008)*, Korea, pp.137-142, by IEEE CS, ISBN: 978-0-7695-3322-3.

Roli F., Giacinto G. & Vernazza G. (2001) Methods for designing multiple classifier systems. In J. Kittler and F. Roli, editors, *Proc. 2nd International Workshop on Multiple Classifier Systems*, Vol. 2096 of Lecture Notes in Computer Science, Cambridge, UK, Springer-Verlag, pp. 78–87.

Sanchez A., Alvarez R., Moctezuma J.C. & Sanchez S. (2006) Clustering and Artificial Neural Networks as a Tool to Generate Membership Functions, *Proceedings of the 16th IEEE International Conference on Electronics, Communications and Computers.*

2

Parameters Determination for Optimum Design by Evolutionary Algorithm

Wen-Jye Shyr
Deparement of Industrial Education and Technology, National Changhua University of Education, Changhua 500, Taiwan, R. O. C.

1. Introduction

The finding a maximum or a minimum function problem under some constraint conditions are called optimization problem. Almost every engineering design problem can be formulated as optimum problems. Solving the optimum problem requires the computation of the global maxima or minima of the objection function. Many heuristic intelligent algorithms had been developed and adapted to several optimal design problems. Heuristic algorithms have merit that they can search the global optimum with a higher probability than deterministic ones. Evolutionary algorithms are stochastic search methods that mimic the metaphor of natural biological evolution and/or the social behavior of species (Shyr, 2008). Obviously, in order to reach this goal makes the search process complicate and the selection of an optimum technique critical. It is a challenge for engineers to design efficient and cost-effect systems without compromising the integrity of the system. The conventional design process depends on the designer's intuition, experience, and skill.

There are several kinds of numerical optimization methods such as neural network, gradient-based search, genetic algorithm, etc (Rao, 1979). Neural network can simulate the relation between the input and output. But it needs samples for training the network first. Sometimes the gradient-based search is fast and efficient, but it is easy to get stuck in local extreme. Compared with them, the genetic algorithm has its special characteristics. No sample is needed for the implementation of genetic algorithm and the most important is that genetic algorithm can derive a global optimum by mutation and crossover technique so as to avoid being trapped in local optima. It is considered as a technique the most suitable for combinatorial optimization design.

The concept of Genetic Algorithm (GA) was first established by Holland (Holland, 1975), based on the mechanism of nature selection and evolutionary genetics. The purpose of the genetic algorithm is to find a better function via some simulation artificial operation process, which includes evaluation, selection, crossover and mutation. Genetic algorithm is used in optimum design because of its efficient optimum capabilities. The genetic algorithm is an efficient tool in the field of engineering education (Bütün, 2005).

2. Optimum design problem formulation

The aim of the optimum design course is to find the best possible combination of solutions, which can be termed as design parameters to maximize or minimize an optimization function.

It is generally assumed in this course that various preliminary analyses have been completed and a detailed design of a concept or a sub problem needs to be carried out. Students should bear in mind that a considerable number of analyses usually have to be performed before reaching this stage of the design optimization problem and it must be stressed because the optimum solution will only be as good as the formulation. Once the problem is properly formulated, good software is usually available to solve it. In this paper, the optimum design software is supported by a genetic algorithm for undergraduate students.

Fig. 1 shows the formulation procedure for the design optimization problems that involve translating a descriptive statement of the problem into a well defined mathematical statement. Detailed steps of formulation procedure are as follows (Arora, 2004):

Step 1: Project/problem statement

The formulation process begins by developing a descriptive statement for the project/problem, which is usually done by the project's owner/sponsor. The statement describes the overall objectives of the project and the requirements to be met.

Step 2: Data and information collection

To develop a mathematical formulation of the problem, students need to gather material properties, performance requirement, resource limits, and other relevant information. Some of the design data and expressions may depend on design variables that are identified in the next step.

Step 3: Identification/definition of design variables

The next step in the formulation process is to identify a set of variables that describe the system, called design variables. The design variables should be independent of each other as far as possible.

Step 4: Identification of a criterion to be optimized

There can be many feasible designs for a system and some are better than others. To compare different designs, it must have a criterion. The criterion must be a scalar function whose numerical value can be obtained once a design is specified. Such a criterion is usually called an objective function for the optimum design problem, which needs to be maximized or minimized depending on problem requirements.

Step 5: Identification of constraints

All restrictions placed on a design are collectively called constraints. The final step in the formulation process is to identify all constraints and develop expressions for them. All these and other constraints must depend on the design variables, since only then do their values change with different trial designs.

3. Fundamentals of genetic algorithm

Genetic algorithm is a numerical optimization technique. More specifically, they are parameter search procedures based upon the mechanics of natural genetics. They combine a Darwinian survival-of-the-fittest strategy with a random. This technique has gained popularity in recent years as a robust optimization tool for a variety of problems in engineering and various problems. The genetic algorithm uses only the function values in the search process to make progress toward a solution without regard to how the functions are evaluated. Continuity of differentiability of the problem functions is neither required nor

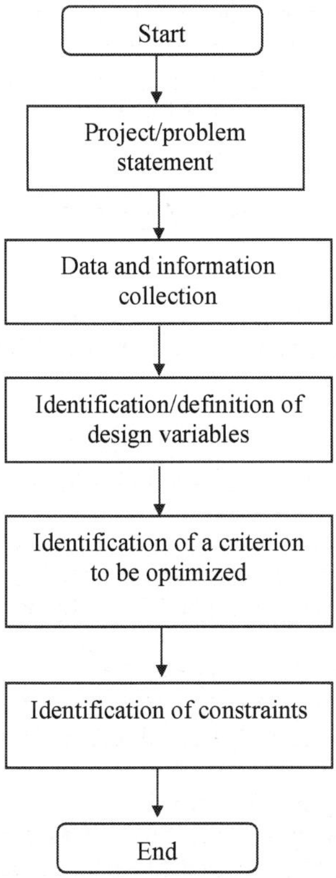

Fig. 1. The formulation procedure for design optimization problems

used in calculations of the genetic algorithm. Therefore, the genetic algorithm is very general and can be applied to all kinds of optimum design problems. In addition, the genetic algorithm determines global optimum solutions as opposed to the local solutions determined by a continuous variable optimization algorithm. The algorithm is easy to use and program since it does not require use of gradients of cost function.

The flow chart of genetic algorithm is given in Fig. 2. The implementation of the genetic algorithm described in this section as follows (Goldberg, 1989; Pan et al., 1995):

Step 1: Initialization

Algorithm is started with a set of solutions (represented by chromosomes) called population. A set of chromosomes is randomly generated. A chromosome is composed of genes.

Step 2: Evaluation

For every chromosome, its fitness value is calculated. Check every chromosome's fitness value one by one. Compared with the present best fitness value, if one chromosome can give better fitness, renew the values of the defined vector and variable with this chromosome and its fitness value. Otherwise, keep their values unchanged.

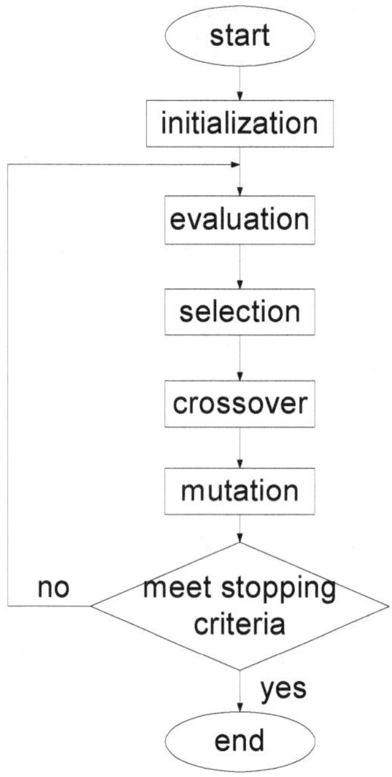

Fig. 2. The flow chart of genetic algorithm

Step 3: Selection
Within the algorithm, population selection is based on the principle of survival of the fittest, which is based on the Darwinian's concept of "Natural Selection"(Dawkins, 1976). A random number generator is used to generate random numbers whose values are between 0 and 1.

Step 4: Crossover
The crossover operation is one of the most important operations in genetic algorithms. The basic idea is to combine some genes from different chromosomes. It is the recombination of bit strings by copying the segments from pairs of chromosomes.

Step 5: Mutation
Some useful genes are not generated in the initial step. This difficulty can be overcome by using the mutation technique. The basic mutation operator randomly generates a number as the crossover position and then changes the value of this gene randomly.

Step 6: Stopping criteria
Steps 2-5 are repeated till the predefined number of generations has been reached. The optimal solution can be generated after termination.

4. The teaching method

The lectures are held in the optimum design laboratory. The teacher explains the conceptions. The examples of genetic algorithm are executed and projected demonstrating the behavior of different optimum design problem. Time is left for the students to run some examples with different parameters realizing an interactive learning process.

The optimum design laboratory serves active problem solving tightly attached to the theoretical material. Each student works on his own computer and solves the optimum design problems by himself. The teacher sets up the problem and gives a permanent guidance. The students build up genetic algorithm programs or combine the programs from given software. The results are then evaluated. Besides worked out examples further programs are also provided. The examination is held in the optimum design laboratory and consists of solving an optimum problem which is assigned by the teacher. The solution is accepted only if the program works in a right way. Genetic algorithm is available during the examination programs.

Interested students may use their knowledge in further optimum design projects. It has to be mentioned that nowadays students are attracted much more by projects connected to optimal control. Students may be better interested in optimum design projects if these are connected somehow to optimal control.

5. Test functions and simulation results

There are three examples examined in this section. Example 1 examined a single variable, and example 2 examined two variables. Three variables are examined in example 3.

Example 1

The objective function of optimum engineering design problems is described as follows (Lindfield & Penny, 1995):

Step 1: Project/problem statement

A manufacturer wishes to produce a wall mounting container which consists of a hemisphere surmounted by a cylinder of fixed height.

Step 2: Data and information collection

The data and information are given as follows: The height of the cylinder is fixed but the common radius of the cylinder and hemisphere may be varied between 2 and 4. The manufacturer wishes to find the radius value which maximizes the volume of the container.

Step 3: Identification/definition of design variables

The two design variables are defined as follows: *r* as the common radius of the cylinder and hemisphere and *h* as the height of the cylinder.

Step 4: Identification of a criterion to be optimized

We can formulate this as an optimization problem by taking *r* as the common radius of the cylinder and hemisphere and *h* as the height of the cylinder. Taking *h*=2 units leads to the objective function

$$\text{Maximize } v = \left(2*\pi*r^3\right)/3 + 2*\pi*r^2 \tag{1}$$

Step 5: Identification of constraints

The radius of the cylinder *r* is between 2 to 4. The defining parameters are as follows: population size=10, probability of crossover=0.6, probability of mutation=0.005 and the generations=20. The simulation of search space is depicted in Fig. 3 and shows the search space performance via genetic algorithm. The simulation result in genetic algorithm is depicted as follows: common radius of the cylinder *r* is equal to 4 and the objective function *v* is equal to 234.5723.

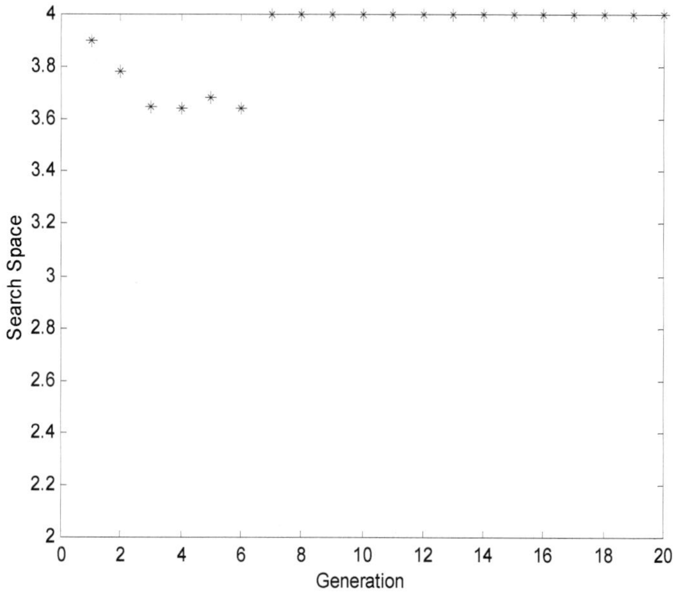

Fig. 3. The search space vs. generation in genetic algorithm (Example 1)

Example 2

The objective function of the optimum design with two variables is described as follows:

$$f(x,y)=x^2+y^2 \tag{2}$$

where $[x,y]=[1\ \ 3;0\ \ 3]$. The population size equals to 20, the probability of crossover is 0.4, the proportion of mutation is 0.05 and the generations are 200.

The solution of this maximization problem is found to be $[x,y]=[3,3]$, and the maximum value of $f(x,y)=18$. The simulation of objective function versus generations is depicted in Fig. 4.

Example 3

The objective function of the optimum design with three variables is described as follows:

$$f(x,y,z)=xyz-xy^2z^2+xy^2z \tag{3}$$

where: $3\le x\le 10$, $2\le y\le 20$, $3\le z\le 7$. The population size equals to 20, the probability of crossover is 0.5, the proportion of mutation is 0.05 and the generations are 200.

For a complicated multivariable function $f(x, y, z)$, it is usually difficult to obtain the global minimum. The genetic algorithm shows its effectiveness to this kind of optimization problem. The solution of this maximization problem is found to be x = 9.804, y =19.946, z = 6.628, and the minimum value of $f(x, y, z)$ = -144200. The simulation of objective function versus generations is depicted in Fig. 5.

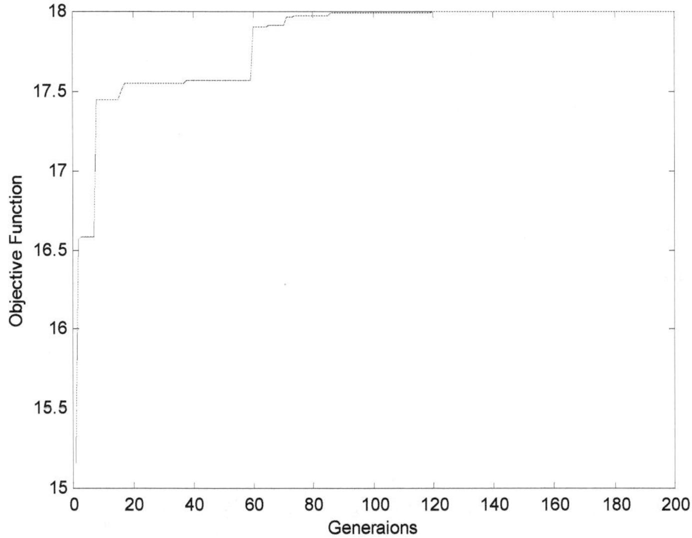

Fig. 4. The simulation of objective function versus generations (Example 2)

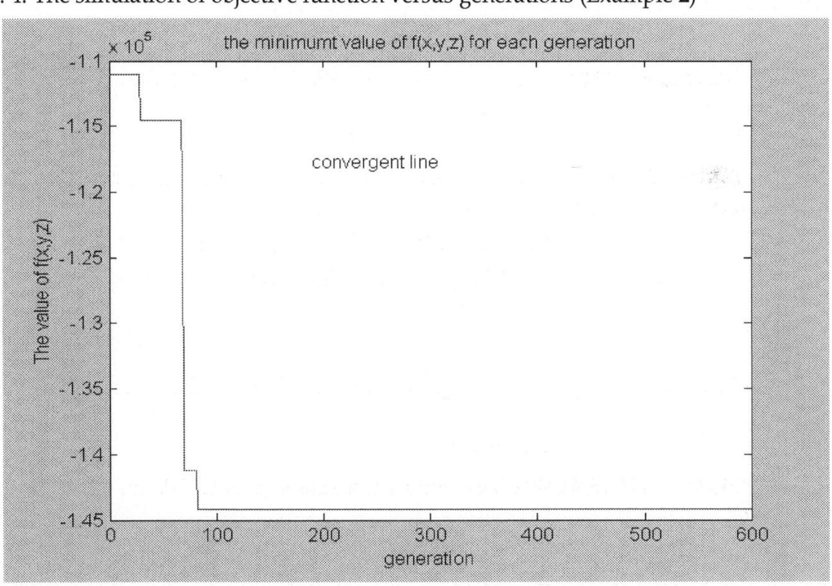

Fig. 5. The simulation of objective function versus generations (Example 3)

These above examples show that the genetic algorithm is effective for solving the optimum design problem.

6. Parameters identification

The identification of suitable adaptive antenna parameters can be carried out using information from optimizing interfence cancellation that can easily be retrieved. The identification of adaptive antenna parameters, as shown in Fig. 6 is performed using the genetic algorithm. The fitness function (Hsu et al., 2005) can be written as follows:

$$AF_n(\theta) = \frac{1}{N}\sum_{n=1}^{N} \alpha \cos[(n-0.5)\psi + \beta_n] \tag{4}$$

where N=number of elements, α =constant amplitude weight for all elements, β_n=phase shifter weight at element n, $\psi = kd\sin\theta = \frac{2\pi}{\lambda} d\sin\theta$, θ = an incidence angle of interfering signal or desired signal, an interfering signal with wavelength λ impinges on any two adjacent sensor elements by a distance d and from a direction θ with respect to array normal. Using the optimization technique, the fitness function cannot exist the imaginary part. As the equation (4) only the real part is left, it is available for searching the optimal solutions using optimization technique.

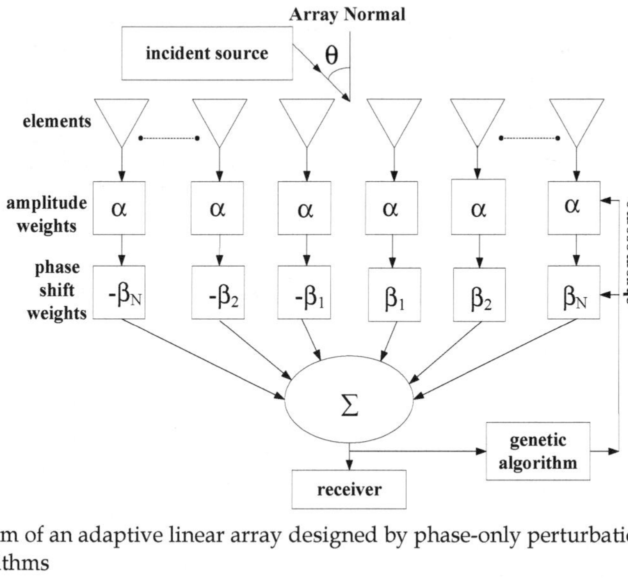

Fig. 6. Diagram of an adaptive linear array designed by phase-only perturbations using genetic algorithms

The values assigned to the necessary variables used by genetic algorithms are as follows: population size P equals to 20; the selected survival rate p_s equals 0.5; the probability of crossover is 0.5; the proportion of mutation is 0.05. In addition, in this problem, we assume a linear antenna array composing of 20 isotropic elements. So, N = 10. The distance d of any two adjacent elements is half of λ. The value of β_n is set between $-\pi$ and π. The unit of β_n is rad. The fitness function is the square of $AF_n(\theta)$in equation (4). The value of α is constant and set between 0.1 and 1. In this case, let α equal 1. Pattern nulling skill can be used to suppress

multiple interferences (including noises). This skill is able to do the cancellation of multiple interferences for different incident directions. One example is given as follows.
The interfering signal's direction is from 40^0 with respect to the array normal. The pattern nulling is derived in the 40^0 interfering direction. The genetic algorithm stops after 250 generations. The result is listed in Table 1. The convergent map is shown in Fig. 7, and the radiation pattern is shown in Fig. 8. This article focuses on the interference cancellation in order to increase the Signal Interference Ratio (SIR). As we know, when we optimized the signal to interference ratio, the noise can be ignored always. Actually, the main purpose of our paper is to propose a method of adjustable canceling interfering signal in the mobile communication. By phase-only perturbation method, the nulling design of an adaptive antenna has been studied by the approach of the genetic algorithm. The excellent nulling results have been derived. In this example, whatever direction the desired signal is from, the SIR has 40 dB at least shown in Fig. 8. For the nulling design, the interferences can be suppressed effectively.

Nulling direction at 40^0	
β_1= -0.364	β_2= -2.229
β_3= -1.394	β_4= 0.195
β_5= -2.977	β_6= 0.402
β_7= 1.149	β_8= 0.622
β_9= -2.016	β_{10}= 0.088

Table 1. The weight vector $[\beta_n]$ for pattern nulling in the interfering directions

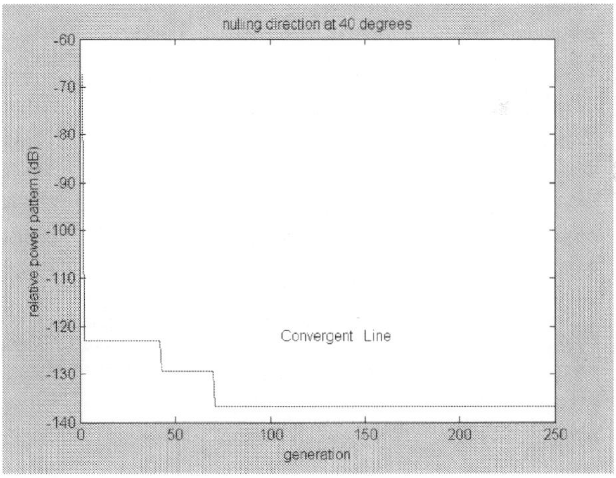

Fig. 7. Relative interference power getting convergent pattern for nulling direction at 40^0

7. Conclusions

Genetic algorithm is global stochastic method based on the mechanism of nature selection and evolutionary genetics. Using genetic algorithm, the extreme value of a function is very easy to be solved as these examples. In this paper, genetic algorithm for identifying adaptive antenna parameter was introduced. Pattern nulling design of adaptive antenna by phase-

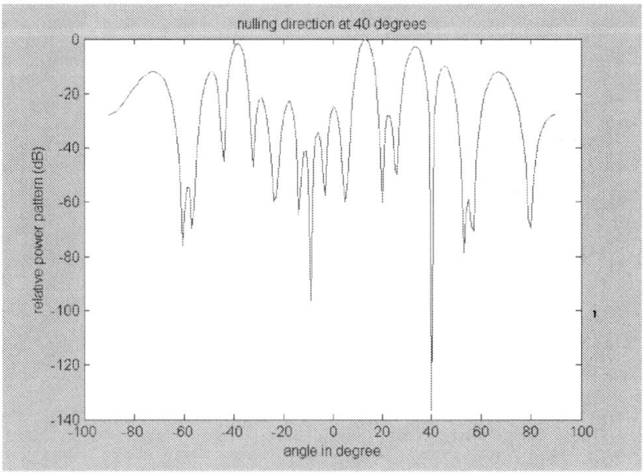

Fig. 8. Adaptive array pattern for single interfering source at 40^0

only perturbations using genetic algorithms is proposed and achieved. This proposed evolutionary algorithm was then successfully applied to the test problems and the adaptive antenna parameter identification, and then proved to be a very promising optimization algorithm for using in optimization problems.

The optimum design problem formulation and the teaching method have been overviewed. Genetic algorithm based optimum design laboratory supported understanding of optimum design problem for engineering education. Studying the optimum design course the students get the experience of solving the optimum design problems by themselves.

8. References

Arora, J. S.(2004). Introduction to optimum design, Elsevier Academic Press. 2nd,.

Bütün, E. (2005). Teaching genetic algorithms in electrical engineering education: a problem-based learning approach, International Journal of Electrical Engineering Education, Vol. 42, Issue 3, pp.223-234.

Dawkins, R. (1976). The selfish gene, Oxford University Press.

Goldberg, D. E. (1989). Genetic algorithms in search optimization and machine learning, Addison- Wesley Publishing Company.

Holland, J. H. (1975). Adaptation in natural and artificial systems, AnnArbor: The University of Michigan Press.

Hsu, C. H., Shyr, W. J. and Kuo, K. K. (2005) .Optimizing interference cancellation of adaptive linear array by phase-only perturbations using genetic algorithms, Lecture Notes in Artificial Intelligence(LNAI), Vol. 3681, pp. 561-567.

Lindfield, G. and Penny, J. (1995). Numerical methods using MATLAB, Prentice-Hall, Inc.

Pan, J. S., McInnes, F. R. and Jack, M. A. (1995). Codebook design genetic algorithms, IEE Electronics Letters, Vol. 31, No.17, pp.1418-1419.

Rao, S. S. (1979). Optimization theory and applications, 2nd.

Shyr, W. J. (2008). Introduction and comparison of three evolutionary-based Intelligent algorithms for optimal design, Proceeding of International Conference on Convergence and Hybrid Information Technology (ICCIT 2008), Vol.2, pp.879- 884.

3

Convergence towards a Dynamic Theory of Linguistics and Semantics

Marius Crisan
University "Politehnica" of Timisoara
Romania

1. Introduction

From the dawn of civilization mankind was aware of the importance of language. We live, think, have knowledge and our being in language. All knowledge of the world and ourselves is expressed and mediated through language. Therefore, it is not surprising that in ancient views language (Greek *logos*) encompassed everything as the soul of the universe, and had mystical and religious dimensions and origins. The term *logos* which literary means "word," "reason," or "plan" denotes a deep concept of divine controlling principle manifested by speech that can be found also in Indian, Persian, and Egyptian theological systems. The opening verses from St. John's Gospel – "In the beginning was the Word, and the Word was with God, and the Word was God." – became a standard quotation in supporting the ancient philosophical conception of language as the universal foundation of life and thought. The philosophical investigation upon the essence of everything led inevitable, at some stage or other, every system of philosophy to consider language and its relation with thinking, cognition, and reality. The early foundations of the systematic study of language can be traced back to Socrates, Plato, and Aristotle in the Western tradition (Modrak, 2001) and to Yāska, Pānini, and Bhartrhari of the ancient Indian Grammar School (Coward, 1980; Matilal, 1985). The merit of these schools of thought is that they realize that understanding the nature of language means understanding ourselves in relation with the universe we live in.

However, the ancient dimensions faded in time, and it is only recently that modern science has begun seriously to investigate language. A considerable research effort was and is still involved. One direction of investigation is conceptual, and has the aim to answer the fundamental philosophical quests regarding the nature, origins, and usage of language. Modern philosophy of language follows the same type of speculative inquiry into language by pure *a priori* reasoning established by the ancients. Its main concern is the development of a theory of meaning and the relationship between language and reality (Lycan, 2000; Malmkjaer, 2009; Morris, 2007). Other topics of interest for philosophers of language are language cognition and language acquisition, generation and speech acts. Here, of particular interest is to understand how language is related to the minds of both the speaker and the hearer. Also, a theory is sought to explain how words are translated into other words.

The other direction is mostly empirical in nature (Sampson, 2002), i.e., based on observation and experimentation, and is specific to modern scientific approach. Initially, the study of language, referred by the term philology, was concerned mainly with the historical development of languages and associated literature in the cultural context. Later, the scientific study of language became known as linguistics. Its main theoretical purpose is the construction of a general theory of the structure of language (grammar) and the study of meaning (semantics) (Aronoff & Rees-Miller, 2003; Fromkin, 2000). Linguistics tries to discover the common elements of all languages or the universals and devise a predictive scientific theory of them. The applied linguistics involves the application of the theory to practical tasks such as language teaching and learning, linguistic competence, and communication (Cook, 2003; Davies & Elder, 2004)

The early attempts in linguistics were oriented towards an idealistic conception of language. Later, the dominant view became the classical premise of structuralism that language is a formal system of discrete symbolic units and their combinations. In Saussure's conception, the language system, called *langue,* is made up of discrete signifying units or signs which externally manifest in different combinations in language use (the speech of an individual), called *parole* (Saussure, 2006). Another essential view of structuralism is the arbitrariness of the connection between the signifier (sound or letter group) and the signified (concept). A similar view that all language is conventional and temporal can be traced back to Aristotle and Plato in the Western tradition and to Indian schools such as Nyāya or Buddhism.

After a period dominated mainly by behaviorist attitudes towards language, modern linguistics became influenced by the view that language is a non-finite but denumerable set that can be defined by an algorithm. Natural languages were considered syntactically rule-governed, and the goal of linguistics became the investigation of these rules. Both statistical and algebraic approaches have been considered with much more emphasis on the latter. In Chomsky's approach (Chomsky, 1957), natural language resembles artificial formal languages and therefore is defined by a finite system of generative rules for each language. The most significant accomplishment is the transformational grammar which uses rules to express relationships among the various elements of a sentence and to generate accordingly the grammatical sentences in a language. The purpose of linguistic analysis of a language L is to make distinction between grammatical sequences and ungrammatical sequences of L and to study the structure of grammatical sequences. In this view, the capability of recognizing the meaningfulness and grammaticality of a potential infinity of sentences can be accounted by the existence of a set of rules for assigning meanings to utterances. These rules are supposed to be innate to humans and form a universal grammar shared by all languages.

Computational linguistics is a precursor of artificial intelligence and originated in the task of using computers to translate texts from other languages (Hutchins & Somers, 1992). Later, the task extended to the study of computer systems for natural language understanding and generation (Mitkov, 2005). Specifically, human-computers interaction became the field of natural language processing (NLP) which has the goal of developing techniques for both speech recognition and synthesis (Huang et al., 2001; Jurafsky & Martin, 2000). An important class of methods for language recognition and generation is based on probabilistic models (Jurafsky & Martin, 2000; Manning & Schütze, 1999), such as n-grams model, hidden Markov and Maximum Entropy model. Given a sequence of units (words, letters, morphemes, sentences, etc.) these models try to compute a probability distribution over possible labels and choose the best label sequence. Another approach in NLP is to use neural networks, in particular self-organizing maps of symbol strings (Kohonen, 2001;

Somervuo, 2003). Still, an important challenge for any NLP approach, which may hinder its success, is the capability of dealing with the dynamic character of language phenomenon. The main progress achieved so far pertains in principal with a concise articulation of language competence rather than providing a working model of language performance. This is the effect of reducing language to the formal or uttered word, which is viewed only as a symbol, carrying information that a computer can store and retrieve. The higher dimensions of language, experienced for instance when the right words are found to express the nuances of a thought, are missed.

Out of dissatisfaction with formal approaches to language, a relatively new trend has manifested in linguistics. This is cognitive linguistics which starts from the fundamental premise that language reflects patterns of thought (Croft & Cruse, 2004; Evans & Green, 2006; Geeraerts & Cuyckens, 2007). In contrast with the Chomskyan approach, where an autonomous separate module for language acquisition is present in the mind, cognitive linguistics assumes that human linguistic ability is conceptual in nature and not different from other cognitive functions. Knowledge of language, being a cognitive process, emerges from language use. Cognitive semantics, as part of cognitive linguistics, goes beyond the classic theories in semantics which try to explain meaning in terms of necessary and sufficient and truth-conditions. Meaning is conceptual, i.e., corresponds with a concept present in the mind and is based on personal understanding. An increasing influence role in the domain is played by the cognitive grammar (Langacker, 2008; Taylor, 2002). According to this view, the mental grammar takes the form of symbolic assemblies, consisting of conventional pairings of form and meaning, without the need of the abstract rules that cannot be naturally discerned in language use. The competence versus performance issue is dissolved as is also dissolved the principled separation between lexicon and grammar. Grammar is an integral part of cognition as the other cognitive abilities. A central place in this theory is occupied by conceptual archetypes. These are related with the grammatical components and lexical classes and play a cognitive role in experiential gestalts. It's interesting to remark the dynamic dimensions introduced by the archetypes such as physical objects, locations, motion of an object through space, events, participants in an event, energy transfer from one participant to another, etc. (Langacker, 2008). A distinct place in the realm of dynamic view in linguistics and semantics is occupied by the Catastrophe Theory proposed by Thom (Thom, 1983), starting from Tesnière's fundamental ideas of actant and valency (Tesnière, 1959). There is a correspondence, in this theory, between the evolution of sentence structures, where the verb has the central role, and the morphogenesis of biological forms. Thom identified a set of archetypal morphologies that play a role in the actantial interactions originated by the verb. The morphogenesis of sentence-structures is described in terms of the number of actants involved by the verb and the evolution of interactions in time.

In recent years, an increased scientific awareness is manifested towards the importance of dealing with the dynamics of phenomena for a deeper understanding in any domain of science. Within cognitive linguistics, the dynamical perspective on linguistic phenomena has been argued by several authors to be a promising alternative to the symbolic paradigm based on logics and algebraic algorithms (Andersen, 2002; Manjali, 1995; Peregrin, 2003; Wildgen, 1986; Wildgen, 2008). Any attempt in explaining natural language remains incomplete unless there is an understanding of its dynamics. The dynamical system theory describes the behavior of complex dynamical systems by employing differential and difference equations. Using the tools offered by this theory, the dynamics modeling of linguistic phenomena can be performed more effectively. Another support to the dynamical approach comes from the new established field of cognitive neurodynamics, which provided evidence that event-related brain potentials reflect a lexical-semantic integration and syntactic process that can be interpreted in terms of dynamical system theory (Graben et al., 2008; Rabinovich et al., 2006; Vogels et al., 2005)

In the above context, a reasonable interest to explore the possibility of using dynamical systems in modeling language and meaning appears motivated. Starting from the premise that natural language phenomena can be viewed as a dynamical system the purpose of this chapter is to investigate the possibility of modeling meaning of words and sentences by superposition of chaotic attractors. In the following sections we present some details of this dynamic approach.

2. Meaning and dynamical systems

The essence of language is to be meaningful. The inquiring into the nature of meaning is one of the most profound philosophical quests for human mind. What is meaning? What it means to mean something? How something meaningful for a person can be known or transmitted to someone else? Several approaches have been proposed for a theory of meaning such as meaning as reference, meaning as truth, meaning as usage, thought and language, a naturalized account of meaning, etc. (Collins, 2001; Greenberg & Harman, 2005; Lycan, 2000; Stainton, 1996). It is not our purpose to analyze these theories here, but some common characteristics can be outlined. All theories of meaning encounter the same difficulty: They try to explain meaning using other meaningful concepts, and for this reason are prone to limitations of one kind or another. In general, since all human knowledge is encompassed within language, in order to explain language we need to use language. However, a way out of this difficulty that can lead also to a certain degree of objectivity is to account the object language in metalinguistic terms. For instance, in formal semantics approaches, a metadescription is obtained by assigning labels to sentence constituents (the syntactic category *S* is replaced by the truth value *t*) and conflating logical terms with lexical categories (Heim & Kratzer, 1998; Nirenburg & Raskin, 2004). Denotational semantics uses mathematical objects to describe the semantics of the system. Emergent semantics principles, in order to establish semantic agreement, are committed to adoption of meta-data representational models (for instance standards like RDF or OWL) (Bozsak et al., 2002). Therefore, meaning has to be described as being something possessing metalinguistic properties. The higher is the degree of such properties the higher the degree of generality of the respective theory of meaning. In our view, we suggest that high-order metalinguistic properties can be provided by taking into account the dynamic role played by the language constituents in the formation of words and sentences.

On the other hand, we have to consider also the following problem. In the classical view, the information content of what a sentence means can be generated from information about the meaning of the sentence's constituents and of the ways they are related to each other. In this concept, natural languages are necessarily compositional. The compositionality constraint has to be satisfied by any theory of meaning for the simple reason that the theory has to show how the meanings of sentences are determined by properties of the simple constituents of the sentences, coupled with the combination or order in which the constituents appear (LePore & Ludwig, 2005). In this context, the proposed dynamic approach tries to answer several fundamental questions (Crisan, 2008; Crisan, 2009b). One is about the formation of meaning. A word is composed of phonemes which are individually uttered by the speaker and individually perceived by the hearer. If the component phonemes of a word are distinct elements in the process of word uttering and perception, how can these distinct elements be cognized as a whole so that the meaning of the word is understood as a resulting composite phoneme-unit? What constitutes the morpheme or the unit of meaning? Do the individual words or even syllables (letters) have a separate meaning by themselves, or meaning is present only when they are combined together? The individual phonemes do not manifest separate meaning by themselves. Only combined together in a word the meaning is revealed. Similarly, the several words, which are supposed to constitute a sentence, only as combined together can convey the unitary meaning at the sentence level. However, the problem is that these phonemes/words are never together in the same time as a whole. They appear in a sequence, one after another. Words containing the same syllables in different order have different meaning or no meaning at all. Yet, the order seems to be less strict for the words in a sentence in order to convey meaning. In principle, the same words can be used in a rephrased sentence to convey the same meaning. One may argue from a structuralist position that it is the last phoneme/word actually perceived combined with the memory of the previous phonemes or words that brings about the meaning as a whole. In other words, the word is nothing more than the phonemes themselves or the whole results from the sum of its parts. But how is such a combination possible which, obviously, should take also into account the order of phonemes in a word or of words in a sentence. What would determine the order of phonemes/words in the absence of an underlying dynamic condition which engenders the unitary meaning? Another problem is to account for the role an individual word might have in sentence- meaning. For instance, not all words refer to a specific thing, or a given word may be used in large varieties of contexts and circumstances. Also, there are causes that may create difficulties such as the similarity/dissimilarity of words' form (polysemy, homonymy, homophony, etc.). From such considerations, we may expect that only a holistic dynamic concept could encompass the nonlinear phenomena of meaning manifestation from sentence's constituents. Verbal communication is made possible because of the presence of similar dynamic linguistic properties in both the speaker and the hearer. It is the role of the dynamic approach to account for such a unifying principle of meaning generation out of the dynamic contribution of the component elements. Therefore, in the dynamic view, we encounter the principle of the gestalt theory that the whole appears greater than the sum of its parts. This is also consistent with the basic principles of cognitive linguistics (Geeraerts & Cuyckens, 2007).

We may start with the assumption that at least one kind of internal states is interrelated with language, or in other words that there is no cognition without the operation of the word. This is not in the sense that we have a thought and then we look for a word with which to express it, or that we have an isolated word which we try to associate with a thought. Our approach assumes that the speaker's purpose is to convey a thought structure, and therefore uses language to encode that structure, hoping that this code will be understood by the hearer. Understanding is equivalent with the formation of a similar thought in the hearer's mind. Thus, meaning appears to be inseparably tied to such concepts as belief, judgment, desire, intention, knowledge, and understanding. Therefore, meaning understanding presupposes the capacity of the receiver to extract and retrieve the thought structure of the transmitter from particular utterances.

Observations may lead to the fact that people do not speak in individual words. Linguistic communication is based on a meaning concept as a whole at the level of indivisible sentences. Although the individual words or even letters have meaning, the sentence is the complete form of a meaningful thought. An ideal receiver has to have the "capacity" to extract meaning from a sentence. This capacity is what qualifies the linguistic competency, and can be described by the cognition of the cognitive properties a sentence has assigned by the transmitter. It is useful to consider the following semantic bearing criteria: (1) semantical competency, (2) expectancy, (3) contiguity in space and time, and (4) transmitter's intention (Matilal, 1985). These cognitive properties are the requirements for defining a grammatical and meaning-bearing sentence. A sentence is said to have semantic competency when the objects denoted by the respective words are compatible one to another. For instance, the sentence "*She sees the light.*" is grammatically acceptable, and has semantic competency, while the sentence "*She hears the color.*" even if it is grammatically acceptable, lacks semantic competency. Semantic expectancy refers to the capacity of an ideal receiver to infer the meaning of an incomplete sentence (utterance). Syntactic expectancy refers to the syntactic property x which has o be assigned to a sentence s when it is not grammatical, in order to make it suitable to convey the meaning. This expectancy is measured by the predictor of the entropy of the entropic source. Contiguity is the property which imposes the absence of any unnecessary spatial (in written text) or temporal (in speech) interval between the words of a sentence. However, there is a difficulty here related with the fact that the same thought can be expressed by the transmitter in different languages and within a language in different paraphrases. On one hand, the thought states of both the transmitter and the receiver are subjective mental states, and on the other hand an objective procedure is required that can provide a 'representation' of those cognition states.

In defining meaning as something that must have a finite and objective significance, we postulate the concept of undivided meaning whole (UMW), which exists internally in the mind (the agent's information level or knowledge base) (Crisan, 2006). This is structured information, and may be similarly conceived as informational structure of an algorithm. A somewhat similar assumption can be found in (Steels & Hanappe, 2006). Even if UMW is a unitary information structure, it is describable rationally in terms of cognitive semantic units. These semantic units are the generating principle of producing the sequence of uttered words. When an agent wants to communicate, it begins with the UMW existing internally in its mind. A sentence (utterance) is significant or meaningful if it can generate knowledge in an ideal receiver (reader or hearer). This knowledge is a result of a reaction mechanism triggered by the series of words in the sentence. When words are uttered producing different sounds in sequence, it appears only to have differentiation. Ultimately, the sound sequence is perceived as a unity or UMW and only then the word meaning, which is also inherently present in the receiver's mind, is identified.

The above described capacity of the receiver to extract meaning from series of words led to another assumption, that the whole word/sentence meaning has to be inherently present in the mind of each agent according to a similar dynamic process. Thus, it can be explained how it is possible the UMW to be grasped by the hearer even before the whole sentence has been uttered. The sounds which differ from one another because of difference in pronouncement cause the cognition of the one changeless UMW without determining any change in it. Sometimes, reasoning may have to be applied to the components of the sentence so that the cognition is sufficiently clear to make possible the perception of the meaning-whole. It appears that the unitary word-meaning is an object of each agent's own cognitive perception. When a word, such as "tree" is pronounced or read there is the unitary perception or simultaneous cognition of trunk, branches, leaves, fruits, etc. in the receiver's mind. Communication (verbal or written) between peoples is only possible because of the existence of the UMW which is potentially perceivable by all and dynamically revealed by words' sounds or symbols.

The concept of UMW is consistent with a more general view, suggested by Bohm, regarding the possibilities for wholeness in the quantum theory to have an objective significance (Bohm, 1990). This is in contrast with the classical view which must treat a whole as merely a convenient way of thinking about what is considered to be in reality nothing but a collection of independent parts in a mechanical kind of interaction. If wholeness and non-locality is an underlying reality then all the other natural phenomena must, one way or another, be consistent with such a model. Natural language generation and understanding is a phenomenon that might be modeled in such a way. UMW is like "active information" in Bohm's language, and is the activity of form, rather than of substance. As Bohm puts it clearly (Bohm, 1990), "...when we read a printed page, we do not assimilate the substance of the paper, but only the forms of the letters, and it is these forms which give rise to an information content in the reader which is manifested actively in his or her subsequent activities." But, similar so called mind-like quality of matter reveals itself strongly at the quantum level. The form of the wave function manifests itself in the movements of the particles. From here, a new possibility of modeling the mind as a dynamical system is considered. In line with Kantian thought, in (Coward, 1980) we find a similar insight, as above, regarding the linguistic apprehension. This is the interplay of two factors of different levels: (a) the empirical manifold of the separate letters or words and (b) the *a priori* synthesis of the manifold which imparts a unity to those elements which would otherwise have remained a mere manifold. According to this kind of observations it appears motivated to use the concept of manifold for modeling the mind as the seat of language generation and understanding. Manifolds are defined as topological spaces possessing families of local coordinate systems that are related to each other by coordinate transformations pertaining to a specific class. They may be seen also as the multidimensional analogue of a curved surface. This property seems suitable to represent both the natural language constraints and semantic content of linguistic objects. The linguistic apprehension is a cognition process that takes place in two phases. First, the separate syllables or words uttered by the transmitter and/or heard by the receiver act as a manifold at the perceptive level. Second, this manifold has to trigger a unitary state of linguistic cognition or UMW. If we want to follow the compositional constraint and account for an integrated meaning at the sentence level we have to postulate the existence of an underlying principle of identity. Without that underlying identity, the sentence's constituents could not be related and remain only separate entities. Such an underlying principle can be identified in the nature of nonlinear dynamic systems that manifest a deterministic chaotic behavior.

Usually, a dynamical system is a smooth action of the real numbers or the integers on a manifold. The manifold is the state space or phase space of the system. Having a continuous function, F, the evolution of a variable x can then be given by the equation:

$$x_{t+1} = F(x_t). \tag{1}$$

The same system can behave either predictably or chaotically, depending on small changes in a single term of the equations that describe the system. Equation (1) can also be viewed as a difference equation ($x_{t+1} - x_t = F(x_t) - x_t$) and generates iterated maps. An important property of dynamical systems is that even very simple systems, described by simple equations, can have chaotic solutions. This doesn't mean that chaotic processes are random. They follow rules, but even the simple rules can produce amazing complexity. In this regard, another important concept is that of an attractor. An attractor is a region of state space invariant under the dynamics, towards which neighboring states in a given basin of attraction asymptotically approach in the course of dynamic evolution. The basin of attraction defines the set of points in the space of system variables such that initial conditions chosen in this set dynamically evolve to a particular attractor. It is important to note that a dynamical system may have multiple attractors that may coexist, each with its own basin of attraction. This type of behavior is suitable for modeling self-organizing processes, and is thought to be a condition for a realistic representation of natural processes.
In our approach, the dynamic continuity can be found in the domain of dynamical systems and chaos theory. The UMW concept and its type of dynamics appear consistent with chaotic attractor modeling. There is a fundamental connection between chaos and information. This view is also supported by other works that demonstrated that a chaotic system can be manipulated to encode symbolic representation of a desirable message (Bollt & Dolnik, 1997; Lai, 2000). Also, in other approaches (Moisl, 2001; Yang, 2003), chaotic attractors are used for coding words and sentences in a process of dynamic interaction.

3. Chaos-based word modeling

In quantum experiments, when particles interact, it is as if they were all connected by indivisible links into a single whole. The same behavior is manifested by the chaotic solutions in an attractor, as we will see in this section. In spite of the apparent random behavior of these phenomena, there is an ordered pattern given by the form of the quantum wave (or potential) in the former case, and by the equations of the dynamic system in the latter.
Let's consider the simplest case of the quadratic iterated map described by the equation:

$$x_{t+1} = a_1 + a_2 x_t + a_3 x_t^2 \tag{2}$$

Even if it is so simple, it is nonlinearly stable and can manifest chaotic solutions. The initial conditions may be drawn to a special type of attractor called a chaotic attractor. This may appear as a complicated geometrical object which gives the form of the dynamic behavior.
In nonlinear dynamics the problem is to predict if a given flow will pass through a given region of state space in finite time. One way to decide if the nonlinear system is stable is to actually simulate the dynamics of the equation. The primary method in the field of nonlinear dynamic systems is simply varying the coefficients of the nonlinear terms in a nonlinear equation and examining the behavior of the solutions. The initial values of the components of the model vector, $m_i(t)$, were selected at random in a process of finding a chaotic attractor. Strange attractors are bounded regions of phase space corresponding to positive Lyapunov exponents. We found more than 100 chaotic attractors. In Table 1 we presented a list of several coefficients along with the Lyapunov exponent for which the chaotic attractors were found by random search (Crisan, 2009a). The initial condition x_0 was selected in the range 0.01 - 1 and lies within the basin in many cases. The Lyapunov

exponent is computed in an iterated process according to the following equation (Sprott, 2003):

$$LE = \Sigma \log_2 |a_2 + 2a_3x_n| \; / N \tag{3}$$

The sum is taken from a value of $n = 1$ to a value of $n = N$, where N is some large number. *LE* gives the rate of exponential divergence from perturbed initial conditions. If the value is positive (for instance, greater than 0.005) then there is sensitivity to initial conditions and a chaotic attractor can manifest. If the solution is chaotic, the successive iterates get farther apart, and the difference usually increases exponentially. The larger the *LE*, the greater the rate of exponential divergence, and the wider the corresponding separatrix of the chaotic region may be. If *LE* is negative, the solutions approach one another. If *LE* is 0 then the attractors are regular. They act as limit cycles, in which trajectories circle around a limiting trajectory which they asymptotically approach, but never reach.

No.	a_1	a_2	a_3	*LE*
1	1.2	-0.9	-0.9	0.3106
2	1.1	-1	-0.6	6.6073
3	1.1	-0.7	-0.9	0.1538
4	0.8	-1.1	-1	0.2805
5	0.7	-1.2	-0.8	0.2001
6	-0.4	-1.2	1.2	0.3144
7	-0.7	-1.1	1.2	0.3033
8	-0.8	-1.1	0.7	6.9382
9	-0.8	-0.9	1.1	0.2214
10	-1.2	-0.9	0.8	0.2793

Table 1. The coefficients values and the Lyapunov exponents for ten attractors of (2)

It's interesting to analyze in more details the behavior of a chaotic attractor. The idea of the self-organizing maps is to project the *N*-dimensional data into something that can be better understood visually. We follow a similar idea in constructing iterated maps. It is convenient to plot the values in the iterated process versus their fifth previous iterate for a more suggestive aspect. In Fig. 1(a) the iterated map for the attractor No. 10 is presented. A remarkable property of the chaotic solutions, as noted above in connection with quantum physics, is the "ballet-like" behavior as iterations progress. Each new dot on the map, representing the solution x_{n+1}, appears in a random position but orderly following the attractor's form.

In Fig. 1(b) the same attractor is shown only after a few iterates (2000). We can observe the sparse distribution of dots but along with the ordered path. This type of behavior is similar with the quantum phenomena, such as the distribution of photons along the interference pattern lines in the two-slit interference experiment, where the photons are emitted in series one after the other. This is also akin to the quality of the perception act (understanding word meaning). It's an observation fact that a word meaning is at first perceived vaguely and then more and more clearly. Thus, through the process of repeated perception or iterations finally the meaning is revealed. Therefore, we may suggest that meaning can be mathematically modeled as a basin of attraction.

Another interesting property is the symmetry between a_1 and a_3 and the corresponding iterated map. Considering again the chaotic attractor $a_1 = -1.2$, $a_2 = -0.9$, $a_3 = 0.8$, a symmetric

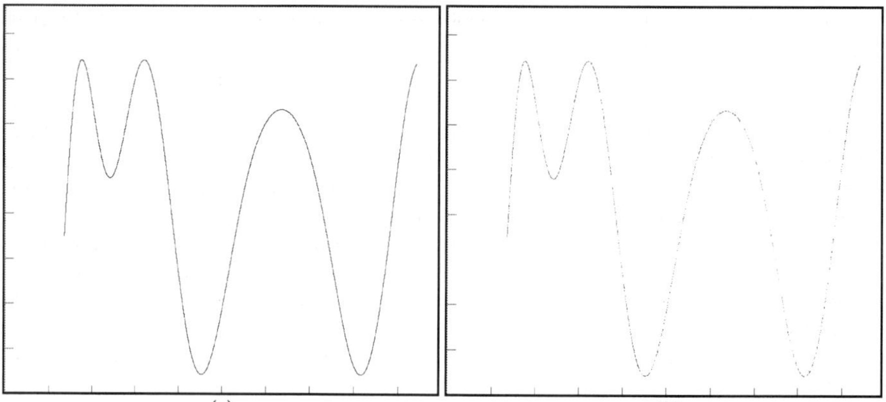

(a) (b)

Fig. 1. (a) Quadratic iterated map of (2). (b) Quadratic iterated map of (2) after 2000 iterates. Note the sparse distribution of dots along the regular pattern of the attractor.

behavior can be obtain for the values $a_1 = 1.2$, $a_2 = -0.9$, $a_3 = -0.8$. There is a large possibility to obtain other attractors by tuning the values of the coefficients. The shape of the attractor changes smoothly with small variations of the coefficients. Even if the interval of variation is rather small, dramatic changes in the shape of the map can be obtained. In Fig. 2(a), the dynamic behavior of (2) can be observed for $a_1 = -1.3$, $a_2 = -0.65$, and $a_3 = 0.8$. If $-1.38 \geq a_1 \geq -0.94$ ($a_2 = -0.9$ and $a_3 = 0.8$) the value of *LE* is negative and fixed point patterns manifest. Trajectories approach a limit cycle for $a_1 = -1.3$, $a_2 = -1$, and $a_3 = 0.9615$. If $a_3 > 0.9615$ the solutions grow unbounded.

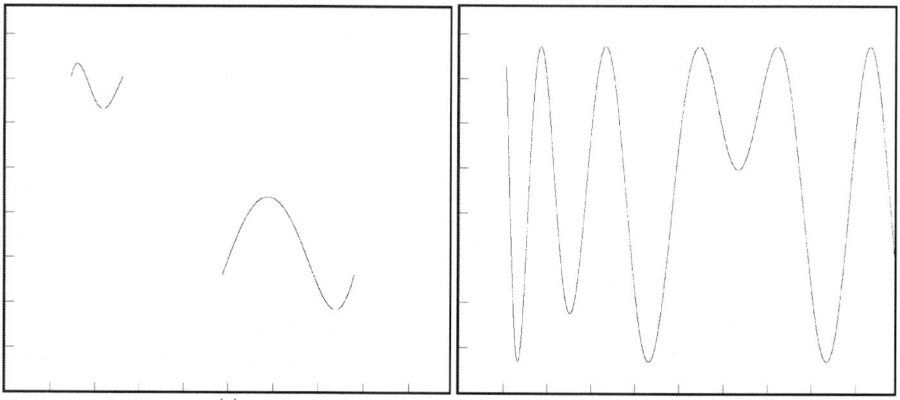

(a) (b)

Fig. 2. (a) The dynamic behavior of (2) for $a_1 = -1.3$, $a_2 = -0.65$, and $a_3 = 0.8$. (b) A different behavior of (2), obtained for $a_1 = -1.3$, $a_2 = -1.06$, and $a_3 = 0.8$.

An important change in shape can be obtained for $a_1 = -1.3$, $a_2 = -1.06$, and $a_3 = 0.8$, with the value of LE = 0.3648, as shown in Fig. 2(b).

The above analysis revealed the fact that chaotic attractors offer dynamic properties that can map in a continuous manner the feature vectors according to some input patterns. In the process of language communication, the dynamics of each phoneme, as it is uttered, has a contribution to the dynamics of the entire word. The goal is to construct a unified word feature that may account for the word meaning or UMW, by encapsulating the phonemes' dynamics into a unitary description of a chaotic attractor.

For a generic word w, composed by a series of m phonemes $p_1p_2...p_m$, the word feature vector is $\boldsymbol{W} = [\boldsymbol{P}_1, \boldsymbol{P}_2,... \boldsymbol{P}_m]$, where $\boldsymbol{P}_i$, $i = 1, m$, are the quadratic maps (2) corresponding to each phoneme. In order to encapsulate the phonemes' dynamics into a resulting attractor at the word level, we may examine two possibilities: (a) to map the phonemes' attractors as coefficients of a higher-order polynomial type equation, and (b) to linearly superpose the phonemes' attractors.

In the first approach, the quadratic maps $\boldsymbol{P}_i$, $i = 1, m$, form the coefficients of the following polynomial type equation,

$$w_{t+1} = k_1 + k_2(P_{1t}w_t + P_{2t}w_t^2 + \dots + P_{mt}w_t^n), \tag{4}$$

where k_1 and k_2 are scale parameters. Eq. (4) describes the chaotic behavior at the word level. Each valid word of length m will determine a corresponding attractor with a unique dynamic behavior. Small variations in the input will be tolerated and recognized with the same meaning, but other illegal combinations will be rejected. For words with higher length, higher-order iterated maps can be used.

A second possibility is to use a linear superposition of $\boldsymbol{P}_i$, $i = 1, m$, of the following form:

$$w_{t+1} = z_1 P_{1t} + z_2 P_{2t} + \dots z_{m-1} P_{m-1t} + P_{mt}, \tag{5}$$

where $z_1,..., z_{m-1}$ are subunitary superposition parameters. These parameters account for the progressive accumulation of the individual phoneme dynamics into the word meaning as the phonemes are uttered in sequence.

In order to exemplify our approach, let's consider the phonemes /*a*/, /*e*/, /*d*/, and /*r*/ as they may form the words *dear* and *dare*. The corresponding feature vectors $\boldsymbol{A} = [a_1, a_2, a_3]$, $\boldsymbol{E}= [e_1, e_2, e_3]$, $\boldsymbol{D} = [d_1, d_2, d_3]$ and $\boldsymbol{R} = [r_1, r_2, r_3]$, are mapped by the following equations:

$$a_{t+1} = a_1 + a_2a_t + a_3a_t^2, \tag{6}$$

$$e_{t+1} = e_1 + e_2e_t + e_3e_t^2, \tag{7}$$

$$d_{t+1} = d_1 + d_2d_t + d_3d_t^2, \tag{8}$$

$$r_{t+1} = r_1 + r_2r_t + r_3r_t^2, \tag{9}$$

where a_t, e_t, d_t, and r_t are the dynamic variables. The four trajectories (6) – (9) are presented in Fig. 3 for the following feature vectors: $\boldsymbol{A}$ = [-0.9, -1.6, 0.6], $\boldsymbol{E}$= [-1, -1, 0.7], $\boldsymbol{D}$ = [0.5, -1.4, -0.6] and $\boldsymbol{R}$ = [0.8, -1.1, -1].

The resulting attractor for the word *dear* is constructed as

$$w_{\text{dear}(t+1)} = k_1+k_2(d_tw_t+e_tw_t^2+a_tw_t^3+r_tw_t^4), \tag{10}$$

and is represented in Fig. 4(a). Similarly, the resulting attractor for the word *dare* appears in Fig. 4(b), according to

$$w_{\mathrm{dare}(t+1)} = k_1+k_2(d_t w_t+a_t w_t^2+r_t w_t^3+e_t w_t^4). \quad (11)$$

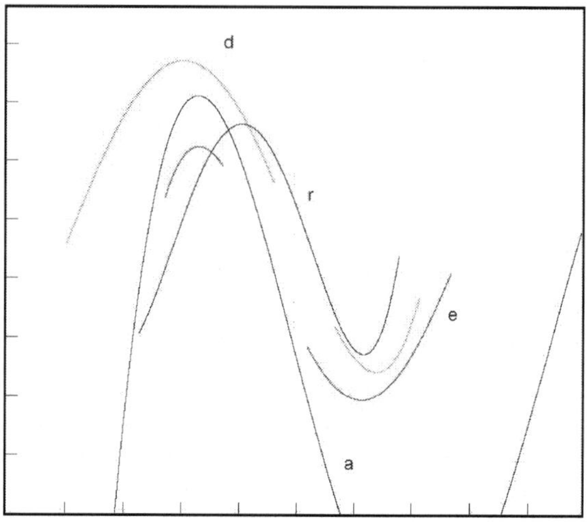

Fig. 3. Chaotic attractors for phonemes /*a*/, /*e*/, /*d*/, and /*r*/.

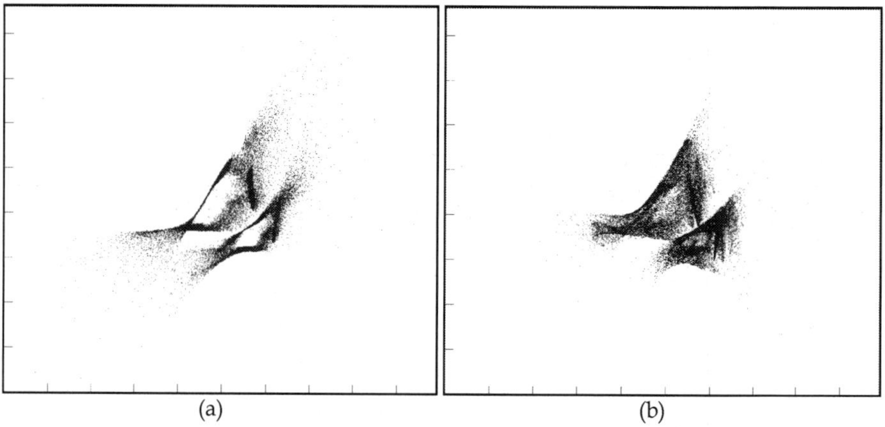

Fig. 4. (a) Chaotic attractor for *dear* according to (10). (b) Chaotic attractor for *dare* according to (11).

There is a clear difference between the dynamics of (10) and (11), although common trajectory patterns can be indentified in both chaotic attractors. This is according to our expectations since both words are composed of the same phonemes. Concomitantly, the meanings encapsulated by the respective words dynamics are clearly different.

In the second approach involving linear superposition, according to (5), the dynamics of the word *dear* is modeled as

$$w_{\mathrm{dear}(t+1)} = z_1 d_t + z_2 e_t + z_3 a_t + r_t, \quad (12)$$

where $z_1 < z_2 < z_3 < 1$. The resulting chaotic behavior is shown in Fig. 5(a). It is interesting to compare the dynamics of (12) with that of (10), for the same word *dear*. They are different because the process of phonemes' encapsulation is linear in (12) and nonlinear in (10). Nonetheless, the dynamic contribution of the word's phonemes is successfully captured in both cases.

A similar linear superposition can be used for the word *dare* in the following form:

$$w_{\mathrm{dare}(t+1)} = z_1 d_t + z_2 a_t + z_3 r_t + e_t , \tag{13}$$

keeping the same superposition parameters as in (12). The dynamics of (13) appears in Fig. 5(b). When comparing to (12), a clear global difference can be noticed concomitantly with the identification of common trajectories patterns.

The simulation results for both linear and nonlinear superposition of phonemes' dynamics have proved the validity of the dynamic approach in modeling meaning and semantics. The model can also account the synthetic interplay between the separate linguistic components and the ultimate unitary manifestation of meaning. The key element in this approach is to emphasize the role of individual phonemes in the formation of the composite phoneme-unit at the word level. In this regard, the above linear superposition enfoldment of the phoneme attractors is suggestive, but the enfoldment process can be further refined as we will exemplify below.

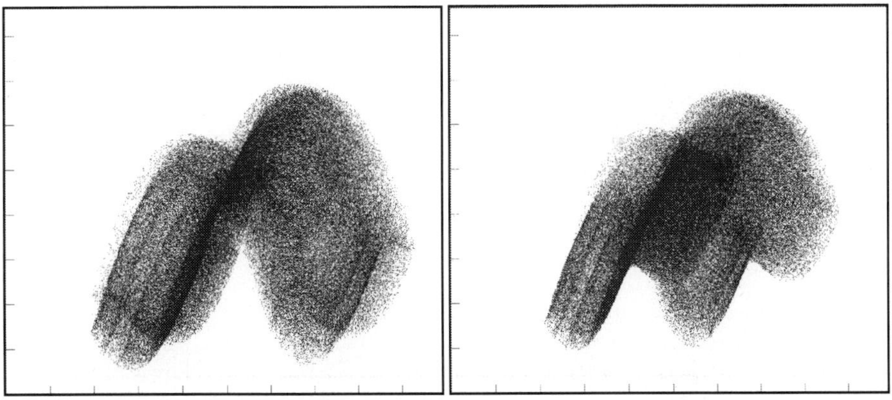

(a) (b)

Fig. 5. (a) Chaotic attractor for *dear* according to (12). (b) Chaotic attractor for *dare* according to (13).

The word is not only a linear sum of the phoneme components but a dynamic compound. Therefore, in a series of phonemes, uttered one after another during the word's generation, the dynamic influence of one phoneme should be manifested in the behavior of the next one in sequence. Then, the influenced of these two phonemes combined is manifested on the next one, and so on. We exemplify this process in the following set of simulations (Crisan, 2009b). We may start from the general form of a two-dimensional non-linear quadratic system:

$$X_{new}(x, y) = A_{00} + A_{01}y + A_{02}y^2 + A_{10}x + A_{11}xy + A_{12}xy^2 + A_{20}x^2 + A_{21}x^2y + A_{22}x^2y^2$$

$$Y_{new}(x, y) = B_{00} + B_{01}y + B_{02}y^2 + B_{10}x + B_{11}xy + B_{12}xy^2 + B_{20}x^2 + B_{21}x^2y + B_{22}x^2y^2 \quad (14)$$

If the coefficients were chosen from the approximate interval [-1 +1] the system would exhibit behavior that was stable or bounded, non-degenerative, non-periodic and deterministically chaotic. This can be a rich source of chaotic attractors suitable for modeling the syllable components of words.

Let's consider a series of three phonemes, say /*o*/, /*r*/, and /*t*/. They can be modeled by equations of type (14) with the values of coefficients as given in Table 2. These values are chosen so that (14) manifests a typical deterministic chaotic behavior. The initial values (x_0, y_0) are selected in the interval (0.001 – 0.5). The dynamics of phoneme /*o*/ can be observed in Fig. 6(a), of phoneme /*r*/ in Fig. 6(b), and of phoneme /*t*/ in Fig. 6(c). There is a rich variety of trajectories in the chaotic behavior which is suitable for the simulation process.

	/*o*/	/*r*/	/*t*/
A_{00}	−0.375	−0.164	0.723
A_{01}	−0.033	0.179	0.883
A_{02}	0.065	0.895	0.178
A_{10}	0.519	−0.377	−0.907
A_{11}	0.533	0.442	−0.419
A_{12}	−0.51	0.106	−0.448
A_{20}	0.255	−0.625	−0.044
A_{21}	−0.822	0.914	−0.08
A_{22}	0.376	−0.117	0.124
B_{00}	0.011	−0.663	0.34
B_{01}	0.032	0.525	−0.169
B_{02}	−0.683	0.43	−0.931
B_{10}	−0.952	−0.075	−0.145
B_{11}	0.229	0.942	−0.876
B_{12}	0.182	0.011	−0.941
B_{20}	−0.046	0.56	0.152
B_{21}	−0.624	−0.728	−0.198
B_{22}	0.032	−0.81	−0.812

Table 2. The Values of Coefficients in (14) for Modeling the Phonemes /*o*/, /*r*/, and /*t*/.

Let's consider next the generation process of the syllable or word *or*. The phoneme /*o*/ is followed immediately in time by the phoneme /*r*/. This means that the attractor of phoneme /*o*/ becomes enfolded in the attractor of phoneme /*r*/ from the very beginning of the word generation. Our premise is that, in order to communicate meaning, an underlying dynamic principle of unifying phonemes in the formation of words has to exist. This is of equally importance for both word generation and recognition.

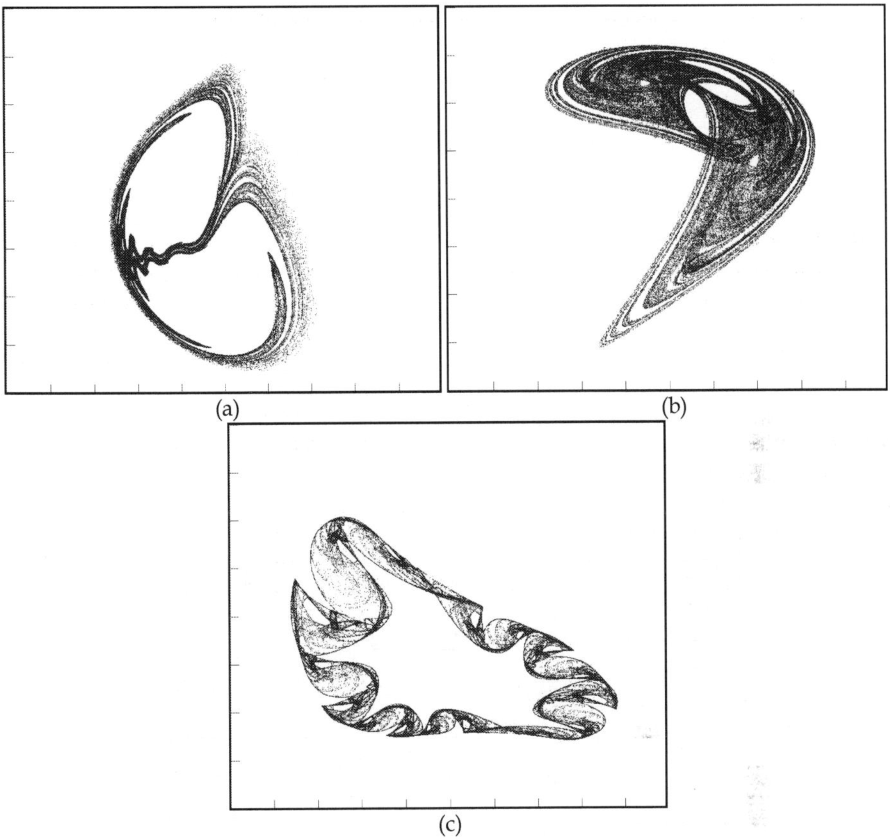

Fig. 6. (a) The dynamics of the phoneme /*o*/. (b) The dynamics of the phoneme /*r*/. (c) The dynamics of the phoneme /*t*/.

Therefore, resuming the above example, the phoneme /*o*/ is generated according to the equation

$$oX_{new}(x, y) = A_{00} + A_{01}y + A_{02}y^2 + A_{10}x + A_{11}xy + A_{12}xy^2 + A_{20}x^2 + A_{21}x^2y + A_{22}x^2y^2 \tag{15}$$

$$oY_{new}(x, y) = B_{00} + B_{01}y + B_{02}y^2 + B_{10}x + B_{11}xy + B_{12}xy^2 + B_{20}x^2 + B_{21}x^2y + B_{22}x^2y^2.$$

The phoneme /*r*/ is generated in a similar iterated process as (15) for the pair $[rX_{new}(x, y), rY_{new}(x, y)]$. Next, in order to account the influence of /*o*/, the values $[rX_{new}(x, y), rY_{new}(x, y)]$ are recomputed, every iteration, according to

$$rX_{\text{new}}(x,y) = w_1\,[rX_{\text{new}}(x,y) + w_2\,oX_{\text{new}}(x,y)]$$

$$rY_{\text{new}}(x,y) = w_1\,[rY_{\text{new}}(x,y) + w_2\,oY_{\text{new}}(x,y)], \tag{16}$$

where w_1 and w_2 are weights. By varying the values of w_1 and w_2 suggestive results of the dynamic influence of /*o*/ upon /*r*/ are obtained. For instance, in Fig. 7(a) the dynamics of the word *or* can be observed for $w_1 = 0.93$ and $w_2 = 0.23$.

Next, it's interesting to study comparatively the dynamics of the syllable *ro*. The phoneme-unit /*ro*/ is generated by a similar equation as (16) of the following form,

$$oX_{\text{new}}(x,y) = w_1\,[oX_{\text{new}}(x,y) + w_2\,rX_{\text{new}}(x,y)]$$

$$oY_{\text{new}}(x,y) = w_1\,[oY_{\text{new}}(x,y) + w_2\,rY_{\text{new}}(x,y)]. \tag{17}$$

The correspondent dynamics can be seen in Fig. 7(b) for $w_1 = 0.9$ and $w_2 = 0.25$.

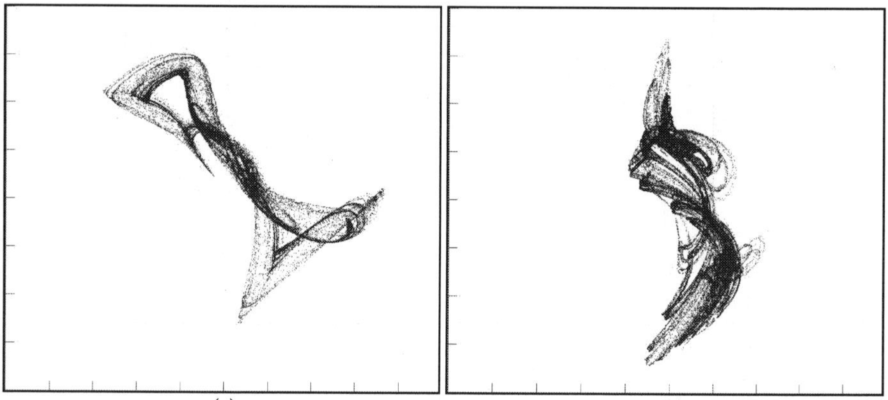

(a) (b)

Fig. 7. (a) The dynamics of the word *or* according to (16). (b) The dynamics of the syllable *ro* according to (17).

The last phoneme in a generated word is dominant because the meaning is revealed only after the last phoneme is uttered. We can observe this effect by considering the influence of the phoneme /t/ upon the previous syllable *or* as in the word *ort*. The following equation models the process,

$$tX_{\text{new}}(x,y) = w_1\,[tX_{\text{new}}(x,y) + w_2\,rX_{\text{new}}(x,y)]$$

$$tY_{\text{new}}(x,y) = w_1\,[tY_{\text{new}}(x,y) + w_2\,rY_{\text{new}}(x,y)], \tag{18}$$

where $[rX_{\text{new}}(x,y), rY_{\text{new}}(x,y)]$ are iterated according to (16). The values of weights are $w_1 = 0.9$ and $w_2 = 0.25$. The dynamic behavior of (18) is presented in Fig. 8(a).

The combined influence of the three attractors can be clearly observed in an interesting pattern. Also, following a similar process, it's interesting to observe the formation of the phoneme-unit *to* in Fig. 8(b), and the dynamics of the word *tor* in Fig. 8(c). Completely different dynamics are obtained in both cases although the initial phonemes are identical. The meaning is determined by the combined effect of all the phonemes' attractors in their order of appearance, in a definite time. Although the phonemes may look like separate entities, as a result of the underlying enfoldment process of their dynamic behavior, the meaning is conveyed as a whole.

The described nonlinear model of attractors' enfoldment is stable and preserves rather well the chaotic behavior of the components. The enfoldment process of the chaotic trajectories of one phoneme into another is clearly demonstrated. This proves to be more refined in modeling the phoneme-unit than the linear superposition as used in (5). However, both methods can provide the resultant chaotic attractor with a clearly distinct pattern for the entire word.

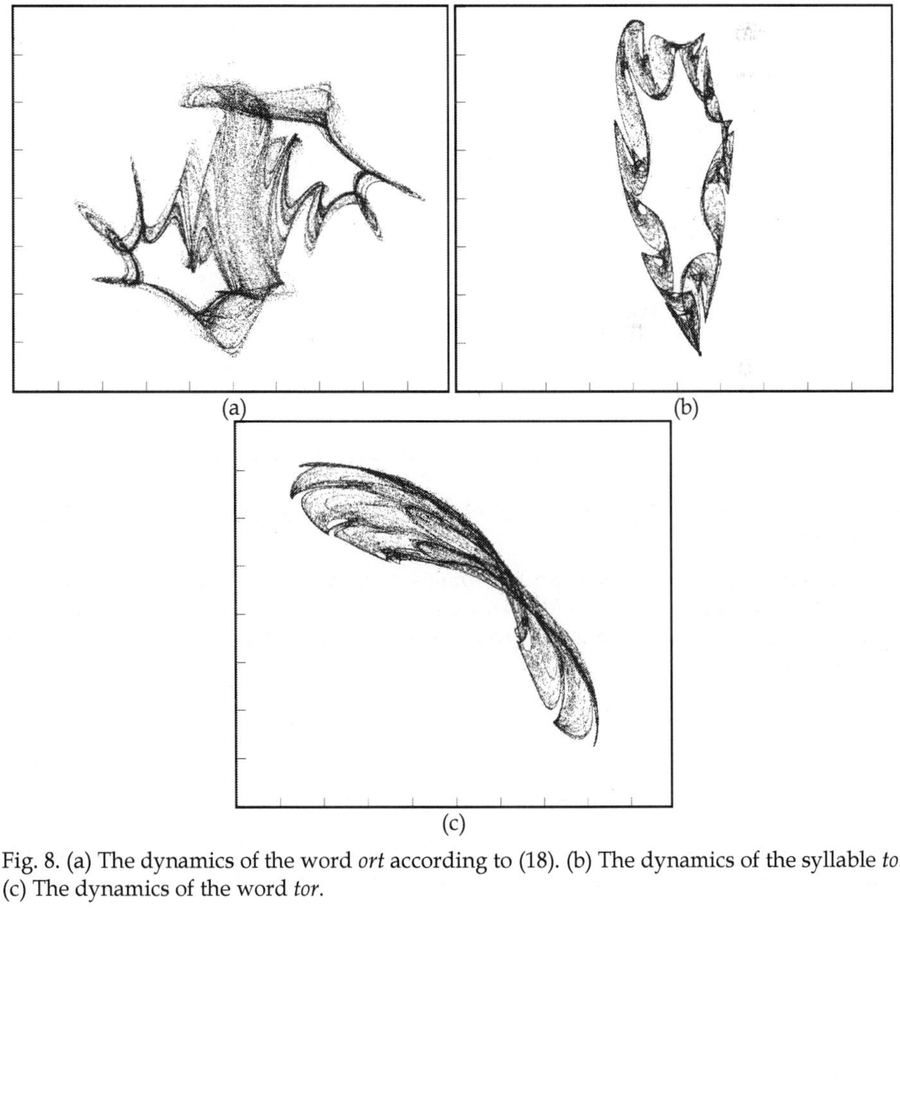

Fig. 8. (a) The dynamics of the word *ort* according to (18). (b) The dynamics of the syllable *to*. (c) The dynamics of the word *tor*.

4. Sentence as the semantic unit of language

We start considering along with other theories of language that the sentence (utterance) is the semantic unit of language. Although the individual words may have meaning this is not complete. Only at the sentence level a complete unitary meaning is revealed. Communication is done with sentences. The individual words have only a conducive role in the formation of the sentence meaning as a unity. The dynamics of the component words of a sentence can be modeled successfully by chaotic attractors. The dynamics of the entire sentence results according to an informational structure which defines the coupling process of the words' attractors and the contribution of each word's dynamics in the ensemble.

The role of the dynamics of each component word can be analyzed considering its relations and position in a sentence. We consider in a general formalization that a word is any phoneme-sequence possessing the property of inflection. Normally, each word takes either a verbal, i.e., conjugational inflection, in which case it is called a verb, or a nominal, i.e., declensional inflection, in which case it is of a non-verbal category (substantives, adjectives, participles, etc.). All the other words which do not have declensional inflections, such as prepositions, may be considered to possess invariant inflection. However, only classifying words in terms of their inflection property is incomplete and does not seem to help much in explaining how the meaning as structured information is conveyed by a sentence. We have to take into account the role of the specific dynamics of each component word in a sentence in relation with other words. Therefore, we suggest the employment of dynamic criteria in defining the notion of a word. The semantic criterion determines the minimum sequence length of the phonemes which convey a meaning. Thus, words may vary in complexity, from the shortest meaning-bearing ones to the more complex compound words. Based on meaningful words, we may define, in general terms, a sentence as being a cluster of words capable to generate a cognitive meaning in a competent receiver (reader or hearer). This concept is further articulated by specifying the dynamic influence and interdependence of words. Here we emphasize the importance of the verb's function in each sentence. Containing a verb is a necessary condition for being a sentence. The verb's role as the organizing centre that distributes the actantial places was discussed in the previous works of Tesnière and Thom (Tesnière, 1959; Thom, 1983). In the present approach we extend this concept by emphasizing the role of the verb's dynamics in forming the sentence-meaning (Crisan, 2009c).

At the sentence level, a similar process of attractor enfoldment as in the case of words can account the formation of UMW. In order to model such a process we need a metalinguistic description. One possibility is to apply the attractor enfoldment process in conjunction with the differentiated cognition model [Crisan, 2006; Matilal, 1985]. According to this concept, we describe cognition as knowing something as something else. In other words, we may know an object by its property to be known. If a certain object x is cognized by another object y, then we write $C(x, y)$. Differentiated-cognition description can be generalized and applied to more complex constructions. For instance, from the sentence

"Adam recites (a) poem." (19)

the meaning can be described in the following terms of cognized objects and properties: *Adam* is cognized by the activity of *reciting* which has a *poem* as object. Thus, cognition appears as a series of descriptions of one object in terms of others. If we use the notation $C(x, y)$ as it was introduced above, the structural cognitive description of the meaning content of (19) is obtained as:

$$C(a, C(r, p)), \tag{20}$$

where a stands for *Adam*, r for *recites*, and p for *poem* respectively. It's interesting to remark the possibility to apply directly the differentiated-cognition model to the X-bar model. We consider again the sentence (19), but using this time a VP representation, since for the sake of simplicity we disregard the verb's inflection information. The head of VP tree is the node V, denoting the verbal element *recites*. This is also the head of the corresponding DCP tree. The specifier of VP is the NP *Adam*, which is the qualifier of the VP node. The V node is cognized with the NP node (complement). The corresponding DCP tree is shown in Fig. 9. The compatibility with the X-bar schema is an advantage that makes the DCP description easily to integrate in the classical syntactic parsers. The semantic description results as follows:

$$C(C(V, NP), C(NP, a)), \tag{21}$$

where a stands for 'agent' which is the qualifying property of the specifier NP.

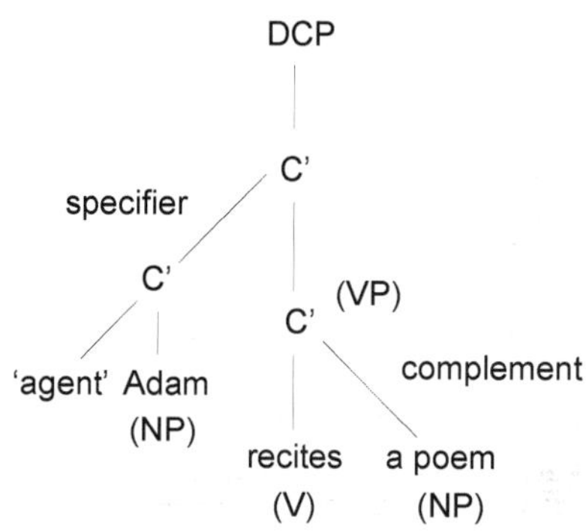

Fig. 9. The corresponding DCP tree of the VP tree of sentence (19) having the verb as the central element.

The verb is modeled by a chaotic attractor that provides a suitable dynamics for making a natural connection to the other words in the sentence. The verb in the head position attracts the other words to it. The two C' nodes in Fig. 9 represent the slots of attraction in the manifold. One slot attracts the nominal element (*Adam*) as agent from one dimension and the other slot attracts the verb's object (*poem*) from another dimension. This approach is in a way consistent with the idea discussed in (Andersen, 2002) of using potential fields associated with each word that influences other words, and subscribes also to the more general view of quantum potential which is regarded as information whose activity is to guide the quantum behavior of particles, as discussed above (Bohm, 1990). We may also note the similitude with the actantial interaction of Thom (Thom, 1959). An interesting proposal for a unifying theory of actants was advanced by Mel'čuk (Mel'čuk, 2004). The Mel'čuk's approach to actants is based on dependency rather than constituency. This means that the structure in which actants appear is determined by dependency relations between terminal elements. Similar dependency structures may result by coupling the attractors according to the DCP description. This is active information that structures the entire sentence as a unity and has to be resident at the receiver's cognitive level.

If the verb's dynamics obeys a potential field behavior as mentioned above the best description is through differential equations. We consider the following differential equations in general form:

$$dx/dt = a_{00} + a_{01}\,y + a_{02}\,y^2 + a_{10}\,x + a_{11}\,xy + a_{20}\,x^2$$

$$dy/dt = b_{00} + b_{01}\,y + b_{02}\,y^2 + b_{10}\,x + b_{11}\,xy + b_{20}\,x^2. \quad (22)$$

This can provide a very rich variety of dynamics according to the values of the coefficients and may suitably model different verb constructs. The feature vector of the verb's component phonemes can be mapped to the twelve coefficients of (22). A remark should be made at this stage. Naturally, in order to model the dynamics of verbs, a similar process of word construct out of component phonemes, as in the previous section, should be considered. However, for the sake of simplicity, in our example, the verb *recites* is modeled directly by (22) according to the following values of coefficients: $a_{00} = 0.2$, $a_{01} = -1$, $a_{02} = 0$, $a_{10} = -0.5$, $a_{11} = 0$, $a_{20} = 0$, $b_{00} = 0$, $b_{01} = 1$, $b_{02} = -1$, $b_{10} = 1$, $b_{11} = 0$, $b_{20} = 0$. The resulting attractor is presented in Fig. 10(a). This attractor is a flow and can act as a connecting principle in forming the sentence meaning by coupling the dynamics of the nominal element and the verb's object.

Next, we suggest that the dynamics of the nominal element can be modeled by a sine-map. This type of map can naturally adapt to the type of dynamics implied by the substance-like nominal element. In the present approach we investigate the following form of sine-map (Okuda & Tsuda, 1994):

$$u_{n+1} = \sin(au_n + bv_n)$$

$$v_{n+1} = \sin(cu_n + dv_n), \quad (23)$$

where the parameters a, b, c, and d can be chosen according to the feature vector of the nominal element. In our case, for the word *Adam* we selected the values: $a = 1$, $b = -1.5$, $c = 1$, and $d = 0.7$. Roughly, these values may correspond to the four component phonemes of the word. The dynamics of (23) is depicted in Fig. 10(b).

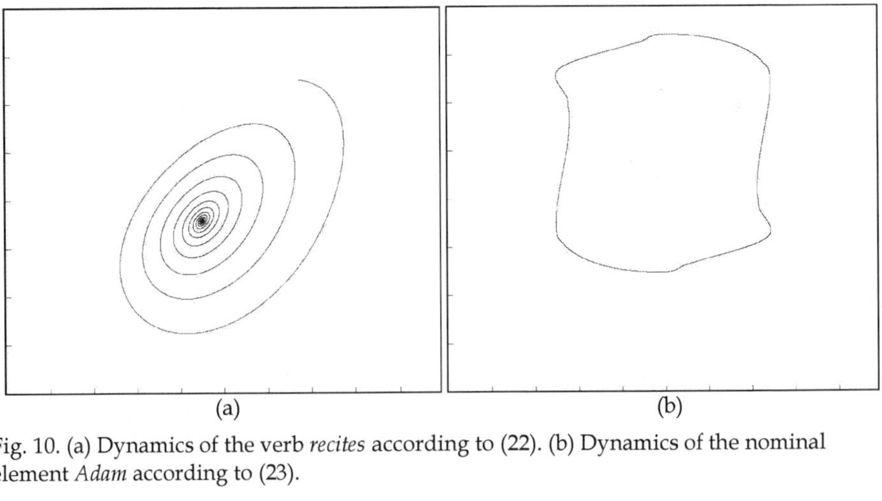

(a) (b)

Fig. 10. (a) Dynamics of the verb *recites* according to (22). (b) Dynamics of the nominal element *Adam* according to (23).

According to the DCP description the verb is the central dynamic element for the entire sentence which couples both the nominal element and verb's object. When the first word in the sentence is uttered this is attracted according to its type of dynamics to the corresponding slot in relation with the verb. Even if the verb is missing, the receiver tends to supply it in order to complete the sentence meaning. In other words, the whole ideas are verbalized. For instance, after the substantive noun *Adam* is uttered, the receiver expects a type of dynamics specific to a verb. This can be modeled by a coupled chaotic system which involves (22) and (23):

$$u_{n+1} = \sin(au_n + bv_n) + k_1x_n$$

$$v_{n+1} = \sin(cu_n + dv_n) + k_1y_n, \tag{24}$$

where k_1 is a coupling constant, and x_n, y_n are the values at the nth iteration of (22) in the discretization process. In Fig. 11(a), the dynamic behavior of the coupled words *Adam recites* is shown for k_1 = 2.5. We can observe a very interesting itinerant motion starting from a cluster like a distorted sine-map (23) to a path influenced by the dynamics of (22). The cluster region is formed dynamically in time and finally emerges into the trajectory of type (22). We can also observe in the cluster several instances of copying the dynamic pattern of (22). The two dynamics naturally fit one to another in a suggestive behavior.
The verb's object can be modeled by another type of dynamics such as a two-dimensional quadratic map of the following form:

$$s_{n+1} = c_{00} + c_{01}t_n + c_{10}s_n + c_{20}\, s_n^2$$

$$t_{n+1} = d_{00} + d_{01}\, t_n + d_{10}\, s_n + d_{02}\, t_n^2, \tag{25}$$

where the eight coefficients can be adjusted to map the word's feature vector. In our example, for the simulation of the verb's object *poem* the values are: c_{00} = 0.8, c_{01} = 0.1, c_{10} = 0.2, c_{20} = -0.4, d_{00} = 0.7, d_{01} = 0.9, d_{10} = 1, d_{02} = -1.2. The attractor is shown in Fig. 11(b).

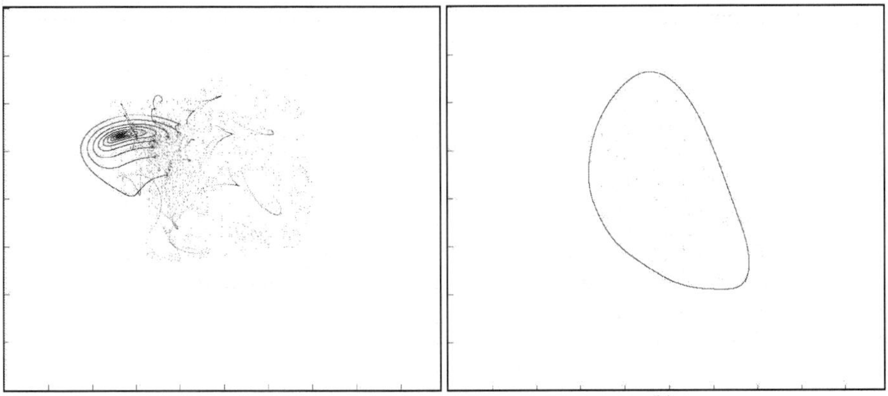

(a) (b)

Fig. 11. (a) Dynamics of the coupled words *Adam recites* according to (24). (b) Dynamics of the verb's object *poem* according to (25).

In the DCP description, the verb dynamics attracts naturally an object. For, instance, when a verb is uttered first, the receiver expects naturally a verb object to follow. This process can be modeled by coupling the systems (22) and (25) as follows:

$$
\begin{aligned}
dx/dt &= a_{00} + a_{01}\, y + a_{02}\, y^2 + a_{10}\, x + a_{11}\, xy + a_{20}\, x^2 + k_2 s_n \\
dy/dt &= b_{00} + b_{01}\, y + b_{02}\, y^2 + b_{10}\, x + b_{11}\, xy + b_{20}\, x^2 + k_2 t_n,
\end{aligned} \tag{26}
$$

where k_2 is a coupling constant. In Fig. 12(a) the dynamics of the coupled words *recites poem* is shown for $k_2 = 0.02$. We can see that the dynamic pattern of the differential equations (22) is preserved and qualified by the chaotic dots due to (25).

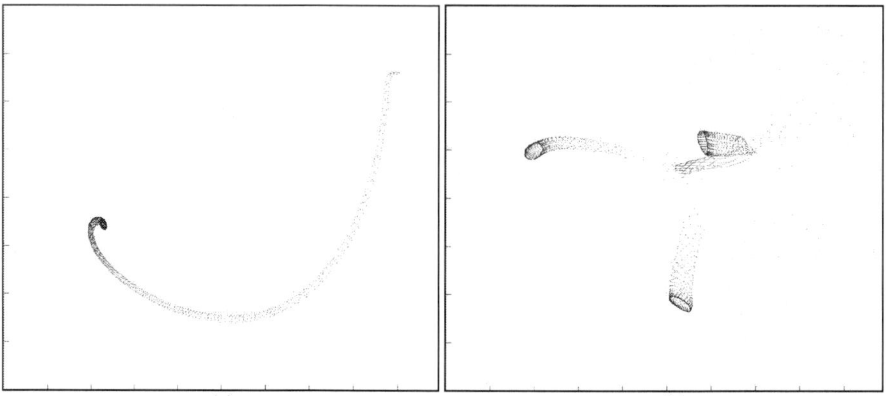

(a) (b)

Fig. 12. (a) Dynamics of the coupled words *recites poem* according to (26). (b) Dynamic behavior of (19) by coupling (24) and (26).

Finally, according to the DCP semantic description (21) we can couple (24) with (26) and obtain the dynamics for the entire sentence (19). The dynamic behavior can be seen in Fig. 12(b) for $k_1 = 0.18$ and $k_2 = 0.33$. We may observe an itinerant motion in the manifold starting from a cluster that finally bursts into three paths that manifest a repeated sequence of patterns similar with (25). This is according to our expectations. The verb dynamics has two slots that naturally have to be filled by the other two actants in the sentence. The final trajectories manifested during the formation of word *Adam* are linked to the verb dynamics. This is responsible for creating an itinerant motion towards the final pattern of the word *poem*. Other interesting patterns are obtained for different combinations of k_1 and k_2, which emphasize either the dynamics of the nominal element or the dynamics of the verb's object. In most cases the itinerant motion between the subject and object is visible. The results support our premise that the verb dynamics is essential in structuring the sentence meaning as a whole.

5. Conclusion

Our purpose was to study the possibility of using dynamical systems in modeling natural language. Of particular interest in any model of meaning, and semantics in general, is to account the interplay process of the empirical manifold of individual phonemes or separate words and the unitary characteristic of meaning as a whole. We started from the premise of UMW and the observation facts of language apprehension and noted a similitude with the chaotic behavior of dynamical systems. The attractor behavior as studied for a series of iterated map seems to be robust enough to accept feature vectors for phonemes that may compose any word of length m in the dictionary. The separate dynamics of the phonemes participate in the manifestation of a unique dynamic behavior of the entire word that may represent the UMW. Two approaches have been proposed for modeling the formation of word's dynamics based on individual phonemes, and the simulation results proved successfully in both cases. At the sentence level, the sentence-meaning is conveyed as a whole and not as the summation of the individual words. This is the result of a cognitive process of assigning cognitive properties by the speaker in order to form a grammatical and meaning-bearing sentence. A competent hearer can extract these cognitive properties of a sentence in a similar cognitive process. This process takes place on the level of sentence-meaning and not on the level of the word-meanings. Only as one hears all of the words of a sentence and grasps the whole sentence by the mind the meaning results in a complete form. The dynamics of this cognitive process is modeled by the enfoldment of chaotic attractors in a similar way as in the case of word's phonemes. The process of meaning communication begins with the UMW in the form of a thought that exists internally in the mind. This UMW determines the configuration for a chaotic attractor. Then, the subattractors for each of the component words are identified and according to the corresponding dynamics for each subattractor the syllables are generated. The same UMW is the generating principle of producing the sequence of words having the sentence-meaning in the speaker's mind, and is also the result of a process of extracting meaning from that sentence in the hearer's mind. Thus, the model preserves the underlying unity of meaning, providing in the same time an account for linguistic communication through series of distinct words. The chaotic attractors corresponding to the sentence's constituent words are enfolded in a resulting chaotic attractor that accommodates the UMW as a unitary information structure. This structure follows the differentiated cognition model based on dependency relations between actants. The sentence-meaning appears as series of cognitions of one object in terms of others, and contains all the information of the component parts but in a higher-order way of integration and completeness. The verb's dynamics plays the central role in the formation of the complete sentence-meaning by creating two slots of attraction for coupling with the dynamics of the subject and the object. This describes naturally the basic structure of the complete UMW of a sentence or thought. In more complex sentences, the subject and the object can be further qualified individually by other properties such as substance-like and spatial-temporal information by coupling their dynamics with the corresponding dynamics of the properties. Even if only one word is uttered, its dynamics determines the corresponding slot of attraction in relation with the verb, and the hearer undergoes a cognitive process involving added word-meanings in order to complete the sentence-meaning. In the case where the single word utterance has the dynamics of a subject, some verbal meaning is added mentally so that the completeness of meaning is achieved. If only the verb is uttered then the complete meaning is mentally perceived by adding a possible subject and even an object according to the context or the cognitive properties suggested by the speaker. In conclusion, in contrast with the classical view which considers language as a collection of independent parts in a mechanical kind of interaction, the logic of the proposed dynamic approach is based on the idea that the meaning-whole is prior to the parts. The simulations results validate this view and encourage us to deepen the research in this direction.

6. References

Andersen, P. B. (2002). Dynamic semiotics. *Semiotica,* Vol. 139 –1/4, 2002, pp. 161-210, ISSN 0037-1998

Aronoff, M. & Rees-Miller, J. (eds.) (2003). *The handbook of linguistics,* Blackwell Publishing, ISBN 1405102527, Oxford/Malden

Bohm, D. (1990). A new theory of the relationship of mind and matter. *Philosophical Psychology,* Vol. 3, No. 2, 1990, pp. 271-286, ISSN 0951-5089

Bollt, E. M. & Dolnik, M. (1997). Encoding information in chemical chaos by controlling symbolic dynamics, *Physical Review E,* Vol. 55, No. 6, June 1997, pp. 6404–6413, ISSN 1539-3755

Bozsak, E., et al. (2002). Kaon - towards a large scale semantic web, *Proceedings of EC-Web 2002,* LNCS, Springer, pp 304–313.

Chomsky, N. (1957). *Syntactic Structures,* Mouton & Co., Publishers, ISBN 3110172798, The Hague

Collins, J. (2001). Truth Conditions Without Interpretation, *Sorites,* Issue #13, pp. 52-71, ISSN 1135-1349.

Cook, G. (2003). *Applied Linguistics,* Oxford University Press, ISBN 9 780194 375986, Oxford

Coward, H. G. (1980). *The Sphota Theory of Language: A Philosophical Analysis,* Motilal Banarsidass, ISBN 8120801814, Delhi

Crisan, M. (2006a). Meaning as Cognition, *Proceedings of the I International Conference on Multidisciplinary Information Sciences and Technologies, InSciT2006,* pp. 369-373, ISBN-10 8461131053, Mérida, Spain, Oct. 2006, Open Institute of Knowledge, Badajoz, Spain

Crisan, M. (2006b). Information Machine and the Gödelian Case. *Scientific Bulletin of "Politehnica" University of Timisoara, Transactions on Automatic Control and Computer Science,* Vol. 51 (65), No.4, 2006, pp. 45-50, ISSN 1224-600X

Crisan, M. (2008). Chaos-Based Meaning Modeling, *Proceedings of the 4th International Conference on Networked Computing and Advanced Information Management, (NCM 2008),* Vol. 2, pp. 314-319, ISBN 9780769533223, Gyeongju, Korea, Sep. 2008, IEEE CS, CPS, Los Alamitos, California

Crisan, M. (2009a). Dynamic Modeling of Natural Language. *Scientific Bulletin of "Politehnica" University of Timisoara, Transactions on Automatic Control and Computer Science,* Vol. 54 (68), No.1, 2009, pp. 39-44, ISSN 1224-600X

Crisan, M. (2009b). Upon Dynamic Natural Language Processing, *Proceedings of the 2009 International Conference on New Trends in Information and Service Science, (NISS 2009),* pp. 487-492, ISBN-13: 9780769536873, Beijing, China, July 2009, IEEE CS, CPS, Los Alamitos, CA

Crisan, M. (2009c). Upon the Dynamic Modeling of Sentence Meaning, *Proceedings of the 5th International Conference on Networked Computing and Advanced Information Management, (NCM 2009),* Seoul, Korea, August, 2009, IEEE CS (in press)

Croft, W. & Cruse, D.A. (2004). *Cognitive Linguistics* (Cambridge Textbooks in Linguistics), Cambridge University Press, ISBN 0521667704, Cambridge/New York

Davies, A. & Elder, C. (eds.) (2004). *Handbook of Applied Linguistics*, Blackwell Publishing, ISBN 0631228993, Oxford/Malden

Evans, V. & Green, M. (2006). *Cognitive Linguistics. An Introduction*, Edinburgh University Press, ISBN 0748618325, Edinburgh

Fromkin, V. A. et al. (2000). *Linguistics: An Introduction to Linguistic Theory*, Blackwell, ISBN 0631197117, Oxford/Malden

Geeraerts, D. & Cuyckens, H. (eds.) (2007). *The Oxford Handbook of Cognitive Linguistics*, Oxford University Press, ISBN 10: 019514378, Oxford/New York

Graben, P. beim, Gerth, S. & Vasishth, S. (2008). Towards dynamical system models of language-related brain potentials. *Cognitive Neurodynamics*, Vol. 2, No. 3, Sept. 2008, pp. 229–255, ISSN 18714080

Greenberg, M. & Harman, G. (2005). *Conceptual Role Semantics. Oxford Handbook of Philosophy of Language*, Ernie Lepore, Barry Smith, eds., Oxford University Press.

Heim, I. & Kratzer, A. (1998). *Semantics in Generative Grammar*, Blackwell, ISBN 0631197133, Oxford

Huang, X., Acero, A. & Hon, H.W. (2001). *Spoken Language Processing: A Guide to Theory, Algorithm and System Development*, Prentice-Hall, ISBN 0130226165, Upper Saddle River, NJ

Hutchins, W. J. & Somers, H. L. (1992). *An introduction to machine translation*, Academic Press, ISBN 012362830X, London

Jurafsky, D. & Martin, J. H. (2000). *Speech and Language Processing: An Introduction to Natural Language Processing, Computational Linguistics, and Speech Recognition*, Prentice-Hall, ISBN 0130950696, Upper Saddle River, NJ

Kohonen, T. (2001). *Self-Organizing Maps*, Springer-Verlag (3rd extended ed.), ISBN 3540679219, Berlin

Lai, Y-C. (2000). Encoding Digital Information Using Transient Chaos, *International Journal of Bifurcation and Chaos*, Vol. 10, No. 4, 2000, pp. 787–795, ISSN 0218-1274

Langacker, R. (2008). *Cognitive Grammar: A Basic Introduction*, Oxford University Press, ISBN 0195331967, New York

Lycan, W. G. (2000). *Philosophy of Language: A contemporary introduction*, Routledge, ISBN 0-415-17116-4, London

Malmkjaer, K. (2009). *The Linguistics Encyclopedia* (3rd edition), Routledge, ISBN 10: 0415424321, London

Manjali, F. (1995). Dynamic Semiotics or the Case for Actantial Case. *Sémiotiques*, No. 6-7, Décembre 1995, pp. 85–97, ISSN 1160-9907

Manning, C. D. & Schütze, H. (1999). *Foundations of Statistical Natural Language Processing*, MIT Press, ISBN 0262133601

Matilal, B. K. (1985). *Logic, Language and Reality*, Motilal Banarsidass, ISBN 81-208-0717-0, New Delhi

Mel'čuk, I. (2004). Actants in semantics and sintax. I: actants in semantics. *Linguistics*, 42-1, 2004, pp. 1-66, ISSN 0024-3949

Mitkov, R. (ed.) (2005). *The Oxford Handbook of Computational Linguistics*, Oxford University Press, ISBN 10: 019927634X, Oxford/New York

Modrak, D. K. W. (2001). *Aristotle's Theory of Language and Meaning*, Cambridge University Press, ISBN 0-521-77266-4, Cambridge/New York

Moisl, H. L. (2001). Linguistic Computation with State Space Trajectories, In: *Emergent Neural Computational Architectures Based on Neuroscience: Towards Neuroscience-Inspired Computing* (S. Wermter, J. Austin & D. Willshaw, ed.), pp. 442-460, Springer, ISBN 3-540-42363-X, London

Morris, M. (2007). *An introduction to the philosophy of language*, Cambridge University Press, ISBN 13 978-0-521-84215-0, Cambridge/New York

Nirenburg, S. & Raskin, V. (2004). *Ontological Semantics*. The MIT Press, ISBN 10: 0-262-14086-1

Okuda, H. & Tsuda, I. (1994). A coupled chaotic system with different time scales: Possible implications of observations by dynamical systems. *International Journal of Bifurcation and Chaos*, vol. 4, no. 4, 1994, pp. 1011–1022, ISSN 0218-1274

Peregrin, J. (ed.) (2003). *Meaning: The Dynamic Turn. Current Research in the Semantics/Pragmatics Interface*, Elsevier, ISBN 0080441874, London

LePore, E. & Ludwig K. (2005). *Donald Davidson: Meaning, Truth, Language, and Reality*, Oxford University Press, ISBN10: 0199251347, Oxford/New York.

Rabinovich, M. et al. (2006). Dynamical principles in neuroscience. *Reviews of modern physics*, Vol. 78, No. 4, 2006, pp. 1213–1265, ISSN 0034-6861

Sampson, G. (2002). *Empirical linguistics*, Continuum International, ISBN 0-8264-4883-6, London/New York

Saussure, F. de. (2006). *Writings in General Linguistics*, Oxford University Press, ISBN 019926144X, Oxford

Somervuo, P. (2003). Speech Dimensionality Analysis on Hypercubical Self-Organizing Maps. *Neural Processing Letters*, Vol. 17-2, April, 2003, pp. 125-136, ISSN 1370-4621

Sprott, J. C. (2003). *Chaos and Time-Series Analysis*, Oxford University Press, ISBN 0198508409, Oxford / New York

Stainton, R.J. (1996). *Philosophical perspectives on language*. Peterborough, Ont., Broadview Press.

Steels, L. & Hanappe, P. (2006). Interoperability through Emergent Semantics. A Semiotic Dynamics Approach. In: *Journal on Data Semantics VI*, pp. 143-167, Springer, ISBN 9783540367123, Berlin/Heidelberg

Taylor, J. R. (2002). *Cognitive Grammar*, Oxford University Press, ISBN 0198700334, Oxford/New York

Tesnière, L. (1959). *Éléments de syntaxe structurale*, Klincksieck, ISBN 2252018615, Paris

Thom, R. (1983). *Mathematical models of morphogenesis*, Ellis Horwood, Halsted Press, ISBN 10: 0470274999, Chichester, New York

Vogels, T.P., Rajan, K., & Abbott, L.F. (2005). Neural Networks Dynamics. *Annual Review of Neuroscience*, Vol. 28, July 2005, pp. 357–376, ISSN 0147006X

Wildgen, W. (1986). Procesual Semantics of the Verb. *Journal of Semantics*, Vol. 5, No. 4, 1986, pp. 321-344, ISSN 0167-5133

Wildgen, W. (2008). The "dynamic turn" in cognitive linguistics. *Studies in Variation, Contacts and Change in English, Vol. 3 – Approaches to Language and Cognition*, 2008, ISSN: 1797-4453

Yang, T. (2003). Dynamics of vocabulary evolution. *International Journal of Computational Cognition*, Vol. 1, No. 1, March 2003, pp. 1–19, ISSN 1542-8060

4

Multiple User-Class Dynamic Stochastic Assignment for a Route Guidance Strategy

Yongtaek Lim
Dept. of Transportation & Logistics, Chonnam National University
Korea

1. Introduction

Traffic information systems have become a major issue in many countries as a modern technology for alleviating traffic congestion in urban areas. Pre-trip or en-route real-time travel information regarding traffic conditions can enhance drivers' knowledge of the situation in road networks and may assist in drivers' decisions such as the choice of departure time, route, and destination. In facts, several papers have shown that traffic information yields benefits to drivers such as travel-time reduction and the avoidance of traffic accidents, among others.

In considering the potential benefits of alternative driver information systems, it is also necessary to evaluate the potential of adverse impacts that improved information may have. Ben-Akiva et al. (1991) explained this phenomenon in terms of three elements: oversaturation; overreaction; and concentration. Among them, overreaction and concentration are the principal causes of adverse effects. Overreaction occurs when drivers' reactions to traffic information cause congestion to transfer from one road to another. It may also generate fluctuations in road usage. Overreaction may occur if drivers respond too sensitively to information on current traffic conditions. Concentration may occur when drivers choose a specific route in a very short period.

In order to implement the strategies of an Intelligent Transportation System (ITS), it is necessary to predict the temporal evolution of the traffic pattern on a congested transportation network, where travel demands and travel costs vary over time and space. For urban areas, dynamic models are mainly considered as they describe how commuters adjust their travel decisions concerning routes and departure times. Moreover, to model the impact of information provision by an ITS, it is necessary to develop a multi-class model given there are different classes of users in a transportation network, who respond in differing ways to traffic information.

In this chapter, a multiple-user-class dynamic stochastic assignment (MDSA) model is introduced to reflect drivers who have varying perceptual errors and varying dynamic traffic behaviors. MDSA is an extended version of a static single-user-class assignment. The driver's route-choice mechanism is based on his/her past experience of the road traffic conditions during prior days of travel. Some information-provision strategies that are involved in a route-guidance system are also introduced for the effective use of the systems.

2. Literature review

One of the basic assumptions in conventional approaches to traffic assignment is that drivers' attributes are identical, i.e., drivers are homogeneous in terms of their attributes. However, this assumption is not realistic in urban traffic conditions: there do exist differences or perceptual errors across drivers. Stochastic approaches to traffic assignment include the variability in drivers' perceptions of costs and seek to minimize the disutility. In stochastic equilibrium models, the costs that are perceived by drivers are considered to be different from the actual costs. The perceived cost is modeled as a random variable. Several approaches have been proposed for formulating and solving the stochastic assignment problem (see Sheffi, 1985). However, simulation-based and proportion-based methods (i.e., methods that are predicated on the proportions of various types of driver, e.g., guided, unguided, etc.) are relatively widespread and accepted in practice.

There are also two kinds of stochastic assignment model: a non-equilibrium-based stochastic assignment model and an equilibrium-based stochastic assignment model. In the first case, a short-run spread of routes between two points is produced without a learning process, whereas, in the second case, a long-run spread of routes is produced with a learning process. Both models reflect the variability of the perceived cost of the routes. In particular, the second case is referred to as a stochastic user equilibrium. The stochastic user equilibrium (SUE) model seeks an equilibrium condition where each user attempts to choose his/her route with the minimum 'perceived' travel cost through a day-to-day learning process; in other words, under the SUE condition, all users stay with their current routes that they perceive to offer the lowest 'perceived' cost to them. By using these stochastic user equilibrium assignment models, we can assess the effect of the traffic information that is provided by the traffic manager.

Breheret et al. (1990) developed a heuristic dynamic assignment model. They assumed that unguided drivers follow an approximate stochastic user equilibrium that is based on the prevailing conditions, whilst guided drivers follow user-optimal routes that are based on current conditions. They reported that the total travel-time decreases until the proportion of guided drivers is 20% and that the benefits for guided drivers are greater than those for unguided drivers. Smith and Russam (1989) also reported a saving of 6-7% in the average journey time for guided drivers, which actually decreased with an increase in the uptake of guidance; unguided drivers also benefited through travel-time reductions of up to 3%. Koutsopoulos and Lotan (1989) assumed that route guidance would reduce the perceptual errors in estimates of the travel times for links; therefore, their model consists of an SUE assignment for two classes with differing variances in the normal distributions with regard to the perceived link costs. An increase in the quality of information resulted in a reduction in the perceptual errors of guided drivers and therefore in a reduction in the travel times. Vuren and Watling (1991) assumed that unguided users were expected to follow an SUE route, whilst equipped drivers were guided via UE (User Equilibrium) or SO (System Optimal) routes. They reported that SO routing benefited unguided drivers at the expense of guided drivers at the levels of uptake that they considered. However, equipped drivers started benefiting as well when their numbers increased: at the highest levels of uptake (greater than 50-70%), guided drivers under SO routing could benefit more than unguided drivers. Baek et al. (1997) and Lim et al. (1997) also suggested a multiple-user-class day-to-day stochastic assignment model and a solution algorithm for reflecting drivers' daily route choice behaviors in the light of traffic information. A numerical example is also presented to illustrate the applications and the assessment of the model.

In conjunction with traffic information, Ta-Yin Hu et al. (1997) simulated daily traffic evolution under real-time information and reactive signal control. They described a day-to-day dynamic simulation-assignment framework to study the interaction between individual decisions, traffic control strategies, and network-flow patterns under real-time information systems. On the other hand, Ben-Akiva et al. (1991) demonstrated some adverse effects of traffic information. They explained that if drivers respond too sensitively to the information provided, potential adverse impacts could occur. Thus, information may lead to an increased travel time and worsen the road network.

The results of prior research, as described above, are obviously rather ambiguous. Hypotheses about route choice and the interactions between guided and unguided drivers might influence the outcomes. However, often the models have used heuristic approaches and they are only valid under rather strong assumptions. These remarks are not intended to belittle the importance of the findings from extant research; they merely show the current problems in understanding and anticipating the behavior of drivers under future route-guidance systems.

3. Model formulation

The model described in this chapter actually consists of two models: a multiple-user-class daily stochastic assignment model and a traffic information model for optimal routing. The multiple-user-class daily stochastic model describes in detail the traffic flow on the road network and drivers' behaviors. The traffic information model sets traffic information for certain control purposes. In this research, some traffic management strategies can be considered with regard to information and then tested in contrived networks. The effects of these information schemes are evaluated through the multiple-user-class daily stochastic model. These two routines execute interactively until mutually consistent traffic flows are obtained.

For the model formulation, we assume the conditions of information provision and travelers' behaviors to be as follows. First, pre-trip and en-route information are provided, the output of which is the optimal route. Second, we define the characteristics of guided and unguided travelers in terms of the size of the perceptual errors. Lastly, guided travelers decide their daily mode and route through information on the projected travel costs.

3.1 Multiple-user-class daily stochastic assignment model

Multiple user-classes (MUC) have more than one class of user, where a class may be defined on the basis of the vehicle type, driver's cost functions, the sections of the network available, etc. A multi-class model is required to take into account differences across drivers or vehicles. To capture the behavioral differences between various types of traveler in terms of information-gathering and compliance with traffic information, a traffic model should incorporate these factors by classifying drivers into different types.

Each class of user is assumed to choose a minimum cost route in accordance with its own definition of cost. MUC would also allow an approximation of the effects of traffic information within an Intelligent Transport System. The guided class of drivers can be assumed to have perfect knowledge of network conditions; thus, the guided class is assumed to follow user-equilibrium (UE) behaviors. However, the unguided class manifests uncertainty with regard to the network states; therefore, this group is assumed to follow the stochastic user-equilibrium (SUE) principle. We may also classify the group by the degree of

guidance. In this research, to take account of MUC, we segment travelers into three groups with respect to the values of a parameter, θ, which is the variance of the guidance. One class is the guided group of drivers, while one of the other two classes is the unguided group of drivers. For the third class of drivers, the variance of the perceived travel time is a fraction of that of the unguided drivers. The three classes are loaded on to the network, one by one.
A stochastic user equilibrium is a more general statement of equilibrium than the conditions of a conventional user equilibrium. In other words, the UE conditions are a particular case of SUE: when the variance in the perception of the travel time is zero, the SUE conditions are identical to the UE conditions. SUE models look particularly attractive in terms of the underlying theory. There are, however, operational and practical difficulties in applying them. The difficulty of an SUE model lies in the convergence properties of a conventional solution algorithm that is based on the convex-combination method. The reasons are twofold. First, the determination of the direction of descent requires, at every iteration, a stochastic network loading. In this step, the link flows are approximately estimated using the law of large numbers rather than computed accurately. The second difficulty with the application of a standard descent algorithm to the minimization of the SUE model is that the move size cannot be optimized since the objective function itself is difficult to compute. To avoid these difficulties, iterative Monte Carlo simulation and the Method of Successive Averages (MSA) are widely used to solve the stochastic user equilibrium problem. MSA is based on a predetermined move size along the direction of descent. In other words, the optimal move size is determined beforehand instead of being attained from the minimization of the objective function.
On the other hand, conventional route-choice models are segmented into multi-nominal logit-based models and probit-based models. In this research, a probit model (Burrell's method), which assumes that the random error of each utility is normally distributed, is used. The computation of the probit choice probabilities used here involves a Monte Carlo simulation procedure.
The day-to-day stochastic assignment requires a modeling of users' dynamic adjustment behaviors, learning and forecasting mechanisms, and reactions to traffic information. Drivers' behaviors vary with the travel cost, which consists of a mean link travel time and variance, which arises from drivers' perceptual errors. In this research, drivers' dynamic route-choice rules are based on the experienced travel time and the predicted travel time that stems from information-provision strategies. The link travel time function is developed as follows.

$$T_a^w(f_a) = (1-\delta)t_a^w(f_a) + \delta s_a^w(f_a) \tag{1}$$

In Eq. (1), $T_a^w(f_a)$ is the total travel cost on link a at day w and comprises of the actual travel cost, $t_a^w(f_a)$, and the predicted cost, $s_a^w(f_a)$. f_a is the flow along link a and δ is a parameter that reflects drivers' behaviors. The sensitivity of drivers to the routing information is tested through an incremental increase in the value of δ. $t_a^w(f_a)$ is the BPR (Bureau of Public Roads) function as shown in Eq. (2) and $s_a^w(f_a)$ is the function of traffic flows in Eqs. (3) and (4).

$$t_a^w(f_a) = t_{ao}^w[1+0.15(\frac{f_a}{c_a})^4] \tag{2}$$

$$s_a^w(f_a) = \beta_1 t_a^w(f_a) + \beta_2 t_a^{w-1}(f_a) + \beta_3 t_a^{w-2}(f_a)\,. \tag{3}$$

$$\sum_{i=1}^{3} \beta_i = 1\,. \tag{4}$$

In the above, t_{ao}^w and c_a are the free-flow travel time and the capacity on link a at day w, respectively. The predicted link travel cost, $s_a^w(f_a)$, is calculated by the moving average method that involves the current and previous link travel-times with a weighting factor of β_i $(i = 1,2,3)$.

3.2 Provision of traffic information

Traffic information plays an important role in drivers' route-choice behaviors and is classified into individual system information and collective system information. Equally, the provision of traffic information also falls into two categories: minimizing the travel cost for the driver (user equilibrium guidance) and minimizing the travel cost for the network as a whole (system optimality guidance). The selection of a route-guidance strategy and its provision to drivers has recently become a key issue for traffic managers. There exist several strategies with respect to management purposes and also exist conflicts of interest between the equipped drivers, who want to improve their travel times, and traffic managers, whose objective is to reduce the overall traffic congestion. One of the solutions to this problem is a strategy that combines the objectives of the user and the system. The three information strategies that are considered in this research are the 'User Optimality [UO] strategy', 'System Optimality [SO] strategy', and 'Mixed Optimality [MO] strategy'. The first strategy, UO routing, is implemented through user equilibrium assignment with an average travel cost on each link as follows.

$$\text{[UO strategy]}\ s_a^w(f_a)\,. \tag{5}$$

For implementing the second strategy, viz., SO routing, a system optimal assignment is performed with a marginal link travel cost as above.

$$\text{[SO strategy]}\ s_a^w(f_a) + f_a \frac{\partial s_a^w}{\partial f_a}\,. \tag{6}$$

Lastly, the mixed optimality strategy that is considered is as follows.

$$\text{[MO strategy]}\ s_a^w(f_a) + \gamma f_a \frac{\partial s_a^w}{\partial f_a}\,. \tag{7}$$

In the above, γ is a parameter between 0 and 1. When γ is 0, the MO routing strategy is equivalent to the UE routing strategy; when γ is 1, it is equivalent to the SO routing strategy. Another important parameter in a traffic information system is the degree of information guidance. Guided travelers determine their routes and modes by the expected travel times and almost no perceptual errors. In contrast, unguided travelers get much more inaccurate information on travel conditions. In the research, we assume that a guided driver follows the user-equilibrium (UE) principle and an unguided driver follows the stochastic user equilibrium (SUE) principle with some variance in the travel time. Thus, the link travel time of an unguided driver can be formulated as:

$$C_a^{w,unguid} \sim N(T_a^w, \theta T_a^w) \quad (8)$$

In the above, $C_a^{w,unguid}$ follows a normal distribution with mean, T_a^w, and variance, θT_a^w. θ is a constant and may be interpreted as the variance of the perceived travel time over link a.

3.3 Solution algorithm

The solution algorithm in the chapter is based on the method of Vuren et al. (1991), which was originally proposed by Vliet et al. (1986) for solving the multi-class user equilibrium assignment problem, and the method of successive averages (MSA) for stochastic network loading with a probit model, which assumes that the random variable is normally distributed with the mean and variance of the link travel time as shown in Eq. (8). MSA is based on a predetermined move size along the direction of descent. Vliet et al. proved that the algorithm converged to a Wardrop equilibrium for each class. The solution algorithm used in the research can be described as follows.

[step 0] Initialization.

Set the iteration number, n=1.

Day: w=1.

Initialize the following.

Information strategy, γ.

Degree of information compliance, δ.

Dispersion parameter of the link travel time for each user-class i, θ_i.

For each user-class i, perform an all-or-nothing assignment based on the initial link travel time, which yields the link flow, f_{ai}^n.

[step 1] Calculate $F_a^n = \sum_i f_{ai}^n$ and the

link cost, $t_a^{w,n}$, corresponding to F_a^n.

[step 2] Traffic information strategy.

2.1 Calculate the predicted link cost, $s_{ai}^{w,n}(f_{ai}^n)$, based on the information strategy.

2.2 Calculate the link travel cost for each user-class, i:

$$T_{ai}^{w,n}(f_{ai}^n) = (1-\delta)t_{ai}^{w,n}(f_{ai}^n) + \delta s_{ai}^{w,n}(f_{ai}^n).$$

[step 3] For each user-class, i:

3.1 Sample a set of link error terms, $\{\varepsilon_{ai}\}$, from the normal distribution by a pseudo-randomization process and set $C_{ai}^{w,n} = T_{ai}^{w,n}(f_{ai}^n) + \varepsilon_{ai}$,

where $\varepsilon_{ai} \sim N(T_{ai}^{w,n}(f_{ai}^n), \theta_{ai} T_{ai}^{w,n}(f_{ai}^n))$.

3.2 Perform an all-or-nothing assignment for this user-class using the randomized costs, $\{C_{ai}^{w,n}\}$, which yields a set of user-class link flows, $\{y_{ai}^n\}$.

3.3 Update the flows for this user-class:

$$f_{ai}^{n+1} = f_{ai}^{n} + (1/n)(y_{ai}^{n} - f_{ai}^{n}).$$

3.4 Set

$$F_{a}^{n+1} = F_{a}^{n} + f_{ai}^{n+1} - f_{ai}^{n}.$$

[step 4] Convergence criterion.
If convergence is attained, stop.
Otherwise, set $n = n+1$ and go to step 1.
[step 5] If $w \geq days$, stop.
Else, $w := w+1$ and go to step 1.

4. Numerical calculations

In order to evaluate the model and information strategies suggested, two example networks are used. The first example involves a simple network with one origin-destination pair that is connected by two routes. The second example is a medium-sized network with several origin-destination pairs; it considers various information strategies in detail.

4.1 A simple network

A numerical example is presented to illustrate the application and assessment of the developed MDSA model. The example network is shown in Figure 1. The input data, such as the link capacity, free-flow cost, and the parameters of compliance and variance, are also shown in Table 1. It is assumed that there is one origin-destination pair from node 1 to node 4 with trip demands of 1500.

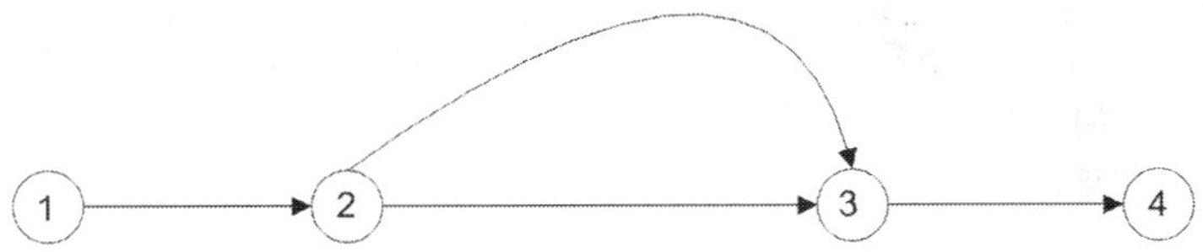

Fig. 1. Simple example network.

Network specification	
Capacity	1000(vehicle/hour)
Free-flow time	60 (sec)
User-class data	
Information compliance (δ)	0.0~1.0 by 0.2
Variance of perception (θ)	0.0/ 0.5/ 1.0
Trip demand (veh/h)	1500
Study period	15 days

Table 1. Input data for the example.

Figures 2 and 3 show the evolution of the total travel-time in the consideration of multiple user-classes in which the parameter, θ, represents the user class. The total travel-time is lower in the early days as the compliance with information increases, that is, as the perceptual error decreases. However, as days elapse, the total travel-time converges to a certain value and no more benefits are realized.

Figure 3 and Table 2 show the variation of the total travel-time with the guidance level and the perceptual error on the first day. It is worth noting that the total travel-time is affected significantly by the perceptual error (θ) and does not decrease as the compliance (δ) with information increases. These results that are derived from the present research show that the effect of the provision of traffic information is influenced by many variables, e.g., the trip-demand level, compliance with information, variance of travel-time perceptions, etc.

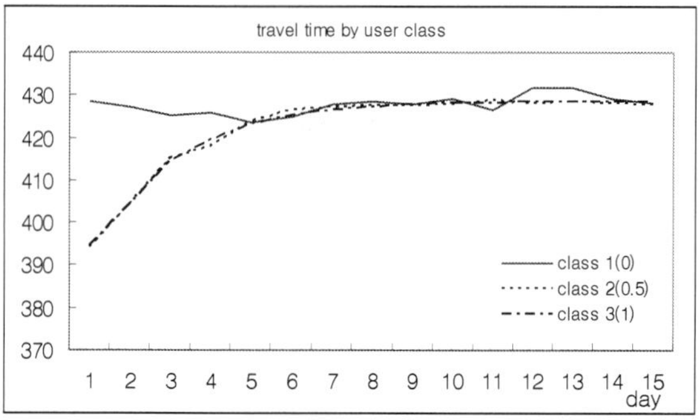

Fig. 2. Variation of the travel time by user class.

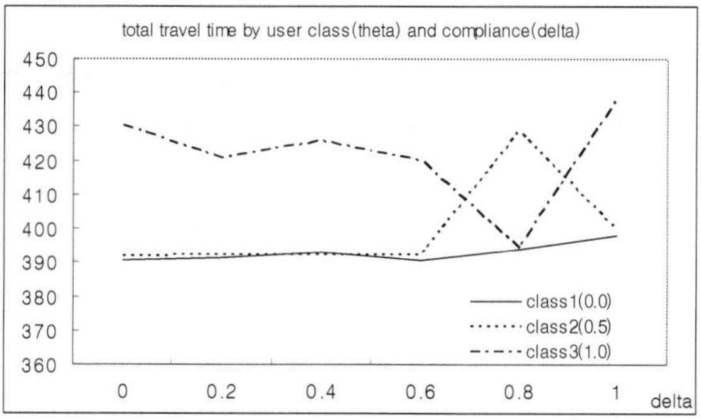

Fig. 3. Variation of the travel time by compliance.

δ	Class 1 (θ=0.0)	Class 2 (θ=0.5)	Class 3 (θ=1.0)
0	390.6	391.7	430.1
0.2	391.3	392	420.8
0.4	392.9	392	425.6
0.6	390.7	392	419.9
0.8	394	428.4	394.3
1	398	399.6	438.1

Table 2. The total travel-time for varying degrees of compliance (δ) for each user-class.

4.2 A large network

The traffic information strategy for multiple user-classes is implemented in more detail with a larger network than in the first example. The network considered is Sioux Falls, SD, USA, which consists of 24 nodes and 76 links. The link impedance is the BPR (Bureau of Public Roads) cost function with the parameters of α (0.15) and β (4).

The effects of information strategies are evaluated under the following scenarios.

Three classes of user: The first class comprises guided drivers. The third class is that of unguided drivers, while the second class refers to drivers who are partially guided/unguided. Each class of drivers aims to minimize its own cost of travel. Guided drivers are provided with perfect information. They totally adhere to the guidance systems; thus, they follow UE behaviors. Unguided drivers, however, in general, fail to do so because of their imperfect knowledge of the traffic conditions; therefore, they follow SUE behaviors. In SUE, the effects of existing errors in journey-time prediction or of drivers imply the lack of complete adherence to guidance. From the viewpoint of the parameter, θ, viz., the variance of the perceived travel time, the UE condition is identical to the SUE condition when θ equals zero. In this research, the three user-classes are assumed to have values of θ of 0.0, 0.4, and 0.8, respectively.

Six different degrees of compliance: To assess the effect of information in terms of the degree of compliance, six different levels are implemented for δ: 0%; 20%; 40%; 60%; 80%; and 100%.

Five different information-provision strategies: γ is a parameter that represents information strategies that range from 0 to 1. When γ is 0.0, User-Optimal (UO) routing is adopted. When γ is 1.0, System-Optimal (SO) routing is adopted. A Mixed-Optimal routing strategy has values that range between 0.0 and 1.0.

Figures 4 and 5 show the evolution of the total travel-time in the consideration of multiple user-classes that have specific values of θ; Figure 4 shows the absolute values, while Figure 5 shows the values normalized with respect to the initial value (at day 1). With guidance, the first class, cls1 in Figure 4, has perfect knowledge of the traffic conditions and the second class, cls2, comes next with some variance of the travel time. Thus, the third class has the highest degree of uncertainty in the network. For each user-class, there exist some fluctuations in the early days. As days elapse, however, their travel-times converge to

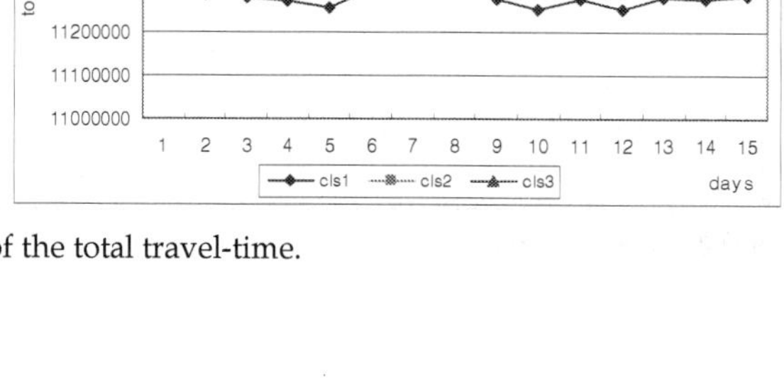

Fig. 4. Variation of the total travel-time.

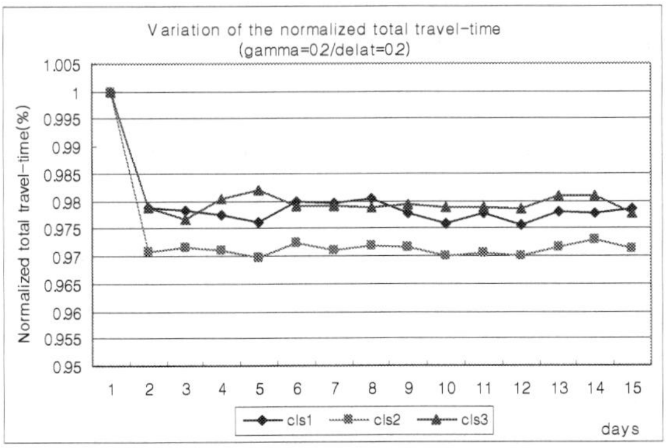

Fig. 5. Variation of the normalized total travel-time.

steady-state values. As one would expect, the first user-class has the lowest value of the total travel-time and the others follow behind with rather insignificant differences between them. After day 1, as shown in Figure 5, the second user-class, relatively speaking, improves its travel time more than the others. Across the three classes, the total travel-time is reduced by 2~4 percentage points with the lapse of time. This benefit comes from the decrease in the perceptual error with respect to the travel time.

Figure 6 and Table 3 depict the relationship between the compliance with traffic information (δ) and the total travel-time for each routing strategy. Note that the effect of routing is expressed as a ratio with respect to the total travel-time under the base case of no compliance with information; thus, values below 1.0 correspond to an improvement in the system performance in comparison with the case of no compliance with traffic information.

As the value of δ increases, as shown in Figure 6, the total travel-times reduce but the differences are not large across information strategies, which are captured as values of gamma (γ):γ=0.0 for the UO strategy and γ=1.0 for the SO strategy. This result implies that

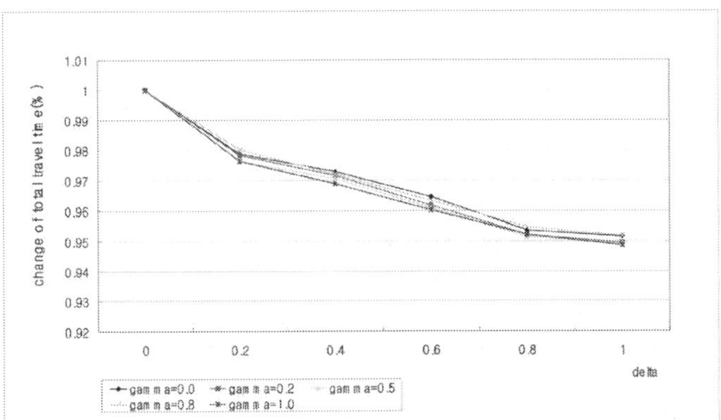

Fig. 6. Relationship of the travel-time reduction to compliance for each strategy.

each routing strategy helps to improve the system. In conjunction with the information effect, Lim et al. (1998) established the adverse impact of traffic information in the case of en-route information provision. When a traffic manager adopts the UO strategy for drivers and the drivers absolutely follow the provided information, the total travel-time even increases above the normalized value of 1.0. Such worsening occurs when drivers switch their routes, which can result in traffic congestion on the alternative route. This phenomenon is a new 'Braess Paradox' that results from the provision of information to drivers. The paradox may arise when traffic managers adopt the UO strategy and drivers take routes for only minimizing their travel times with no consideration of other network users. These worsening cases are also found in some other studies, e.g., Mahmassani et al. (1991), Ben-Akiva et al. (1991), and Emmerink et al. (1995). Ben-Akiva et al. mentioned this kind of adverse effect in more detail. They explained that it may occur on the condition that drivers who receive common information may tend to make similar route-decisions and departure-time decisions, thereby increasing congestion. Fortunately, such worsening did not occur in this research, as shown in Figure 4.

Delta	*Gamma=0.0*	*Gamma=0.2*	*Gamma=0.5*	*Gamma=0.8*	*Gamma=1.0*
0	1	1	1	1	1
0.2	0.978742	0.978298	0.97642	0.980238	0.976377
0.4	0.972921	0.971633	0.970558	0.972052	0.968887
0.6	0.964496	0.961651	0.960782	0.963235	0.960098
0.8	0.953447	0.952067	0.9514	0.954563	0.952074
1	0.951523	0.949395	0.949141	0.951771	0.94855

Table 3. Variation of the total travel-time for each routing strategy and level of compliance.

For different levels of demand, evolutions of the total travel-time are shown in Figure 7 in the case when γ=0.5 and an MO strategy is adopted. Generally, the magnitude of the

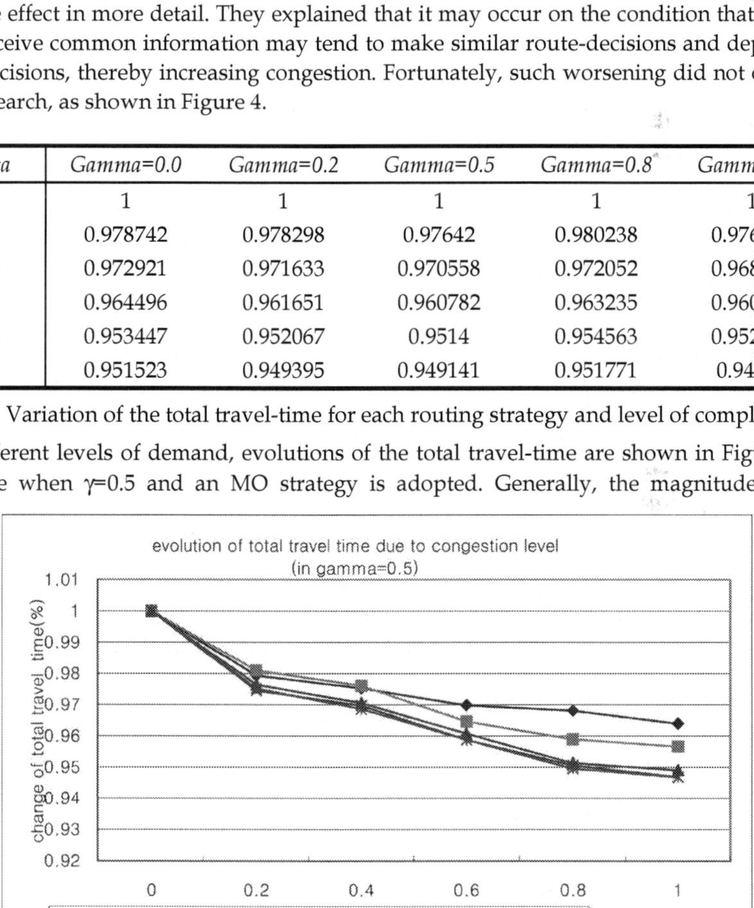

Fig. 7. Evolution of the total travel-time for various levels of congestion.

information effect depends on the value of δ, the degree of compliance. As the figure explains, the more are the drivers who follow the traffic information that is provided by the traffic center, the more benefits we will realize. There, however, exist differences in the information effect as the level of congestion increases. The reason is that when traffic congestion becomes heavier, more routes will be used for minimizing the travel cost. Figure 8 illustrates the evolution of the travel time for each user-class with rising levels of congestion when γ=0.5 and δ=0.6. Similar to Figure 7, in all cases, the travel time saving becomes greater as the level of congestion increases. However, as we would expect, there are also differences between user-classes, although they are not significant.

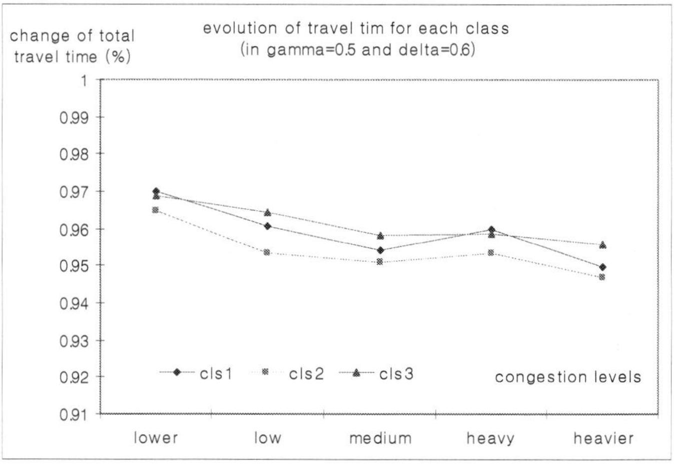

Fig. 8. Evolution of the total travel-time for each user-class.

5. Conclusions

This chapter presents an MDSA model and assesses the effect of traffic information according to the level of information. The MDSA model that is based on previous experiences considers the varying perceptual errors and varying dynamic traffic behaviors of users. Although it may not fully describe the behaviors of travelers, it is accepted here as a reasonable approximation to the long-term average route-choice of travelers under steady-state conditions. The model is also able to more precisely simulate the network conditions than deterministic traffic assignment models in that it is more flexible in reflecting drivers' behaviors. The important results that arise from this study are as follows. Firstly, the results show the traffic patterns of multiple user-classes (MUC) on a link, wherein each class has a unique travel-time. Secondly, this research also shows that the effect of traffic information is influenced by some factors, such as demand conditions, compliance with information, variance of travel-time perceptions, etc. Lastly, the effect of the provision of traffic information exists under the conditions of proper demand, compliance with information, and the variance of travel-time perceptions.

Further studies related to this field of research would include the following issues. Firstly, the effects of traffic information are tested here in normal conditions, not those of traffic incidents. Therefore, it is necessary to evaluate the effects under traffic incidents. Secondly, elastic demands should be considered for representing departure-time and route-choice behaviors.

6. References

Baek, S., Lim, Y., Lim, K. (1997) Multi-class dynamic stochastic assignment. Paper presented at fourth World Congress on Intelligent Transport Systems, Berlin, October

Ben-Akiva, M., De Palma, A., Kaysi, I. (1991). Dynamic network models and driver information system, Transportation Research(A), Vol.25A, 251-266

Breheret, L., Hounsell, N.B. and McDonald, M. (1990) The Simulation of route guidance and traffic incidents, Presented at 22nd Annual Universities Transport Studies Group Conference, Hatfield,UK

Emmerink, R.H., K.W. Axhausen, P. Nijkamp and Rietveld, P. (1995) The potential of information provision in a simulated road transport network with non-recurrent congestion, Transportation Research(C), Vol.3C,293-309

Mahmassani, H.S. and Jayakrishnan, R. (1991) System performance and user response under real-time information in a congested traffic corridor, Transportation Research(A),Vol.25A,293-308

Janson, B. (1991). Dynamic traffic assignment for urban road networks, transportation Research 25B, 143-161

Koutsopoulos, H.N. and Lotan, T. (1990) Motorist information systems and recurrent traffic congestion: sensitivity analysis of expected results, Transportation Research Record 1281, 145-158

Wynter, L.M. (1995) Advances in the theory and application of the muticlass traffic assignment problem, Ph.D. dissertation, Ecole National Des Ponts Et Chaussees

Lim,Y., Baek, S., Lim, K. (1997) Assessment of traffic information with stochastic assignment, EASTS '97 Conference, Oct., 1997, Seoul

Lim,Y., Lee, S. (1998) Traffic management schemes with simulation-based traffic assignment, paper for 8th WCTR, Antwerp, Belgium, July 12-17

Ran, B. and Boyce, D. (1994). Dynamic Urban Transportation Network Models, Lecture Notes in Economics and Mathematical Systems, Springer-Verlag.

Roy Thomas (1991). Traffic Assignment Techniques, Gower publishing company.

Sheffi, Y. (1985). Urban transportation networks: equilibrium analysis with mathematical programming methods, Prentice Hall, New Jersey.

Smith, J.C., Russam, K. (1989) Some possible effects of AUTOGUIDE on traffic in London, IEEE, Toronto, Canada, April

Hu, Ta-Yin, H.,Mahmassani(1997) Day-to-day evolution of network flows under real-time information and reactive signal control, Trnasportation Research 5C,51-69

Vliet, V.D., Bergman, T. and Scheltes, W.H. (1986) Equilibrium traffic assignment with multiple user classes, proceeding of the PTRC Summer Annual Meeting

Vuren, T.V., Vliet, D.V. (1992). Route Choice and Signal Control, Ashgate publishing company.

Vuren, T.V., Watling, D.P. (1991). A multiple user class assignment model for route guidance, TRR 1306.

5

A Framework for Extracting Information from Semi-Structured Web Data Sources

Mahmoud Shaker[1], Hamidah Ibrahim[2],
Aida Mustapha[3] and Lili Nurliyana Abdullah[4]
Department of Computer Science
Faculty of Computer Science and Information Technology
Universiti Putra Malaysia, 43400 Serdang,
Malaysia

1. Introduction

Nowadays, many users use web search engines to find and gather information. User faces an increasing amount of various semi-structured information sources. The issue of correlating, integrating and presenting related information to users becomes important. When a user uses a search engine such as Yahoo and Google to seek a specific information, the results are not only information about the availability of the desired information, but also information about other pages on which the desired information is mentioned. The number of selected pages is enormous. Therefore, the performance capabilities, the overlap among results for the same queries and limitations of web search engines are an important and large area of research. Extracting information from the web data sources also becomes very important because the massive and increasing amount of diverse semi-structured information sources in the Internet that are available to users, and the variety of web pages making the process of information extraction from web a challenging problem. This chapter presents a framework for extracting and classifying semi-structured web data sources. The framework is able to extract relevant information from different web data sources, and classify the extracted information based on a given standard classification. In this chapter, we focus on the Nokia products, as to the best of our knowledge this is the only product that has complete and complex standard classifiers. At the present time, the Internet is general and many people use the Internet to find information. A variety of web pages and the frequently changing of information in web data sources make searching and extracting information very difficult. When Internet users want to get information about Nokia products for example, they first visit search engines such as Yahoo and Google, and then visit all web sites suggested by the search engine. Many researchers such as Guntis Arnicans and Girts Karnitis 2006; Sung Won Jung *et al* 2001; Srinivas Vadrevu *et al* 2007; and Horacio Saggion *et al* 2008 work on extraction of information from web data sources in different domains (traveling, products, business intelligence) but these researches deal with limited web data sources and users still need to use the search engines such as Yahoo and Google to collect more information. We proposed a framework for extracting information from different web data sources. The components of the proposed framework include *Query*

Interface (QI) which is used for accepting user's queries and searching web pages based on the user's queries through search engine, *Information Extraction* (IE) which is used for extracting and classifying the web pages obtained from QI and converting the extracted and classified information into text form, and *Relevant Information Analyzer* (RIA) which is used for determining the relevant information extracted from Information Extraction (IE). The rest of the chapter is organized as follows. In section 2, we explain the concepts related to a typical Information Extraction (IE). In section 3, the previous works related to this research are reported. In section 4, we present the proposed framework. Conclusion is presented in the final section 5.

2. Concepts of Information Extraction (IE)

Information Extraction (IE) is originally the task of locating specific information from a natural language document and is a particular useful sub-area of Natural Language Processing (NLP). The dramatic growth in the number and size of on-line textual information sources has led to an increasing research interest in the information extraction problem (Line Eikvil 1999). Information Extraction is a form of shallow document processing that involves populating a database with values automatically extracted from documents. Over the past decade, researchers have developed a rich family of generic Information Extraction techniques that are suitable for a wide variety of sources from rigidly formatted documents such as HTML generated automatically from a template to natural-language documents (Nicholas Kushmerick 2003). Information Extraction promises to be a sizeable augmentation to the search engines available today, and it can extract precisely the information that the user wants from this set of documents, and provide the user with exactly the information that is required without the level of involvement that this task requires currently (Chia-Hui Chang *et al* 2006). Information Extraction is to discover relevant information without any training (Wolfgang Gatterbauer *et al* 2007). Information Extraction is the identification or pre-processing, consequent or concurrent classification, and structuring into semantic classes making the information more suitable for information processing tasks (Rik De Busser 2006). Information Extraction fills the fields in a table by automatically extracting sub-sequences of human readable text. Sub-sequences are the useful pieces of information in the documents which are taken as input to produce fixed format unambiguous data as output (Line Eikvil 1999; Chia-Hui Chang *et al* 2006). Figure 1 illustrates the taxonomy of Information Extraction which consists of different type of data as input and the approaches that have been proposed for extracting information from semi-structured data. The web tables provide more organized information, summarized information, and conciseness in expressing knowledge (Jeong-Woo Son et al 2008). Therefore, focus is given more on the structure-based which is the main focus of this chapter.

We can differentiate the various Information Extraction approaches by the type of data that are used as origin, namely: (i) structured data, (ii) semi-structured data, and (iii) unstructured data (Katharina Kaiser and Silvia Miksch 2007).

a. Structured Data: Structured data is a meaning of the particular data is assigned as well as it contains sufficient structure to allow unambiguous parsing and recognition of information. Thus, extracting relevant information and the assignment of a meaning can be eased (Katharina Kaiser and Silvia Miksch 2007) as well as quite simple techniques are sufficient for extracting information from structured data provided that the format is known (Line Eikvil 1999).

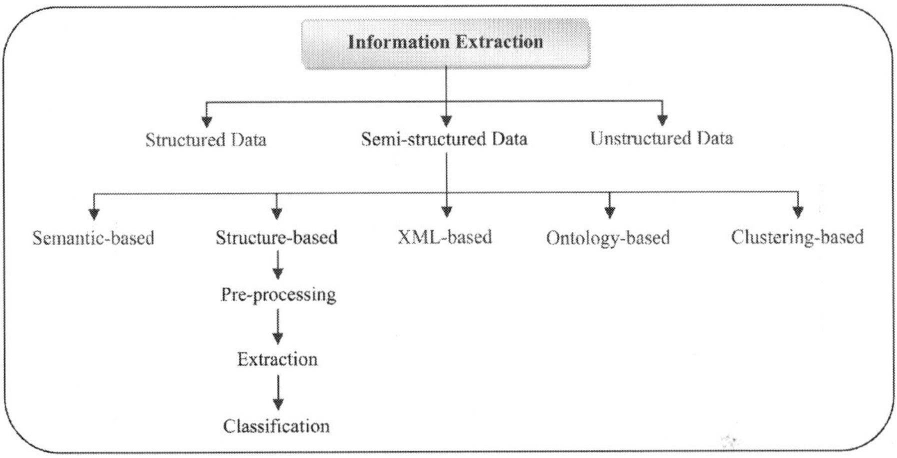

Fig. 1. The taxonomy of Information Extraction

b. Semi-Structured Data: Semi-structure means that it lacks of formatting structured. In semi-structured data, there is no separation between the data and the schema, and the amount of structure used depends on the purpose. No semantic is applied to semi-structured data and analysis of words or sentences is required for extracting the relevant information. XML and HTML pages contain semi-structured data, but HTML is rather more human-oriented or presentation-oriented (Katharina Kaiser and Silvia Miksch 2007). Semi-structured data refers to data with some of the following characteristics (Man I. Lam and Zhiguo Gong 2005):
   - The schema may be implicit in the data and it is not given in advance.
   - The schema may be changing frequently with respect to the size of the data. Therefore, the schema is relatively large.
   - The schema is attributive rather than prescriptive, i.e. it describes the current state of the data.
   - The values of the same attribute may be of differing types and the data is not typed powerfully.
   - The data transfer format may be portable.
   - It can represent the information of some data sources that cannot be constrained by schema.
   - It provides a flexible format for data exchange between different types of databases.

   Information Extraction from semi-structured data such as web pages which contain an enormous quantity of information which is usually formatted for human users is a useful yet complex task and provides a special challenge (Chia-Hui Chang *et al* 2006).

c. Unstructured Data: Unstructured data can be, for example, plain text. It does not imply that the data is structurally incoherent (in that case it would simply be nonsense), but rather that its information is encoded in such a way that makes it difficult for computers to immediately interpret it (Rik De Busser 2006). Linguistic knowledge is required to extract information from unstructured data as well as Natural Language Processing (NLP) techniques are deployed to design rules for locating specific pieces of information or facts in the unstructured data (e.g., text) and using these facts to fill a database (Line Eikvil 1999; Katharina Kaiser and Silvia Miksch 2007).

Information Extraction is performed on unstructured data, semi-structured data, and structured data. Typically, techniques from Natural Language Processing (NLP) are often used for unstructured data and tend to be slow and this can be a problem as the volume of document collections on semi-structured data such as web pages can be large and the extraction is often expected to be performed on the fly. Therefore, NLP techniques are however not well suited for structured and semi-structured data as these techniques require full grammatical sentences (Line Eikvil 1999). The web pages provide a large and growing amount of information stores, which can be reached by manual browsing using a search engine. When a user does a keyword search on a search engine, a large number of web pages may result that might be very time consuming to check through. These web pages are often isolated with no effective connections between them, and respective access service live independently. This scenario motivates the need for information extraction from the web pages which can extract and group information from independent sources (Chia-Hui Chang *et al* 2006). Kostyantyn Shchekotykhin *et al* (2007) explained that much useful information is presented in tabular form on the web pages and Wolfgang Gatterbauer *et al* (2007) showed that extracting information from web tables is possible without reliance on heavy linguistic techniques tuned to the domain of interest in addition to the tables are interesting because they present information in a condensed, rather simple, and well structured way. Tables on the web pages are used for both (i) the genuine purposes that are presenting certain types of data to users which are formatted in rows and columns and (ii) helping construct the layout of a web page. Thus, tables are the richest sources of information on the web pages. David Buttler *et al* (2001) observed in their tests of 50 web sites with over 2000 web pages that the tag <TABLE> is used as object separator (18% of time) more than the other tags such as tag <P> 10% of time, tag <li> 8% of time, tag <hr> 6% of time, tag <ul> 2% of time, tag <DIV> 2% of time, and tag <a> 2% of time. Therefore, the relevant information in a web page that the user needs which must be extracted by IE are found between the tag <TABLE> and </TABLE> (Guntis Arnicans and Girts Karnitis 2006; Fatima Ashraf *et al* 2008). Each table is formatted in rows and columns, whereas it is distinguished in head and body according to meaning. In HTML documents, the tags such as <TABLE>, <TR>, and <TD> are reserved for table structure (Sung-won Jung *et al* 2001). Information Extraction systems do not attempt to understand the text in the input documents but they analyze those portions of each document that contain relevant information. Relevance is determined by predefined domain guidelines which specify what types of information that the system is expected to find (Line Eikvil 1999). Therefore, IE application needs lexicons to start with (e.g. attributes which specify the important information that the user needs to know for identification and utilization of the described objects). Thus, the acquisition and enrichment of lexical or semantic resources is a critical issue in Information Extraction. Standard Classification Scheme is used to identify the entities that have a form of existence in a given domain and specify their essential properties and it is a characterization vocabulary. Information Extraction techniques are then used to locate these entities from the web pages to be presented to the user (B. Chandrasokaran *et al* 1999; Stefan Clepce *et al* 2007).

3. Related works

The previous approaches are organized based on the type of technique used by each approach to extract information i.e. Semantic-based, Structure-based, XML-based, Ontology-based, and Clustering-based. The details of each approach are discussed below.

Semantic-based: With the advent of the Internet, more information is available electronically, and the information on the Internet is generated in textual form which differs from the web page to another in semantics. Semantics generally deals with the relationships between signs and concepts (mental signs). Different kinds of semantics are Lexical Semantics, Statistical Semantics, Structural Semantics, and Prototype Semantics. Srinivas Vadrevu *et al* (2007) have focused on information extraction from web pages using presentation regularities and domain knowledge. They argued that there is a need to divide a web page into information blocks or several segments before organizing the content into hierarchical groups and during this process (partition a web page) some of the attribute labels of values may be missing. **Structure-based**: The structure based approaches employ assumptions about the general structure of tables (i.e., <TABLE> tags) on the web pages (Wolfgang Gatterbauer *et al* 2007; Jeong-Woo Son *et al* 2008). Wolfgang Gatterbauer *et al* (2007) have proposed an approach for extracting information from web tables. Their approach analyzes any given web page for the existence of tabular data, recognizes relations as implied by their spatial arrangement, extracts a number of n-tuples together with hierarchical information about relations between their entries and saves them in structured data format. The task of extracting web tables is formulated as the task of (i) finding all frames for a given web page, (ii) discerning those which adhere to the definition of tables where a 2-D grid is semantically significant from lists and other frames intended for non-relational layout purposes, (iii) transferring the content into a topological grid description in which logical cells are flush with neighboring cells and their spatial relations are explicit. Jeong-Woo Son *et al* (2008) have proposed an approach to discriminate web tables using a composite kernel which combines a parse tree kernel and a linear kernel. They proposed three kinds of features to capture both kinds of web table information which is composed of structural and content ones. First, the parse tree is adopted to reflect the structural information. Second, the content type features are adopted to capture the content information. Finally, they combined both kinds of information using a composite kernel. The main obstacle of their approach comes from the difficulty of generating relevant features for the discrimination. **XML-based**: There are several challenges in extracting information from a semi-structured web page such as the lack of a schema, ill formatting, high update frequency, and semantic heterogeneity of the information. In order to overcome these challenges, some researchers have proposed approaches for transforming the page into a format called Extensible Mark-up Language (XML) (Man I. Lam and Zhiguo Gong 2005). Man I. Lam and Zhiguo Gong (2005) proposed a system which used different methodologies to extract the information. The extraction task is only individual page based. It means that all the fields for the same record are supposed to be contained in the same page. However, in many other situations, the fields may be located in different relevant pages, such as several linked web pages. **Ontology-based**: Ontology is a branch of philosophy and structures of objects, properties, events, processes and relations in every area of reality. Horacio Saggion *et al* (2008) proposed the MUSING project (Multi-industry, Semantic-based next generation business intelligence). The MUSING project needs to cover many semantic categories including locations, organizations and specific business events to help companies that want to take their business overseas and concerned in knowing the best place to exploit. **Clustering-based**: Cluster analysis has been playing an important role in solving many problems in medicine, psychology, biology, sociology, pattern recognition, and image processing. Clustering algorithms attempt to assess the interaction among patterns by organizing patterns into clusters such that patterns within a cluster are more similar to each other than are patterns belonging to different clusters (Fatima Ashraf *et al* 2008). Fatima Ashraf *et al* (2008) have employed clustering techniques for automatic information extraction from HTML documents containing HTML data. They proposed a system which is called ClusTex. They extend the work in Fatima Ashraf and Reda Alhajj (2007) by testing their proposed system in different domains such as Cell phone sales and Marathon schedule. If the tokens of one kind differ from each other in format, then this leads to an incorrect clustering of some tokens.

4. The proposed framework

In this section, we discuss and present the components of the proposed framework for extracting information from semi-structured web data sources. This framework consists of three components, namely: (i) Query Interface (QI), (ii) Information Extraction (IE), and (iii) Relevant Information Analyzer (RIA) as shown in Figure 2. In the following we discuss each of this component in details.

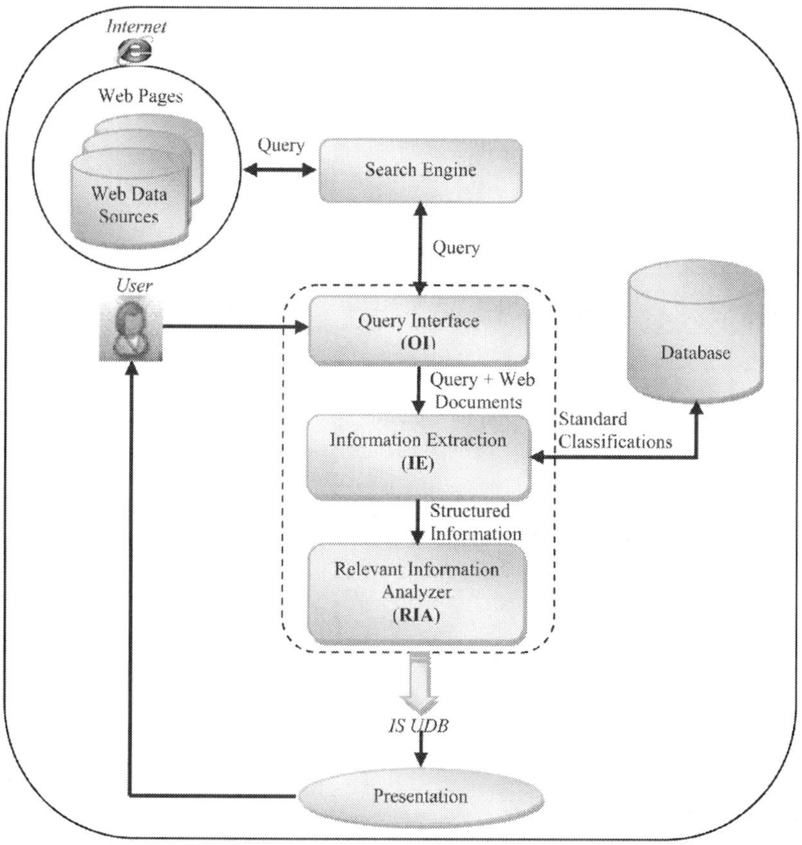

Fig. 2. The proposed framework

4.1 The Query Interface (QI)

The Query Interface is the key entry to the web and tool for accessing information. A user writes a product name (query) in the Query Interface, and the query is send to a search engine which searches the web data sources. The results of the query and web documents are saved in folders by the Query Interface as HTM files. Example of a simple query is shown in Figure 3.

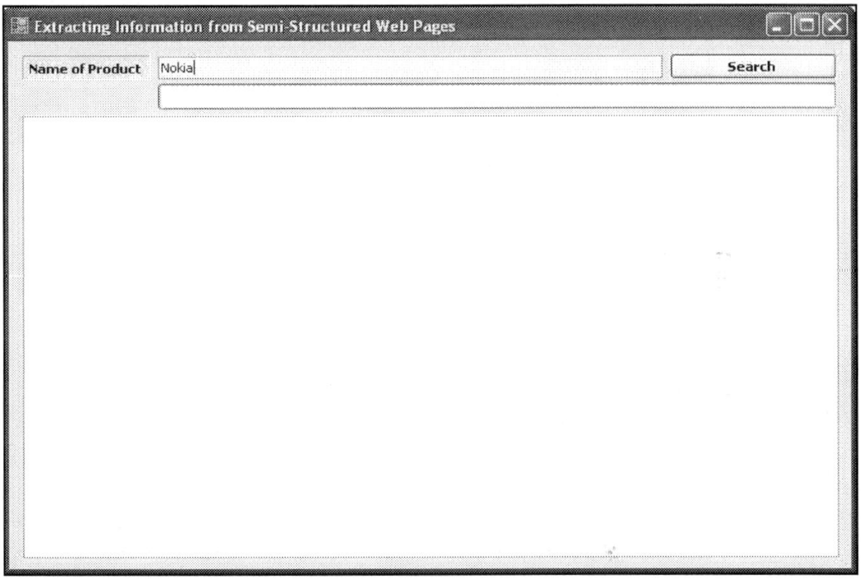

Fig. 3. The Query Interface

Figure 4 illustrates examples of the results of a query and the web documents which are stored in folders.

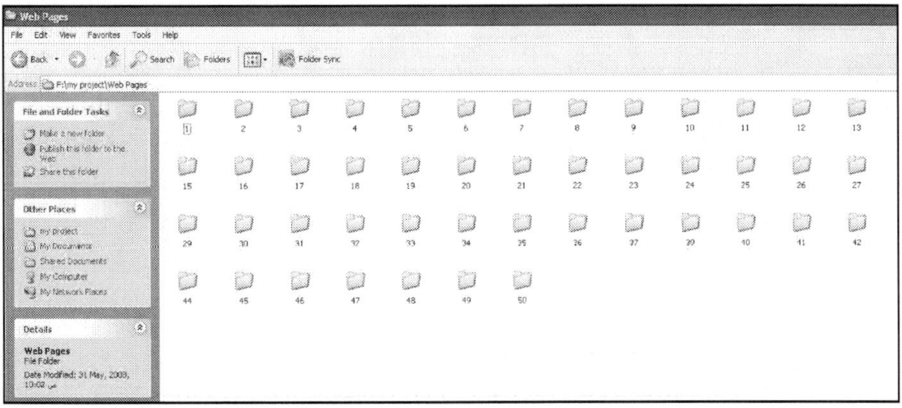

Fig. 4. Examples of results of a query and web documents

4.2 Information Extraction (IE)

The IE extracts and classifies the web pages that are stored in the folders, and converts them into text form. The details steps are discussed below.

Step 1: Based on the standard classification of Nokia products such as General, Size, Display, Ringtones, Memory, Data, Features, and Battery (Guntis Arnicans & Girts Karnitis 2006; Domenico Beneventano & Stefania Magnani 2004) (the attributes are shown in Figure 5) which is stored in database, IE extracts and classifies the web pages. Each kind of product is classified depending on the attributes. Figure 6 illustrates an example of the source code of a web page. IE extracts and classifies only the texts which are found between the tag "<TABLE>" and "</TABLE>". Figure 7 shows an example of information which is saved in an array by IE for matching this information with the standard classification of Nokia products. It illustrates the sub attributes and values of the sub attributes as shown in Figure 8 saved with the symbols "-" and ":" in an array. For example, the sub attribute Brand is saved with the symbol "-" which denotes a sub attribute (web page) and the value Nokia with the symbol ":" which denotes the value of a sub attribute (web page). IE ignores all texts which are not related to the standard classification, that are used for programming HTML web pages such as cellspacing, TBODY, TR, TD, row, href, >, <, /, etc.

Attribute	Index_no
General	1
Size	2
Display	3
Ringtones	4
Memory	5
Data	6
Features	7
Battery	8

Fig. 5. The standard classification of Nokia products

```
<DIV id=pricerunner>
<TABLE style="TEXT-ALIGN: left" cellSpacing=0 cellPadding=0>
 <TBODY>
 <TR>
  <TD class=spec_item>Brand </TD>
  <TD>Nokia </TD></TR>
 <TR>
  <TD class=spec_item>Type </TD>
  <TD>6212 classic </TD></TR>
 <TR>
  <TD class=spec_item>Form factor </TD>
  <TD>Candybar </TD></TR>
 <TR>
  <TD class=spec_item>Color </TD>
  <TD>Black </TD></TR>
 <TR>
```

Fig. 6. Example of the source code of a web page

```
-Brand
:Nokia

-Type
:6212 classic

-Form factor
:Candybar

-Color
:Black
```

Fig. 7. The sub attributes (web page) and values of sub attributes (web page) shown in Figure 7 saved in an array

Step 2: Next IE converts the extracted and classified web page into text form. Figure 8 illustrates the example of the extracted sub attributes and values of the sub attributes, where each line begins with the index of an attribute (the standard classification) that is matched. For example, IE saves the sub attribute *weight* with the index of the attribute *Size*. The matched attributes and sub attributes are then grouped based on the index number. For example, the lines with the index 6 are grouped together as attribute *DATA*, as shown in Figure 9 which illustrates the example of the extracted attributes and sub attributes that are shown in Figure 8 after grouping them based on the index number.
Figure 10 shows the web pages which are extracted, classified, and converted into text form by IE. The texts begin from text 7 until text 37, the IE ignores the web pages which are not related to Nokia products.

```
6- umts
6: Yes

6- hsdpa
6: No

2- weight
2: 123

2- height
2: 87

2- width
2: 78

2- depth
2: 19

8- standbytime(h)
8: 300

8- talktime(m)
8: 240

7- sms
7: Yes

7- email
7: Yes

7- mms
7: Yes

6- bluetooth
6: Yes

6- usb
6: No
```

Fig. 8. The attributes of a web page in a text file with index number of an attribute (the standard classification)

```
2* SIZE
  - weight
      : 123
  - height
      : 87
  - width
      : 78
  - depth
      : 19

3* DISPLAY
  - displaywidth
      : 128
  - displayheight
      : 160
  - lcdsize
      : NA
  - seconddisplay
      : NA

4* RINGTONES
  - voicedialing
      : Yes

5* MEMORY
  - memory
      : NA

6* DATA
  - gprs
      : Yes
  - umts
      : Yes
  - hsdpa
      : No
  - bluetooth
      : Yes
  - usb
      : No

7* FEATURES
  - sms
```

Fig. 9. The attributes of a web page, sub attributes of a web page, and values of sub attributes in a text file after grouping

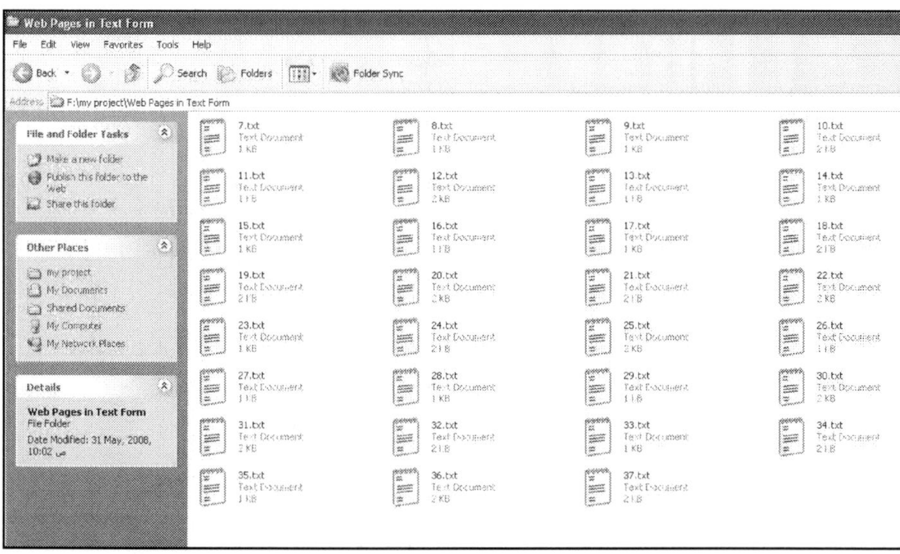

Fig. 10. Web pages in text form

Step 3: Next the IE converts the text (web pages in text form) to structured information. The IE counts the number of extracted sub attributes in each text form, and saves the results in a table. Figure 11 illustrates the number of extracted sub attributes in each text form.

Name of text form	Number of extracted sub attributes in text form
Text 7	24
Text 8	13
Text 9	12
Text 10	13
Text 11	23
Text 12	21
Text 20	42
Text 21	30
Text 22	33
Text 23	1
Text 24	29
Text 25	37
Text 26	22
Text 29	32
...	...
Text 37	28

Fig. 11. The structured information

4.3 Relevant Information Analyzer (RIA)

The function of RIA is to determine the relevant information extracted from Information Extraction (IE) based on the number of attributes available in each text form. The steps performed by RIA are presented below.

Step 1: RIA receives the structured information from IE. Step 2: RIA determines the relevant information extracted from IE based on the number of sub attributes in each text. For example, text 23 has one sub attribute, RIA deletes text 23 because of small number of sub attributes. Sometimes one text (web pages in text form) has the same information found in other text or lesser for the same product, for example text 8 and text 10 have the same number of sub attributes. In this case, RIA deletes one of the texts for reducing the space of storage in the universal database (IS UDB) (Guntis Arnicans & Girts Karnitis 2006). IS UDB receives the rest of the texts from RIA and saved them in universal database. Figure 12 illustrates the results which are displayed to user. A user clicks on any products in the form (Figure 12) then the web sites which have the information about the product appears in a list box (Figure 12).

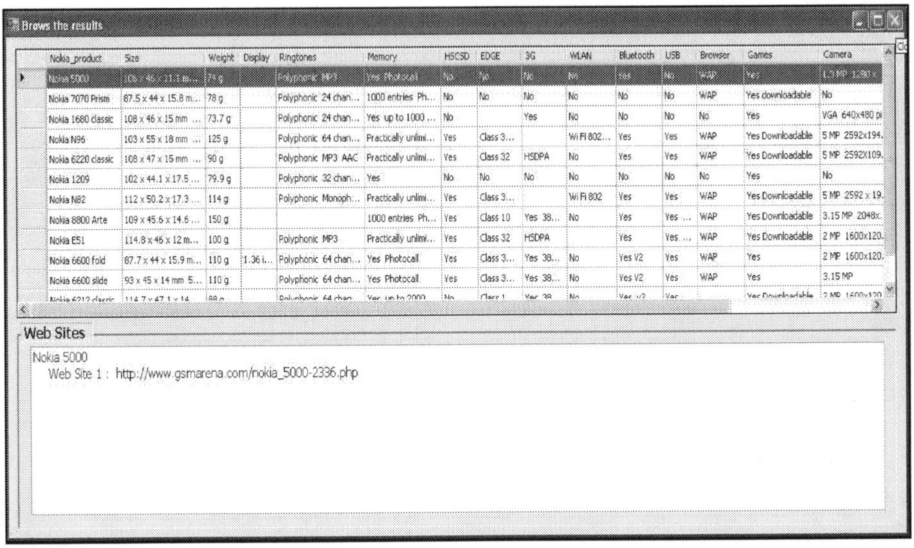

Fig. 12. Browsing the results to user

5. Conclusion

In this chapter, we proposed a framework to search and extract information from different web data sources. The proposed framework provides facilities to the user during search. A user does not need to visit the homepages of companies to get the information about any product, just write the name of product in the Query Interface (QI) and the framework searches all the available web pages related to the text which the user writes in the Query Interface (QI), and the user gets the information with little efforts.

6. References

B. Chandrasokaran, John R. Josophson, and V. Richard Bonjamins (1999). What are Ontologies, and Why Do We Need Them?, *Journal of IEEE Intelligent Systems and Their Applications*, Vol. 14, Issue. 1, pp. 20-26.

Chia-Hui Chang, Mohammed Kayed, Moheb Ramzy Girgis, and Khaled F. Shaalan (2006). A Survey of Web Information Extraction Systems. *Journal of IEEE Transaction on Knowledge and Data Engineering,* Vol. 18, Issue 10, (Oct. 2006) pp. 1411-1428, ISSN: 1041-4347.

David Buttler, Ling Liu, and Calton Pu. 2001. A Fully Automated Object Extraction System for the World Wide Web, *Proceedings of the 21st International Conference on Distributed Computing Systems, Georgia Institute of Technology,* ICDCS, pp. 361-370, ISBN: 0-7695-1077-9, 2001, USA..

Domenico Beneventano and Stefania Magnani (2004). A Framework for the Classification and the Reclassification of Electronic Catalogs, *Proceedings of the 2004 ACM*

Symposium on Applied Computing, pp. 784-788, ISBN: 1-58113-812-1, Nicosia, 2004, Cyprus.

Fatima Ashraf, Tansel Ozyer, and Reda Alhajj (2008). Employing Clustering Techniques for Automatic Information Extraction from HTML Documents. *Journal of IEEE Transactions on Systems, Man, and Cybernetics, Part C: Applications and Reviews*, Vol. 38, (Sept. 2008) pp. 660-673, ISSN: 1094-6977.

Fatima Ashraf and Reda Alhajj (2007). ClusTex: Information Extraction from HTML Pages, *Proceedings of the 21st. International Conference on Advanced Information Networking and Applications Workshops (AINAW'07)*, Vol. 1, pp. 355-360, ISBN: 978-0-7695-2847-2.

Guntis Arnicans and Girts Karnitis (2006). Intelligent Integration of Information from Semi-Structured Web Data Sources on the Base of Ontology and Meta-Models, *Proceedings of the 7th International Baltic Conference*, pp. 177-186, ISBN: 1-4244-0345-6, Vilnius, July 2006, Latvia University, Riga.

Horacio Saggion, Adam Funk, Diana Maynard, and Kalina Bontcheva (2008). Ontology-based Information Extraction for Business Intelligence, In: *Lecture Notes in Computer Science*, pp. 843-856, Springer Berlin, Heidelberg, ISSN: 0302-9743 (Print) 1611-3349 (Online).

Jeong-Woo Son, Jae-An Lee, Seong-Bae Park, Hyun-Je Song, Sang-Jo Lee, and Se-Young Park. 2008. Discriminating Meaningful Web Tables from Decorative Tables using Composite Kernel, *Proceedings of ACM International Conference on Web Intelligence and Intelligent Agent Technology*, Vol. 1, pp. 368-371, ISBN: 978-0-7695-3496-1.

Katharina Kaiser and Silvia Miksch (2007). Modeling Treatment Processes using Information Extraction, In: *Advanced Computational Intelligence Paradigms in Healthcare – 1*, Vol. 48/2007, pp. 189-224, Springer Berlin, Heidelberg, ISSN: 1860-949X (Print) 1860-9503 (Online).

Kostyantyn Shchekotykhin, Dietmar Jannach, and Gerhard Friedrich (2007). Clustering Web Documents with Tables for Information Extraction, *Proceedings of the 4th International Conference on Knowledge Capture*, Canada, pp. 169-170, ISBN: 978-1-59593-643-1.

Line Eikvil (1999). Information Extraction from World Wide Web: A Survey, Norwegian Computing Center, ISBN: 82-539-0429-0.

Man I. Lam and Zhiguo Gong (2005). Web Information Extraction, *Proceedings of IEEE International Conference on Information Acquisition*, pp. 6, ISBN: 0-7803-9303-1, University of Macau, Macao, July 2005, China.

Nicholas Kushmerick (2003). Finite-State Approaches to Web Information Extraction, In: *Information Extraction in the Web Era*, ed. Maria Teresa Pazienza, pp. 77-91, Springer-Verlag Berlin Heidelberg, ISSN: 0302-9743.

Rik De Busser (2006). Information Extraction and Information Technology, In: *Information Extraction: Algorithms and Prospects in a Retrieval Context*, ed. Marie-Francine Moens, pp. 1-22, Springer Netherlands, ISBN: 978-1-4020-4987-3 (Print) 978-1-4020-4993-4 (Online).

Srinivas Vadrevu, Fatih Gelgi, and Hasan Davulcu (2007). Information Extraction from Web Pages using Presentation Regularities and Domain Knowledge. *Journal of World Wide Web*, Springer Netherlands, Arizona State University, USA, Vol. 10, Issue 2, (March 05, 2007) pp. 157-179, ISSN: 1386-145X (Print) 1573-1413 (Online).

Stefan Clepce, Sebastian Schmidt, and Herbert Stoyan (2007). A Hybrid Approach to Product Information Extraction on the Web, In: *Advances in Intelligent Web Mastering*, pp. 68-73. Springer Berlin, Heidelberg, ISBN: 978-3-540-72574-9.

Sung Won Jung, Kyung Hee Sung, Tae Won Park, and Hyuk Chul Kwon (2001). Intelligent Integration of Information on the Internet for Travelers on Demand, *Proceedings of ISIE, IEEE International Symposium*, Vol. 1, pp. 338-342, ISBN: 0-7803-7090-2, Pusin, June 2001, Korea.

Wolfgang Gatterbauer, Paul Bohunsky, Marcus Herzog, Bernhard Krupl, and Bernhard Pollak (2007). Towards Domain-independent Information Extraction from Web Tables, *Proceedings of the 16th International Conference on World Wide Web*, Canada, pp. 71-80, ISBN: 978-1-59593-654-7.

6

A Framework for Localizing Integrity Constraints Checking in Distributed Database

Ali Amer Alwan, Hamidah Ibrahim and Nur Izura Udzir
Department of Computer Science
Faculty of Computer Science and Information Technology
Universiti Putra Malaysia, 43400 Serdang,
Malaysia

1. Introduction

The validity, accuracy, and semantic of data are significant requirements in modern database applications. Semantic data in database is normally represented under the form of integrity constraints. Integrity constraints are properties, typically depending on the nature of the application domain, which must always be satisfied for the data to be considered *consistent*. Maintaining obedience of data with respect to integrity constraints is an essential requirement, since, if some data lacks integrity, then answers to queries cannot be trusted. Databases usually contain massive collections of data that rapidly evolve over time; this makes perfect checking at each update too time consuming a task to be feasible. In this regard, DBMS needs to be extended with the ability to automatically verify that database updates do not introduce any violation of integrity (Martinenghi, 2005; Christiansen & Martinenghi, 2006). The way we pursue here is the so-called *simplification* of integrity constraints. Simplification means to generate a set of integrity tests from the initial constraints whose satisfaction implies the satisfaction of the original constraints in the updated state. The main interest of the simplification process is to obtain a set of integrity tests (simplified forms) that are as easy to evaluate as possible. In this sense, simplification technique is feasible in terms of the cost of evaluating the constraints. *Integrity constraint checking* is the process of ensuring that the integrity constraints are satisfied by the database after it has been updated. Checking the consistency of a database state will generally involve the execution of integrity tests on the database which verify whether the database is satisfying its constraints or not. The problem of checking integrity constraints in database system has been addressed by many researchers, and has been proved to be extremely difficult to implement, particularly in distributed database. This chapter presents a framework for checking integrity constraints in a distributed database by utilizing as much as possible the information at a local site. This is achieved by considering several types of integrity tests and not focusing only on certain type of test as suggested by previous researchers. In addition, an approach for ranking and selecting suitable integrity tests that reduces the amount of data transferred across the network, the amount of data accessed, and the number of sites involved is also presented. The remainder of this chapter is organized as follows. In Section 2, the previous works related to this research are reported.

In Section 3, the basic definitions, notation and examples, which are used in the rest of the chapter, are set out. In Section 4, the components of the proposed framework are described followed by some examples. Conclusion and further research are presented in the final section, 5.

2. Related work

For distributed databases, a number of researchers have looked at the problem of semantic integrity checking. Although many research works have been conducted concerning the issues of integrity constraint checking and maintaining in distributed databases but these works failed to exploit the available information at the target site and explore the various types of integrity tests to ensure local checking can always be achieved. This is briefly shown in Table 1, where column labeled 1, 2, 3, 4, 5, 6, 7, and 8 represent the work by Simon and Valduriez (1986), Qian (1989), Mazumdar (1993), Gupta (1994), Ibrahim *et al* (2001), Ibrahim (2002), Madiraju *et al* (2006), and Soumya *et al* (2008) respectively.

Criteria		1	2	3	4	5	6	7	8
Types of integrity constraints	Domain	√	√	√		√	√		
	Key	√	√	√		√	√		
	Referential	√	√	√	√	√	√		
	Semantic	√	√	√		√	√	√	√
	Transition						√		
Types of tests	Complete	√	√						
	Sufficient		√	√	√	√	√	√	√
	Support								

Table 1. Summary of the Previous Work

The work presented in Simon and Valduriez (1986) constructed a simplification method for integrity constraints expressed in terms of assertions for central databases and extended it to distributed databases. This method produces at assertion definition time, differential pre-tests called compiled assertions, which can be used to prevent the introduction of inconsistencies in the database. The cost of integrity checking is reduced because only data subject to update are checked in this approach.

Qian (1989) argued that most approaches derive simplified forms of integrity constraints from the syntactic structure of the constraints and the update operation without exploiting knowledge about the application domain and the actual implementation of the database. Qian (1989) shows that distributed constraints can be translated into constraints on the fragments of a distributed database, given the definition of the fragmentation, and offers a framework for constraint reformulation. The constraint reformulation algorithm used to derive sufficient conditions can potentially be very inefficient because it searches through the entire space of eligible reformulation for the optimal one. Using heuristic rules to restrict the reformulation step may miss some optimal reformulation.

The work presented by Mazumdar (1993) aims at minimizing the number of sites involved in evaluating the integrity constraints in a distributed environment. In his approach the intention is to reduce the non locality of constraints by deriving sufficient conditions not only for the distributed integrity constraints given, but also for those arising as tests for particular transactions. His method relies on a standard backchaining approach to find the sufficient conditions.

Gupta (1994) presents an algorithm to generate parameterized local tests that check whether an update operation violates a constraint. This algorithm uses the initial consistency assumption, an integrity constraint assertion that is expressed in a subset of first order logic, and the target relation to produce the local test. This optimization technique allows a global constraint to be verified by accessing data locally at a single database where the modification is made. However, this approach is only useful in situations where each site of a distributed DBMS contains one or more intact relations since it does not consider any fragmentation rules.

Ibrahim *et al* (2001) contribute to the solution of constraint checking in a distributed database by demonstrating when it is possible to derive from global constraints localized constraints. They have proved that examining the semantics of both the tests and the relevant update operations reduces the amount of data transferred across the network. The simplified tests have reduced the amount of data that needed to be accessed and the number of sites that might be involved. Ibrahim (2002) extends the work in Ibrahim *et al* (2001) by considering the transition constraints.

The work proposed by Madiraju *et al* (2006) focuses on checking global constraints involving aggregates in the presence of updates. The algorithm takes as input an update statement, a list of global constraints involving aggregates and granules. The sub constraint granules are executed locally on remote sites and the algorithm decides if a constraint is violated based on these sub constraint executions. The algorithm performs constraints checking before the updates and thus saves time and resources on rollback. This approach is limited as they only consider semantic integrity constraints involving both arithmetic and aggregate predicates. Other types of integrity constraints that are important and are frequently used in database applications are not being considered.

Soumya *et al* (2008) proposed a technique to achieve optimization of constraint checking process in distributed databases by exploiting technique of parallelism, compile time constraint checking, localized constraint checking, and history of constraint violations. The architecture mainly consists of two modules: Constraint Analyzer and Constraint Ranker for analyzing the constraints and for ranking the constraints, respectively for systems with relational databases. They achieved optimization in terms of time by executing the constraints in parallel with mobile agents.

From these works, it can be observed that most of the previous works proposed an approach to derive simplified form of the initial integrity constraint with the sufficiency property, since the sufficient test is known to be cheaper than the complete test and its initial integrity constraint as it involved less data to be transferred across the network and always can be evaluated at the target site, i.e. only one site will be involved during the checking process. The previous approaches assume that an update operation will be executed at a site where the relation specified in the update operation is located, which is not always true. For example, consider a relation R that is located at site 1. An insert operation into R is assume to be submitted by a user at site 1 and the sufficient test generated is used to validate the consistency of the database with respect to this update operation, which can be performed locally at site 1. But if the same update operation is submitted at different site, say 2, the sufficient test is no longer appropriate as it will definitely access information from site 1 which is now remote to site 2. Therefore, an approach is needed so that local checking can be performed regardless the location of the submitted update operation. Also, the approach must be able to cater the important and frequently used integrity constraint types.

3. Preliminaries

Our approach has been developed in the context of relational databases. A database is described by a database schema, *D*, which consists of a finite set of relation schemas, $<R_1, R_2, \ldots, R_m>$. A relation schema is denoted by $R(A_1, A_2, \ldots, A_n)$ where *R* is the name of the relation (predicate) with *n*-arity and A_i's are the attributes of *R*. A relational distributed database schema is described as (*D*, *IC*, *AS*) where *IC* is a finite set of integrity constraints and *AS* is a finite set of allocation schemas.

Database integrity constraints are expressed in prenex conjunctive normal form with the range restricted property. A conjunct (literal) is an atomic formula of the form $R(u1, u2, \ldots, uk)$ where *R* is a *k*-ary relation name and each *ui* is either a variable or a constant. A positive atomic formula (positive literal) is denoted by $R(u1, u2, \ldots, uk)$ whilst a negative atomic formula (negative literal) is prefixed by ¬. An (in)equality is a formula of the form *u*1 *OP* *u*2 (prefixed with ¬ for inequality) where both *u*1 and *u*2 can be constants or variables and *OP* $\in \{<, \leq, >, \geq, <>, =\}$. Throughout this chapter the company database is used, as given in Figure 1. This example has been used in most previous works related to the area of constraint checking (Feras, 2006; Ibrahim, 2006; Ibrahim *et al*, 2001; Gupta, 1994).

Schema:

emp(eno, dno, ejob, esal); dept(dno, dname, mgrno, mgrsal); proj(eno, dno, pno)

Integrity Constraints:

Domain Constraint

(*IC*-1) 'The *salary* in relation *emp* must be greater than 0'

$(\forall w \forall x \forall y \forall z)(emp(w, x, y, z) \rightarrow (z > 0))$

Key Constraints

(*IC*-2) '*eno* is the primary key of *emp*'

$(\forall w \forall x1 \forall x2 \forall y1 \forall y2 \forall z1 \forall z2)(emp(w, x1, y1, z1) \wedge emp(w, x2, y2, z2) \rightarrow (x1 = x2) \wedge (y1 = y2) \wedge (z1 = z2))$

(*IC*-3) 'Every department has a unique *dno*'

$(\forall w \forall x1 \forall x2 \forall y1 \forall y2 \forall z1 \forall z2)(dept(w, x1, y1, z1) \wedge dept(w, x2, y2, z2) \rightarrow (x1 = x2) \wedge (y1 = y2) \wedge (z1 = z2))$

Referential Integrity Constraints

(*IC*-4) 'The *dno* of every tuple in the *emp* relation exists in the *dept* relation'

$(\forall t \forall u \forall v \forall w \exists x \exists y \exists z)(emp(t, u, v, w) \rightarrow dept(u, x, y, z))$

(*IC*-5) 'The *eno* of every tuple in the *proj* relation exists in the *emp* relation'

$(\forall u \forall v \forall w \exists x \exists y \exists z)(proj(u, v, w) \rightarrow emp(u, x, y, z))$

(*IC*-6) 'The *dno* of every tuple in the *proj* relation exists in the *dept* relation'

$(\forall u \forall v \forall w \exists x \exists y \exists z)(proj(u, v, w) \rightarrow dept(v, x, y, z))$

(*IC*-7) 'The *mgrno* of every tuple in the *dept* relation exists in the *emp* relation'

$(\forall t \forall u \forall v \forall w \exists x \exists y \exists z)(dept(t, u, v, w) \rightarrow emp(v, x, y, z))$

(*IC*-8) 'The manager salary, *mgrsal*, in the *dept* relation exists in *emp* relation, *esal*'

$(\forall u \forall v \forall w \forall x \exists y \exists z)(dept(u, v, w, x) \rightarrow emp(w, y, z, x))$

General Semantic Integrity Constraints

(*IC*-9) 'Every manager in department *D*1 earns > 4000 '

$(\forall w \forall x \forall y \forall z)(dept(w, x, y, z) \wedge (w = \text{'D1'}) \rightarrow (z > 4000))$

(*IC*-10) 'Every employee must earn ≤ to the manager in the same department'

$(\forall t \forall u \forall v \forall w \forall x \forall y \forall z)(emp(t, u, v, w) \wedge dept(u, x, y, z) \rightarrow (w \leq z))$

(*IC*-11) 'All managers who are working on project *P*3 must earn more than 1000'

$(\forall v \forall w \forall x \forall y \forall z)(dept(v, w, x, y) \wedge proj(x, z, P3) \rightarrow (y > 1000))$

(*IC*-12) 'Any department that is working on a project *P*1 is also working on project *P*2'

$(\forall x \forall y \exists z)(proj(x, y, P1) \rightarrow proj(z, y, P2))$

Fig. 1. The *Company* Static Integrity Constraint

In the database literature, many types and variations of integrity tests have been described (McCune and Henschen, 1989; McCarroll, 1995). The classifications of integrity tests are based on some of their characteristics, as explained below.

a. Based on when the integrity test is evaluated: (i) post-tests - allow an update operation to be executed on a database state, which changes it to a new state, and when an inconsistent result is detected undo this update. The method that applies these integrity tests is called the detection method. (ii) pre-tests - allow an update to be executed only if it changes the database state to a consistent state. The method that applies these integrity tests is called the prevention method.
b. Based on region: (i) local tests - verify the consistency of a database within the local region, i.e. by accessing the information at the local site. The method that adopts these integrity tests is called the local method. (ii) global tests - verify the consistency of a database outside the local region, i.e. by accessing the information at the remote site(s). The method that adopts these integrity tests is called the global method.
c. Based on its properties: (i) sufficient tests - when the test is satisfied, this implies that the associated constraint is satisfied and thus the update operation is safe with respect to the constraint. (ii) necessary tests - when the test is not satisfied, this implies that the associated constraint is violated and thus the update operation is unsafe with respect to the constraint. (iii) complete tests - has both the sufficiency and the necessity properties.

Integrity test based on input	Integrity test based on region	Integrity test based on detection/prevention methods	Integrity test based on its properties
Non-support test	Global test - spans remote site(s)	Post-test - evaluated after an update is performed	Sufficient test
			Necessary test
			Complete test
		Pre-test - evaluated before an update is performed	Sufficient test
			Necessary test
			Complete test
	Local test - spans local site	Post-test - evaluated after an update is performed	Sufficient test
			Necessary test
			Complete test
		Pre-test - evaluated before an update is performed	Sufficient test
			Necessary test
			Complete test
Support test	Global test - spans remote site(s)	Post-test - evaluated after an update is performed	Sufficient test
			Necessary test
			Complete test
		Pre-test - evaluated before an update is performed	Sufficient test
			Necessary test
			Complete test
	Local test - spans local site	Post-test - evaluated after an update is performed	Sufficient test
			Necessary test
			Complete test
		Pre-test - evaluated before an update is performed	Sufficient test
			Necessary test
			Complete test

Table 2. Types of Integrity Tests in Distributed Database

d. Based on the input used to generate the test: (i) non-support tests - these integrity tests are generated based on the update operation and the integrity constraint to be checked, called target integrity constraint, and (ii) support tests - any tests that are derived using other integrity constraints as the support to generate the tests. These types of integrity tests are summarized in Table 2.

4. The proposed framework

Figure 2 illustrates the proposed framework of integrity constraint checking for distributed database systems. This framework is divided into two modules: COMPILE-TIME MODULE and RUN-TIME MODULE which are elaborated in the subsections 4.1 and 4.2, respectively. The proposed framework has been successfully implemented using Visual Basic 6.0 programming language. Each module has been developed and tested with respect to the example database that is considered in this chapter. The major tasks of the framework are to generate the integrity tests for a given update operation, and ranked the selected integrity tests. We do not attempt to discuss in detail the implementation of the components that underpin the framework, but rather present brief results of the implementation of the various components embodied in this framework.

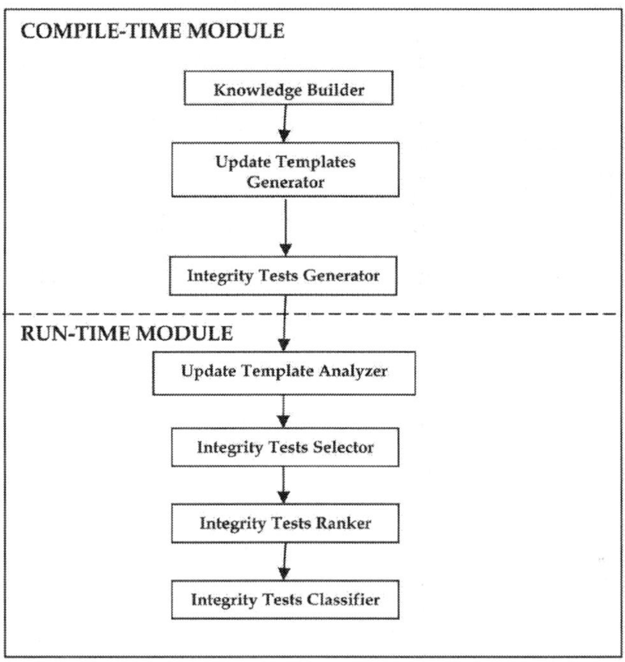

Fig. 2. The Proposed Framework of Constraint Checking

4.1 Components of compile-time module

This module encompasses three components, namely: Knowledge Builder, Update Templates Generator, and Integrity Tests Generator as explained below.

Knowledge Builder: This component analyzes the database schema and integrity constraints for a particular database application. It checks the syntactic correctness of a database schema and extracts some facts that include the names of relations in the database system, names and number of attributes in each relation. In addition, it checks if the input constraints specified by the user are valid and correct with respect to the syntactic formula given in the constraint specification.

Update Templates Generator: The aim of this component is to derive all possible update operations (templates) that might violate a given constraint. The update templates are generated for a particular database by applying the well-known update theorems. These theorems with their proofs can be found in (Nicolas, 1982) and are therefore omitted here.

Integrity Tests Generator: The most important and the essential component in the Compile-Time Module is integrity tests generator. The main operation is to construct the integrity tests by simplifying the integrity constraint which is specified in prenex conjunctive normal form. This component addresses the issue of checking the constraints locally regardless the location of the submitted update operation as elaborated in Section 2. Three types of integrity test are generated by using three different algorithms, namely: complete tests are derived using *Algorithm*-1 proposed by Nicolas (1982); complete/sufficient tests are generated using *Algorithm*-2 proposed by Ibrahim (1998); while support tests are produced using *Algorithm*-3 which is proposed by us. These algorithms adopt the substitution techniques and absorption rules to generate integrity tests (Nicolas, 1982; Ibrahim, 1998). The difference between our algorithm and *Algorithm*-1 and *Algorithm*-2 is that our proposed simplification technique uses other integrity constraints to generate integrity tests while both the *Algorithm*-1 and *Algorithm*-2 used the target integrity constraint (integrity constraint to be checked) as the input. The details of these algorithms are omitted here. Interested readers may refer to Alwan *et al* (2007). Table 3 summarizes the integrity tests generated for the integrity constraints listed in Figure 1 using these algorithms.

In Figure 3 the interface for generating update templates is illustrated for the *Company* database.

Figure 4 presents the interface for the Integrity Tests Generator component that has been implemented for the *Company* database.

4.2 Components of run-time module

The Run-Time Module encompasses four components namely: Update Template Analyzer, Integrity Tests Selector, Integrity Tests Ranker, and Integrity Tests Classifier as elaborated below.

Update Template Analyzer: This component analyzes the syntax of an update operation submitted by a user. It checks that the name of relation and the number of attributes/columns which are specified in the update operation are the same as the name of relation and the number of attributes/columns that appear in the database schema.

Integrity Tests Selector: The main function of this component is to identify the integrity constraints that might be violated given an update operation and select the integrity tests associated to those constraints. This phase is achieved by comparing the real update operation with the update templates that have been generated. This comparison includes checking the name of relation and type of update operation. If both the actual update operation and update template have the same relation name and type of update operation, then the integrity tests of the update template are selected. This is to ensure that only those constraints and their associated integrity tests that might be violated for the given update operation are considered for evaluation.

IC-i	**Update template**	**Integrity test**	**Type of integrity test**
IC-1	insert $emp(a, b, c, d)$	1. $d > 0$	Complete Test
IC-2	insert $emp(a, b, c, d)$	2. $(\forall x2 \forall y2 \forall z2)(\neg emp(a, x2, y2, z2) \vee [(b = x2) \wedge (c = y2) \wedge (d = z2)])$	Complete Test
		3. $(\forall x1 \forall y1 \forall z1)(\neg emp(a, x1, y1, z1))$	Complete Test
		4. $(\exists v \exists w)(proj(a, v, w))$	Support Test
		5. $(\exists t \exists u \exists w)(dept(t, u, a, w))$	Support Test
IC-3	insert $dept(a, b, c, d)$	6. $(\forall x2 \forall y2 \forall z2)(\neg dept(a, x2, y2, z2) \vee [(b = x2) \wedge (c = y2) \wedge (d = z2)])$	Complete Test
		7. $(\forall x1 \forall y1 \forall z1)(\neg dept(a, x1, y1, z1))$	Complete Test
		8. $(\exists t \exists v \exists w)(emp(t, a, v, w))$	Support Test
		9. $(\exists u \exists w)(proj(u, a, w))$	Support Test
IC-4	insert $emp(a, b, c, d)$	10. $(\exists x \exists y \exists z)(dept(b, x, y, z))$	Complete Test
		11. $(\exists t \exists v \exists w)(emp(t, b, v, w))$	Sufficient Test
		12. $(\exists u \exists w)(proj(u, b, w))$	Support Test
	delete $dept(a, b, c, d)$	13. $(\forall t \forall v \forall w)(\neg emp(t, a, v, w))$	Complete Test
		14. $(\forall u \forall w)(\neg proj(u, a, w))$	Support Test
IC-5	insert $proj(a, b, c)$	15. $(\exists x \exists y \exists z)(emp(a, x, y, z))$	Complete Test
		16. $(\exists v \exists w)(proj(a, v, w))$	Sufficient Test
		17. $(\exists t \exists u \exists w)(dept(t, u, a, w))$	Support Test
	delete $emp(a, b, c, d)$	18. $(\forall v \forall w)(\neg proj(a, v, w))$	Complete Test
		19. $(\forall t \forall u \forall w)(\neg dept(t, u, a, w))$	Support Test
IC-6	insert $proj(a, b, c)$	20. $(\exists x \exists y \exists z)(dept(b, x, y, z))$	Complete Test
		21. $(\exists u \exists w)(proj(u, b, w))$	Sufficient Test
		22. $(\exists t \exists v \exists w)(emp(t, b, v, w))$	Support Test
	delete $dept(a, b, c, d)$	23. $(\forall u \forall w)(\neg proj(u, a, w))$	Complete Test
		24. $(\forall t \forall v \forall w)(\neg emp(t, a, v, w))$	Support Test
IC-7	insert $dept(a, b, c, d)$	25. $(\exists x \exists y \exists z)(emp(c, x, y, z))$	Complete Test
		26. $(\exists v \exists w)(proj(c, v, w))$	Support Test
	delete $emp(a, b, c, d)$	27. $(\forall t \forall u \forall w)(\neg dept(t, u, a, w))$	Complete Test
		28. $(\forall v \forall w)(\neg proj(a, v, w))$	Support Test
IC-8	insert $dept(a, b, c, d)$	29. $(\exists y \exists z)(emp(c, y, z, d))$	Complete Test
	delete $emp(a, b, c, d)$	30. $(\forall u \forall v)(\neg dept(u, v, a, d))$	Complete Test
IC-9	insert $dept(a, b, c, d)$	31. $(a <> \text{'D1'}) \vee (d > 4000)$	Complete Test
IC-10	insert $emp(a, b, c, d)$	32. $(\forall x \forall y \forall z)(\neg dept(b, x, y, z) \vee (d \leq z))$	Complete Test
		33. $(\exists t \exists v \exists w)(emp(t, b, v, w) \wedge (w \geq d))$	Sufficient Test
	insert $dept(a, b, c, d)$	34. $(\forall t \forall v \forall w)(\neg emp(t, a, v, w) \vee (w \leq d))$	Complete Test
IC-11	insert $dept(a, b, c, d)$	35. $(\forall z)(\neg proj(c, z, P3) \vee (d > 1000))$	Complete Test
		36. $(\exists x \exists y \exists z)(emp(c, x, y, z) \wedge (d > 1000))$	Support Test
	insert $proj(a, b, P3)$	37. $(\forall v \forall w \forall y)(\neg dept(v, w, a, y) \vee (y > 1000))$	Complete Test
		38. $(\exists z)(proj(a, z, P3))$	Sufficient Test
		39. $(\exists x \exists y \exists z)(emp(a, x, y, z) \wedge (z > 1000))$	Support Test
IC-12	insert $proj(a, b, P1)$	40. $(\exists z)(proj(z, b, P2))$	Complete Test
		41. $(\exists x)(proj(x, b, P1))$	Sufficient Test
	delete $proj(a, b, P2)$	42. $(\forall x)(\neg proj(x, b, P1))$	Complete Test
		43. $(\exists z)(proj(z, b, P2) \wedge (z <> a))$	Sufficient Test

Table 3. Integrity Tests of the Integrity Constraints of the Example Database

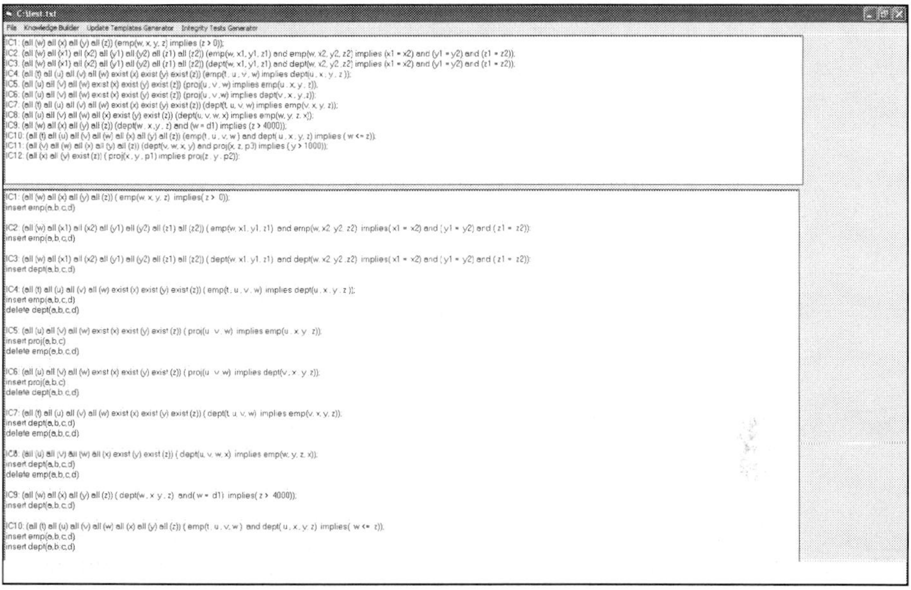

Fig. 3. The List of Update Templates Generated for the *Company* Database

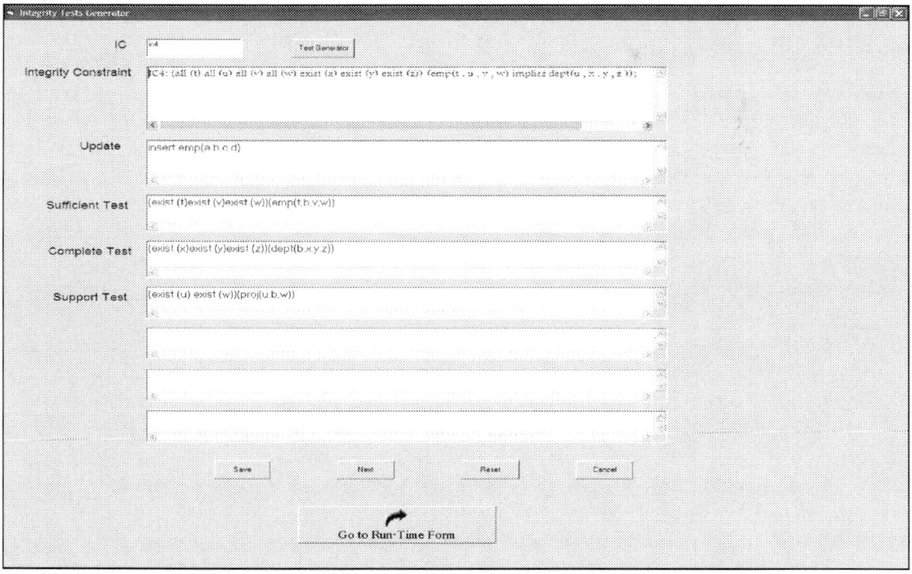

Fig. 4. The Integrity Tests of the Referential Integrity Constraint *IC*-4 for the *Company* Database

Integrity Tests Ranker: The main aim of this component is to rank the selected integrity tests. It attempts to answer the following questions; which test should be selected if there are several alternatives that can be chosen from? What are the criteria that should be measured in order to identify the suitable test?

Most of the works in integrity constraints checking focused on techniques to simplify integrity constraints with the assumption that the simplified forms of the constraints are cheaper than the initial constraints. Thus, the simplified form is evaluated (instead of the initial constraint) to verify the consistency of the database. Moreover, most of the efficiency measurements consider a single cost component and are more applicable for measuring the cost of evaluating integrity constraints in a centralized environment rather than a distributed environment. In addition, most of the previous works consider limited type of integrity tests (complete and sufficient) and depend strictly on the assumption that the update operation is always submitted at the site where the relation specified in the update is located. Thus, their approaches in selecting suitable integrity tests are not general enough. These approaches do not consider support tests and there is no ranking between the types of tests, i.e. all tests are considered the same.

We argue that tests should be ranked as they have different probability of being true or false in a given database state. Thus, we suggest complete test should have the highest priority, followed by sufficient test, and lastly by support test. This is because complete test has both the sufficiency and the necessity properties, sufficient test can only verify for valid database state, and most of the support test is either sufficient test or necessary test. As mentioned in the literature, the amount of data transferred across the network is the most critical factor; therefore we suggest the amount of data transferred to have the highest priority in the ranking model, followed by the number of sites involved, and the amount of data accessed. Based on these arguments, we have proposed a ranking model as shown in Figure 5. Each value in the box, i.e. 1, 2, 3, …, P, is the *rank value* where P is the maximum rank value. The *rank value* of a test, $Test_i$, with respect to T is denoted by $Rank_T$. Similar notation is used for indicating the rank value of a test with respect to σ and $\mathscr{A}$. Thus, we can calculate the total rank value for a given test by simply adding the rank values for each of the parameter, i.e. $Rank\text{-}Test_i = Rank_T + Rank_\sigma + Rank_{\mathscr{A}}$, where T provides an estimate of the amount of data transferred across the network, $\mathscr{A}$ provides an estimate of the amount of data accessed, and σ gives a rough measurement of the amount of nonlocal access necessary to evaluate a constraint or integrity test. The test with the smallest rank value is said to be the suitable test. A test with the lowest total rank value is said to be the most appropriate test. The ranking model is designed as follows:

1. If the amount of data transferred of a given test is 0 (i.e. the test is a local test), then depending on its property, a value of 1, 2, and 3 is assigned to the $Rank_T$ if the test is a complete, sufficient, and support, respectively. Otherwise for each nonlocal test ($T \neq 0$), the tests are ordered according to the value of T and the test with the lowest T, a value of 4 is assigned to its $Rank_T$. The next lowest, a value of 5 is assigned to its $Rank_T$ and so on.
2. If the number of sites involved in checking a given test is 1, then depending on its property, a value of 4, 5, and 6 is assigned to the $Rank_\sigma$ if the test is a complete, sufficient, and support, respectively. The rank value begins with 4 (and not 1, 2, or 3) to show that the number of sites has lower priority than the amount of data transferred. Otherwise, for each test with $\sigma \neq 1$, the tests are ordered according to the number of sites

involved and the test with the lowest σ, a value of 7 is assigned to its Rank$_\sigma$. The next lowest, a value of 8 is assigned to its Rank$_\sigma$ and so on. Also, note that a test with Rank$_\sigma$ = 4 (5 and 6, respectively) will definitely not be assigned a Rank$_T$ = 4 (5 and 6, respectively) since Rank$_T$ = 4 (5 and 6, respectively) indicates that the test is a nonlocal test while Rank$_\sigma$ = 4 (5 and 6, respectively) denotes that the test is a local test. Although they have the same rank value, i.e. 4, but after adding the rank value for both T and σ, the local test will definitely have lower total rank value compared to the nonlocal test.

3. If the amount of data accessed for each of the test is the same, then depending on its property, a value of 7, 8, and 9 is assigned to the Rank$_\mathscr{A}$ if the test is a complete, sufficient, and support, respectively. The rank value begins with 7 (and not 1, 2, ..., 6) to show that the amount of data accessed has the lowest priority compared to the amount of data transferred and the number of sites involved. Otherwise, for each test with different amount of data accessed, these tests are ordered according to the amount of data accessed and the test with the lowest $\mathscr{A}$, a value of 10 is assigned to its Rank$_\mathscr{A}$. The next lowest, a value of 11 is assigned to its Rank$_\mathscr{A}$ and so on. Also, note that a test with Rank$_\mathscr{A}$ = 7 (8 and 9, respectively) can be assigned a Rank$_\sigma$ = 7 (8, 9, ..., P_σ) which indicate that the test is a nonlocal complete test (nonlocal sufficient test and nonlocal support test, respectively) and the amount of data accessed is the same for all the alternative tests.

Parameter/ Type of Test	Complete, *C*	Sufficient, *S*	Support, *Sup*	Remarks
$T = 0$	1	2	3	If $T \neq 0$, the tests are rank accordingly based on the amount of data transferred. Rank value begins with 4, 5, 6, ..., P_T
$\sigma = 1$	4	5	6	If $\sigma \neq 1$, the tests are rank accordingly based on the number of sites involved. Rank value begins with 7, 8, 9, ..., P_σ
$\mathscr{A}_C = \mathscr{A}_S = \mathscr{A}_{Sup}$	7	8	9	If $\mathscr{A}_C \neq \mathscr{A}_S \neq \mathscr{A}_{Sup}$, the tests are rank accordingly based on the amount of data accessed. Rank value begins with 10, 11, 12, ..., $P_\mathscr{A}$.

Note: P_T (P_σ and $P_\mathscr{A}$ respectively) is the maximum rank value assigned to a test based on T (σ and $\mathscr{A}$, respectively).

Fig. 5. The Proposed Ranking Model

To illustrate the ranking model for integrity tests, three scenarios are considered:

i. Centralized database (all relations are located at the same site).
ii. Average case (two relations are located at the same site while the other is located at a different site).
iii. Worst case (each relation is located at different sites).

We assume that *emp* relation contains 500 employees (500 tuples), *dept* relation contains 10 departments (10 tuples), and *proj* relation contains 100 projects (100 tuples).

IC-4 and the insert operation into *emp* relation are used to demonstrate the model, i.e. tests 10 (complete), 11 (sufficient), and 12 (support) are compared.
Based on the result shown in Table 4, complete test, *C*, is selected, as it is the most suitable test for centralized database. Since all tests have similar characteristics with regards to *T* (= 0) and σ (= 1), the only different are the properties of the tests and $\mathcal{A}$. Mazumdar (1993) scatter metric alone is not able to select the suitable test as these tests have the same scatter metric, $\sigma = 1$, while Ibrahim *et al* (2001) will select the test with the lowest $\mathcal{A}$. If the tests have the same amount of data accessed, then no solution is given in Ibrahim *et al* (2001).

Update is submitted at site:	**Location of Relations**		**Rank-$Test_i$**	**Test Selected**
*S*1	*S*1	*emp, dept, proj*	*C* = 1 + 4 + 10 =15 *S* = 2 + 5 + 12 = 19 *Sup* = 3 + 6 + 11 = 20	Test *C*

Table 4. Case (i) Centralized Database

Table 5 presents an average case with several different scenarios. Here, we assume that two of the relations are located at the same site while the other relation is located at a different site, and update operation is submitted at any of these sites. From the results, we observed that local test is always selected regardless the type of the tests. In cases where more than one local test is available, then the tests are rank according to the type and the amount of data accessed (this scenario is similar to the case (i) centralized database discussed earlier).

Update is submitted at site:	**Location of Relations**		**Rank-$Test_i$**	**Test Selected**
*S*1	*S*1 *S*2	*emp, dept* *proj*	*C* = 1 + 4 + 10 = 15 *S* = 2 + 5 + 12 = 19 *Sup* = 4 + 7 + 11 = 22	Test *C*
*S*2	*S*1 *S*2	*emp, dept* *proj*	*C* = 4 + 7 + 10 = 21 *S* = 5 + 7 + 12 = 24 *Sup* = 3 + 6 + 11 = 20	Test *Sup*
*S*1	*S*1 *S*2	*emp, proj* *dept*	*C* = 4 + 7 + 10 = 21 *S* = 2 + 5 + 12 = 19 *Sup* = 3 + 6 + 11 = 20	Test *S*
*S*2	*S*1 *S*2	*emp, proj* *dept*	*C* = 1 + 4 + 10 = 15 *S* = 5 + 7 + 12 = 24 *Sup* = 4 + 7 + 11 = 22	Test *C*
*S*1	*S*1 *S*2	*dept, proj* *emp*	*C* = 1 + 4 + 10 = 15 *S* = 4 + 7 + 12 = 23 *Sup* = 3 + 6 + 11 = 20	Test *C*
*S*2	*S*1 *S*2	*dept, proj* *emp*	*C* = 4 + 7 + 10 = 21 *S* = 2 + 5 + 12 = 19 *Sup* = 5 + 7 + 11 = 23	Test *S*

Table 5. Case (ii) Average Case

Table 6 presents the worst case scenario. In this case each relation is located at different sites. Here, we assume *emp* relation is located at site *S*1, *dept* relation is located at site *S*2, and *proj* relation is located at site *S*3. The test that is selected is the local test (T = 0 and σ = 1). As mentioned earlier, most of the previous works assumed that the update operation is submitted at the site where the relation specifies in the update is located, and thus the sufficient test is always selected. In the ranking model, the suitable test (with the lowest total rank value) is selected and this test can be complete, sufficient or support.

Update is submitted at site:	Location of Relations		Rank-$Test_i$	Test Selected
*S*1	*S*1	*emp*	C = 4 + 7 + 10 = 21	Test *S*
	*S*2	*dept*	S = 2 + 5 + 12 = 19	
	*S*3	*proj*	Sup = 5 + 7 + 11 = 23	
*S*2	*S*1	*emp*	C = 1 + 4 + 10 = 15	Test *C*
	*S*2	*dept*	S = 5 + 7 + 12 = 24	
	*S*3	*proj*	Sup = 4 + 7 + 11 = 22	
*S*3	*S*1	*emp*	C = 4 + 7 + 10 = 21	Test *Sup*
	*S*2	*dept*	S = 5 + 7 + 12 = 24	
	*S*3	*proj*	Sup = 3 + 6 + 11 = 20	

Table 6. Case (iii) Worst Case

Obviously, in some cases, support tests can benefit the distributed database, where local constraint can be achieved. Integrating these various types of integrity tests during constraint checking and not concentrating on certain types of integrity tests (as suggested by previous works) can enhance the performance of the constraint mechanism. Thus, developing an approach that can increase the performance and minimize the cost during the process of constraint checking in the distributed database is important. We have evaluated the model with several cases and several different types of integrity constraints, and in all cases the model is able to select the suitable test as expected.

Integrity Tests Classifier: This component focuses on classifying the integrity tests based on region i.e., into local test or global test. Each test regardless the type can be classified as either local or global depending on where the real update operation is submitted and the location of the relation(s) specified in the integrity tests is located. If the test can be performed locally, then the test is being local. In contrary, when the test needs to transfer data across the network from another site(s) the test is being global. Note that the Integrity Tests Ranker component ranks the integrity tests without selecting any of the tests for evaluation. Only after classification that the test with the lowest total rank value (normally local test) is selected. The *Test Selected* column in tables 4, 5 and 6 is to demonstrate the whole idea of selecting the suitable integrity test to be evaluated from a list of alternative tests. Figure 6 illustrates the interface of the Run-Time Module.

5. Conclusion

In this chapter, we have proposed an approach that performs constraint checking at the target site by utilizing as much as possible the local information to avoid the possibility of transferring data across the network. The novelty of this approach is that local checking can be performed regardless the location of the submitted update operation. This is achieved by having several types of integrity tests and not focusing on certain type of integrity tests as

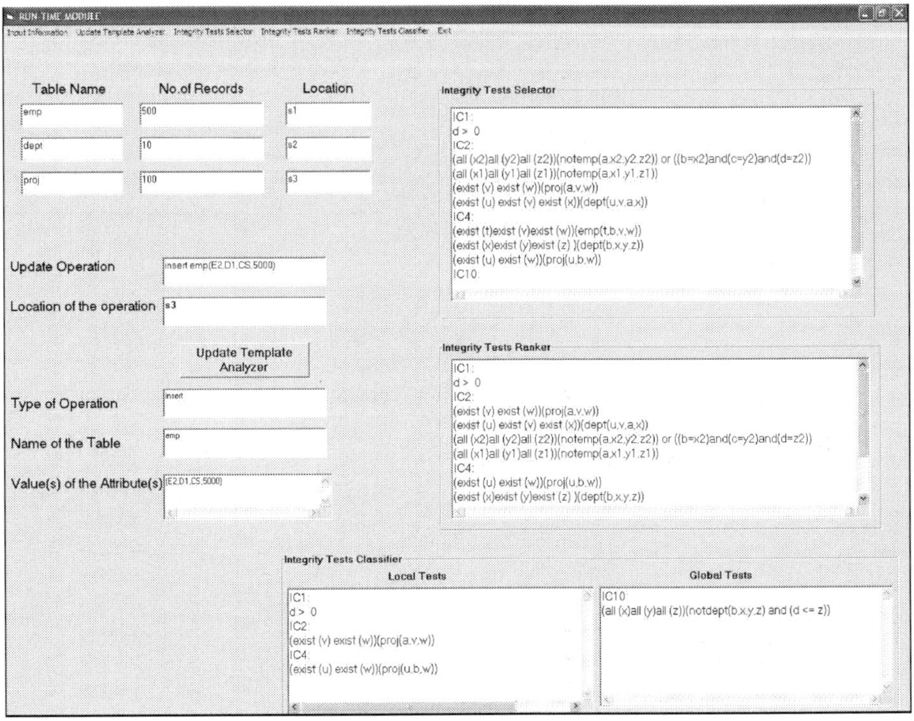

Fig. 6. The Interface of the Run-Time Module

suggested by previous researchers in this area. Also, we have proposed an approach for ranking and selecting suitable integrity tests that reduce the amount of data transferred across the network, the amount of data accessed, and the number of sites involved. Most importantly, we have proved that in most cases, support tests can benefit the distributed database, where local constraint checking can be achieved. Thus, the efficiency of checking constraint process is increased. Both of these strategies are embedded in our proposed framework as presented in this chapter. For future works further enhancement to the proposed approach can be done by considering strategies to maintain the distributed database state when violation occurs. Considering multiple operations or transaction is another area that can be explored where strategies that can minimize the cost of checking the constraints are needed.

6. References

Alwan, A. A.; Ibrahim, H. & Udzir, N. I., (2007). Local Integrity Checking using Local Information in a Distributed Database. *Proceedings of the 1st Aalborg University IEEE.Student Paper Contest 2007 (AISPC'07)*, Aalborg, January 2007, Denmark.

Christiansen H. & Martinenghi D. (2006). On using Simplification and Correction Tables for Integrity Maintenance in Integrated Databases, *Proceedings of the 17th International*

Conference on Database and Expert Systems Applications (DEXA'06), pp. 569 - 576, Krakow, September 2006, Poland.

Feras, A. H. H., (2006). *Integrity Constraints Maintenance for Parallel Databases*. Ph.D. Thesis, Universiti Putra Malaysia, Malaysia.

Gupta A., (1994). *Partial Information based Integrity Constraint Checking*. Ph.D. Thesis, Stanford University, USA.

Ibrahim H. (1998). *Semantic Integrity Constraints Enforcement for a Distributed Database*, Ph.D. Thesis, University of Wales College of Cardiff, Cardiff (UK).

Ibrahim H.; Gray W.A., & Fiddian N.J. (2001). Optimizing Fragment Constraints - A Performance Evaluation, *International Journal of Intelligent Systems - Verification and Validation Issues in Databases, Knowledge-Based Systems, and Ontologies*, Edited by: Ronald, R., John Wiley & Sons Inc.,Vol. 16, No. 3, , 2001, pp. 285 - 306, ISSN 0884-8173.

Ibrahim H. (2002). A Strategy for Semantic Integrity Checking in Distributed Databases, *Proceedings of the Ninth International Conference on Parallel and Distributed Systems*, pp. 139- 144, Republic of China, IEEE Computer Society, December 2002, China.

Ibrahim, H., (2006). Checking Integrity Constraints - How it Differs in Centralized, Distributed and Parallel Databases. *Proceedings of the Second International Workshop on Logical Aspects and Applications of Integrity Constraints*, pp. 563 - 568, Krakow, September 2006, Poland.

Madiraju P.; Sunderraman R., and Haibin W. (2006). A Framework for Global Constraint Checking Involving Aggregates in Multidatabases Using Granular Computing, *Proceedings of IEEE International Conference on Granular Computing (IEEE-GrC'06)*, pp. 506 - 509, Atlanta, May 2006, USA.

Martinenghi, D., (2005). *Advanced Techniques for Efficient Data Integrity Checking*. Ph.D. Thesis, Roskilde University, Denmark.

Mazumdar, S., (1993). Optimizing Distributed Integrity Constraints. *Proceedings of the 3rd International Symposium on Database Systems for Advanced Applications*, pp. 327 - 334, Vol. 4, Taejon, April 1993, Korea.

McCarroll N.F. (1995). *Semantic Integrity Enforcement in Parallel Database Machines*, PhD Thesis, Department of Computer Science, University of Sheffield, Sheffield, UK.

McCune, W. W. & Henschen, L. J., (1989). Maintaining State Constraints in Relational Databases: a Proof Theoretic Basis. *Journal of the Association for Computing Machinery*, Vol. 36 No.1, January 1989, pp. 46 - 68, ISSN:0004-5411.

Nicolas, J. M., (1982). Logic for Improving Integrity Checking in Relational Databases. *Acta Informatica*, Vol. 18, No.3, 1982, pp. 227 - 253, ISSN:0001-5903.

Qian, X., (1989). Distribution Design of Integrity Constraints. *Proceedings of the 2nd International Conference on Expert Database Systems*, pp. 205 - 226, Vienna, Virginia, April 1989, USA.

Simon, E. & Valduriez, P., (1986). Integrity Control in Distributed Database Systems. *Proceedings of the 19th Hawaii International Conference on System Sciences*, pp. 622 - 632, Honolulu, Hawaii, January 1986, USA.

Soumya B.; Madiraju, & Ibrahim H. (2008). Constraint Optimization for a System of Relation Databases, *Proceedings of the IEEE 8th International Conference on Computer and Information Technology (CiT 2008)*, pp. 155 - 160, Sydney, July 2008, Australia.

7

An Agent-Based Software Framework for Robotics and Automation Systems

Franco Guidi-Polanco and Claudio Cubillos
Pontificia Universidad Católica de Valparaíso
Chile

1. Introduction

The concept of "reuse" in software engineering is associated to well design, shorter development times, and easier maintenance of software applications. Today, the bigger reuse unit is given by software frameworks, which offer ready-to-use architectures and code implementations. Several frameworks have been proposed and adopted for a wide variety of traditional application domains (i.e. graphic interfaces, data persistence, web applications, etc.). The robotics and automation is a complex domain where the orientation to get reusable software architectural design has became a center of interest just in the last decade, once complex physiological functions of robots (i.e. sensing, walking, thinking, etc.) have reached certain degree of maturity.

In the field of robotics and automation, current application scenarios consider distributed autonomous cooperative systems, especially aimed to support integration of collaborative societies of devices. Thus, the paradigm is shifted from the single entity that establishes simple perception-planning-reaction interactions with its environment (i.e. detect signals, path planning, reach places), to a colony of autonomous members forced to interact among them in order to accomplish more complex tasks that are unable to be managed solely for each single one. The concept of "member" is used in this context to encapsulate each physical device or virtual process recognizable in the society, which pursues its own individual objectives.

In our vision such systems are conceptualized as a flat interconnection of autonomous and decentralized virtual and robotics agents, where no control hierarchy is enforced, and where each partner takes the initiative to reach to a decision. Agents interact in a peer-to-peer architectural model, and the global behaviour of the system becomes a synergic property of the interaction of their parts.

This work presents a software framework for building automation systems, which promotes different reuse levels. The framework offers a general layered architecture driven by the paradigm of *software agent*. The framework includes an agent platform that satisfies specific requirements in software development for communities of robots and automation devices.

In this paper the architecture is described with more detail, and an example of its application is provided.

2. Related work

The multi-agent system (MAS) paradigm is being adopted to implement control and communication in distributed automation and robotic societies. In such systems, the modelling paradigm is centred in the concept of agent. An agent is a software entity capable to perceive its environment, to evaluate these perceptions against some given design objectives, and to perform some activity in order to reach them, interacting with other similar entities, and acting over its environment. Agents should be designed to exhibit robust operation, even if they are immersed in an open or unpredictably changing environment (Weiss 1999).

In recent years the literature offers several examples of multi-agent architectures and organizations created for domain-specific applications (see (Haibin, 2006), (Dioubate et al. 2008), (Lim et al., 2009), (Rogers et al., 2006) for some examples). These architectures accent the identification of agent's roles and responsibilities, and the description of their interactions and communications. As expected, due to their ad-hoc nature, these architectures are hardly reusable outside their original domains.

In order to improve the reuse of design, some studies establish the convenience of identifying and separating domain-specific aspects from those generic aspects that are common in families of systems. One example is the orientation followed in (Sims et al., 2004) that proposes the reuse of organizational coordination mechanisms across different problem domains and environmental situations. Nevertheless, their work just emphasizes organization and distribution of tasks and goals, while the system's structure is not deeply treated.

An important contribution, in accordance with the latter approach, is the *holonic* paradigm (Valckenaers et al. 2008). This approach, offers an organizational model highly reusable, which can be applied at diverse abstraction levels and replicable in different domains (Jianhui et al., 2004). However, it is a conceptual model that does not specify implementation of concrete services that can be required and reused when developing such systems.

On the other hand, models of agent societies and agent platforms implementations play insufficient attention to the agent's environment, which is an essential part in robotic system's structure. In practice agent architectures fail to adequately identify and consider its role. As indicated in (Weyns et al., 2005), popular frameworks minimize the environment reducing it just to a message transport system or to a brokering infrastructure.

In terms of structure and services, the development of generic agent platforms (e.g. Jade (Bellifemine et al. 1999)) presents concrete architectures with high degree of reusability, but made-up by low-granularity components (commonly, basic communication and directory services), that implement commonly agreed abstract models (e.g. FIPA). Also, these platforms are not designed to satisfy security, connectivity, and scalability requirements originated in the robotic and automation domain (Guidi_Polanco et al. 2004).

The adoption of agent systems as enabling technologies for the development of distributed organizations' infrastructures is currently matter of research. In particular, the agent technology seems not only to satisfy the demand for high flexibility requested by enterprise-wide integration (Rimassa, 2004), but also to provide approaches to support autonomous self-configuration and self-adaptability of their activities in their operational environment.

3. An abstract model for agent-based robotics societies

In the era of Internet, robotic and automation systems are conceived as flat interconnections of autonomous and decentralized decision making/control modules. In such a system, no hierarchy in the decision making is enforced, and each partner takes the initiative to reach a decision. Control modules have decision-making capabilities and coordinate their activities by exchanging data and events according to a peer-to-peer architectural model and common protocols (Brugali & Menga, 2002).

We envision the *agent paradigm* as the software engineering approach to model control modules in such robotic architectures. The arguments in favour of an agent-oriented approach in software engineering for modelling a system can be summarized in the three ideas indicated in (Jennings, 2001): (1) Agent oriented decompositions are an effective way of partitioning the problem space of a complex system; (2) The key abstractions of the agent-oriented mindset are natural means of modelling complex systems; and (3) The agent-oriented philosophy for modelling and managing organizational relationships is appropriate for dealing with the dependencies and interactions that exist in complex systems.

Our approach introduces a layered model that identifies and classifies system's components (i.e. agents and services) accordingly with different granularities. Those components and services that share similar levels of reuse from both, the structural and the organizational point of view, are grouped together. The model is build recognizing at its basis the physical environment, which is virtualized in superior levels, making explicit the way in which agents will interact with it.

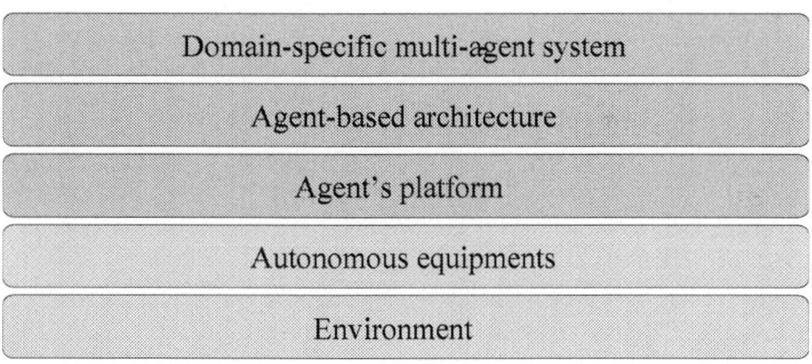

Fig. 1. The layers in a robotic society

This vision is constructed as the abstract model depicted in Figure 1. The abstract model is divided by the following five layers:

a. *Environment*: it is composed by physical objects pertaining or observed in the real world (e.g. objects in mobile robot's environment, wired or wireless communication networks, computational systems in organizations, human operators, etc.), and concepts conventionally adopted for its characterization (e.g. geographical coordinates obtained from a GPS service, temperatures, data transmission latency, water flows measurements, etc.). The physical world is conceptualized as a multidimensional space surrounding agents accomplishing physical-related tasks.
b. *Autonomous Equipments*: represent computing-enabled platforms, such as mobile robots, automated factory machines, or computing devices, which has to be programmed in order to act proactively in the robotic community. Such systems, can offer a wide range

of capabilities expressed in terms of CPU, runtime memory, data storage, data communication, or operating system. These equipments are usually provided with sensors that allow the perception of surrounding relevant variables, actuators to interact with the environment (changing their own position, taking objects, etc.), and communications devices to interchange messages with other equipments. Also, the autonomous equipments provide the runtime environment for the agents, so they must satisfy a set of minimum hardware/software requirements imposed by the agent platform's software (or in an opposite point of view, the agent platforms must be designed to be executed in specific categories of devices).

c. *Agent platform*: corresponds to the software that offers the base classes to build agents, and to virtualize environment-dependent services (e.g. interfaces to peripheral devices, motors, databases, network communication, etc.). It also offers the execution environment that controls the entire agent's life-cycle, and regulates its interactions with other agents and resources. As it was stated above, agent platforms must be designed for their execution in devices with different hardware (e.g. PDAs, mobile phones, desktop computers) and software capabilities (in terms of operating systems and programming languages). A known example of agent platform is JADE (Bellifemine et al., 1999). A comprehensive list of agent platforms can be found in (AgentLink, 2004).
d. *Agent-based architecture*: represent a reusable architecture to support the development of different kinds of agent-based systems. The architecture specifies a set of common services (e.g. directory facilitator, yellow pages, etc.), and a framework of communication/content languages (e.g. ACL (Genesereth and Ketchpel, 1994), KQML (Finin et al., 1993), etc.) and interaction protocols, necessary to achieve interoperability among agents. The services offered by the architecture can be implemented by service agents (such as a yellow-pages agent), or as environment-dependent service (e.g access to some kind of physical device). An example of a particular agent-based architecture is specified by FIPA standards, which was conceived to obtain interoperability between different and generic agent systems (e.g. FIPA Request Interaction Protocol (FIPA, 2002)).
e. *Domain-specific multi agent system* (DSMAS): corresponds to a concrete instance of a multi-agent system, where domain-dependent agents are designed to represent real-world services and systems, and interactions among them are well defined. At this level, agents are often abstractions of real entities pertaining to the application domain. DSMAS architectures can be reused within the scope of the context they were created for. A reusable DSMAS architecture constitutes an agent-based framework for the development of systems within its domain. DSMAS are supported by the services offered by the agent-based architecture. Examples of DSMAS could be a colony of exploration robots, an automated work cell, or a domotic network of devices.

The model proposed above has three main characteristics:

- *Decouples design responsibilities*: the model presents the different aspects related to a multi-agent architecture in a separated way. Therefore, the design responsibilities can be clearly identified and assigned to different development projects or teams.
- - *Promotes high cohesion within each layer*: components within each layer are closely related from the functional and communicational point of view, in such a way that their interactions are optimized.

- *Clearly emphasizes the environment*: traditional agent architectures consider the environment implicitly, in most cases just as a mere communication supplier. In our model, the environment is distinguished as a physical and a virtual one.

4. The G++ Agent Platform

We have developed the G++ Agent Platform, our own software infrastructure for agents' implementation in robotic and automation societies (Guidi-Polanco et al., 2004). In this section, the architecture of the platform is described.

4.1 Design directions

Our work was motivated by the need for creating and integrating autonomous systems through geographical scale cooperation networks, so the following directions guided the design of the G++ Agent Platform:

- *Support for heterogeneous execution hosts:* the size and weight of computers have become considerably smaller, and mobile computers have reached the performance only seen before in desktop computing systems, increasing the range of devices that can be integrated in a distributed automation society. It can include robots, autonomous sensors, PDAs, mobile phones, among others.
- *Support for physical mobility*: some control modules in robotics and automation system are expected to be able to change its position at geographic scale. For example they can run in portable devices carried by its users (e.g. PDAs), or they can be part of inherently mobile systems (e.g. on-board computers in vehicles). This means that connectivity has to be implemented in most cases through wireless networks, and then associated problems such as limited bandwidth and continuity of communications, must be addressed.
- *Support for heterogeneous (wireless) networking*: wireless communication is supported currently by a variety of networking technologies, offering diverse conditions, such as area coverage, bandwidth, cost, or QoS. Even more, not all of the available technologies are present in all geographical places, or they are not always offered with the same configuration at the physical layer. The infrastructure for a global automation system does not have to bet to a convergence in a unique and global-wide technology, but instead it has to be able to manage heterogeneity.
- *Support for heterogeneous systems and resources*: the development of large-scale systems usually requires the integration of new and legacy enterprise resources, such as database systems or old applications. Two strategies are commonly applied to face this integration, if rewriting the application is not possible: wrapping the old application through an extension of its code that allows direct interaction with the external system, or implementing a transducer, which is an interface that translates the external messages in a form suitable for the legacy system, and vice-versa.
- *Support for geographical-scale distribution*: an automation system can integrate systems located in separate geographical places. Although in these days, such integration is possible due to the worldwide coverage of the Internet, it is important to deal with latency times in communications that can be significant in some applications (e.g. direct teleoperation of a robot).

Under such a scenario, the possibility of letting each agent with all the responsibility for its integration with the environment (and consequently, with other peers) implied the agent overload and the replication of complex interaction functionalities. Existing platforms are not suitable to accomplish these requirements.

In the design of the G++ Agent Platform the above requirements are met. Reusability is a property we seek in this architecture, because it has to be applied in different context of robotics and automation, for example the operation of a colony of robots, the organization of virtual teams, or the integration of large-scale inter-factory logistics, among others.

The structure of our agent platform can be appreciated in Figure 2. It is important to state that the G++ Agent Platform is an agent infrastructure not committed to any standard agent architecture (e.g. FIPA), even if compatibility with standard specifications can be obtained adding compatibility modules.

4.2 The architecture of the G++ Agent Platform

The G++ Agent Platform runs over a Java Virtual Machine (JVM) hosted in a computational device. The execution environment of the G++ agent platform provides connectivity services, being responsible for the interactions among all agents. It is also responsible for the virtualization of the physical environment, through the implementation of sensors and actuators interfaces that agents can access. The platform offers two kinds of execution environment implementations, the Container and the Legs module.

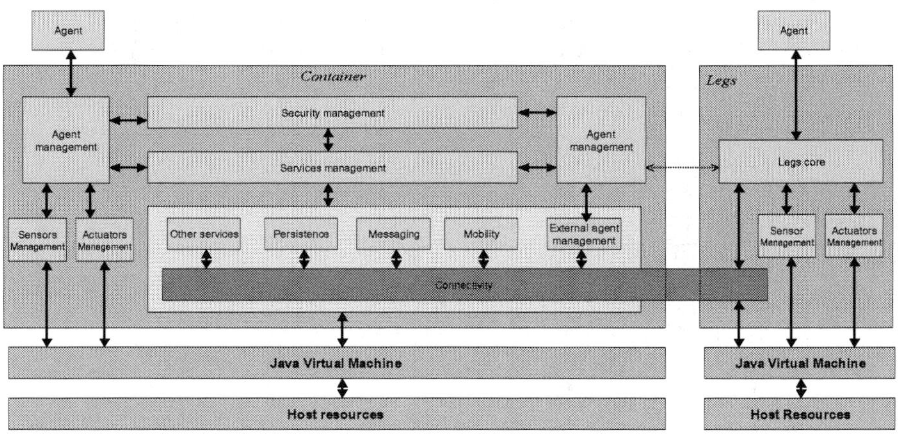

Fig. 2. The G++ platform's architecture.

a. Container

It is the environment for the execution of contained agents. A container runs over a Java Runtime Environment, which allows the access to the resources offered by the host. The container presents to the contained agents common services, such as messaging transport, local event communication, and support for access to external data repositories. Containers implement connectivity services among them for message interchange, and for agent and services migration. They also provide connectivity and state monitoring of external agents, and they instantiate proxies to make transparent the communication between external and internal agents.

b. Legs module

The platform can integrate agents running outside the container. These agents are called external agents or stand-alone agents.

The execution of external agents is allowed by Legs (Local External aGent Support) modules, which are limited execution environments able to host and execute one agent at time. They provide connectivity to a container, and then, to the entire platform. As contained agents, external agents can access all the services provided by the underlying JVM, and some of the communication services offered by the container, but they cannot access other services, such as the agent mobility. External agents can be useful, for example, for the implementation of control systems running on-board of mobile devices with limited capabilities.
The implementation of external agents follows the same structure given for the implementation of contained agents. In fact, if a contained agent does not use resources restricted to contained agents, or host's special resources, it can be transformed in an external agent just launching it from a LEGS module.
In the following subsections, main aspects of the platform are described.

4.2.1 The communication infrastructure

Since early stages of the design, this agent platform has been envisioned as the cornerstone of the distributed architecture for automation systems. In particular, under our conception this environment not only corresponds to the space where agents can perform their duties (as all platforms do), it is also aimed to provide a reliable communication infrastructure that agents can (and should) exploit to interact among themselves in a distributed application. As result, the G++ Agent Platform is able to offer an implementation of a robotic and automation system that will delegate to the own agent's container the conduction of the major communication traffic. So agents can communicate among themselves asking their own container to deliver the message to its destination. Messages are delivered following the best effort policy (i.e. no unnecessary delays are introduced in their expedition), but it is not guaranteed their reception in the right order. This can happen for two main reasons: 1) the latency of the Internet, plus costs incurred in retransmissions of packets naturally tends to increase the time required to transmit a message over long distances, and 2) the interconnections between containers define the paths that messages have to follow from the source to the target, each node acting as a router (the processing time on each container has to be added to the network delays described above). The platform, however, can guarantee the delivery of messages, detecting and informing the sender when they are not arrived within the pre-established time. A time window and a timestamp message field are used in the message for this scope. The time window value can also be infinite, which means no time window is specified. The message timestamp can also be useful to the message receiver, to determine the exact sequence of messages.
The timestamp is a key data to support the quality of the messaging service, but its generation is not easy because requires the adoption of a global time, shared among containers.

4.2.2 Virtual mobility

Virtual Mobility allows agents to be suspended, transported and restored in diverse containers. Mobility can be decided autonomously by the agent, in terms of the moment and destination in which it will be done, or can be enforced by the agent's owner, or by another agent. Mobility is implemented through the serialization of the state of the agent, the transport together with the code (if necessary), and the de-serialization at the destination

container. The platform does not provides support for the serialization of the stack of calling methods, so when this procedure is activated, the agent has to be suspended.
When an agent is moved from its home container to a foreign container, its original agent management system together with the mobility service is responsible to keep trace of the new position of the agent. In such a way, it is possible to implement automatic roaming in the communication to the agent.

4.2.3 Interaction with the environment

The structure of an agent considers a subsystem responsible for achieving information from its environment, where the environment can be virtual, composed by software processes or systems running in a computing device, or physical, as the real world is. For example, a virtual agent can be able to listen to keystrokes, listen to messages sent by other agents, receive network information, or perceive events from the operating system; a robotic agent can be enabled with sonars, infrared range sensors, accelerometers or gyroscopes to perceive the physical environment and its own relationship with it.
On the other hand, agents must be able to act over its environment in order to achieve their goals. The actions can result in a virtual effect, such as the creation of files, the communication of messages to other agents, or physical, as commands over the engine in a wheel-enabled robot.
Sensors and actuators are closely related to the environment because their functionality depends directly on the aspects that they have to detect. In this way, sensors and actuators are device-dependent. However, enabling software agents with specific sensors and actuators can limit their mobility in virtual spaces. The G++ Agent Platform manages sensors and actuators through interface objects that can be attached to agents in runtime. This allows a migrating agent to get access to the specific sensors and actuators offered in each container/platform. This flexibility is obtained providing a common interface for all sensors and actuators that the agent must use to interact with. Also is supported the definition of descriptors to recognize sensors and actuators that the agent could access.
The independence between the agent implementation and its environment makes it possible to follow an evolutionary approach in the development of software agents. In fact, as it is stated in (Arsten et. Al, 1996) complex systems often require development of prototypes and the simulation of the execution. Portability of agents allows new agents to be tested in simulation environments before they are deployed in the real world (e.g. a mobile robot controller). On the other hand, the model well suits for agents based on learning architectures or requiring initial training (such as those based on neural networks), because they can be conditioned for final execution in a simulated environment.

4.2.4 Security

The platform security is focused in the protection of the hosting platform (the container and its agents) from the attacks of potentially malicious visiting agents. The protection of the host is mainly based on trust, and this allows the adoption of a partially open distributed platform. It is *open* because it is possible to add new containers to the network, and each container can admit external agents, coming from other containers of the network. However, this openness is *partial*, because only authorized containers are accepted to join the network, and, potentially, only authorized agents are allowed to visit each host. This approach supposes the container to provide at least two security services, authentication and authorization. Both services are supported by a public key infrastructure (PKI).

5. The Agent-Based architecture for automation and robotics

In this section is described the agent-based software architecture for automation and robotics systems. The architecture follows the abstract model described in Section 3. It provides a set of agent-based meta-services to support advanced communication of the domain-specific systems built on top of it.

This agent-based architecture introduces a communication standard and a set of services to build global automation systems in different domains. The former defines the languages that will be used for exchange of information between entities participating in automation systems. The latter, the set of services that are available for supporting their activity. Three services are offered at this level:

a. *Messaging*: it provides persistence and reliability in direct messaging between senders and well-defined receivers. It is based on based on persistent messages queues, which allows time-decoupled communications among participants
b. *Event distribution*: it implements the asynchronous publish/subscribe communication model. Each container provides local event publication and notification services. The architecture for global automation systems includes agents for the management of distributed subscriptions and notifications.
c. *Service brokering*: it supports dynamic reconfiguration of the relationships between service providers and consumers. Each container provides local event publication and notification services. The architecture for global automation systems includes agents for the management of distributed subscriptions and notifications (that is, among different service points).

The design of the services has explicitly considered the problem of distribution, particularly the unreliability of network connections, which makes indistinguishable crashed components from slow components. This problem, common to all implemented services, was addresses through a mechanism of registration and renewal of the registration with the service provider, that interested users must perform during their lifecycle.

5.1 Messaging service

The messaging service implements reliable messaging delivery among agents, based on *Messenger agents* that extend basic communication capabilities of the G++ Agent Platform. The implementation of the messaging services requires providing each container of the agent society with a messenger agent that interfaces communicating agents with the service. Communicating agents that require to be supported by this service are requested to register themselves with the messenger agent, which maintains a list of agents that are subscribed for the service. Thus, the messenger agent only accepts messages having as target a registered agent, and rejects other messages. Each registration has as parameter the duration of the registration, which represents for how long the agent is interested in being supported by the messaging service. Therefore, the messaging service will be active for each specific communicating agent accordingly to the duration indicated in the registration, but in any moment registrations can be renewed for new periods. The messenger agent accepts messages sent by local agents (i.e. agents pertaining to the same container of the messenger), and delivers them to other agents residing in remote containers. It offers two modalities for delivery: normal delivery, that means the sender only receives an acknowledgement from the local messenger agent indicating that the message has been received by the messaging service, and notified delivery, that allows the sender to receive a notification when the message has finally reached the receiver.

The messaging service is performed through different interaction protocols that regulate the possible conversations between senders and receivers of messages and the messenger agents. Such protocols are:

a. *Subscription request*: performs the registration of an agent with the local messenger for a given period of time.
b. *Subscription renewal*: allows an agent the renewal of a subscription with the messenger for a new period.
c. *Subscription cancel*: an agent subscribed with a messenger can cancel its subscription in any moment, sending a cancel request message.
d. *Activate delivery*: after registration, an agent can request the activation of the message delivery, sending an activate delivery message to the messenger, so queued messages will be delivered to the requesting agent, and further messages received by the messenger will be delivered instantaneously.
e. *Suspend delivery*: an agent can request suspension of delivery of incoming messages at any moment, which means that the messenger agent will stop delivering messages addressed to that agent through it.
f. *Send message*: it is used to transmit a message to a receiver agent using the messaging service supported by messenger agents.
g. *Message Transfer*: it is used by two messengers when exchanging queues of messages.
h. *Message delivery*: this protocol regulates the conversation between a regular agent subscribed to the messaging service and the related messenger agent that has messages to deliver to the former.

5.2 Event distribution service

The communication among components is one of the important problems faced in the development of distributed systems. This is a characteristic of the architectural style of an application, and it can be implemented adopting two approaches (Moro & Natali, 2002): *request/response* and *publish/subscribe*.

The request/response paradigm, is widely adopted in traditional client/server distributed systems such as Web-based applications. However, it results not always adequate, particularly when applications need to continuously collect data generated from large-scale distributed sources, because the network could be overloaded with a high traffic of request and responses. Moreover, if the application includes components running on mobile systems, implementing complete cycles of polling could spend unnecessarily the limited power resource of the device, or could increase the expenses associated to communication traffic.

On the other hand, the publish/subscribe paradigm is claimed to provide the loosely coupled form of interaction required in large-scale systems (Eugster et al., 2003). In this model, components acting as subscribers have the ability to express their interest in some typologies of messages. Thus, they are subsequently notified when publishers generate the messages that match their interest. Using this approach, the communication between publishers and subscribers becomes loosely coupled because both participants do not need to know anything about each other. Communication services implemented over this architecture are usually known as event services.

The core of the event management in our architecture is the *EventBroker* agent, responsible for collecting subscriptions and sending events to the registered subscribers. Subscribers register their interest on events sending a *subscribe* message to the EventBroker agent, without the need to know the effective sources of these events. This subscription information remains stored in the EventBroker, and it is not forwarded to publishers. The event service also provides an *unsubscribe* operation that terminates a subscription. The subscription contains the following information: (1) typology of event of interest; (2) optionally the source of interest; and (3) duration of the subscription.

5.3 Service brokering service

Collaboration among distributed and autonomous control modules is the final objective of our robotics and automation platform. Thus, the whole structure of the framework is built around the idea of a reliable infrastructure for service integration. In part, this can be understood as the objective of classical networking infrastructures, such as DCOM, RMI or CORBA, which is the problem of finding and invoking remote services. However, our architecture does not oversimplify the relationships between the network and the applications, as the cited technologies do. The latter means that the network is seen as a not completely transparent environment, that is, mainly subject to a lack of reliability, with latency and limited bandwidth, in a mutable topology. Our framework explicitly considers that control modules can crash and the system should be aware of such services that become no longer available.

The services brokering service is aimed to establish relationships among the three entities called *client, server* and *service*. The service represents the object of interest that justifies the interaction between the other participants. Services are offered by agents or systems that play the role of servers, which are also responsible for providing, and if it is necessary, for scheduling the accesses to the resources need to perform the service. For example, in an image capture and transmission service, the robotic telecamera agent (server) is responsible for providing and managing the access to the telecamera requested to give the service. In our model, a server is completely free to offer whatever configuration of services, this means that a server can offer only one typology of service, or a wide variety of them. For a specific typology of service, a server could offer concurrently only one instance of service, that is, it can serve just client at time, or it can perform multiples executions simultaneously, depending on the specific implementation and the possibility to share the involved resources (such as external devices, CPU, memory, etc). Any server that joins the system and intends to let clients use its services, must clearly declare this intention by making a long term commitment to taking on a well-defined class of future requests. This declaration is called an *advertisement* and contains a specification of the server capability with respect to the type of request it can accept.

The *ServiceBroker* is the agent of our architectural model that manages a database of advertisements, i.e. it knows the name and location of registered servers, their capabilities, the service interfaces, and the supported communication protocols. When a client agent needs a service that implements a specific interface with specific capabilities, it queries the ServiceBroker for the name of all the available servers in the system that provides that capability. Clients are not supposed to have knowledge about the location of the services they require, they only have to know the name of the ServiceBroker, and direct their requests to it.

The GAP framework adopts the Extensible Markup Language (XML) as the content language to specify capabilities and preferences and to exchange information among distributed control modules over the platform. Description of services expressed in XML documents are exchanged during interactions among interacting agents. The messages that interchange the ServiceBroker with other agents are:

a. *Service advertisement*: it is sent by a server to the ServiceBroker describing the service it want to publish and how long it will be available.
b. *Service request*: contains a description that the client sends to the broker, regarding the characteristics of a requested service.
c. *Broker response*: it corresponds to the answer that the broker returns when dealing with a request coming from a client, indicating references to the services that can satisfy it.
d. *Service advertisement renewal*: allows a server to renew for another period its registration in the ServiceBroker.
e. *Advertisement cancellation*: it is sent by a server to the ServiceBroker that wants to cancel a previous service advertisement.

6. An example of domain-specific multi agent system

For the domain-specific application example, let us consider a colony of mobile robots that have to explore a surface, and cooperate synchronously collecting certain objects, that must be carried to the robots' base. This colony requires the participation of different kinds of autonomous devices:

- Explorers, which are autonomous mobile robots provided with telecameras and grippers, that recognize objects to be collected, and carry them to the nearest transport robot.
- Transport robots: they are autonomous mobile robots that receive the objects collected by explorers and transport them in batches to the colony nest.
- Coordinator: is the autonomous system that receives communication from carriers and coordinates the operation of explorer and transport robots. It operates in a fixed computing device, which is located outside the exploring area, and connected through satellite to the Communicator robot.
- Communicator: is a mobile device that acts as a gateway between the Coordinator and the robots located in the surface to explore.
- Colony Nest: is the computing device that runs messaging and brokering services of the nest.

In this system all the members run a container where operates the agent that implements the own control module. At startup, the containers pertaining to all devices in the surface to explore establish communication among themselves, using a peer-to-peer discovering protocol. Then they register their service capabilities in the ServiceBroker running in the Colony Nest device.

The coordinator, remotely located, creates a data channel with the Colony Nest, using a known IP direction to locate it. Thus, the coordinator asks the service broker located in the Colony Nest for the suitable robotics devices to accomplish the task. From the answer provided by the service broker, the coordinator selects a Communicator device, some explorers and transport robots.

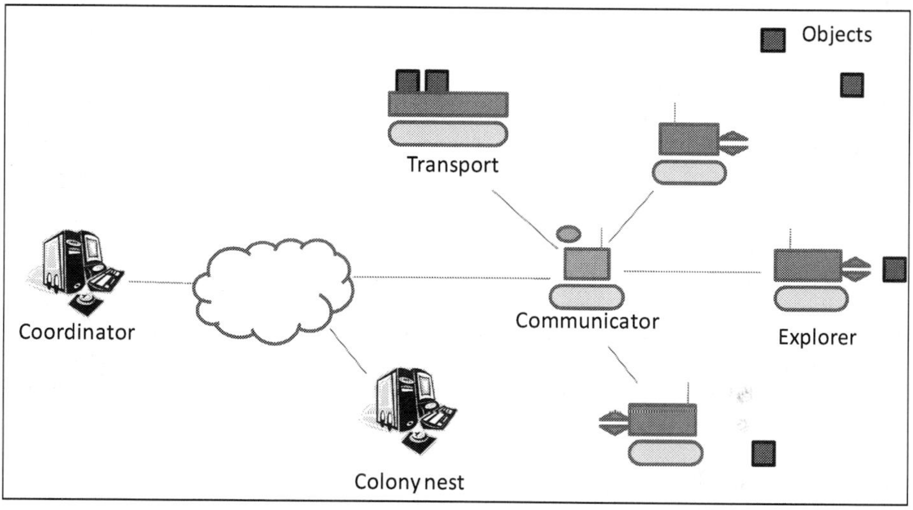

Fig. 2. A colony of explorers.

The Coordinator transmits the mission to each robotic device. The explorers move across the surface detecting objects to be collected, and transmit their positions to the Coordinator. With this information, the coordinator assigns routes to the transport robots, in order to pick up the objects collected by the explorers. If an explorer or transport robot goes out of the communication range, it starts a "turn back home" procedure in order to reestablish communication. If messages had been sent to that robot during the "blackout", they are kept in the messages queue of the MessagingService and transmitted when the device is "visible" again.

The Coordinator could be subscribed in the event broker to listen for certain events, such as mechanical failures. Thus, if a failure message is received, the coordinator can take measures like a replacement for the defective robot.

In the following subsections, the system is described using the model presented in this chapter.

6.1 Environment and autonomous equipments (levels 1 and 2)

The environment is mainly composed by the physical surface that have to be explored, the objects that have to be collected, the obstacles in the route of each robot, etc. Also, available communication networks or global positioning systems that can be accessed by devices are considered part of the environment. In terms of autonomous equipments we have all the devices participating in the colony, including the Coordinator and the Colony Nest devices. Robots are mobile vehicles enabled with sensors (cameras, GPS, encoders, etc.), actuators (engines, grippers, etc.) and communication interfaces (Wi-Fi, satellite, etc.) that must be available for local control modules (robot controllers).

6.2 The agent platform (level 3)

The G++ Agent Platform is used to provide the underlying software infrastructure for the implementation control modules. Each device must provide a Java Runtime Environment where a G++ Container will run. Also, in each robotic device the agent platform must have access to the API (application programming interface) of the available sensors and actuators, in order to build the access to physical components of the robots. The access to the communication stack is obtained, in general cases, through the standard TCP/IP interface provided by the device's operating system.

6.3 Agent-based architecture (level 4)

The agent based-architecture is made-up by all the components required to achieve interoperability among the different participants. For example, the ServiceBroker agent, which is responsible for maintaining the network location (IP address) of each robotic device, and the list of services that them are capable to provide. Another agent that participates in the architecture is the MessengerAgent that supports message queues for reliable delivery of message to mobile robots.

6.4 The domain-specific multi-agent system (level 5)

Each participant in the colony is conceptualized as a software agent, programmed to accomplish its own mission. The implementation requires providing every one of the devices with an agent/control. The control modules can be implemented using different artificial intelligence model. At this level must be also programmed the standard interfaces to the sensors and actuators, and registered locally as service objects in the device's container.

7. Conclusion

In this work we have described our framework for the implementation of distributed robotics and automation systems. Its design was driven by the interest to obtain a decoupled and scalable infrastructure in different application scenarios. This approach emphasizes software engineering aspects of agency, which is a differentiating point when comparing it with other architectures, whose functionalities are more focused in distributed artificial intelligence.

Currently we are developing some case of studies that can help us to test the framework in systems offering different complexity levels.

8. References

Aarsten, A.; Brugali, D. & Menga G. (1996). Designing Concurrent and Distributed Control Systems: an Approach Based on Design Patterns. *Communications of the ACM*, Vol.39, No. 10 (October 1996), pp. 50-58.

AgentLink (2002). Software Products for MultiAgent Systems. Technical Report. *Europe's Network of Excellence for Agent-Based Computing*.

Bellifemine, F.; Poggi, A. & Rimassa, G. (1999). Jade, a FIPA-Compliant Agent Framework. *Proceedings of the 4th Int. Conference on Practical Applications of Intelligent Agents and Multi-Agent Technology*, 1999.

Eugster, P.Th.; Felber, P.A., Guerraoui R. & Kermarrec A.M. (2003). "The Many Faces of Publish/Subscribe". *ACM Computing Surveys,* Vol. 35, No. 2 (June 2003), p. 114-131.

Finin T.; McKay, D.; Fritzson, R. & McEntire, R. (1993) KQML: An Information and Knowledge Exchange Protocol.*Proceedings of the Int. Conference on Building and Sharing of Very Large-Scale Kniowledge Bases,* December 1993.

FIPA (2002). FIPA ACL Message Structure Specification. Standard N. SC00061G, December 2002.

Genesereth M.R. & Ketchpel, S.P. Software Agents. *Communications of the ACM,* Vol 37, No. 7, 1994, p. 48-53.

Haibin Z. (2006). A Role-Based Approach to Robot Agent Team Design. *Proceedings of the IEEE International Conference on Systems, Man and Cybernetics SMC, 2006.* Vol.6 pp.4861-4866, October 2006.

Jennings N.R. (2001). An Agent-Based Approach for Building Complex Software Systems". *Communications of the ACM,* Vol 55 No. 4 (April 2001), p. 35-41.

Jianhui, L.; Kesheng, W.; Hang, G. & Ligang, Q. (2004). An OOT-supported migration approach to holonic robot assembly cell. *Proceedings of the 8th Int. Conference on Computer Supported Cooperative Work in Design, 2004.* Vol.2 pp. 498-501.

Lim, C.S.; Mamat, R. & Braunl, T. (2009) Market-based approach for multi-team robot cooperation. *4th International Conference on Autonomous Robots and Agents, ICARA 2009,* pp.62-67, Feb. 2009.

Mamady, D.; Tan, G.; & Toure M. L. (2008). An artificial immune system based multi-agent model and its application to robot cooperation problem. *Proceedings of the 7th World Congress on Intelligent Control and Automation, WCICA 2008,* pp.3033-3039, June 2008

Moro G. & Natali A. (2002). On the Event Coordination in Multi-Component Systems. *Proceedings of SEKE 2002,* Ischia, Italy.

Odell J.; Van Dyke Parunak H. & Bauer B. (2000) Extending UML for Agents. *Proceedings of the Agent-Oriented Information Systems Workshop at the 17th National Conference on Artificial Intelligence 2000.*

Rogers, T.E.; Sekmen, A.S. & Peng, J. (2006) Attention Mechanisms for Social Engagements of Robots with Multiple People. *The 15th IEEE International Symposium on Robot and Human Interactive Communication, ROMAN 2006,* pp.605-610, Sept. 2006.

Sims, M.; Corkill, D. & Lesser, V. (2004). Separating Domain and Coordination in Multi-Agent Organizational Design and Instantiation, *Proceedings of the International Conference on Intelligent Agent Technology, IAT 2004.*

Valckenaers, P.; Van Brussel, H. & Holvoet, T. (2008). Fundamentals of Holonic Systems and Their Implications for Self-Adaptive and Self-Organizing Systems. *Proceedings of the Second IEEE International Conference on Self-Adaptive and Self-Organizing Systems Workshops, SASOW 2008.,* pp.168-173, Oct. 2008

Weiss, G. (1999) *Multiagent Systems: A Modern Approach to Distributed Artificial Intelligence.* MIT Press, Cambridge, Massachusetts, 1999

Weyns, D.; Schumacher, M.; Ricci, A., Viroli M., & Holvoet T. 'Environments for multiagent systems, State-of-the-art and research challenges'. In Lecture Notes in Computer Science, vol 3374 (2005), Berlin, Heidelberg, Germany.

8

Use of e-Science Environment on CFD Education

Jongbae Moon[1], Jin-ho Kim[2], Soon-Heum Ko[3], Jae Wan Ahn[2], Kum Won Cho[1], Chongam Kim[2], Byoungsoo Kim[4] and Yoonhee Kim[5]

[1]Korea Institute of Science and Technology Information,
[2]School of Mechanical and Aerospace Engineering, Seoul National University,
[3]Center for Computation and Technology, Louisiana State University,
[4]Dept. of Aerospace Engineering, Choongnam National University
[5]Dept. of Computer Science, Sookmyung Women's University
[1,2,4,5]Korea
[3]USA

1. Introduction

'e-Science' represents the global collaborations of people and shared resources to solve new and challenging problems in science and engineering (Hey & Trefethen, 2003) on the basis of the IT infrastructure, typically referred to as the Grid (Foster & Kesselman, 1999). As we can easily infer, e-Science initially meant a virtual environment where a new and challengeable research can be accomplished using latest infrastructures. That virtual environment usually has a form of a web portal page or an independent application with a bunch of computer scientific components inside: high-end application researches include large-scale computations for complex multi-physical mechanisms, coupled works of computation and experiments for design-to-development processes, and/or data-intensive researches. The infrastructure consists of computational and experimental facilities, valuable datasets, knowledge, and so on. Researchers can be referred to as a core component of e-Science environment as their discussions and collaborations are promoted by, managed by and integrated to the environment.

Meanwhile, the meaning of 'e-Science' is becoming broader nowadays. Though e-Science first intended to enrich high-end research activities, it is soon proven to be also effective on academic activities as a cyber education system. (On the other hand, use on inter-disciplinary collaborative researches is not much vitalized as expected, because of diverse preference on internal workflow, I/O and interface among research domains.) Thus, the term 'e-Science' is rather used to represent 'all scientific activities on high performance computing and experimental facilities with the aid of user-friendly interface and system middleware' these days.

As a virtual academic system for aerospace engineering, 'e-AIRS' (e-Science Aerospace Integrated Research System) has been designed and developed since 2005. After three years' development, e-AIRS educational system is finally open, where non-experts can intuitively conduct the full process of computational and experimental fluid dynamic study. Also, the

system is currently under improvement to the research system and eventually would include other physical domains for multi-disciplinary researches.
To develop a cyber education system, we have employed/developed a number of computational and experimental components, as well as lots of middleware modules. They include computer scientific modules (monitoring and scheduling, metadata management, plotting), CFD (Computational Fluid Dynamics) computation tools (mesh generator, visualization software, CFD solver), and remote experiment management tool. Computing and experimental facility pool including resources in Korea, Japan, and Germany are/were connected to e-AIRS server by using Globus (http://www.globus.org). Access Grid Toolkit (http://www.accessgrid.org) is used for open discussion. Services are implemented on a web portal interface, developed by using GridSphere (http://www.gridsphere.org).
Current system is used as lecture materials for undergraduate and graduate fluid dynamic classes. Students get offline lecture on the physical basis of their application target, be trained on how to use the system, and their own simulation on representative fluid dynamic phenomenon through the CFD service in e-AIRS portal. Up to now, more than two hundred students in five universities experienced the use of e-AIRS as their lecture materials and they demonstrated more understand on CFD by using this web portal.
The characteristics and features of e-AIRS educational system will be demonstrated in this chapter. We will first describe how we applied the computer scientific concept (e-Science) to the application domain (fluid dynamics) in detail, including our objective and strategy, design of system and troubleshooting between computer scientist and application researcher. Next, our technology implemented/improved/developed are to be mentioned, including what has been done to develop an optimal system for a specific application domain (fluid dynamics), where we had a hard time in applying currently available computer scientific technology. Then, we will demonstrate how much our product influenced on the education of students majoring in this domain, and will briefly introduce our next goal (professional research system) with current technical trouble.

2. Design of a system

2.1 Motivation

For years, a number of researches have been promoted to conduct aerospace engineering researches/educations under the latest cyber infrastructure. As the representative researches on e-Science, a few projects in the UK e-Science program, a workbench by German Aerospace Center (DLR), a research system by NASA are present. The Distributed Aircraft engine Maintenance Environment (DAME: Jackson et al., 2003) is an UK e-Science pilot project, demonstrating the use of the Grid to implement a distributed diagnostic system for deployment in maintenance applications and environments. The main aim of DAME is to construct a distributed aircraft engine maintenance environment, motivated by the needs of Rolls-Royce and its information system partner Data Systems and Solutions. The Grid-Enabled Optimisation and Design Search for Engineering (GEODISE: http://www.geodise.org) is also one of the UK e-Science pilot projects. It is intended to enable engineers to carry out engineering design search and optimisation involving fluid dynamics, and is bringing together the collective skills of engineers and computer scientists. The Grid-Enabled Computational Electromagnetics (GECEM: http://www.wesc.ac.uk) project aims to use and develop Grid technology to enable large-scale and globally-distributed scientific and engineering research. The focus of GECEM project is collaborative numerical simulation and visualisation between globally-distributed research groups. The Grid-Enabled Wind Tunnel Test System (GEWiTTS: Crowther et al., 2005) project is concerned with the development of a GRID enabled set of communication protocols that enable scientific test equipment and facilities to be networked with computational resources and data storage/visualisation in a secure yet flexible manner. The TENT (Forkert et al., 2000), a simulation environment for DLR, is a component-based framework for the integration of technical applications. The main goal of TENT is the integration of all tools which belong to the typical workflows in a computer aided engineering (CAE) environment and it allows the engineer to design, automate, control, and steer technical workflows interactively. The DARWIN(Walton et al., 2000) is a distributed analysis tool that was developed at the NASA Ames Research Center to support aeronautics design activities. By providing aircraft manufacturers with faster access to wind-tunnel data, the DARWIN system helps to shorten the aircraft design and test process.

Also, there have been a number of trials on developing a cyber education system for fluid dynamic study. E-Fluids (http://www.efluids.com) holds a number of images and videos on various fluid dynamic experiments and computations and it also supports web-based numerical simulation. Java Applets for Engineering Education (http://www.engapplets.vt.edu) includes many Java applets related to fluid dynamics, statics and dynamics. Users can get the source code for all applets. In the Java Virtual Wind Tunnel (http://raphael.mit.edu/Java/), an interactive two-dimensional inviscid CFD simulation of a channel with a bump can be conducted. Users can experiment how the solution evolves with different boundary conditions and numerical schemes.

Though above projects on developing a professional research environment have opened a new scientific frontier on integration of aerospace engineering divisions with IT technology, they also have some weak points in service environment constitution. For example, they are specified for professional engineers and permit only assigned member, so that many general users can not access or use them. There is no user-friendly interface or portal web site for various classes of user groups. Also, for the cyber education system described above, users can easily learn at anytime and anywhere, but there are limitations that simulation and experiment are separated, and they don't have enough resources to conduct many simulations simultaneously.

In consequence, the e-Science environment for any kind of scientific computing including aerospace engineering should be a users' playground, which encourages pioneering trials on their domain science with maximal degree-of-freedom. In this sense, the environment should possess the latest IT technology for application scientists; help various types of researches by conjugating computation, instrumentation and data-driven approach; gather and open as many knowledge as possible; support and encourage the coupling of multiple disciplines; give a detailed guideline on using this environment. Thus, a new e-Science environment is devised to integrate latest IT technology with aerospace engineering discipline and conjunct computation with experiment and existing datasets, in the form of a web portal.

2.2 Objectives and strategies

E-AIRS has been developed and used since 2005 (Kim et al., 2006; Ko et al., 2007), as a product of the Korean e-Science project. The Korean e-Science project has been promoted since 2005 with support from the Korean Ministry of Science and Technology. On the basis of the Korean Grid infrastructure, five research topics were selected as main applications. They include the remote imaging service of an electron microscope, climate information system, molecular simulation, bioinformatics, and the current aerodynamic research system. As can be inferred from its name, e-AIRS first aimed to give a full support on aerospace engineering research process including numerical simulations and instrumental experiments. However, it is soon proven to be very hard to establish a professional research environment without breaking our primary propositions. First, in implementing CFD codes, researchers preferred to import their own solvers without having to change their interfaces according to the formula of system, and suggested diverse GUI designs compatible with their tools. Regarding the instrumental experiments, many valuable data were closely related to national defence, so asked to be protected within an organization. However, it was contradictory to our policy, which is 'to open all information to public and give equal opportunity to all users'. Thus, we have turned our direction to develop a web portal for academic use first and migrate to professional research environment which intensify users' controllability on numerical simulations and allow data protection by restricted user group. Thus, we have determined our objective to construct an easy-to-use cyber education system which includes the full procedure of numerical simulation, remote execution of instrumental experiment with a number of referential datasets, valuable knowledge to academic user. Also, considering the enormous time on building a multi-disciplinary scientific research environment, we first focus on supporting fluid dynamic research activity. As the schematic in Fig. 1 shows, non-experts can intuitively conduct the full process of computational and experimental fluid dynamic study in the e-AIRS educational system. Also, professional users can perform their parametric study on representative fluid dynamic applications.

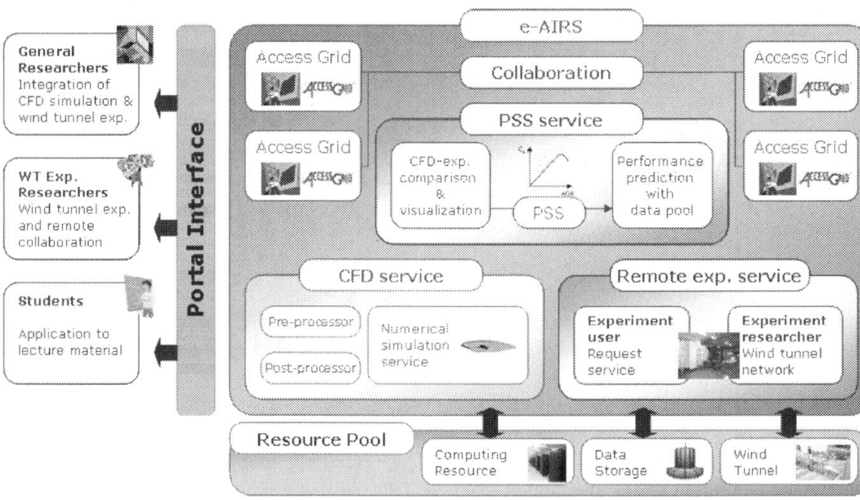

Fig. 1. Schematic of e-AIRS Educational System

The major strategies to establish the above system can be summarized as follows:

- Open to Public: The system should be open to anybody who wants help from us. They should be able to request our service anytime, anywhere. In this reason, the system will be built in the form of a web portal.

- User Interface: Portal interface will be easy enough for non-experts to use intuitively. So, all simulation toolkits are attached in or linked with portal pages. Also, most controllable variables for numerical and instrumental experiments are set up as default values and hidden inside the system to avoid users' mistake.
- Middleware and Core Modules: We focus on integrating application domains and showing our system is running in any cases, not devoting much time on designing and developing new software. We perform a deep survey on available and reliable middleware/application components and minimize the new development.
- CFD Service: Required tools for CFD simulations (i.e., mesh generator, flow simulation code, visualization software) are included in the system. Pre- and post-processing tools are developed in the form of a web application, CFD solver support easy control with automatic parallelization.
- Remote Experiment Service: Considering impossibility to control wind tunnels electronically, the remote experiment service will be asking the experimental operator to conduct specific experiments for users. For this, e-AIRS will facilitate close connection between end-user and experimental operator.
- Integrated Research Service: This service will show the comparison between CFD and experimental results. Furthermore, automated high throughput computing on the selected ranges should be conducted. The system supports automatic parameter sweep and submission of multiple tasks.
- Collaborative Conference: Basically depend on functionality in AGTk. Use various shared applications and give a guideline to use them.

2.3 Brainstorming and conceptual design

As mentioned in the above section, our main strategy is to maximize the use of existing software and focus on integrating them to work. So, a lot of time is spent on filling the list of reliable software components and selecting ones for our system construction.

For portal interface, the main focus would be user-friendliness. So, a long time has been spent on designing detailed user interface and lots of toolkits for web portal development were investigated to select which toolkit will satisfy our design needs. We chose GridSphere as a portal construction package. The GridSphere portlet framework provides a solution to construct an open-source web portal which provides with a friendly and easy to use interface by allowing users to interact with Grid services through standards means such as a web browser. It can also enable developers to quickly develop and package third-party portlet web applications that can be run and administered within the GridSphere portlet container. It supports administrators and individual users to dynamically configure the content based on their requirements. One of the reasons we choose GridSphere is that Gridsphere itself provides grid-specific portlets and APIs for grid-enabled portal development.

CFD service should support pre- and post-processing tools as well as CFD solvers for one-stop CFD service. Also, they shall run through portal page. The selection of CFD tools were rather easy because a CFD group participating in this project already possessed their own tools. As we already had an accurate parallel solver for moderate CFD simulations, this in-house code was used as the core of CFD service. Regarding mesh generator and visualization software, these tools we have possessed were programmed with C language. To let them run through the portal page, they have been ported to Java language and serviced in the form of web applications.

On the other hand, designing a remote experiment service was so hard. First, aerospace engineering experiments were closely related to national defence researches. The security requirement makes instruments hard to open to public service. Thus, moderate-sized supersonic and subsonic wind tunnels possessed by current research group are used to public service. Second, the wind tunnel experiment cannot be digitalized and automated. As all experiments should be done manually, the web portal will support users in requesting specific experiments and getting the resultant data conducted at one of the wind tunnel facilities in the resource pool.

Regarding system construction, we could list a number of middleware available for e-AIRS service. To connect computing infrastructure with e-AIRS system, Globus has been used for Grid setup. Monitoring and scheduling tools will follow resource contributors' choices. Metadata management service and database setup are referenced by previous portal setup experiences. Other components like plotting service and parametric study engine are newly developed.

For collaborative conference, various shared applications are implemented on AGTk. Of these services, the remote visualization was hardest to refer to: though Shared GNUPlot was the only available one, CFD researchers feel hard and uneasy to control this software. Thus, some example scripts are attached to the system to ease CFD visualization.

Designed architecture of e-AIRS system according to above brainstorming is given in Fig. 2.

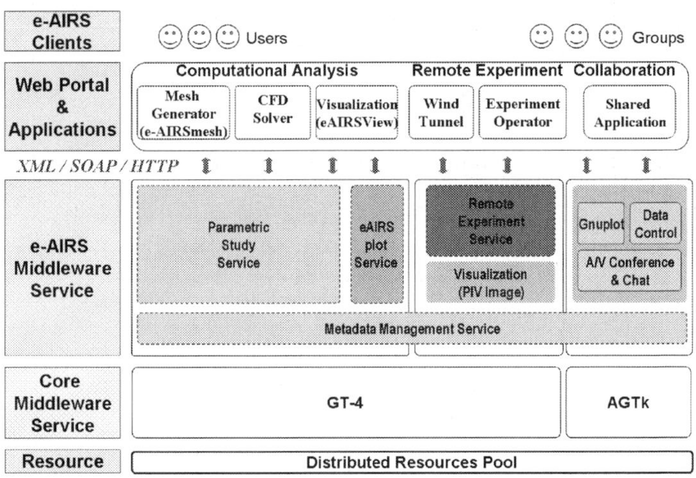

Fig. 2. The Architecture of e-AIRS

3. Development of e-AIRS: infrastructure and general middleware components

3.1 Use of international resource pool

For computing service, e-AIRS first tries to use our own local clusters in KISTI and Seoul National University, Korea, and submits job requests to PRAGMA Grid testbed (http://www.pragma-grid.net) when more resources are required. E-AIRS server requests job execution by using Globus and follows PRAGMA's policy when using international resources. The authors wish to acknowledge the use of the PRAGMA Grid testbed and technical support of many researchers and site administrators at PRAGMA member institutions.

For wind tunnel experiments, e-AIRS utilizes local supersonic and subsonic wind tunnel facilities at Seoul National University. E-AIRS server is connected to control PCs of these equipments to request remote experiments and get resultant data from experimental operators.

3.2 Implementation of core middleware service

3.2.1 Globus

We use the Globus Toolkit to establish cyber environment for CFD simulation because the Globus Toolkit - the de facto standard for open source grid computing infrastructure - is the world's most widely-used set of services and software libraries to support Grids and Grid applications. This Toolkit is freely available in open source format on the Web with applications for security, information infrastructure, resource management, data management, communication, fault detection, portability and more. In many ways, the Globus Toolkit defines Grid computing which enables users to solve a technical or scientific problem that requires a great number of computer processing cycles or access to large amount of data.

We installed Globus Toolkit 4 on our local server to access and submit jobs to computing resources based on Grid. The computing resources are distributed geographically and installed Globus Toolkit 2 or 4. Actually this version of e-AIRS only supports for resources with Globus Toolkit 4 to submit jobs. We are developing an adapter module for Globus Toolkit 2 and 4 so that users can submit jobs to computing resources with different version of Globus Toolkit. e-AIRS uses some Globus components such as WS GRAM for resource management, GridFTP for transferring files, and GSI for security.

A user can log into web portal to solve problems by using Grid environment. Actually, all users should have to get a grid account and proxy to submit a job on Grid environment. However, it is hard to add and manage lots of grid account on each site. So we only use one grid account for all portal users, which means all portal users are mapped into one grid account in e-AIRS system and are sharing one proxy certificate. Even though users share one proxy certificate, it is not much of a problem. Because e-AIRS is a web portal environment and does not support shell environment such as remote terminal using telnet or ssh, so users can't directly access and modify any files.

3.2.2 AGTk (Access Grid Toolkit)

Remote conferencing on e-AIRS is managed by the AGTk (Access Grid Toolkit), and the concept is shown in Fig. 3. When a user needs a remote discussion with other researchers, the user can create a new AG session, and see the session information on the e-AIRS portal. The host can also include participants from the user list on the portal, and the portal server will automatically send e-mail notices to the requested participants. Then, they can participate in the remote conference either by directly accessing the session or by following the link to the session, which is presented on the portal. Fig. 4 shows the interface of the e-AIRS collaboration service.

The AGTk is a powerful system for both remote communication and research data sharing. Detailed AGTk specifications will be omitted in this paper because the AGTk is popular and

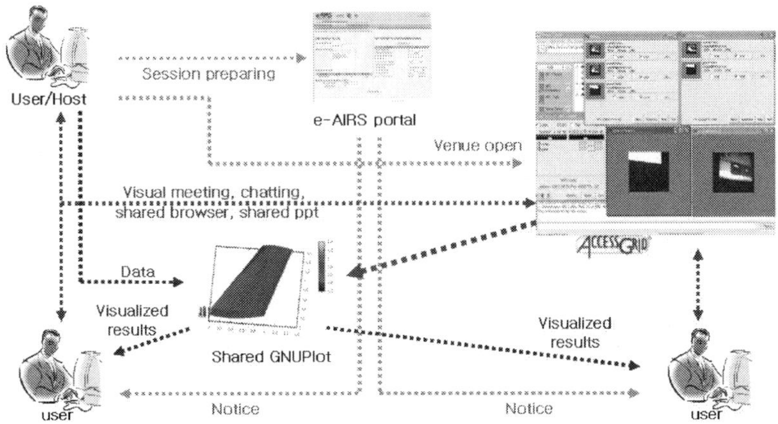

Fig. 3. Overview of the e-AIRS collaboration service

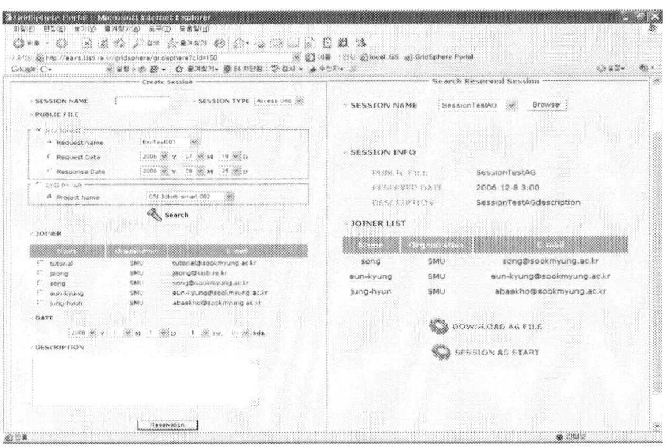

Fig. 4. Interface of the e-AIRS collaboration service

broadly used. Apart from the virtual face-to-face conference and chatting functions, participants in remote conferencing can exploit other shared applications to exchange their ideas and data through AGTk environment. The shared applications include shared PPT, shared browser, shared desktop, shared PDF, and so on. Furthermore, to share research data, the shared GNUPlot software is installed. PIG(Personal Interface to AccessGrid) nodes have been established at Seoul National University, KISTI(Korea Institute of Science and Technology Information), and Sookmyung University.

Because shared desktop on AGTk only supports full screen mode, we developed a module for integrating AGTk and TightVNC which is a free remote control software package. Using TightVNC, Users can see the desktop of a remote machine and control it with your local mouse and keyboard, just like you would do it sitting int the front of that computer. Using this module, users can also view the remote desktop in whole on a screen of smaller size, or users can zoom in the picture to see the remote screen in more detail.

3.3 Formulation of e-AIRS middleware service

3.3.1 MMS (Metadata Management Service)

Because of large amount of numerical data in CFD simulations, the massive data storage should be established separately from the portal server. If the data is saved in the separated storage, it has to be described where certain data is stored. The metadata contains size and type information of the real data, storage server information, and so on. The MMS(Metadata Management System) is integrated management service for this 'metadata and real data' hierarchy. The main roles of MMS can be summarized as follows:

- Creation of metadata
- Storing of metadata onto the meta-DB
- Browsing of metadata when there is a reuse query
- Transfer of real data from the separated server to the portal server

MMS is integrated management service about various data; input data, computational result data, experiment data, and sharing data for collaboration. When user operates his job, his data are accumulated, but user wants to reuse used data and search his data easily. We provide that user only uses projects/cases and system connect selected project/case, DB and real data in remote storage through MMS. User can reuse and analysis whole data easily. If user selects a project, MMS matches cases to the project and connects parameter value of case. Also, since MMS entirely manages data, if user can select a project, user can get computational data and experiment data about the project. e-AIRS service modules call MMS to access the data. MMS is developed as internal web service for security.

Data Storage having real data and DB server are Resource Layer. Portal service, job submission, job monitoring, user management service, e-AIRS internal services are Service Layer. MMS are in Middleware Layer for such services can access and use data in Resource Layer MMS use DB value using wrapper classes which are matching to DB table, and the value of wrapper classes are got/set/updated/deleted by specific web services.

3.3.2 PSS (Parametric Study Service)

Job submission system takes the role of assigning available computing resources to every job when multiple simulations with various input conditions are requested. In e-AIRS, the PSS(Parametric Study Service) supplies not only the assignment of massive computation jobs to resources but also the control of running simulations, using the job scheduling technique. Completed simulation results on various input conditions are then aggregated in a graph by the PSS in order to plot the change of flow characteristics(i.e., lift and drag coefficient profiles) with variation of input parameters(i.e., flow angle of attack, Mach number, Reynolds number).

The PSS is composed of several internal and three external modules. These modules are connected on the Grid services. The EDL(Experiment Description Language) possesses simulation information and it is extended with the reference of RSL(Resource Specification Language) and JSDL(Job Submission Description Language). The EPP(Experiment Parametric Parser) understands the EDL, and effectively creates task units. The ETS(Experiment Task Scheduler) assigns available resources for tasks. An aim of the ETS is to flexibly control tasks according to performance and state of resources and to provide executive environments. The ETD(Experiment Task Dispatchers) bids available resources execute defined tasks.

The Grid information service gives resource information to the PSS internal modules. The experiment information service acquires the metadata from tasks and provides task information to users.

The PSS helps clients acquire additional flow data by simulation. The missing-data-acquisition process proceeds along the following sequence:

1. Choice of the end-cases of data-missing region
2. Generation of the number of sub-cases
3. Automatic submission of additional calculations
4. Final graph-drawing using the validation service.

The PSS consists of four components: a parameter parser, a task generator, a task scheduler, and a task allocator. The parameter parser confirms the user input, and obtains suitable parameter information from the database. The task generator produces sub-cases under the parameter information, and writes sub-case information on the database. The task scheduler checks the status of the computing resources, and the task allocator distributes calculation jobs to the resources of the HTC environment. Fig. 5 shows the overview of the PSS process.

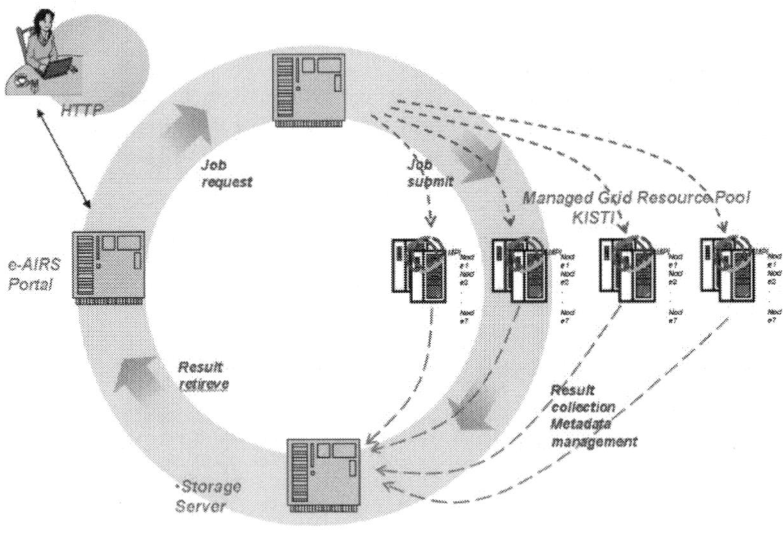

Fig. 5. Overview of automatic job execution of the PSS

3.3.3 Monitoring service

A submitted job is identified by a unique job ID, which can be used for enquiry about the job status. Seven different job states can be presented depending on the current status: queued, stage-in, ready, active, stage-out, done, and failed. Fig. 6 shows the interface of the monitoring service.

With the monitoring service, a user can monitor the latest status of the simulation. The user also can see the convergence history graph for error checking. We developed an error history data module which show error history data that is output of solvers on graph. The convergence history and intermediate results enable the user to judge whether the computational procedure is correct. The user can interrupt the job if it turns out to be wrong. e-AIRS periodically gathers intermediate result files from computing resources by using GridFTP.

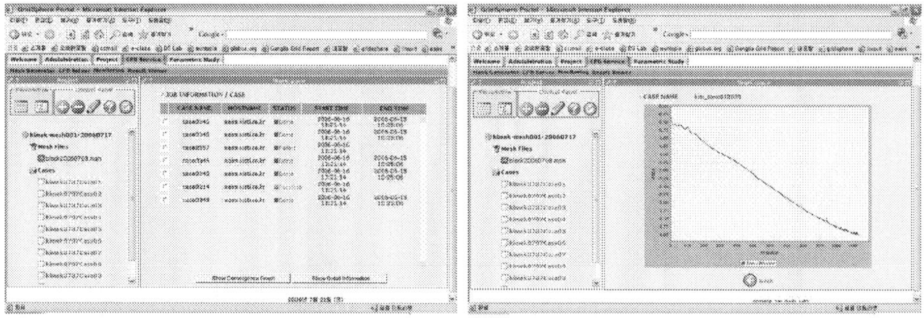

Fig. 6. The monitoring service of e-AIRS

3.3.4 Scheduler

Actually, a scheduler is implemented as a part of PSS. The scheduler fetches a queued job from Database; when a user submits a job, the job is just inserted into a Database and set the field to 'Queued'. And then, the scheduler checks available resource by retrieving RESOURCEINFO table in the Database. The RESOURCEINFO table keeps available queues and status. We should keep dynamic information about available queues, but now set the values manually; we use PRAGMA grid, but there is no global resource broker and scheduler. After the scheduler selects one of resources, it assigns the job into the selected resource. The scheduler assigns queued jobs into first selected resource until the queue is full. If the queue is full, remaining jobs are assigned to the next selected resource.

4. Development of e-AIRS: e-AIRS service components

4.1 CFD software

As application tools, a simple mesh generator and a visualization tool for CFD are developed and attached to a portal in the form of Java applets, and compiled CFD solvers within computing pool are executed using input flow parameters through user interface. They cover the full CFD simulation procedure, seen in Fig. 7.

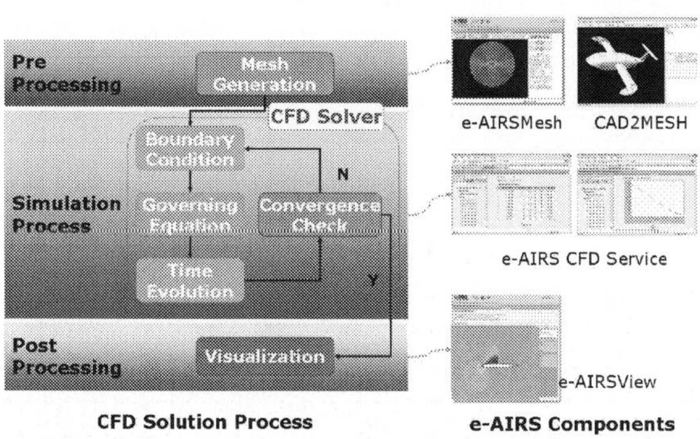

Fig. 7. CFD Service Flow

4.1.1 A mesh generator

The mesh system means the set of discrete cells around the target geometry. CFD simulation tool can obtain the physical values of gas or air on this divided zone, by calculating the numerical fluxes between neighboring spatial cells. Currently, the e-AIRS users can either use their existing mesh system or generate a new mesh on the portal.

To generate the mesh system on the e-AIRS, users need to use two softwares of 'CAD2MESH' and 'e-AIRSmesh'. At first, CAD2MESH captures major line and surface components from CAD data file. CAD2MESH can read CAD files with VRML format and returns those components to e-AIRSmesh input format. Then, e-AIRSmesh generates the mesh system around the body. To construct the mesh system, an algebraic method by a transfinite interpolation technique is used. Also, exponential, hyperbolic tangent, and hyperbolic sine functions are used to distribute grid points.

e-AIRSmesh has a convenient interface to create the model geometry, to make a mesh system, and to specify boundary conditions. Additionally, for easier mesh generation of simple shapes, e-AIRSmesh supports some default mesh templates for standard geometries such as cubical or spherical shape and NACA 4-digit airfoils. CAD2MESH and e-AIRSmesh softwares are shown in Fig. 8.

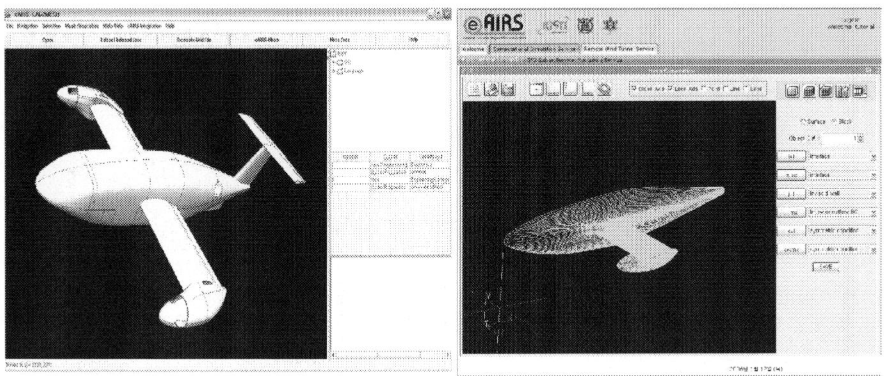

Fig. 8. CAD2MESH and e-AIRSMesh applications

4.1.2 CFD simulation codes

Accurate CFD solver is the core of fluid dynamic simulations. Two in-house CFD solvers for incompressible and compressible flow simulation (Lee et al., 2006; Kim et al., 2003) are imported on e-AIRS. Basically, included CFD codes can conduct parallel simulation and they solve three-dimensional fluid dynamic problems from subsonic to supersonic flow ranges. But, for e-AIRS service, solvers need to be light to enable a number of students to run multiple simulations at the same time within restricted resources. Thus, in e-AIRS, solvers are fixed to solve two dimensional problems by serial processing. Details on solvers are described on above references.

4.1.3 CFD visualization

During and after the computation, all output data in result directory of each case are transferred to a storage server. And, saved resultant data can either be downloaded to users' local machine or visualized through the portal. e-AIRS supports the JAVA-based, free visualization software. As seen in Fig. 9, e-AIRS can visualize the resultant pressure data of the CFD computations with various visualization functions, such as displaying mesh, contour, vector, and boundary plot attributes.

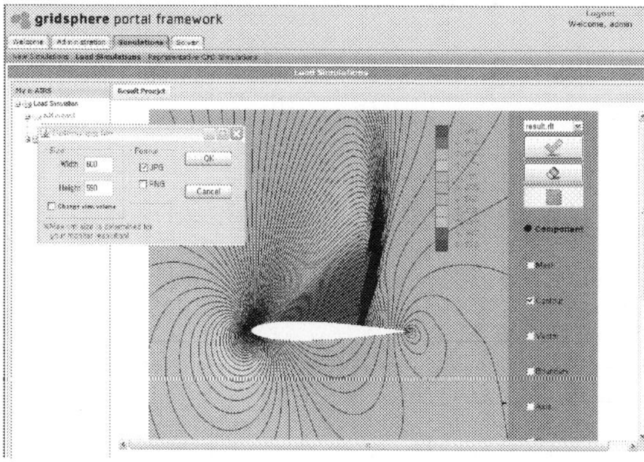

Fig. 9. A data visualization software on the e-AIRS portal

4.2 Components for remote experiment

The remote experiment service consists of three services: the experiment request service, the experiment management service, and the experiment information service. A client can request an experiment through the experiment request service. Then the wind tunnel operator checks newly requested experiments on the experiment management service. This management service offers the detailed information of requested experiment to the operator such as the Reynolds number, the angle of attack, the data form, the test area on the aerodynamic model, and so on. Then the operator can carry out adequate experiments and upload result data files including particle image through web UI. Finally, a client user can browse and check the status of the experiment through the experiment information service. The states are classified as <NEW>, <ON-GOING>, and <FINISHED>. This information service also shows various images with which a user is able to see the result image files conveniently. The figure 9 shows the remote experiment procedures.

The interface of the remote experimental service is composed of various portlets which are developed within the framework of GridSphere. The GridSphere portlet framework provides a solution to construct an open-source web portal. The GridSphere supports standard portlets, and these can be extended to the new portlets. The portlets are implemented in Java and can be modified easily. Regarding experimental service, portal pages cover remote experiment request and information on the result, and Access Grid Toolkit allows the open discussion to that experiment, as in Fig. 10. The AGTk is a powerful system for both remote communication and research data sharing. Apart from the basic face-to-face conference and chatting functions, the participants of remote conferencing can use other shared applications to share their ideas and data. The shared applications are the shared PPT, shared browser, shared desktop, shared PDF, and so on. Furthermore, for sharing of the research data, the shared GNUPlot software is installed. PIG(Personal Interface to AccessGrid) nodes are established in Seoul National University, KISTI(Korea

Institute of Science and Technology Information), Sookmyung University, and KARI(Korea Aerospace Research Institute).

Fig. 10. Remote Experiment Service

5. Use of e-AIRS on academic activities

5.1 Additional support for academic activities

Developed e-AIRS web portal is utilized as lecture materials of undergraduate and graduate classes. Usually, students first learn the basic physics of their application problems in the offline class and get trained on how to use the system. After then, they conduct their numerical simulations through e-AIRS web portal.

Though the tutorial on system usage is given to students, it is insufficient for students to understand the procedure of CFD and fully utilize the whole service within e-AIRS system. Thus, an e-AIRS web page is also developed to let students to review the physics and portal usage by their own. A number of valuable materials on fluid dynamics are stored in the web page. Also, this site provides video tutorials which contain the way of using e-AIRS portal and solving representative fluid dynamic problems, which will be explained in the next section. Features of e-AIRS web pages are given in Fig. 11.

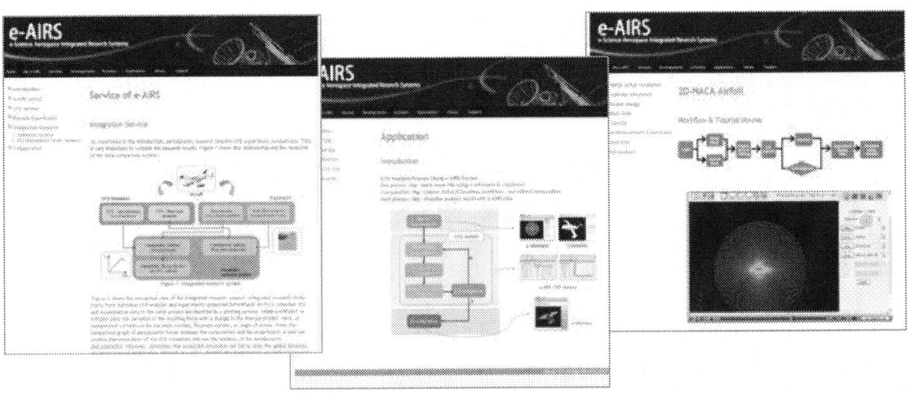

Fig. 11. e-AIRS Web Page (http://eairs.kisti.re.kr/eairs)

5.2 Use of the system on classes

5.2.1 Fluid dynamic applications for students

For the education of students, application problems need to contain various physics of fluids. And, the flow solver is recommended to be light and efficient to reduce total computing time. Thus, two-dimensional compressible and incompressible CFD examples are selected and CFD service on the e-AIRS utilized for the education of undergraduate and graduate students.

For compressible flow analysis, flowfield around NACA0012 airfoil (Fig. 12) is selected as examples. Flow analysis over a NACA0012 airfoil is a conventional example of aerodynamics. In this problem, Mach number and angle of attack are set to be 0.73 and 6 degree. By using 'mesh template' function in e-AIRSmesh, users can make NACA airfoil mesh and impose boundary condition easily. As the flow is in transonic range, a shock wave is formed on upper surface and flow properties change abruptly through the shock.

Likely, the unsteady flow analysis over a cylinder has been selected for the understanding of incompressible flow characteristics. The results (Fig. 13) show the difference of pressure contour and streamlines by the viscous effect. In viscous flows at specific Reynolds numbers, vortices are shed alternatively from the upper and lower surfaces of the cylinder, creating the periodic flow pattern.

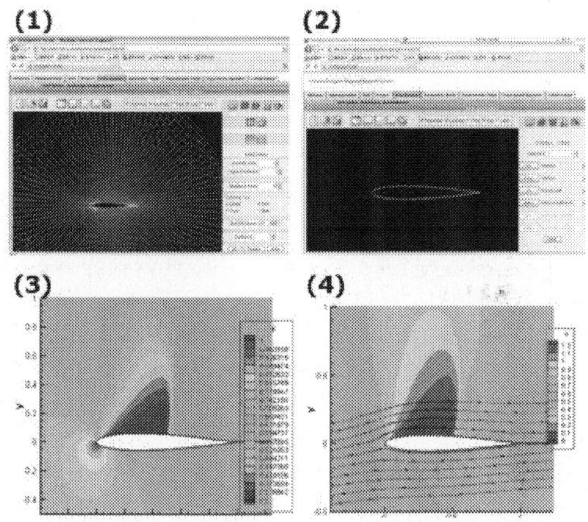

Fig. 12. NACA0012 Airfoil Analyses; (1) Airfoil Mesh System (2) Surface Mesh Points of NACA0012 Airfoil Geometry (3) Pressure Contour around an Airfoil with Transonic Speed (4) Mach Number Contour with Streamline

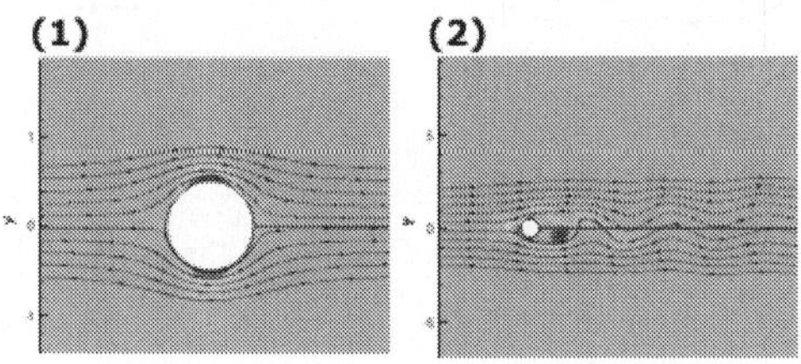

Fig. 13. Vortex Generation on a Cylinder; (1) Inviscid Simulation, Re=140 (2) Viscous Simulation, Re=140

5.2.2 Survey results

Hundreds of students on 6 universities in Korea have experienced this remote lecture on fluid dynamic simulation since 2007. We conducted a survey to 230 students from seven different classes in five universities, about the usefulness of e-AIRS system. Fig. 14 shows the result of the survey. The point 10 is the best and 0 is the worst score. Etc indicates scores lower than six point. We assume that students were satisfied with e-AIRS service if they give more than seven point on each question.

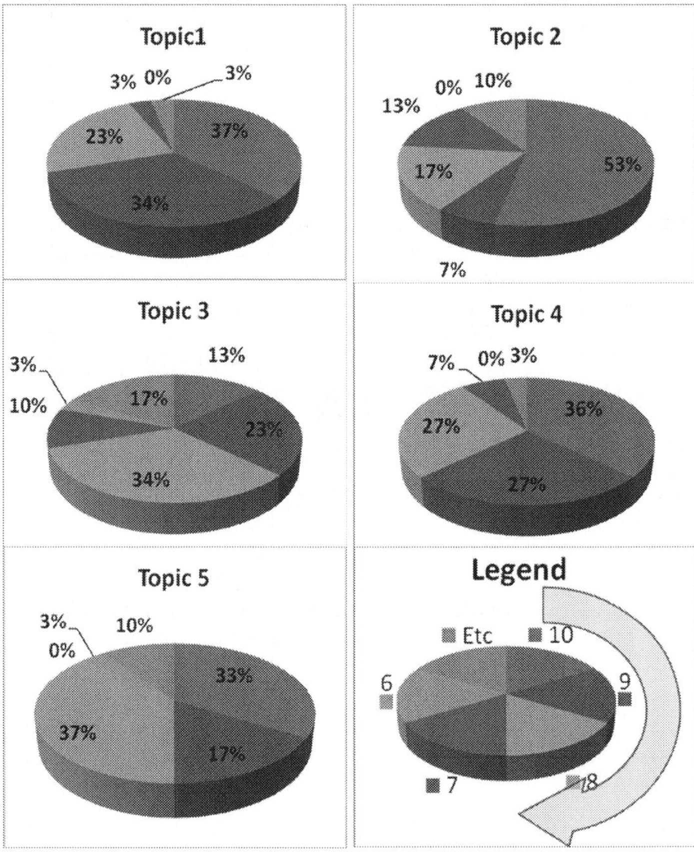

Fig. 14. Graphs of Survey Result;

Topic 1: Increasing the Understanding of CFD Simulation Process

Topic 2: Convenience of Using the Portlet-based Web Portal

Topic 3: Functionality and Convenience of the Mesh Generation

Topic 4: Functionality and Convenience of the CFD Simulation

Topic 5: Functionality and Convenience of the Visualization

As the pie chart illustrates, 94 percent of students said the system helped them to understand the whole process of CFD. Because CFD simulation processes include complex governing equation and CFD techniques, theoretical lectures have a limit to make students understand CFD simulation process. On the other hand, students could easily practice CFD simulation using e-AIRS system, because e-AIRS system provides all components of CFD simulation process.

As indicated in the pie chart, more than 80 percent of the students said that portlet based web portal is convenient. From the survey result, most of students gave high marks for functionality and convenience for mesh generation, CFD simulation, and result data visualization. However, some students required to improve some applet bugs and requested more various CFD solvers and CFD template meshes. Now, Requested opinion was reflected to e-AIRS portal.

6. Ongoing work

Currently, the system is under improvement to the research system by allowing more controllability of advanced users, such as use of users' own application tools within e-AIRS infrastructure. After then, the system will evolve to be the virtual multi-disciplinary research laboratory by implementing more application toolkits in various application domains such as structural dynamics and propulsion.

In the aspect of educational activities, additional various numerical solvers will be adopted. To increase the user pool of e-AIRS, more practical and useful examples should be provided. While e-AIRS has been used for the educational activities of aerospace field only, however, new e-AIRS solvers are planed to launch e-AIRS into the students studying mechanical engineering. In detail, 2-dimensional internal flow solver, 2-dimensional unstructured mesh system will be adopted for the students of the mechanical field.

Moreover, more improvement of e-AIRS performance is promoted including more powerful pre- and postprocessor, 3-dimensional general parallel solver and overset mesh system.

7. Conclusion

E-AIRS components have been investigated and its usefulness has been discussed in this paper. At the early stage, e-AIRS was first designed to support professional aerospace engineering researches through the portal: soon, the system turned the direction to serve as a web portal for academic studies, considering many hardships in developing a professional research system. For convenient use on fluid dynamic study, e-AIRS web portal is designed to give four main services of CFD, remote experiment, parametric study and collaborative conferencing.

In the design of infrastructure and middleware, e-AIRS have focused on rather integrating many available and valuable computer scientific components, than developing modules by our own. Thus, a number of tools such as Globus, Access Grid Toolkit, GridSphere, etc., are used without modification, and middleware developers have invested much endeavour on developing a PSS toolkit.

On the other hand, based on former experiences by CFD component developers, all CFD components are developed by our own. A simple mesh generator and a light visualization software are developed by using Java applet and validated CFD codes are included in the e-AIRS service. For wind tunnel experiment, there has not been any trial on automated experiments. Thus, we have also adopted a conventional manual operation and the portal agents the automatic request by users to a manual instrumental experiment.

Developed system has been used to a number of fluid dynamic classes in undergraduate and graduate schools. To maximize users' conveniences, we have also opened an e-AIRS web page, where a number of valuable knowledge as well as the usage of e-AIRS portal are provided. In the class, students are trained to use e-AIRS system and they conduct representative fluid dynamic simulations. The use of current system made students to understand fluid dynamics more and get motivated on fluid dynamic study.

Now, e-AIRS system goes through a new evolution to the professional fluid dynamic research system, as well as giving more conveniences on educational system. For professional researches, we are allowing more controllability by advanced users, such as use of users' own application tools within e-AIRS infrastructure. After then, the system will evolve to be the virtual multi-disciplinary research laboratory by implementing more application toolkits in various application domains.

8. References

Forkert, T.; Kersken, H.-P.; Schreiber, A.; Strietzel, M. & Wolf, K. (2000). The Distributed Engineering Framework TENT. *Vector and Parallel Processing - VECPAR 2000, LNCS (Lecture Note in Computer Science),* Vol.1981, 38-46, 0302-9743

Foster, I. & Kesselman, C. (2003). *The Grid 2: Blueprint for a New Computing Infrastructure,* Elsevier, 978-1558609334, USA

Hey, T. & Trefethen, A. E. (2003). The Data Deluge: An e-Science Perspective, In: *Grid Computing – Making the Global Infrastructure a Reality,* Berman, F.; Fox, G. & Hey, A. J. G., (Ed.), 809-824, Wiley, 978-0470853191, England

Jackson, T.; Austin, J.; Fletcher, M. & Jessop, M. (2003). Delivering a Grid enabled Distributed Air-craft Maintenance Environment (DAME). *Proceeding of the UK e-Science All Hands Meeting 2003,* pp. 420-427, 1-904425-11-9, UK, September 2003, EPSRC, Swindon

Kim, S.-s.; Kim, C.; Rho, O.-H. & Hong, S. K. (2003). Cures for the Shock Instability: Development of Shock-Stable Roe Scheme. *Journal of Computational Physics,* Vol.185, No.2, 342-374, 0021-9991

Kim, Y.; Kim, E.-k.; Kim, J. Y.; Cho, J.-h.; Kim, C. & Cho, K. W. (2006). e-AIRS: An e-Science Collaboration Portal for Aerospace Applications. *HPCC 2006, LNCS (Lecture Note in Computer Science),* Vol.4208, 813-822, 0302-9743

Ko, S.-H.; Kim, J.; Ahn, J. W.; Yi, J. S.; Kim, C.; Kim, Y.; Cho, K. W. & Choi, D. H. (2007). CFD Researches on the e-AIRS : Korean e-Science Aerospace Research System, *2007 International Conference on Convergence Information Technology (ICCIT 2007),* pp. 815-820, 0-7695-3038-9, Korea, November 2007, IEEE Computer Society, Washington

Lee, J.-S.; Kim, C. & Kim, K. H. (2006). Design of Flapping Airfoil for Optimal Aerodynamic Performance in Low-Reynolds Number Flows. *AIAA Journal,* Vol.44, No.9, 1960-1972, 0001-1452

Walton, J. D.; Filman, R. E. & Korsmeyer, D. J. (2000). The evolution of the DARWIN system, *Proceedings of the 2000 ACM symposium on Applied computing - Volume 2,* pp. 971-977, 1-58113-240-9, Italy, March 2000, ACM, New York

9

The Analytic Hierarchy and the Network Process in Multicriteria Decision Making: Performance Evaluation and Selecting Key Performance Indicators Based on ANP Model

Ming-Chang Lee
Department of Information Management, Fooyin University
Department of Business Administration,
National Kaohsiung University of Applied Sciences,
Taiwan

1. Introduction

AHP is a method for ranking decision alternatives and selecting the best one when the decision maker has multiple criteria (Taylor, 2004). In evaluation n competing alternatives $A_1, A_2, \ldots, A_n$ under a given criterion, it is natural to use the framework of pair-wise comparison by $n \times n$ square matrix from which a set of preference values for the alternatives is derived. Many methods for estimating the preference values from the pair-wise comparison matrix have been proposed and the effectiveness comparatively evaluated. Most of the estimating methods proposed and studied are with the paradigm of the analytic hierarchy process that presumes ratio-scaled preference values. AHP is one of the ways for deciding among the complex criteria structure in different levels. Fuzzy AHP is a synthetic extension of classical AHP method when the fuzziness of the decision maker is considered.

ANP is a new theory that extends the Analytic Hierarchy Process (AHP) to case of dependence and feedbacks introduced by Saaty (1980), with book in 1996 revised and extended in 2001. The ANP makes it possible to deal systematically with all kinds of dependence and feedback in decision system (Fiala, 2001; Chen, 2001). ANP allows for complex interrelationships among decision levels and attributes. The ANP feedback approach replaces hierarchies with networks in which the relationship between levels are not easily represented as higher or lower, dominated or being dominated, directly or indirectly (Meade & Sarkis, 1999). For instance, not only does the importance of the criteria determine the importance of the alternatives, as in hierarchy, but the importance of the alternatives may also have an impact on importance of the criteria (Saaty, 1996). Therefore, a hierarchical representation with a linear top-to-bottom structure is not suitable for complex system (Chung et al., 2005).

In literature, there exists numerous studies conduct with the aim of performing indicators within the boundaries of objective criteria. Sardana (2009) presents a business performance measurement framework, for organizational design, process management, quality management and recipient satisfaction, and defines an appropriate set of performance measures for small or medium enterprise. Hwang (2007) use Data Envelopment Analysis to measure the managerial performance of electronics industry in Taiwan. In multi-criteria decision making (MCDM) model for selecting the collecting centre location in the reverse logistics supply chain model (PLSCM) using the analytical hierarchy process and fuzzy analytical hierarchy process (FAHP) (Anand, et al., 2008). Faisal and Banwet (2009), the ANP, which utilizes the concept of dependence and feedback is proposed as a suitable technique for analyzing IT outsourcing decision. The synergistic integration of two techniques, the analytical network process and data envelopment analysis is application in a multi-phased supplier selection approach (Hasan et al., 2008). Lee (2007) construct an approach based on the analytical hierarchy process and balanced score card. It has four criteria of this study: financial perspective, customer perspective, internal business process perspective, and learning and growth perspective. In model of information system, Ballou et al. (1998) consider four criteria of information products: timeliness, data quality, cost and value. Niemir and Saaty (2004) argues performance indicators have: linked to strategy, quantitative, built on accessible data, easily understood, counterbalanced, relevant, and commonly defined. According the insights of literature a number of criteria have been defined: relevance, reliability, comparability and consistency, understandability and representational quality. As can be seen, the information manufacturing systems criteria (factor) are not independent of each other. Since the criteria (factor) weights are traditionally computed by assuming that the factors are independent, it is possible that the weights computed by including the dependent relations could be different. Therefore, it is necessary to employ analyses which measure and take the possible dependencies among factors into account in the information manufacturing system analysis.

2. Analytical Hierarchy Process (AHP)

2.1 AHP process

The analytic hierarchy process (AHP), developed at the Wharton School of Business by Thomas Saaty (1980), allows decision makers to model a complex problem in a hierarchical structure showing the relationships of the goal, objectives (criteria), sub-objectives, and alternatives (See Figure 1). Uncertainties and other influencing factors can also be included. Figure 1 - Decision Hierarchy AHP allows for the application of data, experience, insight, and intuition in a logical and thorough way. AHP enables decision-makers to derive ratio scale priorities or weights as opposed to arbitrarily assigning them. In so doing, AHP not only supports decision-makers by enabling them to structure complexity and exercise judgment, but allows them to incorporate both objective and subjective considerations in the decision process. AHP is a compensatory decision methodology because alternatives that are deficient with respect to one or more objectives can compensate by their performance with respect to other objectives. AHP is composed of several previously existing but unassociated concepts and techniques such as hierarchical structuring of complexity, pair-wise comparisons, redundant judgments, an eigenvector method for deriving weights, and consistency considerations. The AHP procedure involves six essential steps (Lee et al., 2008).

1. Define the unstructured problem
2. Developing the AHP hierarchy
3. Pair-wise comparison
4. Estimate the relative weights

5. Check the consistency
6. Obtain the overall rating

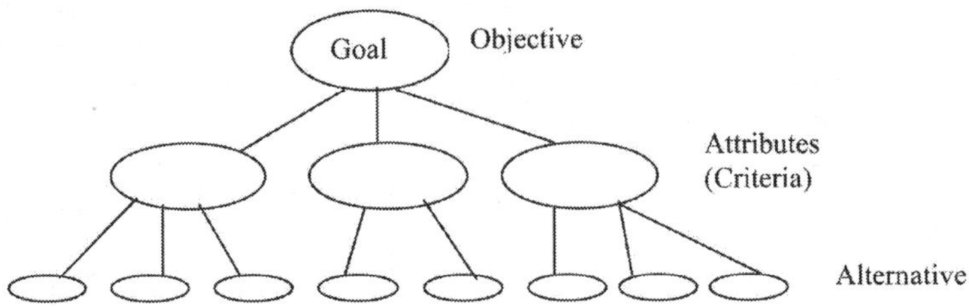

Fig. 1. Hierarchy structure of decision problem

Step 1: Define the unstructured problem
In this step the unstructured problem and their characters should be recognized and the objectives and outcomes stated clearly.

Step 2: Developing the AHP hierarchy
The first step in the AHP procedure is to decompose the decision problem into a hierarchy that consists of the most important elements of the decision problem (Boroushaki and Malczewski, 2008). In this step the complex problem is decomposed into a hierarchical structure with decision elements
Fig.2 represents this structure.

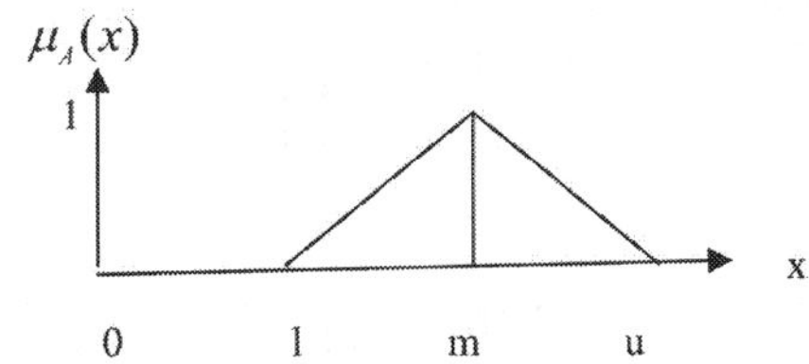

Fig. 2. Triangular membership function

Step 3: Pair-wise comparison
For each element of the hierarchy structure all the associated elements in low hierarchy are compared in pair-wise comparison matrices as follows:

$$A = \begin{bmatrix} 1 & \frac{w_1}{w_2} & \dots \frac{w_1}{w_n} \\ \frac{w_2}{w_1} & 1 & \dots \frac{w_2}{w_n} \\ \cdot & & \\ \frac{w_n}{w_1} & \frac{w_n}{w_2} & \dots 1 \end{bmatrix} \tag{1}$$

Where A = comparison pair-wise matrix,
w_1 = weight of element 1,
w_2 = weight of element 2,
w_n = weight of element n.

In order to determine the relative preferences for two elements of the hierarchy in matrix A, an underlying semantically scale is employs with values from 1 to 9 to rate (Table 1).

Preferences expressed in numeric variables	Preferences expressed in linguistic variables
1	Equal importance
3	Moderate importance
5	Strong importance
7	Very strong importance
9	Extreme importance
2,4,6,8	Intermediate values between adjacent scale values

Table 1. Scales for pair-wise comparison (Saaty, 1980)

Step 4: Estimate the relative weights

Some methods like eigenvalue method are used to calculate the relative weights of elements in each pair-wise comparison matrix. The relative weights (*W*) of matrix *A* is obtained from following equation:

$$A \times W = \lambda_{\max} \times W \tag{2}$$

Where λ_{max} = the biggest eigenvalue of matrix A, I = unit matrix.

Step 5: Check the consistency

In this step the consistency property of matrices is checked to ensure that the judgments of decision makers are consistent. For this end some pre-parameter is needed. Consistency Index (*CI*) is calculated as:

$$CI = \frac{\lambda_{\max} - n}{n-1} \tag{3}$$

The consistency index of a randomly generated reciprocal matrix shall be called to the random index (*RI*), with reciprocals forced. An average *RI* for the matrices of order 1–15 was generated by using a sample size of 100 (Nobre et al., 1999). The table of random indexes of the matrices of order 1–15 can be seen in Saaty (1980). The last ratio that has to be calculated is *CR* (Consistency Ratio). Generally, if *CR* is less than 0.1, the judgments are consistent, so the derived weights can be used. The formulation of *CR* is:

$$CR = \frac{CI}{RI} \tag{4}$$

Step 6: Obtain the overall rating

In last step the relative weights of decision elements are aggregated to obtain an overall rating for the alternatives as follows:

$$w_i^s = \sum_{j=1}^{m} w_{ij}^s w_j \qquad , i = 1, \ldots, n \tag{5}$$

Where w_i^s = total weight of site i,

w_{ij}^{s} = weight of alternative (site) i associated to attribute (map layer) j,

w_j = weight of attribute j,

m = number of attribute,

n= number of site.

2.2 Fuzzy process

2.2.1 A brief introduction to fuzzy set theory

Fuzzy set theory is a mathematical theory designed to model the vagueness or imprecision of human cognitive processes that pioneered. This theory is basically a theory of classes with unship boundaries. What is important to recognize is that any crisp theory can be fuzzified by generalizing the concept of a set within that theory to the concept of a fuzzy set. The stimulus for the transition from a crisp theory to a fuzzy one derives from the fact that both the generality of a theory and its applicability to real world problems are enhanced by replacing the concept of a crisp set with a fuzzy set (Zadeh, 1994).

Generally, the fuzzy sets are defined by the membership functions. The fuzzy sets represent the grade of any element x of X that have the partial membership to A. The degree to which an element belongs to a set is defined by the value between 0 and 1. If an element x really belongs to A if $\mu_A(x) = 1$ and clearly not if $\mu_A(x) = 0$. Higher is the membership value, $\mu_A(x)$, greater is the belongingness of an element x to a set A. The Fuzzy AHP presented in this paper applied the triangular fuzzy number through symmetric triangular membership function. A triangular fuzzy number is the special class of fuzzy number whose membership defined by three real numbers, expressed as (l, m, u).

$$\mu_A(x) = \begin{cases} (x-l)/(m-l), & l \le x \le m \\ (u-x)/(u-m), & m \le x \le u \\ 0 & otherwise \end{cases} \tag{6}$$

Since fuzziness and vagueness are common characteristics in many decision-making problems, a fuzzy AHP (FAHP) method should be able to tolerate vagueness or ambiguity (Mikhailov & Tsvetinov, 2004). In other word the conventional AHP approach may not fully reflect a style of human thinking because the decision makers usually feel more confident to give interval judgments rather than expressing their judgments in the form of single numeric values and so FAHP is capable of capturing a human's appraisal of ambiguity when complex multi-attribute decision making problems are considered (Erensal et al., 2006). This ability comes to exist when the crisp judgments transformed into fuzzy judgments. Zadeh (1965) published his work Fuzzy Sets, which described the mathematics of fuzzy set theory. This theory, which was a generalization of classic set theory, allowed the membership functions to operate over the range of real numbers [0, 1]. The main characteristic of fuzziness is the grouping of individuals into classes that do not have sharply defined boundaries. The uncertain comparison judgment can be represented by the fuzzy number.

2.2.2 Fuzzy AHP process

Step 1: Fuzzy pair-wise comparison matrix

Given a crisp pair-wise comparison matrix (CPM) A, having the values raging from 1/9 to 9, the ceisp PCM is fuzzified using the triangular fuzzy number (l, m u), which fuzzy the original PCM using the conversion number as indicated in the table below (Table 2). In order to construct pair-wise comparison of alternatives under each criterion or about criteria, like that was said for traditional AHP, a triangular fuzzy comparison matrix is defined as follows:

Crisp PCM value	Fuzzy PCM value	Crisp PCM value	Fuzzy PCM value
1	(1 1 1) if diagonal; (1 1 3) otherwise	1/1	(1 1 1) if diagonal; (1 1 3) otherwise
2	(1 2 4)	1/2	(1/4 1/2 1/1)
3	(1 3 5)	1/3	(1/5 1/3 1/1)
4	(2 4 6)	1/4	(1/6 1/4 1/2)
5	(3 5 7)	1/5	(1/7 1/5 1/3)
6	(4 6 8)	1/6	(1/8 1/6 1/4)
7	(5 7 9)	1/7	(1/9 1/7 1/5)
8	(6 8 10)	1/8	(1/10 1/8 1/6)
9	(7 9 11)	1/9	(1/11 1/9 1/7)

Table 2. Conversion of crisp to fuzzy PCM

$$\tilde{A} = (\tilde{a}_{ij})_{n\times n} = \begin{bmatrix} (111) & (l_{12}\ m_{12}\ u_{12})\ldots & (l_{1n}\ m_{1n}\ u_{1n}) \\ (l_{21}\ m_{21}\ u_{21}) & (111) & \ldots & (l_{2n}\ m_{2n}\ u_{2n}) \\ & & & \\ (l_{n1}\ m_{n1}\ u_{n1}) & (l_{n2}\ m_{n2}\ u_{n2})\ldots & (111) \end{bmatrix} \tag{7}$$

Where $\tilde{a}_{ij} = (l_{ij}\ m_{ij}\ u_{ij}), \tilde{a}_{ij}^{-1} = (1/u_{ji}\ 1/m_{ji}\ 1/l_{ji})$

For $i,j = 1,\ldots, n$ and $i \neq j$

Total weighs and preferences of alternatives can be acquired from different method. Two approaches will be posed in resumption.

Step 2: Fuzzy Extent Analysis

Chang's extent analysis: (Chang, 1996)

Different methods have been proposed in the literatures that one of most known of them is Fuzzy Extent Analysis proposed by Chang (1996). The steps of chang's extent analysis can be summarized as follows:

First step: computing the normalized value of row sums (i.e. fuzzy synthetic extent) by fuzzy arithmetic operations:

$$\tilde{s}_i = \sum_{j=1}^{n} \tilde{a}_{ij} \otimes [\sum_{k=1}^{n}\sum_{j=1}^{n} \tilde{a}_{ij}]^{-1} \tag{8}$$

Where ⊗ denotes the extended multiplication of two fuzzy numbers.

Second step: computing the degree of possibility of by following equation:

$$v(\tilde{s}_i \geq \tilde{s}_j) = \sup_{y \geq x}[\min(\tilde{s}_j(x), \tilde{s}_i(y))] \tag{9}$$

which can be equivalently expressed as,

$$v(\tilde{s}_i \geq \tilde{s}_j) = \begin{cases} 1 & m_i \geq m_j \\ \dfrac{u_i - l_j}{(u_i - m_i) + (m_j - l_j)} & l_j \leq u_i, i, j = 1,\ldots,n, j \neq i \\ 0 & otherwise \end{cases} \tag{10}$$

Where $\tilde{s}_i = (l_i \ \ m_i \ \ u_i)$ and $\tilde{s}_j = (l_j \ \ m_j \ \ u_j)$

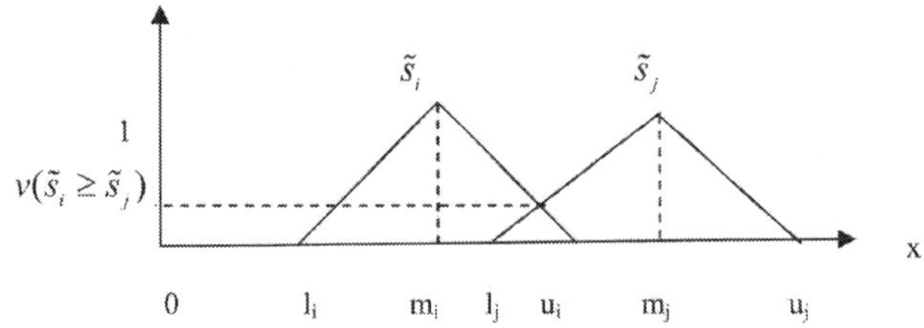

Fig. 3. The degree of possibility of $\tilde{s}_i \geq \tilde{s}_j$

Third step: calculating the degree of possibility of $\tilde{s}_i$ to be greater than all the other (n-1) convex fuzzy number $\tilde{s}_j$ by:

$$v(\tilde{s}_i \geq \tilde{s}_j \ \mid \ j = 1,....,n, j \neq i) = \min_{j\in(1,....,n) j\neq i} v(\tilde{s}_i \geq \tilde{s}_j), \ i = 1,....,n \tag{11}$$

Fourth step: defining the priority vector $W = (w_1,...,w_n)^T$ of the fuzzy comparison matrix $\tilde{A}$ as:

$$w_i = \frac{v(\tilde{s}_i \geq \tilde{s}_j, \ j = 1,...,n; j \neq i)}{\sum_{k=1}^{n} v(\tilde{s}_i \geq \tilde{s}_j, \ j = 1,...,n; j \neq k)} \quad i = 1,...,n \tag{12}$$

Jie, Meng and Cheong's extent analysis: (Jie, Meng and Cheong, 2006)

The fuzzy extent analysis is applied on the above fuzzy PCM to obtain the fuzzy performance matrix. The purpose of fuzzy extent analysis is to obtain the criteria importance and alternative performance by solving these fuzzified reciprocal PCMs.

$$\tilde{w} = (w_1 \ w_2 \qquad w_n)$$

$$\tilde{w}_i = (w_{il} \ \ w_{im} \ \ w_{iu}) \ \ i = 1,....,n \tag{13}$$

$$w_{il} = \sum_{j=1}^{n} a_{ijl} \,/\, \sum_{i=1}^{n}\sum_{j=1}^{n} a_{ijl} \ \ i = 1,....,n$$

$$\tilde{x}_i = (x_{il} \ \ x_{im} \ \ x_{iu}) \ \ i = 1,....,n$$

Step 3: α-cut based method

In this method fuzzy extent analysis is applies to get the fuzzy weights or performance matrix for both alternatives under each criteria context and criteria. After that, a fuzzy weighted sum performance matrix (p) for alternatives can thus be obtained by multiplying the fuzzy weight vector related to criteria with the decision matrix for alternatives under each criteria and summing up obtained vectors $\tilde{p} = \tilde{x}_i * \tilde{w}^T$.

$$\tilde{p} = \begin{bmatrix} (l_1 \ \ m_1 \ \ u_1 \\ (l_2 \ \ m_2 \ \ u_2 \\ \\ (l_n \ \ m_n \ \ u_n \end{bmatrix} \tag{14}$$

Where n is the number of alternative.

According to Wang (1997), in order to checking and comparing fuzzy number, α-cut based method is need for checking and comparing fuzzy number. The α-cut based method 1 stated that if let A and B be fuzzy numbers with α-cut, $A_\alpha = [a_\alpha^-, a_\alpha^+]$ *and* $[b_\alpha^-, b_\alpha^+]$. It say A is smaller than B depend by $A \le B$, if $a_\alpha^- < b_\alpha^-$ and $a_\alpha^+ < b_\alpha^+$. for all $\alpha \in (0,1]$. The advantage of this method is conclusion is less controversial. The α cut analysis is applied to transform the total weighted performance matrices into interval performance matrices which is showed with α Left and α Right for each alternatives as follows:

$$\tilde{p}_\alpha = \begin{bmatrix} (\alpha Left_1 \;\; \alpha Right_1) \\ (\alpha Left_2 \;\; \alpha Right_2) \\ \\ (\alpha Left_n \;\; \alpha Right_n) \end{bmatrix} \tag{15}$$

$$\alpha Left = [\alpha * (m - l)] + l$$

$$\alpha Right = u - [\alpha * (u - m)]$$

Step 4: λ Function and Crisp values Normalization

It is done by applying the Lambda function which represents the attribute of the decision maker that is maybe optimistic, moderate or pessimistic. Decision maker with optimistic attribute will take the medium lambda and the pessimistic person will take the minimum lambda in the range of [0, 1] as follows:

$$c_\lambda = \begin{bmatrix} c_{\lambda 1} \\ c_{\lambda 2} \\ \\ c_{\lambda n} \end{bmatrix} \tag{16}$$

$$c_\lambda = \lambda * \alpha Right + [(1-\lambda) * \alpha Left]$$

Where c_λ is crisp value

Finally, the crisp values need to be normalized, because the elements of different scales.

$$c_{\lambda i} = \frac{c_{\lambda i}}{\Sigma c_{\lambda i}} \tag{17}$$

3. From AHP to ANP

The AHP is comprehensive framework that is designed to cope with the intuitive, the rational, and the irrational when we make multi-objective, multi-criterion, and multi-actor decisions with and without certainty of any number of alternatives. The basic assumption of AHP is the condition of functional independence of the upper part, or cluster (see Figure 4), of the hierarchy, from all its lower parts, and form the criteria or items in each level (Lee & Kim, 2000). In Figure 4, a network can be organized to include source clusters, intermediate clusters and sink clusters. Relationship in network are represented by arcs, where the directions of arcs signify directional dependence (Chang et al., 2006 and Sarkis, 2002). Inner dependencies among the elements of a cluster are represented by looped arcs (Sarkis, 2002). In ANP the hierarchical relation between criteria and alternatives are generalized to networks. Many decision problems cannot be structured hierarchically, because they involve the interaction and dependence of high-level elements on lower-level elements. Not only does the importance of the criteria determine the importance of the alternatives as in a hierarchy, but also the importance of the alternatives themselves determines the importance of the criteria. Thus, in ANP the decision alternatives can depend on criteria and each other as well as criteria can depend on alternatives and other criteria (Saaty, 2001). Technically, in ANP, the system structure is presented graphically and by matrix notations. The graphic presentation describes the network of influences among the elements and clusters by nodes and arcs. The results of pair wise comparisons (weights in priority vectors) are stored to matrices and further to a supper matrix consisting of the lower level matrices. In ANP interdependence can occur in several ways: (1) uncorrelated elements are connected, (2) uncorrelated levels are connected and (3) dependence of two levels is two-way i.e. bi-directional). By incorporating interdependence, Meade and Sarkis (1999) suggest to develop "super-matrix". The super-matrix adjusts the relative importance weights in individual matrices to form a new overall matrix with the eigenvectors of the adjusted relative importance weights.

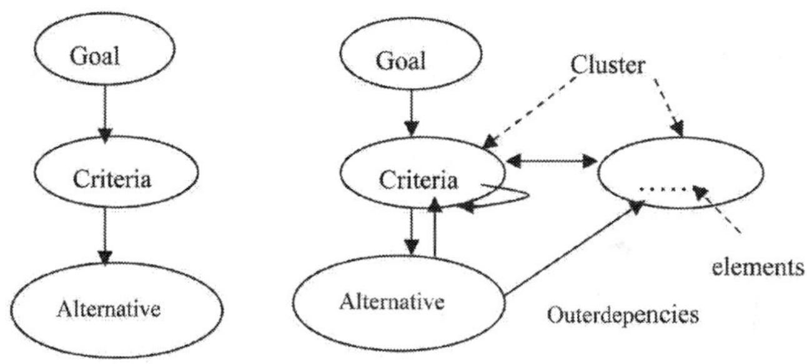

Fig. 4. Hierarchy and network (a) Hierarchy (b) network

3.1 Proposed ANP algorithm

Step 1. model construction and problem structuring: The problem should be stated and be decomposed into a rational system, like a network. The network structure can be obtained by decision-makers through brainstorming or other appropriate methods. An example of the format of network is shown in Figure 4.

Step 2. Pair-wise comparison matrices and priority vectors: In ANP, like AHP, decision elements at each component are compared pair-wise which respect to their importance towards their control criteria. The components (clusters) themselves are also compared pair-wise with respect to their contribution to the goal. Decision makers are asked to respond to a series of pair-wise comparisons where two elements or two components at a time will be compared in terms of how they contribute to their particular level criterion (Meade & Sarkis, 1999). In addition, interdependencies among elements of cluster must also be examined pair-wise; the influence of each element on other elements can be represented by an eigenvector. The relative importance values are determined with Saaty's 1-9 scale (Table 3), where a score of 1 represents equal importance between the two elements and a score 9 indicates the extreme importance of one element (row component in the matrix) compared to the other on (column component in the matrix) (Meade and Sarkis, 1999). A reciprocal value is assigned to the inverse comparison, that is $a_{ij} = 1/a_{ij}$, where $a_{ij}(a_{ji})$ denotes the importance of the *i*th (*j*th) element. Like with AHP, pairwise comparison in ANP is performed in the framework of a matrix, and a local priority vector can be derived as an estimate of the relative importance associated with the elements (or clusters) being compared by solving the following equation:

$$A \times W = \lambda_{max} \times W \tag{18}$$

Where the matrix of pair-wise comparison is A, w is the eigenvector, and λ_{max} is the large eigenvalue of A. Saaty (1980) proposes several algorithms for approximating W. The numerical pair-wise comparison matrices are calculated as per the following equations as, described by Saaty (1980)

$$\tilde{w}_i = \sqrt[n]{\prod_{j=1}^{n} a_{ij}} \tag{19}$$

Where, $\tilde{w}_i$ is the eigenvector of the pair-wise comparison matrix, a_{ij} is the element of the pair-wise comparison matrix.

$$w_i = \tilde{w}_i \Big/ \sum_{i=1}^{n} \tilde{w}_i \tag{20}$$

Equation (20) is to normalize $\tilde{w}_i$

$$\lambda_{max} = \sum_{i=1}^{n} \frac{(Aw)_i}{nw_i} \tag{21}$$

Where, λ_{max} is the eigenvalue.

$$CI = \frac{\lambda_{max} - n}{n-1} \tag{22}$$

$$CR = \frac{CI}{RI} \tag{23}$$

Where, CR denotes the consistency ratio, CI denotes the consistency index, RI denotes the average random consistency index. The value of RI is denoted by the order n of the matrix referring to Table 4.

CR is used to test the consistency of the pair-wise comparison. If the value of CR is less than 0.1, this indicates the pair-wise comparison matrix achieves satisfactory consistency. In this paper, Expert Choice Software (2000) is used to compute the eigenvectors from the pair-wise comparison matrices and to determine the consistency ratios. Another method is discussed by (Chang et. al., 2006). The following three-step procedure is used to synthesize priorities (Chang et al., 2006).

Intensity of importance	Definition	Explanation
1	Equal importance	Two activities contribute equally to the objective
3	Moderate importance	Experience and judgment slightly favor one over another
5	Strong importance	Experience and judgment strongly favor one over another
7	Very strong importance	Activity is strongly favored and its dominance is demonstrated in practice
9	Absolute importance	Importance of one over another affirmed on the highest possible order
2,4,6,8	Intermediate values	Used to represent compromise between the priorities list above
Reciprocal of above non-zero number	If activity i has one of the above non-zero numbers assigned to it when compared with activity j, then j has the reciprocal value when compared with i	

Table 3. Saaty's 1-9 scale for AHP performance

n	1	2	3	4	5	6	7	8	9	10	11
RI	0	0	0.58	0. 90	1.12	1.24	1.32	1.41	1.45	1.48	1.49

Table 4. Average random consistency index (Saaty, 1980)

1. Sum the value in each column of the pair-wise matrix.
2. Divide each element in a column by the sum of its respective column. The resultant matrix is referred to as the normalized pair-wise comparison matrix.
3. Sum the elements in each row of the normalized pair-wise comparison matrix, and divide the sum by the n elements in the row. These final numbers provide an estimate of the relative priorities of the elements being compared with respect to its upper level criterion.

Step 3. Super-matrix formation: The super-matrix concept is similar to the Markov chain process (Saaty, 1996). To obtain global priorities in a system with interdependent influence, the local priority vectors are entered in the appropriate columns of matrix. As a result, a super-matrix is actually a partitioned matrix, where each matrix segment represents a relationship between two clusters in a system. Let the clusters of a decision system be c_k, $k = 1,2,...,n$, and each cluster k has m_k elements, denoted by $e_{k1}, e_{k2},...e_{kmk}$. The local priority vectors obtained in step 2 are grouped and placed in the appropriate positions in a super matrix on the flow of influence from one cluster to another, or from a cluster to itself, as in the loop.

Step 4. Selection of the best alternatives: If the super-matrix formed in step 3 covers the whole network, the priority weights of the alternatives can be found in the column of alternatives in the normalized super-matrix. On the other hand, if a super-matrix only comprises of components that are interrelated, additional calculation must be made to obtain the overall priorities of the alternatives. The alternative with the large overall priority should be the one selection.

The outcome of step 3 is the un-weighted supper-matrix. In order to rank the alternative factors, the limit priority of the alternative factors should be derived through the following process. The un-weighted supper-matrix must first be transformed to a matrix where each of columns is a stochastic column (Saaty, 2006). This is known as the weighted supper-matrix. Then, the weighted supper-matrix must be transformed to a limit matrix which contents the limit priorities of the alternative factors. The alternative factors can then be ranked according to their limit priorities.

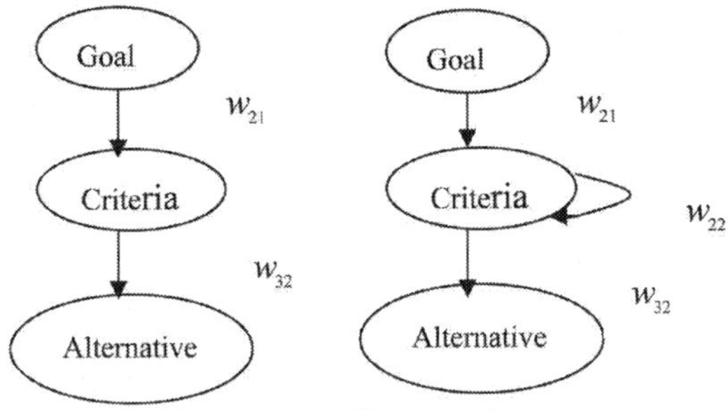

Fig. 5. Hierarchy and network (a) Hierarchy (b) network

$$
W = \begin{array}{cc} & \\ C_1 & \begin{array}{c} e_{11} \\ e_{12} \\ \vdots \\ e_{1m1} \end{array} \\ C_k & \begin{array}{c} e_{k1} \\ e_{k2} \\ \vdots \\ e_{kmk} \end{array} \\ C_n & \begin{array}{c} e_{n1} \\ e_{n2} \\ \vdots \\ e_{nmn} \end{array} \end{array}
\overset{e_{11}\, e_{12} \ldots e_{m1} \ldots e_{k1}\, e_{k2} \ldots e_{kmk} \ldots e_{n1}\, e_{n2} \ldots e_{nmn}}{\begin{bmatrix} W_{11} & W_{1k} & W_{1n} \\ W_{k1} & W_{kk} & W_{kn} \\ W_{n1} & W_{nk} & W_{nn} \end{bmatrix}} \tag{24}
$$

As an example, the super-matrix representation of a hierarchy with three levels as show in Figure 5(a), is as follows:

$$
w_n = \begin{bmatrix} 0 & 0 & 0 \\ w_{21} & 0 & 0 \\ 0 & w_{32} & I \end{bmatrix} \tag{25}
$$

In this matrix, w_{21} is a vector which represents the impact of the goal on the criteria, w_{32} is a matrix that represents the impact of the criteria on each of the alternatives, I is the identity matrix, and zero entries correspond to those elements having no influence. For example give above, if the criteria are interrelated, the hierarchy is replaced with the network shown in Figure 5(b). The interdependency is exhibited by the presence of the matrix w_{22} of the supper-matrix w_n (Saaty, 1996).

$$w_n = \begin{bmatrix} 0 & 0 & 0 \\ w_{21} & w_{22} & 0 \\ 0 & w_{32} & I \end{bmatrix} \tag{26}$$

3.2 Proposed fuzzy ANP algorithm

The process of Fuzzy ANP (FANP) comprises four major steps as follows:

Step 1: Establish model and problem

The problem should be stated clearly and decomposed into a rational system like a network. The structure can be obtained by the opinion of decision makers through brainstorming or other appropriate methods.

Step 2: Establish the triangular fuzzy number

A fuzzy set is a class of objectives with a continuum of grades of membership. Such a set is characterized by membership function, which assigns to each object a grade of membership ranging between zero and one. A triangular fuzz number (TNN) is denoted simply as (l, m, u). The parameters l, m and u, respectively, denote the smallest possible value, the most promising value and the large possible value describe a fuzzy event. Let $[A_{ij}^k]_{n\times n}$ be a represents a judgment of expert k for the relative importance of two criteria C_i and C_j

$$[A_{ij}^k]_{n\times n} = \begin{bmatrix} \tilde{a}_{11}^k & \tilde{a}_{12}^k & \cdots & \tilde{a}_{1n}^k \\ \tilde{a}_{21}^k & \tilde{a}_{22}^k & \cdots & \tilde{a}_{2n} \\ & & & \\ \tilde{a}_{n1}^k & \tilde{a}_{n2}^k & \cdots & \tilde{a}_{nn}^k \end{bmatrix}, \text{k=1, 2, …, m} \tag{27}$$

The triangular fuzzy numbers $\tilde{a}_{ij} = (l_{ij}, m_{ij}, u_{ij})$ and $l_{ij}, m_{ij}, u_{ij} \in [1/9, 9]$ are established as follows:

$$l_{ij} = \min_k(\tilde{a}_{ij}^k),\ m_{ij} = \sqrt[m]{\prod_{k=1}^{m} \tilde{a}_{ij}^k},\ u_{ij} = \max_k(\tilde{a}_{ij}^k) \tag{28}$$

Step 3: Establish the fuzzy Pair-wise Comparison Matrix

From Equation ( ), we have

$$\tilde{A} = (\tilde{a}_{ij})_{n\times n} = \begin{bmatrix} (111) & (l_{12}\ m_{12}\ u_{12})\ldots & (l_{1n}\ m_{1n}\ u_{1n}) \\ (l_{21}\ m_{21}\ u_{21}) & (111) & \ldots\quad (l_{2n}\ m_{2n}\ u_{2n}) \\ & & \\ (l_{n1}\ m_{n1}\ u_{n1}) & (l_{n2}\ m_{n2}\ u_{n2})\ldots & (111) \end{bmatrix} \tag{29}$$

Step 4: α-cut based method and

According to Lious and Wang (1992) and Wang (1997) in order to checking and comparing fuzzy number, α-cut based method is need for checking and comparing fuzzy number. The α can be viewed as a stable or fluctuating condition. The range of uncertainty is the greatest when α = 0. The decision making environment stabilizes when increasing α while, simultaneously, the variance for decision making decreases. Additionally, α can be any number between 0 and 1, an analysis is normally set as the following ten numbers, 0.1, 0.2,…, 1 for uncertainty emulation.

Besides, when α = 0 represents the upper-bound u_{ij} and lower-bound l_{ij} of triangular fuzzy numbers, and while, α =1 represents the geometric meanv m_{ij} .

$$\text{The } \alpha\text{-cut of } \tilde{a}_{ij} = (l_{ij}, m_{ij}, u_{ij}) \text{ is } [L_\alpha(l_{ij}), R_\alpha(u_{ij})] \tag{30}$$

Where $L_\alpha(l_{ij}) = \alpha(m_{ij} - l_{ij}) + l_{ij}$, $R_\alpha(u_{ij}) = u_{ij} - \alpha(u_{ij} - m_{ij})$

$L_\alpha(l_{ij})$ represents the left-end value of α -cut for $\tilde{a}_{ij}$, $R_\alpha(u_{ij})$ represents the right-end value of α -cut for $\tilde{a}_{ij}$

Step 5: λ Function and Crisp Pair-wise Comparison Matrix

Various defuzzication methods are available, and the method adopted herein was derived form Liou and Wang (1992), the method can be clearly express fuzzy perception.

$$g_{\lambda,\alpha}(\tilde{a}_{ij}) = \lambda \times L_\alpha(l_{ij}) + (1-\lambda) R_\alpha(u_{ij}), \quad 0 \le \alpha \le 1, 0 \le \lambda \le 1$$

$$g_{\lambda,\alpha}(\tilde{a}_{ij}) = 1/\, g_{\lambda,\alpha}(\tilde{a}_{ji}), \; 0 \le \alpha \le 1, 0 \le \lambda \le 1 \tag{31}$$

λ can be viewed as the degree of decision maker's pessimism. When λ =0, the decision maker is more optimistic and, thus, the expert consensus is upper-bound u_{ij} of the triangular fuzzy number. When λ =1, the decision maker is pessimistic, and the number ranges froe 0 to 1. However, five numbers 01., 0.3, 0.5, 0.7, and 0.9, are used to emulate the state of mind of decision makers.

The pair-wise comparison matrix is expressed in Equation (32).

$$g_{\lambda,\beta}(\tilde{A}) = g_{\lambda,\alpha}([\tilde{a}_{ij}])_{n\times n} = \begin{bmatrix} 1 & g_{\lambda,\alpha}(\tilde{a}_{12})\ldots & g_{\lambda,\alpha}(\tilde{a}_{1n}) \\ g_{\lambda,\alpha}(\tilde{a}_{21}) & 1 \quad \ldots & g_{\lambda,\alpha}(\tilde{a}_{2n}) \\ & & \\ g_{\lambda,\alpha}(\tilde{a}_{n1}) & g_{\lambda,\alpha}(\tilde{a}_{n2})\ldots & 1 \end{bmatrix} \tag{32}$$

Step 6: Determine Eigenvector and Suppermarix Formation

Let $\lambda_{\max}$ be the eigenvalue of the pair-wise comparison matrix $g_{\lambda,\beta}(\tilde{A})$.

$$g_{\lambda,\beta}(\tilde{A}) \bullet \text{W} = \lambda_{\max} \bullet \text{W} \tag{33}$$

Wheer W denotes the eigenvector of $g_{\lambda,\beta}(\tilde{A})$, $0 \le \alpha \le 1, 0 \le \lambda \le 1$.

4. An illustrative example

4.1 Selecting key performance indicators based on ANP mode

4.1.1 Proposed ANP for Information manufacturing system

The network model developed in order to find out weights of the factors that are to be used in Information manufacturing system performance indicator is shown in Figure 6.

The following criteria have been identified to select relevant performance indicators useful for decision making.

C1. Relevance: A relevant performance indicator provides information to make a difference in decision by helping user to either form prediction about the outcomes of past, present, and future events or to confirm or correct prior expectations. In accounting standard board

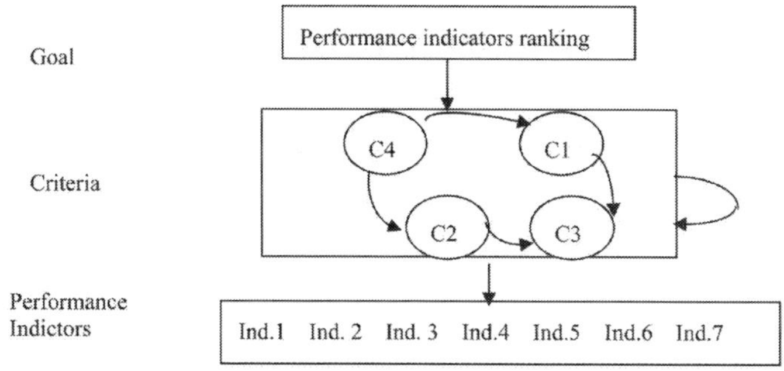

Fig. 6. ANP model for information manufacturing system

(1980), a criteria feature of the relevance has the timeliness, predictive value, and feedback value.

C2: Reliability: Reliability is the ability of a system or component to perform its required functions under stated conditions for a specified period of time. It refers to quality of a performance indicator that assures that it is reasonable free from error and bias and faithfully represents what it purports to represent. In accounting standard board (1980), the reliability of information has verifiability, representational faithfulness, and neutrality.

C3: Comparability and Consistency: Comparability refers to the quality of information related to a performance indicator that enables users to identify similarities and difference between two sets of economic phenomena, while the consistency is the conformity of an indicator from period to period with unchanging policies and procedures. In accounting standard board (1980), Information about a particular enterprise gains greatly in usefulness if it can be compared with similar information about other enterprise and with similar information about the same enterprise for some other period or some other point in time. Comparability between enterprise and consistency in the application of methods over time increase the information value of comparisons of relative economic opportunities or performance.

C4: Understandability and Representational quality: These criteria deals with aspects related to the meaning and format of data collected to build a performance indicator. The performance indicators have to be interpretable as well as easy to understand for user.

The group of performance indicators to be evaluated has been indicated by the top managers of the company.

Ind.1: Actual leather consumptions- Estimated leather consumptions (daily)
Ind.2: Employees' expenses / turnover (monthly)
Ind.3: Number of claims occurred during the process (daily)
Ind.4: Number of supplies' claims (daily)
Ind.5: Number of shifts of the delivery dates of orders / planned orders (daily)
Ind.6: Working minutes for employee / estimated minutes (daily)
Ind.7: Working minutes for department / estimated minutes (daily)

The general sub-matrix notation for Information manufacturing system model used in this study is as follows:

$$w = \begin{matrix} \text{Goal} \\ \text{Criteria} \\ \text{Indictor} \end{matrix} \begin{bmatrix} 0 & 0 & 0 \\ w_1 & w_2 & 0 \\ 0 & w_3 & I \end{bmatrix} \tag{34}$$

Where w_1 is a vector that resents the impact of the goal. w_2 is the matrix that represents the inner dependence of the Information manufacturing system criteria, and w_3 is the matrix that denotes the impact of the criteria on each of the indicators. To apply the ANP to matrix operations in order to determine the overall priorities of the indicator with Information manufacturing system analysis, the proposed algorithm is as follows:

Step 1. Identify Information manufacturing system indicators according to criteria.

Step 2. Assume that there is no dependence among the Information manufacturing system criteria; determine the importance degree of the criteria with 1-9 scale (i.e. calculate w_1).

Step 3. Determine, with 1-9 scale, the inner dependence matrix of each Information manufacturing system criteria with respect to the other criteria (i.e. calculate w_2).

Step 4. Determine the interdependence priorities of the Information manufacturing system criteria (i.e. calculate $w_{criteria} = w_2 \times w_1$).

Step 5. Determine the importance degree of the indicator with respect to each Information manufacturing system criteria with a 1-9 scales (i.e. calculate w_3).

Step 6. Determine the overall priorities of the indicator, reflecting the interrelationships within the manufacturing system criteria (i.e. calculate $w_{indictor} = w_3 \times w_{criteria}$).

4.1.2 Application of the proposed ANP model

Step 1. The problem is converted into a hierarchy structure in order to transform criteria and the indicator into a state in which they can be measured by the ANP technique. The schematic structure established is shown in Figure 6.

Step 2. Assume that there is no dependence among the information manufacturing system criteria; determine the importance degree of the criteria with 1-9 scale is made with respect to the goal. The comparison results are showed in Table 5. All pairwise comparisons in the application are performed by the expert team mentioned in the beginning of this study. In addition, the consistency ration (CR) is provided in the last row of the matrix.

Criteria	C1	C2	C3	C4	Importance degree of information manufacturing system criteria
C1	1	2	3	3	0.447
C2		1	2	3	0.282
C3			1	2	0.163
C4				1	0.105

CR = 0.03

Table 5. Pair-wise comparison of information manufacturing system criteria that there is no dependence along them

$$w_1 = \begin{bmatrix} c1 \\ c2 \\ c3 \\ c4 \end{bmatrix} = \begin{bmatrix} 0.447 \\ 0.282 \\ 0.163 \\ 0.105 \end{bmatrix} \quad (35)$$

Step 3. Inner dependence matrix of each information manufacturing system criteria with respect to the other criteria is determined by analyzing the impact of each criteria on every other criteria using pair-wise comparisons. The dependencies among the information manufacturing system criteria, which are presented schematically in Figure 3, are determined. Based on the inner dependencies presented in Figure 3, pair-wise comparison matrices are formed for the criteria (Table 6)

Criteria	C1	C2	Relative importance weights
C1	1	6	0.857
C2		1	0.142

CR = 0.00

Table 6. The inner dependence matrix of information manufacturing system criteria with respect to C3

Step 4. In this step, the interdependent priorities of the information manufacturing system criteria are calculated as follows:

$$w_{criteria} = w_2 \times w_1 = \begin{bmatrix} 1 & 0 & 0.857 & 0 \\ 0 & 1 & 0.142 & 0 \\ 0 & 0 & 1 & 0 \\ 1 & 1 & 0 & 1 \end{bmatrix} \times \begin{bmatrix} 0.447 \\ 0.282 \\ 0.163 \\ 0.105 \end{bmatrix} = \begin{bmatrix} 0.310 \\ 0.162 \\ 0.086 \\ 0.442 \end{bmatrix} \tag{36}$$

Step 5. In this step, we calculate the importance degrees of the indicators with respect to each criteria. Using Expert Choice software, the eigenvectors are computed by analyzing the matrices and the w_4 matrix.

$$w_3^T = \begin{bmatrix} 0.1220 & 0.1056 & 0.2401 & 0.2407 & 0.1276 & 0.1208 & 0.1047 \\ 0.2690 & 0.3722 & 0.2881 & 0.3089 & 0.3475 & 0.3474 & 0.3329 \\ 0.5070 & 0.3722 & 0.3885 & 0.3089 & 0.3828 & 0.3768 & 0.4082 \\ 0.1067 & 0.1501 & 0.0832 & 0.1416 & 0.1420 & 0.1549 & 0.1543 \end{bmatrix} \tag{37}$$

Step 6. Finally, the overall priorities of the indicator, reflecting the interrelationships within the criteria, are calculated as follows:

$$w_{indictor} = w_3 \times w_2 = \begin{bmatrix} 0.1721 \\ 0.1714 \\ 0.1914 \\ 0.2138 \\ 0.1915 \\ 0.1945 \\ 0.1896 \end{bmatrix} \tag{38}$$

The main results of the ANP application were the overall priorities of the indicators obtained by the synthesizing the priorities of the indicators from the entire network.

4.1.3 Comparing the AHP and ANP results

According the ANP analysis, indicators are ordered as Ind. 4 -Ind. 5 -Ind. 6- Ind. 7 - Ind. 1 - Ind. 2. The sample example is analyze with the hierarchical model given in Figure 5(a) by assuming is no dependence among the criteria.

The overall priorities computed for the alternative are presented below. The same pair-wise comparison matrices are used to compute the AHP priority values. (see Table 7)

$$w_{indictor(AHP)} = w_3 \times w_2 = \begin{bmatrix} 0.2242 \\ 0.2238 \\ 0.2608 \\ 0.2599 \\ 0.2323 \\ 0.2296 \\ 0.2234 \end{bmatrix} \tag{39}$$

In AHP analysis, indicators are ordered as Ind. 3-ind. 4 -Ind. 5 - Ind. 1 – Ind. 2 - Ind. 7.

	Ind. 1	Ind. 2	Ind. 3	Ind. 4	Ind.5	Ind. 6	Ind. 7
Weights in AHP	0.2242	0.2238	0.2608	0.2599	0.2323	0.2296	0.2234
Ranking in AHP	5	6	1	2	3	4	7
Weights in ANP	0.1721	0.1714	0.1914	0.2138	0.1953	0.1945	0.1896
Ranking in ANP	6	7	4	1	2	3	5

Table 7. Weights and ranking of information manufacture systems with AHP and ANP

4.2 Performance evaluation based on ANP model and BSC

4.2.1 Balanced Score Card (BSC)

The BSC is a conceptual framework for translating an organization's vision into a set of performance indicators distributed among four perspectives: Financial, Customer, Internal Business Processes, and Learning and Growth. Indicators are maintained to measure an organization's progress toward achieving its vision; other indicators are maintained to measure the long term drivers of success. Through the BSC, an organization monitors both its current performance (finances, customer satisfaction, and business process results) and its efforts to improve processes, motivate and educate employees, and enhance information systems--its ability to learn and improve. The four perspectives and explained briefly as follows (Kaplan and Norton, 1996)

- Financial perspective: The financial addresses the question of how shareholders view the firm and which financial goals are desired from the shareholder's perspective. The measurement criteria are usually profit, cash flow, ROI, return on invested capital, and economic value added.
- Customer perspective: Customer is the source of business profits; hence, satisfying customer needs is the objective purposed by companies. This perspective provides data regarding the internal business results against measures that lead to financial success and satisfied customers. To meet the organizational objectives and customers expectations, organizations must identify the key business processes at which they must excel. Key processes are monitored to ensure that outcomes are satisfactory.

Internal business processes are the mechanisms through which performance expectations are achieved. Some examples of the core or genetic measures are customer satisfaction, customer retention, new customer acquisition, market position and market share in targeted segment.

- Internal Business process perspective: The objective of this perspective is to satisfy shareholders and customers by excelling at some business process. These are the processes in which the firm must concentrate its efforts to excel. In determining the objectives and measures, the first step should be corporate value-chain analysis. Some examples of the core or genetic measures are innovation, operation and after-sale services.
- Learning and Growth perspective: The objective of this perspective is to provide the infrastructure for achieving the objectives of the other three perspectives and for creating long-term growth and improvement through people, systems and organizational procedures. Some examples of the core or genetic measures are employee satisfaction, continuity, training and skills. The criteria include turnover rate of workers, expenditures on new technologies, expenses on training, and lead time for introducing innovation to a market.

4.2.2 A model of performance evaluation based on ANP and BSC

In order to deal with the performance evaluation problem of enterprise, it is required to employ multiple criteria decision-making methods (MCDM). According to Opricovic and Tzeng (2004), solving MCDM problems is essential to establish evaluation criteria and alternatives, and to apply a normative multi-criteria analysis method in to select a favorable alternative. Since the ANP can be used to select the metrics of the BSC and to help understand the relative importance of metrics. Therefore, the procedures of proposed method are mainly divided the following steps:

Step 1. Define the decision goals

Decision-making is the process of defining the decision goals, gathering relevant information, and selecting the optimal alternative.

Step 2. Establish evaluation clusters

After defining the decision goals, it is required to generate and establish evaluation clusters which is alike a chain of the criteria cluster (purposes), the sub-criteria cluster (evaluators), and the alternatives cluster. Using the theory and methodology of BSC, it creates an adaptive performance evaluation system. According Kanan and Norton (1998), four important factors for evaluating enterprise strategies can be obtained, including: financial perspective (S_1), customer perspective (S_2), Internal Business process perspective (S_3), and Learning and Growth perspective (S_4). In financial perspective, three important factors (sub-critical) are: net asset income ratio (C_{11}), sales net ratio (C_{12}), sales growth ratio (C_{13}). In customer perspective, four important factors (sub-critical) are: customer profitability (C_{21}), market share (C_{22}), customer retention ratio (C_{23}), and customer satisfaction (C_{24}). In Business process perspective, four important factors (sub-critical) are: product improvement (C_{31}), Product Place (C_{32}), product quality (C_{33}), Business process (C_{34}). In Learning and Growth perspective, our important factors (sub-critical) are: employee motivation (C_{41}), Employee Training (C_{42}), Employee satisfaction (C_{43}), Information feedback (C_{44}). As for the alternatives cluster, there are: A_1, A_2, and A_3.

Step 3. Establish network structure

According to step 2, it is assumed that the four selection criteria are independent. Figure 7 illustrates the ANP network component.

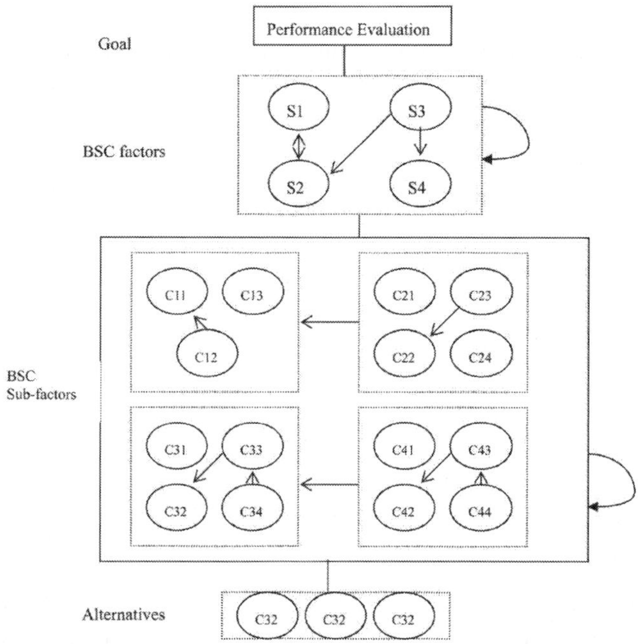

Fig. 7. ANP model for Performance evaluation

Step 4. Pair-wise comparisons matrices and priority vectors

Saaty (1980) proposed several algorithms to approximate W. In this study, Expert Choice (2000) is used to compute the eigenvectors from the pair-wise comparison matrices and to determine the consistency rations.

Step 5. Super-matrix formulation

The super-matrix will be an un-weighted one. In each column, it consists of several eigenvectors which of them sums to one and hence entire column of matrix may sums to an integer greater than one.

In this study, the super-matrix structure is shown in Equation (40). The network model according to the determined criteria is given in Figure 1 W_1 is the local importance degrees of the BSC factors; W_2 is the inner independence matrix of each BSC factor with respect to the other factors by using the schematic representation of the inner dependence among the BSC factors; W_3 is the local importance degrees of the BSC sub-factors; W_4 is the inner independence matrix of each BSC sub-factors with respect to the other sub-factors by using the schematic representation of the inner dependence among the BSC sub-factors; W_5 is the local importance degrees of the alternative strategies with respect to each BSC sub-factors. Also the clusters, which have no interaction, are shown in the supper-matrix with zero (0).

$$\mathbf{W}=\begin{bmatrix} 0 & 0 & 0 & 0 \\ W_1 & W_2 & 0 & 0 \\ 0 & W_3 & W_4 & 0 \\ 0 & 0 & W_5 & I \end{bmatrix} \tag{40}$$

Step 5-1. Calculate W_1

Assuming that there is no dependence among the BSC factors, pair-wise comparison of BSC factor using as 1-9 scale is made with respect to the goal.

$$W_1 = [\,0.447 \;\; 0.282 \;\; 0.1 \;\; 0.105]^T \tag{41}$$

Step 5-2. Calculate W_2

The inner independence matrix of each BSC factor with respect to the other factors is the schematic representation of the inner dependence among the BSC factors. The inner dependence matrix of the BSC factors with respect to S_1, S_2, S_3, S_4.

The inner dependence matrix of the BSC factors (W_2) is found.

$$W_2=\begin{bmatrix} 1.000 & 0.625 & 0.900 & 0.857 \\ 0.068 & 1.000 & 0.000 & 0.142 \\ 0.681 & 0.238 & 1.000 & 0.000 \\ 0.249 & 0.126 & 0.100 & 1.000 \end{bmatrix} \tag{42}$$

Step 5-3. Calculate W_3

In this step, local priorities of the BSC sub-factors are calculated using the pair-wise comparison matrix. A priority vector obtained by analyzing the pair-wise comparison is shown below.

Step 5-4. Calculate W_4

The inner independence matrix of each BSC sub-factor with respect to the other sub-factors is the schematic representation of the inner dependence among the BSC sub-factors.

$$W_3 = \begin{matrix} C_{11} \\ C_{12} \\ C_{13} \\ C_{21} \\ C_{22} \\ C_{23} \\ C_{24} \\ C_{31} \\ C_{32} \\ C_{33} \\ C_{34} \\ C_{41} \\ C_{42} \\ C_{43} \\ C_{44} \end{matrix} \begin{bmatrix} 0.618 & 0.000 & 0.000 & 0.000 \\ 0.242 & 0.000 & 0.000 & 0.000 \\ 0.130 & 0.000 & 0.000 & 0.000 \\ 0.000 & 0.410 & 0.000 & 0.000 \\ 0.000 & 0.311 & 0.000 & 0.000 \\ 0.000 & 0.098 & 0.000 & 0.000 \\ 0.000 & 0.180 & 0.000 & 0.000 \\ 0.000 & 0.000 & 0.513 & 0.000 \\ 0.000 & 0.000 & 0.210 & 0.000 \\ 0.000 & 0.000 & 0.112 & 0.000 \\ 0.000 & 0.000 & 0.164 & 0.000 \\ 0.000 & 0.000 & 0.000 & 0.573 \\ 0.000 & 0.000 & 0.000 & 0.111 \\ 0.000 & 0.000 & 0.000 & 0.242 \\ 0.000 & 0.000 & 0.000 & 0.073 \end{bmatrix} \tag{43}$$

$$W_4=\begin{bmatrix} W_{41} & 0 & 0 & 0 \\ 0 & W_{42} & 0 & 0 \\ 0 & 0 & W_{43} & 0 \\ 0 & 0 & 0 & W_{44} \end{bmatrix} \tag{44}$$

Where

$$W_{41}=\begin{bmatrix} 0.000 & 0.000 & 0.000 \\ 0.333 & 0.000 & 0.000 \\ 0.667 & 0.000 & 0.000 \end{bmatrix} \quad W_{42}=\begin{bmatrix} 1.00 & 0.335 & 0 & 0 \\ 0.00 & 0.349 & 0 & 0 \\ 0.00 & 0.085 & 0 & 0 \\ 0.00 & 0.418 & 0 & 0 \end{bmatrix}$$

$$W_{43}=\begin{bmatrix} 0.228 & 0.331 & 0.000 & 0.206 \\ 0.000 & 0.334 & 0.228 & 0.407 \\ 0.354 & 0.101 & 0.354 & 0.096 \\ 0.418 & 0.234 & 0.234 & 0.291 \end{bmatrix} \quad W_{44}=\begin{bmatrix} 0.564 & 0.083 & 0.256 & 0.413 \\ 0.133 & 0.338 & 0.257 & 0.091 \\ 0.242 & 0.535 & 0.117 & 0.259 \\ 0.060 & 0.043 & 0.376 & 0.239 \end{bmatrix}$$

Step 5-5. Calculate W_5

In this step, local priorities of the four alternatives with respect to each sub--factors are calculated using the pair-wise comparison matrix. A priority vector obtained by analyzing the pair-wise comparison is shown below.

$$W_5=[\, W_{51} \;\; W_{52} \;\; W_{53} \;\; W_{54}] \tag{45}$$

$$W_{51}=\begin{bmatrix} 0.07 & 0.47 & 0.81 \\ 0.65 & 0.08 & 0.07 \\ 0.28 & 0.45 & 0.12 \end{bmatrix} \quad W_{52}=\begin{bmatrix} 0.18 & 0.20 & 0.75 & 0.18 \\ 0.59 & 0.40 & 0.06 & 0.59 \\ 0.23 & 0.40 & 0.19 & 0.23 \end{bmatrix}$$

$$W_{53}=\begin{bmatrix} 0.80 & 0.69 & 0.77 & 0.73 \\ 0.12 & 0.22 & 0.07 & 0.08 \\ 0.08 & 0.09 & 0.16 & 0.19 \end{bmatrix} \quad W_{54}=\begin{bmatrix} 0.40 & 0.12 & 0.75 & 0.69 \\ 0.20 & 0.42 & 0.18 & 0.09 \\ 0.40 & 0.46 & 0.07 & 0.22 \end{bmatrix}$$

Step 6. Limit matrix

After entering the sub-matrices into the super-matrix and completing the column stochastic, the super-matrix is often raised to sufficient large power until convergence occur (Satty, 1996; Meade & Sarkis, 1998). The priority of alternatives, A_1 = 0.478, A_2 = 0.280, A_3 = 0.244.

5. Reference

[1] Anand, M. D., Kumanan, T.S.S, Johnny, M. A., (2008), Application of multi-criteria decision making for selection of robotic system using fuzzy analytic hierarchy process, International Journal of Management and Decision Making, Vol. 9, No. 1, pp. 75-98.

[2] Ballou, D., Wang, R., Pazer, H., and Tayi, G. K., (1998), Modeling information manufacturing systems to determine information product quality, Management Science, Vol. 44. No. 4, pp. 462-484.

[3] Boroushaki, S. and Malczewski, J., (2008), Implementing an extension of the analytical hierarchy process using ordered weighted averaging operators with fuzzy quantifiers in ArcGIS, Computer and Geosciences, Vol. 34, pp. 399-410.

[4] Brans, j. p., Vincke, Ph. And Mareschal, B., (1986), How to select and how to rank projects: the PROMETHEE method, European Journal of Operational Research, Vol. 24, pp. 228-238.

[5] Chang, D. Y., (1996), Applications of the extent analysis method on fuzzy AHP, European Journal of Operation Research, Vol. 95, pp. 649-655.

[6] Chang, S. L., Wang, R. C. and Wang, S. Y. (2006). Applying fuzzy linguistic quantifier to select supply chain partners at different phases of product life cycle, International Journal of Production Economics, 100(2), pp. 348-359.

[7] Chen, Y. W.,(2001), Formulation of a Learning Analytical Network Process, Proceeding of the Sixth International Symposium on The AHP, ISAHP 2001,(Bem-Switzerland), pp. 73-78.

[8] Cheng, W. L. and Li, H., (2004), Contractor selection using the analytic network process, Construction Management and Economics, December, 22, pp. 1021-1032.

[9] Chung, S. F., Lee, A. H. L., and Pearn, W. L.., (2005), Analytical network process (ANP) approach for mix planning in semiconductor fabricator, International Journal of Production Economics, 96, pp. 15-36.

[10] Erensal, Y. C., Oncan, T. and Demircan, M. L., (2006), Determining key capabilities in technology management using fuzzy analytic hierarchy process: a case of Turkey, Information Science, Vol. 176, pp. 2755-2770.

[11] Expert Choice, Expert Choice, Analytical Hierarchy Process (AHP) Software, Version 9.5, Pittsburg, 2000.

[12] Faisal, M. N., Banwet, D. K., (2009), Analysis alternatives for information technology outsourcing decision: an analytic network process approach, International Journal of Business of Information Systems, Vol. 4, No. 1, pp. 47-62.

[13] Fiala, P. and Jablonsky, J., (2001), Performance Analysis of Network Production System by ANP Approach, Proceeding of the Sixth International Symposium on the AHP, ISAHP 2001, (Bem-Switzerland), pp. 101-103.

[14] Hasan, M. A., Shankar, R., Sarkis, J., (2008), Supplier selection in an agile manufacturing environment using data envelopment analysis and analytical network process, International Journal of Logistics Systems and Management, Vol. 4, No. 5, pp. 523-550.

[15] Hwang, S. N., (2007), An application of data envelopment analysis to measure the managerial performance of electronics industry in Taiwan, International Journal of Technology Management, Vol. 40, No, 1/2/3, pp. 215-228.

[16] Jie, L. H., Meng, M. C., and Cheomg, C. W., (2006), Web based fuzzy multi-criteria decision making tool, International Journal of the computer, the Internet and management, Vol. 14, N0. 2, pp. 1-14.

[17] Kaplan, R. S. and Norton, D. P., (1992), The balanced scorecard to work, Harvard Business Review, Vo;. 70, No. 1, pp. 71-79.

[18] Kaplan, R. S. and Norton, D. P., (1996), Using balanced scorecard as a strategic management system,, Harvard Business Review, Vol., 74, No. 1, pp. 75-85.

[19] Lee A. H. I., Chen, W. C. and Chang, C. J., (2008), A fuzzy AHP and BSC approach for evaluating performance of IT department in manufacturing industry in Taiwan, Expert Systems `with Application, Vol. 34, pp. 96-107.

[20] Lee, J. W. and Kim, S. H., (2000), Using analytical network process and goal programming for interdependent information system project selection, Computer and Operations Research, 27, pp. 367-382.

[21] Lee, J. W. and Kim, S. H., (2001), An integrated approach for independent information system projection, International Journal of Project Management, 19, pp. 111-118.

[22] Lee, M. C., (2007), A method of performance Evaluation by Using the Analytic Network Process and Balanced Score Card, Proceedings of the 2007 International Conference

on Convergence Information Technology, 21-23 Nov. IEEE Computer Society pp.235 - 240.

[23] Lious, T. S. and Wang, M. J. J., Ranking Fuzzy Numbers with Integral Value, Fuzzy Sets and Systems, Vol. 50, pp.247-55, 1992.

[24] Meade, L. M. and Sariks, J., (1999), Analyzing organizational project alternatives for agile manufacturing processes: An analytical network approach, International Journal o Production Research, 37, pp. 241-261

[25] Mikhailov, L. and Tsvetinov, P., (2004), Evaluation of services using a fuzzy analytic hierarchy process, Applied Soft Computing, Vol. 5, pp. 23-33.

[26] Niemira, M. P. and Sadty, T. L., (2004), An analytical network process model for financial-crisis forecasting, International Journal of Forecasting, Vol. 20, pp. 578-587.

[27] Nobre, F. F., Trotta, L. T. F., Gomes, L. F. A. M., (1999), Multi-criteria decision making: an approach to setting priorities in health care, Symposium on statistical bases for public health decision making, Vol. 18, No. 23, pp.3345-3354.

[28] Opricovic, S. and Tzeng, G. H.,(2004), Compromise solution by MCDM methods: A comparative analysis of VIKOR and TOPSIS, European Journal of Operational Research, 156, pp. 445-455.

[29] Saaty, T. J. and Vargas, L. G., (1980), Decision Making with the analytic Network process: economics, political, social and technological application with benefits, opportunities, costs and risks, Spring Science + Business, USA

[30] Saaty, T. J, (1996), Decision making in Complex Environments, The Analytical Hierarchy Process for decision Making with Dependence and Dependence and Feedback (USA: RWS Publications).

[31] Saaty, T. L. (1999), Fundamentals of analytic network process, Japan, Kobe: The International Symposium on the Analytic Hierarchy Process.

[32] Saaty, T. L., (2001), The Analytic Network Process: Decision Making With Dependence and Feedback, RWS Publications, Pittsburgh.

[33] Sarkis, J., (2002), Quantitative models for performance measurement system-alternate considerations, International Journal of Production Economics, 86, pp. 81-90.

[34] Saaty, R. W., (2003), The analytical hierarchy process (AHP) for decision making and the analytical network process (ANP) for decision making with dependence and feedback, Creative Decisions Foundation 2003.

[35] Saaty, T. L., (2006), Rank from comparisons and from ratings in the analytic hierarchy/network processes, European Journal of Operational Research, Vol. 168, 2006, pp. 557-570.

[36] Sardana, G. D., (2009), Evaluating the business performance of an SME: a conceptual framework, International Journal of Globalisation and Small Business, Vol. 3, No. 2, pp. 137-159.

[37] Taylor, B. W., (2004), Introduction to Management Science, Pearson Education Inc., New Jersey.

[38] Wang, L. X., (1997), A course in fuzzy systems and control, United States of America, Prentice-Hall.

[39] Zadeh, L. A. (1965), Fuzzy sets, Information and Control, Vol. 8, No. 3, pp. 338-353.

[40] Zadeh, L. A. (1994), Fuzzy logic, neural networks, and soft computing. Communications of the ACM vol. 37, No. 3, pp. 77-84

10

A Cost-Based Interior Design Decision Support System for Large-Scale Housing Projects

Hoon-ku Lee[1], Yoon-sun Lee[2] and Jae-jun Kim[3]
[1]*LIG Engineering and Construction Co., Ltd.*
[2]*Department of Architectural Design, Hanyang University*
[3]*Department of Sustainable Architectural Engineering, Hanyang University*
Korea

1. Introduction

In the early stages of a large-scale housing project, many interior design alternatives remain to be confirmed after a rough review of the costs. In general, interior designers consider the overall concept, colour and style according to floor plans, spaces and elements. However, because they generally do not consider the construction work required, the construction and design characteristics are not connected, and the cost and design properties are controlled separately. This is why the real-time management of cost change is not included in the decision-making process. It is therefore necessary to consider the cost when making decisions on interior design items for an apartment unit plan (Lee et al., 2007).

Rapid advances in information technology are changing the nature of most human activities (Bennett, 2000) and are generating new requirements for clients such as the owner/developer in large-scale housing projects. The clients' requirements are stated in ongoing communications among project participants in the early phase of a project and become embodied in the design phase, during which design alternatives must be selected to meet the clients' requirements while satisfying them in a realistic way. A decision support system for selecting design alternatives is intended to represent design information, document design rationale and manage design changes (Geoffrion, 1987). Many studies on the design phase have focused on the cooperation between various participants such as the architects, engineers and contractors (A/E/C) (Demirkan, 2005; Kalay et al., 1998; Khedro et al., 1994; Lee et al., 2001; Mokhtar et al., 2000), but few studies have examined cooperative systems or decision support systems in which the end-user or client participates in the selection of interior design specifications. In addition, it is unusual to propose a process or database function that accepts and manages the extensive interior design information generated by too many alternatives.

Integrated project systems would help streamline project activities by allowing downstream disciplines to access design information. With this, they could evaluate the design and assess the impact of design decisions on downstream project activities early in the design process (Halfawy & Froese, 2005).

In this chapter, we aimed to devise a system that allows clients to make cost-based decisions suited to their own interior design specifications and that enables the builder to plan resource requirements and budget costs. We describe an information model that supports cost-based decision making in the interior design phase. To do this, we derive the space hierarchy for a large-scale housing project. We also propose a method for building a library of interior design information based on the space hierarchy and interior object information. The proposed model is validated using an example study analysis to show how it supports the decision-making process of various participants in the interior design phase by providing real-time cost information when the interior is initially planned or later changed.

2. A concept of cost-based interior design

2.1 Current interior design procedure

The interior design progresses through the stages of conception, modelling, review, finalisation, detailing, drafting and costing as shown in Fig. 1. Interior designers working on projects come up with design concepts, perform space modelling, review results, fill in details of the finalised design and draft the results, all to calculate the costs for estimates.

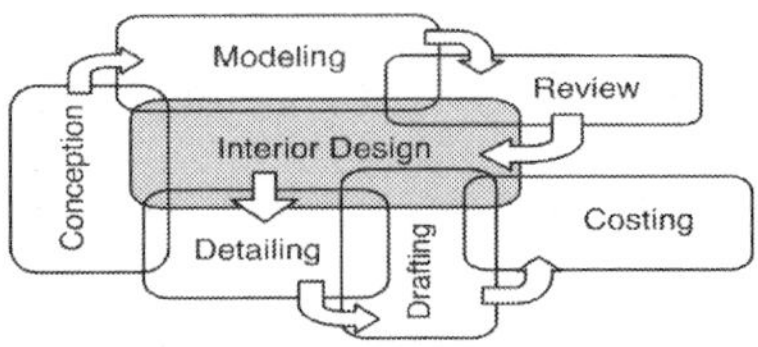

Fig. 1. Interior design phases

In the existing interior design procedure shown in Fig. 2, owners/developers first produce ideas or requests. Then interior designers propose designs and alternatives, and the results are initially reviewed without any consideration of cost. In the detailed design stage, the owner or developer reviews the interior design along with costs.

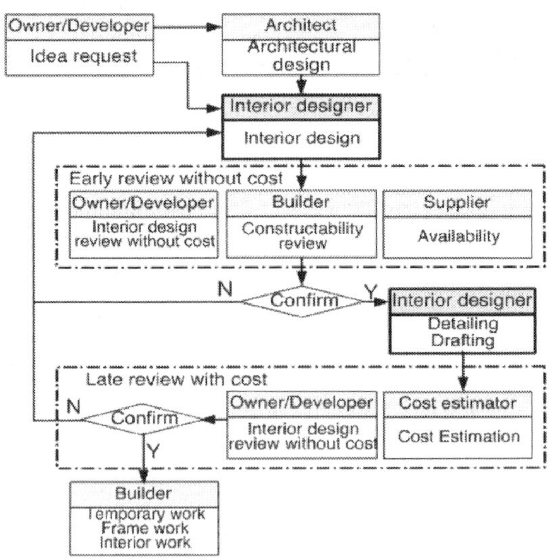

Fig. 2. Current interior design procedure

However, the procedure is a long one, and is subject to many problems in feedback concerning alternative design proposals. During the design stage, design alternatives for finishing materials are based on the planned space and rooms in a unit, according to the demands of the project manager; these alternatives are then incorporated into the unit plan. This process usually generates a good amount of cost information, although it usually fails to manage cost information, one of the fundamental criteria of project performance. Design characteristics and costs are generally not assessed simultaneously as finishing materials are selected because the process is managed on a basis of dualization. Therefore, no cost baseline is determined at each project stage. The interior designer usually does not consider costs generated by the selection of finishing materials, focusing instead on design characteristics such as the concept, color, and pattern for the space or unit plan.

2.2 Proposed cost-based interior design procedure

Recently, experts have started to consider a design-to-cost philosophy to be a necessary requirement for effective project cost management. The design-to-cost method can produce accurate estimates of the cost to produce products or services before the project begins, systematically constraining design goals based on available funds (Michaels & Wood, 1989). Thus, the design-to-cost management strategy and supporting methodologies can achieve an affordable product by treating target cost as an independent design parameter that needs to be achieved during project development. Achieving highly cost-effective results requires assessing costs related to various approaches and design solutions.
Parametric cost estimation models have been developed (Kim et al., 2004). Regression, or multiple regression analysis as it is usually called, is a very powerful statistical tool that can be used as both an analytical and predictive technique for examining the contribution of potential new items to the overall cost estimate reliability (Hegazy et al., 2001). It is not appropriate, however, when describing nonlinear or multidimensional relationships with multiple inputs and outputs (Huyn et al., 1993). In addition, it is difficult to use parametric methods when the number of alternatives tends be infinite, based on the different items of the design.

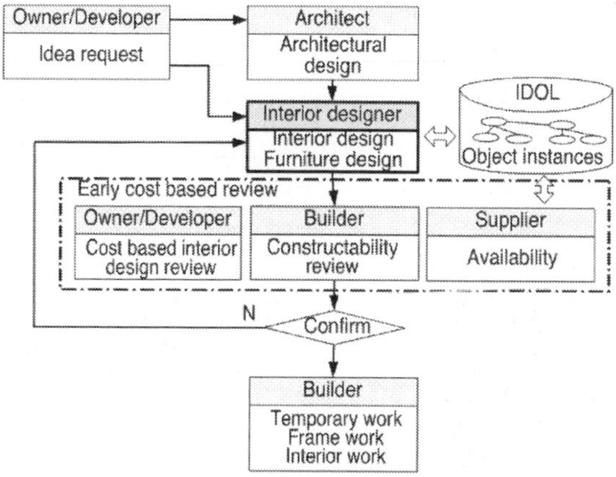

Fig. 3. Proposed cost-based interior design procedure

Therefore, we propose a procedure in which designers use an interior design object library (IDOL) to select an interior design item based on cost. At that point, the total cost for the interior can be reviewed. The builder's constructability review and the suppliers' availability review of the interior design are not included in this study, but the design information stored in the interior design information model can be used in the construction phase.

3. A model for representing interior design information

Various approaches have been proposed to provide structure to product models. Early efforts included the A/E/C building systems model (Turner, 1990) and the general A/E/C reference model (GARM) (Gielingh, 1998). The major standardisation effort in product modelling today is ISO-STEP from the International Standards Organization (Hegazy et al., 2001), and in recent years, researchers in the A/E/C industry have devoted considerable attention to the representation of design information and the management of design changes.

Researchers and practitioners have been investigating improved integration, that is, the continuous and interdisciplinary sharing of data, knowledge and goals among all project participants (Hegazy et al., 2001; Luiten & Tolman, 1997). The architectural information model proposed in these studies manages the creation, modification and exchange of the spatial design information created for all participants in the process for A/E/C purposes (Hegazy et al., 2001). Other studies have proposed building information models from various different perspectives. Anwar (2005) studied methods of structural analysis, modelling and design with structural mechanisms for major members (e.g., foundation, column, beam, wall, slab) in building structures using a structural information model. Choi et al. (2007) provided a building data model including building components such as building, plan, space, ring, wall skeleton, surface and column, for structured floor plans. Figure 4 shows the building project hierarchy (BPH) of a building information model.

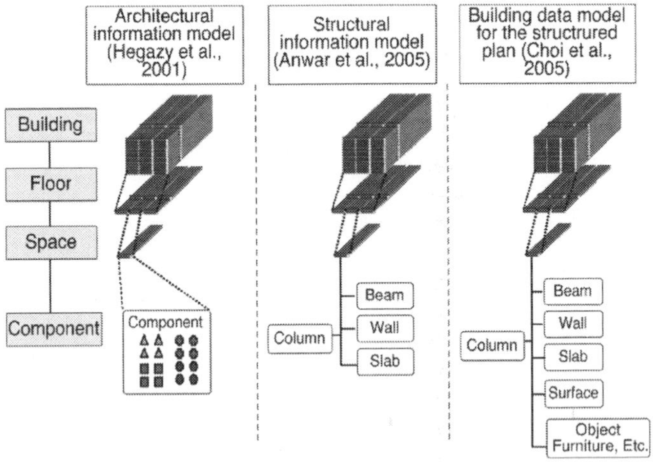

Fig. 4. Building project hierarchy according to the building information model

In this study, the structured floor plan (Choi et al., 2007) was used as the basis of the interior design information for housing projects. The structured floor plan is roughly divided into private space and public space. Its major components are surfaces such as floors, walls and ceilings, and non-surfaces such as furniture, windows, doors and lighting fixtures. These are the major components of private space for an apartment unit plan and serve as the primary focus of this study.

4. A cost-based interior design decision support system

4.1 Roles of an interior design decision support system

4.1.1 Communicating with clients in deciding interior design specifications

The evaluation of design alternatives is an important ongoing phase in the design decision stage and when producing new design concepts. Most design decisions are made intuitively without predicting the actual performance with respect to a variety of parameters such as lighting, energy and comfort (Reichard & Papamichael, 2005). In addition, design decisions are made by expert project participants without regard to the requirements of the occupants in terms of space, element colour, pattern, texture and materials. Consequently, the clients frequently change the interior design when they review the feasibility study and plan the target cost. The added cost, time delay and construction waste generated by such changes lead to claims and waste resources. Therefore, a decision support system must allow client input when the interior design specifications are selected. The owner/developer's requirements lead to design alternatives for each room, and the alternatives are incorporated in space (i.e., the unit plan) in the interior design stage. Also present at this stage is a deluge of cost information, which makes it difficult to generate and manage the costs that predominate in project. Such a problem is also linked to the communication difficulties among the project participants such as the owner/developer, interior designer and builder.

4.1.2 Providing a cost baseline when selecting interior design specifications

Project cost management deals with the procedures to ensure that the project is completed within the approved budget. The Project Management Body of Knowledge explains project cost management as a four-phase process consisting of resource planning, cost estimation, budget establishment and cost control (PMI, 2000). By linking this with the project work breakdown structure (WBS), we propose a cost baseline to control costs during the design phase, which enables the builder to examine resource and cost planning during the interior design phase of a project. Our system reports the changes that a client makes to the interior design, which affect resource planning in the WBS and alter the costs.

4.1.3 Managing an IDOL for integrating design and cost information

To control costs during the interior design phase, interior design information, process characteristics, and cost information must be interrelated. To control the information on the finishes work item generated through the interrelation of the construction and design characteristics, we developed an IDOL. We used a relationship analysis to examine several completed apartment projects to identify interior design objects. The relationships involve spaces, rooms, components (surfaces and non-surfaces), work items, and design • cost • work information. A work item is defined as an interior design object that is integrated with the proposed BPH. For work items, the IDOL includes the surfaces and Non-surfaces design information (colour, material, pattern, texture, image), cost information (quantity, unit, unit price, cost), and work information (specification, size, cad file, work breakdown structure), as shown in Fig. 5. Surfaces include floors, walls and ceilings, while non-surfaces include furniture, windows, doors and lighting fixtures. These are the major components of private space for an apartment unit plan and serve as the primary focus of this study.

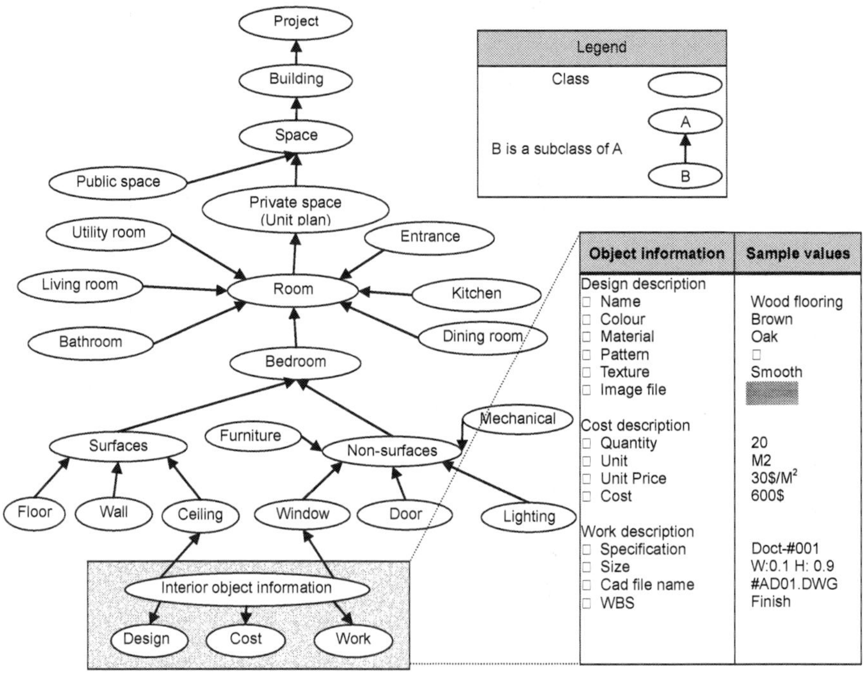

Fig. 5. Hierarchy schematic for interior object information

Once the information is integrated, it can be used by each project participant for his or her particular responsibilities as Fig. 6 suggests. For example, the interior designer reviews the costs and plans several different design alternatives for each room based on the unit plan. The owner/developer can review the project costs for each interior design alternative, and the builder will be able to prepare resource and budget plans for each WBS.

4.2 Schematic of the interior design decision support system

The Interior Design Decision Support System suggested here is capable of controlling interior design costs and supporting client decisions. This is achieved by referring to resource consumption plans from the early phases of a project, and by implementing and using the IDOL database to link the construction and design characteristics for interior design. The procedure involved is shown in Fig. 7, and the components of the system are described in the following section.

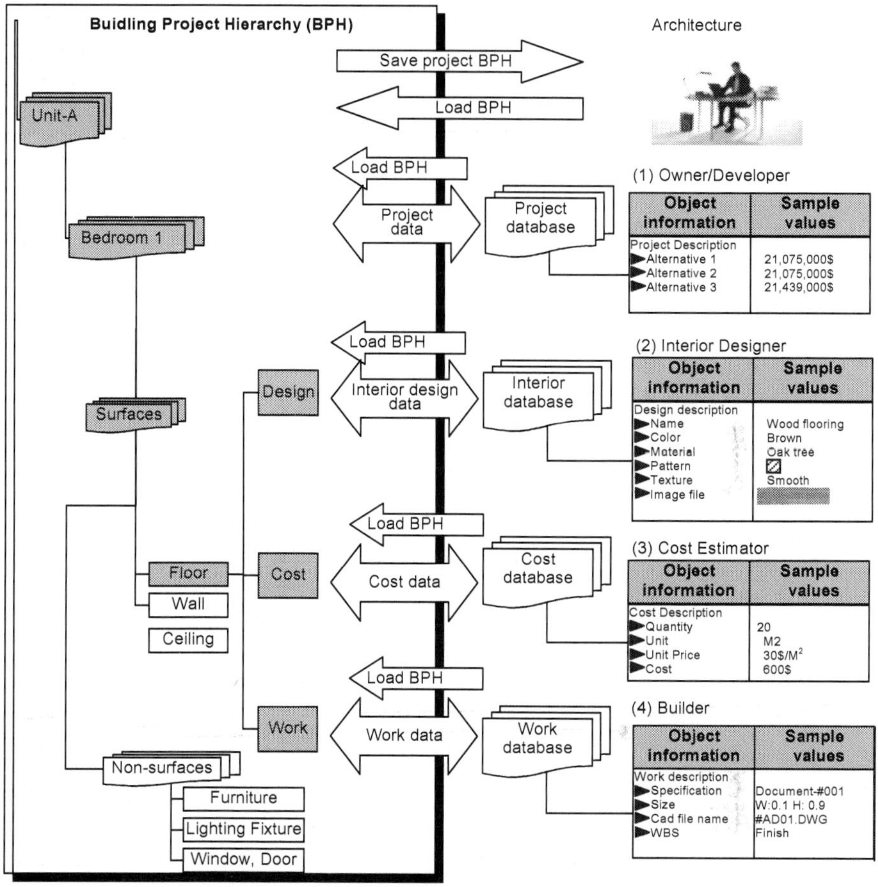

Fig. 6. Multidisciplinary use of the BPH and the IDOL

4.3 Components of the interior design decision support system

4.3.1 Users

The main users of the Interior Design Decision Support System are the client, the interior designer and the builder, who participate in the decision-making process. The interior designer has the responsibility for the interior design process. Once the interior designer selects the default values for the IDOL, clients can change the colour, pattern, texture and material by viewing images of the interior design objects. They can also examine costs, one of the unit measures, on a real-time basis. As shown in Fig. 7, after receiving a BPH from an expert group involving A/E/C, the interior designers select the default values for the IDOL. Then clients are given the task of making selections from the IDOL. With help from a cost estimator, construction costs are estimated for the selected interior design, and in addition, the particulars of the changes in the IDOL are updated and controlled.

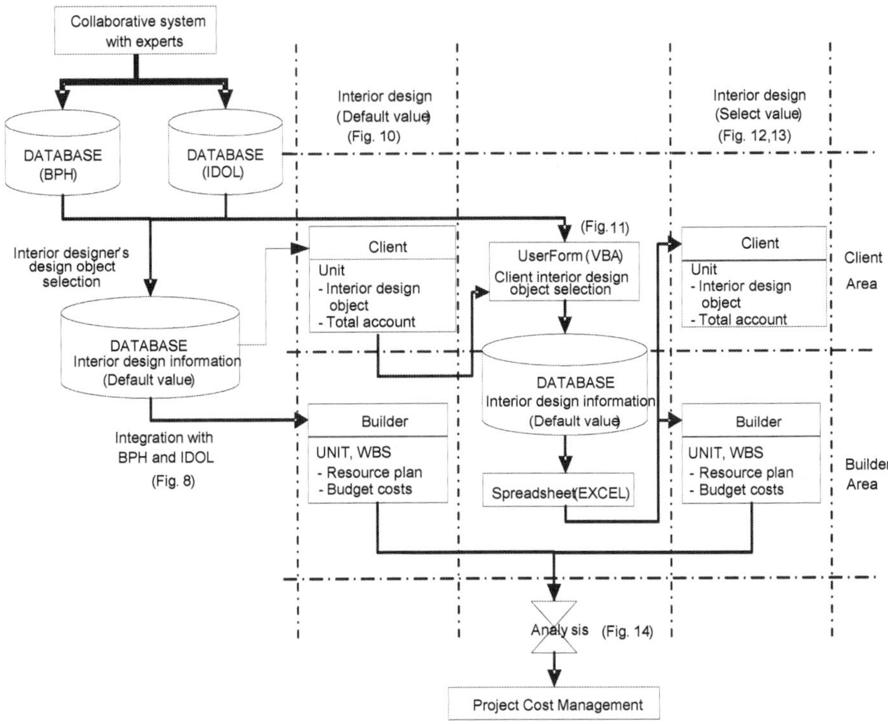

Fig. 7. Schematic of the proposed Interior Design Decision Support System

4.3.2 Decision-making procedure

After the A/E/C group produces the BPH during the detailed design phase, interior designers select the design objects from the IDOL and set the default values for the interior design. Targeting these default values, the clients use the decision support system and make decisions by selecting interior design objects to their requirement from the IDOL. Clients can make decisions either under the constraint of fixed costs (e.g., simply changing the colour of wallpaper), or with the option of variable costs to change the design items.

4.3.3 Information model

The underlying data of the Interior Design Decision Support System are related to the work involved and the costs of the interior specifications. As stated previously, the information on interior design decisions comes from the creation of the IDOL and its integration with the project BPH.

As shown in Fig. 8, the proposed BPH and the IDOL produce interior design information that is integrated after being selected by the client. Here, the IDOL holds the elements such as work items, specification, image, colour, material, unit, unit price and work breakdown structure. The interior design information (the selected value) generated here is displayed and used to meet the requirements of the client and builder.

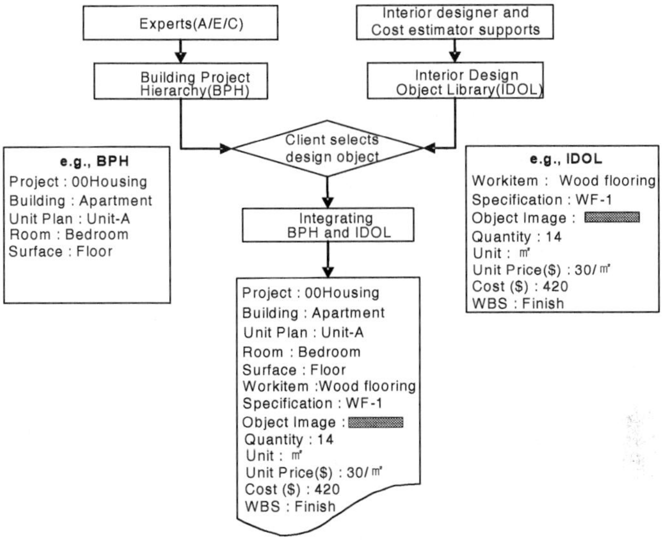

Fig. 8. Integrating the BPH and the IDOL

As seen in Fig. 9, an information model was suggested to integrate the BPH and IDOL that supports cost-based interior design decisions.

5. Example study and application

5.1 Establishing the interior design information (default values)

To set the values for the interior design objects and costs in the early phase, the BPH of the target project is configured in co-operation with the A/E/C experts, and the default values of interior design objects are created with the help of the designer and cost estimator.

The cost of each unit is established when the interior designer inputs the interior design for the units using design objects from the BPH, and the cost estimator inputs the cost estimates for the selected interior design. Figure 10 shows an example of the default values set by the interior designer for each element.

5.2 The client selects the interior design objects

The client makes decisions with the support of the IDOL database, which is linked to the default values. As design objects are selected, the cost is changed accordingly. Using the basic default values, the client selects the interior specifications that their requirements. Two scenarios for changes can be simulated involving the fixed and variable costs.

5.2.1 Fixed cost example

When the client selects the fixed cost condition, he or she can decision making the alternatives provided in the IDOL database, as presented in Fig. 11. The results of these decisions are displayed on a spreadsheet, as shown in Fig. 12. For example, when the client changes the wallpaper pattern, the interior design objects change, although no change in the cost is indicated. Nevertheless, the client can still choose from a variety of alternatives. The information generated in this example is then used in resource planning and project cost management.

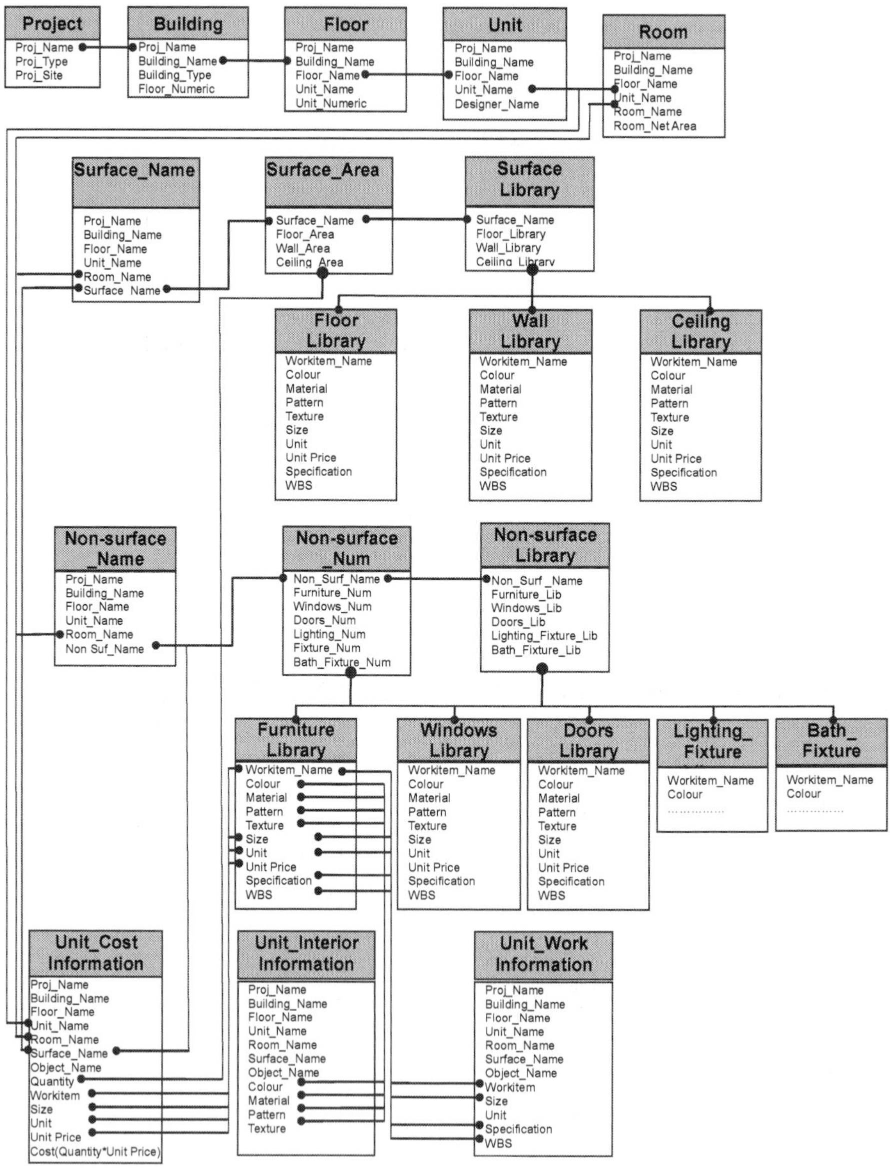

Fig. 9. Interior design information model

Default (1)	Information	Floor	Wall	Ceiling	Decoration	Doors	Fixture	Total
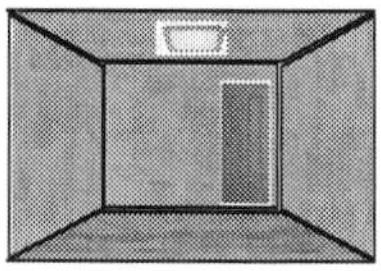	Interior work item	Wood flooring	Wallpaper	Wallpaper	Moulding	Wood door	Lighting fixture	
	Specification	WF-1	WP-1	WP-1	MD-1	0.9*2.0	LF-01	
	Object Image							
	Quantity	14	28	14	15	1	1	
	Unit	M^2	M^2	M^2	M	EA	EA	
	Unit Price ($)	30	5	5	3	250	150	
	Cost ($)	420	140	70	45	250	150	1,075
	WBS	Finish	Finish	Finish	Decoration	Doors	Electric	

Fig. 10. Interior designer-selected values (default values)

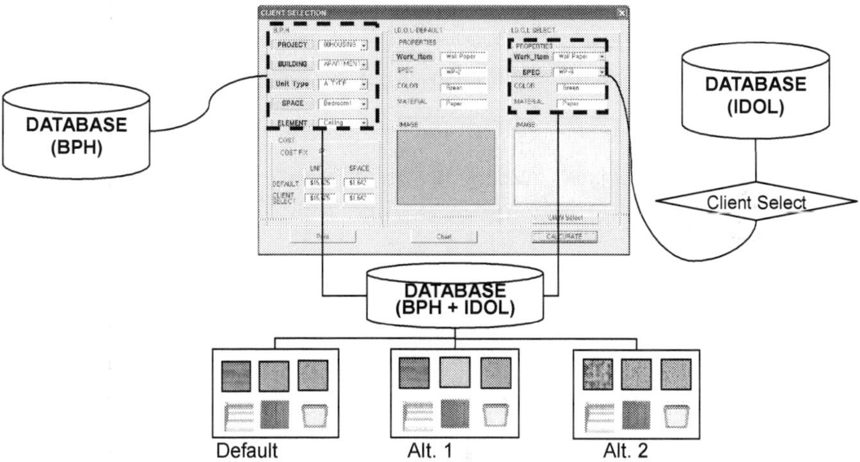

Fig. 11. Decision making the alternatives in IDOL database

Alternative 1	Components	Floor	Wall	Ceiling	Decoration	Doors	Fixture	Total
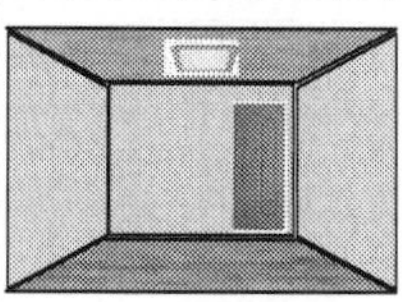	Interior work item	Wood flooring	Wallpaper	Wallpaper	Moulding	Wood door	Lighting fixture	
	Specification	WF-1	WP-2	WP-1	MD-1	0.9*2.0	LF-01	
	Object Image							
	Quantity	14	28	14	15	1	1	
	Unit	M^2	M^2	M^2	M	EA	EA	
	Unit Price($)	30	5	5	3	250	150	
	Cost ($)	420	140	70	45	250	150	1,075
	WBS	Finish	Finish	Finish	Decoration	Doors	Electric	

Fig. 12. Options for the client-selected values under the fixed cost scenario

5.2.2 Variable cost example

Alternatively, the client can select finishes and confirm the final costs on a real-time basis. These decisions are made by selecting from alternatives proposed in the IDOL database when selecting the variable cost option. As Figure 13 shows, when the client changes work items for the floor, wall and ceiling, the cost changes from $1,075 to $1,439. A system example study was run using the default values proposed by the interior designer using the fixed and variable cost options. The change in cost is the difference between the cost of the interior design objects proposed by the interior designer, and the cost of those selected by the client. Under the fixed cost scenario, the client changed the design of wall objects without changing the costs relative to the default values set by the interior designer. With the variable cost option, changing the wood flooring to tile carpet and the wallpaper material from paper to fabric increased the cost to $1,439 from the default value of $1,075.

Alternative 2	Components	Floor	Wall	Ceiling	Decoration	Doors	Fixture	Total
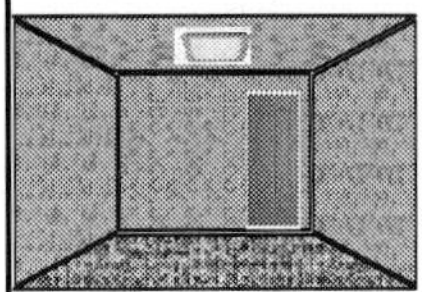	Interior work item	Carpet tile	Wallpaper	Wallpaper	Moulding	Wood door	Lighting fixture	
	Specification	CT-2	WP-3	WP-3	MD-1	0.9*2.0	LF-01	
	Object Image							
	Quantity	14	28	14	15	1	1	
	Unit	M^2	M^2	M^2	M	EA	EA	
	Unit Price($)	50	7	7	3	250	150	
	Cost ($)	700	196	98	45	250	150	1,439
	WBS	Finish	Finish	Finish	Decoration	Doors	Electric	

Fig. 13. Options for the client-selected values under the variable cost scenario

5.3 Application for the client and builder

Considering the needs of the client/builder described in Section 4.1, the interior design objects selected for the target project are integrated for each space and WBS, and the results are displayed for the client and builder. When examining the costs, the client can also check the interior design total project cost by decisions made concerning the unit interior design. The builder can make a project interior construction cost plan and resource consumption plan according to the WBS. The following detailed summaries are produced for the client and builder.

5.3.1 Application for the client

As shown in Fig. 14, the developer or owner can establish a baseline cost of $21,075,000 against which to compare the alternative proposals. Alternative 1 has no cost impact compared to the baseline, while Alternative 2 would increase the project cost by $364,000 due to the interior changes.

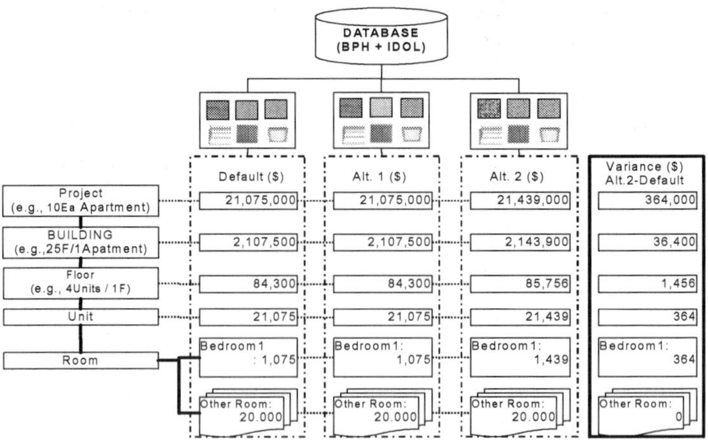

Fig. 14. The total costs according to the changes

5.3.2 Application for the builder

Based on the client's decisions, the builder is provided with cost and resource data according to the WBS (e.g., finishes, doors, windows and furniture), displayed as the amount per construction type as shown in Fig. 15(a). The builder or other agents can also use work items from the spaces as shown in Fig. 15(b).

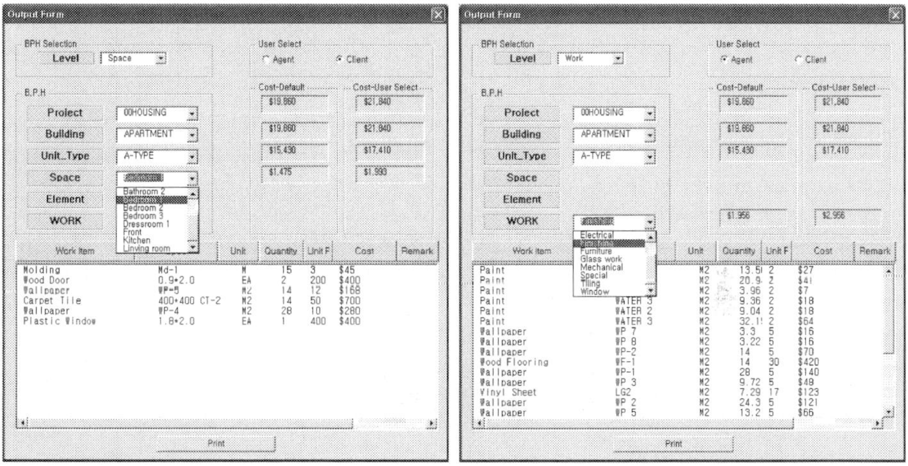

(a) According to WBS (b) According to space resources

Fig. 15. The user interface of default interior design and client-selected items

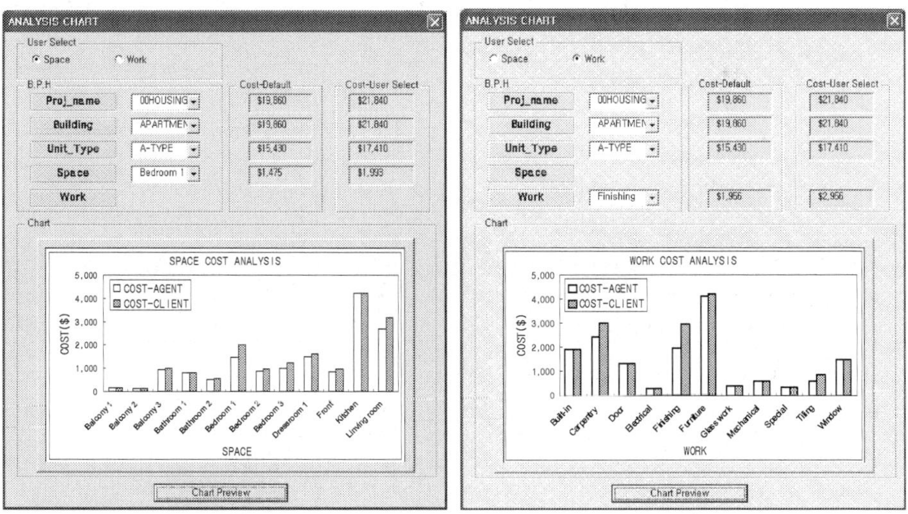

(a) According to space (b) According to works

Fig. 16. Cost analysis charts

The design objects and costs generated here are used as data for managing project costs in the WBS as shown in Fig. 16. By analysing the costs according to the different spaces (Fig. 16(a)) and work (Fig. 16(b)), the builder can make a construction cost plan and resource consumption plan in accordance with the WBS. From the perspective of project cost management, the default cost proposed by the interior designer and the costs determined by client selection can increase the estimate accuracy of the project costs in the early phases of a project.

6. Conclusion

We proposed an interior design decision support system that enables clients to participate in the early phases of the interior design for a housing project. This allows them to select objects (e.g., colours, patterns, material) for the interior design based on the unit measure of costs with input from various A/E/C experts. This also allows the interior designer and cost estimator to check the costs accordingly. The proposed system was implemented using the BPH and IDOL. In an example study, interior design objects and default costs were proposed while examining the fixed and variable cost options.

This study examined how client decisions made during the early design phases and based on restrictions in the interior design can affect a project. An analysis of the results confirmed that our interior design decision support system leads to client satisfaction with the interior design, while enabling clients to manage project costs by providing a cost baseline. Overall, this increases the accuracy of early estimates made during the project concept phase.

Cost and time are both very key indicators for assessing project performance. In the earlier phases of large-scale housing projects, the review of construction costs is important (Kim et al., 2004).

It is not appropriate to state that high-cost interiors designs are good and low-cost ones are not. However, making interior designs or design changes without any consideration of the cost is a source of serious problems for the interior designer and other project participants, especially the owner/developer. Moreover, despite considerable information on costs for alternative proposals selected by interior designers, existing procedures have many problems as seen in a review and feedback of these alternatives.

To address these problems, we investigated various alternative proposals for surfaces (floor, wall and ceiling) and non-surfaces (furniture, windows and doors) on a unit plan basis for large-scale housing development projects, and provided an interior information model. The model was validated through an example study to show how it could be used in the decision-making process by various participants in a construction project. The proposed model is useful in providing a total interior cost review and cost baseline for the developer/owner, a means for cost-based decision making by interior designers, and the interior material information required by builders.

Future studies will focus on the automation of quantity surveying and graphics to reinforce the use of Internet-based decision support systems. In future studies, further subdivision of the design objects characteristics will be necessary, as well as the development of a system that enables clients to make interior design decisions by changing layers, a subject outside the scope of the present study. Additional work is also required to enable interior designers to use the information provided by vendors and suppliers directly, and to provide the information for the procurement phase without any additional processing.

7. References

Anwar, N. (2005). *Component-based, information oriented structural engineering applications.* Journal of Computing in Civil Engineering, Vol. 29 (1), pp 45-57.

Bennett, J. (2000). *Construction the third way: managing cooperation and competition in construction*, Butterworth-Heinemann, Boston, MA.

Björk, B.C. (1989). *Basic structure of a proposed building product model.* Computer Aided Design, Vol. 21 (2) pp 71-78.

Choi, J.W., Kwon, D.Y., Hwang, J.E., & Lertlakkhanakul, J. (2007). *Real-time management of spatial information of design.* Automation in Construction, Vol. 16 (4), pp 449-459.

Dawood, N., Sriprasert, E., Mallasi, Z., & Hobbs, B. (2003). *Development of an integrated information resource base for 4D/VR construction processes simulation.* Automation in Construction, Vol. 12 (2), pp 123-131.

Demirkan, H. (2005). Generating design activities through sketches in multi-agent system. Automation in Construction, Vol. 14 (6), pp 699-706.

Geoffrion, A.M. (1987). *An introduction to structured modelling.* Management Science, Vol. 33, pp 547-588.

Gielingh, W. (1988). *General AEC Reference Model.* ISO TC184/SC4/WG1 doc. 3.2.2.1, ISO, Delft, The Netherlands.

Halfawy, M. & Froese, T. (2005). *Building integrated architecture/engineering/construction systems using smart objects.* Journal of Computing in Civil Engineering, Vol. 19 (2), pp 172-181.

Hegazy, T., Zaneldin, E., & Grierson, D. (2001). *Improving design coordination for building projects.* Journal of Construction Engineering and Management, Vol. 127 (4), pp 322-329.

Huyn, P.N., Geneserth, M.R., & Letsinger, R. (1993). *Automated concurrent engineering in design.* World Computing, Vol. 26 (1), pp 74-76.

ISO (1994). *ISO 10303-1 Part 1: Overview and fundamental principles, International Organization for Standardization*, Geneva, Switzerland.

Kalay, Y.E., Khemluni, L., & Choi, J.W. (1998). *An integrated model to support distributed collaborative design of buildings.* Automation in Construction, Vol. 7 (2-3), pp 177-188.

Khedro, T., Teicholz, P., & Geneserth, M.R. (1994). A framework for collaborative distributed facility engineering. *Proceedings of the 1st Congress of Computing in Civil Engineering*, ASCE, New York, NY, pp 1489-1496.

Kim, G.H., An, S.H., & Kang, K.I. (2004). *Comparison of construction cost estimating models based on regression analysis, neural networks, and case-based reasoning.* Building and Environment, Vol. 39 (10), pp 1235-1242.

Korean National Statistical Office, <http://www.nso.go.kr/>

Lee, E.J., Woo, S.G., & Sasada, T. (2001). *The evaluation system for design alternatives in collaborative design.* Automation in Construction, Vol. 10 (3), pp 295-301.

Lee, H.K., Lee, Y.S., Kim, K.H., & Kim, J.J. (2007). A Cost-based Information Model for an Interior Design in a Large-scale Housing Project, *ICCIT 07, 2007 International Conference on Convergence Information Technology.*

Luiten, G.T.B. & Tolman, F.P. (1997). *Automating communication, in civil engineering.* Journal of Construction Engineering and Management, Vol. 123 (2), pp 113-120.

Mokhtar, A., Beard, C., & Fazio, P. (2000). *Collaborative planning and scheduling of interrelated design changes*. Journal of Architectural Engineering, Vol. 6 (2), pp 66–75.

Project Management Institute (2000). *A Guide to the Project Management Body of Knowledge (PMBOK® Guide)*. Project Management Institute, Singapore.

Reichard, G. & Papamichael, K. (2005). *Decision-making through performance simulation and code compliance from the early schematic phase of building design*. Automation in Construction, Vol. 14 (2), pp 173–180.

Turner, J.A. (1990). *AEC Building Systems Model*. ISO TC184/SC4/WG1 doc. 3.2.2.4, ISO, Delft, The Netherlands.

11

Multimedia Streaming Service Adaptation in IMS Networks

Tanır Özçelebi and Igor Radovanović
Eindhoven University of Technology, Vodafone Netherlands
The Netherlands

1. Introduction

Multimedia services such as video, gaming and music marked the close of the last century and have become inextricably linked with our lives in the current century. The success and popularity of these services was fuelled by the explosive expansion of the Internet and the furious penetration of broadband networks. In particular, the use of multimedia streaming services on portable devices has been popular whenever both the content and the perceived delivery quality have met the expectations of end users.

This chapter of the book does not address content aspects of multimedia streaming services. Such matters are left to media gurus and other researchers. Rather, this chapter focuses on the delivery quality of multimedia streaming services. Particular attention is paid to quality adaptation techniques intended to improve end users' experience of such services.

Our scope includes heterogeneous networks and devices. The solutions presented are applicable to the telecommunications industry.

2. Drivers of quality enhancement

Before we dive deep into quality adaptation of multimedia streaming services, we would like to address *variables* that affect quality and the objective *quality measures*. In order to avoid confusion with the mathematical variables, we will call these variables *drivers* of quality enhancement. Focusing on the drivers will help us identify issues that need to be tackled in order to provide solutions for increasing quality of multimedia streaming services, whereas focusing on the objective quality measures will help us check whether the provided solutions indeed can provide the desired result (which is quality enhancement).

Quality of a multimedia streaming service, as perceived by the end user, is defined as perceived Quality of Service (QoS) and is mainly driven by the two factors. The first factor is *the end-to-end resource availability* required to compose, transport, process and run multimedia streams. This includes the resources in all the devices and networks through which the multimedia stream is flowing. Here one can think of all kinds of end-devices (e.g. PC, gadgets and mobile phones), network devices (e.g. routers, switches and servers) and physical transport media (e.g. copper cable, fiber and ether). The second factor is the *distance*, i.e. the number of hops and the physical distance, between the source and the sink of the multimedia stream (see Fig. 1).

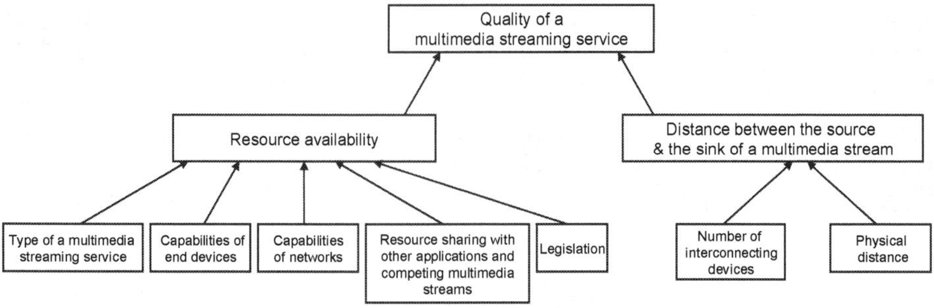

Fig. 1. Quality drivers for multimedia streaming.

The resource availability in turn, is mainly driven by the type of multimedia streaming service, the end-device capabilities, the network capabilities, the presence of other competing multimedia streams and applications, and the legislation regarding multimedia streaming. Let us now elaborate more on these five drivers of resource availability.

2.1 Drivers of resource availability

Not all multimedia streaming services have the same content nor do they all require the same amount of resources to achieve a certain quality. For example, voice, speech and music require throughput of no more than several 10's or 100's of Kbits per second. Other services, like streaming video, may easily require an order, or even two orders of a magnitude higher throughput. Therefore, resource availability is a *relative term* that can be measured only after taking resource requirements into account. Obviously, it is easier to provide better quality of services to those services requiring fewer amounts of resources. Moreover, more instances of such services can be supported simultaneously with the same quality, offering more benefits to both the providers and consumers of those services. Note that resource requirements are varying in time, as explained in Section 4.

Although portable devices like PDA's and smart phones became very resource rich nowadays, the resource availability in those still differs substantially from the desktop PC's and game consoles. Having more resources in the latter types of devices makes it easier to provide better quality for the end users.

Similar arguments hold for networks. Better network QoS can be achieved for packets transmitted over fiber links than for those transmitted over the air as a result of the different characteristics of these two types of physical transport media. For example, the available throughput is affected by the physical attributes of the media such as the amount of attenuation, dispersion and packet losses, the physical distance and the power of the transmitted signal. An important part of this driver is the type of hardware used in the interconnecting devices in the network. Increased packet processing delay in those devices will boost the total packet delay, inherently decreasing QoS in the network[1].

The presence of other competing streams and devices is also a very important quality driver, which affects *availability* of resources in end-devices and networks. After all, what's the point of having ample amount of resources in the end-devices when they are all consumed by other services and applications leaving no room for an additional multimedia service to run?

[1] QoS in networks is defined in Section 3.

Finally, the legislation issue needs to be addressed as well. Having no regulation of media and traffic might lead to a situation where some multimedia streaming services are either unintentionally blocked or intentionally degraded in quality based on the multimedia content and ownership.

2.2 Drivers of distance

After describing the resource availability drivers, we would like to address the drivers of the distance between the source and the sink of the multimedia stream. The first driver, as depicted in Fig. 1, is the physical distance that directly determines the propagation delay in the network. The larger the distance, the larger the propagation delay and thus lower the perceived QoS of the multimedia streaming service. The more interconnecting devices we have the larger the total delay, which addresses the second driver.

3. Objective quality measures

For both providers and consumers of multimedia streaming service, high *perceived QoS* is of utmost importance. The perceived QoS is a subjective measure of the user experience, and is highly correlated with the measured *objective QoS*. The main objective measures used to describe QoS throughout a single multimedia service session are picture Peak Signal-to-Noise Ratio (PSNR), frame refresh rate (video smoothness) and continuousness of multimedia playback (Ozcelebi et al., 2007). Here, a service session is defined as a durable connection between the two end-devices or an end-device and a server. The more efficient the video compression algorithm, the less network bandwidth is needed for a video streaming service to achieve a certain perceived QoS level. Video codecs in the literature such as MPEG2 (ISO/IEC, 2000) and AVC/H.264 (Wiegand et al., 2003) try to achieve such efficient video compression (encoding) such that the perceived QoS of the decompressed (decoded) video is maximized.

Firstly, PSNR is used very commonly as an indicator of this perceived quality. Its value is determined by the power of the pixel noise introduced to the video as a result of lossy compression. As the average power of the pixel errors (mean square error) in video frames introduced during compression increases, the PSNR value decreases. Therefore, assuming ideal transport conditions, higher PSNR value means that a given decoded video at the receiving side is more similar to the original video, i.e. that it is of higher quality.

The second factor determining the perceived QoS is the video frame rate. The human eye perceives our surroundings in a continuous way instead of a frame-by-frame manner as introduced by video technology. This means that as the frame refresh rate of a video decreases, it gets further and further away from what the human eye would perceive. This issue becomes especially troublesome for video scenes with a lot of movement. For a smooth and natural video perception, it is necessary to operate at sufficient frame rates. In practice, 25 fps (frames-per-second) and above is thought to suffice for a decent video experience, although higher frame refresh rates are more suitable for the human perception.

Finally, interruptions during video playback are quite undesirable in terms of perceived QoS and they must be avoided. The receiving side of a video streaming service does some video pre-buffering prior to starting the video playback in order to compensate for possible variations in network throughput and end-to-end delay (i.e. delay jitter). Video playback is started only after the receiving video buffer is at least partially filled (Ozcelebi et al., 2007).

Therefore, there is typically a delay between the time the first video packet is received and the time it is actually displayed on the receiver's screen, called the pre-roll delay, which remedies the negative effects of unpredicted channel behavior. However, if the video encoding rate is higher than the channel throughput for a long period of time, it is possible that the receiver buffer underflows (is emptied) and there are no more video data to display. In this case, the video playback is interrupted and the receiver needs to wait for another pre-roll delay before the video playback can continue, jeopardizing perceived QoS level.

Perceived QoS, in case of multimedia streaming services, is determined by the *intrinsic QoS*, i.e. QoS at the network level. In telecommunications networks, intrinsic QoS of a certain multimedia stream is measured using *throughput, delay, jitter* and *loss-rate*. In order to maximize intrinsic QoS, throughput has to be maximized, whereas delay, jitter and loss-rate have to be minimized, or at least, bounded to a certain limit depending on the service characteristics. The following table describes requirements regarding these intrinsic QoS parameters for 7 different types of services.

Application/ requirement	Reliability	Delay	Jitter	Bandwidth
E-mail	High	Low	Low	Low
File transfer	High	Low	Low	Medium
Web access	High	Medium	Low	Medium
Audio on demand	Low	Low	High	Medium
Video on demand	Low	Low	High	High
Telephony	Low	High	High	Low
Videoconferencing	Low	High	High	High

Table 1. Requirements for high intrinsic QoS of various applications

4. Maximizing perceived QoS

To achieve high perceived QoS, required resources in both the network and the end-devices must be available at *all times* during service provisioning. Moreover, the total delay has to be under a certain minimum level depending on the particular multimedia service. For a voice service it is typically below 150 mSec (on direction), whereas for video it is below 200 mSec. We specifically stress upon this issue since both resource availability and resource requirements fluctuate continuously and substantially during a single session. Resource requirements of a multimedia streaming service may vary drastically in time according to the encoding bitrate and the scene complexity (e.g. amount of spatial pixel variations, temporal movement) in each temporal segment.

Intrinsic QoS can be maximized by combining the usage of proper intrinsic QoS mechanisms with an overprovisioning in the network (Aurrecoechea et al., 1996). Intrinsic QoS mechanisms such as admission control, resource reservation and traffic engineering can be used for this purpose. The pre-requisite for using these intrinsic QoS mechanisms, however, is to have end-to-end control of resources, from the source to the sink of the multimedia stream. Note that this pre-requisite is easily satisfied by telecom operators as they have full control over their networks.

Despite such mechanisms, quality of a telecom multimedia service may still be jeopardized by several factors, e.g. Doppler Effect, shadow fading and multi-path interference in wireless networks. Furthermore, the sink of the multimedia stream is strictly speaking not in the network but in the end-devices, whose resources are not under control of the telecom operators. In the end-devices, resources such as battery, CPU power, memory size and storage space vary in real-time during a single multimedia session, making hard guarantees for a certain level of perceived QoS difficult to achieve.

This problem has become even more acute with the launch of the IP Multimedia Subsystem (IMS) framework as a telecommunications networks initiative (3GPP, 2006). The IMS framework allows usage of the multimedia services from unmanaged access networks that are beyond the operator's control (e.g. WiFi, xDSL). Thus, it is very difficult to control the entire physical bearer infrastructure of the end-to-end channel in a unified way, e.g. by a single operator. This, of course, makes QoS mechanisms such as admission control practically inapplicable. In principle, IMS operators can control call admission in all access networks by enforcing a Service Based Local Policy (SBLP) via the Policy Decision Function (PDF) at the access network border. However, this can be done only if the access network bearer reacts upon the commands from the signaling and control layers in the IMS core, which is generally not the case.

Moreover, even if all IMS networks were somehow controllable, the operators cannot give hard guarantees for resource availability during the whole session due to factors such as fading and interference as explained above. Interference may come from other sessions in the same network technology or signals from different sources that operate in the same frequency band. Some IMS access networks (i.e. 802.11 WiFi networks) utilize the shared Industrial, Scientific and Medical (ISM) frequency band, making them highly vulnerable to interference from other technologies as well, e.g. Bluetooth, microwave oven. These interfering technologies generate errors in real-time packet transmission that are mainly recovered by retransmissions. However, these retransmissions inherently increase latency and decrease effective throughput making provisioning of high perceived QoS extremely difficult.

5. The IMS framework

The IMS is an architectural framework for backward compatible Next Generation Network (NGN) as explained in (ITU, 2009). Backward compatibility implies that the new NGN technology can seamlessly integrate with the legacy one, i.e. 2G and 3G telecom networks and services. The IMS separates functionality of services from the underlying network architecture which means that services offered to the end users are network neutral. This in turn implies that perceived quality of a particular service must be the same irrespective of the network technology used. However, since unmanaged IMS access networks are allowed as well, it becomes much more difficult to achieve the original requirement. The IMS layered architecture is shown in Fig. 2.

The IMS infrastructure allows utilization of IMS services from any IPv6 capable end-device and access network possibly not owned by the telecom operator, as depicted in Fig. 3. These access networks can be unmanageable by telecom operators, meaning they may be unlicensed, non-dedicated and non-deterministic with no QoS control (3GPP, 2006). Therefore, end-to-end QoS reservations may be inapplicable and network bandwidth may

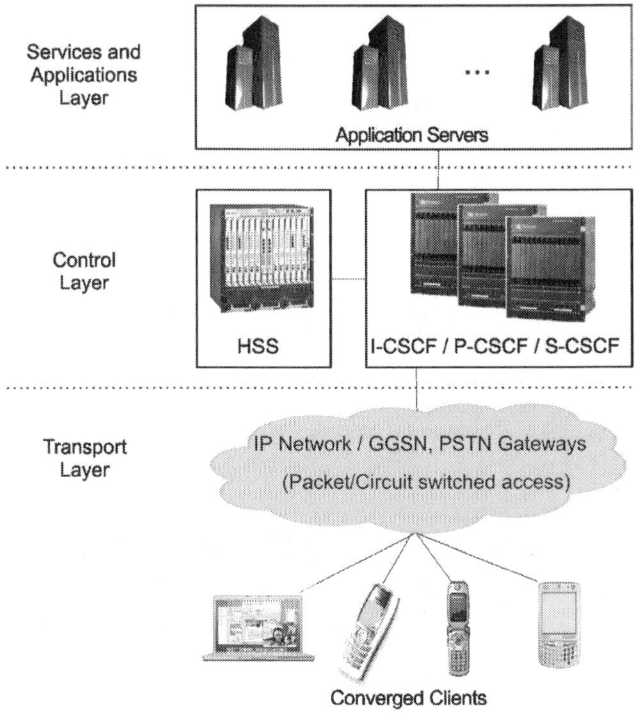

Fig. 2. The IMS layered architecture.

be reserved unnecessarily within the operator's network, since making the same reservation may not be possible in an unmanaged access network. This bandwidth could better be used for other sessions. For example, pure Ethernet-based and public broadband access networks are unmanageable. Therefore, it would not be possible to reserve network resources and guarantee their availability for the duration of a single session, causing perceived QoS to suffer when there is a shortage of network resources.

This is the reason why QoS cannot be guaranteed, and the best-effort QoS model has to be adopted (3GPP, 2006). However, the best-effort QoS model used in the Internet does not support operator's business model that is based on the user's high expectation of the perceived QoS. We strongly believe that in order to satisfy user's expectation, the operators need to adopt *the best of the best-effort QoS model*. This model implies that the best-effort perceived QoS has to be maximized at all times. The way to achieve this goal is described in this chapter. The proposed solution enhances the perceived QoS of multimedia services in the application layer, in situations where the real-time multimedia service QoS cannot be guaranteed in the network layer. The perceived QoS is adapted according to the system overall resource availability. The quantitative value of the system overall resource availability is updated using a signaling mechanism during a single multimedia session. Since the current IMS architecture lacks such a mechanism, as described in the following section, the authors proposed a solution, which is presented in Section 8.

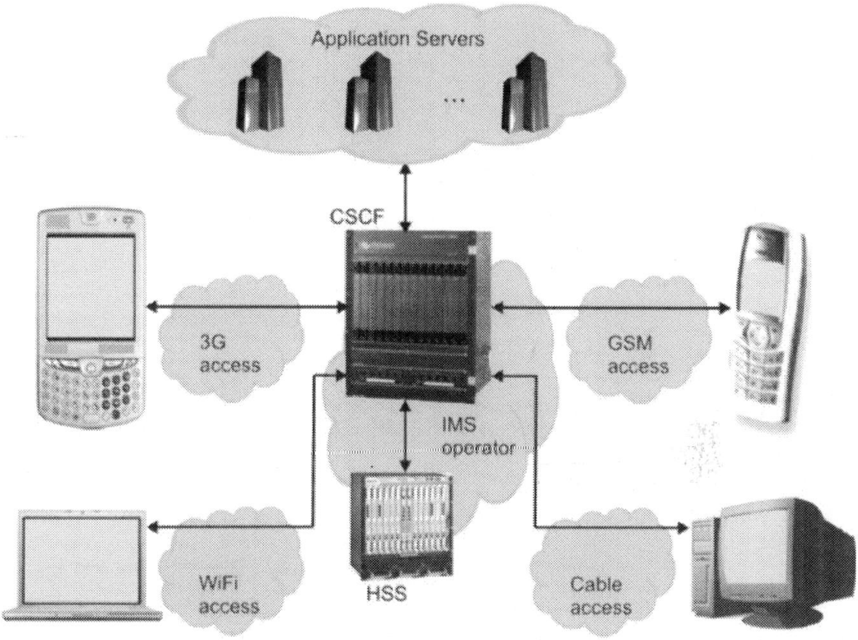

Fig. 3. Architecture of the converged IMS based network.

6. QoS negotiation during the IMS session establishment

In IMS, a call session control is implemented in the signaling and control layers (3GPP, 2006). With the call session control, it is possible to negotiate the QoS parameters of a given session in IMS standard specifications at the beginning of the session using the SIP control messages. QoS parameter negotiation is necessary for the support of variety of end-device types, media codecs, access network technologies and types of user subscriptions. The message flow diagram for such negotiation is shown in Fig. 4.

The caller user equipment (*UE*1) sends a SIP INVITE (Rosenberg et al., 2002) message to the call receiving user equipment (*UE*2) including her proposal for the QoS parameter values. This proposal is checked against the users' subscription credentials and modified if necessary in the Serving-Call Session Control Functions (S-CSCF) serving the two users. The information about the user subscription is sent to S-CSCF by the Home Subscriber Server (HSS). The reason to check for the user's subscription credentials is that the user might not be allowed to use some QoS parameter values due to the type of her subscription.

The reply message (SDP answer) from the call receiving user equipment (*UE*2) includes a set of QoS parameter values that are either the same as the ones received from the S-CSCF (originally sent from *UE*1), or different, depending on the availability of resources in the access network and terminal, media codec type used and the type of user's subscription. This parameter value set is then again checked in the S-CSCF's, which in turn might modify those. Finally, the SIP reply message is forwarded to *UE*1.

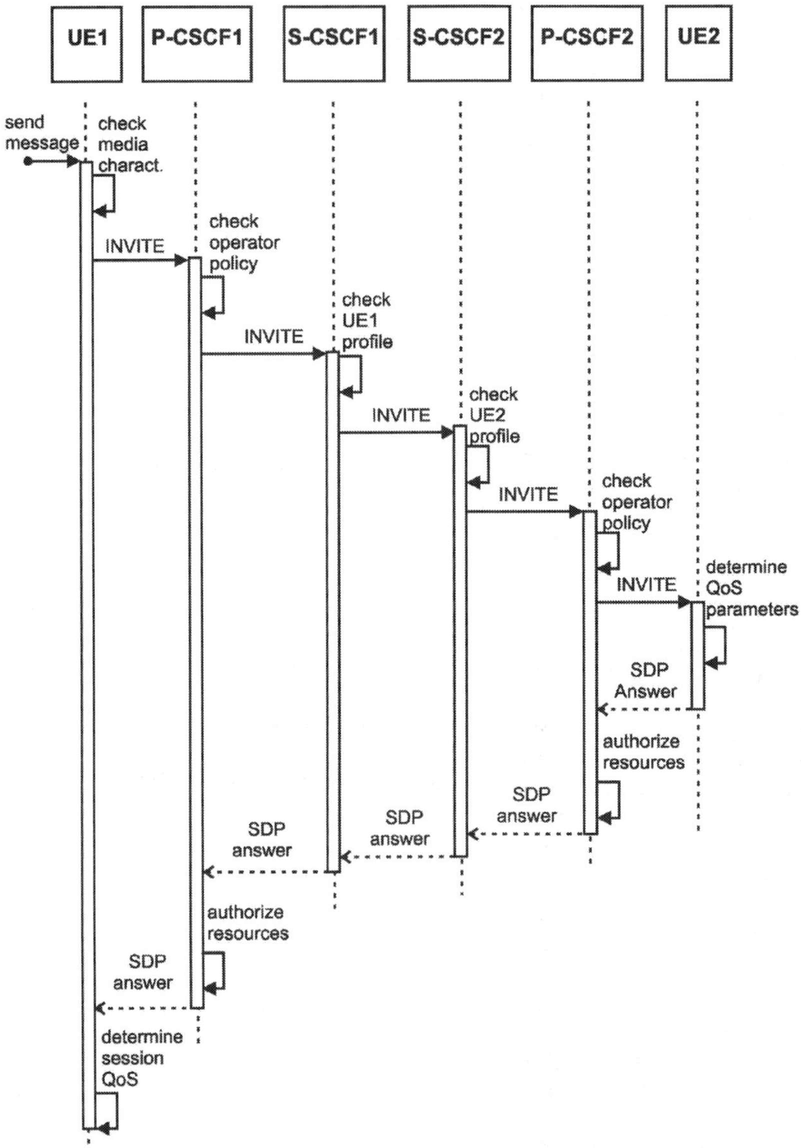

Fig. 4. Message Sequence Diagram showing pre-session QoS negotiation in an IMS network.

Note that, not all the messages such as acknowledgements (ACK) are shown in Fig. 4, for the sake of simplicity. It may take a while before the resource reservation can be finalized at the beginning of a media session, e.g. when the network resources are not available over a specific bearer. Furthermore, after the first QoS offer (see Fig. 4), it is possible that *UE*1

decides to change some session QoS parameters during the same session (e.g. choosing another codec). Therefore, only one QoS negotiation round before the session start may not be enough. *UE*1 can update its QoS offer by sending a SIP UPDATE message that includes the new QoS parameter values. Similarly, *UE*2 can make a new offer with an SIP UPDATE message as well. Therefore, *UE*2 must not inform the caller (by ringing) until the required resources for the session are surely negotiated and reserved. The final values of QoS parameters are set only after *UE*2 sends a 200 OK response to the SIP INVITE message. The quantified QoS parameter values are communicated through the Session Description Protocol (SDP) inside these SIP UPDATE messages.
In reality, the above pre-session QoS negotiation cannot offer a good perceived QoS due to lack of bearer control, nondeterministic networks and interference. In order to achieve enhanced QoS, session QoS parameters need to be renegotiated and modified very often during a single session, adapting to the varying system resource availability in real-time.

7. Literature review on several QoS signaling mechanisms in the IMS

There are several RFCs published by the Internet Engineering Task Force (IETF) that propose resource/capability signaling among end-devices. In (Camarillo et al., 2002), a method that integrates resource management (specifically RSVP) and SIP signaling is introduced in order to make network resource reservation *before the session is established*, i.e. before the called end-device is alerted such that session establishment failures are avoided. However, this RFC proposes no signaling *during* a single session. In our proposed solution it is assumed that reservations may not be possible in the access networks, and therefore the relation with the reservation protocols, like RSVP, is not considered in this work. Furthermore, in our solution, signaling is done during a single session. Another difference is that, we propose an architecture in which information about the resource availability of *both* the end-devices and networks can be transmitted to other interested parties, whereas (Camarillo et al., 2002) gives information about the network resource availability only.
In (Nomura et al., 2006), Internet Media Guides (IMG), i.e. multimedia session descriptions, which can use the SDP format are introduced. However, it is denoted in (Nomura et al., 2006) that SDP syntax causes a huge amount of overhead in delivering IMG metadata over the network and SDP can carry only a small subset of IMG metadata in practical cases (e.g. codec type).
The bandwidth modifier of (Westerlund, 2004) notifies the receiving end-device on the maximum media codec rate to be used and the communication bit-rate required for the bit stream. Thus, (Westerlund, 2004) aims to convey bit-rate information only, without conveying any information about end-device resource availability.
In (Casner, 2003), bandwidth modifiers for RTP Control Protocol (RTCP) are introduced to SDP such that the amount of bandwidth allocated to RTCP in an RTP session is adapted (typically kept below 5% of the overall data rate). We envision that SIP resource availability signaling is preferable for protecting the privacy of resource availability data compared to transport layer protocols (e.g. RTCP), which lack to provide means for authentication, encryption and billing.
An extended SDP protocol for capability declaration (e.g. codec) amongst end-devices to be used in multimedia sessions is introduced in (Andreasen, 2002). It is declared that such capability declarations can be intended for session negotiation, but such session negotiation mechanisms are not described.

In the IMS, it is envisioned that the end-to-end QoS negotiation and resource allocation should be reevaluated during the session depending on requests from the application, network load and link quality (3GPP, 2006). On the other hand, the implementation specifics of such a *QoS renegotiation* mechanism are not provided.

8. Resource availability signaling during a single session and service quality management

As explained in the previous section, the session QoS parameter values have to be renegotiated and modified very often during a single multimedia session in order to adapt the multimedia content quality to the varying resource availability in the system in real-time, maximizing the perceived QoS. This section gives a solution to this problem.

To solve the problem of monitoring resource availability in real time and sending the data which quantitatively describes it, we have introduced two software components for resource availability monitoring and resource availability signaling in real time. Those are the Resource Management (RM) module, and the Resource Availability Server (RAS), respectively. To adapt the multimedia content to the resource availability, we have introduced a Service Quality Management (SQM) software component based on which a real-time adaptation of multimedia communication streaming and stored multimedia data streaming (e.g. video-on-demand) services in the IMS network is made.

The RM module is a crucial part of the proposed resource availability signaling framework. It is responsible for tracking the available device and network resources in real-time. At the receiving device, the RM module publishes the resource availability information in the RAS server in which this information can be accessed by the remote transmitting device. At the transmitting device, the RM is responsible for gathering the resource availability data of the remote receiving device from the RAS. Based on this information, the content quality of the multimedia streaming service can be adapted.

It is the proposed RAS server that is responsible for collecting resource availability information from the receiving end-devices and delivering this information to the transmitting end-devices. Note that in a multimedia communication scenario, e.g. video-conferencing, an end-device can be transmitting multimedia, receiving multimedia, or both.

The proposed SQM module is responsible for adapting the perceived quality of the streamed multimedia service according to the real-time measured resource availability, such that the resource requirements of the streaming service is always kept below or equal to the actual resource availability in the end-devices and in the network. In this way, users are presented with a more reliable and higher quality user experience, where the perceived QoS is boosted when plenty of resources are available and reduced when the resource availability drops. Without adaptation of the perceived QoS, a multimedia session can experience variations in picture and sound quality and re-buffering events (interruptions in playback).

The solution presented here, which includes the introduction of the three software components must be IMS compliant in order to be practically implemented. For the sake of having an IMS compliant architectural solution, we have employed the existing SIP call session control protocol of IMS for resource availability signaling in the architecture we propose. Here it is assumed that the user equipments *UE*1 and *UE*2 have registered to each other's resource availability information at the RAS server. The proposed resource availability signaling and the proposed software components (i.e. RM, RAS and SQM) are depicted in Fig. 5 and Fig. 6.

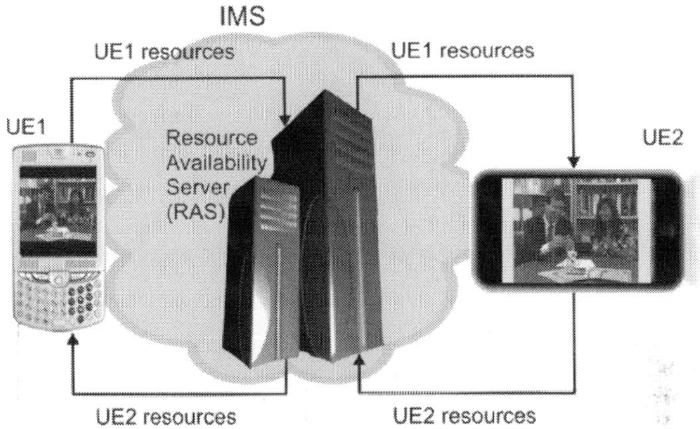

Fig. 5. The proposed system architecture for the mid-session SIP-based resource availability signaling.

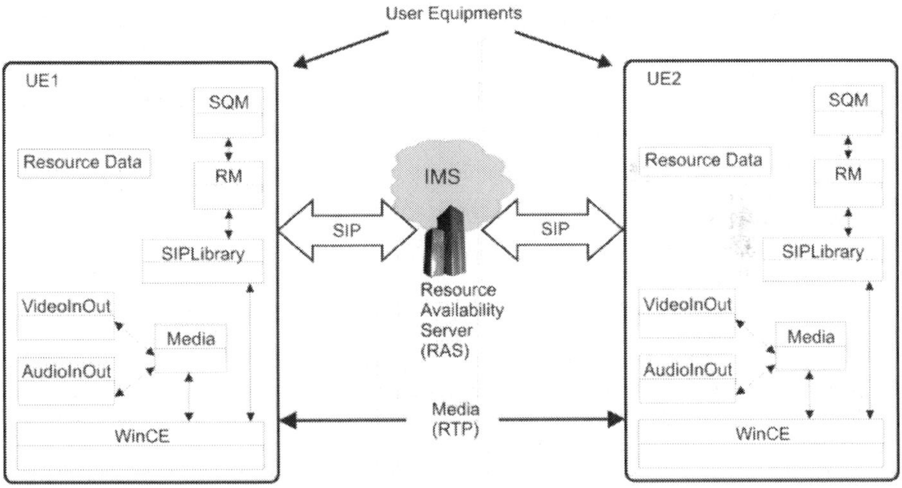

Fig. 6. Deployment view of the user devices and the IMS core.

The resource availability data is carried from *UE*1 and *UE*2 to the RAS and back in the SIP event notification (SIP NOTIFY) messages, as shown in Fig. 6. A resource update is signaled whenever the availability of local resources (e.g. memory, CPU, storage etc.) or the network resources (e.g. bandwidth, jitter etc.) at one end cross critical boundary threshold values. When the resource availability is not changing very fast, resource availability update messages can be quite infrequent. Therefore, the amount of end-device and network resources spent on the resource monitoring and signaling is negligible in the proposed

framework. A worst case scenario is investigated in the next section, where the maximum bitrate adaptation frequency (i.e. inversed minimum response time) of a video encoder is considered as an upper bound on the resource availability update signaling frequency.
The proposed message flow diagram from the end-device to the RAS for the resource availability signaling is depicted in Fig. 7 and our additions to the SIP/SDP parameters as resource indicators are shown in Table 1.

r	::=	"memory" | "CPU" | "storage" | "throughput" | "battery"
t	::=	"Mbytes" | "Kbytes" | "kbps" | "seconds" | "percentage"
a	::=	<resource availability measure>

Table 1. Proposed Additional Resource Data in SDP

After the addition of the proposed resource availability parameters, an example of the SDP resource availability update message is shown in Table 2. Here, both users will be aware of each other's local and network resources and SQM can use this information to adapt the multimedia content in order to maximize the perceived QoS.

```
NOTIFY sip:abc.somename.com SIP/2.0
Via: SIP/2.0/UDP abc.tue.nl:5060;branch=z9hG4bKnashds7
Max-Forwards: 70
To: Bob <sip:server.somename.com>
From: Bob <sip:abc.somename.com>;tag=456248
Call-ID: 843817637684230@998sdasdh09
CSeq: 1826 NOTIFY
Contact: <sip:abc@192.0.2.4>
Expires: 7200
Content-Type: application/sdp
Content-Length: 131

v= RM/1.45
o= abc 5876768686868 7698798797979 IP 1.2.3.4
s= 123456789
i= Resource update to presence server
c= IN IP4 1.2.3.4
b= 100 kbps
k= none

r= memory
i= free memory status
t= kbytes
a= 12450

r= battery
i= battery charge remaining
t= percentage
a= 86
--msg ends--
```

Table 2. Example SDP with Resource Data.

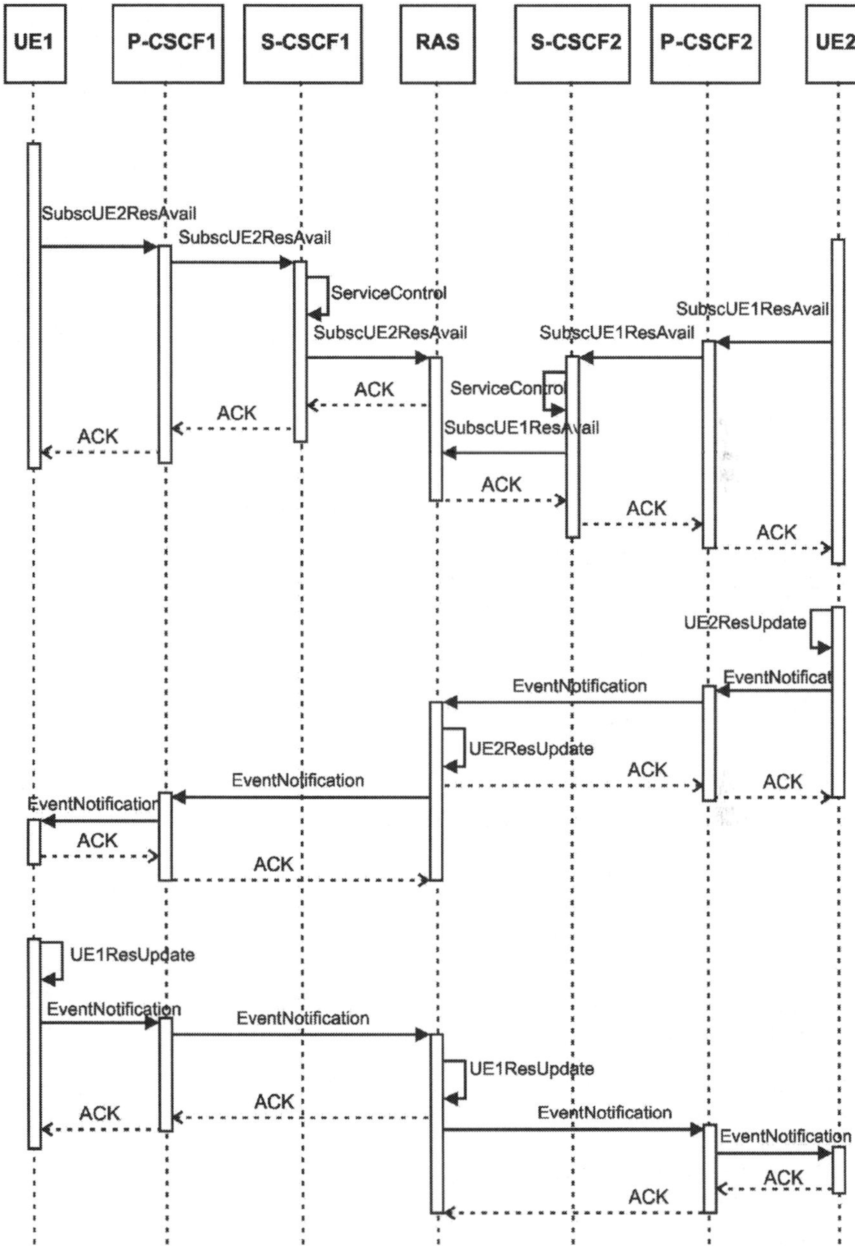

Fig. 7. Message Sequence Diagram showing SIP based resource availability update signaling.

9. Overhead of the signaling mechanism

For the proposed solution to be practically implementable, it is important that the introduced signaling overhead is negligible when compared to the original multimedia data. The maximum overhead caused by the proposed signaling mechanism will be in case the resource availability is done at the maximum adaptation speed of the multimedia codec used. Video encoders are slow in changing their encoding rates compared to channel variations due to limitations imposed by buffer management strategies of latest video encoders such as (VBV) model (Zhao & Kuo, 2003) of MPEG and the Hypothetical Reference Decoder (HRD) model (Ma et al., 2003) in AVC/H.264. Since we cannot adapt the video quality at a speed higher than the adaptation response time of the codec, resource availability signaling frequency must not be higher than the codec response time. Video adaptation algorithms need at least one group of pictures (GOP) - a frame sequence in a given structure - in order to converge to a target bit rate every time the video is adapted and at most 1 GOP per second is taken as a rule of thumb in order to achieve high compression efficiency. Such an approach would allow 1 adaptation per second in the worst case. Therefore, we assume that resource availability is done on a one update per second basis in the worst case, and the network overhead caused by this signaling is measured to be around 8 kbps, as shown in Fig. 8. The signaling overhead is zero before the session starts, and it increases to 8 kbps on average per session after the session is initiated. Note that this overhead of 8 kbps is very small compared to the average encoding bitrate of a decent quality video.

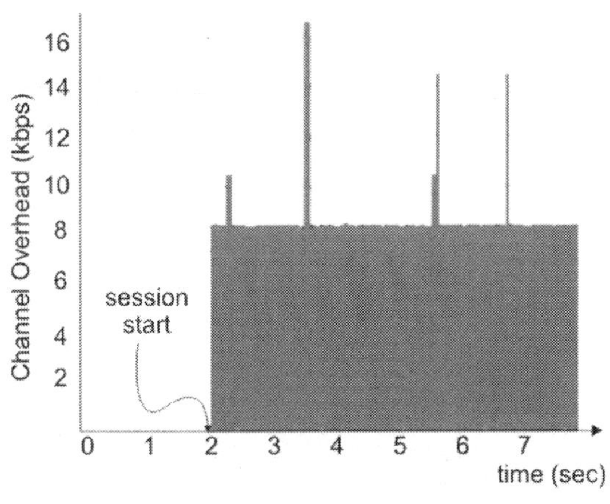

Fig. 8. Resource availability signaling channel overhead in the worst case scenario (signaling period: 1 sec.).

For an analysis of how many IMS sessions can be supported with the introduced signaling framework, it is time to look at some literature. In (Vingarzan et al., 2005), the design and implementation of an Open IMS core has been done and the load on the IMS core network and the proxies due to SIP message flow is investigated. In an IMS network with 100,000 subscribers, 1/3 of the subscribers are assumed to be online and registered simultaneously at a typical instant and 1/16 of these subscribers are assumed to be engaged in a multimedia session with an average duration of 180 seconds. In this case, the system would have to support 11,57 calls per second and the Open IMS core would have to process around 81 SIP messages per second (7 SIP messages for each multimedia call setup). In their experimental results, it was shown that a simple Intel Pentium 4 processor running at 3GHz (HyperThreaded) is enough to do the tasks of all IMS core components at once (i.e. I-CSCF, S-CSCF, P-CSCF and HSS) and still handle 120 SIP messages per second (around 17 calls per second). Considering the above data, in a worst case scenario of the proposed architecture, i.e. when each and every one of the active users has to adapt their multimedia within a given second, around 2000 SIP messaging events would need to be handled by the IMS core. This is quite realizable in a real-life deployment of the IMS core network since i) all components (CSCF's and HSS's) of the system normally reside on different hardware nodes in a deployed IMS core, ii) using multiple instances of the same component (e.g. multiple S-CSCF's) is very common for load-balancing, and iii) the state-of-the-art processors of today (e.g. multi-core processors) are much more powerful than a 3GHz Intel Pentium 4 processor. Clearly, in a more realistic case, the resource availability signaling overhead decreases even further when the resource signaling is done based on critical thresholds as described in the previous section.

The RAS is an additional server unit that can be implemented as an AS and it is independent of the IMS CSCF. Therefore, the existence of RAS does not put any computational overhead on the CSCF's.

10. Experimental results

In our experiments, we have separately demonstrated signaling from the multimedia transport. The reason for this is that running multimedia on the PCs rather than on the PDAs offered more freedom for experimenting with the adaptation of the perceived QoS.

10.1 Signaling scheme

For demonstrating our signaling scheme we have implemented the RAS server in a PC, whereas the RM software components were installed in the 2 PDAs running the WinCE operating system. Between the two PDA's we have established a multimedia communication session (see Fig. 5).

To start the session, the PDA applications use the SIP INVITE message. The multimedia flow is started after the ACK is received from the caller. The multimedia communication session ends up with a SIP BYE message which terminates the media session. Resource availability data from each PDA is transported to the RAS module using our SIP NOTIFY messages with the new header fields introduced in Table 1.

An example snapshot of the RAS interface is shown in Fig. 9. Here the real-time resource availability data of both end-devices is shown on a display, quantifying a remaining battery power (BT in %), storage space (ST in MBytes) and the available dynamic memory size (MM in MBytes).

Fig. 10 shows a snapshot of the User Interface (UI) of the client test application in the PDA. The top left menu is used to make a call or to exit the application. The first line shows the local IP address and the port number. The local and the remote resource availability data are displayed in the second and the last line, respectively.

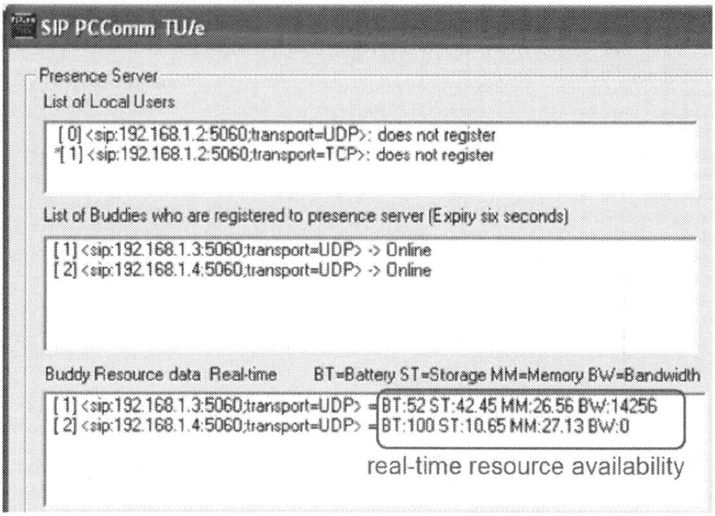

Fig. 9. A snapshot of the RAS log interface.

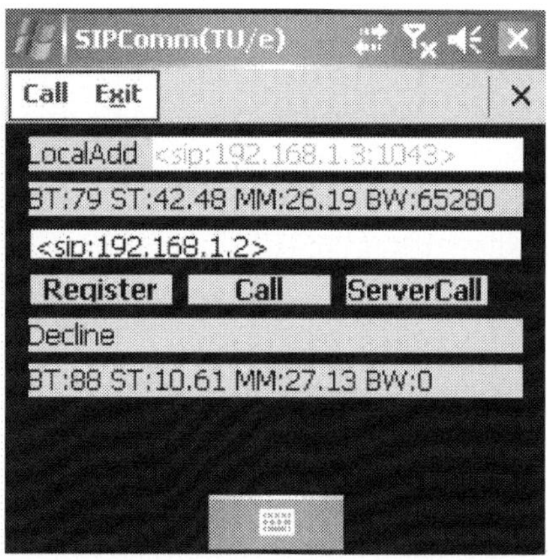

Fig. 10. A snapshot of a user interface of the PDA.

10.2 Multimedia adaptation

To demonstrate the effect of the multimedia content quality adaptation during a single session in order to increase the perceived QoS, we have installed the source of the multimedia stream in a PC and the sink in a laptop, both running the Windows XP operating system (see Fig. 11). To emulate the effects of bandwidth variation during a single multimedia session we have introduced a Linux Router on which Linux Advanced Routing and Traffic Control is implemented. Finally, we have compared the perceived QoS of the received multimedia with and without content quality adaptation during a single session. The multimedia session between the PCs is carried over Real-time Transport Protocol (RTP).

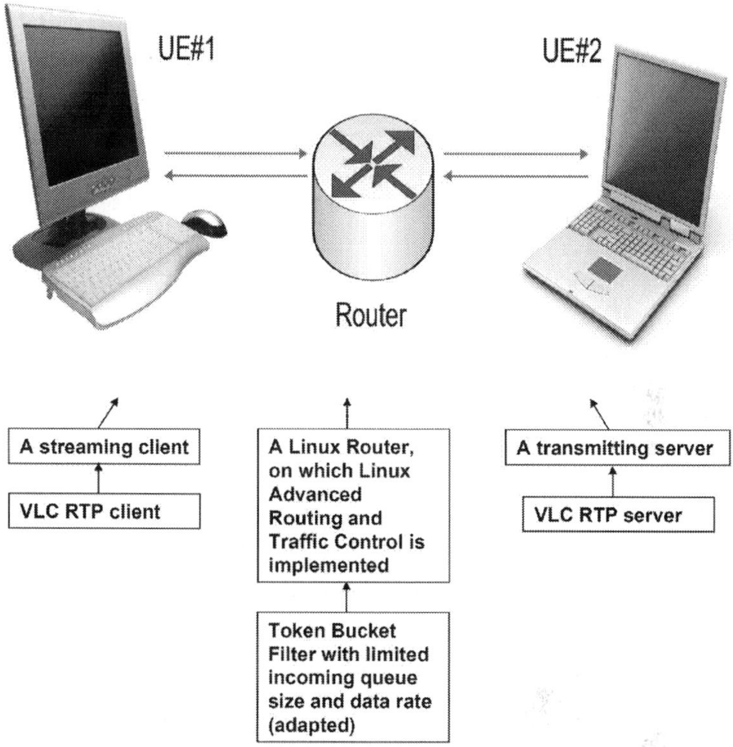

Fig. 11. Traffic controlled video streaming system setup.

Based on the signaling information, quality of the multimedia stream content has to be adapted to maximize the perceived QoS. However, such adaptation cannot be done arbitrarily, since multimedia codecs have their own limitations in changing the encoding bit rate on-the-fly even in the case of scalable codecs or the bit stream switching. Therefore, in multimedia content quality adaptation, adaptation speed should not be higher than that of the multimedia codec. In (DeVito et al., 2006), it is argued that video adaptation algorithms in the literature need up to 3 groups of pictures (GOP) in order to converge to a target bit rate every time the video is adapted. Here a GOP is defined as a frame sequence of a given structure in a video stream, whose first frame is an intra-coded (I) frame. Furthermore, it is also denoted in (DeVito et al., 2006) that the size of a GOP has to be kept large in an encoded video bit stream in order to attain reasonable compression efficiency and 1 GOP per second is taken as a rule of thumb, which would allow 1 adaptation in every 3 seconds for the other rate controllers in the literature and 1 adaptation per second for the advanced rate controller of (DeVito et al., 2006). Therefore, we assume that the maximum video adaptation frequency is 1 adaptation per second for typical videos. Updating resource availability at the speed higher than the adaptation speed would result in *no* improvement of the perceived QoS. Moreover, resource consumption in the network and end-devices will be higher.

We controlled the instantaneous maximum throughput from *UE*2 (a laptop computer) to *UE*1 (a desktop computer) by means of a Linux router in the middle as shown in Fig. 11, on which a Linux Advanced Routing and Traffic Control (LARTC, 2009) script is run to employ a Token Bucket Filter (Perez & Valenzula, 2005) as the traffic shaper (bandwidth limiter).

For our experiments, we encode the video at different target bitrates at different time intervals according to the channel throughput determined by the router. Let the maximum data throughput through the router be *R* kbps in a given time interval. We encode the corresponding video segment at a lower target bitrate than *R* considering a typical 25% – 30% channel overhead due to Ethernet/IP/UDP/RTP headers involved.

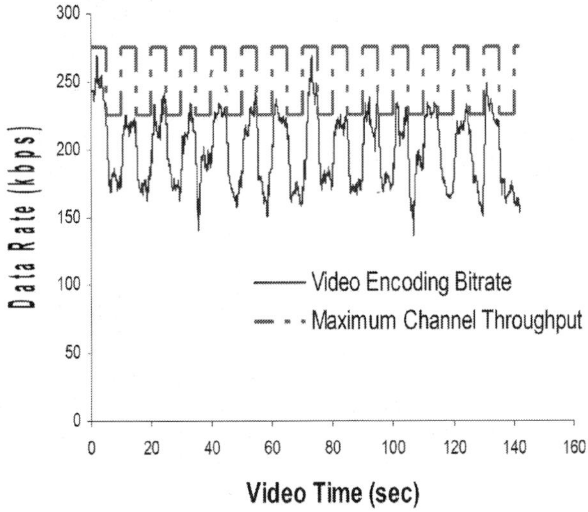

Fig. 12. Maximum channel throughput vs proposed adaptive video encoding bitrate graph (an example case)

Having a limited incoming queue size, the router drops any UDP packet that overflows its incoming queue. The multimedia sender is not aware of the bandwidth variation causing video packet losses. If there are no retransmissions at the sender, perceived video quality loss will be considerable unless the video encoding rate is kept to the reasonable values. In Fig. 12, the encoding bitrate for a video of 142 seconds length can be seen as it changes over time together with the network resource availability (i.e. maximum channel throughput). As the maximum channel throughput alternates between 275 kbps and 225 kbps in 5 second intervals, the video encoding rate is changed accordingly (alternated between 220 kbps and 180 kbps) in the proposed scheme, achieving an average encoding rate of 200 kbps.

The traffic control script applied for this purpose is given in Table 2 where the uplink throughput limit for the outgoing eth0 interface of the LINUX router is alternated between 225 kbps and and 275 kbps as explained above. The parameter limits and burst denote the maximum number of bytes that can be queued waiting for tokens (the queue size) and the bucket size (maximum possible number of tokens instantaneously available).

```
tc qdisc add dev eth0 root tbf rate 275kbit limit 150kb burst 10kb
sleep 5
tc qdisc change dev eth0 root tbf rate 225kbit limit 150kb burst 10kb
sleep 5
tc qdisc change dev eth0 root tbf rate 275kbit limit 150kb burst 10kb
...
tc qdisc change dev eth0 root tbf rate 225kbit limit 150kb burst 10kb
sleep 5
tc qdisc del dev eth0 root tbf rate 225kbit limit 150kb burst 10kb
```

Table 3. Linux Advanced Routing and Traffic Control script applied for the adaptive streaming experiment

The comparison of an example frame from the original video, the proposed solution and the nonadaptive solution can be seen in Fig. 13-15. When the perceived QoS of the standard nonadaptive video (average 200 kbps) solution with the proposed adaptive video (average 200 kbps) solution, the perceived QoS is enhanced in the proposed scheme as shown in Fig. 13-15 and the continuity of the video playback at the client side is satisfied only in the adaptive encoding case.

11. Summary

Thanks to a rapid increase in the number of both fixed and mobile Internet users, networked multimedia services have become an important part of our daily lives over the last decade. The availability of broadband connectivity in both homes and offices has allowed users to access multimedia content without bandwidth concerns and with a high degree of perceived quality. Furthermore, the wide availability of powerful and relatively inexpensive end user equipment through which high quality multimedia services can be enjoyed (such as personal computers) has considerably diminished concerns relating to device capability and resource availability.

Fig. 13. Original uncompressed video

Fig. 14. Constant bitrate coding and transmission (avg: 200 kbps)

Fig. 15. Proposed adaptive coding and transmission (avg: 200 kbps)

The recent introduction of "fast" telecom data services (e.g 3G) made it possible to introduce the experience of streaming multimedia content into the telecom community. This is however not straightforward from a technical perspective and a number of challenges need to be addressed. In contradistinction to the fixed broadband situation, bandwidth in mobile telecoms networks is expensive. This makes it difficult in such networks to utilize overprovisioning methods in support of multimedia streaming services. In addition, resources in mobile user equipment (battery, CPU etc) are often quite limited. It is therefore difficult to guarantee adequate resource availability throughout a single multimedia session. Despite this, telecom users are now able to stream multimedia content to their equipment depending on the real-time availability of their network and end device resources. The introduction of IMS networks has made it possible for users residing in unmanaged access networks (such as WiFi, xDSL) to access these services. However, it is not possible for the operator to apply network-level QoS mechanisms (such as admission control) on such unmanaged access networks. Perceived QoS guarantees become infeasible in this case. This chapter presents a framework for monitoring and signaling resource availability and for QoS adaption in support of devices, used over heterogeneous, IMS-based networks, which have variable resource availability and which lack QoS support. This enables the user experience of accessing real-time multimedia services on such devices and across such networks to be enhanced. An extended IMS architecture with additional system components is proposed in the context of the framework presented. Network and end device resource availability during a single session is monitored and communicated in real time and the encoding bitrate is adapted accordingly.

The system components proposed in this context are the Resource Manager, the Resource Availability Server and the Service Quality Manager. The proposed enhanced systems architecture is IMS compliant. The real time resource availability data is conveyed by means of the SIP protocol. Experimental results have shown that the proposed method can substantially improve the perceived quality of real-time streaming over IMS networks. The same approach can be applied to other real-time services having similar requirements, e.g. online gaming.

12. References

3GPP. (2006) Digital Cellular Telecommunications System (Phase 2+), Universal Mobile Telecommunications System (UMTS), IP Multimedia Subsystem (IMS), *Stage 2, V7.6.0, TS 23.228, 3GPP,* December 2006.

Andreasen, F. (2002). Session Description Protocol (SDP) Simple Capability Declaration, RFC 3407, October 2002.

Aurrecoechea, C. ; Cambell, A. & Hauw, L. (1996). A survey of QoS architectures, *Proceedings of the 4th IFIP International Conference on Quality of Service,* Paris, France, March 1996.

Camarillo, G. ; Marshall, W. & Rosenberg, J. (2002). "Integration of Resource Management and Session Initiation Protocol (SIP)", *RFC 3312,* October 2002.

Casner, S. (2003). Session Description Protocol (SDP) Bandwidth Modifiers for RTP Control Protocol (RTCP) Bandwidth, *RFC 3556,* July 2003.

De Vito, F. ; Ozcelebi, T. ; Sunay, O. ; Tekalp, M. ; Civanlar, R. & De Martin, J. C. (2006). Per-GOP Bitrate Adaptation for H.264 Compressed Video Sequences, *in L. Atzori et al. (Eds.): LNCS 3893,* pp. 198-206, Springer-Verlag Berlin Heidelberg 2006.

ISO/IEC. (2000). ISO/IEC 13818: 'Generic coding of moving pictures and associated audio (MPEG-2)', 2000.

ITU. (2009). http://www.itu.int/ITU-T/ngn/index.phtml, June 2009.

LARTC. (2009). http://lartc.org/, June 2009.

Ma, S. ; Gao, W. ; Wu, F. & Lu, Y. (2003). Rate control for JVT video coding scheme with HRD considerations, *Proceedings of the IEEE International Conference on Image Processing (ICIP),* vol. 3, pp. III_793-III_796, September 2003.

Nomura, Y. ; Walsh, R. ; Luoma, J-P. ; Asaeda, H. & Schulzrinne, H. (2006). A Framework for the Usage of Internet Media Guides (IMGs), *RFC 4435,* April 2006.

Perez, D. & Valenzuela, J.L. (2005). Performance of a token bucket traffic shaper on a real IEEE 802.11 test-bed, *Proceedings of the 16th IEEE International Symposium on Personal, Indoor and Mobile Radio Communications*, vol.3, pp.1931-1935, 11-14 September 2005.

Rosenberg, J. ; Camarillo, G. ; Johnston, A. ; Peterson, J. ; Sparks, R. ; Handley, M. & Schooler, E. (2002). "SIP: Session Initiation Protocol," *RFC 3261*, June 2002.

Vingarzan, D. ; Weik, P. & Magedanz, T. (2005). Design and Implementation of an Open IMS Core, *in T. Magedanz et al. (Eds.) LNCS 3744*, pp. 284-293, Springer-Verlag Berlin Heidelberg 2005.

Westerlund, M. (2004). A Transport Independent Bandwidth Modifier for the Session Description Protocol (SDP), *RFC 3890*, September 2004.

Wiegand, T.; Sullivan, G. & Luthra, A. (2003). Draft ITU-T recommendation and final draft international standard of joint video specification, *ITU-T Rec.H.264 | ISO/IEC 14496-10 AVC*, May 27, 2003.

Zhao, L. & Kuo, C.-C. J. (2003). Buffer-constrained R-D optimized rate control for video coding, *Proceedings of the IEEE International Conference on Acoustic, Speech and Signal Processing*, Hong Kong, pp. III_89 -III_92, April 6-10, 2003.

12

Secure and Mobile Multimedia Convergence

Alex Talevski and Vidyasagar Potdar
Curtin University of Technology
Australia

1. Introduction

In the Information Technology and Telecommunication (IT&T) world, convergence refers to the move towards the use of a single united interaction medium and media as opposed to the many that we use today. IT&T Convergence aims to enable telecommunications services that are concurrently coupled with enterprise and internet data. The ability to concurrently visualize a concept via sound, images, video, graphs and diagrams while communicating greatly enhances interaction. Communication is more pleasing, meaningful, effective and efficient. This allows for actions to be taken with greater understanding, precision and speed as a response to just-in-time requirements from distributed locations. Therefore, data and telecommunications convergence promises a wide range of possible solutions that will increase productivity and flexibility, and provide new opportunities for modern enterprises.
Converged voice and data services have rapidly emerged as a popular alternative to existing telecommunications networks and computer services. Many sources (Phil & Cary, 2009; Stallings, 2004; Deloitte, 2009; Grant, 2005) indicate that converged voice and data networks of various forms are rapidly growing across industry in the last 5 years. However, converged telecommunications and data services have been largely isolated to static environments where fixed Personal Computers (PC) and network connections are used in conjunction with various software tools that simulate pseudo converged sessions. Generally, data presented on the internet and in enterprise applications is not available on telecommunications networks and computer devices and vice-versa. Computer Telephony Integration (CTI), Voice Over Internet Protocol (VoIP) and Interactive Voice Response (IVR) systems form cornerstone technologies behind IT&T convergence.
This chapter proposes a secure and mobile multimedia convergence solution.

1.1 Computer Telephony Integration (CTI)

Telephone and computer systems are two technologies that impact many aspects of our daily lives. These technologies drive the world's economy and are central to the operation of virtually every enterprise. Computer Telephony Integration (CTI) is defined as the integration between computers and telephony systems (Strathmeyer, 1996). CTI technologies bridge the features of computers such as data handling, media processing and graphical user interface with telephone features such as call handling and routing. Currently, CTI is predominantly used to drive software-based Private Automatic Branch eXchange (PABX) systems. However, CTI is heading toward the convergence of both data and voice services over data networks.

1.2 Voice over Internet Protocol (VoIP)

Voice over Internet Protocol (VoIP) (also termed IP Telephony) refers to the transport of voice traffic over data networks. Using VoIP, carrier grade voice communication is digitized and routed in discrete IP packets through a data connection. VoIP is particularly useful when there is limited or financially prohibitive access to alternative telephony networks. Telephone calls can be transmitted with little or no loss in functionality, reliability, or voice quality. VoIP has rapidly emerged as a popular alternative to existing telephony networks (Darlington, 2007; Deloitte, 2009). However, to date, VoIP has been a solution that is mostly used as an alternative medium to carry-out cost-effective long-distance telephone calls.

1.3 Interactive Voice Response Telecom (IVR)

IVR systems provide computer controlled telephone answering and routing functions, as well as facilities for the collection and provision of information. Interactive voice and keypad driven menus allow callers to request information and respond to prompts. Based on developer defined configuration, IVR devices route calls to the appropriate place or system. These systems may use a mixture of human and computer interaction which is provided live, pre recorded by an attendee or digitally synthesized sound to convey information to the caller.

Unfortunately, industry has failed to make the most of CTI, VoIP and IVR technologies. Current use of these technologies has been limited to purely telephony applications like telephone conversations and conferencing. Existing systems rarely provide a flexible and integrated approach where more than telecommunication services are provided. Hence, this chapter proposes a flexible approach that integrates the features of CTI, VoIP, and IVR technologies.

2. Media convergence

Telecommunications and data convergence is required as a consequence of the increased flexibility that businesses demand (Hui & Matthews, 2004). Media convergence aims to enable distributed virtual collaboration environments that would provide all industries and consumers with a new and powerful means for collaboration. From an enterprise perspective, converged telecommunications and data services for its employees, partners and end customers is essential.

Converged voice and data services have rapidly emerged as a popular alternative to existing telephony networks. This chapter proposes a foundation for converged voice, video and data solutions. A media convergence solution must have the following key properties;

- **Telecommunications -** Private Automatic Branch eXchanges (PABX) that facilitate call management and routing.
- **Computing -** Graphical User Interfaces (GUI) help visualize interaction through converged telecommunications and computing features such as user interfaces, images, sounds, animations, videos, graphs and tables. Access to enterprise data, applications, services and networks further enhances communication.
- **Convenience -** Traditionally, enterprise applications allow users to access corporate data in a static location using a personal computer. However, accessibility of the proposed feature-rich converged services via a variety of devices in the context of a single converged session offers enterprises great power and flexibility. Such systems must be as convenient as a mobile telephone is for everyday communication.

- **Mobility -** People are no longer desk-bound. Enterprises have to consider the growing population of mobile users that would benefit from the next generation of IT&T services. As more sophisticated wireless devices emerge, the demand for mobile two-way communication will rise dramatically. Flexible, rich access to telecommunications services is crucial in order to achieve optimum performance. New technologies offer innovative features that result in better ways of doing business. Therefore, it is necessary to consider the restrictions imposed by this platform.
- **Functionality -** Current mobile computing devices have powerful hardware, utilize large graphical interfaces and offer network connectivity. With these features, the demand for media and function rich services and multi-way communication on the move will rise dramatically. A novel solution that provides convergence functions on the move is required.
- **Interface -** Desired content must be delivered directly to devices concurrently and interchangeably in a number of formats. Interaction may be performed through various devices and their interfaces (Dual-Tone Multi-Frequency (DTMF), keyboard / mouse, touchscreen, pen etc) and/or through voice driven commands interchangeably. Speech recognition and biometrics (Juang, 1999) aid user interaction.
- **Flexibility -** Due to the diverse nature of this environment, a flexible and adaptive approach is required. However, a problem faced in developing a system such as the one discussed is the complexity of service integration that occurs on the different layers of telecommunications services, telephony networks, computer systems and data networks. Flexible solutions are needed due to the requirement to deploy such solutions in quite diverse roles and environments and unclear, lacking and/or evolving existing enterprise systems. In order to develop a flexible solution that exhibits the required solution properties, a re-configurable service oriented architecture must be employed.

3. Development approach

In order to satisfy the key properties outlined earlier, we propose the following features;

Telecommunications

- Full Public Branch eXchange (PBX) services
- Telephone calling functions
- Teleconferencing features
- Call forwarding
- Message bank
- Simple Message Service (SMS)
- Call history
- Contacts repository

Computing

- Graphical User Interface (GUI)
- Internet
- eMail
- Voice over Internet Protocol (VoIP)
- Enterprise applications
- Instant Messaging (IM) including presence services

- Interactive Voice Response Telecom (IVR)
- Global Positioning System (GPS) including location services

Convenience

- The proposed system may be employed to access a variety of telecommunications and computer services via a telephone or computing device.
- Interaction is available via various access devices (TV, PC, PDA, telephone, mobile phone, web and others) both wired and wireless.
- Voice / data transportation mediums (IP, Wi-Fi, Bluetooth, GPS, GPRS, UMTS etc) both wired and wireless connection that is carrier, device and network independent.
- Voice over Internet Protocol (VoIP) including a variety of transportation protocols and encodings (H323, SIP, IAX etc).
- Public Switched Telephone Network (PSTN) and the Plain Old Telephone Service (POTS) services.
- No dependence on specialized hardware devices.

Mobility

- Available and accessible on common telephones, mobile phones and PDAs.
- Conforms to the screen size, processing power, memory, storage and battery life of mobile devices.

Functionality

- Data handling, media processing and graphical user interfaces coupled with telephone features such as call management and routing.
- Full telecommunications and teleconferencing features coupled with whiteboarding, file sharing, instant messaging, meeting and presentation management.
- Customised switchboard intelligent call forwarding and voice mail features are used to manage calls as required.
- Access to enterprise and internet data
- Profiles, contact information, favourites, history
- Voice mail

Interface

- Concurrent streaming media (voice, video, web and data) where interaction can be performed using web, voice, SMS, video, data and instant messaging interfaces.
- Automatic Speech Recognition (ASR)
- Dual Tone Multi Frequency (DTMF)
- Biometrics
- Transparent voice / data switchover

Flexibility

- Proven open technologies with a focus on wide compatibility.
- Re-configurable component-based framework which constitutes the skeletal support that is used as the basis for constructing the solution.
- Simplified software construction, customisation, integration and evolution.
- Complimenting components that can operate as a composite or individually.
- Flexible access to telecommunications services and enterprise and internet data.
- Allows prompt awareness and response to enterprise triggers

We aim to promote converged multimedia collaboration in an easy and convenient manner. Therefore, this proposal focuses on an open extensible architecture that uses a mobile thin client approach to allow converged service access via a range of devices and network connections with no specialized hardware or software.

4. Media Convergence Centre (MC^2)

Our proposed Media Convergence Centre (MC^2) (Figure 1) allows users to participate in a converged multimedia collaboration network using a variety of interaction devices in an easy and convenient manner. A thin client approach is adopted to allow access via a range of devices and connections with no specialized software or hardware. Calls, conferences and data services are provided over wired and wireless telephony and data networks. Interaction can be performed using voice, video, and data streams. The MC^2 (Figure 1) is composed of the following key components MC^2 Communicator, Convergence Centre, Switchboard, Conference, Call, Interact and Services.

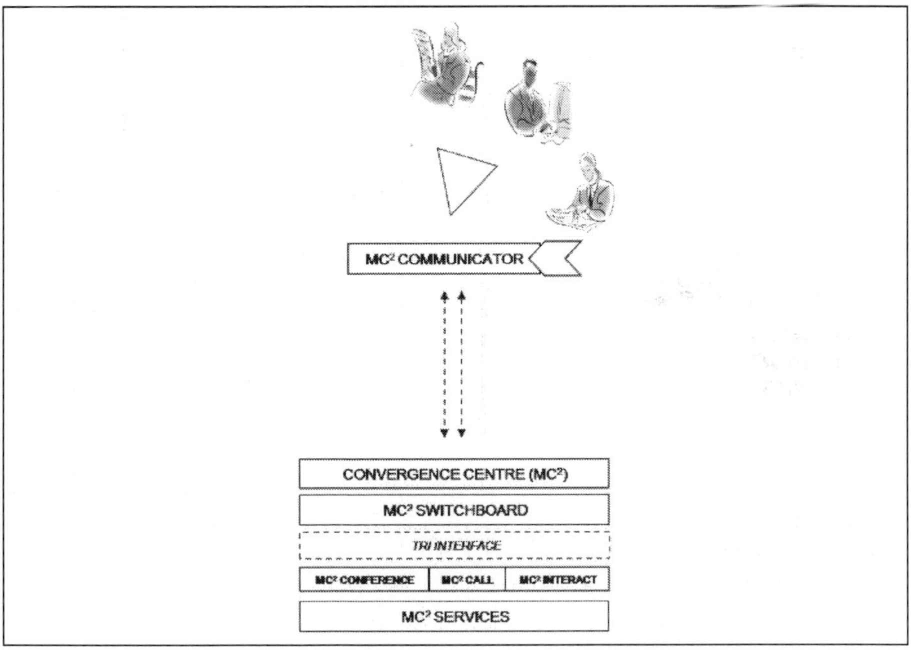

Fig. 1. Media Convergence Centre (MC^2)

4.1 MC^2 Switchboard

A MC^2 Communicator (Figure 2) focuses on a thin client that is available using a browser and web connection and/or a telephone. As most enterprises have both telecommunications and internet facilities, it is intended to provide collaboration functions just like a telephone provides telecommunications services. The solution aims to facilitate mobile telephony, conferencing, video interaction, instant messaging, SMS and all other MC^2 services outlined below. Furthermore, it is imperative that this client allows users to utilise their call forwarding, contacts, history etc. The MC^2 Communicator provides access to the MC^2 Switch board and MC^2 Conference, MC^2 Call, MC^2 Interact and MC^2 Services via an concurrent and interchangeable Tri-Interface. The solution utilises a number of existing technologies such as JWChat, Ajax, Punjab, Jabber Agi and Asterisk arranged in the following way;

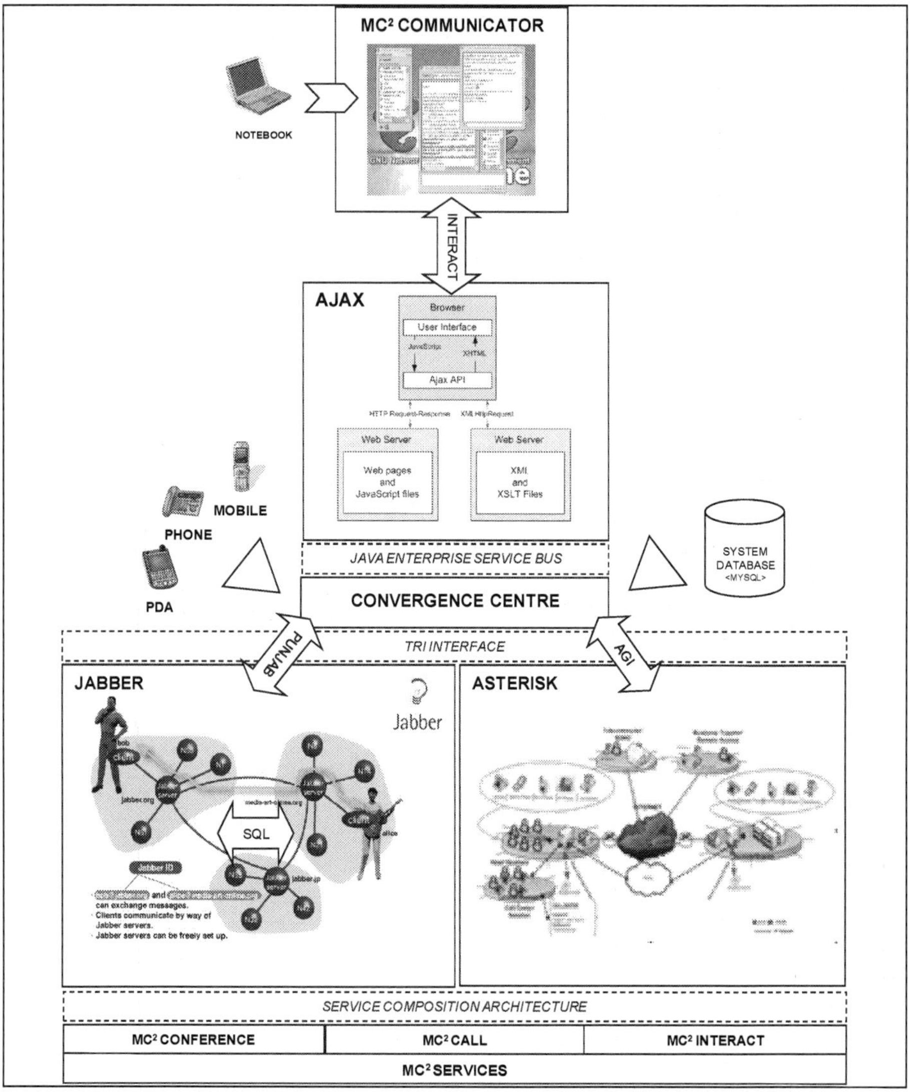

Fig. 2. Media Convergence Centre (MC^2)

4.2 MC² Switchboard

The MC² Switchboard (Figure 2) is a web-based tool for managing phone calls. It contains traditional switchboard properties.

4.3 MC² Conference

The MC² Conference (Figure 2) utilizes a thin-client approach. It provides an integrated web conferencing suite. PSTN, GSM and VoIP are integrated in a single session. The solution gives the ability to view and control the status of all participants in a conference. It is possible to interact using voice, video and data. In particular, presentation sharing and flow control as well as file sharing (with version control) are available to enhance the conference experience.

4.4 MC² Call

Full telephony services as per Public Switched Telephone Network (PSTN) and Plain Old Telephone Service (POTS). MC² Call (Figure 2) is available on any browser or telephony device.

4.5 MC² Interact

The MC² Interact (Figure 2) services provide a reconfigurable Interactive Voice Response Telecom (IVR) that enables selected computer controlled telephone answering functions, collection of information and interactive menus for callers to use to input data using the telephone keypad or voice prompts. Based on user defined steps, commands and responses to prompts, calls are routed to a configured place or data. Users can create, change and remove multiple MC² Interact maps. Figure 4 illustrates a high level architecture of the MC² Voice Access to Data (VAD) (Talevski & Chang 2009) solution which provides access to enterprise and internet data The plugin services used here interact with the user using voice prompts and/or a web interface and access other components, services and repositories as required. Sample vEmail, vFinance, vStocks, vWeather, and vNews plugin services are illustrated.

4.6 MC² Services

To demonstrate the feasibility of such a solution (Figure 2) we developed the following services as IVR plugins. It is possibly to develop virtually any enterprise or internet service as a MC² Interact services. A web interface is provided to personalize and optimize the solution.

- **vEMail Service -** Emails can be accessed at any time and followed up instantly. The vEMail voice plugin hosts a Post Office Protocol (POP) email service where high priority emails can be forwarded for voice access. The vEMail voice plugin reads out each email using a clear voice. The user may interact with the vEMail voice plugin by telephone key tones. MC² Interact allows the automatic browsing of emails without user intervention. It is possible to reply to emails with predefined email templates and forward messages to predefined contacts immediately. Users may manage their email messages by saving, moving and deleting selected items. It is also possible to customize the way that the system performs and to manage emails contacts and template messages via an easy to use web interface.
- **vStocks Service -** Live Australian Stock Exchange (ASX) values can be heard at the user's convenience. The vStocks service reads out detailed information on each user's

individually predefined stocks. Stock list navigation is performed using telephone key tones. MC[2] Interact allows the browsing of stock data without user intervention. The vStocks service is able to announce each stock's trade date, time, change, previous close, day high, day low, and volume. Users may customize the stock properties they wish to hear to suit their individual preferences.

- **vWeather Service -** Live Bureau of Meteorology (BOM) weather forecasts can be accessed at any time. The vWeather service reads out detailed weather information for a user's predefined city or town. Weather forecasts are read out for up to one week in advance. Forecast information, days high and days low are given for each day. Users may customize their city to suit their individual preferences and travel arrangements. MC[2] Interact allows the weekly weather forecast to be read out without user intervention.
- **vNews Service -** Live Rich Site Summary (RSS) News feeds can be heard at a preferred occasion based on a user's preference. The vNews service reads out each news item as requested by the users telephone key tone interaction or automatically.

An N-Tier distributed platform and component based computing architecture is proposed using the following technologies and tools (Figure 2);

- **Asterisk -** Asterisk (Digium, 2009) is an open source software PBX that can be programmed to create custom applications. Our system uses the java-based Application Gateway Interface (AGI) to trigger custom classes that handle incoming connections.
- **Java -** Java provides a platform independent environment that has wide support. Java (Sun, 2009) was used to interface the tools mentioned and implement the solutions in this system. Enterprise Java Beans are a suitable for the development of distributed and heterogeneous component systems. These technologies were proposed because the Asterisk AGI has wide Java support and many existing libraries and frameworks that interface the soft-switch functions of Asterisk.
- **AT&T TTS -** The AT&T Text-To-Speech (TTS) (AT&T, 2009) engine generates high quality synthesized voice from text. It is integrated through the Asterisk AGI interface. Using the AT&T TTS is it possible to adopt different dialogue files to simulate accents from different nationalities.
- **Speex -** This product (Speex, 2009) provides Automatic-Speech-Recognition (ASR) functions. Asterisk's extended scripting commands make use of Speex to take voice commands from a user.
- **Hibernate -** Hibernate (Hibernate, 2009) is a high performance object / relational mapping service for Java. It uses interfaces that have defined via mapping documents to convert between the Object Oriented (OO) to the Relational Database Management Systems (RDBMS).
- **MySQL -** In order to persist hibernate objects we us the MySQL RDBMS (MySQL, 2009).
- **JWChat -** A full featured, web-based Jabber client. Written using AJAX (JWChat, 2009).
- **AJAX -** Asynchronous JavaScript and XML, is a Web development technique for creating interactive web applications (Ajax, 2009).
- **PunJab -** A HTTP, jabber client interface that allows persistent client connections to a jabber server (Punjab, 2009).
- **Jabber -** A collection of open, XML-based protocol for instant messaging and presence Information. Used by over ten million people Worldwide (Jabber, 2009).

- **IAX** - The Inter-Asterisk Exchange protocol (IAX) (IAX, 2009) was created as an alternative signalling protocol to SIP and H.323. IAX has full signalling and media transfer capabilities that can be used with any type of streaming data (including video). Libiax is a library to take care of the low level network functions. This library was constructed by the makers of Asterisk, and is commonly used by open source IAX clients. The code modifications necessary to support encryption were mostly required within libiax.
- **Cryptlib** - Cryptlib is an powerful, general purpose open-source cryptography package designed to provide security services to applications. Its main purpose is to provide cryptography functions that can be integrated into applications (Cryptlib, 2009).

Clearly, the critical problem in achieving converged IT&T services is being able to combine the many differing technologies and applications that operate computer and telecommunications systems. Furthermore, it is of critical importance that convergence services provide access to enterprise systems.

5. Service composition

The ability of systems to adapt or be adapted to disparate enterprise requirements and environmental changes is referred to as their flexibility (Booch, 1994). A flexible system is needed due to the requirement for a system to be deployed in converged enterprise (diversity) and to be flexible to evolving requirements (uncertainty) (Booch, 1994). Versatile systems exhibit generic and function rich properties as a response to growing enterprises' demand for rapid and frequent development, maintenance, customization and evolution. Convergence needs to facilitate such enterprise growth through integrated telecommunications and computer systems.

Service-based software engineering is a way of raising the level of abstraction for software development so that software can be built by easily reusing previously designed, implemented and refined converged services. Composite architectures that incorporate enterprise services are formed using a Service-Oriented Architecture (SOA) as a standardized way of connecting loosely-coupled systems such as the many that already exist in the computing and telecommunications areas.

Re-configurable service oriented architectures promote simplified software evolution in complex environments. They can be used to provide the glue between enterprise business applications and multi-modal forms of converged business communication to access a variety of telecommunications and data services.

Using a reconfigurable plug and play component-based framework as a basis for the creation and modification of software, it is possible to construct, customize, integrate and evolve convergence solutions in a straightforward way.

5.1 Service architecture

The following framework promotes simplified software construction, customisation, integration and evolution of convergence solutions. The framework allows the solution to easily integrate existing enterprise and internet applications and newly implemented components as communication / interaction services. Services may be added and removed dynamically as per business requirements. This allows for prompt awareness and response to enterprise triggers.

At the highest level, MC^2 behaves as an IVR entrypoint. As illustrated below (Figure 3), voice plugin discovery, query, identification and invocation are used to situate, define, describe and utilize available telecommunications and computing services. Once a service plugin has been identified it is assigned access telephone number and appropriate voice/video/data interface. Upon activation, and during execution, each voice plugin governs user interaction and the provision of its converged services.

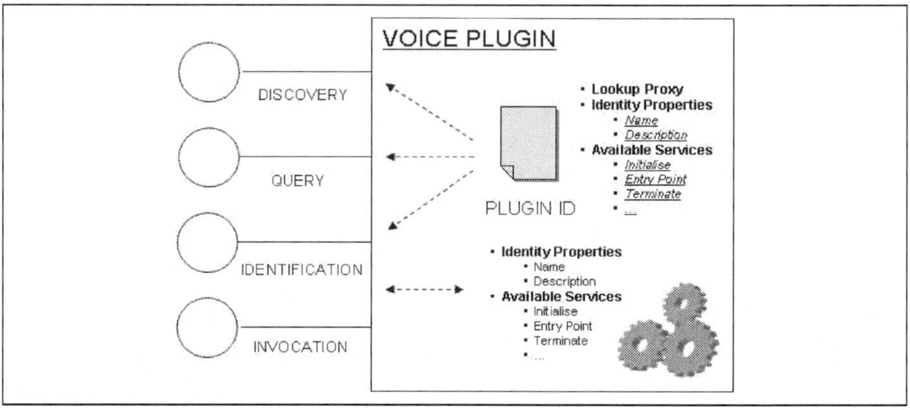

Fig. 3. Converged Service

The plugin architecture defines the following component interface;

- **Discovery** - Plugin discovery is used to find, identify, describe and use available voice plugins. In order to locate plugins, the MC2 Interact server broadcasts a request for a voice plugin lookup service. Each voice plugin responds to this request with a lookup proxy.
- **Query** - The MC2 Interact host is able to query the voice plugin lookup service for available services.
- **Identification** - The voice plugin lookup service is used to define voice plugin characteristics.
- **Invocation** - When a voice plugin is selected via the IVR the MC2 Interact host dynamically binds to the voice plugin and invokes its entrypoint. The voice plugin then takes over interaction control and performs its identified services.

Figure 4 illustrates a high level architecture of the Interact portion of the MC2 proposal. It provides access to enterprise and internet data using an Interactive Voice Response (IVR) system and concurrent web interface. The plugin services used here interact with the user using voice prompts and/or a web interface and access other components, services and repositories as required. Sample vEmail, vFinance, vStocks, vWeather, and vNews plugin services are illustrated.

6. Security

Corporate customers are generally more security conscious. They require that potential new technologies are proven not to be a security risk. Most current converged and VoIP-based offerings do not offer a practical security solution. However, an important aspect behind the corporate success of the telecommunications and data convergence is security. As these technologies become more heavily integrated into the workplace, so too do the

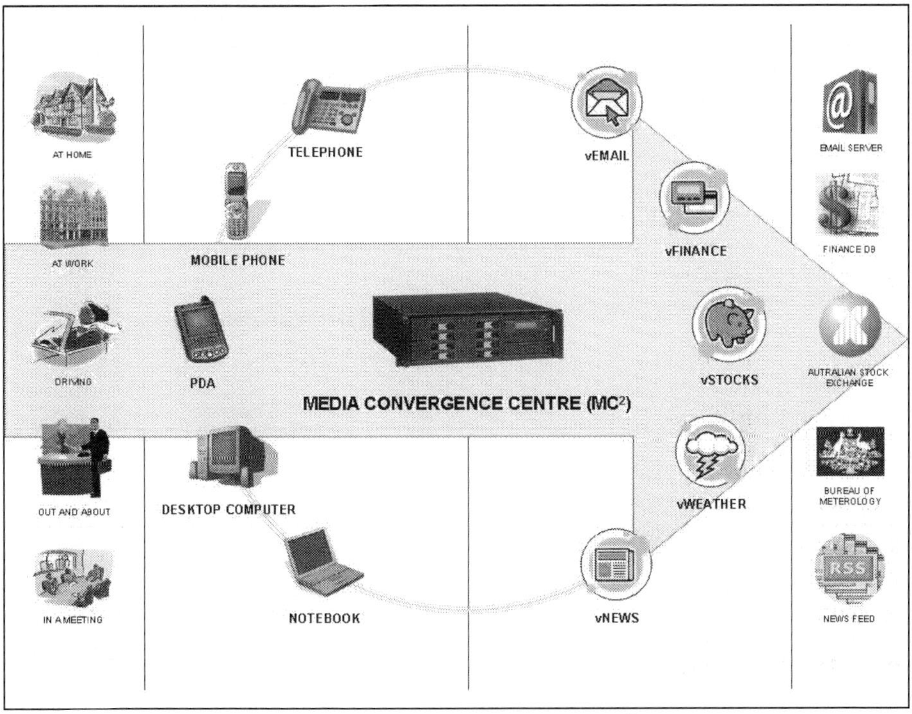

Fig. 4. MC2 Interact

opportunities for hackers. Converged information is generally routed unsecured through data packets on a public network. There is software that can capture, reconstruct and/or modify these sensitive interactions which opens numerous security concerns as follows (Bilby, 2009):

- Eavesdropping and recording phone calls
- Tracking calls
- Stealing confidential information
- Modifying phone calls
- Making free phone calls
- Pranks / Practical jokes
- Board room bugging
- Sending spam (voice or email)

There are currently very few practical security standards available to secure converged telecommunications and computing services on mobile devices.. Furthermore, many enterprises that have adopted converged technology have not been able to effectively secure these solutions as a result of multi-vendor incompatibilities (Gohring, 2009). To alleviate this, it is necessary to add some form of protection, such as encryption, at the transport or network layer. By incorporating security at each level of the network, it makes successful attacks much more difficult. Simply breaking one type of security will not expose the entire network; it would require multiple levels of protection to be compromised. However incorporating multilevel security would incur additional cost, which should be considered.

To allow multi-vendor solutions to interoperate it is essential that such solutions are integrated into a mobile convergence standard. There have been many attempts to provide secure services for the major convergence protocols (Abad, 2003; Arkko & Carrara, 2004; IAX, 2009). Unfortunately, these systems typically suffer from the following problems:

- Complicated to deploy and maintain
- Rely on proprietary and/or incompatible solutions
- Require an existing Public Key Infrastructure (PKI) and/or other resources
- Experience Significant routing problems when passing through NAT

6.1 Encryption algorithms

In order to provide secure transmission of data, it is necessary to offer confidentiality and authentication. In other words, data must be valid and should not be available nor disclosed to unauthorized parties.

In order to support different codecs, the encryption algorithm must be able to support variable length data payloads where the amount of data per frame is likely to be short but send at a high frequency (approximately 30-100 bytes 50 times per second).

As the data payload is relatively small, it would be advantageous to use an encryption method that will not increase the size of the data to be sent. Any small increases in size will add significant overhead to the transmission.

The Inter-Asterisk Exchange protocol (IAX) was created as an alternative signalling protocol to SIP and H.323. It provides full converged media transfer capabilities. The block diagrams below give a basic description of the structure of the IAX software layers and an added security layer (Figure 5). After the converged data has been encoded, it is intercepted and encrypted before being sent across the network. At the receiver's side, the data is decrypted, and passed back through the normal IAX processing stack.

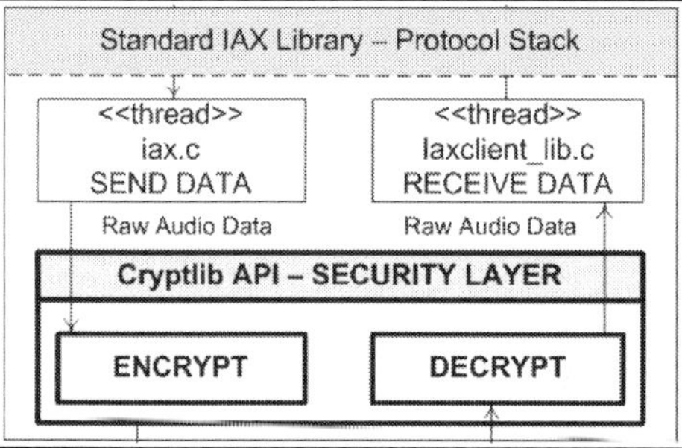

Fig. 5. Modified IAX Architecture Diagram

7. Conclusion

IT&T convergence refers to the move towards the use of a single united interaction medium and media as opposed to the many that we use today. Such convergence aims to enable telecommunications services that are concurrently coupled with enterprise and internet data. This new found visibility greatly enhances interaction through sound, images, video, graphs and diagrams. Communication is more pleasing, meaningful, effective and efficient. Therefore, enterprises can take actions as a response to market drivers much more quickly and with greater precision. Data and telecommunications convergence promises a wide range of possible solutions that will increase productivity and flexibility, and provide new opportunities for modern enterprises. This chapter proposed a secure and mobile multimedia convergence solution.

8. References

Abad, I., "Secure Mobile VoIP", in Microelectronics and Information Technology, Royal Institute of Technology: Stockholm, 2003, p. 137.

Ajax, "AJAX Home", On-line at: http://www.ajax.org/#home (2009).

Arkko, J., Carrara, E., RFC3830 - MIKEY: Multimedia Internet KEYing. Internet Engineering, 2004.

AT&T, "AT&T TTS", On-line at: http://www.research.att.com/viewProject.cfm?prjID=315 (2009)

Booch, G., Object-Oriented Analysis and Design with Applications (Second Ed.), Benjamin / Cummings, Redwood City, Calif, 1994.

Bilby, D., "Voice over IP: What You Don't Know Can Hurt You", On-line at: http://www.security-assessment.com/files/presentations/VOIP_What_You_Don%27t_Know_Can_Hurt_You.ppt (2009).

Cryptlib, "Cryptlib Home", On-line at: http://www.cryptlib.com/ (2009).

Darlington, R., "What is multimedia convergence and why is it so important", On-line at: http://www.rogerdarlington.co.uk/Multimediaconvergence.html (2007).

Deloitte, "Getting off the Ground: Why the move to VoIP is a decision for all CXOs", On-line at: http://www.deloitte.com/dtt/budget/0,1004,cid%253D67263,00.html (2009).

Deloitte, "Protecting the digital assets : 2006 TMT Security Survey", On-line at: http://www.deloitte.com/dtt/budget/0,1004,cid%253D67263,00.html (2009).

Digium, "Asterisk Home", On-line at: http://www.asterisk.org/ (2009).

Grant, M., "Voice Quality Monitoring for VoIP Networks", Calyptech Pty. Ltd., Melbourne, 2005.

Gohring, N., "Sysadmins express concerns on VoIP security", On-line at:: http://www.techworld.com/security/news/index.cfm?newsID=6030&pagtype=samechan (2009).

Hibernate, "Hibernate Home", On-line at: http://www.hibernate.org/ (2009).

Hui, M. C., Matthews, H.S., "Comparative analysis of traditional telephone and Voice-over-Internet Protocol (VoIP) systems", In Proceedings of the IEEE International Symposium on Electronics and the Environment, 2004.

IAX, "IAX Encryption", On-line at: http://voip-info.org/wiki/view/IAX+encryption (2009).

IAX, "IAX Specification", On-line at: http://www.rfc-editor.org/authors/rfc5456.txt (2009).

Jabber, "Jabber Home", On-line at: http://www.jabber.org/ (2009).

Juang, B.H., "Advances and challenges in speech, audio and acoustics processing for multimedia communications" In Proceeding of the International Symposium on Signal Processing and Its Applications, Brisbane, Australia, 1999.

JWChat, "JWChat Home", On-line at: http://blog.jwchat.org/jwchat/ (2009).

MySQL, "MySQL Home", On-line at: http://www.mysql.com/ (2009).

Phil, S., Cary, F., You Don't Know Jack About VoIP, Queue, 2004, 2(6), p. 30-38.

Punjab, "Punjab Home", On-line at: http://code.stanziq.com/punjab (2009).

Speex, "Speex Home", On-line at: http://www.speex.org/ (2009).

Stallings, W., Data and Computer Communications (Seventh Ed.), Pearson Educational International, 2004.

Strathmeyer, C. R., "An Introduction to Computer Telephony", IEEE Communications Magazine, 35(5), May 1996, pp. 106–11.

Sun, "Java Home", On-line at: http://java.sun.com/ (2009).

Talevski, A., Chang, E., 'Reconfigurable Software Architecture for Voice Access to Data Services', In Proceedings of the International Conference on Digital EcoSystems and Technologies, Cairns, Australia, 2007.

13

Resource Scheduling Scheme for Multimedia Service Provisioning in Ubiquitous Environment

Dong Cheul Lee[1], Bok Kyu Hwang[1] and Byungjoo Park[2]
[1]*KT,*
[2]*Hannam University*
Republic of Korea

1. Introduction

In telecommunication industry, field resources had many tasks to visit customers and have provided network provisioning services. In the meantime, the amount of tasks and the diversity of customer's needs were overwhelming and the available human resources were not sufficient. To solve this problem, many telecoms had transformed field environment into ubiquitous environment. Thus, the resources carried a portable hand held device so that they could get detail information of the tasks and could transmit the results of the task at anywhere after they finished the task. Also, they could enable or disable the operation of network interfaces remotely. Furthermore, telecoms had adopted work team based appointment reservation system to manage the human resource's schedules. By using this system, call center operators could take customer calls, arrange appointments, and assign the tasks to work teams for service provisioning. And each resource could retrieve the task which was assigned to its team.

However, this system has several disadvantages. First, the operators can not know precise time when the resource can visit the customer site. Second, the resources retrieve tasks which were assigned to their team by themselves so that the tasks might not be distributed evenly. Third, if an urgent task, which should be done quickly, has assigned to a team, work managers should find suitable resources quickly because there is no time to wait until the resources retrieve the task by them selves. However, work managers do not have enough information to decide which resources would be the best to finish the task quickly.

There have been many studies about resource scheduling. Since a resource should visit a customer site, modeling this problem can be treated as a vehicle routing problem (Laporte et al., 2000). To find a near optimal solution for this, CVRPTW(Capacitated-Vehicle Routing Program with Time Window) (Schumitt et al., 2004) and the fast local search and guided local search (Tsang & Voudouris, 1997) which simplifies a complicated real world problem to a similar simple well-known theoretical model were suggested. However, these static scheduling approaches were not efficient in dynamic environment. British Telecom had suggested several dynamic scheduling method, such as dynamic scheduling (Lesant et al., 2000) and dynamic scheduler for work manager (Lesant et al., 1998), but they were not suitable for the operators who should arrange visiting time and assign tasks in real time. We propose an individual resource scheduling system especially to address resource scheduling challenge in ubiquitous and dynamic environment for provisioning multimedia services at telecom.

2. Resource scheduling problem

Previously, telecoms had used a work team based scheduling system which was assigning tasks to work teams as described in Fig. 1. When a customer requests a service, an operator in a call center searches suitable work teams. Those work teams should have been in charge of the work regions which includes the customer site because work regions are managed by work teams. Also, the total number of allocated tasks of the teams should not exceed maximum allocation count. To prevent concentrated allocations to a team, maximum allocation counts are managed by team hourly. After the operator selected a suitable team among the teams which satisfying a work region constraint and a maximum allocation count constraint, the task is assigned to the team so that any available resources in the team can dispatch the task and offers the service to the customer. While they are processing their tasks, work managers are monitoring the progress of the tasks, and re-schedule the delayed task if necessary.

However, as we mentioned before, this scheduling approach has several disadvantages since the scheduling process is based on the work team. Therefore, we propose individual resource based scheduling process which assigns tasks to the resource directly as described in Fig 1. In this process, when a customer requests a service, the operator searches suitable resources to deliver the service. Since work regions are managed by resources in this process, the selected resource should have been in charge of the work region which includes the customer site. Work regions are small enough not to make the resources travel for a long time. Also, the resources that have available time slot can be chosen by the system to assign the task and the time slot is managed per 15 minutes.

3. System architecture

To tackle individual resource scheduling challenge, we designed the system architecture as shown in Fig. 2. The Schedule Visualizer works as an interface between operators and the scheduling system and visualizes the schedules of resources. It gets schedule data from the Schedule Manager after the Schedule Manager computes an optimal solution for selecting the resources using the Human Resource Manager, the Task Duration Estimator, and the Driving Time Estimator. The resources input their day off, holiday duty, night shift, and business trip information to the Human Resource Manager. The Task Duration Estimator estimates the duration of a task before the reousrce actually does the task. Also, the Driving Time Estimator estimates the resource's moving time from one customer site to another before they actually move.

3.1 Task Duration Estimator

When a customer requests a service to a call center operator, the operator should be able to estimate the duration of the task to reserve the resource's schedule. Arrival time of the resource can be easily known since a customer wants specific visit time. However, the finish time of the task is hard to estimate since the duration of a task can vary with the resource's experience, service type, and provided network facilities.

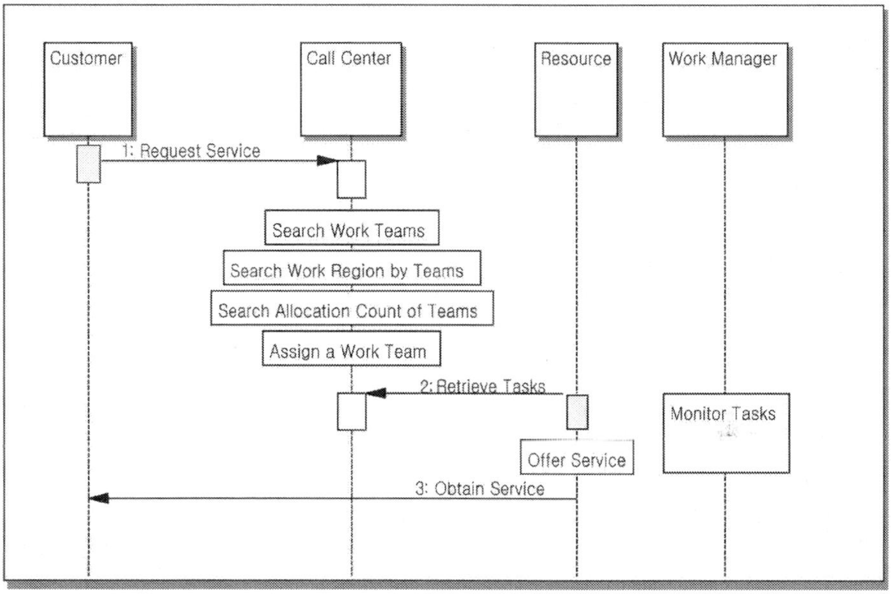

(a) The work flow of the work team based scheduling scheme

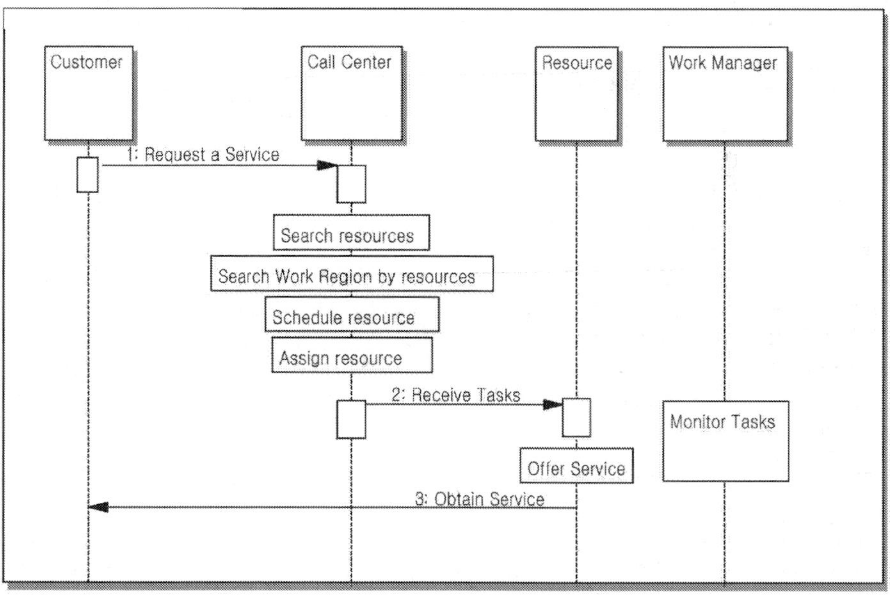

(b) The work flow of the individual resource based scheduling scheme

Fig. 1. The work flow comparisons between previous and suggested schemes

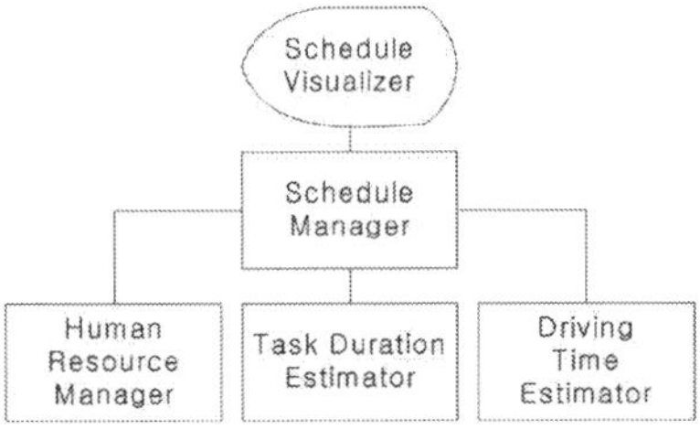

Fig. 2. System Architecture

The Task Duration Estimator can estimate the duration of a task by using statistical data. It calculates and stores the mean duration of previous tasks for each task type and resource. The task types can be classified by the service and the network facility. The multimedia services includes POTS, broadband, IP TV, and VoIP. And the network facilities are classified into FTTH, hybrid FTTH, xDSL, IP-xDSL, and Fast Ethernet. Furthermore, the duration can be varied by the day of the week and a time zone. The time zone is classified into forenoon, afternoon, and night. As a result, the mean duration $\mu(n)_{dur}$ is managed by resource ID, the service type, the facility type, the day of the week, and the time zone. And it is calculated as follows:

$$\mu(n)_{dur} = \frac{\sum_{i=1}^{n} \tau(i)_{ft} - \tau(i)_{at}}{n} \tag{1}$$

$\tau(i)_{ft}$ means the time when the resource had completed the ith task and it can be obtained when the resource had finished its task and sent the result to the system. $\tau(i)_{at}$ means the time when the resource had arrived at a customer site for the ith task and it can be obtained when the resource had arrived at a customer site and notify the system of its arrival time. Whereas n is the total number of tasks with same resource ID, service type, facility type, day of the week, and time zone in latest one month.

3.2 Driving Time Estimator

Even though call center operators can estimate the duration of the task by using the Task Duration Estimator, they should also consider departure time of the resource from a previous customer site. Therefore, they should also estimate the time to travel from a previous customer site to a next customer site. However, the driving time is hard to estimate since it can vary with moving distance, moving velocity. Also, there can be many uncertainties such as weather and traffic conditions.

The Driving Time Estimator estimates the driving time of the resource from one customer site to another by using statistical data. It calculates and stores mean velocity for each resource. The velocity of a resource for ith task υ_i can be calculated as follows:

$$\upsilon_i = \frac{\delta_i}{\tau(i)_{at} - \tau(i-1)_{ft}} \tag{2}$$

δ_i means the previous resource's driving distance from i-1th customer site to ith site. To find δ_i, we used a Geographic Information System (GIS) with traffic function enabled. Since we can get the addresses of customers, the Driving Time Estimator converts the addresses to coordinates and computes the driving distance between two points by using GIS. Like the Task Duration Estimator, the driving time can be varied by the day of the week and a time zone. As a result, the mean $\mu(n)_{vel}$ velocity is managed by resource ID, the day of the week, and the time zone. And it is calculated as a harmonic mean (Bian & Tao, 2008) like an equation (3).

$$\mu(n)_{vel} = \frac{1}{\frac{1}{n}\sum_{i=1}^{n}\frac{1}{v_i}} \tag{3}$$

n is the total number of tasks with same resource ID, day of the week, and a time zone in one month. If a resource started the first task on a day, $\tau(0)_{ft}$ means nine O'clock since they had started their work at that time. Also, δ_1 means the distance from their local office to a customer site. Therefore, when an operator wants to assign a task to a resource, the Driving Time Estimator calculates the distance from the current location of the resource to the location of the tasks by using a GIS. Also it can estimate the driving time by dividing the mean velocity $\mu(n)_{vel}$ into the distance.

3.3 Human Resource Manager

The Human Resource Manager manages a day off, a holiday duty, a night shift, and business trip information of the resources. It is used for searching the available resources at a specific date by the Schedule Manager. If they had a day off or a business trip on a certain day, they are excluded from a resource pool at that time. On the other hand, if they put in a holiday duty or the night shift, they are included in the pool at that time.

3.4 Schedule Manager

Call center operators should search a suitable resource when they assign a task. If they choose a resource without any consideration at their convenience, they can not manage resource's schedule efficiently. However, finding a suitable resource by themselves is hard due to there are many factors to consider.

The Schedule Manager searches a near optimal resource for a task. It uses *find_resource*() algorithm to find a solution. The input value of the algorithm consists of $\tau(i)_{at}$, service type, and work region. These values can be obtained while the operator talks over with a customer. It uses the Driving Time Estimator and the Task Duration Estimator to estimate the departure time and finish time for each resource. Also, the Human Resource Manager is used for excluding resources that don't work on weekday and including resources who work on holiday or at night.

3.5 Schedule Visualizer

Call center operators should be able to identify and monitor resource's schedule. The Schedule Visualizer displays resource's schedule and interacts with the operators. It represents the schedule as a Gantt Chart so that the operator can identify the status of the tasks. It also helps the work managers identify the task that is not likely to be completed on time so that they can rearrange the next task of the resource.

Algorithm *find_resource*($\tau(i)_{at}$, *servicetype, workregion*)
BEGIN
1. DEFINE *wlist* , *templist* as resource's list;
2. IF($\tau(i)_{at}$ ==*holiday*) THEN store *resources* who are responsible for a holiday duty into *wlist*;
   ELSE IF($\tau(i)_{at}$ ==*night*) THEN store *resources* who are responsible for a night shift into *wlist*;
   ELSE store *resources* who don't have a day off or are not on a business trip into *wlist*;
3. exclude *resources* who are not in charge of the *servicetype* from *wlist*;
4. exclude *resources* who are not responsible for the *workregion* from *wlist*;
5. *templist=wlist*;
6. DEFINE *stime* as the departure time for the task, *ftime* as the finish time of the task;
7. FOR(each *resource t* in *templist*)
   BEGIN
   stime= $\tau(i)_{at}$ -DrivingTimeEstimator();
   ftime= $\tau(i)_{at}$ +TaskDurationEstimator();
   IF time between *stime* and *ftime* is in other schedules of *t* THEN exclude *t* from *templist*;
   END
8. IF *templist* is NULL THEN RETURN *wlist*;
9. IF *templist* has *resources* having no task THEN exclude *resources* who have tasks from *templist*;
10. delete *resources* from *templist* except top 5 *resources* with shortest (*driving time+task duration*);
11. IF(gap of (*driving time+task duration*) of *resources* in *templist* is within 10 min) THEN delete *resources* from *templist* except *resource* with minimum tasks;
12. ELSE delete *resources* from *templist* except a *resource* with shortest (*driving time+task duration*);
13. RETURN *templist*;

Algorithm *find_resource*()

4. Implementation

The resource scheduling system consists of PC client, PDA client, application server, EAI server, and database server as shown in Fig. 3.

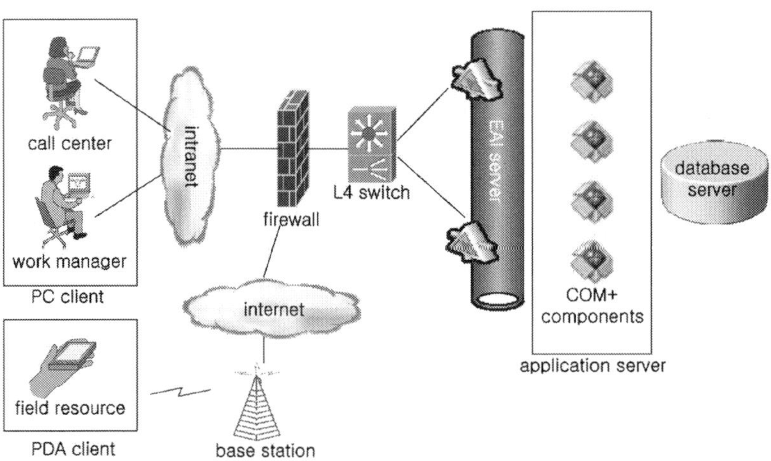

Fig. 3. Implementation

The PC client is used by call center operators and work managers at local offices. They can get a suitable resource when assigning a task to a resource. They can also monitor the current status of the tasks whether there are delayed tasks. It is implemented as C/S method on .NET framework.

Field resources use the PDA clients when they process their tasks. They notify the application server of their arrival time and finish time by using the client. If an operator has assigned a task to a resource, the application server sends a short message to the client so that they can recheck their schedule and retrieve detail information from the server by using the client. The PDA client communicates with the application server on WiBro or CDMA2000 1x or EVDO network. It uses Windows Mobile .NET platform and MS SQL CE 2.0 DBMS. And it is implemented with C# .NET.

The Driving Time Estimator and the Task Duration Estimator and the Schedule Manager and the Human Resource Manager are implemented in the application server as COM+ components. The server communicates with other systems or the clients via the EAI server. BizTalk Server 2004 is used for the EAI server. Both servers operate on Windows Server 2003 platform and load balanced by using L4 switch and protected by a firewall. Server applications are implemented with C# .NET.

The database server stores tasks, schedules, and resources information from the application server and it uses MS SQL Server 2005 as a DBMS. Periodically executed stored procedures are registered as SQL Server jobs for calculating and storing the average durations of the tasks and the average driving velocities of the resources.

The system has been used at a telecom in Korea for scheduling field resources in specific area. To analize the efficiency of the system, we compared density distribution between previous and suggested scheme as shown in Fig. 4. The density distribution shows how many resources have done how many tasks in a day. The data were collected for one month, three times. The number of resources and tasks in the figure were modified for security reasons. Fig. 4 (a) shows the distribution of work team based scheduling scheme. We can identify that most resources can process 3~5 tasks in a day. Fig. 4 (b) shows the distribution of individual resource based scheduling scheme. We can identify that most resources can process 5~7 tasks in a day. Thus the resources can process about 2 more tasks in this environment. Therefore, we conclude that the resource can process more tasks by using our system.

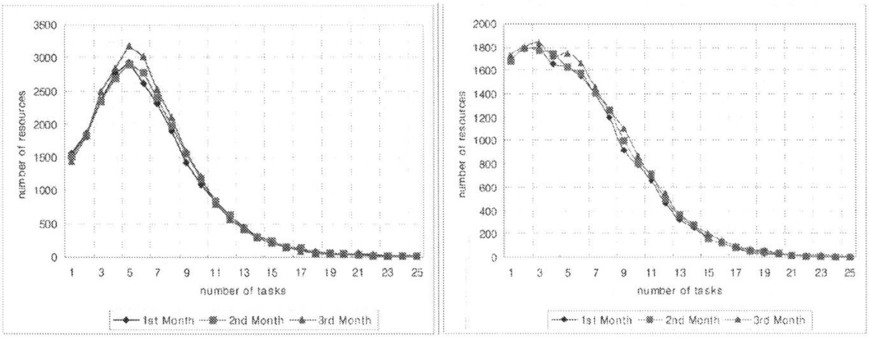

Fig. 4. The density distribution comparisons between work team based scheduling scheme and resource based scheduling scheme

5. Conclusion

We proposed the resource scheduling system for multimedia service provisioning in ubiquitous environment. To solve this problem, we designed five modules which are the Task Duration Estimator, the Driving Time Estimator, the Schedule Visualizer, the Human Resource Manager, and Schedule Manager. They were implemented in a telecom, and the resources at the telecom could process more tasks after adopting the system. As a future work, we will improve the system to solve not only telecom's resource scheduling problem but also other resource scheduling problems.

6. References

Bian, W. & Tao, D. (2008) Harmonic mean for subspace selection, *19th International Conference on Pattern Recognition*, pp. 1–4, DOI:10.1109/ICPR.2008.4760987.

Laporte, G.; Gendreau, M.; Potvin, J.Y. & Semet, F. (2000) Classical and modern heuristics for the Vehicle Routing Problem, *International Transactions in Operational Research*, Vol. 7, Issue 4-5, pp. 285-300, DOI:10.1111/j.1475-3995.2000.tb00200.x.

Lesaint, D.; Azarmi, N.; Laithwaite, R. & Walker, P. (1998) Engineering Dynamic Scheduler for Work Manager, *BT Technology Journal*, Vol. 16, No. 3, pp. 16-29.

Lesant, D. ; Voudouris, C. & Azarmi, N. (2000) Dynamic Workforce Scheduling for British Telecommunications plc, *INTERFACES*, Vol 30, No. 1, January-February, pp. 45-56.

Schumitt, L.J.; Aflaki, J.; Pitts, S.T. & Kamery, R.H. (2004) An Emphasis on Heuristics Combined with GA to Improve the Quality of the Solutions: Some Methods Used to Solve VRPs and VRPTCs, *Proceedings of the Academy of Information and Management Sciences*, Vol. 8, Num. 1, pp. 53-58.

Tsang, E. & Voudouris, C. (1997) Fast Local Search and Guided Local Search and Their Application to British Telecom's Workforce Scheduling Problem, *Operations Research Letters*, Vol. 20, Issue 3, pp. 119-127, DOI:10.1016/S0167-6377(96)00042-9.

14

Promoting Socio-Cultural Values Through Storytelling Using Animation and Game-Based Edutainment Software

Nor Azan Mat Zin[1], Nur Yuhanis Mohd Nasir[1] and Munirah Ghazali[2]
[1]*Universiti Kebangsaan Malaysia,*
[2]*Universiti Sains Malaysia,*
Malaysia

1. Introduction

Rapid advancement in the field of Information Communication Technology (ICT) has also changed the landscape of education and entertainment. Instructions can now be delivered through well designed interactive multimedia application software. Multimedia technology enables instructional delivery through effective learning strategies such as digital storytelling using 2D or 3D animation or animated cartoons, simulation and digital games. Animation in the form of cartoons, anime and animated feature films are popular forms of entertainment and widely used in various fields such as advertisement, entertainment, education and science. In Japan, animation is known as Anime. Research showed that anime is an art that can help adolescents shape and build their identities based on their favorite anime (Mahar, 2003). Anime can also help develop various skills and abilities among children (Frey & Fisher, 2004). Therefore we can use animation based edutainment software to educate children about their socio-cultural values while entertaining them with interesting folklore at the same time.

Literature has always played an important role in our lives, especially from the cultural aspect, since it is rich with educational messages and socio-cultural values to be imparted to the people in a society. However, the emphasis placed on learning of sciences and technology at school has caused neglect to the formal teaching of literature except for the few hours allocated in language lessons and for students who take social science courses. Furthermore, local children are more familiar with Western's literature as presented by folktales and stories in Hollywood made movies such as *Robin Hood, Sleeping Beauty* and *Cinderella.* To promote local literature to the younger 'Net' generation, a more attractive way is needed, one of which is with the help of current available information technology tools. In this chapter we discuss the research carried out to develop edutainment software with contents from the Malay literature to help promote society's socio-cultural values to the younger 'Net' generation.

2. Traditional Malay literature and socio-cultural values

Traditional Malay literature is rich in variety and of beautiful forms which are differentiated based on their structures and contents. Folktales or folk stories, *syair* and *peribahasa* are some examples of Malay literature which are considered as part of Malay cultural heritage (Muhammad, 2000; Braginsky, 2004).

Folktales are stories from yesteryear or a world of fantasy which usually consists of magical elements such as talking animals, fairies and healing powers (Thompson, 1978). The story contains custom elements that reflect a particular culture since the creation of these types of stories were influenced by factors such as geographical areas, languages, and social interaction. However, migration, religious preaching, trading, explorations and wars have caused stories to cross borders and spread throughout continents. That is why similar stories could be found in multiple locations around the world. However, the same stories may have slight differences due to modifications made to suit particular people where the story had reached (Thompson, 1978).

Stories were created for knowledge transfer and sharing (Machado et al., 2001; Madej, 2003). Before printing technology existed, storytelling were carried out verbally by storytellers. During those times, storytelling used to be practiced and has sociologically affected people around the globe (Thompson, 1978; Madej, 2003; Garzotto & Forfori, 2006). Storytelling was an activity during leisure time where old folks told stories to others especially young children for the purpose of educating them on matters related to culture, taboos, customs, and beliefs. Stories are capable of stimulating cognitive skills of listeners and emotionally influence them (Brand & Donato, 2001).

Syair, on the other hand, was created to narrate and express tales through rhythmic reading. The word "syair" originated from Arabic word "syi'r" which means "poetry". *Syair* then, is basically a traditional Malay poetry (Muhammad, 2000; Braginsky, 2004; Abdul Rahman, 1997). It was popular for educational purposes as well as for entertainment and religious activities among the Malays since the 15th century. Table 1 shows the different genres of *syair* in traditional Malay literature.

Narrative *Syair*	**Non-narrative *Syair***
Romance	Religious
Historical	Advice
Religious	Others
Cynical	

Table 1. Genres of Malay *syair*

Peribahasa, another category of Malay literature are traditional verbal expressions similar to the English "sayings" (Fanany & Fanany, 2003). Metaphors are used in sentences to deliver the meanings of an expression or saying in a subtle and indirect way. For example, a *peribahasa "Ada gula ada semut"* which translated in English as "When there is sugar, there are also ants" refers to places with potential for making profits where many people are likely to gather. "*Bagai enau dalam belukar*" is another saying, which means "like an enau tree in a jungle" an advice against selfishness. The metaphor Enau is a palm tree growing tall in tropical forest, always managing to outgrow its shoots over other trees. These *peribahasa* were old sayings of advice, derived from observations of surrounding world consisting of elements such as trees and animals or things of daily use.

Socio-cultural values of a society as embedded in its literature are passed down through generations via oral storytelling and later on documented in books. However, the process of modernization and national development including usage of modern technology and changes in educational curriculum has caused our society to neglect our literature. Most college students and school children no longer understand *peribahasa* or *syair* and are not familiar with local folklores or folk stories. The metaphors and terms used are unknown to them. We believe that multimedia technology can be used to promote traditional literature and hence socio-cultural values to the current Net generation. Animation and digital storytelling can help users visualize ancient terms and metaphors used in literature besides presenting content in an interesting, lively and dynamic manner.

3. Education and multimedia

In this era of ICT, multimedia-based contents such as digital games, animated stories and edutainment software are popularly in demand. Interactive information presentations and activities are designed to attract users, especially children. Multimedia with interactive elements allows users to actively interact with a system or a software. In the early 1990's, when ICT was accepted as a new way of communicating and knowledge sharing, the Malaysian government introduced the Smart School concept. Schools were provided with computers and educational software. Thus the demand for local content-based educational software has prompted research supported by government funding in software development.

The term "edutainment" was coined from the words "education" and "entertainment". Drawing from what the original words meant, edutainment is thus a concept for fun learning. Buckingham (2005) has defined edutainment as a hybrid genre that relies heavily on visual material and on more informal, less didactic styles of address. When using edutainment software, students will get to learn through the use of entertainment (Egloff, 2004; Klein, 2007). Children who enjoy learning will loosen up and learn better thus enable them to take things more easily and became more motivated to put forth effort without resentment and such software motivates students to explore topics in greater depths (Okan, 2003; Prensky, 2007).

Using ICT, multimedia-based education can be realized in a variety of ways, for examples through interactive story telling, simulation, games and animated story. Animation in the form of cartoons, anime and animated feature films are a popular form of entertainment, which can therefore be used as a means for education which is entertaining at the same time. Usually, children are animation-enthusiasts and easily drawn into watching animated-content programs. Folk stories, *syair* and *peribahasa* which used to be presented verbally or in printed forms can now be delivered and shared with other people using today's multimedia technology. Multimedia-based content for educational purposes will create a new dimension for traditional literature. By ensuring a program or software is suitable for young viewers, good values could reach them if the content of the program is designed to fit them. Presenting literature using multimedia technology is a way to revive traditional socio-cultural values.

3.1 Socio-cultural development

Social responsibility includes the development of social skills, ethics, characters, way of living with others and responsibility for furthering the common good (Berman, 1997). Transmitting good moral values could influence socio-cultural development. In general, education through teachers at school is seen as a commonplace idea to transmit values but with various media available today, teachers will have to compete with other influences in the young people's lives (Haydon, 2006). These influences could be from parents, siblings, peers and media such as television. In today's ICT era, people including children are becoming more IT-dependent. They spend much of their time playing computer games and socializing with other people virtually. Therefore, children today are more exposed to digital materials which are being communicated through digital media. This certainly has influence on children's cognitive and socio-cultural development.

3.2 Media influence on socio-cultural development

Development is fostered by the interaction between a child who is cognitively maturing and actively constructing meaning from his or her experiences and the media is seen as one of the forces that influence the child's conceptions of the social world (Berman, 1997). Television for instance can serve as models for children, portraying family members managing their relationships and conflict effectively through weekly family series (Berman, 1997; Douglas, 1996). However, some programs have been reported to have negative values such as violence, aggressive behaviors and disrespect to parents or adults, which has to a certain extent influenced behaviors of our young generation today.

Various researches have shown that a child could be influenced by listening to stories and watching animated stories or anime (Mahar, 2003; Frey & Fisher, 2004). The influence could either be positive or negative, depending on the contents viewed. There are quite a number of children's animated television series which are based on superheroes stories involving violence and fighting scenes. This could convey wrong ideas to a child that a problem can be solved through aggression because children tend to imitate what they see and hear, including from television. Violence presented on screen such as movies or video games could lead to children's belief that being aggressive is a good way to get what they want (Haninger et al., 2004; Center on Media and Child Health, 2008).

Additionally, studies (Adam et al., 1999) have shown that many movies from Disney Studio and other production houses had influenced children negatively in certain aspects, such as smoking and alcohol abuse. A Review of 40 selected studies on smoking in the movies showed that smoking in movies increases adolescent smoking initiation. Exposure to movie smoking makes viewers' attitudes and beliefs about smoking and smokers more favorable and has a dose-response relationship with adolescent smoking behavior (Haydon, 2006). Through ICT which is available today, various resources could be accessed via the Internet and CD-ROMs. With a combination of text, audio, graphics and animation, computer technology enriches education in a way that traditional teaching media such as books, video, role-plays and so forth might look irrelevant and tedious (Okan et al., 2003). Children are now increasingly using media at schools, with family or friends. Research has also found that playing games is the most common way of users ages 2 to 18 years old using computers (Wartella et al., 2000).

Nonetheless, it is not the medium (media) itself that affects children's perceptions, attitudes or awareness but the content with which they carry out activities with specific conditions and goals (Berman, 1997; Wartella et al., 2000). Therefore, content developers should be more sensitive when creating a product especially for children and adolescents users so that positive messages are transmitted and also to bring about behavioural change by engendering specific socio-cultural attitudes and acceptable behaviours to them.

4. Animation

One of multimedia element is animation. Animation is often used in edutainment software for its capabilities to minimize users' cognitive load and enable users to focus on a long-duration presentation (Jamaluddin & Zaidatun, 2003). Animation is defined as an art of movement expressed with static images. This illusion of movement is achieved by rapidly displaying frames of still images in a sequence (Kerlow, 2000).

Malaysia imported a lot of animation series from the United States and Japan. Some contents of imported animations are not suitable for local viewing in terms of the cultural values. During the 1980s and 1990s, locally produced short animation movies based on local folk stories were aired on education television channel. They were meant to educate children on moral values. The stories were "The Legend of a Mouse deer", "Mouse deer and a Monkey", "The Wise Crow" and "The Greedy Lion". Later in 1995 and 1998, "Usop Sontorian" and "Silat Lagenda" were produced. Usop Sontorian was Malaysia's first animation television series while the latter was a full-length digital animated movie (Perpustakaan Negara Malaysia, 2001). Currently there are efforts to produce local animation stories, an example of which is *Upin and Ipin,* a 3D animated story of twin brothers and their activities with family and friends.

In the following sections we discuss the research on designing and developing *MyEduTale,* an edutainment software based on Malay literature of folk stories, *syair* and *peribahasa* as the contents which aims to motivate socio-cultural awareness among children.

5. Research objectives

This study were carried out to design and develop edutainment software, *MyEduTale* (short for Malaysian Edutainment Folktale software) using Malay literature as contents. 2D animation was used for storytelling, in addition to interactive games, puzzles and activity modules. Specifically, the objectives of this research were to identify suitable method for the research of designing and developing a literature-based socio-cultural edutainment software focusing on moral and value aspects and to develop a conceptual model of the edutainment software. This research was also to recreate and present local folktales, folk stories, *peribahasa* and *syair* in the form of 2D animation created using simple and fast animation technique and interactive multimedia technology. The prototype software was also evaluated for usability in the aspects of user satisfaction, effectiveness and ease of use.

6. Research method

The research method identified and used was based on ADDIE Instructional Design (ID) model, taking into consideration the animation development processes of pre-production, production and post-production (see Fig. 1). ID model was used because we were designing instructional and entertainment software. The detailed explanation of the process, activities and output involved is further explained and shown in research framework, Figure 2.

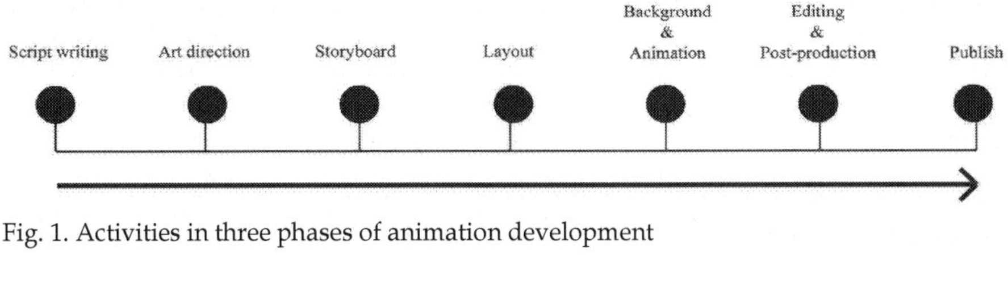

Fig. 1. Activities in three phases of animation development

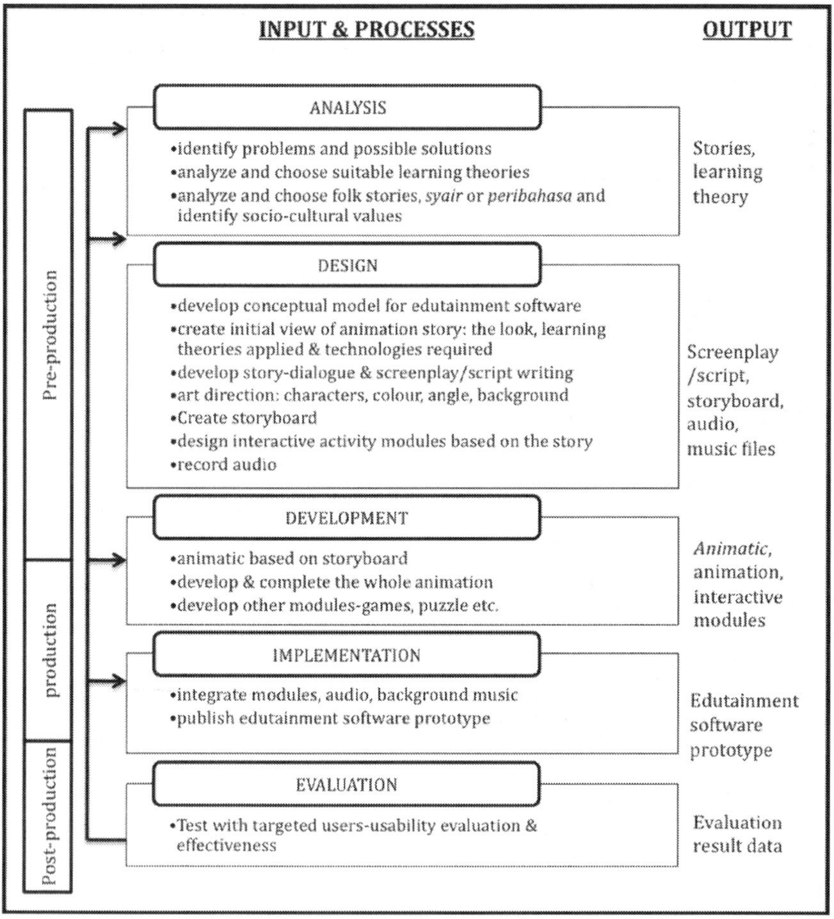

Fig. 2. Research framework

7. Design and development

The design and development process involves development of the conceptual model (Fig. 3) for the edutainment software, story development, screenplay or scriptwriting, storyboarding, character development, design and development of supporting elements and interactive module and animating (Nor Azan & Nur Yuhanis, 2007).

There are five components in the model, the first is the content. *MyEduTale* uses Malay literature of folktales, syair and peribahasa, as the content to educate users on socio-cultural values through story telling. Local folktale were chosen because learning using local-based content will be much easier for users to identify themselves through the course materials (Halimah et al., 2000). Folktale were also chosen because children love to listen to stories so it will be fun for them to learn through a content which is presented in the form they love

(Halimah et al., 2000; Madej, 2003) Furthermore, stories could help children to develop new experience and construct the meaning of their lives through stories (Madej, 2003).

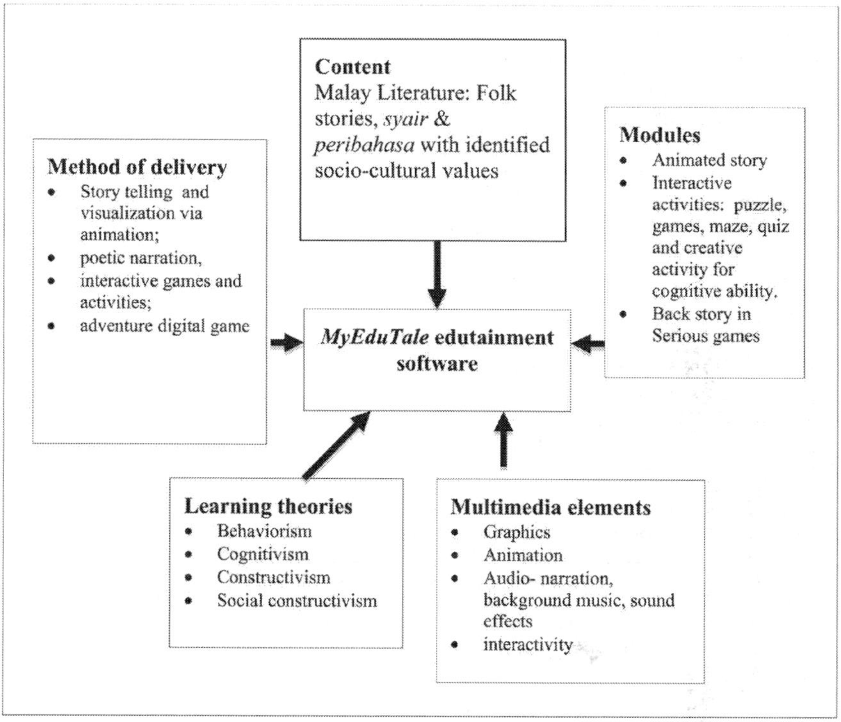

Fig. 3. The conceptual model of *MyEduTale* edutainment software

The second component is the learning theories. Learning theories applied in designing the activities in *MyEduTale* are behaviorism, cognitivism including constructivism and social constructivism. The purpose of applying these theories is to ensure the effectiveness of learning process using these edutainment software. Behaviorism states that learning happens when one receives stimulus or motivation (Ratten & Ratten, 2007). This theory is applied in "Know your characters " module. Four modules use cognitive learning theory which stated that learning is a process that combines previous and new information to solve problem (Schiffman & Kanuk, 2000). The modules are "Test your understanding", "Lost House", "Arrange the pictures" and "Create your own story ending" where users need to think of the correct answers and strategies for the challenges in each of module. Social constructivism is the learning theory applied in "Animated story" module. According to this theory, learning process happens when there is interaction between human, his behavior and environment (Davis, 2006). The last theory used in *MyEduTale* is constructivism which is applied in "Create your own story ending" module. Learning is said to happen when new knowledge or information is developed by the learner (Garde, 2007).

The third component in the model is the method of delivery which includes storytelling using animation, poetic narration, interactive games and activities and adventure games.

The fourth component is the multimedia elements. Since *MyEduTale* is meant to be an edutainment software for children, it is developed using multimedia elements of animation, graphic, various types of audio and interactive elements. MyEduTale are user-oriented environment, meaning that all modules in the software are provided with uniform and consistent interactive features and navigation elements so that users will be at ease to navigate from one module to another. Children tend to be attracted to dynamic, colourful and beautiful elements so multimedia is the best tool to get them into focusing on the content.

The fifth element is the modules available in *MyEduTale*. There are several modules in each *MyEduTale* edutainment software. The main module is a 2D animated story the module called "Animated story". Other modules are activity modules created based on the animated story. They are interactive activities of games, puzzle, maze, quiz, and creative activity. The activity modules in *MyEduTale* provide users with exercises and games. Garcia-Barcena & Garcia-Crespo (2006) and Liu & Chun (2007) reported in their researches that students are motivated to learn in a game-based learning environment. The activity modules are meant to review and reinforce users' understanding towards the message embedded in the animated story. In *MyEduTale*, there are several games or activity modules which are based on the main stories. These modules comprise of a simple drag and drop game (Know your characters), a quiz module consisting of ten comprehension questions (Test your understanding), maze game (Lost House), (Finding lost objects), picture puzzle (Arrange the pictures) and a story writing module where users can create and rewrite their own story ending for the folk story (Create your own story ending). This last module was desined to help users to be creative and imaginative by having them write the story ending the way they wish the story to end because children love reading their own stories (Halimah et al., 2000). Of all these activities, the picture puzzle module is the most challenging activity which requires users to rearrange pieces of cut pictures into one complete perfect picture. The level of complexity of activities increase from one module to another, from the simplest activity to suit younger-aged users to the most difficult activity for older users and those who like more mind-challenging activity.

There are four different versions of *MyEduTale* edutainment prototypes developed in this research. They are either folktale or story with 2D animation storytelling and interactive activity modules, a wholly 2D animation *syair*, an animated collection of *peribahasa*, and a serious game (game for education) prototypes, all have contents representing the Malay literature.

7.2 Story development

Folk stories, *syair* and *peribahasa* were studied and compared to identify for socio-cultural values. Two folk stories, "Si Bangau yang Membalas Budi" (The crane that rewards good deeds) and "Sumpah Sang Kelembai" (The curse of Sang Kelembai) were selected. The first story revolves around an era of yesteryear and consists of magical elements of a talking Bangau (flamingo) and its transformation into a human form. The setting of the story is in a rural Malay village. Based on the original storyline, a script was written with dialogues for each and every character in the story. The story started with panning around the village area to indicate the type of surrounding environment or the setting of scene of the story. Then, two of the main characters are introduced with a scene showing how they earn their living. This is to highlight the fact that the characters are people who live near poverty. As the story moves on, enter the third character, the flamingo. Since this is a folktale, talking animal is not an oddity but is logical to the mind as does the flamingo's ability to communicate verbally with the human characters. As the story progresses, the fourth character is revealed and the central messages designed to be delivered through the story are shown bit by bit until the end of the story. Towards the resolution of the story, the climax is shown to create suspense. The ending of the story is narrated by a voice to ensure that all messages or moral of the story are transferred to the audience. The moral of the story include good deeds will be rewarded, don't break promises and be kind to people as well as animals.

The second story was about a poor woodcutter, Badek who was one day given some magical seeds by an unknown old witch, Sang Kelembai who magically disappear after saying that the man can become rich and made him promise to help other poor and needy people. Eventually Badek became a rich farmer as a result of selling his produce grown from the magic seeds. However, he forgot his promise, became arrogant and turned away poor or old people who came for his help. His friends were all rich people. One day during his daughter's wedding, an old woman who was actually Sang Kelembai was prevented from joining the feast. She wont leave until she meet Badek. Badek came to see the old lady, recognized her as the witch and remembered his promise, but unfortunately it was too late for regrets. The story ended with Sang Kelembai cursing Badek into a human stone. The moral of this story is that one must always be humble and help others in need.

One version of the software is a serious game using the folktale of Awang Miskin as the backstory. Awang Miskin was an orphan boy who lives with his mother. He wanted to be a learned man. In this game, players will help Awang Miskin pass through many obstacles in his adventure or quest for learning. The moral of the story and the game is hard work pays and players get to play many games at different levels which represent Awang Miskin's knowledge levels. Other values are also embedded in each game level.

The *syair* choosen was about an orphan girl who was mistreated by her stepmother. The girl was finally rescued from the house by a magic swing and was found by a prince whom she married at the ending of the story. This *syair* is a story told through poetic narration (similar to singing) using animation from beginning until the end. As for *peribahasa,* a few were selected based on the ease of visualizing them using animation. The animation tell the meaning of each *peribahasa*. Basically animation help in visualizing the *peribahasa* for easier understanding of their meanings.

7.3 Character development

The story "The Crane that Rewards Good Deeds" has four main characters which are an old man named "Pak Mat", Pak Mat's wife; "Mak Som", a talking flamingo and a young beautiful lady named "Mariam". Besides all these four characters, there are a few supporting characters towards the end of the story, which are the villagers. The main characters in Sang Kelembai are the farmer and Sang Kelembai. There are other characters such as the villagers and the farmer's wife and daughter. The syair has two main characters, the orphaned girl and the cruel stepmother. Supporting characters include the girl's father, the king and the prince. The main character for the serious game software is Awang Miskin. All characters were designed based on local identity in terms of physical appearance, attires, and styles. Figures 4, 5 and 6 are illustrations of the main human characters of each story while Figure 7 shows a traditional Malay house based on Malay architectural structure. The first step in designing these characters was to sketch on papers. Then, all characters and props were designed, developed and edited directly in the graphic software Adobe Illustrator and Adobe Photoshop. However, most of the characters and props were developed and edited directly using Macromedia Flash MX Professional 2004.

Fig. 4. Three main characters in "The Crane that Rewards Good Deeds" developed using Macromedia Flash MX Professional 2004.

Fig. 5. Characters in "The curse of Sang Kelembai" (the first character is a poor Badek while second is a rich Badek, a beggar and Sang Kelembai)

Fig. 6. The main character in serious game, Awang Miskin.

Fig. 7. Screen shot of a scene showing the Malay village house of Pak Mat and his wife.

7.4 Development of supporting elements

Elements such as audio and background graphics were inserted in the animation stories to make the presentation of the story more attractive and interesting. Most graphics were created directly in Macromedia Flash MX Professional 2004 while a few were edited in Adobe Photoshop and Adobe Illustrator. Different audios were used for different situations and according to the mood of the scene. Types of audio used for the animation story were background music, dialogues, narration, poetic narration and sound effects. These audio files were recorded and edited using Cool Edit Pro Version 2.00. The background music used were Malay folk songs. Types of audio used are background music, dialogues, narration, poetic narration and sound effects. These audio files were either self-recorded or taken from available commercial sources. Audio editing was done using Cool Edit Pro Version 2.00.

Background music used in *MyEduTale* were folk and children songs reproduced by the Ministry of Unity, Culture, Arts and Heritage (KeKKWa). Titles of some of the songs used are "Burung Kakak Tua", "Chan Mali Chan" and "Bulan". As for graphics, most of the elements were created directly in Macromedia Flash MX Professional 2004 while the rest were edited in Adobe Photoshop and Adobe Illustrator.

7.5 Animation process

The animation process was carried out using Macromedia Flash MX Professional 2004. Limited animation technique (see Fig.8) was used since this technique allows development of animation in shorter times. A character is broken down into a few different parts and each part can be reused many times. For example, a human character can be divided into the head, hair, body, left hand, right hand, left leg and right leg. This can help save work space memory and time taken for drawing. Every part is saved as objects in Flash library.

Fig. 8. Limited animation technique: graphics of a character were broken into several movable pieces for movement manipulation.

On stage in Flash, each part of a completed character is placed in different layers so that every part in each layer can be animated in different ways (Fig.9). A layer in Flash cannot have more than one graphic if the graphic is to be given moving effect. To create movement, frame is manipulated to give the best quality animation. The frame rate of the animated stories in *MyEduTale* is 25 fps (25 frames are played in a second). Figures 10 to 14 are typical sample screen shots from each type of edutainment software developed in this research.

Fig. 9. Screen shot of a workspace during animation process in Macromedia Flash MX 2004

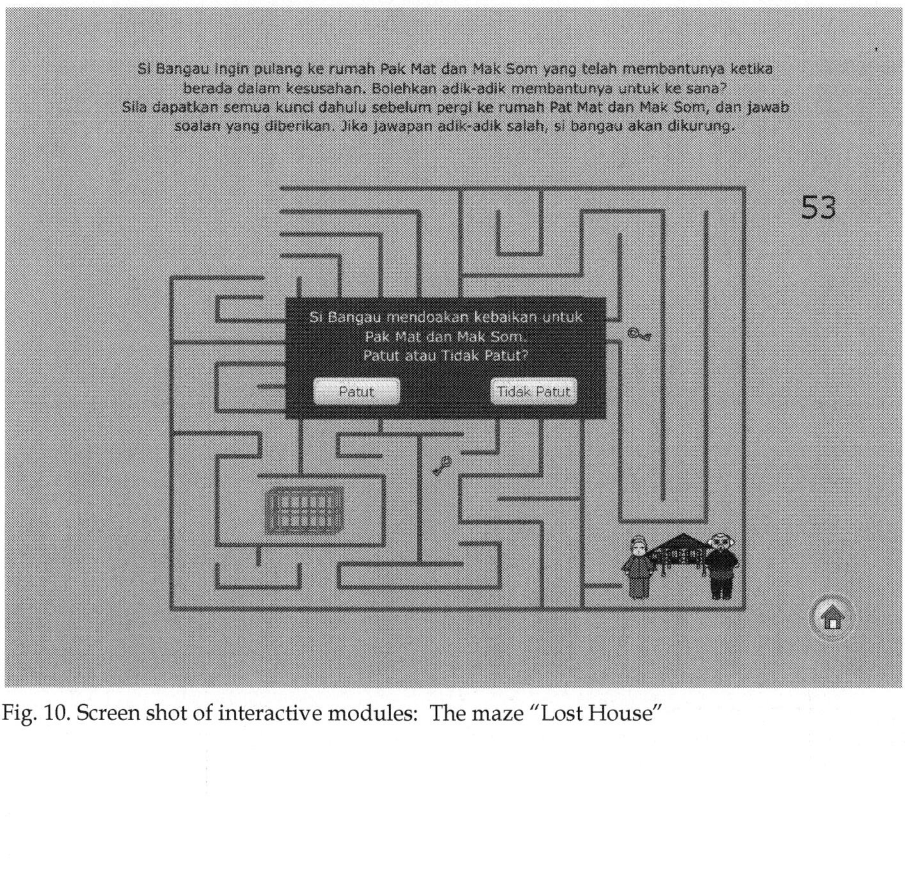

Fig. 10. Screen shot of interactive modules: The maze "Lost House"

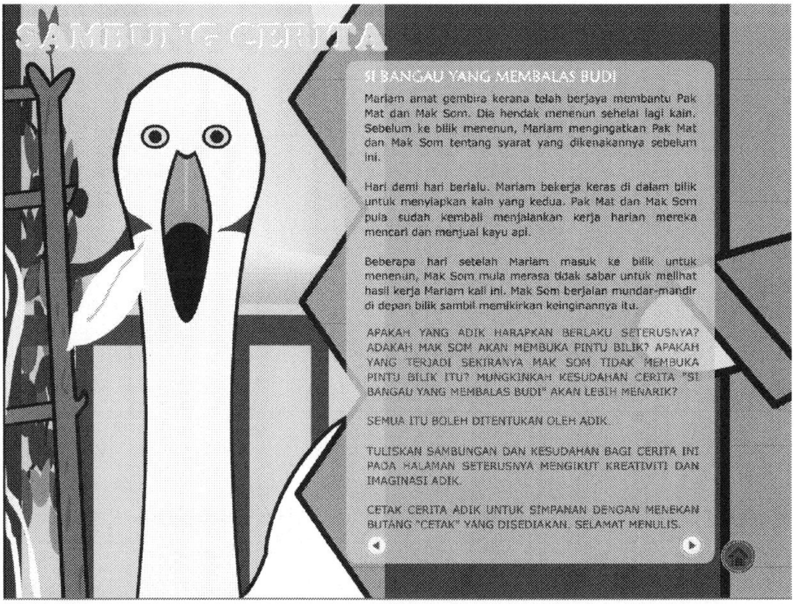

Fig. 11. Creative module "Create your own ending"

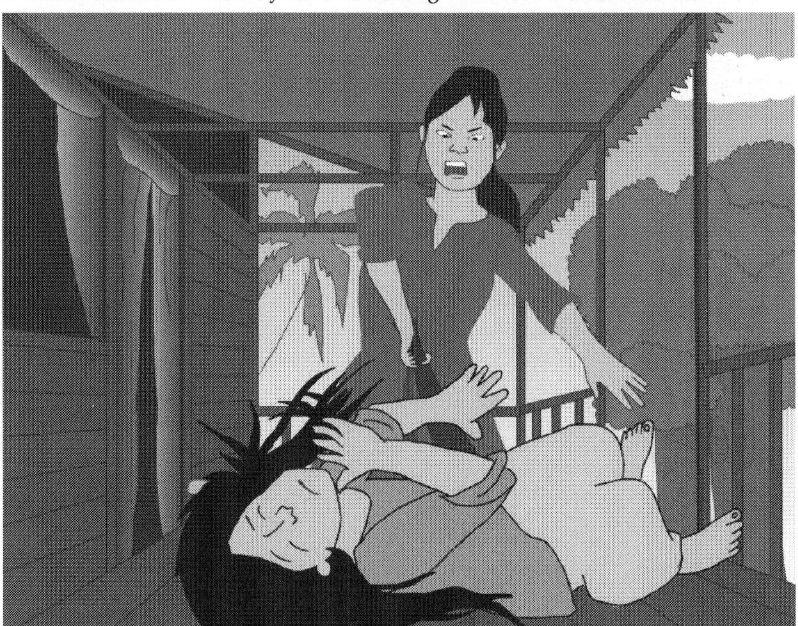

Fig. 12. A screen shot from "The magic Cradle" *syair*.

Fig. 13. A screen shot from *Peribahasa* " Where there is sugar, there are ants".

Fig. 14. A screen shot from the serious game software.

8. Evaluation of *MyEduTale*

Evaluation of the software as an alternative tool in socio-cultural education is not carried out because longer time is needed to observe any behavioural change due to exposure to values embedded in the software. Furthermore, our concern in this research is on the design of the software as a tool to teach socio-cultural values, so we only evaluate users understanding of the message in the software through their perception of software effectiveness and usability testing of the interface design.

One of the *MyEduTale* prototype with the story "The Crane that Rewards Good Deeds" was tested on 30 users who were children ages 5 to 12 years old. The testing sessions were conducted in groups to get users' opinions and acceptance towards the software (Nor Azan & Nur Yuhanis, 2008.).

Users were allowed to explore the software on their own while being observed by the researcher to see how engaged they were while using it. Usability questionnaires were distributed to them after they have completed all the modules in MyEduTale. The scale used in the questionnaire is based on Likert Scale from 1 to 5, with scale 1 for "totally disagree" or "very poor" and scale 5 for "totally agree" or "very good". Findings from the testing indicated that 92% of users were satisfied using the software. 93% users reported that *MyEduTale* is easy to use while 95% agreed that the software is effective in delivering the intended values through the story and reinforced with the activity modules. Effectiveness of the software was rated at 4.8 out of 5, on Likert scale.

Our observations throughout the testing found that girls were more engaged and concentrated more on the 2D animated story and simpler activity modules while boys were more attracted to activity modules especially the maze and puzzle modules. Nevertheless, every user went through watching the animated folktale from beginning until the end and explored every module in *MyEduTale*. Respondents were also interviewed to get their personal opinions on *MyEduTale*.

Through questionnaires, observation and interviews, it is found that the most favourable module in *MyEduTale* is the maze game, while animated folktale module comes next, followed by the quiz, picture puzzle, story ending writing and finally drag and drop activity module. In terms of the physical look and appearances, respondents were all satisfied with the colour-scheme as well as the graphics in *MyEduTale*. However, respondents also commented on the challenge aspect of activity modules which they suggested could be improved by making it more interesting and challenging. On the whole, it is found that majority of respondents who evaluate *MyEduTale* gave positive responses and showed great interest towards the edutainment software. Other software prototypes are still being evaluated.

9. Conclusion

MyEduTale is developed to motivate socio-cultural awareness among children aged 5 to 12 years old using Malay literature. Literature used includes folktale or folk story, *syair* and *peribahasa* which have socio-cultural values in the form of morals of the story intended and designed to be transferred to users mainly through 2D animation. The values included are: do not break promise, be kind to people as well as animals, help those in need, work hard, and good deeds will be rewarded.

We have used Malay literature as contents for various types of edutainment software based on our conceptual model. Folktales which used to be the medium for educating people a very long time ago is reconstructed in this research for the exact same purpose, which is to educate people through stories. Designed to suit current technology savvy users' preferences using multimedia elements, an edutainment software provides an alternative for moral and socio-cultural education that aims to educate young children to adopt good values. In addition, the software can help to revive the popularity of local folktales among younger generations.

Findings from the software evaluation indicated positive signs for software acceptance, therefore it is hoped that *MyEduTale* can be an example for similar research on education using other literature heritage. Future research can look into other types of literature and stories or folklores to be used as edutainment software content.

10. References

Abdul Rahman Kaeh. (1997) *Syair madhi: Citra Melayu Nusantara,* Perpustakaan Negara Malaysia (National Library Of Malaysia), ISBN 98362187, Kuala Lumpur

Adam, O., Goldstein, R. A. S., & Glen, R. N. (1999). Tobacco and Alcohol Use in G-Rated Children's Animated Films. *JAMA.* 282(13), pp.1228-1229, ISSN 0098-7484

Berman, S. (1997). *Children's Social Consciousness and the Development of Social Responsibility,* State University of New York, ISBN 0791431983, New York

Braginsky, V. (2004) *The heritage of traditional Malay literature: A historical survey of genres, writings and literary views.* KITLV Press, ISBN 9067182141, Leiden

Brand, S.T. & Donato, J. (2000). *Storytelling in Emergent Literacy: Fostering Multiple Intelligence,* Delmar Cengage Learning. 0766814807, New York

Buckingham, D. & Scanlon, M. (2005). Selling. Learning: Towards a political economy of edutainment media. *Media, Culture and Society,* 27,1, pp. 41-58. DOI: 10.1177/0163443705049057, ISSN 0163-4437

Center on Media and Child Health, Children's Hospital Boston. (2004-2008). Violent Video games http://cmch.tv/mentors/hotTopic.asp?id=65, (access on 16 November 2008)

Davis, A. (2006). Theories used in IS Research: Social Cognitive Theory. http://www.istheory.yorku.ca/socialcognitivetheory.htm. (access on 30th March 2007)

Douglas, W. (1996). The fall from grace? The modern family on television". *Communication Research.* 23, 6, pp. 675-702. DOI: 10.1177/009365096023006003

Egloff, T.H. (2004). Edutainment: A case study of interactive CD-ROM playsets. *Computers in entertainment,* 2, 1, pp. 1. ISSN 1544-3574

Fanany, I. & Fanany, R. (2003). *Wisdom of the Malay Proverbs.* Dewan Bahasa dan Pustaka, ISBN 9789836277473/9836277471, Kuala Lumpur

Frey, N. & Fisher, D. (2004). Using graphics novels, anime and the Internet in an urban high school. *English Journal,* 93, 3, pp. 19. ISSN 0013-8274

Garcia-Barcena, J. & Garcia-Crespo, A. (2006). Game Based Learning: A Research on Learning Content Management Systems. *Proceedings of 5th WSEAS International Conference on Education and Educational Technology.*pp. 541-592, ISSN 1790-5117, ISBN 960-8457-57-2

Garde, S., Heid, J., Haag, M., Bauch, M., Weires, T. & Leven, F.J. (2007). Can design principles of traditional learning theories be fulfilled by computer-based training systems in medicine: The example of CAMPUS. *International Journal of Medical Informatics,* 76, pp. 124-129. DOI:10.1016/j.ijmedinf.2006.07.009

Garzotto, F. & Forfori, M. (2006). FaTe2: storytelling edutainment experiences in 2D and 3D collaborative spaces, *Proceedings of the 2006 conference on Interaction design and children,* pp. 113 - 116, DOI http://doi.acm.org/10.1145/1139073.1139102, Tampere, Finland, *June 07 - 09, 2006,* ACM, New York

Halimah Badioze Zaman, Norhayati Abdul Mokti, Nor Azan Mat Zin, Munir, Tengku Mohd Tengku Sembok & Mohamed Yusoff. (2000) Motivating literacy through MEL: A multimedia based tutoring system. *The New Review of Children's Literature and Librarianship,* 6, 2000, pp. 125-136, ISSN 1361-4541

Haninger, K., Ryan, M. S., & Thompson, K. M. (2004). Violence in teen-rated video games. *Medscape General Medicine.* 6, 1, http://www.hsph.harvard.edu/kidsrisk/images/MGMvideogames.pdf, 2004. (online, access on 10 November 2008),

Haydon, G. (2006) *Values in Education.* Continuum International Publishing Group, ISBN 0826492711, London

Jamaluddin Harun & Zaidatun Tasir. (2003). *Multimedia Dalam Pendidikan,* PTS Publication, ISBN 9831929616, Bentong

Kerlow, I. V. (2004) *The art of 3-D computer animation and imaging,* John Wiley & Sons Inc., ISBN 0-471-43036-6 (3rd edition), New York

Klein, T. (2007). Animated Appeal: A Survey of Production Methods in Children's Software. *Animation Studies,* 2, pp. 1-8. ISSN 1930-1928

Liu, E. Z. F. & Chun, H. L. (2007). Education Computer Games for Instructional Purposes: Current Status and Evaluative Indicators. Proceedings of the 6th WSEAS International Conference on E-ACTIVITIES (E-Learning, E-Communities, E-Commerce, E-Management, E-Marketing, E-Governance, Tele-Working / E-ACTIVITIES'07), pp: 161-165, ISBN: 978-960-6766-22-8, Tenerife, Spain,December 14-16 2007, WSEAS Press, Tenerife

Machado, I., Paiva, A. & Prada, R. (2001). Is the wolf angry or... just hungry?, *Proceedings of the Fifth International Conference on Autonomous Agents,* pp. 370 – 376. ISBN 1-58113-326-X, Montreal, Quebec, Canada, May 28-Jun1 2001, ACM, New York

Madej, K. (2003). Towards digital narrative for children: From education to entertainment. A historical perspective, *ACM Computers in Entertainment,* 1, 1, pp. 1-17, ISSN 1544-3574

Mahar, D., (2003). Bringing the outside in: One teacher's ride on the Anime highway. *Language Arts,* 81, 2, (Nov 2003) pp. 110-117, ISSN 0360-9170

Muhammad Haji Salleh. (2000) *Puitika sastera Melayu,* Dewan Bahasa dan Pustaka, ISBN 967-942- 236-4 (Edisi Kedua), Kuala Lumpur

Nor Azan Mat Zin & Nur Yuhanis Mohd Nasir. (2007). Edutainment Animated Folk Tales Software to Motivate Socio-Cultural Awareness. *Computer Science Challenges: Proceedings of 7th WSEAS International Conference on Applied Computer Science,* pp. 310-315, ISBN 9789606766152, Venice, Italy, Nov 21-23 2007.WSEAS Press, Venice

Nor Azan Mat Zin & Nur Yuhanis Mohd Nasir. (2008). Evaluation of Edutainment Animated Folk Tales Software to Motivate Socio-Cultural Awareness. *Proceedings of the Third International Conference on Convergence and Hybrid Information Technology (ICCIT08),* vol. 1, pp. 315-319, ISBN 978-0-7695-3407-7, Busan, Korea, November 11-13, IEEE Computer Society, Washington DC, USA

Okan, Z. (2003). Edutainment: Is learning at risk?, *British Journal of Educational Technology,* 34, 3, pp. 255-264, ISSN 0007-1013

Perpustakaan Negara Malaysia (2001). Filem animasi: Silat Lagenda. http://www.pnm.my/yangpertama/Seni_Filemanimasi.htm. (access on 5 April 2007)

Prensky, M. (2007) *Digital Game-Based Learning,* Paragon House, ISBN 1557788634, MN, USA.

Ratten, V., & Ratten. H. (2007). Social cognitive theory in technological innovations. *European Journal of Innovation Management,* 10, 1, pp. 90-108, ISSN 1460-1060

Schiffman, L. & Kanuk, L. (2006). *Consumer behavior,* Prentice Hall, New Jersey, ISBN 0131869604

Thompson, S. (1978). *The folktale,* University of California Press ISBN 0520035372, Berkerly and Los Angeles, CA

Wartella, E., O'Keefe, B., & Scantlin, R. (2000). Children and interactive media: A compendium of current research and directions for the future. Menlo Park, CA: Markle Foundation. http://www.markle.org/news/digital_kids.pdf

15

A New Auto Exposure System to Detect High Dynamic Range Conditions Using CMOS Technology

Quoc Kien Vuong, Se-Hwan Yun and Suki Kim
Korea University, Seoul
Republic of Korea

1. Introduction

Recently, Image Signal Processing (ISP) has become an interesting research field, along with the development and emergence of various image capturing systems. These image systems include digital still cameras, surveillance systems, webcams, camcorders, etc... ISP is any form of signal processing for which the input is an image, such as photographs or frames of video; the output of image processing can be either an image or a set of characteristics or parameters related to the image. Most image-processing techniques involve treating the image as a two-dimensional signal and applying standard signal-processing techniques to it. ISP helps visually optimize raw output images captured with image sensors located in image systems.

For most of such devices, auto exposure (AE) has become one major function which automatically adjust the amount of incident light on the image sensor so as to utilize its full dynamic range, or for proper exposure. To control the amount of incident light, cameras adjust the aperture, shutter speeed, or both. If the expsoure time is not long enough, output images will appear darker than actual scenes, which is called under-exposure. On the other hand, if the exposure time is too much, output images will appear much brighter than actual scene, which is called over-exposure. Both cases result in a loss of details and image would pocess a bad quality. Only at an appropriate exposure can a camera provide good pictures with the most details.

Many AE algorithms have been developed (Liang et al., 2007), (Shimizu et al., 1992), (Murakami & Honda, 1996) and (Lee et al., 2001) to deal with high-contrast lighting conditions. Some of them employ fuzzy method while others use various ways of segmentation. However, most of these algorithms have some drawbacks on either their accuracy or on the complexity, or both while estimating lighting conditions.

According to the research (Liang et al., 2007), it is difficult to discriminate back-lit conditions from front-lit conditions using histogram methods (Shimizu et al., 1992) and (Murakami & Honda, 1996). Further simulations in this paper shows that the tables and criteria used to estimate lighting conditions are confusing and not consistent. These methods tend to address only excessive back-lighting and front-lighting conditions as well as how to distinguish between these two conditions.

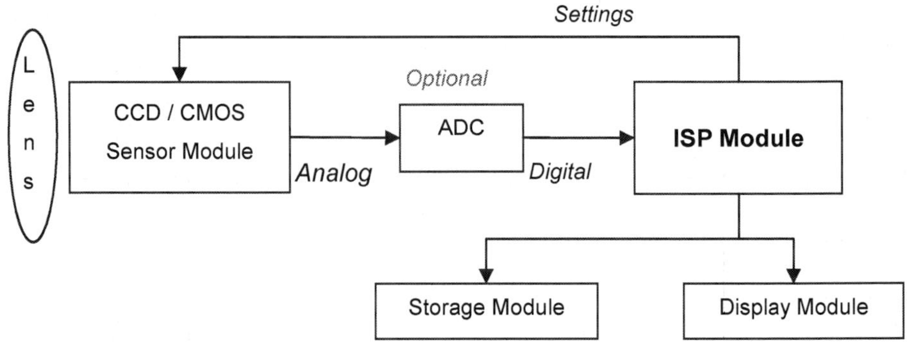

Fig. 1. Simplified block diagram of an image capturing system

Other algorithms such as (Murakami and Honda, 1996) and (Lee et al., 2001) used fixed-window segmentation methods to estimate the brightness and lighting conditions. The main drawback of these algorithms is the in-flexibility. Most of these algorithms, including (Liang et al., 2007) assume that there is a main object in each image; therefore, they can not work well with images that have no main objects, only normal sceneries, or images in which a main object is not located at the centre. Furthermore, the gain coefficients for each region in a picture are different, hence color and brightness distortion may occur.

In (Kao et al., 2006), multiple exposure methods were presented to improve the dynamic range of output pictures. Simulation results showed that its algorithm might easily lead to color inconsistency and bad chromatic transitions.

This paper introduces a new approach to control AE which can be used to determine the degree of contrast lighting employing a simple and quick method which is presented in Section 3. Section 4 describes how to decide if the condition is normal lit, excessive back lit or just a condition with a high dynamic range. Then the algorithm uses a simple multiple exposure mechanism to improve the dynamic range of the output image so that more details can be revealed. In Section 5, simulation results are presented. Finally, conclusions are given in Section 6.

3. AE algorithm for lighting-condition detection

3.1 Lighting condtion detecting

Lighting conditions can be generally classified as normal-lit, excessive back-lit or high contrast. A back lighting condition is a scene in which light sources are located behind the whole scenery or main objects. In this case, the brightness of the background is much higher than that of the main object. A high contrast lighting condition is a scene that consists of many regions of very different brightness levels. Front lighting conditions can also be considered as high contrast lighting. These are the conditions in which light sources are located in front of and somehow close to the main object and therefore, the brightness of that main object is much higher than that of the background.

Usually, it is not very difficult at all to capture images of normal lit or normal illuminated scenes. However, in the cases of excessive back-lit and high contrast lighting conditions, output images may lose a significant amount of details. A picture taken in such a condition may contain regions that are much darker or brighter than the actual ambient scene. If the exposure value is set such that dark objects and regions look bright enough to see, then other bright objects and regions will be too bright or over-exposed. On the contrary, if the exposure value is set such that bright objects and areas become adequately bright enough to human eyes, then other objects and areas will be too dark or under-exposed to distinguish each separate detail. Estimating litghting conditions accurately can help a camera device decide how to compensate its exposure value for better output pictures.

To determine the degree of lighting conditions, the proposed method uses the relationship between the mean value and median value of an image.

The mean value is simply the average component value of all elements in an array, or particularly of all pixels in an image. A component can be a color component (R, G, or B) or the brightness level.

The median value is the value of the middle element in a sorted array. This array is an array of brightness levels of all pixels in an image. Note that since the element at the middle is taken into account, the array can be sorted either ascendingly or descendingly without affecting the value of the middle element. Fig. 2 illustrates the difference between these two values.

Original array

158	250	85	203	70	89	110	105	120

Mean value: 132

Sorted array

70	85	89	105	110	120	158	203	250

Median value: 110

Fig. 2. Mean and median values of an array

According to Fig. 2, although the average value is somewhere in the middle of the range, the median value is much smaller than the mean value. This is because the number of small value elements outweights that of large value ones. For a sorted large-size array, if the values of all elements increase or decrease steadily, the difference between the mean and the median values is not significant. However, if the values of all items increase or decrease abruptly somewhere within the array, then the middle item may have a very large or very small value, depending on the outweighing number of large-value or small-value elements. This leads to a significant difference between the mean and the median values.

The idea of estimating the relationship between the mean and median values of an array can be applied to lighting condition detection. Since the total number of pixels in an image is very large, that idea will be even more accurate and applicable. In the case of normal lighting conditions, the brightness level of all pixels follows a steady distribution throughout the whole color and brightness ranges of each image. Therefore, the mean value just differs a little from the median value. On the contrary, in the cases of high contrast lighting and back lighting conditions, for under- or appropriate exposure value, the median value of the brightness levels tends to reside in the small-value section and hence, it differs much from the average value of the whole array of all pixels.

Fig. 3 illustrates the use of the relationship between these two values in detecting illuminating conditions. Note that Bl_{mean} and Bl_{med} denote the mean and the median value of the brightness level, respectively, D_L denotes the difference between the two values, and D_{thres} denotes the threshold value.

(a) Normal-lighting

$Bl_{mean} = 112$

$Bl_{med} = 103$

$D_L = 9 < D_{thres}$

(b) Back-lighting

$Bl_{mean} = 118$

$Bl_{med} = 79$

$D_L = 39 > D_{thres}$

(c) High Contrast Lighting

$Bl_{mean} = 120$

$Bl_{med} = 100$

$D_L = 20 \geq D_{thres}$

Fig. 3. Bl_{mean}, Bl_{med} and D_L in different lighting conditions

The next issue is to decide the value of brightness level of an image. Unlike most high end camera systems, low end camera platforms employ CMOS image sensors that produce output images in the RGB form. Most conventional systems perform the conversion from RGB to another color space such as YCbCr in order to reveal the luminance value Y. However, since the green component (G) contributes the most to the brightness of an image, G can be used directly as the brightness level without introducing much difference from Y. This can help reduce the complexity and processing time of the overall architecture. Experimental results of (Liang et al., 2007) demonstrate the similarity between Y and G. Referring back to Fig. 3, all brightness values (Bl_{mean}, Bl_{med}) are exactly values of Y (luminance) component of each image. The following table provides corresponding brightness values in term of G component for images in Fig. 3.

Image	Bl_{mean}		Bl_{med}		D_L	
	G	Y	G	Y	G	Y
(a)	111	112	103	103	8	9
(b)	116	118	76	79	40	39
(c)	120	120	99	100	21	20

Table 1. G and Y component as brightness level of images in Fig. 3

In brief, the G component of an RGB image will be used as the luminance when estimating lighting conditions. It is the relationship between the mean and median G values of an image to be used as the criterion to judge illuminating conditions. For under- and properly exposed pictures, if the difference between these two values is minor, the scene is normal lit; otherwise the scene is excessive back-lit or it pocesses a high dynamic range illumination. This relationship will be used in the AE mechanism to help control the exposure value depending on lighting conditions. In term of implementation, the hardware required to compute the mean and median value is simple and among basic blocks. Thus, this method is really effective in terms of processing time and implementation.

3.2 Auto exposure

The proposed AE method addresses image capturing systems that employ CMOS image sensor and that have limited capabilities. According to (Liang et al., 2007) and (Kuno et al., 1998), the relationship between the luminance value and the exposure factors can be expressed as:

$$Bl = k \times L \times G \times T \times (F/\#)^{-2} \tag{1}$$

where Bl is the brightness level of the captured image, k is a constant, L is the luminance of the ambient light, G is the gain of the automatic gain control, $F/\#$ is the aperture value, and T is the integration time.

This basic equation is used in combination with Bl_{mean}, Bl_{med}, D_L, and D_{thres} to enhance the proposed modified AE algorithm.

Let Bl_n and Bl_{opt} denote the brightness levels of the current frame and the frame taken with optimal exposure time. For a certain scene and when both frames are taken continuously within a very short time, L and G remain almost the same. For most cell phones and surveillance cameras employing CMOS technologies, the aperture is fixed at its maximum value, thus $F/\#$ is constant. The exposure function (1) for the current frame and the frame taken with optimal exposure time are:

$$Bl_n = k \times L \times G \times T_n \times (F/\#)^{-2} \tag{2}$$

$$Bl_{opt} = k \times L \times G \times T_{opt} \times (F/\#)^{-2} \tag{3}$$

where T_n and T_{opt} are the current and optimal integration time values.

By dividing (2) by (3), the relationship between Bl_n and Bl_{opt} can be expressed as:

$$\frac{Bl_n}{Bl_{opt}} = \frac{k \times L \times G \times T_n \times (F/\#)^{-2}}{k \times L \times G \times T_{opt} \times (F/\#)^{-2}} \tag{4}$$

$$[Bl_n / Bl_{opt}] = [T_n / T_{opt}] \tag{5}$$

$$\log_2 Bl_n - \log_2 Bl_{opt} = \log_2 T_n - \log_2 T_{opt} \tag{6}$$

$$\log_2 T_{opt} = \log_2 T_n - \log_2 Bl_n + \log_2 Bl_{opt} \tag{7}$$

The proposed algorithm uses Bl_{mean} to control AE based on the idea of mid-tone in an iterative way. The mid-tone idea assumes that the optimal exposure value should be around 128 which is the middle value of the range [0, 255]. However, unlike (Liang et al., 2007), in this paper, the optimal brightness level is not fixed. Bl_{opt} may be changed according to the lighting conditions. Besides, since the camera response is not totally linear, the actual values in each condition are obtained by performing a series of experiments. A lot of pictures were taken under different lighting conditions in order to obtain the most suitable optimal values of Bl_{opt} for normal lighting, back lighting or high contrast lighting conditions, and lighting conditions when the current picture is over exposed. These optimal values are expected to be close to the mid-tone value 128, which means that the values of $\log_2 Bl_{opt}$ should be close to $\log_2 128=7$.

Let Bl_{opt}^{norm} denote the optimal brightness level in the case of normal-lit conditions with low exposure time, Bl_{opt}^{bkdr} denote the optimal value in the case of back lighting or high contrast lighting conditions with low exposure time, and let Bl_{opt}^{over} denote the optimal value in the case of over exposure.

In real implementation, (7) is convenient for data to be stored in look-up tables (LUT). The values of Bl_{mean}, Bl_n, and T_n all reside in the range [0..255], which means that there are only 256 possible values for each of these variables. Therefore, for each variable, a LUT can be used to store the corresponding logarithm value of each possible value. Other operators in (7) are just simple additions and subtractions which consume little hardware and processing time. The mid-tone range Bl_{mt} is [100, 130]. After capturing the first frame, the values of Bl_{mean} and Bl_{med} are calculated and are used to decide the value of Bl_{opt} as described in Fig. 4. After this stage, the optimal exposure time is obtained using (7). Note that due to the non-linearity of sensors, this mechanism is supposed to be carried out iteratively until Bl_{mean} falls into Bl_{mt}. Different appropriate values of Bl_{opt} help reduce the number of iterations instead of just one common Bl_{opt} for all lighting conditions.

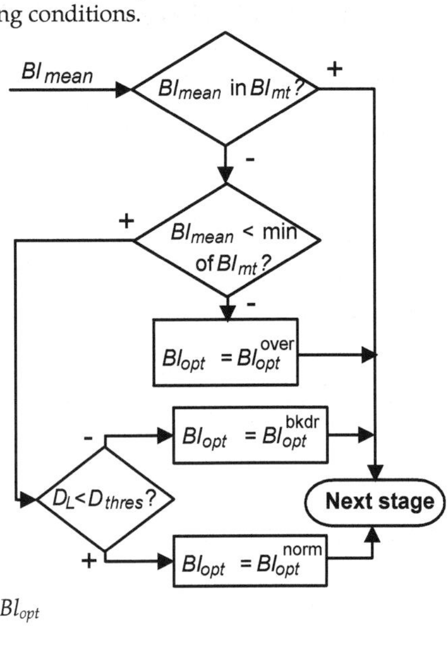

Fig. 4. Deciding value for Bl_{opt}

4. Multiple exposure

Multiple exposure is supposed to enhance the details of an output picture by fusing multiple images of the same scene taken at different exposures. In general, multiple image fusion is really difficult to implement in terms of both complexity and speed. Image fusion also barely provides good enough quality. The main reason is image fusion involves in only luminance signal control since this mechanism is based on images of different exposure values. It is therefore hard to estimate the relationship between the luminance and the chromatic channels which is required to maintain good and real colors in the fused output image. So far it is well-known that only human eyes can do all these functions the best and in a really miracle way. Several multiple exposure algorithms have been introduced but in most cases, they tend to increase hardware cost and decrease color performance.

For low end camera systems, multiple exposure would not be a good choice due to those above reasons. The solution is to equip them with better sensors that have better dynamic range. However, this would also increase the cost. On the contrary, one more reason that limits multiple exposure performance is that existing algorithms don't consider lighting conditions when fusing images. In order to overcome those problems and make multiple exposure applicable to low end systems, this paper proposes a simple algorithm taking into account the lighting condition. The general idea of multiple exposure is described in Fig. 5. Note that the modified Bl_{mt} is [90, 130] and is slighly different from standard Bl_{mt}.

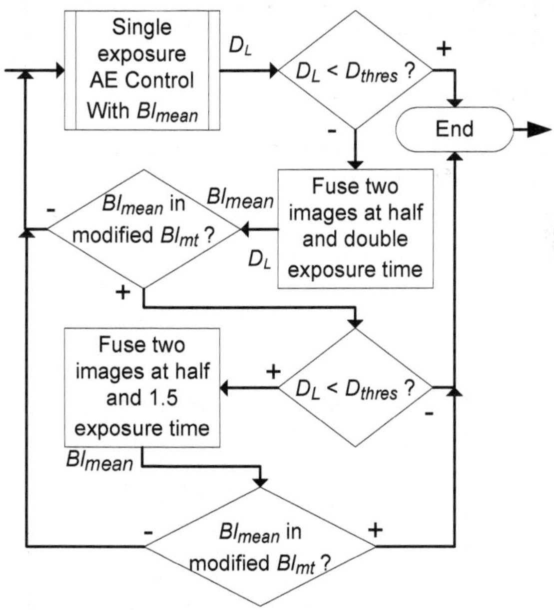

Fig. 5. Multiple exposure algorithm

The two images are simply fused together as follows:

$$F_X(x,y) = (F_X^{lo}(x,y) + F_X^{hi}(x,y)) / 2 \tag{8}$$

where $F_X(x, y)$ is the color value of the pixel (x, y), X is either R, G, or B component, *lo* is low exposure and *hi* is high exposure. This step includes just one basic function, which is simple and easy to implement.
The multiple exposure mechanism can bring more details to dark areas and over-exposed areas. The frame taken with a lower exposure time provides details; on the other hand, the frame taken with a higher exposure time brightens the fused image.
This multiple exposure mechanism is also important to lighting condition estimation. By judging the difference values between the mean and median brightness values of an image before and after fusion, the degree of high contrast lighting can be revealed as excessive back lighting (back lighting) or just high contrast lighting.

5. Simulations

Simulations were carried out using a simple platform employing CMOS image sensors (CIS) with parameter values as follows:

$D_{thres} = 20$ $\log_2 Bl_{opt}^{norm} = 6.8$ $\log_2 Bl_{opt}^{bkdr} = 7$

$\log_2 Bl_{opt}^{over} = 6.36$ $Bl_{mt} = [100,130]$ Modified $Bl_{mt} = [90:130]$

Fig. 6 illustrates results of the stage of automatic exposure including the multiple exposure function since this function helps decide accurately lighting conditions. All lighting conditions were addressed during evaluation. According to Fig. 6, in the case of high dynamic range scenes, only after one image fusion can the system decide if the picture is just high contrast lit or excessive back-lit.
Simulation results show that the proposed AE algorithm can detect lighting conditions accurately and does not require much computation. Furthermore, the algorithm is independent from the position of the light source and can work well with images with or without a main object.
Because of the non-linear characteristics of CMOS sensors, sometimes it requires that the AE algorithm be iterated more than once since the first calculated exposure value does not return a value in the range of Bl_{mean} in Bl_{mt}. Therefore, the overall AE mechanism may include more than one adjusting time.
Tables 2 - 4 demonstrate simulation results for all cases of lighting conditions. Both Y channel (luminance component in the YCbCr format) and G channel are observed. Simulation results show that G component can be used as the luminance of an image without any significant difference. Furthermore, the lighting condition of each scene is correctly detected as its real condition. In most cases, the number of times the AE mechanism is iterated is less than two. This indicates that the proposed algorithm provides a high accuracy rate and fastens the overall performance.
Table 2 describes simulation results of back-lit conditions. The values of D_L after AE controlling and after fusion show that fused images provide more details than un-fused ones. This ability is very useful for camera systems that employ CMOS image sensors with limited dynamic range.
In Table 3, scenes possessing high dynamic range (HDR) conditions are evaluated. After AE controlling, the multiple exposure mechanism is carried out twice. The values of D_L also indicate that fused images provide more details than un-fused ones.

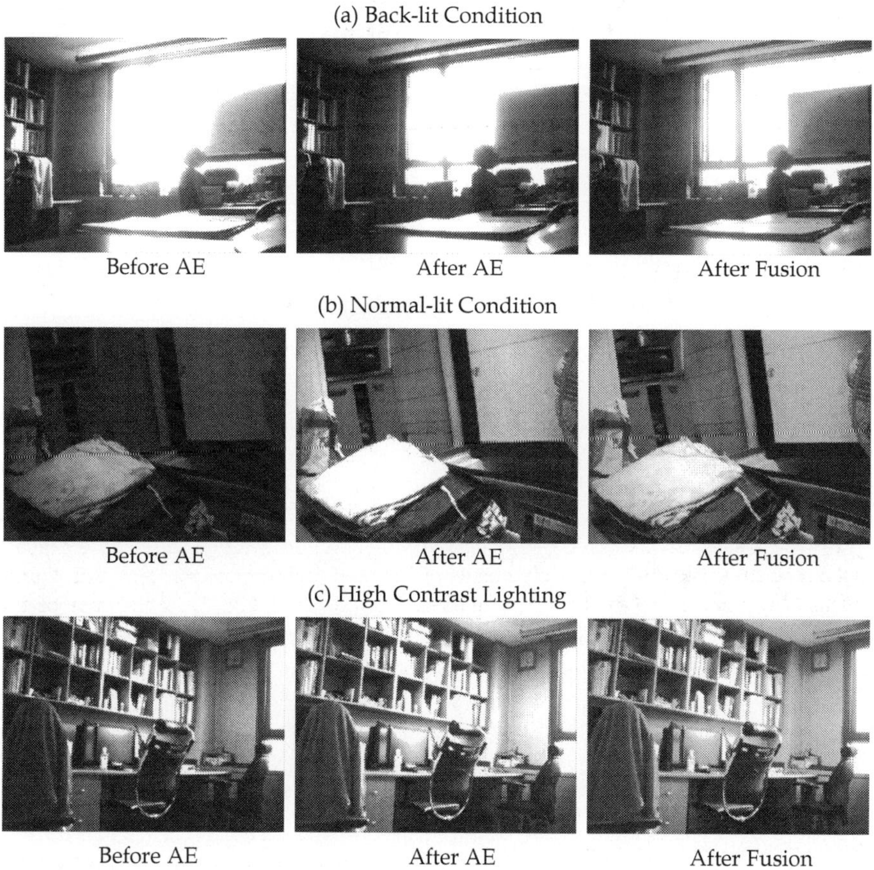

Fig. 6. Simulations with AE algorithm

Scene	Starting Values		Times	After AE			After Fusion		
	Bl_n	D_L		D_L	Bl_n Y	Bl_n G	D_L	Bl_n Y	Bl_n G
(1)	156	8	1	40	118	116	27	123	122
(2)	130	27	1	42	107	104	29	115	112
(3)	160	-6	1	39	121	121	22	121	120
(4)	173	-78	2	39	111	111	24	114	114
(5)	87	49	1	45	115	114	31	119	117

Table 2. Evaluation of back-lighting conditions

Table 4 describes simulation results of images taken in normal-lit conditions. The simulation also shows further values of these pictures after fusing using two images taken at half and 1.5 times the optimal exposure time. These experiment results indicate that this multiple exposure mechanism can also provide more details in output images for surveillance systems.

Scene	Starting Values		Times	After AE			After Fusion		
				D_L	Bl_n		D_L	Bl_n	
	Bl_n	D_L			Y	G		Y	G
(1)	84	22	2	21	120	120	12	109	109
(2)	22	13	2	32	106	100	19	112	105
(3)	77	29	2	25	115	114	13	107	106
(4)	169	-33	2	30	117	116	19	111	111
*(5)	37	15	1	45	121	112			

Table 3. Evaluation of high contrast lighting conditions

*night scene taken with the system's maximum exposure value; thus no fusion was carried out after AE.

Scene	Starting Values		Times	After AE			After Fusion		
				D_L	Bl_n		D_L	Bl_n	
	Bl_n	D_L			Y	G		Y	G
(1)	79	-3	1	-11	117	115	-14	110	109
(2)	82	14	1	14	105	104	8	99	99
(3)	8	3	3	15	109	106	8	99	98
(4)	40	11	1	15	107	111	9	101	104
*(5)	3	1	1	0	42	39			

Table 4. Evaluation of normal lighting conditions

*night scene taken with the system's maximum exposure value.

The proposed algorithm was also applied on a hi-end digital still camera (DSC) in combination with a computer-based software for experiments. Eventhough the CCD of the DSC has a much better dynamic range than the CIS, this method still improved the ability of estimating lighting conditions as well as details of output pictures. Simulations were carried out with the same scene but under different lighting conditions to illustrate the performance of the algorithm as depicted in Fig. 7 and Fig. 8. In the case of normal-lighting (Fig. 8b), the built-in and the proposed mechanisms introduced relevant outputs in terms of exposure and details.

Evaluations were performed under the condition of no flash for better comparisons. Although the proposed algorithm can only slightly improves the performance of the DSC, it still helps estimate lighting conditions accurately.

6. Conclusion

A new AE algorithm with lighting condition detecting capability has been introduced. The proposed architecture mainly addresses platforms employing CMOS Image Sensor, most of which have limited capabilities. However, the new and simple method for estimating lighting conditions is also widely applicable to other hi-end platforms.

The proposed algorithm can quickly estimate an appropriate exposure value after a small number of frames. It can also improve the accuracy and enhance the details of output images, owing to the simple multiple exposure mechanism.

Using the new mechanism to detect lighting conditions, the system is flexible and can work well with most images without being affected by the positions of light sources and main objects. Since the algorithm is not computationally complicated, it can be fitted in most CMOS platforms that have limited capabilities such as cell phones and/or surveillance cameras.

Before AE $Bl_{mean} = 73$
$Bl_{med} = 23$
$D_L = 50 > D_{thres}$

After AE $Bl_{mean} = 104$
$Bl_{med} = 62$
$D_L = 42 > D_{thres}$

After Fusion $Bl_{mean} = 106$
$Bl_{med} = 69$
$D_L = 37 > D_{thres}$

DSC Auto Mode $Bl_{mean} = 75$
$Bl_{med} = 25$
$D_L = 50$

Fig. 7. Back-lighting/excessive lighting condition with DSC

In the future, the multiple exposure method should be further improved so that no luminance cast is introduced and the degree of lighting conditions can be more precisely estimated. Furthermore, besides AE, there are two other important ISP functions: AF, and AWB. Future research would focus on implementing these two functions such that the relationship between the mean and the median values of each color channel can be further exploited, thus the resource and the result of AE stage can be re-used to reduce the computing time and the hardware required.

7. References

Kao, W. C.; Hsu, C. C.; Kao, C. C. & Chen, S. H. (2006). Adaptive exposure control and real-time image fusion for surveillance systems. *Proceedings of IEEE Int. Symposium on Circuits and Systems*, vol. 1-11, pp. 935-938, Kos, Greece, May 2006.

Kuno, T.; Sugiura, H. & Atoka, M. (1998). A new automatic exposure system for digital still cameras. *IEEE Trans. Consum. Electron.*, vol. 44, pp. 192-199, Feb. 1998.

Lee, J. S.; Jung, Y. Y.; Kim, B. S. & Ko, S. J. (2001). An advanced video camera system with robust AF, AE, and AWB control. *IEEE Trans. Consum. Electron.*, vol. 47, pp. 694-699, Aug. 2001.

Fig. 8. High dynamic range and normal-lighting conditions with DSC

Liang, J. Y.; Qin, Y. J. & Hong, J. L (2007). An auto-exposure algorithm for detecting high contrast lighting conditions. *Proceedings of the 7th Int. Conf. on ASIC*, vols. 1 and 2, pp. 725-728, Guilin, Peoples R. China, Oct. 2007.

Murakami, M. & Honda, N. (1996). An exposure control system of video cameras based on fuzzy logic using color information. *Proceedings of 5th IEEE Int. Conf. on Fuzzy Systems*, vols 1-3, pp. 2181-2187, Los Angeles, Sep. 1996.

Shimizu, S.; Kondo, T.; Kohashi, T.; Tsuruta, M. & Komuro, T. (1992). A new algorithm for exposure control based on fuzzy logic for video cameras. *IEEE Trans. Consum. Electron.*, vol. 38, pp. 617-623, Aug. 1992.

16

Security Architecture for Sensitive Information Systems

Xianping Wu, Phu Dung Le and Balasubramaniam Srinivasan
Monash University
Australia

1. Introduction

The use of information has become a pervasive part of our daily life; we have become "... an information society" (Gordon & Gordon, 1996). Employees use information to make personal choices and perform basic job functions; managers require significant amounts of it for planning, organizing and controlling; corporations leverage it for strategic advantage. Since the application of computers in administrative information processing began in 1954 (Davis & Olson, 1985), computers have become a key instrument in the development of information processing. The rapid development of information technology (IT) has helped to firmly establish the general attitude that information systems are a powerful instrument for solving problems.

Utilizing these emerging technologies, however, is not without problems. People start considering their sensitive information when it is transmitted through open networks; managers begin worrying about using forged information for business plans; and corporations worry about customer and investor confidence if they fail to protect sensitive information. Protecting sensitive information has consequently become a top priority for organizations of all sizes.

Despite this priority, the majority of existing sensitive information systems (Bacon & Fitzgerald, 2001; Bhatia & Deogun, 1998; Hong et al., 2007) focus on performance and precision of data retrieval and information management. A number of techniques are employed to protect information systems; however, in many cases, these techniques are proving inadequate. For example, while several information systems (Beimel et al., 1999; Cachin et al., 1999; Gertner et al., 1998; Gertner et al., 2000) use the add-ons security features to provide information confidentiality (which allow users to share information from a data media while keeping their channel private), these security measures are insufficient.

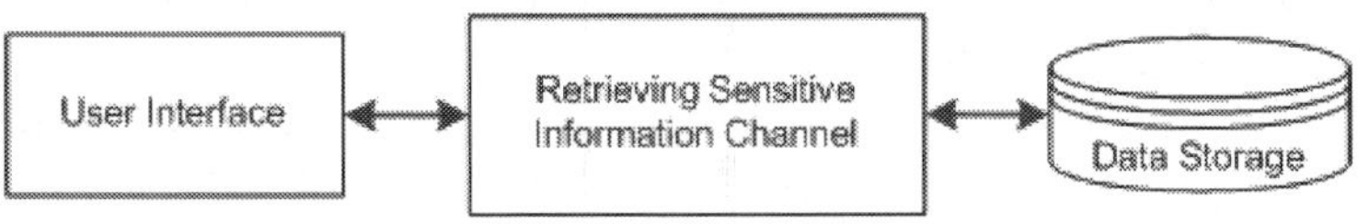

Fig. 1. The Architecture of Generic Sensitive Information Systems

As shown in Fig.1, generic sensitive information systems consist of - *communication channel*, *user interface* and *sensitive information storage* - three major components, and they are all potential targets for adversaries wanting to benefit from security weaknesses. Therefore, in following sections, existing approaches, main issues and limitations relating to sensitive information protection are investigated.

1.1 Related work and limitations

According to the process of sensitive information retrieving, several security aspects need to be studied. Firstly, securing *communication channel,* it applies cryptography and security tunnels to protect message between entities. Secondly, securing *user interface,* it uses authentication mechanisms to prevent unauthorized access to sensitive information. Thirdly, securing *sensitive information storage,* it uses cryptographic keys to encrypt all sensitive information before storing it.

1.1.1 Securing communication channel

In cryptography, a confidential channel is a way of transferring data that is resistant to interception, but not necessarily resistant to tampering. Conversely, an authentic channel is a way of transferring data that is resistant to tampering but not necessarily resistant to interception (Tienari & Khakhar, 1992). Interception and tampering resistance is best developed through communication channel.

In order to reach the interception resistance goal, all communication is scrambled into ciphered text with a predetermined key known to both entities to prevent an eavesdropper from obtaining any useful information. In order to achieve the tampering resistance goal, a message in a communication is assembled using a credential such as an integrity-check to prevent an adversary from tampering with the message.

In this section, the different approaches of securing communication channel are investigated, and their pros and cons are evaluated. The investigation is conducted by subdividing *communication channel* into unicast channel and multicast channel

Secure Communication in Unicast Channels: With the recent development of modern security tools to secure bidirectional communication between two entities, many protocols, such as Internet Protocol Security (IPsec) (Atkinson, 1995), Secure Sockets Layer (SSL), Transport Layer Security (TLS) (Dierks & Rescorla, 2008; Freier et al., 1996) and Secure Real-time Transport Protocol (SRTP) (Lehtovirta et al., 2007), have been proposed in the literature to address the problems and challenges of a secure unicast *communication channel.* One of the most important factors in unicast *communication channel* protection is the cryptographic key. The issues of key distribution and key type, therefore, determine the security of the unicast communication channel.

IPsec and SSL/TLS are the most famous, secure and widely deployed among all the protocols for protecting data over insecure networks. IPsec is a suite of protocols for protecting communications over Internet Protocol (IP) networks through the use of cryptographic security services. It supports network-level peer authentication, data origin authentication, data integrity, data confidentiality (encryption), and replay protection. However, in IPsec, communication is protected by session keys, and the security of a session key is guaranteed by long-term shared keys. Therefore, once the long-term keys are compromised, the security of IPsec is under threat. As Perlman and Kaufman (2001) indicated, IPsec is vulnerable to dictionary attack, due to the pre-shared long-term keys, and Ornaghi and Valleri (2003) demonstrated it in a BlackHat conference.

Moreover, in IPsec, the long-term shared keys involve into key exchange protocol to generate session keys. According to information entropy (Gray, 1990), the uncertainty of key materials decreases when the use of the key materials in generation session keys is frequent. This leads to the key materials (that is, the long-term shared keys) being exposed.

SSL/TLS are cryptographic protocols that provide security and data integrity for unicast communications over insecure networks to prevent eavesdropping, tampering, and message forgery by employing pre-shared master secret (long-term shared key). That the master secret remains truly secret is important to the security of SSL/TLS. However, in the protocol design, the usage of master secret involves multiple phases, such as session key generation, certificate verification and cipher spec change (Wagner & Schneier, 1996).

On the top of the above concerns, the SSL/TLS protocols suffer from different types of flaws (Micheli et al., 2002): identical cryptographic keys are used for message authentication and encryption, and no protection for the handshake, which means that a man-in-the-middle downgrade attack can go undetected. Although a new design of SSL/TLS overcomes a few flaws, as (Bard, 2004; Wagner & Schneier, 1996) state, an attacker can use plaintext attacks to break SSL/TLS protocols due to the long-term shared identical cryptographic keys.

Secure Communication in Multicast Channels: As group-oriented communication systems become more widespread, sensitive information confidentiality is an issue of growing importance for group members. To achieve confidential communication in a multicast channel, cryptographic keys are employed to secure the multicasted contents. The keys (or the group key) must be shared only by group members. Therefore, group key management is important for secure multicast group communication. In modern group key management - Logical Key Hierarchy (LKH) (Harney & Harder, 1999), One-way Function Tree (OFT) (Sherman & McGrew, 2003), Iolus (Mittra, 1997) - for sensitive information systems requires group keys to have a number of characteristics: group key secrecy, backward secrecy, forward secrecy and group key independency. In addition, modern management also requires flexible and efficient rekeying operations and privacy for group members (Kim et al., 2004).

However, Challal and Seba (2005) imply that the major problems of group key management are confidentiality, authentication and access control. Also, there are no solutions to dedicate privacy protection for group members and confidentiality for sensitive information systems. Moreover, when a user joins a group, the new group keys are unicast to the user encrypted by a pre shared long-term key. It raises risks of sensitive information systems associated with the compromise of the long term key.

1.1.2 Securing user interface

The common security mechanism to protect *user interface* in sensitive information systems is authentication. Authentication is "the process of confirming or denying a user's claimed identity, which can be proved by knowledge, possession and property factors" (Meyers, 2002). This form of security uses measures such as security tokens (something users have), passwords (something users know) or biometric identifiers (something users are).

Kerberos (Steiner et al., 1988) is a representative knowledge factor based authentication protocol which allows individuals communicating over a non-secure network to prove their identity to one another in a secure manner. In the original design of Kerberos, session keys exchange used long-term shared keys. Although researchers (Erdem, 2003; Harbitter & Menascé, 2001; Sirbu & Chuang, 1997) proposed the use of public key cryptography to enhance security for key exchange and authentication, the long-term shared key is still a limitation of Kerberos-based information systems (Kohl et al., 1994). In 2008, Cervesato et al. (2008) pointed out that man-in-the-middle attack can breach Kerberos-based information systems.

Other authentication factors based authentication protocols suffer security threats when the physical devices (security tokens and smart card) are lost or stolen or the biometric sources (fingerprint and retinal pattern) are compromised. Moreover, privacy is another concern; how biometrics, once is collected, can be protected.

By briefly investigating the extant authentication approaches in sensitive information systems, there is no proper technique to protect *user interface* in the process of sensitive information retrieving. Moreover, the extant authentication approaches are not able to manage dynamic group member authentication and authorization while allowing individuals to share their sensitive information without sacrificing privacy.

1.1.3 Securing sensitive information storage

Data encryption is a security mechanism to protect sensitive information at rest. It depends on a long-term shared key to cipher all critical information at rest (*sensitive information storage*). For example, IBM employs symmetric keys in z/OS to protect the sensitive information documents, and uses public keys to wrap and unwrap the symmetric data keys used to encrypt the documents. With this technique, IBM claims that many documents can be generated using different encryption keys (Boyd, 2007).

Similar mechanisms are also used for Oracle Database and Microsoft SQL Server, which conduct critical information protection via long-term shared keys. The security of the IBM mechanisms relies on public key infrastructure; if the public key pairs are disclosed, no matter how many different encryption keys are used to protect information, the whole information system will be compromised. In addition, the security of Oracle and Microsoft mechanisms depend on a long-term database master key; the sensitive information may be revealed if the database systems are breached.

It can be seen that no technique can ensure privacy protection, and also that the security of those techniques relies on long-term keys and public keys. Also, none of the existing approaches to protecting information storage can manage dynamic ownership of sensitive information (for example, in the case that a user loses the asymmetric key in z/OS or that the ownership of sensitive information is changed in a database).

1.1.4 Summary

Sensitive information systems consist of three major components: *communication channel, user interface* and *sensitive information storage*; the protection of these three components equates to the protection of sensitive information itself. Previous research in this area has been limited due to the employment of long-term shared keys and public keys. Currently, no complete security solution exists to help protect sensitive information in the three components. Issues such as dynamic sensitive information ownership, group authentication and authorization and privacy protection also create challenges for the protection of sensitive information systems.

In response to these limitations, we therefore propose a novel security architecture for sensitive information systems to tackle the problems and challenges.

1.2 Organization of the chapter and contributions

The rest of the chapter is organized as follows: Section 2 proposes formal security architecture for sensitive information systems. Section 3 details the components of the proposed secure architecture. Section 4 gives a formal and thorough security analysis and discussion of the components. Section 5 concludes and provides future researcher directions.

Contributions: This research contributes to the development of the body of knowledge surrounding sensitive information protection. Its contributions include the following:

- Formal definition and cryptographic properties proofs of dynamic keys
  This thesis offered a first formal definition of dynamic keys with the following proved cryptographic properties: dynamic key secrecy, former key secrecy, key collision resistance and key consistency. The formal definition and the cryptographic properties can also be used as a guide to design new dynamic key generation algorithms. More importantly, the formal definition gives a distinct semantic notion to distinguish dynamic keys from other cryptographic keys, such as session keys, one-time pad and long-term keys.
- A new proposed security architecture for sensitive information systems
  This research proposed a novel security architecture by the employment of dynamic key and group key theories to overcome the security threats and concerns of sensitive information systems in the components of *communication channel, user interface* and *sensitive information storage*. The architecture can be applied to security applications all sectors, including the business, healthcare and military sectors, to protect sensitive information.

As a result of these contributions, we claim that the proposed security architecture for sensitive information systems protects *communication channel, user interface* and *sensitive information storage*. The architecture provides strong authentication and authorization mechanisms to conduct dynamic membership of groups and individuals to share or access sensitive information. It also prevents legal users accessing unauthorized sensitive information against internal security threats. The architecture achieves strong protection for sensitive information at rest in order to overcome security threats that compromise credentials of information systems. Furthermore, it is able to handle dynamic information ownership. Finally, the proposed architecture achieves privacy protection and includes a feature to detect and prevent intrusion.

2. Security architecture for Sensitive Information Systems (SecureSIS)

2.1 Dynamic key theory

A dynamic key is a single-use symmetric key used for generating tokens and encrypting messages in one communication flow. Each key is a nonce, which stands for number used once (Anderson, 2001). The use of dynamic keys introduces complications, such as key synchronization, in cryptographic systems. However, it also helps with some problems, such as reducing key distribution and enhancing key security. There are three primary reasons for the use of dynamic keys in sensitive information protection.

First, securing sensitive information by using long-term symmetric keys makes sensitive information systems more vulnerable to adversaries. In contrast, using dynamic keys makes attacks more difficult. Second, most sound encryption algorithms require cryptographic keys to be distributed securely before enciphering takes place. However, key distribution is one of the weaknesses of symmetric key algorithms. Although asymmetric key algorithms do not require key distribution, they are, in general, slow and susceptible to brute force key search attack. This situation can be improved by using asymmetric key algorithms once only to distribute an encrypted secret. Dynamic keys can then be generated based on the secret and other key materials. This process can improve the overall security considerably. Last, but not least, security tokens can be generated by either long-term symmetric keys or nonce dynamic keys. Even though both methods generate variational tokens every time, the dynamic key method is more difficult to break than the long-term key method.

In accordance with the primary reasons for using dynamic keys in sensitive information protection, it is necessary to have an unambiguous and formal definition. The notion of a one-way function (Menezes et al., 1996) is used for reference. This is defined as "... a function f such that for each x in the domain of f, it is easy to compute $f(x)$; but for essentially all y in the range of f, it is computationally infeasible to find any x such that $y = f(x)$." Formally, a function $f:\{0,1\}^* \rightarrow \{0,1\}^*$ is one way if, and only if, f is polynomial time computable, and for any probabilistic polynomial time algorithm A, the probability that A successfully inverts $f(x)$, for random $x \in_R \{0,1\}^{|x|}$, is negligible (Talbot & Welsh, 2006). Therefore, dynamic keys can be defined as follows:

Definition 2.1 (Dynamic Keys) Dynamic keys $DK = \{dk_i \mid i \in N\}$ are synchronously offline generated by a special one-way function $f(.)$ in two entities P and Q based on a form of pre-shared secret (s). Concisely:

$$DK = \{f^i(forms\ of\ s) \mid i \in \mathbb{N}\} \tag{1}$$

where,

$$\forall x, y(x \neq y), \neg(\exists f^i(x) = f^i(y)) \tag{2}$$

The special one-way function dynamic key generation scheme (Kungpisdan et al., 2005; Li & Zhang, 2004) has been proposed. However, the formal proofs have never been given; consequently, having formally defined dynamic keys, the cryptographic properties of dynamic keys are discussed and proved.

One of the most important security requirements of dynamic keys theory is key freshness. This means a generated dynamic key must be guaranteed to be new and able to be used only once. Furthermore, a dynamic key should be known only to involved entities. Therefore, four important security properties of dynamic keys (dynamic key secrecy, former key secrecy, key collision resistance and key consistency) are given.

Suppose that a set of dynamic keys is generated n times and the sequence of successive dynamic keys is $DK = \{dk_1, dk_2, ..., dk_n\}$ and $f(.)$ is a special one-way function to generate DK. The properties are:

Theorem 2.1 (Dynamic Key Secrecy) Dynamic key secrecy guarantees that it is computationally infeasible for an adversary to discover any dynamic key $\forall i \in \mathbb{N}, dk_i \in DK$.

Proof: From the definition it is apparent that the key generation algorithm is a one-way function. The dynamic key generation function therefore inherits the properties of the one-way function with the consequence that "for any probabilistic polynomial time algorithm A, the probability that A successfully inverts $f(x)$, for random $x \in_R \{0,1\}^{|x|}$, is negligible". Thus, it is computationally infeasible for an adversary to discover any dynamic key. □

Theorem 2.2 (Former Key Secrecy) Former key secrecy ensures that an adversary, who knows a contiguous subset of used dynamic keys (say $\{dk_0, dk_1 ... dk_i\}$), cannot discover any subsequent dynamic keys dk_j, where dk_j is the newest generated and $i < j$.

Proof: Assuming n dynamic keys, let B_i denote the event of selecting a dynamic key from dynamic key i (dk_i). Notice that $\sum_{i=1}^{n} B_i$ form a partition of the sample space for the experiment of selecting a dynamic key. Let A denote the event that the selected dynamic key is compromised. Therefore, based on Bayes' rule, the probability that dk_j is compromised is $Pr(B_j \mid A) = \frac{Pr(B_j)Pr(A \mid B_j)}{\sum_{i=1}^{n} Pr(B_i)Pr(A \mid B_i)}$. According to the argument in the proof of Theorem 2.1, it is computationally infeasible for an adversary to discover any dynamic key. In other words, given a fresh dynamic key dk_j, the probability of this key being compromised is $Pr(A \mid B_j) = 0$, and $Pr(B_j \mid A) = 0$. Even if a contiguous subset of used dynamic keys becomes known, the security of subsequent fresh keys will not be affected. □

Theorem 2.3 (Key Collision Resistance) Key collision resistance means that given a dynamic key generation algorithm, $f(.)$, and two initial seeds, S_X and S_Y ($S_X \neq S_Y$), the probability of key collision is negligible.

Proof: Let λ be the probability of dynamic key collision with two different initial seeds. The probability of no key collision can then be characterized by a Poisson Distribution (Scheaffer, 1994): $Pr(y) = \frac{\lambda^y}{y!} e^{-\lambda}, y = 0,1,2....$ Where $y = 0$, no key collision event can occur and we have $Pr(0) = \frac{\lambda^0}{0!} e^{-\lambda} = e^{-\lambda}$. Since $f(x)$ is a special one-way function, then the probability of $Pr(0)$ converges towards 1 and $\lambda \approx 0$. The value is negligible and completes the proof. □

Theorem 2.4 (Key Consistency) Key consistency guarantees to produce sequential, consistent, dynamic keys DK, if given the same $f(.)$ and an initial seed.

Proof: Given the same $f(.)$ and an initial seed, two entities P and Q can generate one set of dynamic keys. Let B denote the event of having distinct initial seeds for two entities. $\overline{B}$ is the complement of B, which has same initial seeds for both entities. Let A denote the event of producing the same output under $f(.)$. From Theorem 2.3, the probability of the two distinct inputs, S_X and S_Y, and the $f(.)$ producing the same output is negligible. The probability of producing the same output by a given $f(.)$ and two distinct seeds therefore converges towards 0. Hence, $Pr(B \mid A) \approx 0$. Since $\overline{B}$ is the complement of B, according to additive and multiplicative rules of probability, we have $Pr(A) = Pr(AB) + Pr(A\overline{B})$. Thus, $Pr(\overline{B} \mid A) = 1 - Pr(B \mid A)$. It follows $Pr(\overline{B} \mid A) \approx 1$. Therefore, given the same seeds and $f(.)$, the two entities can generate the same set of dynamic keys. □

2.2 Security architecture

Security architecture (SecureSIS) consists of four "tangible" components: dynamic key management (DKM) , user-oriented group key management (UGKM) (Wu et al., 2008b), authentication and authorization management (AAM) (Wu et al., 2009) and sensitive information management (SIM) (Wu et al., 2008a), and two "intangible" components: security agreement (SA) and security goals (Goals). DKM is the security foundation of

SecureSIS. It manages dynamic keys for other components to secure *communication channel*, *user interface* and *sensitive information storage* in the process of sensitive information retrieving.

In SecureSIS, two sets of dynamic keys are employed for engaging users (U) to protect their sensitive information and privacy. One is dynamic data key set DK_X, which is used to integrate with (encrypt) sensitive information at rest. Another is dynamic communication key set DK_Y, which is used to secure communication and generate tokens for authentication. In addition, there is no sensitive information at rest for "tangible" components. Hence, only one set of dynamic keys (component dynamic keys) conducts the security of communication channel among components.

UGKM is a membership management in SecureSIS. It is a novel hybrid group key management approach to govern dynamic membership and protect user privacy and multicast communication secrecy. Together with DKM, unicast communication channel for individuals and multicast communication channel for group members are protected.

AAM manages authentication and authorization for individuals and group members to protect user interface. The employment of DKM and UGKM makes the AAM secure and flexible to deal with group authorization, individual privacy protection.

SIM uses dynamic data keys to integrate with sensitive information at rest in order to protect sensitive information storage. It guarantees the breach of SIS does not have negative impact on the security of sensitive information itself. Also, SIM manages sensitive information ownership by applying UGKM to ensure the utility of sensitive information.

SA component guarantees the security of sensitive information in SecureSIS, if, and only if the sensitive information satisfies the agreement.

Goals component is security expectations of SecureSIS. According to the process of sensitive information retrieving, this component consists of user interface's goal, communication channel's goal and sensitive information storage's goal.

In order to protect sensitive information (called ***I***), the security architecture, SecureSIS, can be characterized as follows:

Definition 2.2 (SecureSIS) Security architecture is defined as a union of the following sets:

$$SecureSIS = [U, AAM, UGKM, SIM, DKM, SA, Goals] \quad (3)$$

where,

i. U is a set composed of engaged users who require sensitive information ***I***.
ii. AAM is a set of authentication and authorization management objects for verifying U and allowing U to delegate authorization in order to protect *user interface*.
iii. UGKM is a user-oriented group key management object for providing secure *communication channel* in order to secure ***I*** sharing among subsets of U.
iv. SIM is a set of sensitive information management objects for protecting *sensitive information storage*.
v. DKM is a set of dynamic key management objects for providing and managing dynamic keys of U, AAM, UGKM and SIM.
vi. SA stands for the security agreement associated with ***I***. It is a notional inner relationship between U and ***I***.
vii. Goals represents security goals of architecture regarding ***I*** protection.

To illustrate the conceptual architecture based on the definition of SecureSIS, AAM, UGKM, SIM and DKM can be thought as "tangible" objects to protect ***I***. These objects are therefore components of SecureSIS architecture. In addition, SA and Goals are "intangible", thus, the tangible conceptual architecture is illustrated in Fig. 2.

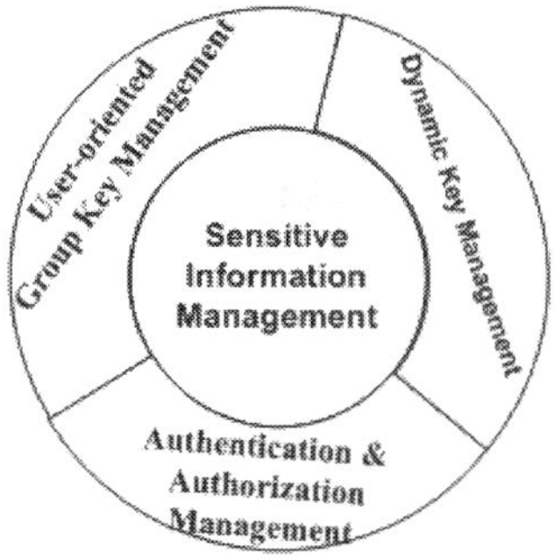

Fig. 2. Tangible Conceptual Architecture of SecureSIS.

The set of engaged users, U, is a key component in SecureSIS. Every user owns or shares sensitive information. To protect sensitive information, the security of each single user needs to be scrutinized. In order to protect the privacy of each individual, U is classified into two categories: passive users, ω, and active users, ϖ. Passive user is inert and infrequently joins and leaves the system. In SecureSIS, ω does not share its own sensitive information with others, but accesses the sensitive information of ϖ. Active user is vigorously and frequently joins and leaves the system. ϖ needs to share sensitive information with ω therefore, it needs high privacy protection. Meanwhile, by a request, ω can be transformed into ϖ and vice versa ($\omega \cap \varpi = \varnothing$).

SecureSIS is split into several administrative areas. Each area has a local secure group controller (LSGC) associated with a subgroup to manage ***I*** sharing and accessing. The controllers together constitute a multicast group (UGKM) that maintains group key consistency by exchanging group information dynamically and securely. The communication structure of SecureSIS is shown in Fig.3.

In SecureSIS, the SA is the "contract" that governs the relationships between sensitive information ***I*** and owners (U) in a secured transaction (for example, information accessing and sharing). The SA classifies sensitive information into a number of levels following information classification, and then assigns access rules to each information object.

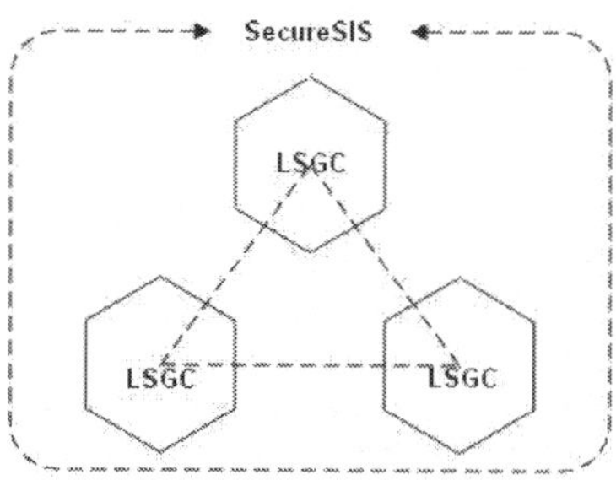

Fig. 3. The Structure of SecureSIS.

When designing security architecture for sensitive information systems, sensitive information protection is the primary consideration. Sensitive information must be stored safely (*sensitive information storage*), transmitted securely (*communication channel*) and made available only to authenticated and authorized (*user interface*) users. Such desires can be defined as security goals of SecureSIS.

User Interface's Goal (UIG): Sensitive information must only be disclosed to legitimate users with proper permissions and genuine sensitive information systems.

Communication Channel's Goal (CCG): Sensitive information must be identically maintained during transmission via open networks.

Sensitive Information Storage's Goal (SISG): Sensitive information must be stored securely and satisfy the requirement that only privileged users can understand and retrieve the information.

3. Security architecture components

3.1 Dynamic Key Management (DKM)

The reason for the employment of two sets of dynamic keys is that dynamic data keys are only used to integrate into sensitive information at rest (encryption), and dynamic communication keys are used only for token generation and commination protection. The two sets of dynamic keys are independent. According to the single-use nature and cryptographic properties of dynamic keys, the breach of one set of dynamic keys does not compromise the security of SecureSIS. Formally:

Definition 3.1 (Dynamic Key Management) Dynamic keys management is a quadruple $[DK_X, DK_Y, CDK, G(.)]$, where:

i. DK_X is a set composed of dynamic data keys $\{dk_{Xi} \mid i \in \mathbb{N}\}$ of users for securing sensitive information storage. Given $u_n \in U$, the dynamic data key set for user u_n is:

$$DK_X = \{dk_{Xi}.u_n \mid i \in \mathbb{N}\} \tag{4}$$

ii. DK_Y is a set composed of dynamic communication keys of users for protecting user interface and communication channel. Given $u_n \in U$, the dynamic communication key set for user u_n is:

$$DK_Y = \{dk_{Yj}.u_n \mid i \in \mathbb{N}\} \tag{5}$$

iii. CDK is a set composed of dynamic keys of each components for securing communication between DKM and AAM & SIM. Given $aam_m \in AAM, dkm_k \in DKM \text{ and } sim_n \in SIM$, the component dynamic key set for aam_m, dkm_k and sim_n is $\{cdk_i.aam_m \mid i \in \mathbb{N}\}$, $\{cdk_j.sim_n \mid i \in \mathbb{N}\}$ and $\{cdk_l.dkm_k \mid i \in \mathbb{N}\}$, respectively.

iv. $G(.)$ is a dynamic key generation scheme. It generates dynamic keys synchronously with U and other components in SecureSIS.

In order to make good use of dynamic key properties, the following agreements apply:

- For users, a user sharing DK_X and DK_Y with SecureSIS does not necessarily mean that the user has registered and is legitimate.
- For users, dynamic data keys do not involved in any communication. The keys are strictly used to wrap and unwrap sensitive information only.

- For both users and "tangible" objects, dynamic communication keys are used to generate security tokens and encipher communications.
- For objects, dynamic communication keys of users are generated via DKM, and transmitted securely via dynamic communication keys of objects.
- For both users and objects, a network failure caused by asynchronous dynamic communication keys will trigger a network fault heal event (Ngo et al., 2010). The event can be performed via negotiating dynamic key counters $\{Yj \mid j \in N\}$.

3.2 User-oriented Group Key Management (UGKM)

Every user in SecureSIS is managed via this component, and it applies a hierarchical structure to secure multicast communication channel. It is a top-down structure and consists of a root, subgroups (SG), clusters (C) and leaves (associated with users U).

The passive users ω are initially aggregated into clusters, at the upper level, called subgroups. Each cluster selects one of its members as the cluster leader to be the representative. The active users ϖ cannot join clusters, but virtual clusters. Each virtual cluster is a virtual container to accommodate involved ω and ϖ. When an active user joins, a member (passive user) of a closed cluster forms a virtual cluster under the same subgroup node. The member (passive user) is called virtual leader for the virtual cluster. The component is characterized as follows:

Definition 3.2 (User-oriented Group Key Management) User-oriented group key management is a septuple $[\omega, \varpi, C, VC, L, VL, Alg(U)]$, where:

i. VC (virtual cluster) is a set composed of virtual containers to accommodate involved ω and ϖ. An active user can only join (belong to) one virtual cluster; however, a passive user can belong to a subset of virtual clusters, such that,

$$
\begin{aligned}
&\forall \varpi_i \in \varpi, \exists! vc_j \in VC : \varpi_i \in vc_j \\
&\forall \omega_i \in \omega, \exists \, at\ least\ one\ vc_j : \omega_i \in \bigcup_{j \in N} vc_j
\end{aligned}
\tag{6}
$$

ii. L (leader) is a set composed of leaders $L \subset \omega$ for authentication as representatives of clusters, used in AAM.
iii. VL (virtual leader) is a set composed of virtual leaders $VL \subset \omega$ for constructing virtual clusters and managing key operations.
iv. $Alg(U)$ is a suite of algorithms that manages U join and leave rekeying operations.

3.2.1 Key tree structure

As discussed in Section 1.1.1, since the drawbacks of the existing multicast communication channel approaches. The UGKM scheme must guarantee privacy protection for group members and confidentiality for sensitive information systems. It must also be suitable for groups with a large number of members. Therefore, UGKM is a two-tier hybrid group key management that focuses on privacy protection and confidentiality of sensitive information. Fig.4. depicts the logical structure of UGKM.

UGKM is divided into two levels: the passive user level (key tree distribution scheme) and the active user level (contributory group key management scheme). The passive user level consists only of passive users who participate in sensitive information sharing and accessing of other active users. As mentioned in Section 2.2, if a passive user wants to share its

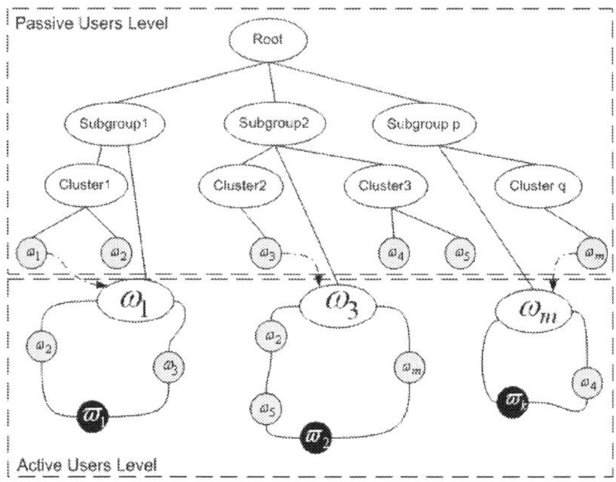

Fig. 4. Logical Structure of UGKM

sensitive information, the user must transform into an active user. When an active user joins the system, one of passive users will be promoted to leader to construct a dynamic virtual cluster under the subgroup.

3.2.2 Member join

In SecureSIS, users are categorized into passive and active users. Also, active users can only join virtual clusters. Therefore, there are three scenarios: an active user joins the system, a passive user joins a cluster and a passive user joins an existing virtual cluster.

Active User Joins. When an active user (ϖ_1 in Fig. 5) wishes to join the group, it applies the active user level key distribution agreement. Since a new virtual cluster is created, it does not need backward secrecy and the join procedure starts with an active user join request:

i. First, ϖ_1 contacts a LSGC, and the LSGC forwards the request to AAM for authentication via a secure unicast channel.
ii. After successful verification, one of the passive users (say ω_1) is selected as a leader. Then ω_1 constructs a dynamic virtual cluster $vc_i \in VC$ that connects all relevant members (say ω_2, ϖ_1 and ω_3).

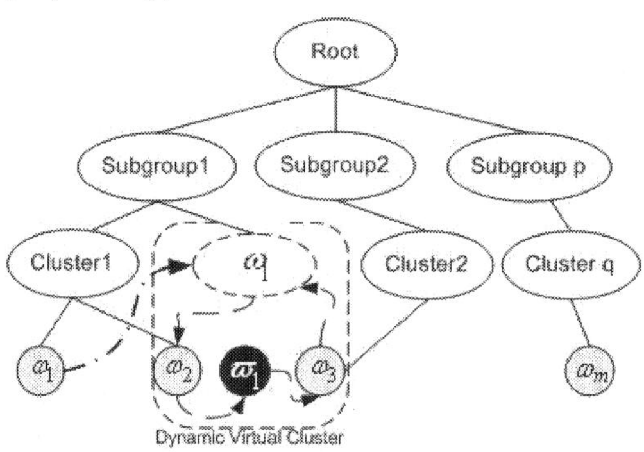

Fig. 5. User Join.

iii. All members of vc_i then start to contribute secrets and generate a virtual cluster key. The key is synchronized with a LSGC for sharing sensitive information among members based on virtual cluster key generation algorithm.

When an active user joins, a new virtual cluster is created and a virtual cluster key is contributed by all group members. The passive user (leader) has all relevant group keys and the LSGC knows the new virtual cluster key. Consequently, the rekeying operation does not take place. In other words, an active user join action does not affect whole group, and the virtual cluster leader takes responsibility for sensitive information forwarding.

Passive User Joins Cluster. When a passive user (for example, ω_m in Fig. 5.) wants to join the group, it applies the passive user level key distribution agreement. Backward secrecy must be guaranteed to prevent the new member from accessing previous group communications. The join procedure starts with passive user join request:

i. First, ω_m contacts the nearby LSGC, and the LSGC forwards the request to AAM for authentication via a secure unicast channel.
ii. After successful verification, the LSGC updates group keys for backward secrecy and unicast the new group keys for ω_m encrypted by the dynamic communication key of ω_m.

Passive User Joins Existing Virtual Cluster. If a passive user (ω_m in Fig. 5.) wants to join an existing virtual cluster, it needs to apply contributory group key management. For backward secrecy, the old virtual cluster key must be replaced with new contributed key:

i. First, ω_m contacts the nearby LSGC and the LSGC forwards the request to AAM for authentication via a secure unicast channel.
ii. After successful verification, a new virtual cluster key is generated by the leader and ω_m via the virtual cluster key generation algorithm.
iii. Once the new virtual cluster key is generated the leader broadcasts the new keys in the virtual cluster and informs the LSGC.

No matter whether the joining user is active or passive, if the user wishes to join a virtual cluster, contributory group key management is applied. Therefore, no rekeying operation occurs. To protect the privacy of active users, when a passive user wants to join an existing virtual cluster, the passive user needs access permission from the active user in the virtual cluster.

3.2.3 Member leave

Similar to the join operation, there are three scenarios for the member leave operation: an active user leaves the system, a passive user leaves the system or a passive user leaves an existing virtual cluster.

Active User Leaves. Suppose an active user (ϖ_1 in Fig. 5) wants to leave the system. It does not need forward secrecy, because virtual clusters are containers for active users. When the active user leaves, the virtual cluster is destroyed.

Passive User Leaves Cluster. If a passive user (for example, ω_m in Fig. 5) wants to leave cluster, it needs to apply a passive user level key distribution agreement. Forward secrecy must be guaranteed to prevent the leaving user from accessing future group communications. The leave operation begins with a passive user leave request:

i. First, ω_m sends a leave request to the LSGC.

ii. Upon receipt, the LSGC triggers a key update for other group members and unicasts new group keys to the involved cluster users with their dynamic communication keys.

Passive User Leaves Existing Virtual Cluster. If a passive user (for example, ω_3 in Fig. 5) wants to leave the virtual cluster, the virtual cluster will not be destroyed (which is the case should an active member leave). However, to ensure backward secrecy, the virtual cluster key needs to be updated. This action does not affect other group members.

i. First, ω_3 sends a leave request to the leader ω_1. ω_1 removes ω_3 from the member list and then updates LSGC.
ii. The LSGC then triggers the virtual cluster key generation algorithm to generate a new virtual cluster keys with existing members in the virtual cluster.

Passive users leaving several virtual clusters at the same time follow the procedure for this algorithm. However, when the passive user wants to leave the system, the procedure will apply group key tree management. Because the passive user does not "provide" sensitive information for virtual cluster members, the passive user does not have any impact on the virtual cluster. For forward secrecy, only a new virtual cluster key is required.

3.2.4 Periodic rekeying operation

The periodic rekeying operation is a process to renew group keys in the system for security purposes. It does not relate to either join or leave key operations. After a period of time, the group keys become vulnerable to key compromise and cryptanalysis attacks. This operation helps the system to reduce those risks. Because active users know virtual cluster keys rather than group keys, the periodic rekeying operation applies to passive users only.

3.3 Authentication and authorization management

Authentication and authorization are two interrelated concepts that form the security component of *user interface*. This component conducts security by co-operating with UGKM and DKM. It can be characterized as follows:

Definition 3.3 (Authentication and Authorization Management AAM) Authentication and authorization management is a quadruple $[U, EID, Proto, v(u_i, eid_j)]$, where:

i. EID is a set composed of enciphered identities for all registered users U.
ii. Proto is a set composed of protocols for authenticating the legitimacy of U and allowing U to delegate authorization in SecureSIS. (It consists of Initialization, Logon and AccessAuth, a suite of protocols).
iii. $v(u_i, eid_j)$ is a verification function that associates a Boolean value with a user $u_i \in U$ and an enciphered identity $eid_i \in EID$. Such checking defines the legitimacy of a user u_i with regard to the eid_j.

3.3.1 Initialization protocol

For every user registered in the system, the LSGC generates a unique random identity associated with the user. Separate from dynamic keys management, the unique identity generation takes place only in the LSGC. Given $aam \in AAM$ (an authentication and authorization management object) and $dkm \in DKM$ (a dynamic key management object), the protocol is described as follows:

i. A user $u_i \in U$ registers with the system, *dkm* generates a unique random identity id_i for the user u_i and two unique random secrets. (The two unique secrets are secretly distributed to the user u_i for generating dynamic communication keys and dynamic data keys.)

ii. *dkm* uses the hash value of the first dynamic communication key and index i of the user to encipher the unique number as eid_i. Precisely:

$$EDI = \bigcup_{i=1}^{N} \{id_i\}h(i, dk_{Y0}.u_i) \tag{7}$$

The generation of id_i can be varied depending on the security requirement. As suggested, multi-factor authentication provides stronger security for *user interface*. Therefore, we suggest that the id_i can be formed by a combination of a biometrics factor (fingerprint or DNA sequence), a possession factor (smart card) or a knowledge factor (passwords).

3.3.2 Logon protocol

Logon protocol is used as a first security shield to protect sensitive information systems. Once a user successfully verifies with a LSGC, the user is able to request and join a group. In other words, before joining a group, a user must be authenticated as a legitimate user. The protocol is depicted as follows:

i. First, a user sends a request to $aam \in AAM$, $\{logon\_request, h(i, dk_{Y(j-1)}.u_i)\}dk_{Yj}.u_i$.

ii. After understanding the received packet, *aam* uses $h(i, dk_{Y(j-1)})$ as a key K to decipher eid_i. If, and only if, the enciphered value is same as id_i, then the user is legitimate, and the user can make further requests, such as to join a group or to access sensitive information.

iii. Subsequently, *aam* sends back a challenge to verify itself to the user.

iv. When the user leaves the system, the current dynamic communication key of the user is used to generate a new key $K' = h(i, dk_{Y(j+n)}.u_i)$, and produce a new eid_i' to replace the old eid_i, where n is a natural number, indicating the number of messages performed by the user in the system ($eid'_i \leftarrow \{\{eid_i\} \sim K\}K'$).

3.3.3 AccessAuth protocol

The AccessAuth protocol offers an authentication and authorization mechanism for sensitive information sharing among groups and users. It enables privacy protection whereby owners can take full control of their sensitive information. The protocol also manages group-to-group, group-to-individual, individual-to-individual and individual-to-group authentication and authorization.

Before depicting the protocol, participant classification is given to clarify that participant p_m and p_n can be either a group or an individual. Formally:

Definition 3.4 (Participant Classification PC) PC is a triple, $[P, T, \varsigma]$, where P is a set of participant objects and T is an enumeration of $\{single, group\}$, and $\varsigma : P \rightarrow T$ is the participant classification mapping.

When the classification type is $T: single$, P acts as an individual user $P \subseteq U$. When type is $T: group$, P is representative of a cluster $c_i \in C \cup VC$ where $P \subseteq L \cup VL$. In other words, P is a leader of c_i (a cluster or a virtual cluster). The protocol is described as follows:

i. p_m generates a token $h(I_n\_request, dk_{Y(j-1)}.p_m)$ and sends it together with a request (sensitive information of p_n) to the LSGC. Note that if p_m has the status of $T: group$, the p_m will be the representative (leader) of a group.
ii. After understanding the request and verifying the token, aam in the LSGC checks for permission based on the security agreement (SA) of sensitive information.
iii. After obtaining the token and query from aam, p_n can delegate permissions on each selective portion of information according to the query and generate a new token $h(I'_n\_response, dk_{Yj}.p_n)$. This token is sent back in the response message to aam to be ciphered by the next dynamic communication key.
iv. When aam receives and verifies the token from p_n, p_m is able to retrieve the sensitive data. If p_m has the status of $T: single$, the sensitive information will be unicast to p_m, otherwise, the sensitive information is multicast to the group and encrypted by the group key (either a cluster key or a virtual cluster key).

3.4 Sensitive information management

One of the most important technological challenges, that sensitive information systems facing today, is keeping sensitive content secure when it is shared among internal and external entities. In this component, dynamic keys are used to integrate with sensitive information ***I*** in order to help guard against the unauthorized disclosure of ***I***. The sensitive information is stored in a form of cipher (encrypted sensitive information, named EI), in another words, no plaintext is kept in SecureSIS. Also, each ***I*** is encrypted by a different dynamic data key, and all these dynamic data keys are encrypted by current dynamic data key (encrypted dynamic data keys, named EDK). Therefore, only the owner of sensitive information possesses the correct and latest dynamic data key. The privacy of owner thus is maintained in SecureSIS. The SIM component is formally characterized as follows:

Definition 3.5 (Sensitive Information System SIM) Sensitive information management is a quadruple $[RI, CI, EL, f(I)]$, where:

i. RI is a set composed of indices for collected critical information ***I***.
ii. CI is a union of sets of encrypted sensitive information (EI) and encrypted dynamic data keys (EDK), where, EI is produced using dynamic data keys of sensitive information owner u_n, $EI = \bigcup_{i,j \in \mathbb{N}} \{I_j\} dk_{Xi}.u_n, I_j \in I$ and, EDK is generated using current dynamic data keys of sensitive information owner to encrypt the keys used to encipher the information. It can be symbolized as: $EDK = \bigcup_{i,j \in \mathbb{N}} \{\{dk_{Xi}.u_n\} dk_{XC}.u_n, h(EI_j)\}, EI_j \in EI$.

   Meanwhile, $dk_{XC}.u_n$ is a current dynamic data key of u_n. It is specified in order to encrypt and decrypt the dynamic data keys (EDK). The encrypted keys are stored in the header of EI.
iii. EL stands for emergency list; a set of relationship objects O. Each $o_i \in O$ contains a user $u_i \in U$, a nominated cluster $c_n \in C$, an allocated auditing cluster $c_a \in C$ and an encrypted dynamic data key. At the cost of triggering an automatic audit, EL is used in an emergency to gain access to sensitive information ***I*** of users that would normally be inaccessible. $EL = \bigcup_{i \in \mathbb{N}^*} u_i, c_{n \mapsto i}, c_{a \mapsto i}, \{dk_{XC}.u_i\} K_{combine}$, where $K_{combine}$ is a combination key of

leaders l_n and l_a, which represent cluster $c_{n\mapsto i}$ and $c_{a\mapsto i}$ respectively, and $K_{combine} = h(h(n, dk_{Yj}.l_n), h(a, dk_{Yk}.l_a))$.

iv. *f(I)* is a symmetric cryptographic function that employs dynamic data key $dk_{Xi}.u_j$ to encipher/decipher sensitive data *I* and dynamic data keys.

3.4.1 SIM structure

Sensitive information management objects contain encrypted sensitive information and other supportive information. Each record or file of a user is enciphered with different dynamic data keys. Letting $ci_i.u_j \in CI$ be an object of CI, the structure of a SIM object is illustrated as in Fig. 6.

In regard to the architecture of SecureSIS, several administration areas form a multicast group (UGKM) and each area is managed by a LSGC associated with a subgroup. Also, RI, defined in SIM, is a set of indexes for collected sensitive information. The sensitive information of a user can therefore be stored in different SIM objects. In other words, fragmented sensitive information of a user can be transferred from different geographic locations and located by RI.

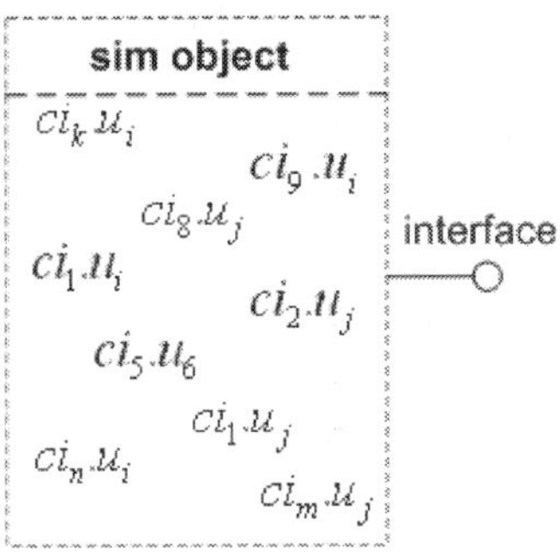

Fig. 6. Structure of a SIM Object.

3.4.2 Dynamic membership operations

When a user registers with the system, the user must agree and choose a trusted participant, either a joined cluster or a nominated cluster. The chosen participant will be added to the emergency list (EL). This confidentiality "overrides" rule allows an authenticated cluster in an emergency to gain access to sensitive information of users which would normally be inaccessible. The rule also solves the problem of information accessibility when a user permanently leaves the system. In other words, dynamic ownership of sensitive information is provided.

Meanwhile, the maintenance of the list EL is important. EL Update is an operation that updates the new nominated cluster or encrypted dynamic data keys to a relationship object $o_i \in O$. There are two events to trigger EL update. First, when a user requests a change of the nominated trust cluster, the system will allocate a new audit cluster and generate a new combination key by leaders of the new nominated cluster and the allocated audit cluster. Second, when the dynamic communication keys of the leaders are changed, the encrypted user dynamic data keys will be updated. The EL update operation ensures the list is up-to-date in order for it to be used for authentication in emergency access situations or when the user permanently leaves.

Emergency Access. It is necessary when a user is not able to authenticate with the system and the user has authorized the nominated cluster as a trust participant. In an emergency circumstance, the user's sensitive information can be accessed via the attendant audit cluster. Given $c_n \in C \cup VC$ as a nominated cluster for user $u_n \in U$ and $c_a \in C$ as an audit cluster, we have $l_n \in c_n$ and $l_a \in c_a$ as a leader of corresponding clusters. For an emergency access, the procedure is described as follows:

i. An emergency access event occurs.
ii. The leader of the nominated cluster sends a request to the system together with a token.
iii. The system looks at the EL and sends a request to the corresponding audit cluster in order to have a response and a token.
iv. After the system gathers two tokens from the nominated and audit clusters, the system will recover user u_n dynamic data key and encipher it with the dynamic communication key of l_n. The sensitive information of user u_n will then be sent to the nominated cluster c_n.

User Permanently Leaves. When a user permanently leaves the system, the user either removes selected owned sensitive information or leaves it as "orphan" information. When orphan information exists in the system, the nominated cluster takes control of the information.

The procedure is the same as in the emergency access procedure steps i-iii. The last step is to use the dynamic data key of the leader l_n to encipher the leaving user's dynamic data keys.

4. Security analysis and discussion on secureSIS

4.1 Security of DKM

Definition 3.1 demonstrates that two sets of dynamic keys are necessary to ensure security when protecting the sensitive information of users. The dynamic communication key set $\{dk_{Yj} \mid j \in \mathbb{N}\}$ protects communication channel and user interface, while the dynamic data key set $\{dk_{Xi} \mid i \in \mathbb{N}\}$ secures sensitive information storage.

Because dynamic keys possess dynamic key secrecy, former key secrecy and key collision resistance properties, a corollary can be made.

Corollary 4.1 Because SecureSIS uses two sets of dynamic keys, even if one set of dynamic keys were to be disclosed, the security of the proposed system would not be compromised.

Proof: Based on mutual information, $I(A;B) = \sum Pr(A;B)\log(\frac{Pr(A;B)}{Pr(A)P(B)})$, if $A = DK_X$ and $B = DK_Y$, then we have $I(DK_X;DK_Y) = \sum Pr(DK_X;DK_Y)\log(\frac{Pr(DK_X;DK_Y)}{Pr(DK_X)P(DK_Y)})$, and, according to key collision resistance, the probability of dynamic keys collision is negligible. In other words, generated two sets of dynamic keys with two independent unique seeds guarantee that DK_X is independent of DK_Y. Hence, according to probability theory, if, and only if A and B are independent, will $P(DK_X;DK_Y) = P(DK_X)P(DK_Y)$. If that is the case, then, we have $I(DK_X;DK_Y) = \sum Pr(DK_X;DK_Y)\log(\frac{Pr(DK_X;DK_Y)}{Pr(DK_X)P(DK_Y)}) = 0$, which is equivalent to saying that one disclosed set of dynamic keys cannot reveal any information about another set of dynamic keys. □

Because a set of dynamic keys has no impact on another set of dynamic keys in DKM, a corollary can be claimed.

Corollary 4.2 The use of two sets of dynamic keys in SecureSIS can achieve intrusion detection and prevention.

Proof: Let A denote an adversary. By observing network traffic, A obtains a subset of used dynamic keys and a number of used tokens. According to dynamic key secrecy and former key secrecy, new dynamic keys are computationally infeasible based on obtained keys and tokens. Should A try to penetrate the system with obtained information, the action will be detected immediately, because dynamic keys can only be used once. In addition, although the actions of A compromise one set of dynamic keys, because of Corollary 4.1, the other set of dynamic keys will still be secure and unaffected. The security of the sensitive information is maintained and the proof is complete. □

4.2 Security of UGKM

Group key secrecy renders the discovery of any group key computationally infeasible for a passive adversary. In UGKM, group keys are generated by the key server (DKM) randomly in the passive user tier; this guarantees group key secrecy. However, in the active user tier, as defined, all active users belong to virtual clusters, and contributory group key management is applied to secure multicasting critical contents. The discussion in Section 3.2 on group keys gives an algorithm that generates virtual cluster keys for all involved members; a corollary can now be devised to show that UGKM also has a group key secrecy feature.

Corollary 4.3 The contributed virtual cluster key is computational infeasible.

Proof: Assume a virtual cluster $vc_n \in VC$ consists of one active user ϖ_m and n-1 passive users $vc_n \in VC, vc_n = \{\varpi_m, involved\sum \omega_i\}$. The virtual cluster key K_{vc} is formed by contributing the intermediate key $ik_i = f(dk_{Y_j}.u_i) \bmod p$ (the dynamic communication key) of each user $u_i \in vc_n$. Let K and IK be virtual cluster keys and intermediate key spaces respectively. Then, if an adversary obtains all intermediate keys $IK = \{ik_i \mid i \in \mathbb{N}\}$, the probability of breaching the contributed K_{vc} is:

$$Pr(K \mid IK) = Pr(K = K_{vc}; IK = ik_1) + Pr(K = K_{vc}; IK = ik_2) + \ldots + Pr(K = K_{vc}; IK = ik_n) \quad (8)$$

Thus we have, $Pr(K \mid IK) = \sum_{i=1}^{n} Pr(K = K_{vc}; IK = ik_i) = \sum_{i=1}^{n} Pr(K = K_{vc} \mid IK = ik_i) Pr(IK = ik_i)$. The contributed secret $dk_{Y_j}.u_i$ has all the cryptographic properties of dynamic keys and the special function $f(.)$ has the property of $\forall x, y (x \neq y), \neg\exists f(x) = f(y)$ (Definition 2.1). Therefore, the probability of generating each intermediate key $ik_i = f(dk_{Y_j}.u_i) \bmod p$ is $\frac{1}{p}$. In other words, the generated intermediate key is uniformly distributed over the interval $[0, p-1]$, and we have $Pr(IK = ik_i) = \frac{1}{p}$. Therefore, Eq. 8 is $\frac{1}{p}\sum_{i=1}^{n} Pr(K = f(ik_1 ... ik_n) \mid IK = ik_i)$.

There are n intermediate keys in vc_n, so, given an intermediate key, the probability of guessing $Pr(K = ik_1...ik_n \mid IK = ik_i) = \frac{1}{n}$. Thus, $Pr(K \mid IK) = \frac{1}{p}\sum_{i=1}^{n}\frac{1}{n} = \frac{1}{p}$. The contributed virtual cluster key $K = K_{vc}$ is therefore uniformly distributed over the interval $[0, p - 1]$. The contributed virtual cluster key is computationally infeasible; the proof is complete. □

Forward secrecy guarantees that knowledge of a contiguous subset of old group keys will not enable the discovery of any subsequent group keys. In other words, forward secrecy prevents users who have left the group from accessing future group communication. Forward secrecy is demonstrated in the active user tier by the member leave operation.

In the active user leave operation, each virtual cluster has only one active user and the existence of the active user determines the existence of the virtual cluster. When the active user leaves the virtual cluster, the cluster is destroyed. Operations involving active users consequently do not need forward secrecy. However, when a passive user leaves an existing virtual cluster, forward secrecy is necessary. As described in Section 3.2.3, a corollary can be made.

Corollary 4.4 Forward secrecy is guaranteed in virtual clusters.

Proof: Suppose ω_n is a former virtual cluster member. Whenever a leaving event occurs as a result of a passive user leaving an existing virtual cluster operation, a new K_{vc} is refreshed, and all keys known to leaving member ω_n will be changed accordingly. The probability of ω_n knowing the new K_{vc} is $Pr(new\ K_{vc} \mid K_{vc})$. According to Corollary 4.3, virtual cluster keys are uniformly distributed. The old K_{vc} and new K_{vc} are therefore independent and we have $Pr(new\ K_{vc}, K_{vc}) = Pr(new\ K_{vc})Pr(K_{vc})$, then $Pr(new\ K_{vc} \mid K_{vc}) = Pr(new\ K_{vc})$. Therefore, the probability of knowing the old K_{vc} and being able to use it to find the new K_{vc} is the same as finding the new K_{vc}. In other words, ω_n has the same level of information of the new virtual cluster key as an adversary. Forward secrecy is satisfied in operations involving virtual clusters; the proof is complete. □

Backward secrecy ensures that a new member who knows the current group key cannot derive any previous group key. In other words, backward secrecy prevents new joining users from accessing previous group content. Backward secrecy is achieved in the active user tier through the member join operation. In the active user join operation, when an active user joins the group, a new virtual cluster is created and consequently there are no previous virtual cluster keys to be taken into consideration; in this situation, backward secrecy is not a concern. However, when a passive user joins an existing virtual cluster operation, backward secrecy needs to be considered. As described in Section 3.2.4, a corollary can be made.

Corollary 4.5 Backward secrecy is guaranteed in virtual clusters.

Proof: Similar as Corollary 4.4.

4.3 Security of AAM

The proposed AAM manages the security of SecureSIS by adopting DKM and UGKM to protect user interface. It allows users to authenticate themselves to have fine-grain control over portions of their critical information. AAM offers secure authentication and flexible authorization for individuals and group members. AAM consists of an Initialization protocol, a Logon protocol and the AccessAuth protocol. In this section, the Logon protocol, as a representative, is examined to show the security in *user interface* protection.

In order to verify the security of each protocol, Spi calculus (Abadi, 1999; Abadi & Gordon, 1997) is used to evaluate the security of AAM. The approach is to test that a process $P(x)$ does not leak the input x if a second process Q cannot distinguish running in parallel with $P(M)$ from running in parallel with $P(N)$, for every M and N. In other words, $P(M)$ and $P(N)$ are indistinguishable for the process Q.

In order to investigate the Logon protocol, the protocol needs to be first abstracted into Spi calculus:

i. $u_i \rightarrow aam:\{logon\_req, h(i, dk_{Y(j-1)}.u_i)\}dk_{Yj}.u_i$ on $c_{ua}, c_{ua} \in C$.

ii. $aam \rightarrow dkm:\{key\_req, i\}cdk_l.aam$ on $v_{ad}, v_{ad} \in V$.

iii. $dkm \rightarrow aam:\{dk_{Yj}.u_i\}cdk_{l+1}.aam$ on $v_{da}, v_{da} \in V$.

iv. $aam \rightarrow u_i:\{logon\_req, h(logon\_req, dk_{Yj}.u_i)\}dk_{Y(j+1)}.u_i$ on $c_{au}, c_{au} \in C$.

It is assumed there are n users and each user has a public input channel (C). Informally, an instance of the protocol is determined by a choice of involved entities. More formally, an instance is a triple *[w,t,I]* such that w and t are entities, such as users and SecureSIS component objects, and ***I*** is a message. Moreover, F is an abstraction representing the behaviours of any entities after receipt of the message from the protocol. Meanwhile, messages between *aam* and *dkm* occur in private communication channels (*V*) (steps ii and iii). The proof is the same as the public communication channels steps i and iv. Therefore, in this discussion, the proof of messages i and iv is given. In the Spi calculus description of the Logon protocol, given an instance (w, t, I), the following process corresponds to the role of users and the LSGC (AAM and DKM).

$$\begin{aligned} Send_{w,t} &\triangleq \overrightarrow{c_{wt}}\langle\{logon\_req, h(w, dk_{Y(j-1)}.u_w)\}dk_{Yj}.u_w\rangle \mid c_{tw}(x_{cipher}).case\ x_{cipher}\ of \\ &\{x, H(y_p)\}dk_{Y(j+1)}.u_w\ in\ let\ (x, y_{nonce}) = y_p\ in\ [x\ is\ logon\_req][y_{nonce}\ is\ dk_{Yj}.u_w]\ in\ F \end{aligned} \tag{9}$$

The process $Send_{w,t}$ describes one entity (users) processing an output message i) in parallel with an input message iv). It is a process parameterised by entities w and t. Formally, we view $Send_{w,t}$ as a function that map entities w and t to processes, called abstractions, and treat w and t on the left of $\triangleq$ as bound parameters. For the process $Recv_t$, it describes one entity (LSGC) processing an input message iv) in parallel with an output message i).

$$\begin{aligned} Recv_t &\triangleq c_{wt}(y_{cipher}).case\ y_{cipher}\ of\ \{x, H(y_p^1)\}dk_{Yj}.u_w\ in\ let(x, y_{nonce}^1) = y_p^1 \\ &in\ [x\ is\ w][y_{nonce}^1\ is\ dk_{Y(j-1)}.u_w] \mid \overrightarrow{c_{tw}}\langle\{logon\_req, h(logon\_req, dk_{Yj}.u_w)\}dk_{Y(j+1)}.u_w\rangle \end{aligned} \tag{10}$$

The processes $Sys(I_1 \ldots I_m)$ describes the whole protocol (message i and iv) with m instances. The channels c_{wt} and c_{tw} are public channels. The processes send a logon request under the dynamic communication key $dk_{Yj}.u_w$ and receive LSGC challenge information under the dynamic communication key $dk_{Y(j+1)}.u_w$. Besides, $(vdk_{Yj}.u_w)$ and $(vdk_{Y(j+1)}.u_w)$ achieve the effect that only entity w and t have the dynamic communication keys. Let $\bigcup_{x \in 1..m} P_x$ be $m-way$ composition $P_1 \mid \ldots \mid P_m$, and $\underline{(vdk_{Yj}.u_{wx})}\underline{(vdk_{Y(j+1)}.u_{wx})}$ stand for $(vdk_{Yj}.u_{w1})\ldots(vdk_{Yj}.u_{wm})(vdk_{Y(j+1)}.u_{w1})\ldots(vdk_{Y(j+1)}.u_{wm})$ we have:

$$Sys(I_1...I_m) \triangleq (c_{wt})(c_{tw})(\underline{vdk_{Yj}.u_{wx}})(\underline{vdk_{Y(j+1)}.u_{wx}})\{\bigcup_{x\in 1..m}(Send_{wx,tx} \mid !Recv_{tx})\} \tag{11}$$

The replication of the receiving processes $\bigcup_{x\in 1..m}!Recv_{tx}$ means that every entity is ready to play the role of receiver in any number of runs of the protocol in parallel. Therefore, the protocol can be simultaneous, even though same entity may be involved in many instances. We now examine one instance of the protocol. Let $\equiv$ be structural equivalence by combining Eq. 9 and 10, we have Eq. 11 rewritten as:

$$\begin{aligned} Sys \equiv\ & (vdk_{Yj}.u_w)(vdk_{Y(j+1)}.u_w)c_{wt}(y_{cipher}).case\ y_{cipher}\ of\{x, H(y_p^1)\}dk_{Yj}.u_w\ in\ let(x, y_{nonce}^1) = y_p^1 \\ & in\ (x\ is\ w)(y_{nonce}^1\ is\ dk_{Y(j-1)}.u_w) \mid \overline{c_{wt}}\left\langle \{logon\_req, h(w, dk_{Y(j-1)}.u_w)\}dk_{Yj}.u_w \right\rangle \mid \\ & c_{tw}(x_{cipher}).case\ x_{cipher}\ of\ \{x, H(y_p)\}dk_{Y(j+1)}.u_w\ in\ let\ (x, y_{nonce}) = y_p \\ & in\ (x\ is\ logon\_req)(y_{nonce}\ is\ dk_{Yj}.u_w)\ in\ F \mid \overline{c_{tw}}\left\langle \{logon\_req, h(logon\_req, dk_{Yj}.u_w)\}dk_{Y(j+1)}.u_w \right\rangle \end{aligned} \tag{12}$$

Based on the reaction relation and reduction relation rules,

$$\begin{aligned} Sys & \mapsto (vdk_{Yj}.u_w)(vdk_{Y(j+1)}.u_w)F(logon\_req, h(logon\_req, dk_{Yj}.u_w), h(w, dk_{Y(j-1)}.u_w)) \\ & \mapsto F(logon\_req, h(logon\_req, dk_{Yj}.u_w), h(w, dk_{Y(j-1)}.u_w)) \end{aligned} \tag{13}$$

The processes have not revealed the information of *logon_req* and tokens. In the Logon protocol, the tokens are generated with the dynamic communication keys of users. According to the cryptographic properties of dynamic keys, the dynamic communication keys of users are equivalent to random numbers as well as the tokens. Consequently, a specification is given by revising the protocol. After applying reaction relation and reduction relation rules, we have $Sys_{spec} \mapsto F(logon\_req, random, random)$. This is equivalent to Sys (noted as $Sys(I_1...I_m) \simeq Sys(I_1...I_m)_{spec}$). In other words, $Sys(I_1...I_m)$ and $Sys(I_1...I_m)_{spec}$ are indistinguishable to an adversary. Thus this protocol has two important properties as proved:

- Authenticity: entity B always applies F to the message that entity A sends, and an adversary cannot cause entity B to apply F to other messages. In other words, $Sys(I_1...I_m) \simeq Sys(I_1...I_m)_{spec}$ for any message.
- Secrecy: The message cannot be read in transit from entity A to entity B, if, and only if F does not reveal the message, then the whole protocol does not reveal the message.

4.4 Security of SIM

The security of SIM is conducted by two sets of dynamic keys. The first set of dynamic keys (dynamic communication keys) is a security shield that is used to protect *communication channel* and *user interface*. The second set of dynamic keys (dynamic data keys) is the security core of SIM. This set only protects *sensitive information storage* and integrates with sensitive information stored in cipher form; it is never involved in the protection of *communication channel* and *user interface*.

According to Section 3.4, SIM offers the following security features:

- Every data entry operation yields different EI.
- Every transaction triggers EDK updates.
- Any data altered results in a new EI and a new set of EDK.

- Only the owner of sensitive data has the correct dynamic key to decipher the data.
- Only in an emergency circumstance is a nominated cluster, overseen by an auditing cluster, able to access the sensitive information of users.
- Any "orphan" sensitive information is managed by a nominated cluster overseen by an auditing cluster.

Intuitively, because the above facts protect sensitive information in storage, it would appear that sensitive information is secure and protected, even should the storage be breached. Therefore, a corollary can be made.

Corollary 4.6 Even if the security of one user is breached in SIM, the security of other users and sensitive information will not be compromised.

Proof: Suppose that S is a sample space possessing enciphered sensitive information. Events $B_1, B_2, \ldots B_n$ partition S, and we have $B_1 \cup B_2 \cup \ldots \cup B_n = S$. Due to SIM security features, the occurrence of events B_i and B_j are independent. Therefore, $B_i B_j = \varnothing$ for any pair i and j. Let B_j denote the event that disclosed information comes from user u_j and $Pr(B_i) > 0, i \in \mathbb{N}$. Let A denote the event that the sensitive information is compromised. According to the conditional probability of compromised information B_j given event A is one, $Pr(B_j \mid A) = 1$. Apply Bayes' law, we have:

$$Pr(B_j \mid A) = \frac{Pr(B_j)Pr(A \mid B_j)}{\sum_{i=1}^{n} Pr(B_i)Pr(A \mid B_i)} \tag{14}$$

and thus,

$$\begin{aligned} Pr(B_j)Pr(A \mid B_j) &= \sum_{i=1}^{n} Pr(B_i)Pr(A \mid B_i) \\ &= Pr(B_1)Pr(A \mid B_1) + Pr(B_2)Pr(A \mid B_2) + \ldots + \\ &\quad Pr(B_j)Pr(A \mid B_j) + Pr(B_{j+1})Pr(A \mid B_{j+1}) + \ldots + \\ &\quad Pr(B_{n-1})Pr(A \mid B_{n-1}) + Pr(B_n)Pr(A \mid B_n) \end{aligned} \tag{15}$$

and then,

$$Pr(B_1)Pr(A \mid B_1) + \ldots + Pr(B_{j-1})Pr(A \mid B_{j-1}) + Pr(B_{j+1})Pr(A \mid B_{j+1}) + \ldots + Pr(B_n)Pr(A \mid B_n) = 0 \tag{16}$$

Since, $\forall Pr(B_i) > 0$, then conditional probability of compromising sensitive information of others is zero. We have $Pr(A \mid B_1) + \ldots + Pr(A \mid B_{j-1}) + Pr(A \mid B_{j+1}) + \ldots + Pr(A \mid B_n) = 0$. Therefore, even when one user is compromised in SIM, the probability of breaching other sensitive information is zero; the proof is complete. □

4.5 SecureSIS goals discussion

Based on the proofs of Theorems 2.1-2.4 and Corollaries 4.1-4.6, the proposed security architecture satisfies the security requirements. By using the theorems and corollaries already presented, in this section, we prove that SecureSIS also meets its intended security goals.

Proof of User Interface's Goal. *User interface* is protected by a combination of AAM, DKM and UGKM. According to the discussion on AAM, any user $\forall u_i \in U$ can prove u_i to

SecureSIS by adopting dynamic communication keys securely. Also, for any sensitive information $\forall I_i \in I$, if the user u_i provides proof to SecureSIS with full permission to I_i, then the user u_i possesses the information. In addition, if user u_i possesses the information, then u_i has full control of it. Moreover, the Logon protocol in AAM, which guarantees that, as long as there is a correlated token (signature), SecureSIS will believe that the action is performed by user u_i. Furthermore, as was discussed in the Logon protocol on AAM a challenge-response message is returned by using the dynamic communication key of user u_i to generate a token in order to verify the genuineness of SecureSIS. According to the cryptographic properties of dynamic keys and the security of AAM, sensitive information is only disclosed to legitimate users with proper permissions and genuine SecureSIS. □

Proof of Communication Channel's Goal. The security of *communication channel* is managed by the use of dynamic communication keys (DKM) and group keys (UGKM). As discussed in Section 3.3.3, it ensures that $\forall u_i \in U$ believes received sensitive information is identically maintained in transit. Using the AccessAuth protocol, every message among entities is assembled with a unique token. Because of the features of DKM and UGKM, the keys needed to protect communication are secure. Every message received by SecureSIS can then be verified. Consequently, we have that sensitive information is identically maintained during transmission via open networks in SecureSIS. □

Proof of Sensitive Information Storage's Goal. The security of *sensitive information storage* is attained by SIM participating with DKM and UGKM. if $\forall u_i \in U$ possesses the information, the user has full control of it. In other words, the user can decipher EI_j. Hence u_i believes possessed sensitive information is genuine in sensitive information storage, and ensures that sensitive information is stored securely and only privileged users can understand and retrieve sensitive information in SecureSIS. □

5. Conclusion and future work

Protecting sensitive information is a growing concern around the globe. Securing critical data in all sectors, including the business, healthcare and military sectors, has become the first priority of sensitive information management. Failing to protect this asset results in high costs and, more importantly, can also result in lost customers and investor confidence and even threaten national security. The purpose of this research was to develop a security architecture able to protect sensitive information systems.

Sensitive information systems consist of three components: *communication channel, user interface* and *sensitive information storage*; the protection of these three components equates to the protection of sensitive information itself. Therefore, this research contributes to the development of the body of knowledge surrounding sensitive information protection. Its contributions include the following:

- Formal definition and cryptographic properties proofs of dynamic keys.
- A new proposed security architecture for sensitive information systems.

This research has opened up avenues for further work. These include i) investigation into the use of dynamic keys for intrusion prevention and detection; and ii) the design and development of new dynamic key algorithms.

This research has presented a security architecture that overcomes the limitations of existing security approaches in protecting sensitive information. The architecture has also

demonstrated the feature of intrusion prevention and detection by the employment of two sets of dynamic keys. This mechanism has yet to be studied formally and systematically. It could be further investigated and proposed as a new component for SecureSIS.
Another direction for future research could involve the design of new cryptographic algorithms in order to enhance the security of sensitive information systems. This current research has enabled the formal definition of dynamic keys and regulated the cryptographic properties of dynamic keys. Future work might involve the testing of these definitions to further demonstrate their appropriateness when guiding the design of new dynamic key generation algorithms.

6. References

Abadi, M. (1999). Secrecy by typing in security protocols. *Journal of the ACM, Vol: 46,* No. 5, pp, 749 - 786. ISSN: 0004-5411

Abadi, M, & Gordon, AD. (1997). A calculus for cryptographic protocols: the spi calculus. *Proceedings of* the *4th ACM conference on Computer and Communications Security,* pp.36-47, ISBN: 0-89791-912-2, Zurich, Switzerland, 1997, ACM, New York

Anderson, RJ. (2001). *Security Engineering: A Guide to Building Dependable Distributed Systems,* John Wiley & Sons, ISBN: 978-0-470-06852-6, New York

Atkinson, R. (1995). *Security Architecture for the Internet Protocol* (No. RFC 1825): Network Working Group, The Internet Engineering Task Force.

Bacon, CJ, & Fitzgerald, B. (2001). A systemic framework for the field of information systems. *ACM SIGMIS Database Vol: 32,* No. 2, pp, 46 - 67. ISSN: 0095-0033

Bard, GV. (2004). *The vulnerability of ssl to chosen-plaintext attack* (No. 2004/111): Cryptology ePrint Archive.

Beimel, A, Ishai, Y, Kushilevitz, E, & Malkin, T. (1999). One-way Functions are Essential for Single-Server Private Information Retrieval. *Proceedings of* the *31st Annual ACM Symposium on Theory of Computing,* pp.89-98, ISBN: 1-58113-067-8, Atlanta, Georgia, USA, 1999, ACM, New York

Bhatia, SK, & Deogun, JS. (1998). Conceptual clustering in information retrieval. *IEEE Transactions on Systems, Man, and Cybernetics, Vol: 28,* No. 3, pp, 427-436. ISSN: 1083-4419

Boyd, G. (2007). IBM Encryption Facility for z/OS. Retrieved 28 April, 2008, from ftp://ftp.software.ibm.com/common/ssi/rep_sp/n/ZSD01450USEN/ZSD01450USEN.pdf

Cachin, C, Micali, S, & Stadler, M. (1999). Computationally Private Information Retrieval with Polylogarithmic Communication, In: *Advances in Cryptology,* J Stern (Ed.), pp. 402-414, Springer Berlin / Heidelberg, ISBN: 978-3-540-65889-4, London, UK

Cervesato, I, Jaggard, AD, Scedrov, A, Tsay, J-K, Christopher, & Walstad. (2008). Breaking and fixing public-key Kerberos. *Information and Computation Vol: 206,* No. 2-4, pp, 402-424. ISSN: 0890-5401

Challal, Y, & Seba, H. (2005). Group Key Management Protocols: A Novel Taxonomy. *International Journal of Information Technology Vol: 2,* No. 1, pp, 105-118. ISSN: 1305-2403

Davis, GB, & Olson, MH. (1985). *Management Information Systems: Conceptual Foundations, Structure, and Development,* Mcgraw-Hill, ISBN: 0070158282, New York

Dierks, T, & Rescorla, E. (2008). *The Transport Layer Security (TLS) Protocol (V1.2)* (No. RFC 5246): Network Working Group, The Internet Engineering Task Force.

Erdem, OM. (2003). High-speed ECC based Kerberos Authentication Protocol for Wireless Applications. *Proceedings of* the *IEEE Global Telecommunications Conference*, pp.1440-1444, ISBN: 0-7803-7974-8, 2003, IEEE, Danvers, MA

Freier, AO, Karlton, P, & Kocher, PC. (1996). *The SSL Protocol (V3.0)*: Transport Layer Security Working Group.

Gertner, Y, Goldwasser, S, & Malkin, T. (1998). A Random Server Model for Private Information Retrieval, In: *Randomization and Approximation Techniques in Computer Science,* M Luby, JDP Rolim & MJ Serna (Ed.), pp. 200-217, Springer Berlin / Heidelberg, ISBN:3-540-65142-X, London, UK

Gertner, Y, Ishai, Y, Kushilevitz, E, & Malkin, T. (2000). Protecting data privacy in private information retrieval schemes. *Journal of Computer and System Sciences Vol: 60,* No. 3, pp, 592-629. ISSN: 0022-0000

Gordon, SR, & Gordon, JR. (1996). *Information Systems: A Management Approach,* The Dryden Press, Harcourt Brace College Publishers, ISBN: 9780471273189, Orlando, Florida

Gray, RM. (1990). *Entropy and Information Theory,* Spinger-Verlag, ISBN: 0-387-97371-0, New York

Harbitter, A, & Menascé, DA. (2001). The performance of public key-enabled kerberos authentication in mobile computing applications. *Proceedings of* the *8th ACM conference on Computer and Communications Security,* pp.78-85, ISBN: 1-58113-385-5, Philadelphia, PA, USA, 2001, ACM, New York

Harney, H, & Harder, E. (1999). *Logical Key Hierarchy Protocol*: Network Working Group, The Internet Engineering Task Force.

Hong, W-S, Chen, S-J, Wang, L-H, & Chen, S-M. (2007). A new approach for fuzzy information retrieval based on weighted power-mean averaging operators. *Computers & Mathematics with Applications Vol: 53,* No. 12, pp, 1800-1819. ISSN: 0898-1221

Kim, Y, Perrig, A, & Tsudik, G. (2004). Tree-based group key agreement. *ACM Transactions on Information and System Security, Vol: 7,* No. 1, pp, 60 - 96. ISSN: 1094-9224

Kohl, JT, Neuman, BC, & T'so, TY. (1994). The Evolution of the Kerberos Authentication System. *Proceedings of* the *Distributed Open Systems,* pp.78-94, ISBN: 0-8186-4292-0, 1994, IEEE Computer Society Press

Kungpisdan, S, Le, PD, & Srinivasan, B. (2005). A Limited-Used Key Generation Scheme for Internet Transactions. *Lecture Notes in Computer Science, Vol: 3325,* No., pp, 302-316. ISSN: 0302-9743

Lehtovirta, V, Naslund, M, & Norman, K. (2007). *Integrity Transform Carrying Roll-Over Counter for the Secure Real-time Transport Protocol (SRTP)* (No. RFC 4771): Network Working Group, The Internet Engineering Task Force.

Li, Y, & Zhang, X. (2004). A Security-Enhanced One-Time Payment Scheme for Credit Card. *Proceedings of* the *14th International Workshop on Research Issues on Data Engineering: Web Services for E-Commerce and E-Government Applications,* pp.40-47, ISBN: 0-7695-2095-2, Washington, DC, USA, 2004, IEEE Computer Society

Menezes, A, Oorschot, PCV, & Vanstone, SA. (1996). *Handbook of Applied Cryptography*, CRC Press, ISBN: 9780849385230, California

Meyers, RA. (2002). *Encyclopedia of Physical Science and Technology*, Academic Press, ISBN: 9780122274107, Michigan

Micheli, AD, Brunessaux, S, Lakshmeshwar, S, Bosselaers, A, & Parkinson, D. (2002). *Investigations about SSL*: MATRA Systèmes & Information, NOKIA Research Centre, K.U.Leuven Research & Development and British Telecommunications.

Mittra, S. (1997). Iolus: A framework for scalable secure multicasting. *Proceedings of* the *ACM SIGCOMM Computer Communication Review*, pp.277-288, ISBN: 0146-4833, New York, 1997, ACM, New York

Ngo, HH, Wu, XP, Le, PD, & Wilson, C. (2010). Dynamic Key Cryptography and Applications. *Journal of Information System Security, Vol: 10*, No. 3, pp, 161-174 ISSN: 1816-3548

Ornaghi, A, & Valleri, M. (2003). Man in the middle attacks Las Vegas, NV,USA: Black Hat.

Perlman, R, & Kaufman, C. (2001). Analysis of the IPSec Key Exchange Standard. *Proceedings of* the *10th IEEE International Workshops on Enabling Technologies: Infrastructure for Collaborative Enterprises, 2001*, pp.150-156, ISBN: 0-7695-1269-0, Cambridge, MA, USA, 2001, IEEE

Scheaffer, RL. (1994). *Introduction to Probability and Its Applications*, Wadsworth Publishing Company, Duxbury Press, ISBN: 0-534-23790-8, Washington

Sherman, AT, & McGrew, DA. (2003). Key Establishment in Large Dynamic Groups Using One-Way Function Trees. *IEEE Transactions on Software Engineering, Vol: 29*, No. 5, pp, 444-458. ISSN: 0098-5589

Sirbu, M, & Chuang, J. (1997). Distributed authentication in Kerberos using public key cryptography. *Proceedings of* the *Network and Distributed System Security*, pp.134-141, ISBN: 0-8186-7767-8, San Diego, CA, USA, 1997, IEEE Computer Society Washington, DC, USA

Steiner, J, Neuman, C, & Schiller, JI. (1988). Kerberos: An Authentication Service for Open Network Systems. *Proceedings of* the *Winter 1988 Usenix Conference*, pp.191-200, Dallas, Texas, 1988,

Talbot, J, & Welsh, D. (2006). *Complexity and Cryptography-An Introduction*, Cambridge Univeristy Press, ISBN: 9780521852319, New York

Tienari, M, & Khakhar, D. (1992). *Information network and data communication*, Amsterdam, Elsevier Science Pub. Co., ISBN: 9780444702142, Espoo, Finland

Wagner, D, & Schneier, B. (1996). Analysis of the SSL 3.0 protocol. *Proceedings of* the *2nd USENIX Workshop on Electronic Commerce*, pp.4-17, Oakland, California, 1996, USENIX Association

Wu, XP, Le, PD, & Srinivasan, B. (2008a). Dynamic Keys Based Sensitive Information System. *Proceedings of* the *9th International Conference for Young Computer Scientists*, pp.1895-1901, ISBN: 978-0-7695-3398-8, Zhang Jia Jie, China, 2008a, IEEE Computer Society

Wu, XP, Ngo, HH, Le, PD, & Srinivasan, B. (2008b). A Novel Group Key Management Scheme for Privacy Protection Sensitive Information Systems. *Proceedings of* the

International Conference on Security and Management, pp.93-99, ISBN: 1-60132-085-X, Las Vegas, Vevada,USA, 2008b, CSREA Press

Wu, XP, Ngo, HH, Le, PD, & Srinivasan, B. (2009). Novel Authentication & Authorization Management for Sensitive Information Privacy Protection Using Dynamic Key Based Group Key Management. *International Journal of Computer Science & Applications, Vol: 6*, No. 3, pp, 57-74. ISSN: 0972-9038

17

A Study on Sensor Node Capture Defence Protocol for Ubiquitous Sensor Network

Yong-Sik Choi and Seung Ho Shin
Dept. of Computer Science and Engineering,
University of Incheon
South Korea

1. Introduction

Ubiquitous computing in being actively researched and one of the main technologies in ubiquitous computing environments is recognized as RFID and Sensor system. The RFID and Sensor system has much benefit but simultaneously has some problems such as user's privacy violation. USN (Ubiquitous Sensor Network) is a key to build ubiquitous computing environment, and it has been drawing attentions. Sensor node collects data through observation or detection as being installed at various places. Sensor node is to be placed at where an attacker can easily access.

This exposure raises the possibility of sensor node capture attach to dig encrypted secret, to change programming or control with ill intention. Thus, this is to study the basis of technology that USN technology can be actualized by drawing and suggesting fragility and requirements in security that can happen in USN, and by suggesting the direction of security service centered on safe key distribution, certification and node capture defense technology.

For the control of key that can be used for the certification of sensor node or encryption of sensed information, the researchers suggest a key control method and security protocol to defend against sensor node capture by applying PKI (Public Key Infrastructure) method to Hash Lock. For the control of key that can be used for the certification of sensor node or encryption of sensed information, the researcher have used MetaID as a secret key by applying PKI method to Hash Lock based on the difficulties in calculating inverse function of one-way hash function. Sensor is certificated by a registered open key (meta ID) and the meta ID creates the only key (k) of each sensor with meta ID = H(k). At this time, H( ) is Hash function. To transmit data safely, transmission node transmits data by encrypting data using link key, and the node that receives the data decodes it with its own secret key. All transmission nodes receive the certification of receiving nodes by transmitting their own data. Distributed secret key is re-encrypted on a regular basis regardless of the loss of key to raise safety and provides resilience against sensor capture.

The composition of this paper is as follows: in the second chapter, USN, Key management technology and Hash Lock Approach as related researches. In the third chapter, the design of security protocol using PKI will be presented. In the fourth chapter, experimental environment will be presented and there will be the conclusion in the final chapter.

2. Related work

2.1 Ubiquitous Sensor Network

USN(Ubiquitous Sensor Network) is a wire and wireless network, which consists of several sensor nodes deployed in a certain field. Sensor node should have the functions of computation, sensing and wireless communication. The number of sensor network is about 10~10,000 and its location is flexible depending on its necessity. Because the price per sensor node is not expensive, it is easy to embody sensor network. As sensor network standardizations, sensor interface standardization (IEEE 1451) and sensor network standardization (802.15.4) are being performed. Especially, ZigBee is characterized by low power and low cost, thus, with 2GHz -based wireless home network, it is possible to connect 255 device within 30m radius in a speed of 250kbs [1], [6].

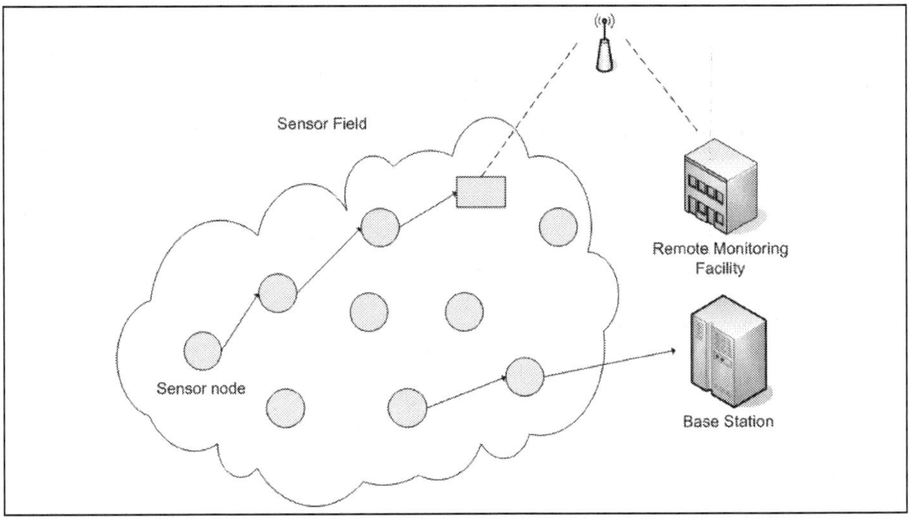

Fig. 1. Ubiquitous Sensor Network Architecture

2.2 Key management

Key control protocol plays the role to construct safe communication infra and to create secret key that are necessary for various security protocols by establishing the reliable relationship between sensor nodes, which are temporarily installed under the condition without reliable sensor or infra [2].

As key control mechanisms, there are pairwise key, random key pre-distribution, public key infrastructure and hierarchical key management [3].

As a shared key in network, pairwiae key is used in encoding and authentification, providing effectiveness and simplification. However, the damage caused by node capture may affect entire network, and thus, additional key renewal protocol is required [3], [4].

Before installation random key pre-distributions receive random number of keys from the previously created key pool. It uses the key if neighboring key and common key exist, but it establishes link key through the connected neighboring node if they do not exist. In this method, depending on the density of sensor network, the entire network may not be entirely connected. Furthermore, because it is a pre-distribution method, it is impossible to provide the newness of key.

Public key infrastructure provides hardware-based public key through the selections of proper algorithm, parameter and optimal embodiment. Although it suggests the application of public key technology in order to distribute low-frequency key, public key-based structure should be established in advance [4], [5].

Hierarchical key management includes hop by hop message encoding / decoding process by the key, which is distributed between nodes in advance according to the characteristic of hierarchical communication structured, suggesting the processing process of sensor addition/deletion. But intermediate node saves key in proportion to the number of child node, it require the capacity to create key. It cannot provide the resilience for sensor capture [3].

2.3 Hash Lock approach

The Hash-Lock approach proposed by Weis et all. Use the concept of locking and unlocking the tag to allow access. The security of the Hash-Lock approach uses the principle based on the difficulty of inverting a one-way hash function. The scheme makes use of a back-end database to provide correct reader to tag identification and the concept of meta-ID stored in each tag. To lock the tag the reader sends a hash of a random key, as the meta-ID, to the tag. i.e. meta-ID<-hash(key). The reader then stores the meta-ID and key in the back end database. While locked, the tag only responds with the meta-ID when queried. As shown in Fig. 2, to unlock the tag, the reader will query the tag for the meta-ID. The reader will then use the meta-ID to lookup a key and ID for the tag in the database. If the meta-ID is found, the reader then sends the key to the tag in an attempt to unlock the tag. The tag hashes the key and compares the results against the meta-ID stored in the tag [2], [3], [6].

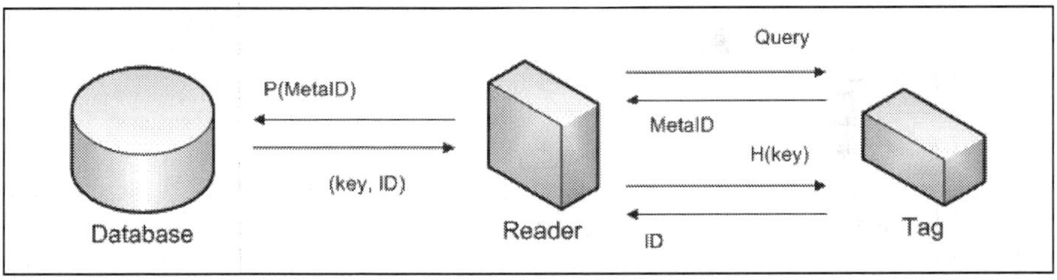

Fig. 2. Hash Locking Protocol

2.4 Hash function algorithm

The Cryptographic hash functions are playing very important roles in modern cryptology, such as checking the integrity of information or increasing the efficiency of authentication code and digital signature. When compared with general hash functions used in non cryptographic computer applications, although both cases are functions from domain to range, they are different from each other in several important aspects. Also, the hash function outputs the value called hash value or have code of fixed length by the input of messages having random length. More strictly, the hash function h correspond text alignment of random length as n bit text alignment of fixed length [5], [7].

When domain is called D and range is called R, the function d h: D -> R(|D| > R) is a many-to-one corresponding function. Accordingly, the collision exists for the hash function in general. For example, assuming function h as the one having input value of t bit and output value of n bit, the number of input values while h has randomness corresponds to each output value. Accordingly, two input values selected at random with probability 2^{-n} comes to have same output value regardless of the t value.

The handling process of most has functions is the repetitive one hashing the input of random length by divided processing of successive fixed blocks. First, the input X becomes padded to become a multiple of block length and divided from X1 to t number of blocks as Xt. The hash function h is described as follows.

$$\begin{aligned} &H_0 = IV \\ &H_i = f(H_{i-1}, X_i), \\ &1 \le i \le t, \\ &h(X) = H_t \end{aligned} \tag{1}$$

Here, f is the compress function), Hi is the chaining variable between i-1 and i, while IV is the initial value. The general structure of repetitive hash function using compressed function is in the Fig. 3.

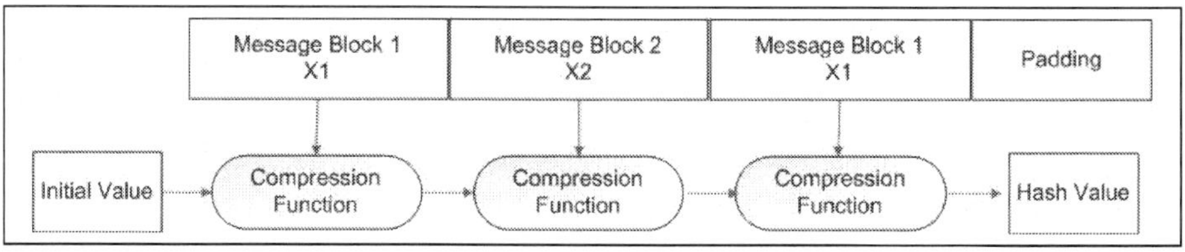

Fig. 3. Structure of the Hash-Function with recurrent

The calculation of hash value is dependent on the chain variable. While starting the hash calculation, this chain variable comes to have the fixed initial value expressed as the part of algorithm. The compressed function renews this chain variable by getting the message block as input until it becomes hashed. This process gets repeated in cycles for all message blocks, and the last value gets output as hash value on the same message. The hash function gets classified into 3 types depending on which structure is used as internal compressed function [8].

1. Hash-Functions based Block Cipher
2. Hash-Functions based Modular Calculation
3. The other Hash-Functions

The exclusive hash function has fast processing speed, and they're the functions specially designed for hashing regardless of other system sub factors. The exclusive hash function proposed until today has the structure based on MD4 designed by Rivest in 1990. There are MD5, SHA-1, RIPEMD-160 and HAVAL for hash functions of MD series being widely used at this time.

When a specific hash function is assigned, although it is ideal to verify the lowest limit on complications attacking the hash function for the establishment of safe hash functions, such method is not known for the most part in reality and the applicable known complication of the attack is considered as the security of hash function for the most part. If hash value is assumed as uniform probability variable, the following are well-known facts.

For the n bit hash function h, the guessing attack to discover preimage and second preimage with 2^n operation. For the attacker that is able to select messages, the birthday attack is able to discover the collision message pair M, Mt with about $2^{n/2}$ operation.
If n bit hash function satisfies the following two characteristics, it serves as an ideal security. Once the hash value is given, the discovery of preimage and second preimage requires 2^n operation.

3. Design of security protocol

In order to transmit data safely, transmission node transmits data by encoding it with link key, and the node that receives data decodes its own secret key. All transmission nodes certify received nodes by transmitting their own data. Distributed secret key is recreated and distributed in a certain cycle regardless of the loss of key.
For the network, which has the recovery power of sensor node capture, it makes copy on network, sends all packets via various independent passes, inspects consistency of the node receiving packet, excludes captured node from network, erases the information contained in sensor, and stops its function if sensor receives the password saved in its own data field.

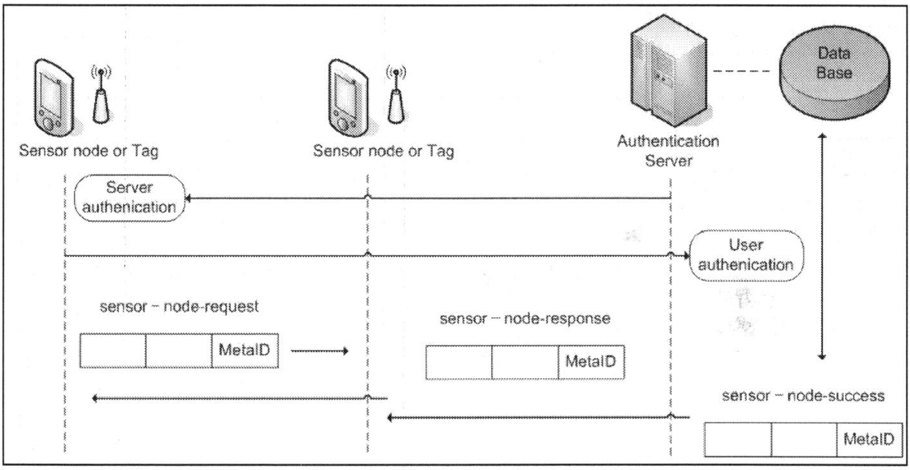

Fig. 4. The security protocol

[Step 1]
Authentication server creates and registers private key and public key using ECC(Elliptic Curve Crypto) about sensor node. Authentication server requires transmission of MetaID packet.
[Step 2]
Sensor node that receipt of message is response sensor-node-response message.
[Step 3]
Reader or sensor node is Authentication key generate by P(MetaID). And send a value.
{sep_ID, P(MetaID)} = Value
[Step 4]
Sensor node is response sensor-node-response packet using hash value.

[Step 5]
Reader or sensor node compare authentication database with receipt value and if value agrees. It is valid sensor node. Transmit key, ID to sensor node.

4. Experimental environment

4.1 Experimental

Implementation controls of Sensor nodes data transmission /reception cycle. The composition of implementation is as follows: Serial communication, node commander, topology view, data log and staticstic view.
Fig. 6 sensor data shows the process. Data created in sensor node is moved through its own routing path and is concentrated on base node. Data of base node is passed on middleware that handles RFID/data of sensor node through serial communication. It is stored to database.

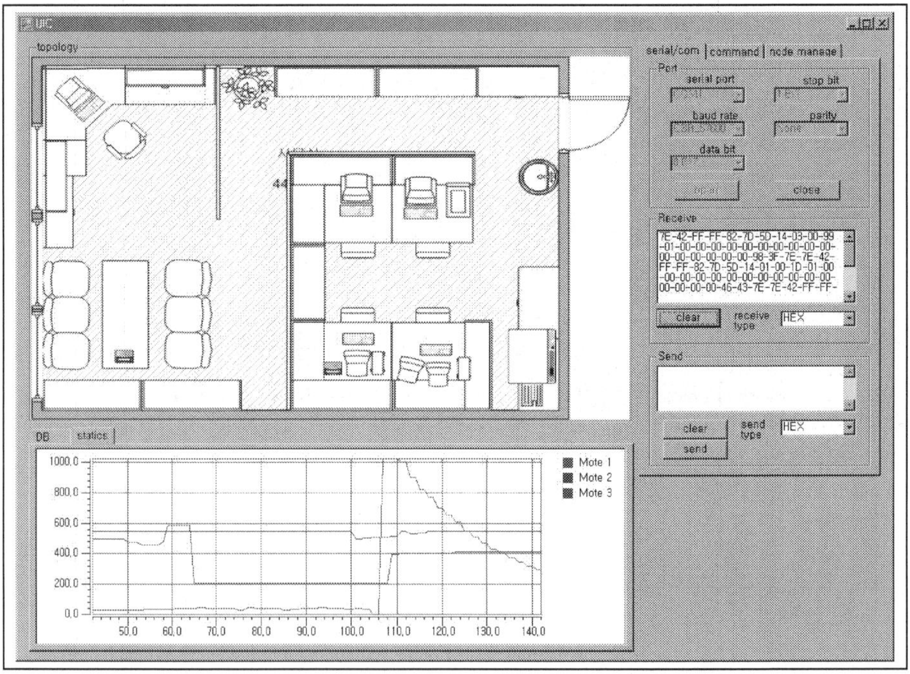

Fig. 5. The implementation architecture

It undergoes filtering to form statistics /analysis module and sensor topology mesh. And then, the user does command in sensor through sensor Commander and changes establishment of sensor.
Fig. 7 shows class diagram. It is RFID/Sensor node data collecting prototype class. For data collecting, we do not consider data pattern escape limit. With Simplex 1:n network satisfied and through application, what is planed is the command with structure simplified to architecture broadcast.

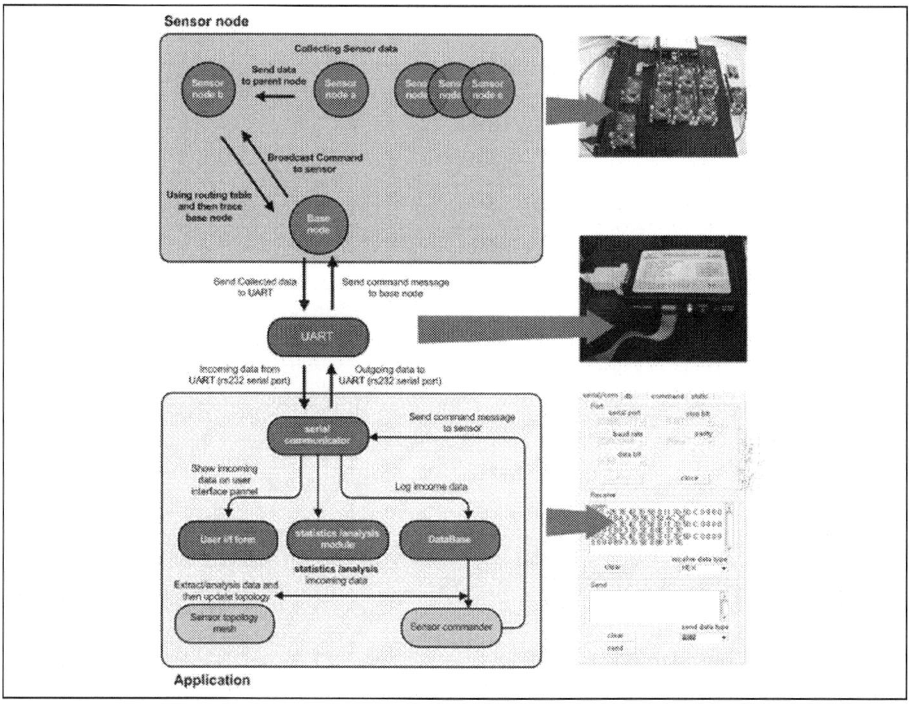

Fig. 6. Data flow

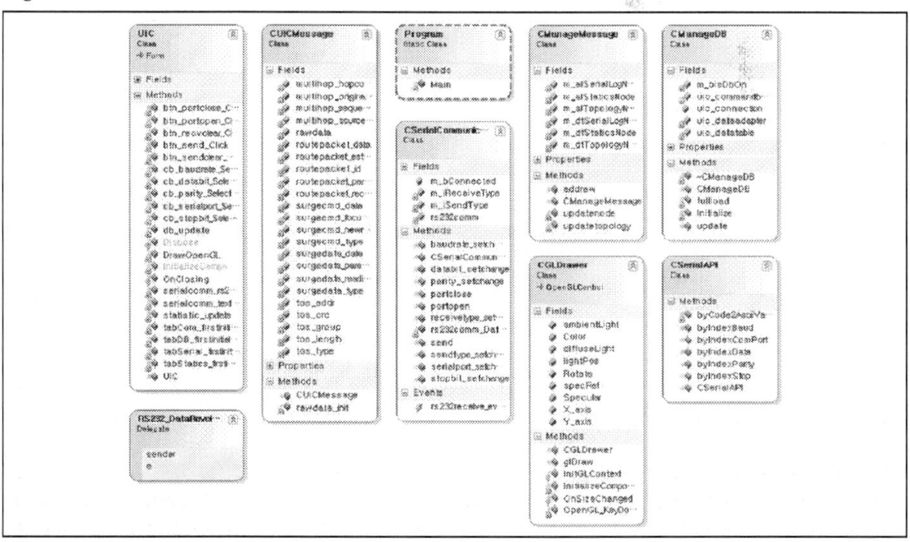

Fig. 7. Class diagram

4.2 Design of sensor node data modules

4.2.1 Data logging

Data, coming from Serial terminal, filters communication codes before inserted to CManageDB instance. Input is divided and use history node for pure log that stores occurrence data, using info node to keep dynamic topology and storing by history node and info node to database. Like Fig. 8. Stored data can be used in data sending/receipt state and network state analysis between sensor nodes.

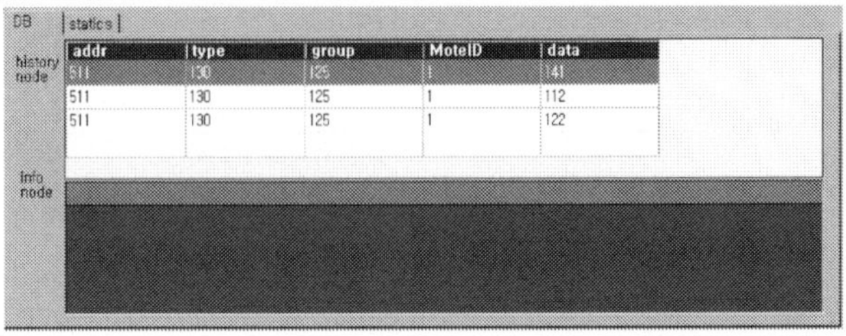

Fig. 8. Data logging

4.2.2 Serial communication

Data collected from sensor nodes, performing serial communication through PC's RS232 cable gathers on middleware. Data collection method of PC is established in serial communication form of Fig. 9. The establishment of sensor module except variable port of PC is 1 stop bit, 57600 baud rates, none parity and 8 data bits.

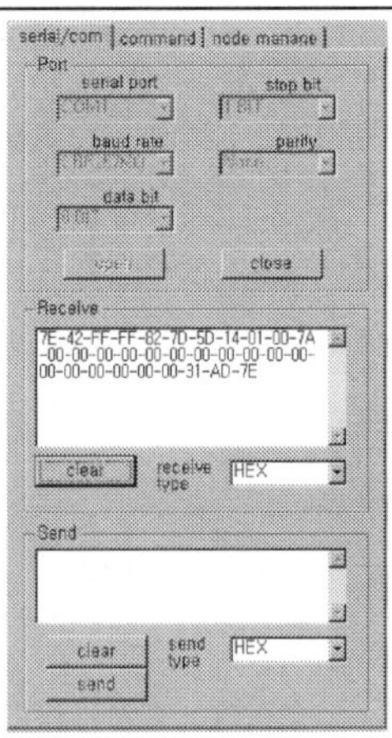

Fig. 9. Serial communication form

4.3 Sensor modules load code

Unnecessary transmission of information is possible because TinyOS mote msg can be commonly used. Therefore, we propose light lite mote msg. We have recorded lite mote msg in each sensor module, developing Mote hex image that is supposed to be loaded in sensor module to do sending-receive in addition. It is in Fig. 10 and we have composed network in 1:N.

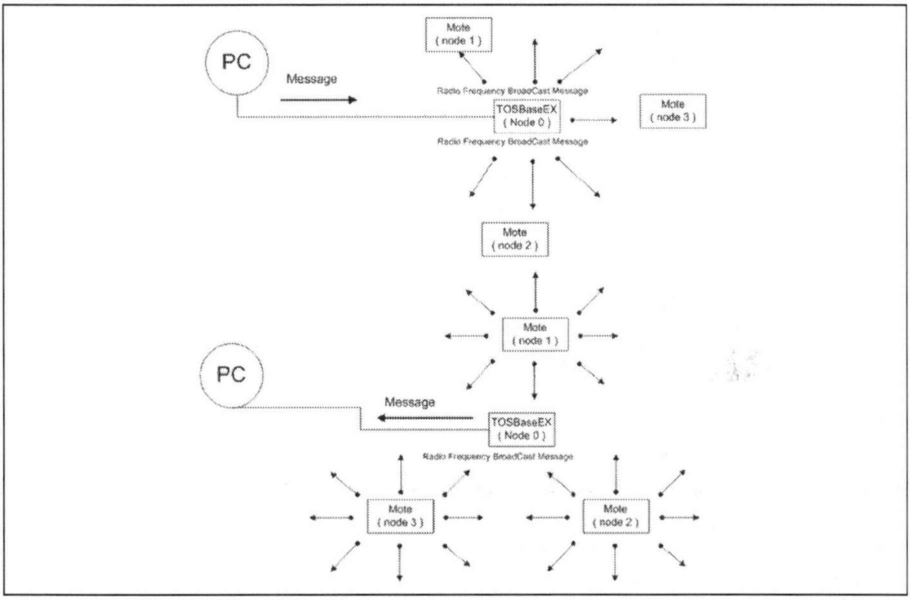

Fig. 10. Mote msg operability

4.4 Arrangement sensor nodes

We have collected data for compose reciprocity network and location of each sensors and pattern in each sensors.

We have arranged sensor nodes with Fig. 11 to collect sensor data. Sensors node compose network and collected data in limited area.

5. Conclusion

Sensor network is applied to various fields from the special application fields such as wild environment monitoring, industrial machine measurement and military-purpose measurement to the daily application fields such as fire monitoring and pollution monitoring.

Ubiquitous computing can be actualized by drawing and suggesting fragility and requirement in security that can happen in ubiquitous environment, and by suggesting the direction of security service centered on safe key distribution, certification and sensor node capture defense technology. In the proposed cryptosystems we use a new security protocol. For the control of key that can be used for the certification of sensor node or encryption of sensed information, the researchers suggest a key control method and security protocol to defend against sensor node capture by applying PKI method to Hash Lock. Drawing security weakness that may occur in the network environment and its requirement and suggesting the direction of security service can realize sensor network technology.

In a nutshell, it measures the target precisely and collects and delivers the safe information.

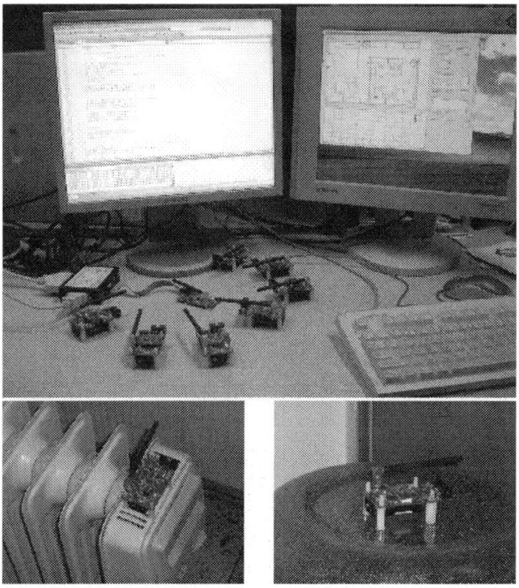

Fig. 11. Layout sensor and data caputure

6. References

[1] I.F.Akyiliz, W.Su, Y.Sankarasubramaniam and E. Cayirci, "A survey on sensor network", IEEE Communication Magazine, pp 102-114, 2002.

[2] A. Perrig, R. Szewczyk, V. Wen, D. Culler and J. D. Tygar, "SPINS: Security Protocols for Sensor Network", Wireless Network Journal(WINE), September 2002.

[3] W. Du, J. Deng, Y. S. Han and P. Varshney, "A Pairwise Key Pre-distribution Scheme for Wireless Sensor Network", 10th ACM Conference on Computer and Communications Security (CCS), October 2003.

[4] J. Staddon, S. Miner, and M. Franklin, "Self-Healing Key Distribution with Revocation", Proceedings of 2002 IEEE Symposium on Security and Privacy (S&P2002), May 2002.

[5] Haiyun Luo, Petros Zefros, Jiejun Kong, Songwu Lu, and Lixia Zhang, "Self-securing Ad Hoc Wireless Networks", 7th IEEE Symposium on Computers and Communication (ISCC '02), July 2002.

[6] K. Takaragi, M. Usami, R. Imura, R. Itsuki, T. Satoh, "An ultra small individual recognition security chip," Micro, IEEE Nov/Dec 2001 Pages 43 - 49, Volume 21, Issue 6

[7] ZigBee Alliance Document 03522 : Security Service Specification, December 2004.

[8] J. Hoffstein, J. Pipher, J. H. Silverman, "NTRU: A Ring-Based Public Key Cryptosystem." Lecture Notes in Computer Science, 1423:267, 1998.

18

Theory and Practice of Program Obfuscation

Xuesong Zhang, Fengling He and Wanli Zuo
JiLin University
China

1. Introduction

Software piracy has long been a confusing challenge to the software industry; especially with the popularity of the Internet today, this threat is growing more seriously. As a valuable form of data, software represents significant intellectual property. However, reverse engineering of software code by competitors may reveal important technological secrets, bring great harm to software developers and software providers. Because of this deterministic and self-cleared behaviour, as well as the environmental dependency property, when running under a malicious host, software may be accessed and modified by infinite resources and tools, all useful information would be definitely exposed to the attacker, which brings about great difficulty to software protection.

Along with the intensification of software market competition, technology theft poses another threat to the intellectual property rights protection. The competitors may analyze and collect the key technology or algorithm in the software through reverse engineering, which will quickly narrow the technology gap. They can also adjust their strategy according to the weakness or leakage explored from the software, and then they can use them to carry on some attacks, resulting in malicious competition. In some cases, the competitors may even do not need to understand the software internal working principle, they can directly extract the key code and integrated it into their own software to effectively enhance their competitiveness, thus seize the market share.

Clearly, there is a strong need for developing more efficient and effective mechanisms to protect software from becoming the victim of reverse engineering. Among those major approaches developed by different researchers, program obfuscation seems to be one of the most promising techniques. The concept of obfuscation was first mentioned by Diffie and Hellman (1976). When introducing the public-key cryptosystem, they claimed that, given any means for obscuring data structures in a private-key encryption scheme, one could convert this algorithm into a public-key encryption scheme.

Informally, obfuscation is a kind of special translation process. It translates a "readable" program into a function equivalent one, but which is more "unreadable" or harder to understand relatively. This kind of translation has the widespread potential applications both in cryptography and software protection, such as designing homomorphic public-key cryptosystems, removing random oracles from cryptographic protocols and converting private-key encryption schemes into public-key ones etc. in cryptography, or preventing reverse engineering (Collberg et al. (1997, 1998a, 1998b)), defending against computer viruses (Cohen (1993), Josse (2006)), protecting software watermarks and fingerprints

(Collberg & Thomborson (2000), Naccache et al. (1999)) and providing security of mobile agents (D'Anna et al. (2003), Hohl (1998)) etc. in software protection. The main difference between these two research directions is: the former is based on information theory, its goal is to try to get an obfuscator with well-defined and provable security, while the later is based on software engineering, though lacking the firm ground for estimating to what extent such methods serve the purpose, it does increase program complexity, bring barriers to program understanding.

The chapter is structured as follows: Section 2 reviews various forms of formal definition of obfuscators put forward by different researchers and the corresponding positive and negative effect on the possibility of such obfuscator. Part of this section refers to the survey made by Wyseur (2009). Section 3 gives a systemic description of software obfuscation based on software engineering perspective, it is mainly composed of the concept and taxonomy developed by Collberg et al. (1997), and it also includes some most recently new research results. In Section 4 and Section 5, we propose two Java program obfuscating method respectively, namely the call-flow obfuscation and instruction obfuscation. Section 6 concludes the paper.

2. Obfuscation theory

2.1 Notations

*PPT*denotes probabilistic polynomial-time Turing machine. For *PPT* A and any input x the output $A(x)$ is a random variable. $A^M(x)$ denote the out put of A when executed on input x and oracle access to M .We will write $|A|$ to denote the size of A. For a pair of Turing machines A and B, $A \approx B$ denotes their equivalence, i.e. $A(x) = B(x)$ holds for any input x .Function $f : N \to [0,1]$ is negligible if it decreases faster than any inverse polynomial, i.e. for any $k \in N$ there exists n_0 such that $f(n) < 1/n^k$ holds for all $n \geq n_0$. We use $neg(\cdot)$ to denote unspecified negligible function.

2.2 Definitions of obfuscation

The first contributions towards a formalization of code obfuscation were made by Hada (2000), who presented definitions for obfuscation based on the simulation paradigm for zero knowledge. The main difference between the obfuscation definition and the simulation-based definition used in (black-box) cryptography, lies in the type of objects the adversary interacts with. In the obfuscation case, it is a comparison between (white-box) interaction to an implementation of the primitive, and the interaction with an oracle implementation (black-box). In the tradition cryptography case, it is between an oracle implementation of the cryptographic primitive, and an idealized version. This new concept is captured by the Virtual Black-Box Property (VBBP). Informally, obfuscators should satisfy the following two requirements: (1) functionality: the new program has the same functionality as the original one and (2) Virtual Black-Box Property: whatever one can efficiently compute given the new program, can also be computed given oracle access to the original program. The functionality requirement is a syntactic requirement while the virtual black-box property represents the security requirement that the obfuscated program should be unintelligible. The definition of obfuscation was firstly formalized by Barak et al. (2001).

Definition 1 (Obfuscator): A probabilistic algorithm O is an obfuscator if the following three conditions hold:

- Functionality: $\forall P \in \mathcal{P}$, $O(P)$ has the same function as P.
- Polynomial slowdown: There is a polynomial p, such that for every P, $|O(P)| \le p(|P|)$, and if P halts in t steps on some input x, then $O(P)$ halts in $p(t)$ steps on input x.
- Virtual Black-Box Property: Given access to the obfuscated program $O(P)$, an adversary should not be able to learn anything more about the program P, than it could learn from oracle access to P.

The Virtual Black-Box Property was defined in several different notions by Barak et al. (2001).

Predicate-based obfuscation

In this notion, an adversary aims to compute some predicate on the program P. In this sense, the virtual black-box property captures that for any adversary and any Boolean predicate π, the probability that an adversary is able to compute $\pi(P)$ given the obfuscation $O(P)$ should be comparable to the probability that a simulator S is able to compute $\pi(P)$ when given only oracle access to P. Roughly speaking, this guarantees that the adversary A does not have any advantage of white-box access, compared to a black-box simulation, hence the obfuscation does not leak any extra information on $\pi(P)$.

Definition 2 (Predicate-based Virtual Black-Box Property): An obfuscator O satisfies the Predicate-based Virtual Black-Box Property if for any predicate π and for any (polynomial time) adversary A, there exists a (polynomial time) simulator S, such that for $\forall P \in \mathcal{P}$:

$$|\Pr[A(1^{|P|}, O(P)) = \pi(P)] - \Pr[S_A^P(1^{|P|}) = \pi(P)]| \le neg(|P|),$$

where the probabilities are taken over the coin tosses of A, S, and O.

As pointed out by Barak et al. (2001) and Hohenberger et al. (2007), the predicate definition does give some quantifiable notion that some information (i.e., predicates) remains hidden, but other non-black-box information might leak and compromise the security of the system. This lead to a stronger notion of "virtual black-box".

Distinguisher-based obfuscation

This notion of obfuscation is based on computational indistinguishability, and does not restrict what the adversary is trying to compute. For any adversary given the obfuscated program $O(P)$, it should be possible to construct a simulator S (with only oracle access to P) that is able to produce a similar output. This notion of similarity is captured by a distinguisher D.

Definition 3 (Distinguisher-based Virtual Black-Box Property): An obfuscator O satisfies the distinguisher-based Virtual Black-Box Property if for any (polynomial time) adversary A, there exists a (polynomial time) simulator S, such that that for $\forall P \in \mathcal{P}$:

$$|\Pr[D(A(O(P))) = 1] - \Pr[D(S^P(1^{|P|})) = 1]| \le neg(|P|),$$

where D is a distinguisher, and the probabilities are taken over the coin tosses of A, S, and O.

This notion of security is quite similar to the notion of semantic security for (black-box) cryptographic schemes. As pointed out by Wee (2005), this removes the need to quantify over all adversaries, as it is necessary and sufficient to simulate the output of the obfuscator. To avoid trivial obfuscation, Hofheinz et al. (2007) extended the distinguisher-based definition by giving the distinguisher oracle access to the functionality P. This leads to a very strong notion of obfuscation.

The above definitions are defined for cryptography purpose, however, for most program obfuscation in real world, this virtual black-box condition is too strong. For ordinary software, it is usually supplied with a user manual specifying its functionality. That is, the adversary knows the function the program compute. The aim of obfuscation in this case is not to hide any property of the program which refers to its functionality, but to make unintelligible the implementation of these functional properties in a particular program. This lead to a non black-box definition – Best-possible obfuscation (Goldwasser & Rothblum (2007)).

Best possible obfuscation

Best possible obfuscation makes the relaxed requirement that the obfuscated program leaks as little information as any other program with the same functionality (and of similar size). In particular, this definition allows the program to leak non black-box information. Best-possible obfuscation guarantees that any information that is not hidden by the obfuscated program is also not hidden by any other similar-size program computing the same functionality, and thus the obfuscation is (literally) the best possible.

Definition 4 (Distinguisher-based Best-possible Obfuscation): An obfuscator O is said to be a best possible obfuscator if there exists a (polynomial time) simulator S, such that for any two programs $P_1, P_2 \in \mathcal{P}$ that compute the same function, and $|P_1|=|P_2|$, such that:

$$|\Pr[D(O(P_1))=1]-\Pr[D(S(P_2))=1]|\leq neg(|P_1|),$$

where D is a distinguisher, and the probabilities are taken over the coin tosses of S and O.

Instead of requiring that an obfuscator strip a program of any non black-box information, this definition requires only that the (best-possible) obfuscated program leak as little information as possible. Namely, the obfuscated program should be "as private as" any other program computing the same functionality (and of a certain size). A best-possible obfuscator should transform any program so that anything that can be computed given access to the obfuscated program should also be computable from any other equivalent program (of some related size). A best-possible obfuscation may leak non black-box information (e.g. the code of a hard-to-learn function), as long as whatever it leaks is efficiently learnable from any other similar-size circuit computing the same functionality.

While this relaxed notion of obfuscation gives no absolute guarantee about what information is hidden in the obfuscated program, it does guarantee (literally) that the obfuscated code is the best possible. It is thus a meaningful notion of obfuscation, especially when we consider that programs are obfuscated every day in the real world without any provable security guarantee. In this sense, it may be conjectured that best possible obfuscation is more closed to software protection obfuscation.

Apart from these three definitions above, there are other notions of obfuscation, such as that based on computational indistinguishability, satisfying a relation or computing a predicate, we refer Barak et al. (2001), Hofheinz et al. (2007), Hohenberger et al. (2007), Kuzurin et al.(2007), Wee (2005) for more details.

2.3 Negative results

In their seminal paper, Barak et al. (2001) show that it is impossible to achieve the notion of obfuscation according to Definition 2, that is, it is impossible to construct a generic obfuscator for all family of programs P. This is proved by constructing a family of functions F which is inherently unobfuscatable in the sense that there exists some predicate $\pi : F \rightarrow \{0,1\}$ that can be computed efficiently when having access to an obfuscated implementation $O(f)$ of $f \in F$, but no efficient simulator can compute $\pi(f)$ much better than by random guessing, given solely oracle access to f. This result follows from the following paradox.

- If one-way functions exist, then there exists an inherently unobfuscatable function ensemble.
- The existence of an efficient obfuscator implies the existence of one-way functions.

As a result of the above, it can be concluded that efficient obfuscators do not exist.

Due to the paradox, every cryptographic primitive that implies the existence of a one-way function, implies the existence of a respectively unobfuscatable primitive. This applies to digital signature schemes, symmetric-key encryption schemes, pseudo-random function ensembles, and MAC algorithms.

Goldwasser and Kalai (2005) argued in the predicate-based notion of obfuscation to hold in the presence of auxiliary input. They observe that this is an important requirement for many applications of obfuscation, because auxiliary input comes into play in the real world. They prove that there exist many natural classes of functions that cannot be obfuscated with respect to auxiliary input (both dependent and independent auxiliary input).

Wee (2005) explored obfuscation of deterministic programs under the strong (distinguisher-based) notion of obfuscation, and concluded that deterministic functions can be obfuscated if and only if the function is learnable. Hofheinz et al. (2007) also remarked that any family of deterministic functions must be approximately learnable to be obfuscatable (in their augmented strong notion of obfuscation). Hence, it is not possible to obfuscate (deterministic) pseudo-random functions under their definition.

On non black-box definition, Goldwasser and Rothblum (2007) show that if there exist (not necessarily efficient) statistically secure best-possible obfuscators for the simple circuit family of 3-CNF circuits, then the polynomial hierarchy collapses to its second level, and give the impossibility result for (efficient) computationally best-possible obfuscation in the (programmable) random oracle model.

2.4 Positive results

A positive result on obfuscation was presented prior to the first formulation of definitions for obfuscation. Canetti (1997) presented a special class of functions suitable for obfuscation under very strong computational assumptions, that works for (almost) arbitrary function distributions. In subsequent work, Canetti et al. (1998) presented a construction suitable for obfuscation under standard computational assumptions, which is proved secure for uniform function distribution. Both results are probabilistic and technically very sophisticated.

Lynn et al. (2004) explored the question of obfuscation within an idealized setting – the random oracle model, in which all parties (including the adversary) can make queries to a random oracle. The heart of their construction is the obfuscation of a point function. A point function $I_\alpha(x)$ is defined to be 1 if $x = \alpha$, or 0 otherwise, and they observed that in the random oracle model point functions can be obfuscated, leading to obfuscation algorithms for more complex access control functionalities. Under cryptographic assumptions, it is also known how to obfuscate point functions without a random oracle. Canetti (1997) showed (implicitly) how to obfuscate point functions (even under a strong auxiliary-input definition), using a strong variant of the Decisional Diffie-Hellman assumption. Wee (2005) presented a point function obfuscator based on the existence of one-way permutations that are hard to invert on a very strong sense. Wee also presented a construction for obfuscating point functions with multi-bit output, which are point functions $I_{\alpha,\beta}(x)$ that evaluate to β on input α, and to 0 on any other input.

Most of the obfuscation definitions presented above, are either too weak for or incompatible with cryptographic applications, have been shown impossible to achieve, or both. Hohenberger et al. (2007) and Hofheinz et al. (2007) present new definitions which have a potential for interesting positive results. Hohenberger et al. introduce the notion of average-case secure obfuscation, based on a distinguisher-based definition that allows families of circuits to be probabilistic. They present a probabilistic re-encryption functionality that can be securely obfuscated according to this new definition. Similarly, Hofheinz et al. present another variant of a distinguisher-based definition. The deviation is that they consider probabilistic functions and select the function to be obfuscated according to a distribution. Their new notion is coined average obfuscation. The goal is to consider obfuscations for specific applications, and they demonstrated the obfuscation of an IND-CPA secure symmetric encryption scheme that results into an IND-CPA secure asymmetric scheme. Similar results hold for the obfuscation of MAC algorithms into digital signature schemes.

3. Heuristic obfuscation

Despite the fundamental results so far from theoretical approaches on code obfuscation, their influence on software engineering of this branch is minor: security requirements studied in the context of cryptographic applications are either too strong or inadequate to many software protection problems emerged in practice. Everybody dealing with program understanding knows that, in many cases, even small programs require considerable efforts to reveal their meaning. This means that there exists the possibility of some weakly secure obfuscators. Program obfuscation is received more attention gradually exactly based on this viewpoint in software engineering in the last decade. The practical goal of obfuscation is then to make reverse engineering uneconomical by various semantic preserving transformations, it is sufficient that the program code be difficult to understand, requiring more effort from the attacker than writing a program with the same functionality from scratch.

Early attempts of obfuscation aim at machine code level rewriting. Cohen (1993) used a technique he called "program evolution" to protect operating systems that included the replacement of instructions, or small sequences of instructions, with ones that perform semantically equal functions. Transformations included instruction reordering, adding or removing arbitrary jumps, and even de-inlining methods. However, it was until the appearance of the paper by Collberg et al. (1997), software engineering community became acquainted with obfuscation. They gave the first detailed classification of obfuscating transformations together with the definition of some analytical methods for quality measures.

3.1 Types of obfuscation

Lexical obfuscation

This involves renaming program identifiers to avoid giving away clues to their meaning. Since the identifiers have little semantic association with program itself, their meaning can be inferred from the context by a determined attacker, lexical obfuscation has very limited capability and is not alone sufficient. Typical Java obfuscators such as SourceGuard[1] and yGuard[2] etc. all implement this kind of obfuscation. It is worth noting that, in order to mislead the analyzer, Jaurora[3] randomly exchange identifiers instead of scramble them, thus, has the more secrete property. Chan et al. (2004) bring forward an advanced identifier scrambling algorithm. They utilize the hierarchy characteristic of jar package, i.e. a sub package or a top-level type (classes and interfaces) may have the same name as the enclosing package. Sequentially generated identifiers are used to replace those original identifiers in a package, and the generation of identifiers is restarted for every package. They also use the gap between a Java compiler and a Java virtual machine to construct source-code-level rules-violation, such as illegal identifiers, nested type names. However, this kind of source-code-level rules-violation can be repaired at bytecode level by some automated tools (Cimato et al. (2005)).

Data obfuscation

This transformation targets at data and data structures contained in the program, tries to complicate their operations and obscures their usage, such as data encoding, variable and array splitting and merging, variable reordering, and inheritance relation modifying. Among them, the array reconstruction method receives more attention in recent years. Array splitting, merging, folding, and flattening was discussed by Collberg (1998a) in detail. Further researches are also carried out later, such as generalized array splitting method (Drape (2006)), composite function based indexing method(Ertaul & Venkatesh (2005)), homomorphic function based indexing method (Zhu (2007)), and class encapsulated array reconstruction method (Praveen & Lal (2007)) etc. Data obfuscation is especially useful for protecting object-oriented application since the inheritance relation is crucial to software architecture undestanding. Sonsonkin et al. (2003) present a high-level data transformations of Java program structure – design obfuscation. They replaced several classes with a single class by class coalescing, and replaced a single class with multiple classes by class splitting. They hold that, if class splitting is used in tandem with class coalescing, program structure would be changed very significantly, which can hide design concept and increase difficulty of understanding.

Control Obfuscation

This approach alters the flow of control within the code, e.g. reordering statements, methods, loops and hiding the actual control flow behind irrelevant conditional statements. This form of obfuscation can be further divided into two categories, dynamic dispatch and opaque predicate. For the dynamic dispatch, Wang et al. (2001) proposed a dynamic dispatch model based on the fact that aliases in a program drastically reduce the precision of static analysis of the program. Chow et al. (2001) transformed a program to flat model by dividing it into basic blocks, and embed into it an intractable problem with respect to computational complexity theory. Consequently, to determine the target address is equivalent to solving the intractable problem. Toyofuku et al. (2005) assigned each method with a unique ID. During program execution, the control flow will randomly points to any method, and whether the target method will execute or not is based on the comparison

[1] http://www.4thpass.com/
[2] http://www.yworks.com/products/yguard/
[3] http://wwwhome.cs.utwente.nl/~oord/

between the method's ID and a global variable that is updated after each method execution. An opaque predicate is a conditional expression whose value is known to the obfuscator, but is difficult for an adversary to deduce statically. For the construction of opaque predicate, Collberg's (1998b) algorithm is based on the intractability property of pointer alias, Venkatraj's (2003) algorithm is based on well-known mathematical axioms and probability distribution, Palsberg's (2000) algorithm is based on data structure correlation, while Drape's (2007) algorithm is based on program slicing information.

Prevention obfuscation

This transformation is quite different in flavor from control or data transformation. In contrast to these, their main goal is not to obscure the program to human reader. Rather, it is designed to make known automatic deobfuscation techniques more difficult, or to explore known problems in current deobfuscators or decompilers, e.g. junk bytes insertion. Some dynamic dispatching methods inherently have this capability. Batchelder and Hendren (2007) proposed a number of prevention transformation techniques for Java program by exploiting the semantic gap between what is legal in source code and what is legal in bytecode. The methods include converting branches to jsr instructions, disobeying constructor conventions, and combining try blocks with their catch blocks etc., all which lead to the decompilers failing to decompile the bytecodes. Instead of obfuscating the program itself, Monden et al. (2004) gave an idea for obfuscating the program interpretation. If the interpretation being taken is obscure and thus it can not be understood by a hostile user, the program being interpreted is also kept obscure since the user lacks the information about "how to read it."

3.2 Quality of obfuscation

According to Collberg (1997), there are four main metrics measure the effectiveness of an obfuscating transformation in terms of potency, resilience, cost, and stealth. Potency measures the complexity added to the obfuscated program. Resilience measures how well the transformation holds up under attack from an automatic deobfuscator. Cost measures the execution time/space penalty of obfuscating a program. Stealth measures how much the obfuscated code looks like the original one and how well it fits in with the other code. These proposed measures are known as analytical methods, since they extract information by taking obfuscation algorithms parameter, source program and obfuscated program. Utilizing these metrics, Wroblewski (2002) gave a thorough comparison of different obfuscation algorithms based on source code level transformation. Dyke and Colin (2006) proposed an obfuscation method at assembly-code level and did a similar comparison work. Karnick et al. (2006) developed an analytical method based on these metrics to evaluate the strength of some commercial Java obfuscators.

The drawback of these metrics is that they do not define exactly to what extent the difficulty or hardness it takes to understand the obfuscated program compared to the original one for an analyzer. This is partially due to the considerable gap between theory and practice of program obfuscation (Kuzurin et al. (2007)). The formal definition of obfuscation for cryptography purpose is not suitable for most program protection applications in real world. Thus, how to clearly reveal the most important common properties required in any software obfuscation and give the corresponding effective measure metrics still need a long road to run.

4. Call-flow obfuscation

Linn and Debray (2003) proposed the concept of branch function in their native code tamper-proofing algorithm. Unconditional branch instructions are converted to calls to a branch function. The branch function will transfer execution to the original target based on information of stack, which will prevent a disassembler from identifying the target address, thus resist to static analysis effectively. Unfortunately, this algorithm is only applicable to native code which can access and modify its own stack, but not suitable to Java byte code. As a control obfuscation algorithm, the proposed scheme generalized this idea and apply it to Java object-oriented language. One instance method invocation in Java language can be interpreted as a kind of special unconditional jump in assembly language level, and all those methods invocation can be transformed to a unified style, so long as they have the same parameter and return type. This form of transformation will lead to a strong obfuscation result by further using of alias and method polymorphism. This kind of obfuscation algorithm is called as call-flow obfuscation. In Fig. 1, the codes of some methods in user defined class are extracted and embedded into some object's methods in the object pool. All the objects in the class pool are inherited from the same super class, and their relations are either paternity or sibling. Each object's *DoIt* method is the mergence of more than two methods in user defined classes. When the program going to execute one merged method which is originally defined in user defined class, a request is sent to the class pool, and the class pool will return one object whose method is executed instead according to the request parameter. Since objects in the class pool are up cast to their common base type, which object's *DoIt* method will really execute can only be ascertained at runtime. Static analyze of this kind of single level type with dynamic dispatch inter-procedure points-to is PSPACE hard (Chatterjee et al. (2001)).

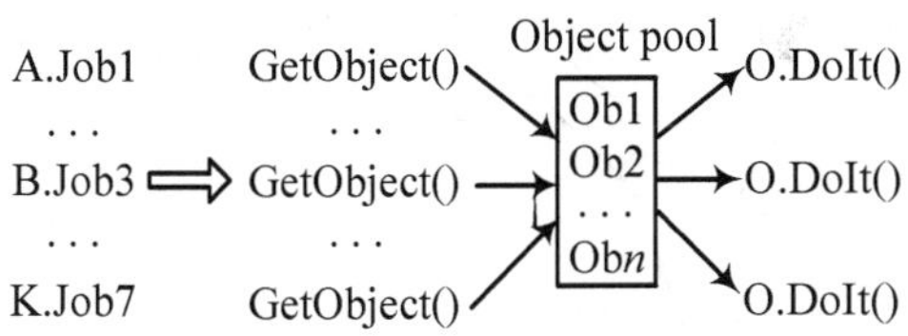

Fig. 1. The object pool model

4.1 Obfuscation algorithm

In Java language, an application consists of one or more packages, and it may also use some packages in the standard library or other proprietary libraries. The part of a program that will be obfuscated by the obfuscation techniques is called the obfuscation scope. In this section, obfuscation scope only refers to those packages developed by the programmer himself.

The obfuscation algorithm mainly consists of three steps, namely the invocation format unification, inter-classes method merging, and object pool construction.

Invocation format unification

The parameters and return types defined in a method of a program are usually different from each other. In order to perform inter-classes method merging, their invocation formats should be unified. The two classes import in Fig. 2 are used for this purpose. They encapsulate the parameters and return type for any method. In these two classes, all non-primitive data types are represented by some items in the object array *aO*. The *ParamObject* has a few more Boolean fields than the *ReturnObject*, they are used to select the execution branch after multiple methods have been merged. In this case, there are three flags in *ParamObject*, which means at most four different methods can be merged into one *DoIt* method. The interface *DoJob* declares only one method *DoIt*, which uses *ParamObject* as its formal parameter and *ReturnObject* as its return type. All the methods to be merged will be eventually embedded into the *DoIt* method of some subclasses inherited from *DoJob*.

```
public class ParamObject {
  public double[] aD;  public float[] aF;
  public long[] aL;    public int[] aI;
  public short[] aS;   public byte[] aY;
  public char[] aC;    public boolean[] aB;
  public Object[] aO;
  boolean flag1, flag2, flag3;
}
public iterface DoJob {
   public ReturnObject DoIt (ParamObject p);
}

public class ReturnObject {
  public double[] aD;  public float[] aF;
  public long[] aL;    public int[] aI;
  public short[] aS;   public byte[] aY;
  public char[] aC;    public boolean[] aB;
  public Object[] aO;
}
```

Fig. 2. Unification of invocation format

```
public class A {
  public int DoJobA1(int x)
  public long DoJobA2(double x, double y)
}

public class B {
  public int DoJobB1(int x, int y)
  public char DoJobB2(String s)
  public boolean DoJobB3(boolean b, char c)
}

{
   a = new A();   b = new B();
   a.DoJobA1(10);   b.DoJobB3(false, 'A');
}
```

Fig. 3. The original classes definition and method invocation

```
public class DoJob1 implements DoJob {
  public ReturnObject DoJob(ParamObject p) {
    ReturnObject o = new ReturnObject();
    if(p.flag1){  //DoJobB2  } else if(p.flag2){  //DoJobA1  } else{  //Garbage code  }
    return o;
  }
}
```

Fig. 4. Inter-classes method merging

Inter-classes method merging

In determining which method can be merged, factors such as inheritance relation and method dependency relation must take into consideration. Methods in the following scope should not be obfuscated.

- Method inherited from (implements of an abstract method or overrides an inherited method) super class or super interface that is outside of the obfuscation scope.
- Constructor, callback function, native method and finalize method
- Method declaration with throws statement
- Method which access inner-class
- Methods whose internal codes invoke other non-public methods, which inherited from super class or super interface that is outside of the obfuscation scope.

Fig. 4 shows a possible merging instance of two classes defined in Fig. 3. Method *DoJobA1* and *DoJobB2* which belong to class *A* and class *B* respectively are merged into one *DoIt* method. Since it only needs two flags in this instance, other flags in the *ParamObject* can be used to control the execution of garbage code, which forms a kind of obfuscating enhancement. (The garbage code here refers to the code that can executes normally, but will not destroy the data or control flow of the program.)

When carry on method merging, three special situations need handling.

Method polymorphism: If the merged method is inherited from super class or super interface that is within the obfuscation scope, all methods with the same signature (method name, formal parameter type and numbers) in the inherited chain should also be extracted and embedded into some *DoIt* methods respectively.

Method dependency: The merged method invokes other methods defined in current class or its super class, eg. an invocation to *DoJobA2* inside method *DoJobA1*. There are two approaches to this situation:

- If *DoJobA2* is a user-defined method, it can be merged further, otherwise, its access property is modified to public, and the following action is taken the same as the second approach.
- The invocation is transformed to the standard form by adding a qualifier in front of the invocated method, i.e. *DoJobA2* is converted to *a. DoJobA2*. The qualifier *a* is an instance of class *A* which is put into the object array of *ParamObject* as an additional parameter.

  Field dependency: The merged method uses the field defined in current class or its super class. There are also two approaches:
- Class qualifier can be added before the fields accessed by this method, which is similar to the second approach in method dependency. But this is not suitable for the non-public field inherited from super class that is outside of the obfuscation scope.
- This solution adds *GetFields* and *SetFields* method for each class. The *GetFields* returns an instance of *ReturnObject* which includes fields used by all methods that are to be merged, and this instance is put into the object array of the *ParamObject*. Code in *DoIt* method can use this parameter to refer to the fields in the original class. After the execution of *DoIt*, an instance of *ReturnObject* is transferred back by invoking the *SetFields* method which making changes to the fields in the original class.

Object pool construction

A lot of collection data types provided by JDK can be used to construct the object pool, such as List, Set and Map etc. However, these existing data types have standard operation mode, which will divulge some inner logical information of the program. The universal hashing is a desired candidate to construct the object pool here.

The main idea behind universal hashing is to select the hash function at random from a carefully designed class of functions at the beginning of execution. Randomization guarantees that no single input will always evoke worst-case behavior. Due to this randomization property, the algorithm can behave differently on each execution, even for the same input, guaranteeing good average-case performance for any input.

Definition 5: Let H be a finite collection of hash functions that map a given universe U of keys into the range $\{0,1,\cdots,m-1\}$. Such a collection is said to be universal if for each pair of distinct keys $k,l \in U$, the number of hash functions $h \in H$ which $h(k)=h(l)$ is at most $|H|/m$.

One construction algorithm for a universal class of hash functions is: Choosing a prime number p large enough so that every possible key k is in the range 0 to $p-1$, inclusive. p is greater than the number of slots in the hash table m, Let Z_{p1} denote the set $\{0,1,\cdots,p-1\}$, and let Z_{p2} denote the set $\{1,2,\cdots,p-1\}$. For any $a_1 \in Z_{p1}$ and $a_2 \in Z_{p2}$, the following equation makes up of a collection of universal hashing functions.

$$h_{a_1,a_2}(k) = ((a_1 k + a_2) \bmod p) \bmod m$$

The universal hashing table is used to store all instances of classes inherited from *DoJob*. If collision occurs, second level hashing table is established in the corresponding slot. The randomizahion characteristic of universal hashing enables us to assign different values to a_1 and a_2 each time the program start. According to this characteristic, any expressions can be constructed based on a_1 and a_2, and be used as the key to access hashing table. In this case, the key is no longer a constant, and better information hiding result obtained. Fig. 5 shows the structure of hashing table. In which, instance of class *DoJob9* is stored by key *keym,* and the same instance is acquired by key *keyl.* Notice that the key used to store an object is different from the key to request the same object, their relation and hashing table itself may be protected by other data or control obfuscating algorithm. In Fig. 6, invocation to class *A*'s mehod *DoJobA1* is replaced by invocation to *DoIt* method in one of *DoJob*'s subclass.

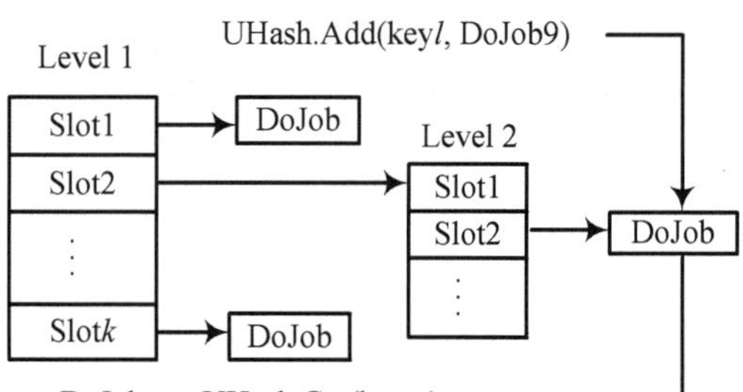

Fig. 5. Structure of hashing table

However, using key to access hashing table directly will cause some problem when in face of method polymorphism. Consider the inherited relation in Fig. 7, if all methods in class *A* are extracted and embedded into some *DoIt* methods, method extraction should be performed during each method overridden in subclasses of *A*. Due to the complexity of points-to analysis, it's hard to determine which instance *a* will refers to in the statement of *a.DoJob1*. As a result, it still cannot be determined that which key should be used to access the hashing table. Under this situation, one method *GetIDs* should be appended to the super class *A*. *GetIDs* will return an array includes all keys corresponding to those methods in current class which have been merged into the object pool. If subclass overrides any method of parent class, the *GetIDs* method should also be overridden. Fig. 7 shows the return arrays of each class corresponding to the left side. All IDs of the overridden method have the same position in the array as the original method in super class. In this way, the statement *a.DoJob1* can be replaced by invocation to *Uhash.Get* with the first element in the array as the parameter.

```
DoJob1 dojob = new DoJob1();
UHash.Add( 217, dojob);
...
//a.DoJobA1(10)
ParamObject p = new ParamObject();
int[] i = new int[1];    i[0] = 10;
p.al = d;    p.flag2 = true;
DoJob dojob = UHash.Get( 3 * a1+ a2 + 13 );
ReturnObject r = do.DoIt(p);
```

Fig. 6. Invocation to class *A*'s mehod *DoJobA1* is replaced by invocation to *DoIt* method in one of *DoJob*'s subclass

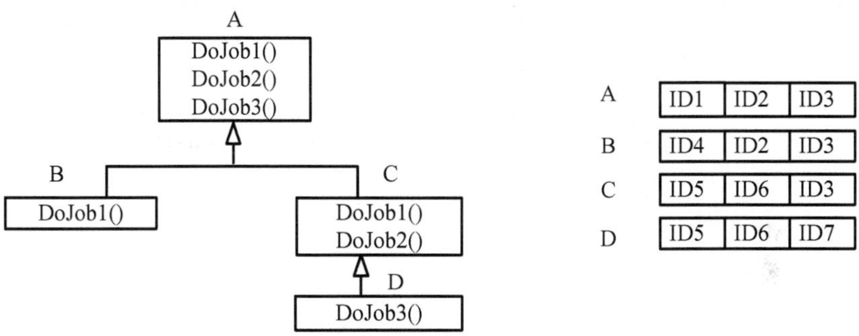

Fig. 7. Method polymorphism and return array

4.2 Obfuscating enhancement

In order to perform effective attack, which instance each *DoJob* references to should be precisely located. Since all objects added into the object pool have been upcast to their super class *DoJob*, and different keys are used to store and access the same object in hashing table. It is not feasible to clarify all the call-flows in a program relying solely on static analysis. However, frequently accessing of hashing table, and the if-else block partitioned according to flag in *DoIt* method still leak some useful information to a malicious end user. These information may be used as the start point of dynamic attack. There are many mechanisms to hide these information.

Multi-duplication: This approach makes multi duplication to some merged methods. Each duplication is transformed by different algorithm to have distinct appearance, such as parameter type conversion, variable or array compressing and decompressing, splitting and merging. Wenever a merged method is executed, the same functionality can be realized whatever object is selected.

Method interleaving: Since methods merged into the same *DoIt* are branch selected by the flag value, bears the obvious block characteristic. Further action may be taken to interleave these blocks, obscuring their boundaries. The Boolean type flags can be obscured at the same time, e.g. importing opaque predicate, replacing one Boolean type with two or more integer types.

Random assignment of parameters: Since only parts of the fields in *ParamObject* are used during one execution of a merged method, they may be used to perform pattern matching attack by malicious users. Those unused fields can be randomly assigned any value before invocating to *DoIt*, and further action can be taken to add some garbage codes which reference to these fields.

Hashing table extension: This aproach extends some slots to insert new objects. The parameters used in *DoIt* method of these newly inserted object are different from the *DoIt* method of objects that have already existed. When a slot that includes more than one objects is located by the given key, the return object is randomly selected from those in this slot. Before entering the corresponding execution branch according to the given flag, a check will be made to ensure whether those formal parameters in *ParamObject* are valid or not, including fields used by following instructions should not be null, and fields not used should be null. If parameter mismatch found, an exception is thrown. Now the *DoIt* invocation code is enclosed in a loop block (Fig. 8), and following instructions will not be executed until a success invocation to the *DoIt* method.

```
while(true){
   try{
      dojob = UHash.Get( 572 );
      r = do.DoIt(p);
      break;
   }catch(ParamMismatchException e){
      continue;
   }
}
```

Fig. 8. The *DoIt* method invocation model after hashing table extension

Dynamic adjusting of object pool: Multi-rules can be adapted simultaneously to construct the object pool. At the program start point, one operation rule is randomly selected, and a new thread is introduced by which readjust the operation rule once in a while. The key used to access object pool should also be modified along with the rule change. Clearly, combined with the previous mechanism, this enhancing measure can withstand dynamic analysis to a certain extent.

4.3 Experimental result

We extend the refactor plugin in Eclipse, and apply this scheme to five java programs. Currently, only the basic obfuscating method is implemented, excluding those enhanced mechanisms such as multi-duplication, method interleaving etc. Some of the programs are Java applets which will never terminate without user interference. Their execution time is only measured in finite cycles. For example, the ASM program will simulate the stock market forever, and the corresponding execution time given in Table 1 is based on the first thirty cycles.

Table 1 indicate that, the program size increasing ratio after obfuscating lies between 1.11 and 1.62. With the size growing of the original program, the ratio presents a downward trend. The reason lies in the fact that all newly-inserted codes are mainly used for object pool definition and operation, while the codes used for method merging and invocations are relatively few. The largest execution time decline is no more than 6%. In fact, some of the merged methods are invoked more than 10000 times, such as the *join* method in MultiSort. However, since all objects in the object pool have been initialized soon after program starts. Once accessed, the object pool will only return an object which has already been instantiated. And at the same time, the classes *ParamObject* and *ReturnObject* are directly inherited from Object, apart from the need for loading, linking and initialization during their first creation, the follow-up instantiation is only a small amount of work. Thus, the proposed scheme has little performance influence on the original program.

Program	Description	Method Merged		Before Obf.	After Obf.	Ratio
WizCrypt	File encryption tool	8	Jar file size (byte)	13755	21892	1.58
			Execution time (sec)	50.46	51.25	1.02
MultiSort	Collection of fifteen sortin algorithms	17	Jar file size (byte)	14558	23497	1.62
			Execution time (sec)	102.06	107.83	1.06
Draw	Draw random graphs	11	Jar file size (byte)	16772	26123	1.56
			Execution time (sec)	6.12	6.23	1.02
ASM	Artificial stock market	29	Jar file size (byte)	87796	97149	1.11
			Execution time (sec)	31.20	32.38	1.04
DataReport	Report generator	22	Jar file size (byte)	59030	68555	1.17
			Execution time (sec)	8.71	9.15	1.05

Table 1. Experimental result by using only the basic obfuscation method

5. Instruction obfuscation

The concept of obfuscated interpretation was motivited by Monden et al. (2004). They employed a finite state machine (FSM) based interpreter to give the context-dependent semantics to each instruction in a program, thus, attempts to statically analyze the relation between instructions and their semantics will not succeed. In fact, our proposed method is similar to this technique. However, the FSM interpretation unit is hardware implemented, its state transition rule cannot change any more once being embedded. Further more, in order to maintain the same state at the top of any loop body in a translated program, a sequence of dummy instructions must be injected into the tail of the loop. These dummy instructions will destroy the correctness of the stack signature, which means it is very hard (if not impossible) to implement the translation of a Java program after which the translated program can still runs normally. In our scheme, the mapping rule is more generally defined, which can be easily changed at will. Because there is no need to insert dummy instructions, it is extremely easy to make a translated program looks like a normal program whether by reverse engineering or runtime inspection.

The core idea of this framework is to construct an interpreter *W*, which carries out obfuscated interpretations for a given program *P*, where *P* is a translated version of an original program P_0 written in Java bytecode. The obfuscated interpretation means that an interpretation for a given instruction c is not fixed; specifically, the interpretation for c is determined not only by c itself but also by other auxiliary input to W (Fig. 9).

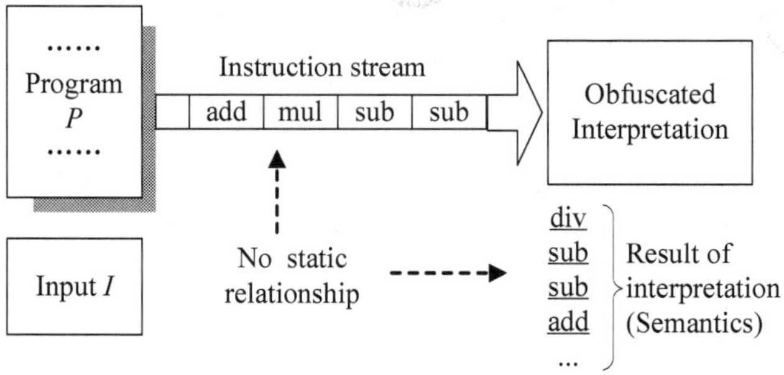

Fig. 9. Obfuscated interpretation concept

In order to realize the obfuscated interpretation in W, a permutation mechanism is employed that takes input as an instruction c where each permutation makes a different interpretation for c. Since the interpretation for a particular type of instruction varies with respect to permutation definitions, we call such W a permutation-based interpreter. In this framework, W is built independent of P_0; thus, many programs run on a single interpreter W, and any of the programs can be easily replaced to a new program for the sake of updating.

5.1 Framework for obfuscated interpretation

Overview

The following diagram (Fig. 10) shows brief definitions of materials related to W.

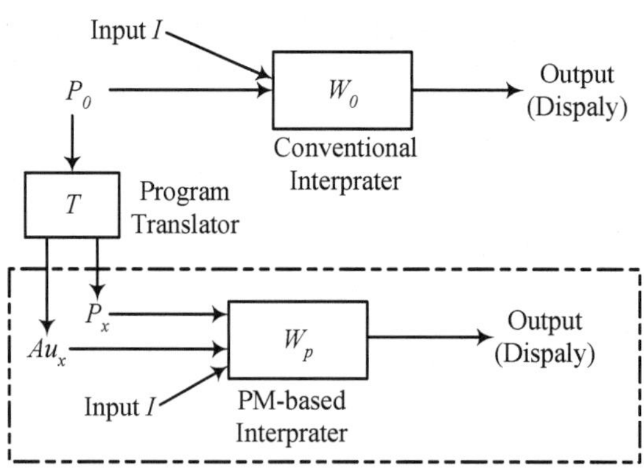

Fig. 10. Obfuscated interpretation framework

P_0: is a target program intended to be hidden from hostile users. Let us assume that P_0 is written in bytecode, where each statement in P_0 consists of a single opcode and (occasionally) some operands.

W_0: is a common (conventional) interpreter for P_0 such as a Java Virtual Machine.

P_x: is a "translated program" containing encoded instructions whose semantics are determined during execution according to the auxiliary input Au_x. This P_x is an equivalently translated version of P_0, i.e., P_x has the same functionality as P_0.

I: is an input of P_0 and P_x. Note that P_0 and P_x take the same input.

W_p: is a permutation-based interpreter that can evaluate encoded instructions of P_x according to the auxiliary input Au_x. This W_p is an extension of W_0 with a permutation unit. Each W_p has a unique key which is used to decrypt Au_x.

T: is a program translator that automatically translates P_0 into P_x with respect to the randomly created one-to-many map among all possible instructions.

Au_x: is the one-to-many mapping rule that describe how one opcode map to the others generated randomly by T when translating a program. The content of Au_x is encrypted by the same key as that of W_p.

In this framework, it is assumed that W_p is hidden from the end user as much as possible, e.g., it is integrated with the Java Virtual Machine. However, P_x must be delivered to the user and put in an accessible area so as to enable it to update. Each W_p should be equipped with a different key so that an adversary cannot easily guess one W_p's interpreter after having "cracked" some other W_p's interpreter.

Permutation Unit

The permutation unit denoted as W_p can be defined as follows:

$\sum = \{c_0, c_1, \ldots, c_{n-1}\}$ is the input alphabet.

$\Psi = \{\underline{c_0}, \underline{c_1}, \ldots, \underline{c_{n-1}}\}$ is the output alphabet.

$\prod = \{\pi_0, \pi_1, \ldots, \pi_{n-1}\}$ is the auxiliary input alphabet. It is decrypted from Au_x using the key owned by W_p.

$\lambda_i : \sum \times \prod \rightarrow \Psi$ is the output function.

$\Lambda = (\lambda_0, \lambda_1, \ldots, \lambda_{n-1})$ is the n -tuple of all output functions. Λ is the specification of a W_p that defines a dynamic map between obfuscated instructions.

Based on Monden et al. (2004), there are four types of design choices for the interpreter, which are dependent upon the instruction set used for P_x. Let $InsP_0$ and $InsP_x$ be the instruction sets for P_0 and P_x,. In Type 1 design, the instruction set for P_x is the same as that for P_0, so $InsP_x = InsP_0$. In the rest of this section, we focus on this design type. Let us assume $InsPx = \sum \cup O$ where elements $c_i \in \sum$ are obfuscated instructions, and $o_i \in O$ are non-obfuscated instructions. This means, P_x contains both c_i and o_i, and, if the permutation unit recognizes $c_i \in \sum$ as input then its semantics is determined by the auxiliary input π_i, otherwise an input $o_i \in O$ is directly passed to the execute unit. Each underlined symbol c_i in Ψ denotes the normal (untranslated) semantics for the correspondingly-indexed opcode c_i in $\sum$.

Here is a simple example of W_p where

$\sum = \{iadd, isub, imul, idiv\}$

$\Psi = \{iadd, isub, imul, idiv\}$

$\prod = \{0, 1, 2, 3\}$

$\Lambda = (\lambda_0(iadd, 0) = \underline{isub}, \lambda_0(isub, 0) = \underline{isub}, \lambda_0(imul, 0) = \underline{iadd}, \lambda_0(idiv, 0) = \underline{imul}, \lambda_1(iadd, 1) = \underline{idiv}, \lambda_1(isub, 1) = \underline{imul}, \lambda_1(imul, 1) = \underline{idiv}, \lambda_1(idiv, 1) = \underline{isub}, \lambda_2(iadd, 2) = \underline{iadd}, \lambda_2(isub, 2) = \underline{iadd}, \lambda_2(imul, 2) = \underline{isub}, \lambda_2(idiv, 2) = \underline{idiv}, \lambda_3(iadd, 3) = \underline{imul}, \lambda_3(isub, 3) = \underline{idiv}, \lambda_3(imul, 3) = \underline{imul}, \lambda_3(idiv, 3) = \underline{iadd})$

This W_p takes an encoded opcode $c_i \in \{iadd, isub, imul, idiv\}$ as an input, translates it into its semantics (cleartext opcode) $\underline{c_i} \in \{\underline{iadd}, \underline{isub}, \underline{imul}, \underline{idiv}\}$ according to π_i, and outputs $\underline{c_i}$. Fig. 11

shows an example of interpretation for an instruction stream given by this W_p. Obviously, even this simple permutation has the ability to conduct an obfuscated interpretation.

c_i	π_i		$\underline{c}_i$
iadd	3		imul
imul	0		iadd
idiv	2	⟶	idiv
imul	1		idiv
isub	2		iadd

Fig. 11. Instruction stream interpretation

When concerning the other design types, the input alphabet $\sum$ and the auxiliary input alphabet $\prod$ is larger, which will eventually resulting to a more complex W_p.

Program Translator

The translator T can be defined based on interpreter W_p:

$\sum' = \Psi = \{\underline{c}_0, \underline{c}_1, \ldots, \underline{c}_{n-1}\}$ is the input alphabet.

$\Psi' = \sum = \{c_0, c_1, \ldots, c_{n-1}\}$ is the output alphabet.

$\prod = \{\pi_0, \pi_1, \ldots, \pi_{n-1}\}$ is the auxiliary output alphabet. It is encrypted by the key of W_p to get Au_x.

$\lambda'_i : \sum' \rightarrow \Psi' \times \prod$ is the output function.

$\Lambda' = (\lambda'_0, \lambda'_1, \ldots, \lambda'_l)$, is a tuple of all possible output functions. Its item count l is determined by the permutation rule, and is larger than n by far.

The definition above shows that λ'_i is a one-to-many function. This non-deterministic characteristic is the key idea to make each translation of P_0 different from the other.

In order to make P_x pass Java's bytecode verifier, bytecode that can substitute each other without causing any stack or syntactic errors must be classified into subgroups carefully according to their operand type and operand number. For example, the four instructions *iadd, isub, imul* and *idiv* belong to the same group, because they all pop two integers, perform relevant operation, and then push the integer result back into the stack. Each of them form a one-to-many relation to the others (including the instruction itself). Thus, the input (and output) alphabet is partitioned into many sub groups according to their features, such that symbols $c_0, c_1, \ldots, c_{a-1}$ are in the first group G_1 and the symbols $c_a, c_{a+1}, \ldots, c_{b-1}$ are in the second group G_2, and so on.

During program translation, T only accepts those input instructions that belong to $\sum'$. For each accepted instruction, the following actions are performed:

- Decide the sub group G_j this instruction belongs to.
- Search for all $\lambda_k, \ldots, \lambda_{k+l} \in \Lambda$ that output $\underline{c}_i$ in G_j.
- Randomly select m, k m $k + l$, extract c_m and π_m from λ_m, and put them into Ψ' and $\prod$ respectively.

Fig. 12 shows an example of program translation corresponding to W_p of Fig. 11. As shown in Fig. 12, the output is considerably different from the input of Fig. 11. This means that given a program P_0, each time a different P_x is produced even for the same W_p. In other words, this framework can guarantee that each installed copy of a program is unique. More precisely, each installed copy differs enough from all other installed copies to ensure that successful attacks on its embedded copyright protection mechanism cannot be generalized successfully to other installed copies.

$\underline{c}_i$		c_i	π_i
imul		idiv	0
iadd		isub	2
idiv	→	isub	3
idiv		iadd	1
iadd		idiv	3

Fig. 12. Example of T: $P_0 \rightarrow P_x$

5.2 Implementation

We now consider some implementation issues of our framework on mobile phones. The platform of choice in this setting is Mysaifu JVM[4]. It is an open source Java Virtual Machine runs on the Windows mobile platform. It's runtime Java library is based on the GNU Classpath[5] whose target is to be fully compatible with the core of JDK1.5.

Auxiliary Input

When Mysaifu JVM opens a jar file, it loads all the class files into memory, and perform bytecode verification by iterating through all methods at the same time. JVM also load a few system classes such as JavaLangSystem, JavaLangString, JavaLangThread, JavaLangClass etc. immediately after startup. Then, the main class is executed by JVM interpreter. The best place to embed our Type 1 permutation unit into JVM is right in front of the verifier.

There are two places to store Au_x. One is in the jar manifest file as an extended option, the other one is in the class file itself as an attribute. In the former case, filename and relevant permutation rule must be included in Au_x, and when faced with incremental update, the correspondence between filename and permutation rule should also be updated, which will call for much more effort to do. In the latter case, we can replace any class file freely, without worry about the permutation rule. Because a Java virtual machine implementation is permitted to silently ignore any or all attributes in the attributes table of a code attribute, the attribute we added which include Au_x will not cause any error in a third party JVM. Here the latter one is the desired choice for this implementation.

In this target, SIM card number is used as the key to encrypt Au_x. When JVM find the given attribute in one code attribute table, it will decrypt the attribute info, and use this info to translate some instructions in the corresponding method. In this way, the obfuscated java software will be interpreted correctly in the modified JVM.

Experimental Result

We have implemented our framework by Visual Studio 2005 and Eclipse 3.2M.

The Java bytecode instructions are divide into two classes:

- Simple instructions (Table2): Instructions that can be substitute each other. They are classified into seven subgroups further. Subgroups that contain less than five instructions are omitted.

  Local storage related instructions (Table 3): In order to pass the check by bytecode verifier, a data-flow analysis is needed to guarantee that the local variable referenced by the submitted instruction has already been defined and initialized. Since the

[4] http://www2s.biglobe.ne.jp/~dat/java/project/jvm/

[5] http://www.gnu.org/software/classpath/

Subgroup	Instructions	Subgroup	Instructions
1	iconst_m1	4	fadd
	iconst_0		fsub
	iconst_1		fmul
	iconst_2		fdiv
	iconst_3		frem
	iconst_4		
	iconst_5	5	dadd
2	iadd		dsub
	isub		dmul
	imul		ddiv
	idiv		drem
	irem	6	ifeq
	iand		ifne
	ior		iflt
	ixor		ifle
3	ladd		ifgt
	lsub		ifge
	lmul	7	if_icmpeq
	ldiv		if_icmpne
	lrem		if_icmplt
	land		if_icmple
	lor		if_icmpgt
	lxor		if_icmpge

Table 2. Simple instruction subgroups

Subgroup	Instructions	Subgroup	Instructions
1	iload_0	2	istore_0
	iload_1		istore_1
	iload_2		istore_2
	iload_3		istore_3
3	lload_0	4	lstore_0
	lload_1		lstore_1
	lload_2		lstore_2
	lload_3		lstore_3
5	fload_0	6	fstore_0
	fload_1		fstore_1
	fload_2		fstore_2
	fload_3		fstore_3
7	dload_0	8	dstore_0
	dload_1		dstore_1
	dload_2		dstore_2
	dload_3		dstore_3

Table 3. Local storage related instruction subgroups

instructions like iload n, istore n etc. have two bytes length, while the instructions in Table 3 are one byte in length, substitution of the two different length instructions will affect all the following local variable's address, which leads to a more complicated processing, these instructions are also omitted.

We applied our scheme to five java programs (Table 4 and 5). It can be seen that about 10 percent of instructions are replaced by other instructions in the same group in Table 4, while only about 1 percent of instructions are replaced by other instructions in the same group in Table 5 for local storage related instructions. The file size in the second line of Table 4 gets smaller after obfuscated. This is due to the compress algorithm of jar compressed the obfuscated files more effectively. In fact, some of the class files inside the jar become bigger than the original.

Program	Size (bytes)		Total instructions	Substituted instructions
	Before obfuscation	After obfuscation		
Example.jar	111580	112480	2218	157
Imageviewer.jar	4137	4099	369	34
Jode.jar	530491	551630	83051	9909
Jbubblebreaker.jar	187795	189978	5718	649
JHEditor	77036	79942	11896	1545

Table 4. Simple instruction obfuscation

Program	Size (bytes)		Total instructions	Substituted instructions
	Before obfuscation	After obfuscation		
Example.jar	111580	112097	2218	25
Imageviewer.jar	4137	4196	369	11
Jode.jar	530491	565753	83051	2981
Jbubblebreaker.jar	187795	189086	5718	183
JHEditor	77036	79231	11896	567

Table 5. Local storage related instruction obfuscation

All the results in Fig. 13, 14, 15,16 are obtained by the following Mysaifu JVM settings:
Max heap size: 2M

- Java stack size: 32KB
- Native stack size: 160KB
- Verifier: Off

In debug mode, the max load delay is less than 10%, while most load delay is lower than 6% in release mode. When these programs are ready to run, their efficiency is the same as those original programs. Thus, our proposed scheme has little performance influence on the original program.

To some extent, this framework is a mixture of obfuscation, diversity, and tamper-proofing techniques. Each instruction is a one-to-many map to its semantics which is determined by the auxiliary input at runtime. Due to the fact that each output function λ_i can be defined independently based on different W_p, the translation space is very large. Only for Table 2, there will be $7! \times 8! \times 8! \times 5! \times 5! \times 6! \times 6! \approx 5.1e10^{22}$ different rules (translators) approximately. Further more, suppose a program contains seventy instructions within

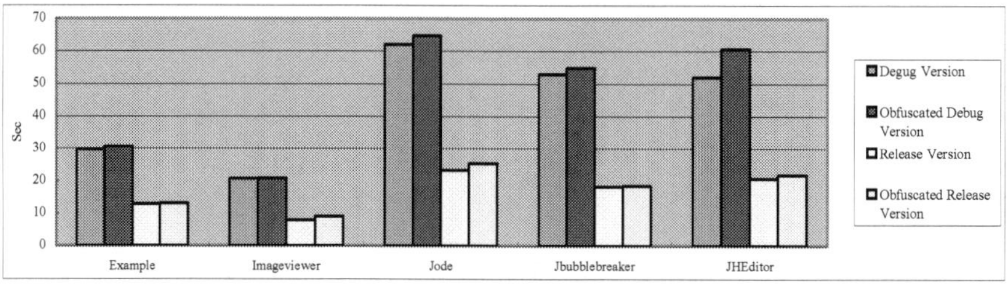

Fig. 13. Load time of simple instruction obfuscation in the Pocket PC 2003 SE Emulator

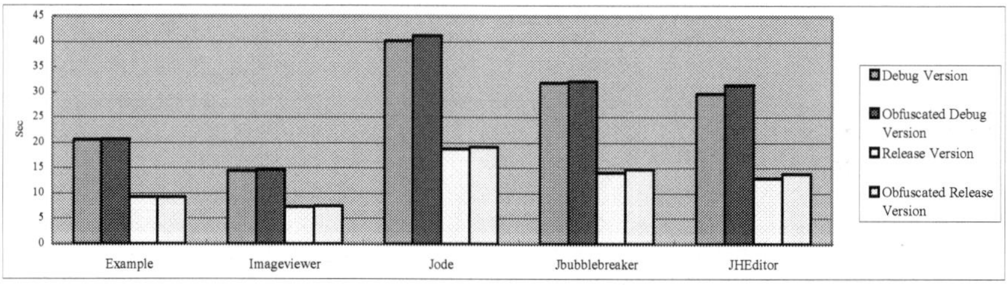

Fig. 14. Load time of simple instruction obfuscation in Dopod P800 mobile phone

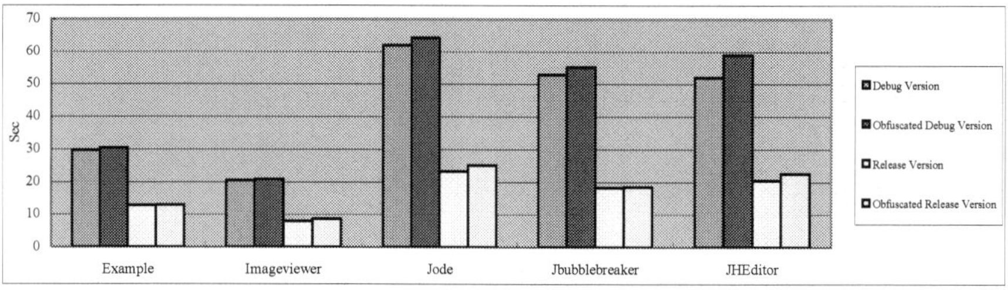

Fig. 15. Load time of local storage related instruction obfuscation in the Pocket PC 2003 SE Emulator

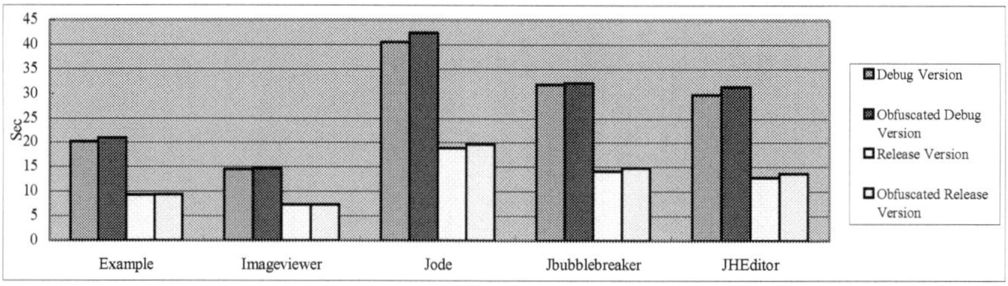

Fig. 16. Load time of local storage related instruction obfuscation in Dopod P800 mobile phone

which each ten instructions belongs to a distinct subgroup. Then there would be $10^7 \times 7 \times 8 \times 8 \times 5 \times 5 \times 6 \times 6 \approx 4$ e 10^{12} different versions even for a single interpreter. The translated program P_x can also be seen as an encrypted version. Not knowing the precise map among instructions, tampering it will definitely lead to the program's undefined behavior. An malicious users who tries to decompile the translated program only get the wrong semantics, he cannot reveal the real algorithm or design model.
The effective way to attack this framework is to crack Au_x. Once the SIM card number is obtained, the auxilary input Au_x can be easily decrypted. Using SIM card number as the enryption key is the most vulnerable weaknpoint of this model, it still need further study to establish a more secure way to protect Au_x.

6. Conclusion

Since Collberg's (1997) and Barak's (2001) seminal papers, program obfuscation has received considerable attentions over the last decade. As a result, a variety of formal definitions and practical methods of obfuscation have been developed. This chapter provides a brief survey of this progress on both the context of cryptography and software engineering. As a relatively less expensive method, despite the impossibility in cryptography, obfuscation does introduce the difficulty to reverse engineering. In this sense, it is still one of the promising techniques on software protection. In Sections 4, a call-flow obfuscation method is presented for Java program, which is also applicable to any other object oriented language. At the final section, an instruction obfuscation framework target at mobile phone Java applications is discussed. Different from personal computer platform, the JVM run in embedded system is usually customized according to different mobile phone hardware model, which leads to a large variety of JVMs. This kind diversity of JVM indicates that it is feasible and easy to apply the framework to the protection of mobile Java program.

7. References

Barak, B., Goldreich, O., Impagliazzo, R. ,Rudich, S., Sahai, A., Vadhan, S., Yang K. (2001). On the (Im)possibility of Obfuscating Programs. *Proceedings of the 21st Annual International Cryptology Conference on Advances in Cryptology,* pp. 1-18, Santa Barbara, 2001 Aug. 19-23, Springer-Verlag, California.

Batchelder, M., Hendren, L. (2007). Obfuscating java: The most pain for the least gain, *Proceedings of the International Conference on Compiler Construction, Lecture Notes in Computer Science,* vol. 4420, 2007, pp. 96-110, Springer, Berlin.

Canetti, R. (1997). Towards Realizing Random Oracles: Hash Functions That Hide All Partial Information, *Advances in Cryptology - CRYPTO 1997, Lecture Notes in Computer Science,* vol. 1294, pp. 455–469, London, UK, 1997, Springer-Verlag.

Canetti, R., Micciancio, D., Reingold, O. (1998). Perfectly One-Way Probabilistic Hash Functions (Preliminary Version). *Proceedings of the 30th ACM Symposium on Theory of Computing (STOC 1998),* pages 131–140. ACM Press.

Chan, J.T. , Yang, W. (2004). Advanced obfuscation techniques for Java bytecode, *Journal of Systems add Software,* Vol. 71, No.2, pp. 1~11.

Chatterjee, R., Ryder, B.G., Landi, W. (2001). Complexity of Points-To Analysis of Java in the Presence of Exceptions. *IEEE Transactions on Software Engineering,* Vol. 27, pp. 481-512.

Chow, S., Gu, Y., Johnson, H., Zakharov, V.A. (2001). An Approach to the Obfuscation of Control-Flow of Sequential Computer Programs, *Proceedings of the 4th International Conference on Information Security*, pp. 144-155.

Cimato, S., Santis, A.D., Petrillo, U.F. (2005). Overcoming the obfuscation of Java program by identifier renaming, *Journal of Systems and Software*, Vol. 78, pp. 60-72.

Collberg, C., Thomborson, C., Low, D. (1997). A Taxonomy of Obfuscating Transformations. Tech. Report, #148, University of Auckland.

Collberg, C., Thomborson, C., Low, D. (1998a). Breaking Abstractions and Unstructuring Data Structures, *Proceedings of IEEE International Conference on Computer Languages*, pp. 28-38.

Collberg, C., Thomborson, C., Low, D. (1998b). Manufacturing cheap, resilient and stealthy opaque constructs. *Proceedings of the 25th ACM SIGPLAN-SIGACT Symposium on Principles of Programming Languages*, pp. 184–196, San Diego, California, US.

Collberg, C., Thomborson, C. (2000). Watermarking, tamper-proofing, and obfuscation tools for software protection. Technical Report TR00-03, The Department of Computer Science, University of Arizona.

Cohen, F.B. (1993). Operating system protection through program evolution. *Computers and Security*, Vol. 12, pp. 565–584.

Diffie, W., Hellman, M. (1976). New directions in cryptography, *IEEE Transactions on Information Theory*, Vol. 22, No. 6, pp.644–654.

Drape, S. (2006). Generalising the array split obfuscation, *Information Sciences Journa*, Vol. 177, No. 1, pp. 202-219*l*, Elsevier, Department of Computer Science, University of Auckland, March 2006.

Drape, S., Majumdar, A., and Thomborson, C. (2007). Slicing Obfuscations: Design, Correctness, and Evaluation, *Proceedings of the Seventh ACM Workshop on Digital Rights Management (ACM-DRM 2007) (Part of the Fourteenth ACM Conference on Computer and Communications Security (ACM-CCS 2007))*, pp.70-81, October 29 - November 2, 2007. Alexandria, VA, USA. ACM Press.

Dyke, V., Colin, W. (2006). Advances in low-level software protection, PhD thesis, Oregon State University.

D'Anna, L., Matt, B., Reisse, A., Van Vleck, T., Schwab, S., LeBlanc, P. (2003). Self-Protecting Mobile Agents Obfuscation Report, Report #03-015, Network Associates Laboratories.

Ertaul, L., Venkatesh, S. (2005). Novel Obfuscation Algorithms for Software Security, *Proceedings of the 2005 International Conference on Software Engineering Research and Practice*, pp.209-215, June, Las Vegas.

Goldwasser, S., Kalai, Y.T. (2005). On the Impossibility of Obfuscation with Auxiliary Input. *Proceedings of the 46th Symposium on Foundations of Computer Science (FOCS 2005), IEEE Computer Society*, pp. 553–562, Washington, DC, USA.

Goldwasser, S., Rothblum, G. (2007). On Best-Possible Obfuscation, *Lecture Notes in Computer Science*, vol. 4392, pp.194–213,Springer-Verlag.

Hada, S.(2000). Zero-Knowledge and Code Obfuscation. In Tatsuaki Okamoto, editor, Advances in Cryptology - ASIACRYPT 2000, volume 1976 of Lecture Notes in Computer Science, pages 443–457, London, UK, 2000. Springer-Verlag.

Hofheinz, D., Malone-Lee, J., Stam, M. (2007). Obfuscation for Cryptographic Purposes. *Proceedings of 4th Theory of Cryptography Conference (TCC 2007), Lecture Notes in Computer Science,* vol. 4392, pp. 214–232. Springer-Verlag.

Hohenberger, S., Rothblum, G., Shelat, A., Vaikuntanathan, V. (2007). Securely Obfuscating Re-Encryption. *Proceedings of 4th Theory of Cryptography Conference (TCC 2007), Lecture Notes in Computer Science,* vol. 4392, pp. 233–252, Springer-Verlag.

Hohl, F. (1998) . Time limited blackbox security: protecting mobile agents from malicious hosts, *Mobile Agents and Security, Lecture Notes in Computer Science,* Vol. 1419, pp. 92–113. Springer, Heidelberg.

Josse, S. (2006). How to assess the effectiveness of your anti-virus. *Computer Virology,* 2006,Vol. 2, pp.51-65, Springer Paris.

Karnick, M., MacBride, J., McGinnis, S., Tang, Y., Ramachandran, R. (2006). A Qualitative analysis of Java Obfuscation, *Proceedings of 10th IASTED International Conference on Software Engineering and Applications,* Dallas TX,USA, November 13-15, 2006.

Kuzurin, N., Shokurov, A., Varnovsky, N., Zakharov, V. (2007). On the Concept of Software Obfuscation in Computer Security, *Lecture Notes in Computer Science,* Springer-Verlag, vol.4779, pp.281-298.

Linn, C., Debray, S. (2003). Obfuscation of executable code to improve resistance to static disassembly. *ACM Conference on Computer and Communications Security,* pp. 290-299, Washington D.C.

Lynn, B., Prabhakaran, M., Sahai, A. (2004). Positive Results and Techniques for Obfuscation. *Advances in Cryptology - EUROCRYPT 2004, Lecture Notes in Computer Science,* vol. 3027, pages 20–39. Springer-Verlag.

Monden, A., Monsifrot, A., Thomborson, C. (2004). A framework for obfuscated interpretation, *Australasian Information SecurityWorkshop (AISW2004),* ed. P. Montague and C. Steketee, ACS, CRPIT, vol. 32, pp. 7–16.

Naccache, D., Shamir, A., Stern, J. P. (1999). How to copyright a function? , *Lecture Notes in Computer Science,* vol.1560, pp. 188–196, March 1999,Springer

Palsberg, J., Krishnaswamy, S., Kwon, M., Ma, D., Shao, Q., and Zhang, Y., (2000). Experience with software watermarking. *Proceedings of 16th IEEE Annual Computer Security Applications Conference (ACSAC'00).* IEEE Press, p308-316. New Orleans, LA, USA, 2000.

Praveen, S., Lal, P.S. (2007). Array Data Transformation for Source Code Obfuscation. *Proceedings of World Academy of Science, Engineering and Technology (PWASET)* Vol.21 MAY 2007, ISSN 1307-6884.

Sosonkin, M., Naumovich, G., Memon, N. (2003). Obfuscation of design intent in object-oriented applications. *Proceedings of the 3rd ACM workshop on Digital rights management,* pp. 142–153, New York, NY, USA, 2003, ACM Press.

Toyofuku, T., Tabata, T., Sakurai, K. (2005). Program Obfuscation Scheme using Random Numbers to Complicate Control Flow, *Proceedings of the First International Workshop on Security in Ubiquitous Computing Systems (SecUbiq`05), Lecture Notes in Computer Science (LNCS),* Vol. 3823, pp. 916-925.

Venkatraj, A. (2003). Program Obfuscation, MS Thesis, Department of Computer Science, University of Arizona.

Wang, C., Hill, J., Knight, J.C., Davidson, J.W. (2001). Protection of software-based survivability mechanisms, *Proceedings of the 2001 conference on Dependable Systems and Networks, IEEE Computer Society*, pp. 193-202.

Wee, H. (2005). On Obfuscating Point Functions, *Proceedings of the 37th ACM Symposium on Theory of Computing (STOC 2005)*, pp. 523–532, New York, NY, USA, 2005. ACM Press.

Wyseur, B. (2009). White-Box Cryptography, PhD thesis, Katholieke Universiteit Leuven.

Wroblewski, G. (2002). General Method of Program Code Obfuscation, PhD thesis, Wroclaw University of Technology, Institute of Engineering Cybernetics.

Zhu, F. (2007). Concepts and Techniques in Software Watermarking and Obfuscation, PhD Thesis, University of Auckland.

19

Systematic Generation of An Irreducible Polynomial of An Arbitrary Degree m over $\mathbb{F}_p$ Such That $p > m$

Hiroaki Nasu[1], Yasuyuki Nogami[1], Yoshitaka Morikawa[1], Shigeki Kobayashi[2] and Tatsuo Sugimura[2]
[1]Okayama University,
[2]Shinshu University
Japan

1. Introduction

There are many studies for generating irreducible polynomials (L. M. Adleman & H. W. Lenstra (1986)) – (Ian. F. Blake et al., (1993)). This is because irreducible polynomials play critical roles in the cases such as constructing extension field or generating random sequence. The problem of generating irreducible polynomial is theoretically interesting and have attracted many scientists and engineers. Those previous works are roughly classified by the objective: one is arbitrary – degree and the other is efficient for fast arithmetic operations in extension field. This paper is related to the former. As an application of the proposed method, the authors consider variable key – length public key cryptography (M. Scott (2006)).

Adleman et al. (L. M. Adleman & H. W. Lenstra (1986)) have shown that an irreducible polynomial of degree m over $\mathbb{F}_p$ with an arbitrary pair of p and m is generated by using a Gauss period normal basis (GNB) in $\mathbb{F}_{p^m}$ and Shoup shown almost the same idea (V. Shoup (1990)). Because, as introduced in Gao's paper (S. Gao (1993)), a GNB in $\mathbb{F}_{p^m}$ always exists for an arbitrary pair of p and m such that $4p$ does not divide $m(p-1)$. However, they do not explicitly give a concrete generating algorithm. Of course, their calculation costs are not explicitly evaluated. Their methods are based on the minimal polynomial determination and efficiently using Newton's formula (R. Lidl & H. Niederreiter (1984)). On the other hand, the authors (K. Makita et al., (2005)) have explicitly given efficient generating algorithms in which characteristic $p = 2$ is only dealt with. These algorithms (K. Makita et al., (2005)) determine the minimal polynomial of TypeII ONB in $\mathbb{F}_{2^m}$ quite fast; however, if TypeII ONB does not exist in $\mathbb{F}_{2^m}$, it does not work. Thus, our previous works restrict not only degrees but also the characteristic to 2. Using Newton's formula and a certain special class of Gauss period normal bases in $\mathbb{F}_{p^m}$, this paper gives a concrete algorithm that efficiently generates an irreducible polynomial of degree m over $\mathbb{F}_p$ for an arbitrary pair of m and $p > m$. When $p > m$, it is automatically satisfied that $4p$ does not divide $m(p-1)$. The restriction $p > m$

comes from using Newton's formula. When one uses the distributive law instead, the proposed algorithm can avoid the restriction.

The main idea is as follows. Just like the previous works (L. M. Adleman & H. W. Lenstra (1986)), (V. Shoup (1990)), if we have arithmetic operations in $\mathbb{F}_{p^m}$, for a proper element a in $\mathbb{F}_{p^m}$ we can calculate its minimal polynomial $M_\alpha(x)$ with respect to the prime field $\mathbb{F}_p$, where a proper element means that it belongs to $\mathbb{F}_{p^m}$ but not to its proper subfield. It is well-known that $M_\alpha(x)$ becomes an irreducible monic polynomial over $\mathbb{F}_p$ and the coefficients of $M_\alpha(x)$ are systematically calculated from its vector representation by Newton's formula (V. Shoup (1990)), (R. Lidl & H. Niederreiter (1984)). In order to carry out multiplications in $\mathbb{F}_{p^m}$ without using an irreducible polynomial of degree m over $\mathbb{F}_p$, this paper uses cyclic vector multiplication algorithm (CVMA) (Y. Nogami et al., (2003)).

As previously described, this paper uses a special class of Gauss period normal bases (GNB). The special class normal basis is given from TypeI ONB (Y. Nogami et al., (2003)). In what follows, we call it TypeI-X NB (TypeI eXtended normal basis). The authors have proposed a multiplication algorithm for TypeI-X NB, it is cyclic vector multiplication algorithm (CVMA) (Y. Nogami et al., (2003)). It is noted that CVMA can calculate a multiplication in $\mathbb{F}_{p^m}$ without explicitly preparing an irreducible polynomial of degree m over $\mathbb{F}_p$ as the modulus polynomial of $\mathbb{F}_{p^m}$. Arithmetic operations in extension field $\mathbb{F}_{p^m}$ is defined by an irreducible polynomial $f(x)$ over $\mathbb{F}_p$ of degree m in which $f(x)$ is often called the modulus polynomial of $\mathbb{F}_{p^m}$. Using CVMA for TypeI-X NB, this paper shows an efficient algorithm for generating an irreducible polynomial of an arbitrary degree m over an arbitrary prime field $\mathbb{F}_p$ such that $p > m$. It uses Newton's formula. In other words, this paper explicitly gives an efficient algorithm for the ideas introduced by (L. M. Adleman & H. W. Lenstra (1986)), (V. Shoup (1990)). After that, this paper shows that the proposed algorithm can quite efficiently determine the minimal polynomial of TypeI-X NB in $\mathbb{F}_{p^m}$. The proposed algorithm has the following features: 1) it efficiently determines the minimal polynomial of the special class normal basis (TypeI-X NB), 2) its calculation complexity does not closely depend on the size of characteristic p, 3) its calculation cost is clearly given with degree m, thus we can estimate how much calculation time the proposed algorithm needs, 4) it can generate primitive polynomials if $(p^m - 1)$ is factorized as the product of prime numbers, and 5) as compared to distinct degree factorization based irreducibility testing algorithm (J. Gathen & D. Panario (2001)) and the case using the distributive law instead of Newton's formula, it generates an irreducible polynomial much faster.

As an application, this paper considers variable key – length public key cryptography in which one fixes characteristic p within the word length of the processor concerned and varies degree m appropriately.

Throughout this paper, #SADD, #SMUL and #SINV denote the number of additions, multiplications, and that of inversions in $\mathbb{F}p$, respectively. In this paper, a subtraction in $\mathbb{F}p$ is counted up as an addition in $\mathbb{F}p$. p and m denote characteristic and extension degree, respectively, where p is a prime number. $\mathbb{F}_{p^m}$ denotes the m-th extension field over $\mathbb{F}p$ and $\mathbb{F}^*_{p^m}$ denotes the multiplicative group in $\mathbb{F}_{p^m}$. $X \mid Y$ means that X divides Y. Without any additional explanation, lower and upper case letters show elements in prime fields and extension fields, respectively, and a Greek character shows a zero of modulus polynomial. Polynomials in this paper are all monic polynomials.

2. Fundamentals

In this section, we briefly go over several classes of irreducible polynomials over $\mathbb{F}_p$.

2.1 Irreducible binomial

The well-known optimal extension field (OEF) adopts an irreducible binomial as the modulus polynomial (D. Bailey & C. Paar (2000)). We can easily prepare an irreducible binomial by the following theorem (R. Lidl & H. Niederreiter (1984)).

Theorem 1 There exist irreducible binomials in the form $x^m - s$, $s \in \mathbb{F}_p$ if and only if each prime factor of m divides $p-1$ and $4 \mid (p-1)$ when $4 \mid m$. ■

For example, let m be a prime, if the following relation holds, $x^m - s$ becomes irreducible over $\mathbb{F}_p$.

$$s^{(p-1)/m} \neq 1. \tag{1}$$

According to Theo.1, in this case $p - 1$ must be divisible by the prime number m. Therefore, when m is large, irreducible binomials of degree m over $\mathbb{F}_p$ are quite restricted corresponding to p.

2.2 Irreducible trinomial

Irreducible trinomials have been studied especially for characteristic $p = 2$. For an arbitrary pair of p and m, irreducible trinomials do not always exist (E. Berlekamp (1968)). In addition, it is not explicitly known when the following trinomial becomes irreducible over $\mathbb{F}_p$.

$$x^m + ax^n + b, \quad a, b \in \mathbb{F}_p. \tag{2}$$

In general, in order to generate an irreducible trinomial in the form of Eq.(2), we need irreducibility tests with changing the parameters a, b, and n. Therefore, when both p and m are large, searching an irreducible trinomial becomes quite time-consuming.

2.3 Variable transformation

According to the following theorems (R. Lidl & H. Niederreiter (1984)), (Y. Nogami et al., (1999)), we can generate higher degree irreducible polynomials with corresponding variable transformations.

Theorem 2 For an irreducible polynomial $f(x)$ of degree m over $\mathbb{F}_p$, if and only if $f(x)$ satisfies

$$x^{(p^m-1)/k} \not\equiv 1 \bmod f(x) \tag{3}$$

for a certain prime number k such that k divides $p^m - 1$, $f(x^k)$ becomes irreducible over $\mathbb{F}_p$. ■

Theorem 3 For an irreducible polynomial $f(x)$ of degree m over $\mathbb{F}_p$, if and only if the $(m-1)$-th coefficient is not 0, $f(x^p - x)$ becomes irreducible over $\mathbb{F}_p$. ■

Based on these theorems, we can generate infinite number of irreducible polynomials of degree mk^i (R. Lidl & H. Niederreiter (1984)) and mp^i (Y. Nogami et al., (1999)), respectively; however, prime degree irreducible polynomials are not generated. In addition, we need a certain seed irreducible polynomial $f(x)$.

2.4 Cyclotomic irreducible polynomial

According to the next theorem, we can easily obtain all one irreducible polynomial $(x^{m+1}-1)/(x-1)$ (T. Sugimura & Y. Suetugu (1991)). The coefficients of $(x^{m+1}-1)/(x-1)$ are all one, therefore it is called all one polynomial of degree m.

Theorem 4 All one polynomial $(x^{m+1}-1)/(x-1)$ of degree m is irreducible over $\mathbb{F}_p$ if and only if the following conditions are both satisfied.

1. $m + 1$ is a prime number, therefore m is even.
2. p is a primitive element in $\mathbb{F}_{m+1}$, where note that $m + 1$ is a prime number, $\mathbb{F}_{m+1}$ denotes the prime field of order $m + 1$. ■

Sugimura et al. introduced all varieties of the cyclotomic irreducible polynomials (T. Sugimura & Y. Suetugu (1991)); however, as shown in the above theorem, the degree is a certain even number. In other words, odd degree irreducible polynomials can not be obtained as cyclotomic polynomials.

2.5 Distinct degree factorization

We can generate an irreducible polynomial $f(x)$ of a certain prime degree m over $\mathbb{F}_p$ by randomly preparing a polynomial of degree m over $\mathbb{F}_p$ and then testing its irreducibility over $\mathbb{F}_p$. For this irreducibility test, we can apply the distinct degree factorization (DDF) (E. Berlekamp (1968)). In the case that the degree m is a prime number, DDF checks the following relation:

$$f(x) \mid (x^{p^m} - x)/(x^p - x). \tag{4}$$

Noting that this paper mainly deals with characteristic p larger than m, $f(x)$ is irreducible over $\mathbb{F}_p$ if and only if $f(x)$ satisfies Eq.(4). This calculation requires polynomial multiplications and modulo operations, therefore it becomes more time-consuming as characteristic p and degree m become larger. Moreover, the possibility that a polynomial $f(x)$ of degree m becomes irreducible over $\mathbb{F}_p$ is about $1/m$. Therefore, when we apply such an irreducibility testing algorithm for generating an irreducible polynomial, it becomes a probabilistic problem. Since the calculation Eq.(4) needs $\mathcal{O}(m^{2.7} \log p)$ multiplications in $\mathbb{F}_p$ when we apply the well-known Karatsuba method for polynomial multiplications and the binary method for the exponentiation x^{p^m}(D. Knuth (1981)), generating an irreducible polynomial of degree m over $\mathbb{F}_p$ needs $\mathcal{O}(m^{3.7} \log p)$ multiplications in $\mathbb{F}_p$. Therefore, when both p and m are large, it will be a quite time-consuming operation.

2.6 Recursive generation

If we have an irreducible polynomial, we can recursively generate a lot of irreducible polynomials of the same degree (A. J. Menezes, editor (1993)); however, we need an irreducible polynomial as a generator.

2.7 Minimal polynomial determination

If we have the arithmetic operations in $\mathbb{F}_{p^m}$, we can generate an irreducible polynomial as the minimal polynomial of an arbitrary proper element in $\mathbb{F}_{p^m}$. If an element belongs to $\mathbb{F}_{p^m}$but not to its proper subfield, the element is called proper element in $\mathbb{F}_{p^m}$. In general, the arithmetic operations are defined by the modulus polynomial that is a certain irreducible polynomial of degree m over $\mathbb{F}_p$; however, some extension fields do not explicitly need an irreducible polynomial of degree m such as TypeII AOPF (Y. Nogami et al.,(2005)). TypeII AOPF adopts TypeII optimal normal basis (ONB).
The authors (K. Makita et al., (2005)) have proposed efficient algorithms for determining the minimal polynomial of TypeII ONB (Y. Nogami et al., (2005)). TypeII ONB only exists in the following extension fields $\mathbb{F}_{p^m}$.
Theorem 5 TypeII ONB exists in $\mathbb{F}_{p^m}$ if and only if p and m satisfy (1) and either (2a) or (2b):
1. $2m + 1$ is a prime number.
2.a p is a primitive element in $\mathbb{F}_{2m+1}$.
2.b The order of p mod $2m + 1$ is m and $2 \mid (m - 1)$. ■

The algorithms proposed in (K. Makita et al., (2005)), in which the case of $p = 2$ is only dealt with, are quite fast; however, they have the following problems:

- They determine the minimal polynomial of TypeII ONB in $\mathbb{F}_{2^m}$. In other words, if TypeII ONB does not exist in $\mathbb{F}_{2^m}$, they does not generate an irreducible polynomial of degree m over $\mathbb{F}_2$.
- They do not generate an irreducible polynomial over $\mathbb{F}_p$ for an arbitrary pair of p and m.

Adleman et al. (L. M. Adleman & H. W. Lenstra (1986)) and Shoup (V. Shoup (1990)) have introduced that an irreducible polynomial of degree m over $\mathbb{F}_p$ with an arbitrary pair of p and m can be generated by using a GNB in $\mathbb{F}_{p^m}$; however, they do not give any explicit algorithms. Of course, their calculation costs are not explicitly evaluated. Thus, this paper explicitly gives an algorithm that generates an irreducible polynomial of degree m over $\mathbb{F}_p$ by using a GNB in $\mathbb{F}_{p^m}$. In addition, the calculation cost is explicitly given. It is applied for an arbitrary pair of p and m.

3. Irreducible polynomial generation

This section introduces the idea and algorithms.

3.1 Main idea

In this section, we introduce a special class of Gauss period normal bases (GNB). The special class normal basis is given from TypeI ONB (Y. Nogami et al., (2003)). In this paper, we call it TypeI-X NB (TypeI eXtended normal basis). The authors have proposed a multiplication algorithm named cyclic vector multiplication algorithm (CVMA) (T. Yoshida et al., (2006)). It is also available for TypeI-X NB. It is noted that CVMA calculates a multiplication in $\mathbb{F}_{p^m}$ without explicitly preparing an irreducible polynomial of degree m over $\mathbb{F}_p$ as the modulus polynomial of $\mathbb{F}_{p^m}$. Using CVMA with TypeI-X NB, this paper shows an efficient algorithm for generating an irreducible polynomial of an arbitrary degree m over an arbitrary prime field $\mathbb{F}_p$. After that, it is shown that the proposed algorithm quite efficiently determines the minimal polynomial of TypeI-X NB in $\mathbb{F}_{p^m}$.

3.2 Minimal polynomial

Let us briefly go over the fundamentals of minimal polynomial. Let α be a proper element in $\mathbb{F}_{p^m}$. Then, its minimal polynomial $M_\alpha(x)$ is given as

$$M_\alpha(x) = \prod_{i=0}^{m-1} (x - \alpha^{p^i}) \tag{5a}$$

$$= x^m + a_{m-1}x^{m-1} + \cdots + a_1 x + a_0, \tag{5b}$$

where $a_{m-1}, \ldots, a_1, a_0$ are in $\mathbb{F}_p$. $M_\alpha(x)$ becomes a monic irreducible polynomial of degree m over $\mathbb{F}_p$ (R. Lidl & H. Niederreiter (1984)). When the degree m is large, it is too time-consuming to directly develop Eq.(5a) into Eq.(5b) with the distributive law; however, if m is smaller than p, we can systematically obtain each coefficient of $M_\alpha(x)$ by Newton's formula as described in the next section. As previously introduced, the restriction thus comes from using Newton's formula.

3.3 Minimal polynomial and Newton's formula

First, we define the notation $\mathrm{Tr}^{[n]}(\alpha)$ as follows.

Definition 1 For a proper element a in $\mathbb{F}_{p^m}$, consider its m conjugates as follows:

$$\{\alpha, \alpha^p, \cdots, \alpha^{p^{m-1}}\}. \tag{6}$$

Let $1 \leq n \leq m$, $\mathrm{Tr}^{[n]}(\alpha)$ is defined as

$$\mathrm{Tr}^{[n]}(\alpha) = \sum_{0 \leq i_1 < i_2 < \cdots < i_n \leq m-1} \alpha^{p^{i_1}} \alpha^{p^{i_2}} \cdots \alpha^{p^{i_n}}. \tag{7}$$

■

According to the Newton's formula (R. Lidl & H. Niederreiter (1984)), (V. Shoup (1990)), each coefficient of the minimal polynomial $M_\alpha(x)$ that is defined by Eqs.(5) is systematically given by

$$\begin{aligned} a_{m-n} &= (-1)^n \mathrm{Tr}^{[n]}(\alpha) \\ &= n^{-1} \left\{ -\mathrm{Tr}^{[1]}(\alpha^n) + \sum_{i=1}^{n-1} (-1)^{i+1} \mathrm{Tr}^{[i]}(\alpha) \mathrm{Tr}^{[1]}(\alpha^{n-i}) \right\} \end{aligned} \tag{8}$$

where $1 \leq n \leq m$ and $\mathrm{Tr}^{[1]}(\alpha^{n-i})$ is the trace of $\alpha^{n-i}$with respect to $\mathbb{F}_p$. As shown in Eq.(8), we need to calculate n^{-1}. Therefore, the above equation can be applied for the case that $p > m$. Newton's formula needs a lot of trace calculations, for which TypeI-X NB is also efficient because it is a normal basis (R. Lidl & H. Niederreiter (1984)).

3.4 A special class of Gauss period normal bases

Let us consider a special class of type-h$\langle k,m \rangle$ Gauss period normal bases as follows (T. Yoshida et al., (2006)).

Let km+1 be prime and suppose that p is a primitive element in $\mathbb{F}_{km+1}$. Then, let ω be a primitive (km + 1) fist root of unity, ω belongs to $\mathbb{F}_{p^{km}}$. The conjugates of ω form a TypeI ONB as follows.

$$\{\omega, \omega^p, \cdots, \omega^{p^{km-1}}\}. \tag{9}$$

Then, consider a special class of GNB as

$$\{\gamma, \gamma^p, \cdots, \gamma^{p^{m-1}}\}, \quad \gamma = \sum_{j=0}^{k-1} \omega^{p^{jm}}. \tag{10}$$

In this paper, we call the normal basis Eq.(10) TypeI-X normal basis (TypeI-X NB). A lot of studies about GNB have been done (M. Nöcker (2001)), (R. Granger (2005)). Gao (S. Gao (1993)) has discussed from the viewpoints of normal basis and self dual normal basis in detail. According to Gao's paper (S. Gao (1993)), TypeI-X NB in $\mathbb{F}_{p^m}$ always exists for an arbitrary pair of p and m such that $4p$ does not divide $m(p-1)$. The authors also checked it experimentally (T. Yoshida et al., (2006)). In the next section, how to carry out a multiplication with TypeI-X NB is introduced.

3.4.1 Multiplication with TypeI-X NB

A multiplication $Z = XY$ with TypeI-X NB in $\mathbb{F}_{p^m}$ is carried out by the algorithm shown in Fig 1. It is named cyclic vector multiplication algorithm (CVMA) (Y. Nogami et al., (2003)). The authors have improved CVMA several times (T. Yoshida et al., (2006)), (Y. Nogami et al., (2005)). In Fig 1. $\langle\cdot\rangle$ means $\cdot$ mod $km + 1$.

Input: $X = \sum_{i=0}^{m-1} x_i \gamma^{p^i}, \; Y = \sum_{i=0}^{m-1} y_i \gamma^{p^i}$.

Output: $Z = XY = \sum_{i=0}^{m-1} z_i \gamma^{p^i}$.

Preparation:

1. Determine k such that TypeI ONB exists.
2. For $0 \le i \le m$, $q[i] \leftarrow 0$.
3. For $0 \le t \le m-1$ and $0 \le h \le k-1$, $g\left[\langle p^{t+hm} \rangle\right] \leftarrow t+1$.
4. $g[0] \leftarrow 0$.

Procedure:

For $0 \le i \le m-1$, $q[i+1] \leftarrow x_i y_i$.
For $0 \le i < j \le m-1$, {
  $M \leftarrow (x_i - x_j)(y_i - y_j)$,
  For $0 \le h \le k-1$, {
    $q\left[g[\langle p^i + p^{j+hm} \rangle]\right] \leftarrow q\left[g[\langle p^i + p^{j+hm} \rangle]\right] + M$.
  }
}
For $0 \le i \le m-1$, $z_i \leftarrow kq[0] - q[i+1]$.

(End of algorithm)

Fig. 1. CVMA in $\mathbb{F}_{p^m}$ with TypeI-X NB

This algorithm needs the following cost:

$$\#\text{SMUL} = \frac{m(m+1)}{2} + 1, \tag{11a}$$

$$\#\text{SADD} = \frac{m(m-1)(k+2)}{2} + m. \tag{11b}$$

The well–known Karatsuba method calculates a polynomial multiplication of degree m with $\mathcal{O}(m^{1.7})$ $\mathbb{F}_p$–multiplications (D. Knuth (1981)); however, in this case we need a certain modulus polynomial of degree m over $\mathbb{F}_p$. On the other hand, CVMA does not need such an irreducible polynomial of degree m over $\mathbb{F}_p$; however, extension degree m is preferred to be small.

3.5 Minimal polynomial determination with CVMA

Using CVMA, as Sec.3.3 we can determine the minimal polynomial$M_\alpha(x)$ of a proper element $\alpha \in \mathbb{F}_{p^m}$.

a. Calculate α^i and then $\mathrm{Tr}^{[1]}(\alpha^i)$, where $1 \leq i \leq m$.

b. Calculate the coefficients a_i, $0 \leq i \leq m-1$.

Noting that TypeI-X NB Eq.(10) is a normal basis, $\mathrm{Tr}^{[1]}(\alpha^i)$ is calculated by $m-1$ additions in $\mathbb{F}_p$ with the vector coefficients of α^i. When a vector is represented with a normal basis, its trace is calculated by adding all of the vector coefficients. In addition, whether or not the element is a proper element in $\mathbb{F}_{p^m}$ is easily checked from its vector coefficients. For an arbitrary proper element α, determining its minimal polynomial $M_\alpha(x)$ takes the following calculation cost.

For the operation (a),

$$\#\text{SMUL} = (m-1)\left(\frac{m(m+1)}{2} + 1\right), \tag{12a}$$

$$\#\text{SADD} = (m-1)\left(\frac{m(m-1)(k+2)}{2} + m\right) + m(m-1). \tag{12b}$$

In detail, for α^i, $1 \leq i \leq m$, we need $m-1$ multiplications in $\mathbb{F}_{p^m}$ with CVMA. Then, for $\mathrm{Tr}^{[1]}(\alpha^i)$, we need $m-1$ additions in $\mathbb{F}_p$. In total, we need Eqs.(12). For the operation (b),

$$\#\text{SMUL} = \#\text{SADD} = \frac{m(m-1)}{2} + (m-1), \tag{13a}$$

$$\#\text{SINV} = m-2. \tag{13b}$$

The calculation cost Eqs.(13) is given from Eq.(8). The operations (a) and (b) need $\mathcal{O}(m^3)$ and $\mathcal{O}(m^2)$ $\mathbb{F}_p$-multiplications, respectively. Thus, the major computation is for the operation (a).

By the way, since the proposed algorithm is based on the minimal polynomial determination, it can be applied for generating a primitive polynomial. In detail, if p^m-1, that is the order of $\mathbb{F}^*_{p^m}$, is factorized as the product of prime numbers, we can prepare a primitive element in $\mathbb{F}_{p^m}$ as a proper element α (R. Lidl & H. Niederreiter (1984)). Then, using a primitive element, the proposed algorithm generates a primitive polynomial of degree m over $\mathbb{F}_p$. In the next section, applying one of the basis elements shown in Eq.(10) as a proper element in $\mathbb{F}_{p^m}$, we improve the operation (a).

3.6 Minimal polynomial of TypeI-X NB

Using γ defined in Eq.(10), that is a proper element in $\mathbb{F}_{p^m}$ and its conjugates form the TypeI-X NB Eq.(10), we calculate its minimal polynomial $M_\gamma(x)$. According to Eq.(8) and CVMA Fig 1., the minimal polynomial $M_\gamma(x)$ is calculated by the algorithm Fig 2.
In Fig 2., Tr $[i]$ denote $\mathrm{Tr}^{[1]}(\gamma^i)$, $1 \le i \le m$, respectively. In addition, $x[j]$, $0 \le j \le m-1$ denote the vector coefficients of γ^{i-1}, $2 \le i \le m$ in each loop from line 7: to line 18:. Since TypeI-X NB is a normal basis, traces are efficiently calculated as shown at line 17:. Lines 1:, 2:, and 3: are preparations for CVMA in $\mathbb{F}_{p^m}$. From line 9: to line 17:, $\gamma^{i-1} \times \gamma$, $1 \le i \le m$ is calculated by modifying CVMA. This calculation is quite simpli_ed because the vector representation of the input γ is (1, 0, 0, ... , 0). Then, at line 18: $\mathrm{Tr}^{[1]}(\gamma^i)$ is calculated. At line 16:, noting that k is small (T. Yoshida et al., (2006)), $kq[0]$ is calculated with k¡1 additions in $\mathbb{F}_p$. Thus, the calculation cost for the operation (a) becomes

$$\#\text{SMUL} = 0, \tag{14a}$$

$$\begin{aligned}\#\text{SADD} &= (m-1)(m-1) + (m-1)(m-1)k + (m-1)(k-1) + m(m-1) + (m+1)(m-1) \\ &= (m-1)(mk + 3m - 1).\end{aligned} \tag{14b}$$

In the right hand side of Eq.(14b), the five terms correspond to line 11:, 13:, 16:, 17:, and 18:, respectively. Thus, the operation (a) does not need any multiplications in $\mathbb{F}_p$, therefore the major computation is changed to the operation (b) shown from line 20: to line 26: in Fig 2., which needs $\mathcal{O}(m^2)$ $\mathbb{F}_p$-multiplications. Line 23: corresponds to Eq.(8). In detail, its calculation cost is evaluated as Eq.(13).
As shown in Fig 2., the proposed algorithm needs to calculate the indexes such as $\langle 1 + (p^{j+mt}) \rangle$; however, these indexes can be previously calculated when extension degree m is small. Of course, we can directly write down the program with the previously calculated indexes, therefore, the calculation cost for these indexes is not taken into account in this paper. By the way, according to Gao's paper (S. Gao et al., (2000)), when parameter k is even and divisible by p, TypeI-X NB becomes a self dual normal basis and thus $M_\gamma(x)$ is the minimal polynomial of the self dual normal basis in $\mathbb{F}_{p^m}$.
As introduced in Sec.1, we can of course calculate $M_\gamma(x)$ with the distributive law instead of Newton's formula as follows.

$$M_\gamma(x) = (x-\gamma)(x-\gamma^p)\cdots(x-\gamma^{p^{m-1}}). \tag{15}$$

In order to develop Eq.(15) in this case, we need $\times\gamma^{p^i}$ $m(m-1)/2$ times. Its calculation cost becomes

$$\#\text{SMUL} = 0, \tag{16a}$$

$$\#\text{SADD} = \frac{m(m-1)}{2}(mk + 3m - 1). \tag{16b}$$

Thus, it needs $\mathcal{O}(m^3)$ $\mathbb{F}_p$–additions. It does not need any $\mathbb{F}_p$–multiplications; however, the proposed algorithm becomes faster than using the distributive law as extension degree m becomes larger.

Input: $\gamma = (1, 0, 0, \cdots, 0) \in \mathbb{F}_{p^m}$.

Output: $M_\gamma(x) = x^m + \sum_{i=0}^{m-1} g_i x^i, \; g_i \in \mathbb{F}_p$.

Determine k such that TypeI ONB exists.
For $0 \le t \le m-1$ and $0 \le h \le k-1$, $g\left[\langle p^{t+hm}\rangle\right] \leftarrow t+1$.
$g[0] \leftarrow 0$.
$\mathrm{Tr}\,[1] \leftarrow -1$. For $2 \le t \le m$, $\mathrm{Tr}\,[t] \leftarrow 0$.
$x\,[0] \leftarrow 1$. For $1 \le t \le m-1$, $x\,[t] \leftarrow 0$.
$g_{m-1} \leftarrow 1$. For $0 \le t \le m-2$, $g_t \leftarrow 0$.
For $2 \le i \le m$, {
    For $0 \le j \le m$, $q[j] \leftarrow 0$.
    $q[1] \leftarrow x\,[0]$, $N \leftarrow 0$.
    For $1 \le j \le m-1$, {
        $M \leftarrow x[0] - x[j]$,
        For $0 \le h \le k-1$, {
            $q\left[g\left[\langle 1 + p^{j+hm}\rangle\right]\right] \leftarrow q\left[g\left[\langle 1 + p^{j+hm}\rangle\right]\right] + M$.
        }
    }
    $M \leftarrow kq[0]$.
    For $0 \le j \le m-1$, $z_j \leftarrow M - q[j+1]$.
    For $0 \le j \le m-1$, $N \leftarrow N + x\,[j]$. $\mathrm{Tr}\,[i] \leftarrow -N$.
}
For $2 \le i \le m$, {
    $M \leftarrow 0$,
    For $1 \le j \le i-1$, {
        $M \leftarrow M - g_{m-j}\mathrm{Tr}\,[i-j]$,
    }
    $g_{m-i} \leftarrow i^{-1}\,(M - \mathrm{Tr}\,[i])$.
}

(End of algorithm)

Fig. 2. Calculation of the minimal polynomial $M_\gamma(x)$

4. Consideration

This section shows some experimental results and comparison.

4.1 Experimental result and comparison

The authors have simulated the proposed algorithm on Pentium4 (1.7GHz) using C++ programming language and NTL (NTL). The authors also simulated the DDF-based irreducibility test which is introduced in Sec.2 and the case using the distributive law.

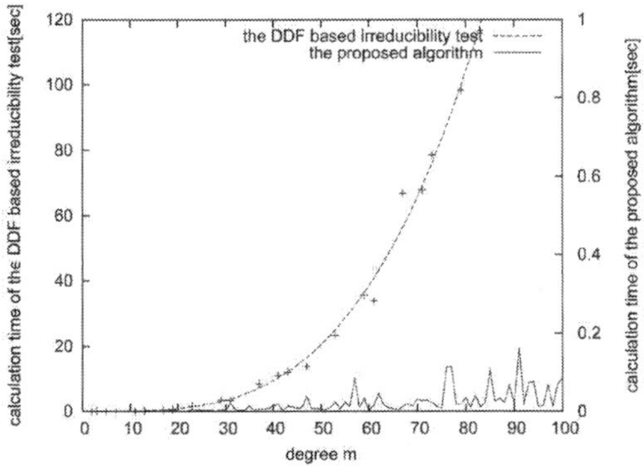

Fig. 3. The average computation time for generating an irreducible polynomial with the DDF-based irreducibility test and the proposed algorithm with p_1.

Let p_1 and p_2 be respectively given as follows:

$$p_1 = 65479 \text{ (16-bit)}, \tag{17}$$

$$p_2 = 1021076650872657639182783768587758285335306012183 \text{ (160-bit)}. \tag{18}$$

- For the proposed algorithm, the authors measured the average computation time for generating an irreducible polynomial of degree m over $\mathbb{F}_p$ by changing m from 2 to 100 with p_1 and p_2.
- For the DDF-based irreducibility test, inputting randomly generated polynomials of degree m over $\mathbb{F}_p$, the authors measured the average computation time for generating an irreducible polynomial with p_1 and the following prime degrees:

$$\{2,3,5,7,11,13,17,19,23,29,31,37,41,\\ 43,47,53,59,61,67,71,73,79,83\}, \tag{19}$$

  and then with p_2 and the following prime degrees:

$$\{7,11,13,17,19,23,29,31,37,41,43,47\}. \tag{20}$$

  Note that the irreducibility test is carried out by Eq.(4) when m is a prime number.
- For the case using the distributive law, the authors also measured the computation time for generating an irreducible polynomial of degree m over $\mathbb{F}_p$ by changing m from 2 to 100 with p_1.

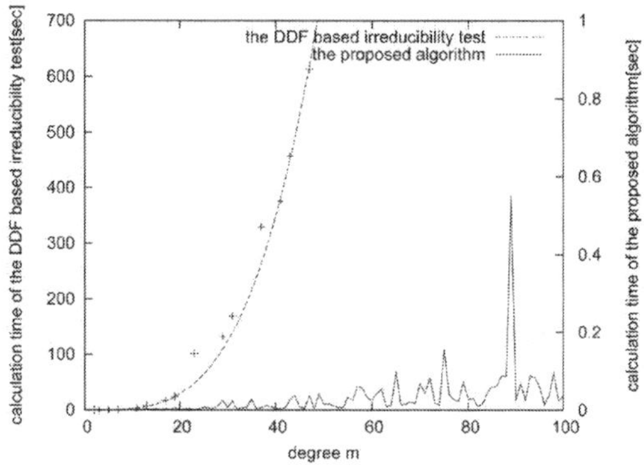

Fig. 4. The average computation time for generating an irreducible polynomial with the DDF-based irreducibility test and the proposed algorithm with p_2.

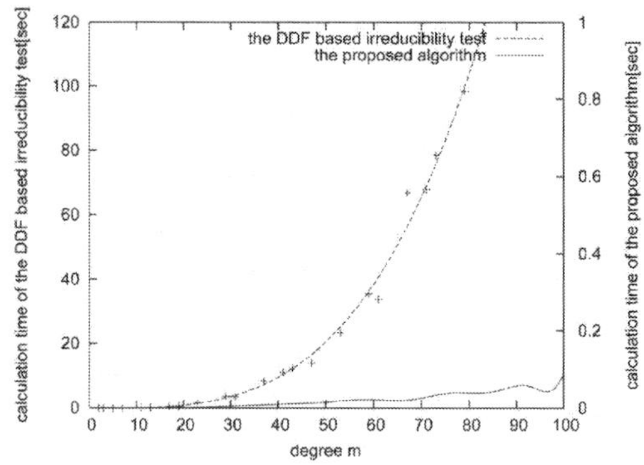

Fig. 5. The Bezier curve for the proposed algorithm in Fig 3.

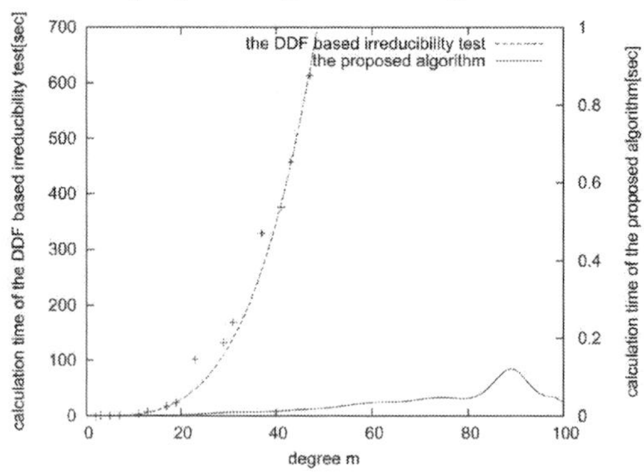

Fig. 6. The Bezier curve for the proposed algorithm in Fig 4.

The reason why the authors choose p_1 and p_2 given above is that the former does not need multi−precision arithmetic operations and the latter is sufficient secure size for elliptic curve

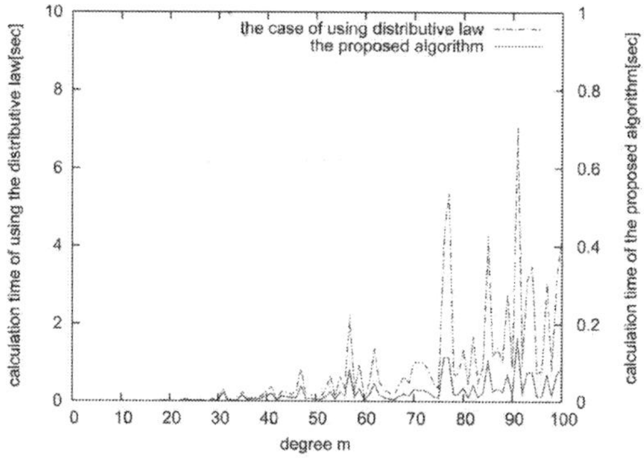

Fig. 7. The average computation time for generating an irreducible polynomial with the distributive law as Eq.(15) and the proposed algorithm with p_1.

cryptography (A. J. Menezes (1993)). Fig 3., Fig 4. and Fig 7. show the result. In Fig 3. and Fig 4., for example, when m = 83 with p_1, the proposed algorithm took 0.011 seconds with the parameter k = 2 and the DDF-based irreducibility test took 117 seconds. The proposed algorithm is about 10^4 times faster. As shown in the graphs, there are a few cases that the proposed algorithm is not very fast. For example, when m = 77 and 78 with p_1, the proposed algorithm took 0.115 and 0.019 seconds, respectively. The latter case is quite faster than the former. It is because of the parameter k. In the former case, k was 30, on the other hand, in the latter case, k was 4. Thus, the parameter k is preferred to be small. Of course, since the calculation cost of the proposed algorithm is clearly given as Eqs.(13) and Eqs.(14), in advance we can easily estimate how much calculation time the proposed algorithm needs. When the characteristic is p_1, the average of k's was 13.6. When the characteristic is p_2, the average was 12.8.

Fig 7. shows the comparison of the proposed algorithm and the case using the distributive law. For example, when m = 83 with p_1, the proposed algorithm took 0.011 seconds and the case using the distributive law took 0.496 seconds. The proposed algorithm is about 45 times faster. Fig 7. shows that the proposed algorithm is faster than using the distributive law. Therefore, using Newton's formula is better; however, it restricts p and m such that $p > m$.

As compared to the DDF-based irreducibility test, the proposed algorithm does not depend on the size of the characteristic p. It is because the calculation cost of the DDF-based irreducibility test depends on the size of p as introduced in Sec.2.5; however, that of the proposed algorithm does not. Therefore, as shown in Fig 3. and Fig 4., when p is large, the proposed algorithm generates an irreducible polynomial much faster than using the DDF-based irreducibility test. Fig 5. and Fig 6. are the Bezier curves for the data of the proposed algorithm in Fig 3. and Fig 4., respectively.

5. Conclusion

This paper has shown an efficient algorithm for generating an irreducible polynomial of an arbitrary degree m over an arbitrary prime field $\mathbb{F}_p$ such that $p > m$.

6. References

L. M. Adleman and H. W. Lenstra (1986). Finding irreducible polynomials over finite fields, *Proc. Of the eighteenth annual ACM Symp. on Theory of computing*, pp. 350-355.

Ian. F. Blake, S. Gao, and R. Lambert (1993). Constructive problems for irreducible polynomials over finite fields, *Proc. of the third Canadian workshop on Information theory and applications*, pp. 1-23.

M. Scott (2006). Scaling security in pairing-based protocols, available at http://mirror.cr.yp.to/eprint.iacr.org/2005/139.pdf, Cryptology Archive, ePrint.

V. Shoup (1990). New algorithms for finding irreducible polynomials over finite fields, *Math. of Comp.* vol. 54, pp. 435-447.

S. Gao (1993). Normal Bases over Finite Fields, *Doctoral thesis*, University of Waterloo, Ontario, Canada.

R. Lidl and H. Niederreiter (1984). Finite Fields, Encyclopedia of Mathematics and Its Applications, Cambridge University Press.

K. Makita, Y. Nogami, and T. Sugimura (2005). Generating Prime Degree Irreducible Polynomials by Usig Irreducible All-One Polynomial over F_2, *Electronics and Communications in Japan*, Part III : Fundamental Electronic Science, vol. 88, no. 7, pp. 23-32.

Y. Nogami, A. Saito, and Y. Morikawa (2003). Finite Extension Field with Modulus of All-One Polynomial and Representation of Its Elements for Fast Arithmetic Operations, *IEICE Trans.*, vol. E86-A, no. 9, pp. 2376-2387.

D. Bailey and C. Paar (2000). Optimal Extension Fields for Fast Arithmetic in Public-Key Algorithms, *Proc. Asiacrypt2000*, LNCS 1976, pp.248-258.

T. Yoshida, H. Katou, Y. Nogami, and Y. Morikawa (2006). Extension fields for an arbitrary pair of the characteristic and extension degree, *Proc. of Computer Security Symposium 2006 (CSS2006)*, pp. 43-48, in Japanese.

J. Gathen, and D. Panario (2001). Factoring Polynomials Over Finite Fields: A Survey, *J. Symbolic Computation*, vol. 31, pp. 3-17.

E. Berlekamp (1968). Algebraic Coding Theory, McGraw-Hill.

Y. Nogami, K. Tanaka, T. Sugimura, and S. Oshita (1999). Deriving In_nite Number of Irreducible Polynomials by Variable Transformation $x^p - x + s$, *Trans. of IEICE (A)*, vol. J82-A, no. 4, pp. 587-590, in Japanese.

T. Sugimura and Y. Suetugu (1991). Considerations on Irreducible Cyclotomic Polynomials, *Electronics and Communications in Japan*, Part3, vol. 74, no. 4, pp.106-113.

D. Knuth (1981). The Art of Computer Programming, *vol.2: Seminumerical Algorithms*, Addison-Wesley.

A. J. Menezes, editor (1993). Applications of Finite Fields, *Kluwer Academic Publishers*, Boston, MA.

Y. Nogami, S. Shinonaga, and Y. Morikawa (2005). Fast Implementation of Extension Fields with TypeII ONB and Cyclic Vector Multiplication Algorithm, *IEICE Trans. Fundamentals*, vol. E88-A, no. 5, pp. 1200-1208.

M. Nöcker (2001). Data Structures for Parallel Exponentiation in Finite Fields, available at http://deposit.ddb.de/.

R. Granger (2005). On Small Degree Extension Fields in Cryptology, available at http://www.cs.bris.ac.uk/Publications/Papers/2000527.pdf.

S. Gao, J. Gathen, D. Panario, and V. Shoup (2000). Algorithms for exponentiation in finite fields, *J. Symb. Comput.* 29, no. 6, pp. 879-889.

A Library for doing Number Theory., http://www.shoup.net/ntl/

A. J. Menezes (1993). Elliptic Curve Public Key Cryptosystems, *Kluwer Academic Publishers.*

20

Efficient Pairings on Twisted Elliptic Curve

Yasuyuki Nogami, Masataka Akane,
Yumi Sakemi and Yoshitaka Morikawa
Okayama University
Japan

1. Introduction

Recently, pairing-based cryptographic applications such as ID-based cryptography (D. Boneh et al. (2001)) and group signature authentication (T. Nakanishi & N. Funabiki (2005)) have received much attentions. In order to make these applications practical, pairing calculation needs to be efficiently carried out. For this purpose, several efficient pairings such as Tate (H. Cohen & G. Frey (2005)), Ate (F. Hess et al. (2006)), twisted Ate (S. Matsuda et al. (2007)), and *subfield-twisted* Ate (A. J. Devegili et al. (2007)), (M. Akane et al. (2007)) have been proposed. Consider an elliptic curve E: $y^2 = x^3 + ax + b$, a, b, $\in \mathbb{F}_p$ and let its order $\#E(\mathbb{F}_p)$ be a prime number r for simplicity. Then, let the embedding degree be k, r divides $p_k - 1$ but not divide $p_i - 1$, $1 \leq i < k$. Moreover, r^2 divides $\#E(\mathbb{F}_{p^k})$ and thus *pairing* is considered on r-*torsion* group of $E(\mathbb{F}_{p^k})$.

Tate, Ate, and twisted Ate pairings can be roughly classiffied by the inputs for Miller's algorithm (F. Hess et al. (2006)). In general, as the inputs, Miller's algorithm needs two rational points and the number of calculation loops. Tate pairing $\tau(\cdot, \cdot)$ uses rational points $P \in E(\mathbb{F}_p)$ and $Q \in E(\mathbb{F}_{p^k})/rE(\mathbb{F}_{p^k})$, and the number of loops of Miller's algorithm is $\lfloor \log_2 r \rfloor$. Tate pairing mainly uses P for elliptic curve additions and line calculations in the loops. Q is used only for assignment calculations. The output of Miller's algorithm is denoted by $f_{r,P}(Q)$. Ate pairing $\alpha(\cdot, \cdot)$ uses rational points $P \in E(\mathbb{F}_p)$ and $Q \in E[r] \cap \mathrm{Ker}(\phi - [p])$, but the number of loops is $\lfloor \log_2(t-1) \rfloor$, where ϕ is Frobenius map for rational point, $E[r]$ is the subgroup of rational points of order r, and t is the Frobenius trace of $E(\mathbb{F}_p)$, that is $\#E(\mathbb{F}_p) = r = p+1-t$. The number of loops is about half of that of Tate pairing; however, Ate pairing mainly uses Q elliptic curve additions and line calculations in the loops. The output of Miller's algorithm is denoted by $f_{t-1,Q}(P)$ and thus plain Ate pairing is slower than Tate pairing.

In the case that the embedding degree k is equal to $2e$, $3e$, $4e$, $6e$, where e is a positive integer, it is known that an isomorphic map exists between a certain subgroup of $E(\mathbb{F}_{p^k})$ and *subfield-twisted* curve $E'(\mathbb{F}_{p^e})$. Let E : $y^2 = x^3 + b$, $b \in \mathbb{F}_p$ be Barreto-Naehrig curve whose embedding degree is 12, Devegili et al. (A. J. Devegili et al. (2007)) accelerated Ate pairing by using *subfield-twisted* BN curve $E'(\mathbb{F}_{p^2})$ and OEF (optimal extension field) technique (D. Bailey & C. Paar (2000)), where the twisted BN curve is given by E': $y^2 = x^3 + bv^{-1}$ and v is a quadratic and cubic non residue in subfield $\mathbb{F}_{p^2}$. Denoting the isomorphic map

from $E'(\mathbb{F}_{p^2})$ to the corresponding subgroup of $E(\mathbb{F}_{p^{12}})$ by ψ_6, it calculates $f_{t-1,\psi_6(Q')}(P)^{(p^{12}-1)/r}$, $P \in E(\mathbb{F}_p)$, $Q' \in \psi_6^{-1}(E[r] \cap \mathrm{Ker}(\phi - [p]))$ for which *subfield- twisted* curve E' $(\mathbb{F}_{p^2})$ and Q' are efficiently used. In this case, since the twist degree d = k=e is 6, it is called *sextic* twist.
In this paper, first let us suppose

$$\mathbb{G}_1 = E[r] \cap \mathrm{Ker}(\phi - [1]), \tag{1a}$$

$$\mathbb{G}_2 = E[r] \cap \mathrm{Ker}(\phi - [p]), \tag{1b}$$

where E is a pairing-friendly curve of embedding degree k = $2e$, $3e$, $4e$, $6e$. Let E' be degree d = k/e twisted curve over $\mathbb{F}_{p^e}$. Then, one can consider an isomorphic map between $E(\mathbb{F}_{p^k})$ and $E'(\mathbb{F}_{p^e})$. Denoting it from $E'(\mathbb{F}_{p^e})$ to $E(\mathbb{F}_{p^k})$ by ψ_d, consider $\mathbb{G}'_1 = \psi_d^{-1}(\mathbb{G}_1)$ and $\mathbb{G}'_2 = \psi_d^{-1}(\mathbb{G}_2)$. Using $Q' \in \mathbb{G}'_2$ and $P' \in \mathbb{G}'_1$, this paper proposes a new Ate pairing that calculates

$$\alpha(Q', P') = f_{t-1,Q'}(P')^{(p^k-1)/r}, \tag{2}$$

namely *cross twisted* (Xt) Ate pairing. Compared to plain Ate pairing and the previous work (A. J. Devegili et al. (2007)), Xt-Ate pairing can substantially use arithmetic operations in subfield $\mathbb{F}_{p^e}$, thus it leads to quite efficient implementation of Ate pairing. After that, this paper shows a simulation result by using BN curve and *sextic twist*. When order r is a 254-bit prime number, it is shown that Xt-Ate pairing with BN curve is carried out within 14.0 milli-seconds for which the authors uses Pentium4 (3.6GHz), C language, and GNU MP library (GNU MP). Compared to the previous *subfield-twisted* Ate pairing (A. J. Devegili et al. (2007)), Xt-Ate pairing made the algorithmic implementation and cost evaluation much clearer.
Throughout this paper, p and k denote characteristic and embedding degree, respectively. $\mathbb{F}_{p^k}$ denotes k-th extension field over $\mathbb{F}_p$ and $\mathbb{F}^*_{p^k}$ denotes the multiplicative group in $\mathbb{F}_{p^k}$. $X \mid Y$ and $X \nmid Y$ mean that X divides and does not divide Y, respectively.

2. Fundamentals

In this section, let us briefly go over some fundamentals of elliptic curve, twist technique, Ate pairing, and Miller's algorithm.

2.1 Elliptic curve

Let $\mathbb{F}_p$ be prime field and E be an elliptic curve over $\mathbb{F}_p$ defined as

$$E : y^2 = x^3 + ax + b, \;\; a, b \in \mathbb{F}_p. \tag{3}$$

$E(\mathbb{F}_p)$ that is a set of rational points on the curve, including the *infinity point* $\mathcal{O}$, forms an additive Abelien group. Let $\#E(\mathbb{F}_p)$ be its order, consider a large prime r that divides $\#E(\mathbb{F}_p)$. The smallest positive integer k such that r divides $p_k - 1$ is especially called *embedding degree*. One can consider pairings such as Tate and Ate pairings over $E(\mathbb{F}_{p^k})$. $\#E(\mathbb{F}_p)$ is usually given as

$$\#E(\mathbb{F}_p) = p + 1 - t, \tag{4}$$

where t is the Frobenius trace of $E(\mathbb{F}_p)$.

2.2 Twist technique

When embedding degree k is equal to $2e$, where e is a positive integer, from Eq.(3) the following quadratic-twisted elliptic curve E' is given.

$$E' : y^2 = x^3 + av^{-2}x + bv^{-3}, \ a, b \in \mathbb{F}_p, \tag{5}$$

where v is a quadratic non residue in $\mathbb{F}_{p^e}$. Then, between $E'(\mathbb{F}_{p^e})$ and $E(\mathbb{F}_{p^{2e}})$, the following isomorphism is given.

$$\psi_2 : \begin{cases} E'(\mathbb{F}_{p^e}) & \to E(\mathbb{F}_{p^{2e}}), \\ (x, y) & \mapsto (xv, yv^{3/2}). \end{cases} \tag{6}$$

In this case, E' is called *quadratic-twisted* curve.

In the same, when embedding degree k satisfies the following conditions, we can respectively consider the twisted curves.

- $k = 3e$ (cubic twist)

$$E : y^2 = x^3 + b, \ b \in \mathbb{F}_p, \tag{7a}$$

$$E' : y^2 = x^3 + bv^{-2}, \tag{7b}$$

where v is a cubic non residue in $\mathbb{F}_{p^e}$ and $3 \mid (p - 1)$.

$$\psi_3 : \begin{cases} E'(\mathbb{F}_{p^e}) & \to E(\mathbb{F}_{p^{3e}}), \\ (x, y) & \mapsto (xv^{2/3}, yv). \end{cases} \tag{7c}$$

- $k = 4e$ (quatic twist)

$$E : y^2 = x^3 + ax, \ b \in \mathbb{F}_p, \tag{8a}$$

$$E' : y^2 = x^3 + av^{-1}x, \tag{8b}$$

where v is a quadratic non residue in $\mathbb{F}_{p^e}$ and $4 \mid (p - 1)$.

$$\psi_4 : \begin{cases} E'(\mathbb{F}_{p^e}) & \to E(\mathbb{F}_{p^{4e}}), \\ (x, y) & \mapsto (xv^{1/2}, yv^{3/4}). \end{cases} \tag{8c}$$

- $k = 6e$ (sextic twist)

$$E : y^2 = x^3 + b, \ b \in \mathbb{F}_p, \tag{9a}$$

$$E' : y^2 = x^3 + bv^{-1}, \tag{9b}$$

where v is a quadratic and cubic non residue in $\mathbb{F}_{p^e}$ and $3 \mid (p - 1)$.

$$\psi_6 : \begin{cases} E'(\mathbb{F}_{p^e}) & \rightarrow E(\mathbb{F}_{p^{6e}}), \\ (x, y) & \mapsto (xv^{1/3}, yv^{1/2}). \end{cases} \tag{9c}$$

When one uses Barreto-Naehrig curve that is a class of *pairing-friendly* curve, one can apply any quadratic, cubic, quatic, or sextic twist because its embedding degree is equal to 12. As described in the following sections, sextic twist is the most efficient for pairing calculation. Eqs.(6), (7c), (8c), and (9c) are summarized as

$$\psi_d : \begin{cases} E'(\mathbb{F}_{p^e}) & \rightarrow E(\mathbb{F}_{p^{de}}), \\ (x, y) & \mapsto (xv^{2/d}, yv^{3/d}). \end{cases} \tag{10}$$

Thus, when twist degree d is even, x-coordinate $x\,v^{2/d}$ belongs to proper subfield $\mathbb{F}_{p^{k/2}}$ because $v^{2/d} \in \mathbb{F}_{p^{k/2}}$. In addition, when d = 2 or 4, the coefficient of x of the twisted curve E' can be written as $av^{-4/d}$.

2.3 Ate pairing

Let $P \in \mathbb{G}_1$ and $Q \in \mathbb{G}_2$, Ate pairing α is defined as a bilinear map:

$$\alpha : \begin{cases} \mathbb{G}_2 \times \mathbb{G}_1 & \rightarrow \mathbb{F}^*_{p^k}/(\mathbb{F}^*_{p^k})^r \\ (Q, P) & \mapsto f_{t-1,Q}(P)^{(p^k-1)/r}, \end{cases} \tag{11}$$

where $\mathbb{G}_1$ and $\mathbb{G}_2$ are denoted by

$$\mathbb{G}_1 = E[r] \cap \mathrm{Ker}(\phi - [1]), \tag{12a}$$

$$\mathbb{G}_2 = E[r] \cap \mathrm{Ker}(\phi - [p]). \tag{12b}$$

$E[r]$ denotes a subgroup of order r in $E(\mathbb{F}_{p^k})$ and $[i]$ denotes i times scalar multiplication for a rational point. ϕ denotes Frobenius endomorphism, i.e.,

$$\phi : E \rightarrow E : (x, y) \mapsto (x^p, y^p), \tag{13}$$

where x and y are x-coordinate and y-coordinate of a rational point, respectively. In general, $A = f_{t-1,Q}(P)$ is calculated by Miller's algorithm (H. Cohen & G. Frey (2005)) and then so-called *final exponentiation* $A^{(p^k-1)/r}$ follows.

2.4 Miller's Algorithm

Several improvements for Miller's algorithm have been given. Barreto et al. proposed BKLS algorithm. Algorithm 1. shows the calculation flow of the BKLS algorithm for $f_{s,Q}(P)$. It consists of functions shown in Table 1.

In this algorithm, main computation part is Step 4, Step 5, Step 7 and Step 8. In this paper, let Step 4 and Step5 be *main routine*, and let Step 7 and Step 8 be *sub routine*. In the case of Ate pairing, $P(x_P, y_P) \in \mathbb{G}_1$, $Q(x_Q, y_Q) \in \mathbb{G}_2$, $s = t - 1$, and then $f_{s,Q}(P)$ becomes an element in $\mathbb{F}^*_{p^k}$.

As shown in the algorithm, elliptic curve addition and doubling that use rational points in $E(\mathbb{F}_{p^k})$ needs arithmetic operations in $\mathbb{F}_{p^k}$. If it has *subfield-twisted* curve such as Eq.(5), it can be efficiently reduced to subfield arithmetic operations by isomorphic maps such as Eq.(6). Thus, twist degree d is preferred to be large such as 6, that is *sextic* twist. When the d is even number, the denominator calculations in Algorithm 1. can be ignored.

Algorithm 1 : BKLS Algorithm

Input : $s, P \in \mathbb{G}_1, Q \in \mathbb{G}_2$

Output : $f_{s,Q}(P) \in \mathbb{F}_{p^k}$

Procedure :

$f \leftarrow 1$
$T \leftarrow Q$
for $i \leftarrow \lfloor \log_2 s \rfloor$ downto 1 do:
  $f \leftarrow f^2 \cdot l_{T,T}(P)/l_{2T,\mathcal{O}}(P)$
  $T \leftarrow T + T$
  if $s_i = 1$ then:
    $f \leftarrow f \cdot l_{T,Q}(P)/l_{T+Q,\mathcal{O}}(P)$
    $T \leftarrow T + Q$
  end if
end for
return f

s_i :	i-th bit of s from the lowest bit.
$l_{T,T}$:	the tangent line at T.
$l_{T,Q}$:	the line passing through T and Q.
$l_{2T,\mathcal{O}}$:	the vertical line passing through $2T$.
$l_{T+Q,\mathcal{O}}$:	the vertical line passing through $T+Q$.

Table 1. Notations in Algorithm 1.

3. Main proposal

In this section, a new fast pairing, namely *cross twisted* (Xt-) Ate pairing, is proposed.

3.1 Xt–Ate pairing

Supposing that the pairing-friendly curve E has a degree $d = k/e$ twist and E' be a d-th twisted curve such as Eq.(5). From the discussion in Sec.2.3, Ate pairing α is given as

$$\alpha : \begin{cases} \mathbb{G}_2 \times \mathbb{G}_1 & \rightarrow \mathbb{F}^*_{p^k}/(\mathbb{F}^*_{p^k})^r \\ (Q, P) & \mapsto f_{s,Q}(P)^{(p^k-1)/r}. \end{cases} \tag{14}$$

On the ohter hand, Xt-Ate pairing is proposed as

$$\alpha' : \begin{cases} \mathbb{G}'_2 \times \mathbb{G}'_1 & \rightarrow \mathbb{F}^*_{p^k}/(\mathbb{F}^*_{p^k})^r \\ (Q', P') & \mapsto f_{s,Q'}(P')^{(p^k-1)/r}, \end{cases} \tag{15}$$

Main routine (Step 4&5 in Algorithm 1)

Procedure	Computation
1. $[2]T$	$\lambda \leftarrow (3x_T^2 + a)/(2y_T)$
	$x_{2T} \leftarrow \lambda^2 - 2x_T$
	$y_{2T} \leftarrow (x_T - x_{2T})\lambda - y_T$
2. f^2	$f \leftarrow f^2$
3. $f \cdot l_{T,T}(P)$	$l_{T,T}(P)$
	$\leftarrow (x_P - x_T)\lambda - (y_P - y_T)$
	$f \leftarrow f \cdot l_{T,T}(P)$
4. $f/l_{2T,\mathcal{O}}(P)$	$l_{2T,\mathcal{O}}(P) \leftarrow x_P - x_{2T}$
	$f \leftarrow f/l_{2T,\mathcal{O}}(P)$

Sub routine (Step 7&8 in Algorithm 1)

Procedure	Computation
1. $T+Q$	$\lambda \leftarrow (y_Q - y_T)/(x_Q - x_T)$
	$x_{T+Q} \leftarrow \lambda^2 - x_Q - x_T$
	$y_{T+Q} \leftarrow (x_Q - x_{T+Q})\lambda - y_Q$
2. $f \cdot l_{T,Q}(P)$	$l_{T,Q}(P)$
	$\leftarrow (x_P - x_Q)\lambda - (y_P - y_Q)$
	$f \leftarrow f \cdot l_{T,Q}(P)$
3. $f/l_{T+Q,\mathcal{O}}(P)$	$l_{T+Q,\mathcal{O}}(P) \leftarrow x_P - x_{T+Q}$
	$f \leftarrow f/l_{T+Q,\mathcal{O}}(P)$

where P' is a point of $\mathbb{G}_1' = \psi_d^{-1}(\mathbb{G}_1) \subset E'(\mathbb{F}_{p^{12}})$ and Q' is a point of $\mathbb{G}_2' = \psi_d^{-1}(\mathbb{G}_2) \subset E'(\mathbb{F}_{p^2})$. Here, it is most importatnt thisng that the next equation is hold,

$$\alpha'(Q', P') = \alpha(Q, P). \tag{16}$$

The main feature of Xt-Ate pairing is that the isomorphic map ψ_d^{-1} is to P as $P' = \psi_d^{-1}(P)$. In other words, $P \in E(\mathbb{F}_p)$ is extended to $P' \in E'(\mathbb{F}_{p^k})$ and $Q \in E(\mathbb{F}_{p^k})$ is compressed to $Q' \in E'(\mathbb{F}_{p^e})$. Thus, the authors named it *cross twisted* (Xt-) Ate pairing. Fig 1. shows the key map of Xt-Ate pairing with $\mathbb{G}_1'$ and $\mathbb{G}_2'$. In spite of the inputted points P' and Q' on the twisted curvce, the miller loop s is given by $t - 1$, where t is the trace of $E(\mathbb{F}_p)$. The following three lemmas lead to Eq.(16).

Lemma 1.

$$d(p^e - 1) \mid (p^k - 1)/r. \tag{17}$$

Proof: From the definition of embedding degree,

$$r \nmid (p^e - 1). \tag{18}$$

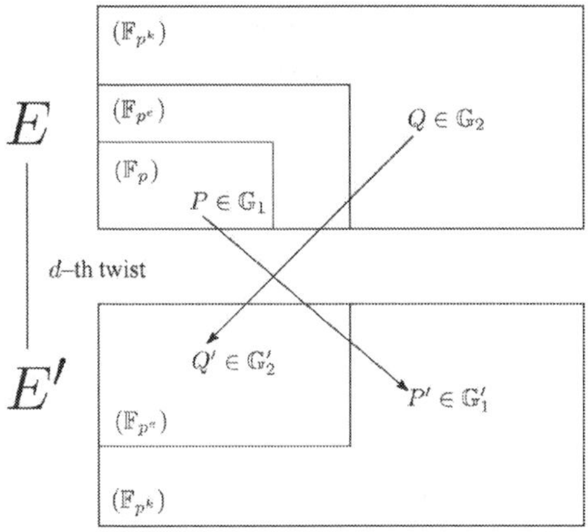

Fig. 1. Xt-Ate pairing with $\mathbb{G}'_1$ and $\mathbb{G}'_2$

Then, we have

$$\begin{aligned}\frac{(p^k-1)/r}{p^e-1} &= \left(p^{(d-1)e}+p^{(d-2)e}+\cdots+1\right)/r \\ &= \left(\sum_{i=1}^{d} p^{(d-i)e}\right)/r \\ &= \left(\sum_{i=1}^{d}(p^{(d-i)e}-1)+d\right)/r.\end{aligned} \tag{19}$$

Since $d \mid (p-1)$ and $\gcd(d, r)$=1, this lemma is shown. ■

Lemma 2.

$$l_{T',T'}(P')^{(p^k-1)/r} = l_{T,T}(P)^{(p^k-1)/r}, \tag{20}$$

$$l_{T',Q'}(P')^{(p^k-1)/r} = l_{T,Q}(P)^{(p^k-1)/r}. \tag{21}$$

Proof: Using T', $Q' \in \mathbb{F}_{p^e}$ such that $T = \psi_d(T')$ and $Q = \psi_d(Q')$, the slopes $\lambda_{T,T}$ and $\lambda_{T,Q}$ are written as

$$\begin{aligned}\lambda_{T,T} &= \frac{3x_T^2+a}{2y_T} \\ &= \frac{3\left(x_{T'}v^{2/d}\right)^2+a}{2x_{T'}v^{3/d}} \\ &= \frac{3x_{T'}^2+a/v^{4/d}}{2x_{T'}}\cdot\frac{v^{4/d}}{v^{3/d}} \\ &= \frac{3x_{T'}^2+a'}{2x_{T'}}\cdot v^{1/d} \\ &= \lambda_{T',T'}\cdot v^{1/d},\end{aligned} \tag{22a}$$

$$\begin{aligned}\lambda_{T,Q} &= \frac{y_Q - y_T}{x_Q - x_T} \\ &= \frac{y_{Q'}v^{3/d} - y_{T'}v^{3/d}}{x_{Q'}v^{2/d} - x_{T'}v^{2/d}} \\ &= \frac{y_{Q'} - y_{T'}}{x_{Q'} - x_{T'}} \cdot \frac{v^{3/d}}{v^{2/d}} \\ &= \frac{y_{Q'} - y_{T'}}{x_{Q'} - x_{T'}} \cdot v^{1/d} \\ &= \lambda_{Q',T'} \cdot v^{1/d}.\end{aligned} \tag{22b}$$

Thus, regardless of whether or not $T = Q$, we have

$$\lambda_{T,Q} = \lambda_{T',Q'} v^{1/d}. \tag{23}$$

Then, we have

$$\begin{aligned}l_{T,Q}(P) &= (x_P - x_T)\lambda_{T,Q} - (y_P - y_T) \\ &= (x_{P'}v^{2/d} - x_{T'}v^{2/d})\lambda_{T',Q'}v^{1/d} \\ &\qquad - (y_{P'}v^{3/d} - y_{T'}v^{3/d}) \\ &= (x_{P'} - x_{T'})\lambda_{T',Q'}v^{3/d} - (y_{P'} - y_{T'})v^{3/d} \\ &= l_{T',Q'}(P') \cdot v^{3/d}.\end{aligned} \tag{24}$$

Since $v \in \mathbb{F}_{p^e}$, the following equation holds.

$$\left(v^{3/d}\right)^{(p^e-1)d} = \left(v^{(p^e-1)}\right)^3 = 1. \tag{25}$$

Therefore, according to Lemma 1, $v^{3/d}$ of Eq.(24) becomes 1 at *final exponentiation* of Xt-Ate pairing. Thus, this lemma is shown. ■

Lemma 3.

$$l_{T',\mathcal{O}}(P')^{(p^k-1)/r} = l_{T,\mathcal{O}}(P)^{(p^k-1)/r}. \tag{26}$$

Proof: Since the following equation holds,

$$\begin{aligned}{}_{T,\mathcal{O}}(P) &= x_P - x_T \\ &= x_{P'}v^{2/d} - x_{T'}v^{2/d} \\ &= (x_{P'} - x_{T'}) \cdot v^{2/d} \\ &= l_{T',\mathcal{O}}(P') \cdot v^{2/d}.\end{aligned} \tag{27}$$

Note $v \in \mathbb{F}_{p^e}$, we have

$$\left(v^{2/d}\right)^{(p^e-1)d} = \left(v^{(p^e-1)}\right)^2 = 1. \tag{28}$$

Therefore, according to Lemma 1, $v^{2/d}$ of Eq.(27) becomes 1 at *final exponentiation* of Xt-Ate pairing. Thus, this lemma is shown. ■

$F_{t\text{-}1,Q}(P)$ is calculated with $l_{T,T}(P)$, $l_{T,Q}(P)$, and $l_{T,\mathcal{O}}(P)$. Therefore, according to Lemma 2 and Lemma 3, Eq.(16) is shown.

3.2 Calculation procedure

Suppose the following d-th twisted curve E' over $\mathbb{F}_{p^e}$.

$$E' : y^2 = x^3 + a'x + b', \ a', b' \in \mathbb{F}_{p^e}. \tag{29}$$

Noting that $P' \in \mathbb{G}_1' \subset E'(\mathbb{F}_{p^k})$ and $Q' \in \mathbb{G}_2' \subset E'(\mathbb{F}_{p^e})$, Xt-Ate pairing is computed by Algorithm 2.. In practice, the *main routine* (Step 4&5 in Algorithm 2) and the *sub routine* (Step 7&8 in Algorithm 2) are computed as follows. First, compute

$$\lambda_{T',T'} = \frac{3x_{T'} + a'}{2y_{T'}}, \tag{30a}$$

$$\lambda_{T',Q'} = \frac{y_{Q'} - y_{T'}}{x_{Q'} - x_{T'}}. \tag{30b}$$

Algorithm 2 : Xt–Ate pairing

Input : $s = t - 1, P' \in \mathbb{G}_1', Q' \in \mathbb{G}_2'$

Output : $\alpha'(Q', P') = f_{s,Q'}(P')^{(p^k-1)/r}$

Procedure :

1. $f \leftarrow 1$
2. $T' \leftarrow Q'$
3. for $i \leftarrow \lfloor \log_2 s \rfloor$ downto 1 do:
4. $\quad f \leftarrow f^2 \cdot l_{T',T'}(Q)/l_{2T',\mathcal{O}}(P')$
5. $\quad T' \leftarrow T' + T'$
6. $\quad$ if $s_i = 1$ then:
7. $\quad\quad f \leftarrow f \cdot l_{T',Q'}(P)/l_{T'+Q',\mathcal{O}}(P')$
8. $\quad\quad T' \leftarrow T' + Q'$
9. $\quad$ end if
10. end for
11. $f \leftarrow f^{(p^k-1)/r}$
12. return f

Regardless of whether or not $T' = Q'$, we have

$$x_{T'+Q'} = \lambda^2_{T',Q'} - x_{Q'} - x_{T'}, \tag{31a}$$

$$y_{T'+Q'} = (x_{Q'} - x_{T'+Q'})\lambda_{T',Q'} - y_{Q'}, \tag{31b}$$

and the next line calculations are computed as

$$l_{T',Q'}(P') = (x_{P'} - x_{Q'})\,\lambda_{T',Q'} - (y_{P'} - y_{Q'}), \tag{32a}$$

$$l_{T',\mathcal{O}}(P') = x_{P'} - x_{T'}. \tag{32b}$$

Every calculation excluding the one multiplication shown in Eq.(32a) are carried out in subfield $\mathbb{F}_{p^e}$. Thus, most of this algorithm is efficiently carried out by subfield arithmetic opearations in $\mathbb{F}_{p^e}$. Note that the Eq.(32a) needs the multiplication between elements in $\mathbb{F}_{p^e}$ and $\mathbb{F}_{p^{k/\gcd(d,2)}}$. When the twist degree d is even number, it has a little advantage. Of course, when the d is even, as previously introduced, the calculation of Eq.(32b) can be ignored. The *main rutine* and the *sub routine* of Xt-Ate pairing can be written as the following algorithms.

Main routine (Step 4&5 in Algorithm 2)

Procedure	Computation
1. $[2]T'$	$\lambda \leftarrow (3x_{T'}^2 + a')/(2y_{T'})$
	$x_{2T'} \leftarrow \lambda^2 - 2x_{T'}$
	$y_{2T'} \leftarrow (x_{T'} - x_{2T'})\lambda - y_{T'}$
2. f^2	$f \leftarrow f^2$
3. $f \cdot l_{T',T'}(P')$	$l_{T',T'}(P')$
	$\leftarrow (x_{P'} - x_{T'})\lambda - (y_{P'} - y_{T'})$
	$f \leftarrow f \cdot l_{T',T'}(P')$
4. $f/l_{2T',\mathcal{O}}(P')$	$l_{2T',\mathcal{O}}(P') \leftarrow x_{P'} - x_{2T'}$
	$f \leftarrow f/l_{2T',\mathcal{O}}(P')$

Sub routine (Step 7&8 in Algorithm 2)

Procedure	Computation
1. $T' + Q'$	$\lambda \leftarrow (y_{Q'} - y_{T'})/(x_{Q'} - x_{T'})$
	$x_{T'+Q'} \leftarrow \lambda^2 - x_{Q'} - x_{T'}$
	$y_{T'+Q'} \leftarrow (x_{Q'} - x_{T'+Q'})\lambda - y_{Q'}$
2. $f \cdot l_{T',Q'}(P')$	$l_{T',Q'}(P')$
	$\leftarrow (x_{P'} - x_{Q'})\lambda - (y_{P'} - y_{Q'})$
	$f \leftarrow f \cdot l_{T',Q'}(P')$
3. $f/l_{T'+Q',\mathcal{O}}(P')$	$l_{T'+Q',\mathcal{O}}(P') \leftarrow x_{P'} - x_{T'+Q'}$
	$f \leftarrow f/l_{T'+Q',\mathcal{O}}(P')$

3.3 Cost evaluation

We evaluate the calculation cost of Xt-Ate pairing. In order to simplify the cost evaluation, we only take the calculation costs for multiplication, squaring, and inversion in finite field into account. Notations in Table 2. are used.

Let the calculation costs of *main routine* and *sub routine* in Algorithm 2 be TMAIN and TSUB, respectively. When the number of the calculation loops of Miller's algorithm is $\lfloor \log_2 s \rfloor$, Xt-Ate pairing excluding the final exponentiation needs the following cost.

$$(\lfloor \log_2 s \rfloor - 1)\text{TMAIN} + (\text{Hw}(s) - 1)\text{TSUB}, \tag{33}$$

−1's in the above equation denote that it is no needed to calculate for the most significant bit. When d is even such as 2, 4, and 6, TMAIN and TSUB are given as

$$\begin{aligned} \text{TMAIN} &= 2S_e + 2M_e + I_e + M_{e,k/\gcd(d,2)} + S_k + M_k, \\ \text{TSUB} &= S_e + 2M_e + I_e + M_{e,k/\gcd(d,2)} + M_k. \end{aligned} \quad (34)$$

When d = 3, since the vertical line calculation is needed, they becomes

$$\begin{aligned} \text{TMAIN} &= 2S_e + 2M_e + I_e + M_{e,k/\gcd(d,2)} + S_k + 2M_k, \\ \text{TSUB} &= S_e + 2M_e + I_e + M_{e,k/\gcd(d,2)} + 2M_k. \end{aligned} \quad (35)$$

Following the cost evaluation manner of (S. Matsuda et al. (2007)), (F. Hess et al. (2006)), $M_{2^i3^je}$ be $3^i5^jM_e$, $M_{i,j} = (j/i)M_i$, and $S_i = M_i$ for simplicity. Then, we have Table 3. Suppose that $\text{Hw}(s) \approx \lfloor \log_2 s \rfloor / 2$, $M_{5e} = 15M_e$, and roughly $I_i = 7M_i$, we have Table 4.

M_i, S_i, I_i :	the calculation costs of a multiplication, squaring, and inversion in $\mathbb{F}_{p^i}$, respectively.
$M_{i,j}$:	the calculation cost of a multiplication between two elements in $\mathbb{F}_{p^i}$ and $\mathbb{F}_{p^j}$, where i divides j.
$\text{Hw}(s)$:	the Hamming weight of s.

Table 2. Notations for cost evaluation

d	TMAIN	TSUB
2	$11M_e + I_e$	$7M_e + I_e$
4	$22M_e + I_e$	$12M_e + I_e$
3	$19M_e + I_e$	$13M_e + I_e$
6	$34M_e + I_e$	$18M_e + I_e$

Table 3. Calculation costs of TMAIN and TSUB for Xt-Ate pairing

$\lfloor \log_2 p \rfloor$	$\lfloor \log_2 r \rfloor$	k	d	cost
384	256	8	4	$14784\,M_1$
256	256	10	2	$44352\,M_1$
256	256	12	6	$20396\,M_1$

Table 4. Calculation costs of Xt-Ate pairing

4. Efficiency of Xt-Ate pairing

This section shows the efficiency of Xt-Ate pairing.

4.1 Comparison of pairings

Table 5. shows the comparison of the input parameters of Miller's algorithm between various pairings.

pairing	s	A	B
plain Tate	r	$E(\mathbb{F}_p)$	$E(\mathbb{F}_{p^k})$
Twisted Ate (S. Matsuda et al. (2007))	$(t-1)^e \mod r$	$E(\mathbb{F}_p)$	$E(\mathbb{F}_{p^k})$
plain Ate	$t-1$	$E(\mathbb{F}_{p^k})$	$E(\mathbb{F}_p)$
Xt–Ate	$t-1$	$E'(\mathbb{F}_{p^e})$	$E'(\mathbb{F}_{p^k})$

Table 5. Input parameters of $f_{s,A}(B)$

Consider the inputs for Miller's algorithm calculating $f_{s,A}(B)$ with s,A, and B. In detail, the number of calculation loops of Miller's algorithm is given by $\lfloor \log_2 s \rfloor$, the point A is used for a lot of calculations, and the point B has little effect on the efficiency. Therefore, plain Tate pairing uses A 2 $E(\mathbb{F}_p)$. Twisted Ate pairing (S. Matsuda et al. (2007)) uses $(t-1)^{k/d}$ (mod r) as s. For cyclotomic families such as Barreto-Naehrig curve, $(t-1)^e$ (mod r) is smaller than $t-1$ in general. Thus, twisted Ate pairing is more efficient than plain Tate pairing.
Ate pairing made the number of the calculation loops of Miller's algorithm, that is $t-1$, smaller than that of Tate pairing but it uses $A \in E(\mathbb{F}_{p^k})$. Thus, plain Ate pairing is not superior to Tate pairing. However, Ate pairing generally uses $A \in E'(\mathbb{F}_{p^{k/d}})$ instead of that in $E(\mathbb{F}_{p^k})$.
Xt-Ate pairing is more efficient than the Ate pairing. It uses $B \in \mathbb{G}_1' = \psi_d^{-1}(\mathbb{G}_1)$, where $\mathbb{G}_1 \subseteq E(\mathbb{F}_p)$. Xt-Ate pairing does not calculates $l_{T,Q}(P)$ by eq.(37) and it calculates $l_{T',Q'}(P')$ by eq.(32a) for Miller's algorithm since every calculation is carried out over twisted curve E'.
It is noted that Xt-Ate pairing uses $\mathbb{G}_2'$ and $\mathbb{G}_1'$; however, for pairing-based cryptographic applications such that a lot of scalar multiplications are needed, $\mathbb{G}_1 \subseteq E(\mathbb{F}_p)$ and $\mathbb{G}_2'$ should be used for them. Appropriately using isomorphic map ψ_d and ψ_d^{-1}, not only Xt-Ate pairing but also scalar multiplications will be efficiently carried out.
As the most recent works, Vercauteren (F. Vercauteren (2008)), Lee et al. (E. Lee et al. (2008)), and the authors (Y. Nogami et al. (2008)) have proposed efficient Ate pairings, namely *optimal pairing, R-Ate pairing, Xate pairing*, respectively. They have reduced the number of the calculation loops of Miller's algorithm less than $t - 1$. For their works, *cross-twist* technique can be efficiently applied.

4.2 Xt-Ate pairing for BN curve

In order to show the efficiency of Xt-Ate pairing, this subsection considers Barreto-Naehrig (BN) curve (P. S. L. M. Barreto & M. Naehrig (2006)) of 254-bit prime order with $k = 12$ and $d = 6$. Since *sextic twist* is efficiently applied, embedding degree 12 is one of the most competitive research targets. As a typical feature of BN curve, characteristic p, order r, and Frobenius trace t are given by using an integer variable χ as

$$p(\chi) = 36\chi^4 - 36\chi^3 + 24\chi^2 - 6\chi + 1, \tag{36a}$$

$$r(\chi) = 36\chi^4 - 36\chi^3 + 18\chi^2 - 6\chi + 1, \tag{36b}$$

$$t(\chi) = 6\chi^2 + 1. \tag{36c}$$

For BN curve, Devegili et al. (A. J. Devegili et al. (2007)) proposed an improved Ate pairing whose Miller's algorithm calculates elliptic curve operations of $\mathbb{G}_2' \in E'(\mathbb{F}_{p^2})$. Then, $\mathbb{G}_2'$ is isomorphic to G_2 with ψ_6 defined by Eq.(9c), for every loop of Miller's algorithm, it needs to calculate $l_{T,Q}(P)$ as follows:

$$\begin{aligned} l_{T,Q}(P) &= (x_P - x_Q)\lambda_{T,Q} - (y_P - y_Q) \\ &= (-y_P) + (x_P \cdot \lambda_{T',Q'})z + (y_{T'} - x_{T'} \cdot \lambda_{T',Q'})z^3. \end{aligned} \tag{37}$$

This calculation needs 3 times $\mathbb{F}_p$ multiplications. On the other hand, Xt-Ate pairing needs 9 times $\mathbb{F}_p$ mutiplications to calculate $l_{T',Q'}(P')$. Thus, in this view point, Devegili et. al. work is more efficient than Xt-Ate pairing.

Though the Devegili et. al. work restricts the parameters of pairing friendly curve. As also introduced in (A. J. Devegili et al. (2007)), (Y. Sakemi et al. (2008)), (M. Akane et al. (2007)), χ of small Hamming weight is efficient for not only Miller's algorithm but also final exponentiation. Table 6. shows all χ's of Hamming weight 3 that gives 254-bit prime order BN curve. Note that, in this case, there are no χ's of Hamming weight 2 such that order r becomes 254-bit prime number.

χ	Hw(s)	E
$2^{62}+2^{35}+2^{24}$	12	$y^2=x^3+10$
$2^{62}+2^{55}+1$	12	$y^2=x^3+7$
$-2^{62}-2^{41}-2^{23}$	12	$y^2=x^3+13$

Table 6. χ of small Hamming weight that gives 254-bit prime order BN curve

5. Simulation

This section shows a simulation result of Xt-Ate pairing.

5.1 Parameters of pairing-friendly curve

In this simulation, the authors used the following χ and BN curve,

$$\chi = 2^{62} + 2^{35} + 2^{24}, \tag{38}$$

$$E : y^2 = x^3 + 10, \tag{39}$$

then $r = \#E(\mathbb{F}_p)$ becomes 254-bit prime number and the order of $\mathbb{F}_{p^{12}}$ becomes 3048-bit number.

5.2 Representation of extension field

This simulation First, the authors prepared $\mathbb{F}_{p^4}$ with type-⟨1, 4⟩ Gauss period normal basis (GNB) (H. Cohen & G. Frey (2005)) and also $\mathbb{F}_{p^3}$ with type-⟨2, 3⟩ GNB. Then, the authors prepared $\mathbb{F}_{p^{12}}$ as *tower field* $\mathbb{F}_{(p^4)^3}$by towering ⟨2, 3⟩ GNB over $\mathbb{F}_{p^4}$ (Y. Nogami & Y. Morikawa (2003)). For multiplication with GNB, the authors implemented our previous work *cyclic vector multiplication algorithm* (CVMA) (H. Kato et al. (2007)). For example, CVMA calculates a multiplication in $\mathbb{F}_{(p^m)^n}$ by

$$M_{mn} = \frac{n(n+1)}{2} M_m = \frac{mn(m+1)(n+1)}{4} M_1. \tag{40}$$

For inversions in extension field and prime field, the authors implemented Itoh-Tsujii inversion algorithm (T. Itoh & S. Tsujii (1988)) and *binary extended* Euclidean algorithm (D. Knuth (1981)), respectively. Since GNB is normal basis, one can easily prepare arithmetic operations in subfields $\mathbb{F}_{p^2}, \mathbb{F}_{p^4}, \mathbb{F}_{(p^2)^3}$. Table 7. shows the timing of each operation.

[unit:μs]

extension field	operation type	254–bit p
$\mathbb{F}_p$	M_1	0.65
	I_1	8.30
$\mathbb{F}_{p^2}$	M_2	1.65
	I_2	11.5
$\mathbb{F}_{p^4}$	M_4	4.40
	I_4	20.4
$\mathbb{F}_{p^6}$	M_6	7.84
	I_6	32.2
$\mathbb{F}_{p^{12}}$	M_{12}	21.5
	I_{12}	80.7
	S_{12}	19.6

Table 7. Timings of each arithmetic operation

5.3 Final exponentiation

Using several Frobenius mappings, the final exponentiation is carried out as Algorithm 3. (A. J. Devegili et al. (2007)), where we note that the exponent $(p^{12}-1)/r$ is factorized as

$$(p^{12}-1)/r = (p^2+1)(p^6-1)\frac{p^4-p^2+1}{r}. \tag{41}$$

f^{p^i}'s shown in Algorithm 3. are given by Frobenius mappings. In the case of BN curve of embedding degree 12, referring to (A. J. Devegili et al. (2007)), final exponentiation is carried out by Algorithm 3. Note that Frobenius maps such as f^{p^i} in Algorithm 3. do not need any arithmetic operations because GNB is normal basis.

From Algorithm 3., it is found that the exponentiations of χ and χ^2 needs hard exponentiations such as binary method (square and multiply method). The calculation cost of an exponentiation closely depends on the binary representation of the exponent.

The calculation cost of final exponentiation Algorithm 3. is evaluated as

$$\begin{aligned} &\{4 + \lfloor \log_2 \chi \rfloor + \lfloor \log_2 \chi^2 \rfloor\} S_{12} \\ &+\{17 + \mathrm{Hw}(\chi) + \mathrm{Hw}(\chi^2)\} M_{12} + 2I_{12}. \end{aligned} \tag{42}$$

Substituting $S_{12} = 0.9M_{12}$ and $I_{12} = 4M_{12}$ that is base on the simulation result Table 7., we have

$$\{28.6 + 2.7\lfloor \log_2 \chi \rfloor + \mathrm{Hw}(\chi) + \mathrm{Hw}(\chi^2)\}M_{12}. \tag{43}$$

Algorithm 3 : Final exponentiation
Input : f given by $f_{t-1,Q'}(P')$, χ, p
Output : $f^{(p^6-1)(p^2+1)(p^4-p^2+1)/r}$
Procedure :
1. $f \leftarrow f^{p^6} \cdot f^{-1}$
2. $f \leftarrow f^{p^2} \cdot f$
3. $a \leftarrow (f^6)^{\chi} \cdot (f^5)^{p^6}$
4. $b \leftarrow a^p$
5. $b \leftarrow a \cdot b$
6. compute f^p, f^{p^2}, and f^{p^3}
7. $c \leftarrow b \cdot (f^p)^2 \cdot f^{p^2}$
8. $f \leftarrow f^{p^3} \cdot (c^6)^{\chi^2} \cdot c \cdot b \cdot (f^p \cdot f)^9 \cdot a \cdot f^4$
9. return f

5.4 Simulation result

Table 8. shows the simulation result. Xt-Ate pairing of 254-bit and 3048-bit security levels is carried out within 14.0 milli-seconds. Thus, it is shown that *cross twist* technique is quite efficient for Ate pairing. The authors simulated Xt-Ate pairing using Eq.(38) with the computational environment Table 9.

6. Conclusion

In this paper, supposing

$$\mathbb{G}_1 = E[r] \cap \mathrm{Ker}(\phi - [1]), \tag{44a}$$

$$\mathbb{G}_2 = E[r] \cap \mathrm{Ker}(\phi - [p]), \tag{44b}$$

where E was a pairing-friendly curve of embedding degree $k = 2e, 3e, 4e, 6e$, then denoting the isomorphic map from $E'(\mathbb{F}_{p^e})$ to $E(\mathbb{F}_{p^k})$ by ψ_d, we considered $\mathbb{G}'_1 = \psi_d^{-1}(\mathbb{G}_1)$ and $\mathbb{G}'_2 = \psi_d^{-1}(\mathbb{G}_2)$. Using $Q' \in \mathbb{G}'_2$ and $P' \in \mathbb{G}'_1$, this paper proposed a new Ate pairing that calculates

$$\alpha(Q', P') = f_{t-1,Q'}(P')^{(p^k-1)/r}, \tag{45}$$

namely *cross twisted* (Xt) Ate pairing. Compared to plain Ate pairing and Devegili's work, Xt-Ate pairing could substantially use arithmetic operations in subfield $\mathbb{F}_{p^e}$, thus it lead to quite efficient implementation of Ate pairing. Then, this paper showed a simulation result by using BN curve and *sextic twist*. When order r was a 254-bit prime number, it was shown that Xt-Ate pairing with BN curve was carried out within 14.0 milli-seconds for which the authors used Pentium4 (3.6GHz), C language, GNU MP library.

[unit:ms]

Xt–Ate pairing	
Miller's algorithm	8.80
final exponentiation	4.49
total	13.3
elliptic curve scalar multiplication†	
$\mathbb{G}_1 \in E(\mathbb{F}_p)$‡	2.65
$\mathbb{G}'_2 \in E'(\mathbb{F}_{p^2})$	7.02
exponentiation†	
$\mathbb{G}_3 \in \mathbb{F}^*_{p^{12}}$	7.88

†with 254–bit random scalars/exponents.

‡ *Projective coordinate* is used.

Table 8. Timings of operations with 254-bit prime order BN curve

CPU	Pentium4 3.6GHz
cash size	2048KB
OS	Linux 2.6.21
Language	C
compiler	gcc 4.2.1
option	-O3 -march=pentium4 -fforce-mem
library	Gnu MP 4.2.1 (GNU MP)

Table 9. Computational environment

7. References

D. Bailey and C. Paar (2000). Optimal Extension Fields for Fast Arithmetic in Public-Key Algorithms, *Proc. Asiacrypt2000*, LNCS 1976, pp. 248-258.

P. S. L. M. Barreto, and M. Naehrig (2006). Pairing-Friendly Elliptic Curves of Prime Order, *Proc. of SAC2005*, LNCS 3897, pp. 319-331.

D. Boneh, B. Lynn, and H. Shacham (2001). Short signatures from the Weil pairing, *Proc. of Asiacrypt2001* , LNCS 2248, pp. 514-532.

H. Cohen and G. Frey (2005). Handbook of Elliptic and Hyperelliptic Curve Cryptography, *Discrete Mathematics and Its Applications*, Chapman & Hall CRC, pp. 280-285, p. 458.

A. J. Devegili, M. Scott, and R. Dahab (2007). Implementing Cryptographic Pairings over Barreto-Naehrig Curves, *Proc. of Pairing 2007*, LNCS 4575, pp. 197-207.

GNU MP. GNU Multiple Precision Arithmetic Library, http://gmplib.org/

F. Hess, N. Smart, and F. Vercauteren (2006). The Eta Pairing Revisited, *IEEE Trans. Information Theory*, pp. 4595-4602.

T. Itoh and S. Tsujii (1988). A Fast Algorithm for Computing Multiplicative Inverses in $GF(2^m)$ Using Normal Bases, *Inf. and Comp.*, vol. 78, pp. 171-177.

D. Knuth (1981). The Art of Computer Programming, *vol. 2: Seminumerical Algorithms*, Addison-Wesley.

E. Lee, H. Lee, and C. Park (2008). Efficient and Generalized Pairing Computation on Abelien Varieties, IACR ePrint archive, available at http://eprint.iacr.org/2008/040.

S. Matsuda et al. (2007). Optimised versions of the Ate and Twisted Ate Pairings, IACR, ePrint, available at http://eprint.iacr.org/2007/013.pdf

T. Nakanishi and N. Funabiki (2005). Verifier-Local Revocation Group Signature Schemes with Backward Unlinkability from Bilinear Maps, *Proc. of Asiacrypt2005*, LNCS 3788, Springer-Verlag, pp. 443-454.

Y. Nogami and Y. Morikawa (2003). A Fast Implementation of Elliptic Curve Cryptosystem with Prime Order Defined over F_{p^8}, *Memoirs of the Faculty of Engineering Okayama University*, vol. 37, no. 2, pp. 73-88.

M. Akane, H. Kato, T. Okimoto, Y. Nogami, and Y. Morikawa (2007). An Improvement of Miller's Algorithm in Ate Pairing with Barreto-Naehrig Curve, *Proc. of Computer Security Symposium 2007 (CSS2007)*, pp. 489-494.

M. Akane, H. Kato, T. Okimoto, Y. Nogami, and Y. Morikawa (2007). Efficient Parameters for Ate Pairing Computation with Barreto-Naehrig Curve, *Proc. of Computer Security Symposium 2007 (CSS2007)*, pp. 495-500.

H. Kato, Y. Nogami, T. Yoshida, and Y. Morikawa (2007). Cyclic Vector Multiplication Algorithm Based on a Special Class of Gauss Period Normal Basis, *ETRI Journal*, vol. 29, no. 6, pp. 769 - 778, available at http://etrij.etri.re.kr/Cyber/servlet/BrowseAbstract?paperid=RP0702-0040

Y. Nogami, M. Akane, Y. Sakemi, H. Kato, and Y. Morikawa (2008). Integer Variable χ-based Ate Pairing, *Proc. of Pairing 2008*, LNCS 5209, pp. 178-191.

Y. Sakemi, H. Kato, M. Akane, T. Okimoto, Y. Nogami, and Y. Morikawa (2008). An Improvement of Twisted Ate Pairing Using Integer Variable with Small Hamming Weight, *The 2008 Symposium on Cryptography and Information Security (SCIS)*, Jan. 22-25.

F. Vercauteren (2008). Optimal Pairings, IACR ePrint archive, available at http://eprint.iacr.org/2008/096.

21

An Improvement of Twisted Ate Pairing with Barreto-Naehrig Curve by using Frobenius Mapping

Yumi Sakemi, Hidehiro Kato, Yasuyuki Nogami and Yoshitaka Morikawa
Okayama University
Japan

1. Introduction

Recently, pairing-based cryptographic applications such as ID-based cryptography (Boneh et al., 2001) and group signature scheme (Nakanishi & Funabiki, 2005) have received much attention. In order to make it practical, various pairings such as Ate pairing (Cohen & Frey, 2005), *subfield-twisted* pairing (Matsuda et al., 2007) and *subfield-twisted* Ate pairing (Devegili et al., 2007) have been proposed. This paper focuses on *twisted-Ate* pairing with Barreto-Naehrig (BN) curve (Barreto & Naehrig, 2005). As a typical feature of BN curve whose embedding degree is 12, its characteristic p, its order r, and Frobenius trace t are respectively given with *integer variable* χ as follows.

$$p(\chi) = 36\chi^4 - 36\chi^3 + 24\chi^2 - 6\chi + 1, \tag{1a}$$

$$r(\chi) = 36\chi^4 - 36\chi^3 + 18\chi^2 - 6\chi + 1, \tag{1b}$$

$$t(\chi) = 6\chi^2 + 1. \tag{1c}$$

Pairing calculation usually consists of two parts, one is Miller's algorithm calculation and the other is so-called *final exponentiation*. Let E be BN curve of characteristic p, Miller's algorithm of *twisted-Ate* pairing calculates $f_{s,P}(Q)\, f_{s,P}(Q)$, where s is given by $(t-1)^2 \bmod r$, P and Q are rational points in certain subgroups of order r in $E(F_p)$ and $E(F_{p^{12}})$, respectively. In this case, $(t-1)^2 \bmod r$ becomes

$$(t-1)^2 \bmod r = 36\chi^3 - 18\chi^2 + 6\chi - 1 \tag{2}$$

it corresponds to the number of iterations of Miller's algorithm. In addition, the hamming weight of $(t-1)^2 \bmod r$ is preferred to be small for Miller's algorithm to be fast carried out. This paper proposes an improvement of Miller's algorithm.
In the improvement, we use the following relations:

$$\begin{aligned}(t-1)^2 &\equiv 36\chi^3 - 18\chi^2 + 6\chi - 1 \\ &\equiv 6\chi^2(6\chi - 3) + 6\chi - 1 \equiv p(6\chi - 3) + 6\chi - 1 \bmod r,\end{aligned} \tag{3}$$

,where $p \equiv t-1=6\chi^2 \bmod r$ .First, calculate $f_{6\chi-3,P}(Q)$ by Miller's algorithm, then calculate $f_{6\chi-1,P}(Q)$ by using the result of the preceding calculation. Then, using the result, calculate $f_{p,(6\chi-3)P}(Q)$ for which Frobenius mapping in extension field $F_{p^{12}}$ with respect to prime field F_p is efficiently applied. In detail, since p is the characteristic of F_{p^m}, Frobenius mapping does not need any arithmetic operations when the extension field has fast Frobenius mapping such as OEF (Bailey & Paar, 1998). After that, the authors show some simulation results from which we find that the improvement shown in this paper efficiently accelerates *twisted-Ate* pairing including *final exponentiation* about 14.1%.

Throughout this paper, p and k denote characteristic and extension degree, respectively. F_{p^k} denotes k-th extension field over F_p and $F_{p^k}^*$ denotes its multiplicative group.

2. Fundamantals

This section briefly reviews elliptic curve, *twisted-Ate* pairing, and divisor theorem.

2.1 Elliptic curve and BN curve

Let F_p be prime field and E be an elliptic curve over F_p. $E(F_p)$ that is the set of rational points on the curve, including the *infinity point* O, forms an additive Abelian group. Let $\#E(F_p)$ be its order, consider a large prime number r that divides $\#E(F_p)$. The smallest positive integer k such that r divides p^k-1 is especially called *embedding degree*. One can consider a pairing such as Tate and Ate pairings on $E(F_{p^k})$.

Usually, $\#E(F_p)$ is written as

$$\#E(F_p)=p+1-t, \tag{4}$$

where t is the Frobenius trace of $E(F_p)$. Characteristic p and Frobenius trace t of Barreto--Naehrig (BN) curve (Barreto & Naehrig, 2005) are given by using an integer variable χ as Eqs.(1). In addition, BN curve E is written as

$$E(F_p): y^2 = x^3 + b, \quad b \in F_p \tag{5}$$

whose embedding degree is 12. In this paper, let $\#E(F_p)$ be a prime number r for instance.

2.2 Twisted ate pairing with BN curve

Let ϕ be Frobenius endomorphism, i.e.,

$$\phi: E(F_{p^{12}}) \to E(F_{p^{12}}): (x,y) \to (x^p, y^p), \tag{6}$$

Then, in the case of BN curve, let G_1 and G_2 be

$$G_1 = E[r] \cap \mathrm{Ker}(\phi - [1]), \tag{7a}$$

$$G_2 = E[r] \cap \mathrm{Ker}([\xi_6]\phi^2 - [1]) \tag{7b}$$

where ξ_6 is a primitive 6-th root of unity and let $P \in G_1$ and $Q \in G_2$, *twisted-Ate* pairing $\alpha(\cdot,\cdot)$ is defined as

$$\alpha(\cdot,\cdot):\begin{cases} G_1 \times G_2 \to F^*_{p^{12}}/(F^*_{p^{12}})^r \\ (P,Q) \mapsto f_{s,P}(Q)^{(p^{12}-1)/r}. \end{cases} \tag{8}$$

$A = f_{s,P}(Q)$ is usually calculated by Miller's algorithm (Devegili et al., 2007), then so--called *final exponentiation* $A^{(p^{12}-1)/r}$ follows. The number of calculation loops of Miller's algorithm of *twisted-Ate* pairing with BN curve is determined by $\lfloor \log_2 s \rfloor$, where *s* is, in this case, given by

$$s = (t-1)^2 \bmod r = 36\chi^3 - 18\chi^2 + 6\chi - 1. \tag{9}$$

It is said that calculation cost of Miller's Algorithm is about twice of that of final exponentiation.

2.3 Divisor

Let *D* be the principal divisor of $Q \in E$ given as

$$D = (Q) - (O) = (Q) - (O) + div(1). \tag{10}$$

For scalars $a, b \in Z$, let *aD* and *bD* be written as

$$aD = (aQ) - (O) + div(f_{a,Q}), \quad bD = (bQ) - (O) + div(f_{b,Q}), \tag{11}$$

where $f_{a,Q}$ and $f_{b,Q}$ are the rational functions for *aD* and *bD*, respectively. Then, addition for divisors is given as

$$aD + bD = (aQ) + (bQ) - (O) + div(f_{a,Q} \cdot f_{b,Q} \cdot g_{aQ,bQ}), \tag{12a}$$

where $g_{aQ,bQ} = l_{aQ,bQ}/v_{aQ+bQ}$, $l_{aQ,bQ}$ denotes the line passing through two points aQ, bQ, and v_{aQ+bQ} denotes the vertical line passing through $aQ+bQ$. Moreover, the following relation holds.

$$a(bD) = \sum_{i=0}^{a-1}(bQ) - a(O) + div(f_{b,Q}^a \cdot f_{a,bQ}). \tag{12b}$$

Thus, let (*a*+*b*)*D* and (*ab*)*D* be written as

$$(a+b)D = ((a+b)Q) - (O) + div(f_{a+b,Q}), \tag{13a}$$

$$(ab)D = (abQ) - (O) + div(f_{ab,Q}). \tag{13b}$$

we have the following relation.

$$f_{a+b,Q} = f_{a,Q} \cdot f_{b,Q} \cdot g_{aQ,bQ}, \quad f_{ab,Q} = f_{b,Q}{}^a \cdot f_{a,bQ} = f_{a,Q}{}^b \cdot f_{b,aQ}. \tag{14}$$

Miller's algorithm calculates $f_{s,Q}$ efficiently.

3. Main proposal

First, this section briefly goes over Miller's algorithm. Then, an improvement of *twisted-Ate* pairing with BN curve of embedding degree 12 is proposed.

3.1 Introduction of Miller's algorithm

Several improvements for Miller's algorithm have been given. Barreto et al. proposed *reduced* Miller's algorithm. **Fig. 1** shows the calculation flow of *reduced* Miller's algorithm for $f_{s,P}(Q)$. It consists of functions shown in **Algorithm 1** and **Algorithm 2,** *see* **Table 1.**

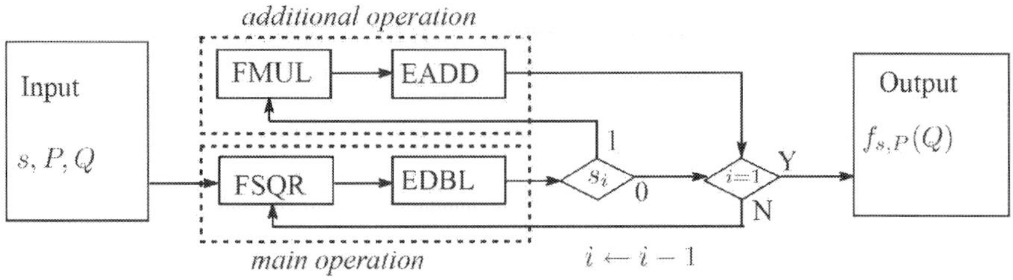

Fig. 1. Calculation flow of Miller's algorithm

In the case of *twisted-Ate* pairing, let $P \in G_1$, $Q \in G_2$ and s be given by Eq.(9), $f_{s,P}(Q)$ becomes an element in $F_{p^k}^*$. In **Fig. 1,** s_i is the i-th bit of the binary representation of s from the lower, FMUL and FSQR denote multiplication and squaring over $F_{p^{12}}$, EADD and EDBL denote elliptic curve addition and doubling over G_1. As shown in the algorithm, *main operation* is repeated $\lfloor \log_2 s \rfloor$ times but *additional operation* is only carried out when s_i is 1. Thus, the calculation cost of Miller's Algorithm can be reduced by reducing the number of *additional operations.*

Input:	$T \in G_1, Q \in G_2$
Output:	f, T
	FSQR
1.	$\lambda_{T,T} \leftarrow (3x_T^2)/(2y_T)$
2.	$l_{T,T}(Q) \leftarrow (x_Q - x_T)\lambda_{T,T} - (y_Q - y_T)$
3.	$f \leftarrow f^2 \cdot l_{T,T}(Q) / v_{T+T}(Q)$
4.	return f
	EDBL
5.	$x_{2T} \leftarrow \lambda_{T,T}^2 - 2x_T$
6.	$y_{2T} \leftarrow (x_T - x_{2T})\lambda_{T,T} - y_T$
7.	Return $T \leftarrow 2T$

Algorithm 1. FSQR and EDBL of Fig. 1

3.2 Proposed method

$f_{A,P} = f_{B,P}$ means $f_{A,P}{}^{(p^{12}-1)/r} = f_{B,P}{}^{(p^{12}-1)/r}$ in what follows, where $f_{A,P}$ and $f_{B,P}$ are the rational functions of divisors, respectively. Miller's algorithm of *twisted-Ate* pairing with BN curve calculates $f_{s,P}(Q)$, where s is given as

$$s = (t-1)^2 = 36\chi^3 - 18\chi^2 + 6\chi - 1 \bmod r. \tag{15}$$

Input:	$P \in G_1, Q \in G_2$
Output:	f, T
	FMUL
1.	$\lambda_{T,P} \leftarrow (y_P - y_T)/(x_P - x_T)$
2.	$l_{T,P}(Q) \leftarrow (x_Q - x_P)\lambda_{T,P} - (y_Q - y_P)$
3.	$f \leftarrow f \cdot l_{T,P}(Q) / v_{T+P}(Q)$
4.	return f
	EADD
5.	$x_{T+P} \leftarrow \lambda_{T,P}^2 - x_T - x_P$
6.	$y_{T+P} \leftarrow (x_P - x_{T+P})\lambda_{T,P} - y_P$
7.	return $T \leftarrow 2T$

Algorithm 2. FMUL and EADD of Fig. 1

s_i:	the i-th bit of the binary representation of s from the lower.
$l_{T,T}$:	the tangent line at T.
$l_{T,P}$:	the line passing through T and P.
v_{T+T}:	the vertical line passing through $2T$.
v_{T+P}	the vertical line passing through $T+P$.
$\lambda_{T,T}$:	the slope of the tangent line $l_{T,T}$.
$\lambda_{T,P}$:	the slope of the line $l_{T,P}$.

Table 1. Notations used in **Algorithms 1, 2,** and **3**

$r(\chi)$	χ	Hw(s*)
254 Bits	$2^{62}+2^{46}+2^{29}$	83
	$2^{64}+2^{35}+2^{24}$	82
	$2^{62}+2^{55}+1$	36
	$-2^{62}-2^{41}-2^{23}$	43

* $s = (t-1)^2 \bmod r = 36\chi^3-18\chi^2+6\chi-1$

Table 2. χ of small Hamming weight that gives BN curve of 254 bits prime order

The proposed method calculates $f_{s,P}(Q)$ using the following relations:

$$p \equiv t-1 = 6\chi^2 \bmod r, \tag{16a}$$

$$s \equiv 6\chi^2(6\chi-3)+6\chi-1 \equiv p(6\chi-3)+6\chi-1 \bmod r. \tag{16b}$$

Using χ of small Hamming weight, first calculate $f_{6\chi-3,P}(Q)$ and then calculate $f_{6\chi-1,P}(Q)$ by using the result of the preceding calculation. Then, by calculating $f_{p,(6\chi-3)P}(Q)$ for which Frobenius mapping is efficiently applied, the number of *additional operations* is substantially reduced. In detail, let $\chi' = 2\chi-1$, calculate $f_{\chi',P}(Q)$ by Miller's algorithm. Then, calculate $f_{6\chi-3,P}(Q)$ as

$$f_{6\chi-3,P} = f_{\chi',P}^3 \cdot g_{\chi'P,\chi'P} \cdot g_{2\chi'P,\chi'P}. \tag{17}$$

Since 6 χ-1=(6 χ-3)+2, $f_{6\chi-1,P}(Q)$ is given as

$$f_{6\chi-1,P} = f_{6\chi-3,P} \cdot f_{2,P} \cdot g_{(6\chi-3)P,2P}. \tag{18}$$

Then, calculate $f_{(6\chi-3)\cdot 6\chi^2,P}$ by using $f_{6\chi-3,P}$. **Algorithm 3** shows Miller's algorithm whose initial value of *f* is *f*'. Though it can be calculated by **Algorithm 3** as

$$f_{(6\chi-3)\cdot 6\chi^2,P} = f_{6\chi^2,(6\chi-3)P}\,|_{f'=f_{(6\chi-3),P}}, \tag{19}$$

according to Eq.(16a), this paper calculates it by **Algorithm 3** as follows.

$$f_{(6\chi-3)\cdot 6\chi^2,P} = f^{6\chi^2}_{(6\chi-3),P} \cdot f_{6\chi^2,(6\chi-3)P}\,|_{f'=1} = f^{p}_{(6\chi-3),P} \cdot f_{6\chi^2,(6\chi-3)P}\,|_{f'=1} \tag{20}$$

Finally, we have

$$f_{6\chi^2(6\chi-3)+6\chi-1,P} = f_{(6\chi-1),P} \cdot f^{p}_{(6\chi-3),P} \cdot (f_{6\chi^2,(6\chi-3)P}\,|_{f'=1}) \cdot g_{(6\chi-1)P,(6\chi-3)P}. \tag{21}$$

The proposed method has the following advantages.

- χ of small hamming weight efficiently works.
- It can reduce a multiplication in $F_{p^{12}}$ at Step6 of **Algorithm 3** by Frobenius mapping.

Input:	$P \in G_1, Q \in G_2, f' \in F_{p^{12}}$
Output:	$f_{\chi,P'}(Q)$
1.	$f \leftarrow f', T \leftarrow P$
2.	For $i = \lfloor \log_2(s) \rfloor$ downto 1 :
3.	$\quad f \leftarrow f^2 \cdot l_{T,T}(Q) / v_{T+T}(Q)$
4.	$\quad T \leftarrow 2T$
5.	$\quad$ If $s_i = 1$, then :
6.	$\quad\quad f \leftarrow f \cdot f' l_{T,P}(Q) / v_{T+P}(Q)$
7.	$\quad\quad T \leftarrow T + P$
8.	return f

Algorithm 3. Miller's Algorithm whose initial value of f is f'.

4. Experimental result

In order to show the efficiency of the proposed method, the authors simulated *twisted-Ate* pairing with BN curve of order $r \approx 2^{254}$. In this simulation, the authors used χ and BN curve shown in **Table 3. Table 4** shows the simulation result.

As a reference, **Table 5** shows timings of multiplication (mul), inversion (inv) in each subfield of $F_{p^{12}}$ and squaring (sqr) in $F_{p^{12}}$. According to **Table 4**, in the cases of $r \approx 2^{254}$, the proposed method reduced the calculation times of Miller's algorithm by 18.0%.

size of p, r	254 bits
BN curve	$y^2=x^3+10$
χ	$2^{64}+2^{35}+2^{24}$
Hw(s)	82
Hw(χ)	3

Table 3. Parameters of *twisted-Ate* pairing

p, r		254 bits
Miller's part	Conventional	14.5
	Proposed	11.8
final exponentiation		4.45
Total	Conventional	19.0
	Proposed	16.3
Elliptic curve scalar multiplication*	$G_1 \in E(F_p)$**	2.31
	$G_2 \in E'(F_{p^2})$	7.01

* Average timings with random scalars and exponents of
** *Projective coordinates* are used.
Remark : Pentium4 (3.6GHz), C language, and GMP 4.2.2 library are used.

Table 4. Comparison of timings [ms]

F_p	mul	0.65
	inv	8.43
F_{p^2}	mul	1.65
	inv	11.4
F_{p^4}	mul	4.39
	inv	19.6
F_{p^6}	mul	7.78
	inv	32.4
$F_{p^{12}}$	mul	21.6
	inv	80.3
	sqr	19.7

Remark: Pentium4 (3.6GHz), C language, and GMP 4.2.2 library are used.

Table 5. Timings of operations in subfield (p: 254 bit prime number)[μs]

5. Conclusion

This paper has proposed an improvement of *twisted-Ate* pairing with Barreto-Naehrig curve so as to efficiently use Frobenius mapping with respect to prime field. Then, this paper showed some simulation result by which it was shown that the improvement accelerated *twisted-Ate* pairing *including final exponentiation* about 14.1%.

6. Acknowledgement

This work is supported by ``Strategic Information and Communications R&D Promotion Programme" from the Ministry of Internal Affairs and Communications, Japan.

7. References

Bailey, D. & Paar, C. (1998). Optimal Extension Fields for Fast Arithmetic in Public-Key Algorithms, *Proceedings of CRYPT'98*, pp.472-485, ISBN: 978-3-540-64892-5, USA, August 1998, Springer-Verlag, Santa Barbara, California

Barreto, P. S. L. M. & Naehrig, M. (2006). Pairing-Friendly Elliptic Curves of Prime Order, *Proceedings of SAC2005*, pp. 319-331, ISBN: 978-3-540-33108-7, Canada, August 2005, Springer-Verlag, Kingston

Boneh, D.; Lynn, B. & Shacham, H. (2001). Short signatures from the Weil pairing, *Proceedings of Asiacrypt2001*, pp. 514-532, ISBN: 978-3-540-42987-6, Australia, December 2001, Springer-Verlag, Gold Coast

Cohen, H. & Frey, G. (2005). *Handbook of Elliptic and Hyperelliptic Curve Cryptography*, Chapman & Hall CRC, ISBN: 1584885181

Devegili, A. J.; Scott, M. & Dahab, R. (2007). Implementing Cryptographic Pairings over Barreto-Naehrig Curves, *Proceedings of Pairing2007*, pp. 197-207, ISBN: 978-3-540-73488-8, Japan, July 2007, Springer-Verlag, Tokyo

GNU Multiple Precision Arithmetic Library, http://gmplib.org/

Hess, F.; Smart, N.; & Vercauteren, F. (2006). The Eta Pairing Revisited, *IEEE Trans. Information Theory*, Vol. 52, No. 10, October 2006, pp. 4595-4602, ISSN: 0018-9448

Matsuda, S.; Kanayama, N; Hess, F.; & Okamoto, E. (2007). Optimised Versions of the Ate and Twisted Ate Pairings, *Proceedings of 11th IMA International Conference*, pp. 302-312, ISBN: 978-3-540-77272-9, UK, December 2007, Springer-Verlag, Cirencester.

Nakanishi, T. & Funabiki, N. (2005). Verifier-Local Revocation Group Signature Schemes with Backward Unlinkability from Bilinear Maps, *Proceedings of Asiacrypt2005*, pp. 443-454, ISBN: 978-3-540-30684-9, India, December 2005, Springer-Verlag, Chennai

22

An Improvement of Cyclic Vector Multiplication Algorithm

Hidehiro Kato, Yasuyuki Nogami, Tomoki Yoshida, Kenta Nekado, Shoichi Takeuchi, and Yoshitaka Morikawa
Okayama University
Japan

1. Introduction

Pairing-based cryptographic applications such as ID-based cryptography (Boneh et al., 2001) and group signature authentication (Nakanishi & Funabiki, 2005) have received much attentions. Such an application needs a pairing-friendly elliptic curve and arithmetic operations in a certain extension field F_{p^m}. The extension degree is especially called *embedding degree*. In general, corresponding to the pairing-friendly curve, characteristic p is restricted so as to satisfy a certain condition and m is fixed to a certain positive integer. For example, Barreto-Naehrig (BN) curve (Barreto & Naehrig, 2005) and Freeman curve (Freeman, 2006) are well known pairing - friendly curves. In the case of BN curve, characteristic p needs to be given with an integer χ as

$$p = 36\chi^4 - 36\chi^3 + 24\chi^2 - 6\chi + 1 \tag{1}$$

and m is fixed to 12. In the case of Freeman curve,

$$p = 25\chi^4 - 25\chi^3 + 25\chi^2 - 10\chi + 3 \tag{2}$$

and embedding degree m is fixed to 10. In order to make those cryptographic applications practical, definition field F_{p^m} needs to have fast arithmetic operations, especially multiplication. However, some of these restrictions cannot satisfy the conditions for fast arithmetic operations inversely.

Optimal extension field (OEF) (Bailey & Paar, 1998) has fast arithmetic operations and is widely used (Devegili et al., 2007). Since OEF uses Karatsuba-based polynomial multiplication and an irreducible binomial as the modular polynomial, a multiplication in OEF is efficiently carried out. However, in order to construct F_{p^m} as OEF, each prime factor needs to divide p - 1. It is a critical condition for Freeman curve, for example, because characteristic p of Freeman curve is given by Eq.(2) and thus can never satisfy it. On the other hand, type-<k,m> Gauss period normal basis (GNB) can be easily prepared in F_{p^m} whenever 4p does not divide $m(p$ - 1) (Kato et al., 2007). As previously introduced, m is relatively small than p, therefore this condition is always satisfied. In addition, the authors have proposed an efficient multiplication algorithm using GNB (Kato et al, 2007). It is called *cyclic vector multiplication algorithm* (CVMA). In the previous work (Kato et al, 2007), CVMA is quite efficient when m is small such as for the use of pairing-based cryptographic applications. However, the calculation cost of CVMA becomes worse as k becomes larger. As shown in (Kato et al, 2007), most of cases have small k within 5 but it sometimes becomes large.

In this paper, a symmetric feature that appears in the calculation of CVMA is first introduced. Then, based on the feature, an improvement of CVMA is proposed. From some simulation results, it is shown that the improved CVMA efficiently carries out a multiplication in extension field even if parameter k is large.

Throughout this paper, p and m denote the characteristic and the extension degree, respectively, where p is a prime number. F_{p^m} denotes an m-th extension field over F_p. Without any additional explanation, lower and upper case letters show elements in prime field and extension field, respectively, and a Greek alphabet shows a zero of modular polynomial. In this paper, a subtraction in F_p is counted up as an addition in F_p. M_1, A_1 and D_1 denote the calculation costs of a multiplication, addition and doubling in F_p.

2. Fundamentals

This section briefly reviews Gauss period normal basis, cyclic vector multiplication algorithm (CVMA), and then shows a problem of CVMA.

2.1 Gauss period normal basis

Type-<k,m> Gauss period normal basis in F_{p^m} is defined with an integer k as follows (Gao, 1993).

Definition 1 *Let* $km + 1$ be *a prime number not equal to p and suppose that* $\gcd(km/e,m) = 1$, *where e is the order of p modulo* $km + 1$. *Then, for any primitive k-th root θ of unity in* F_{km+1},

$$\gamma = \sum_{i=0}^{k-1} \beta^{\theta^i} \tag{3}$$

generates a normal basis $\{ \gamma, \gamma, \ldots, \gamma^{p^{m-1}} \}$ *in* F_{p^m}, *where β is a* $(km + 1)$*-st root of unity that belongs to* F_{p^e}. *This normal basis Eq.(3) is called type-*<k,m> *Gauss period normal basis.* ■

For an arbitrary extension degree m, there is an infinite number of k's such that $km + 1$ becomes a prime number. It is well-known as the Dirichlet's theorem on arithmetic progressions(Apostol, 1976). Moreover, when p is odd and $4p$ does not divide $m(p - 1)$, it is known that type-<k,m> Gauss period normal basis with a certain integer k always exists for an arbitrary pair of p and m (Gao, 1993).

2.2 TypeI-X GNB and CVMA

Consider a class of Gauss period normal basis of which the order e shown in Def.1 is km+1. When k is equal to 1, it is typeI optimal normal basis (Cohen & Frey, 2005), thus in what follows we call the class of Gauss period normal basis *typeI–X* (typeI eXtended) GNB.

The authors have shown a multiplication algorithm with typeI–X Gauss period normal basis called *cyclic vector multiplication algorithm* (CVMA) (Kato et al., 2007). Fig.1 shows CVMA with typeI-X GNB in F_{p^m}. In the algorithm Fig.1, <x> denotes x mod $km + 1$

The calculation cost of CVMA is given by

$$\left\{\frac{m(m+1)}{2}+1\right\}M_1+\left\{\frac{m(m-1)(k+2)}{2}+m\right\}A_1, \tag{4}$$

where M_1 and A_1 denote the calculation costs of a multiplication and an addition in F_p, respectively. Different from OEF (optimal extension field) that restricts the characteristic p and extension degree m (Bailey & Paar, 1998)[1], our proposed multiplication algorithm, that is CVMA, is widely applicable since it is based on Gauss period normal basis (Kato et al, 2007). Especially, CVMA is efficient when extension degree m is small.

Input: $X = \sum_{i=0}^{m-1} x_i \gamma^{p^i}, Y = \sum_{i=0}^{m-1} y_i \gamma^{p^i}$.

Output: $Z = XY = \sum_{i=0}^{m-1} z_i \gamma^{p^i}$.

Preparation:

Determine k that satisfies the conditions in Def.1.
for $i = 0$ to m do
$q[i] \leftarrow 0$
for $t = 0$ to $m - 1$ do
for $h = 0$ to $k - 1$ do
$g[<p^{t+hm}>] \leftarrow t + 1$
$g[0] \leftarrow 0$

Procedure:

for $i = 0$ to $m - 1$ do
$q[i+1] \leftarrow x_i y_i$
for $i = 0$ to $m - 2$ do
for $j = i+1$ to $m - 1$ do
$M_{ij} \leftarrow (x_i - x_j)(y_i - y_j)$
for $h = 0$ to $k - 1$ do
$q[g[<p^i+p^{j+hm}>]] \leftarrow q[g[<p^i+p^{j+hm}>]] + M_{ij}$
for $i = 0$ to $m - 1$ do
$z_i \leftarrow kq[0] - q[i+1]$

(End of algorithm)

Fig. 1. CVMA with TypeI-X Gauss period normal basis in F_{p^m}

2.3 A problem in conventional CVMA

As shown in Eq.(4), the calculation cost of CVMA depends on the integer k. In general, A_1 is much smaller than M_1; however, if k is large, it will not be negligible. As shown in our previous work (Kato et al, 2007), the minimal integer k such that the conditions for type I-X Gauss period normal basis tends to be small such as within 5 but sometimes becomes large. When we can appropriately set the parameters p and m such that the corresponding minimal integer k becomes small, it will not be a critical problem. However, when these parameters are restricted as pairing-based cryptographies, it is out of options for CVMA. Thus, for such a case, this paper shows an improvement of CVMA.

3. Improvement of CVMA

This section shows an improvement of CVMA by which the number of F_p-additions needed for a multiplication in F_{p^m} with CVMA is efficiently reduced.

[1] Each prime factor must divide p-1.

3.1 Pre-Computation

According to the original CVMA Fig.1, the temporary data M_{ij} shown at Step 3 of the procedure is prepared with corresponding to i and j. Then, at Step 5, it is added to k coefficients among $q[l]$, $0 \leq l \leq m$.

The k coefficients to which the temporary data M_{ij} is added are determined from not only I and j but also p and m. It can be previously computed. In order to explain the basic idea, let us consider the following simple example. Let (p, m, k) be (41, 3, 6), respectively, and let X, Y be given as

$$X = x_0\gamma + x_1\gamma^p + x_2\gamma^{p^2}, \tag{5a}$$

$$Y = y_0\gamma + y_1\gamma^p + y_2\gamma^{p^2}. \tag{5b}$$

Suppose that not only x_0y_0, x_1y_1, x_2y_2 but also M_{01}, M_{02}, M_{12} have been calculated as the temporary values, then we need to calculate $q[0]$, $q[1]$, $q[2]$, and $q[3]$. In this case, those temporary values are used as

$$q[0] = 0, \tag{6a}$$

$$q[1] = x_0y_0 + M_{01} + 2M_{02} + 3M_{12}, \tag{6b}$$

$$q[2] = x_1y_1 + 2M_{01} + 3M_{02} + M_{12}, \tag{6c}$$

$$q[3] = x_2y_2 + 3M_{01} + M_{02} + 2M_{12}, \tag{6d}$$

Note that M_{01}, M_{02}, and M_{12} are given as

$$M_{01} = (x_0 - x_1)(y_0 - y_1), \tag{7a}$$

$$M_{02} = (x_0 - x_2)(y_0 - y_2), \tag{7b}$$

$$M_{12} = (x_1 - x_2)(y_1 - y_2), \tag{7c}$$

In our previous work (Kato et al, 2007), it has been shown that $q[0]$ becomes 0 when k is even. As shown in Eqs.(6), six M_{01}'s in total are added to $q[1]$, $q[2]$, and $q[3]$. M_{02}'s and M_{12}'s are similarly added to $q[1]$, $q[2]$, and $q[3]$. Thus, it is found that the number of additions increases as k becomes larger.

Based on Eqs.(6), consider the following $m \times {}_mC_2$ matrix given from the coefficients related to k:

$$\begin{pmatrix} 1 & 2 & 3 \\ 2 & 3 & 1 \\ 3 & 1 & 2 \end{pmatrix}. \tag{8}$$

As shown in Eq.(8), finite field theory often demonstrates such a symmetric feature. In what follows, we consider how to reduce the number of such additions. Such a matrix can be previously computed because it only depends on p, m, and k.

3.2 Improvement with tree structure

Eq.(8) can be decomposed as

$$\begin{pmatrix} 1 & 2 & 3 \\ 2 & 3 & 1 \\ 3 & 1 & 2 \end{pmatrix} = \begin{pmatrix} 1 & 0 & 1 \\ 0 & 1 & 1 \\ 1 & 1 & 0 \end{pmatrix} + \begin{pmatrix} 0 & 2 & 2 \\ 2 & 2 & 0 \\ 2 & 0 & 2 \end{pmatrix}. \tag{9}$$

Thus, the decomposed equation also has the symmetric feature. Then, consider C_{101}, C_{011}, and C_{110} as

$$C_{101} = M_{01} + 2M_{12}, \tag{10a}$$

$$C_{011} = M_{02} + 2M_{01}, \tag{10b}$$

$$C_{110} = M_{12} + 2M_{02}. \tag{10c}$$

The lower suffixes correspond to the column vectors of the first matrix of the right-hand side of Eq.(9) and thus it is led from Eq.(9). Then, using C_{101}, C_{011}, and C_{110}, $q[1]$, $q[2]$, and $q[3]$ are calculated by

$$q[1] = x_0 y_0 + C_{101} + C_{110}, \tag{11a}$$

$$q[2] = x_1 y_1 + C_{110} + C_{011}, \tag{11b}$$

$$q[3] = x_2 y_2 + C_{101} + C_{011}, \tag{11c}$$

Though Eqs.(6) needs 18 additions, Eqs.(11) needs only 12 additions. This example is one of the most efficient cases. However, since the lower suffixes are efficiently controlled with *tree structure*, this technique can be widely applied for more general cases. In other words, using *tree structure*, $q[0]$ to $q[m]$ are systematically recomposed with temporary calculated values such as C_{110}, C_{101}, and C_{011}.

4. Simulation

In order to show the efficiency of the improvement, this section simulates the improved CVMA with some practical parameter settings.

4.1 Parameter settings

This section considers a more practical case. Since pairing-based cryptographies often considers 158-bit characteristic p and extension degree $m = 6$, for simulation we consider $m = 6$ and the following p:

$$p = 218673105437695088256450591/ \\ 949649001738589593793. \text{ (158bit)} \tag{12}$$

In this case, the minimal k that satisfies the conditions for the existence of type I-X Gauss period normal basis in F_{p^6} is 12. Noting that k is even in the same of the preceding example, consider $q[1]$ to $q[6]$ in this case. Then, the $m \times {}_mC_2$ becomes

$$\begin{pmatrix} 0 & 2 & 2 & 3 & 2 & 3 & 3 & 1 & 3 & 1 & 0 & 3 & 3 & 1 & 3 \\ 2 & 3 & 3 & 1 & 3 & 0 & 2 & 2 & 3 & 3 & 3 & 1 & 1 & 0 & 3 \\ 3 & 3 & 1 & 0 & 3 & 2 & 3 & 3 & 1 & 0 & 2 & 2 & 3 & 3 & 1 \\ 3 & 1 & 2 & 3 & 1 & 3 & 3 & 1 & 0 & 2 & 3 & 3 & 0 & 2 & 3 \\ 1 & 0 & 3 & 2 & 3 & 3 & 1 & 2 & 3 & 3 & 3 & 1 & 2 & 3 & 0 \\ 3 & 3 & 1 & 3 & 0 & 1 & 0 & 3 & 2 & 3 & 1 & 2 & 3 & 3 & 2 \end{pmatrix}. \tag{13}$$

In this case, it is decomposed as Eq.(14).

$$\begin{pmatrix} 0&2&2&2&2&2&2&0&2&0&0&2&2&0&2 \\ 2&2&2&0&2&0&2&2&2&2&2&0&0&0&2 \\ 2&2&0&0&2&2&2&2&0&0&2&2&2&2&0 \\ 2&0&2&2&0&2&2&0&0&2&2&2&0&2&2 \\ 0&0&2&2&2&2&0&2&2&2&2&0&2&2&0 \\ 2&2&0&2&0&0&0&2&2&2&0&2&2&2&2 \end{pmatrix} + \begin{pmatrix} 0&0&0&1&0&1&1&1&1&1&0&1&1&1&1 \\ 0&1&1&1&1&0&0&0&1&1&1&1&1&0&1 \\ 1&1&1&0&1&0&1&1&1&0&0&0&1&1&1 \\ 1&1&0&1&1&1&1&1&0&0&1&1&0&0&1 \\ 1&0&1&0&1&1&1&0&1&1&1&1&0&1&0 \\ 1&1&1&1&0&1&0&1&0&1&1&0&1&1&0 \end{pmatrix}. \tag{14}$$

Thus, while the original CVMA needs

$$21M_1 + 210A_1, \tag{15a}$$

the improved CVMA needs

$$21M_1 + 86A_1 + 15D_1. \tag{15b}$$

4.2 Simulation result

Let characteristic p be 158-bit prime, Table 1 shows calculation costs and simulation results of the original CVMA for some pairs of extension degree m and k, Table 2 shows those of the improved CVMA. The simulation result shows that the improved CVMA becomes more efficient than the original.

extension degree m	parameter k	without the improvement†	with the improvement†
6	1	(21,50,-)	-
	2	(21,60,-)	-
	6	(21,120,-)	(21,80,15)
	12	(21,210,-)	(21,86,15)
12	1	(78,198,-)	-
	2	(78,343,-)	(78,321,1)
	6	(78,528,-)	(78,393,36)
	12	(78,660,-)	(78,426,60)

†(21, 80, 15) denotes $21M_1 + 80A_1 + 15D_1$, for example.

Table 1. Calculation cost of CVMA

5. Conclusion

This paper has first introduced *cyclic vector multiplication algorithm* (CVMA) that is a multiplication algorithm in extension field. Then, it was also introduced that CVMA was

extension degree m	parameter k	without the improvement [μs]‡	with the improvement [μs]‡
6	1	(21,50,-)	-
	2	(21,60,-)	-
	6	(21,120,-)	(21,80,15)
	12	(21,210,-)	(21,86,15)
12	1	(78,198,-)	-
	2	(78,343,-)	(78,321,1)
	6	(78,528,-)	(78,393,36)
	12	(78,660,-)	(78,426,60)

‡The authors used Pentium4 (3.6GHz), C language, and GMP4.2.2 library.

Table 2. Timing of a multiplication with CVMA

useful under the tight restrictions of *pairing-based cryptographies*. Then, this paper pointed out a problem about the calculation cost of CVMA. For this problem, this paper proposed an improvement. According to some simulation results, it was shown that the improvement made CVMA much more efficient.

6. References

Apostol, T. (1976). *Introduction to Analytic Number Theory*, Springer-Verlag, ISBN: 978-0-387-90163-3

Bailey, D. & Paar, C. (1998). Optimal Extension Fields for Fast Arithmetic in Public-Key Algorithms, *Proceedings of CRYPT'98*, pp.472-485, ISBN: 978-3-540-64892-5, USA, August 1998, Springer-Verlag, Santa Barbara, California

Barreto, P. S. L. M. & Naehrig, M. (2006). Pairing-Friendly Elliptic Curves of Prime Order, *Proceedings of SAC2005*, pp. 319-331, ISBN: 978-3-540-33108-7, Canada, August 2005, Springer-Verlag, Kingston

Boneh, D.; Lynn, B. & Shacham, H. (2001). Short signatures from the Weil pairing, *Proceedings of Asiacrypt2001*, pp. 514-532, ISBN: 978-3-540-42987-6, Australia, December 2001, Springer-Verlag, Gold Coast

Cohen, H. & Frey, G. (2005). *Handbook of Elliptic and Hyperelliptic Curve Cryptography*, Chapman & Hall CRC, ISBN: 1584885181

Devegili, A. J.; Scott, M. & Dahab, R. (2007). Implementing Cryptographic Pairings over Barreto-Naehrig Curves, *Proceedings of Pairing2007*, pp. 197-207, ISBN: 978-3-540-73488-8, Japan, July 2007, Springer-Verlag, Tokyo

Freeman, D. (2006). Constructing pairing-friendly elliptic curves with embedding degree 10, *Proceedings of ANTS-VII*, pp. 248-258, ISBN: 978-3-540-36075-9, Germany, July 2006, Springer-Verlag, Berlin

Gao, S. (1993). Normal Bases over Finite Fields. *Doctoral thesis*, Waterloo, Ontario, Canada GNU Multiple Precision Arithmetic Library, http://gmplib.org/

Kato, H.; Nogami, Y. & Morikawa, Y. (2007) Cyclic Vector Multiplication Algorithm Based on a Special Class of Gauss Period Normal Basis. *ETRI Journal*, Vol. 29, No. 6, December 2007, 768-778, ISSN: 1225-6463

Nakanishi, T. & Funabiki, N. (2005). Verifier-Local Revocation Group Signature Schemes with Backward Unlinkability from Bilinear Maps, *Proceedings of Asiacrypt2005,* pp. 443-454, ISBN: 978-3-540-30684-9, India, December 2005, Springer-Verlag, Chennai

23

A Wireless Sensor Network for Field Hockey Performance Analysis

Shamala Subramaniam, Mohammed Ahmed Almoqry, Sangeetha Thavamani, Roger Canda, Mohamed Othman and Zuriati Zulkarnain
University Putra Malaysia
Malaysia

1. Introduction

The tracking of human movement has indeed become a central issue in acquiring optimized and strategy based solutions in various domains of applications. The utilization of technology in the enhancement of tracking players in a team sport is an evident applications which should utilize sensors. The game of field hockey is a sports requiring two main cohesive human movement. The first being individual and the second representing the group dynamics. Groups in the game of field hockey represents micro-human network formation and of the entire eleven players on the field. Among the pertinent sports technology utilized by field hockey teams is based on video visualization and the capturing of the player movement (Lu, 2007). In order to gain a clear understanding of the situation on the ground, it is becoming vital to observe from close range, using remote sensing devices placed in the area of interest. However, there are only a few movement tracking systems available today, and most of these systems are wired which tend to pose constraints in terms of movement (Wang, 2005). There are also a constrained number of wireless sensor available today to track human movements. Among the developed solutions is a wearable wireless sensor network to capture human movement (Wang, 2005). The system was tested on dance performance. In this research the advantages were for the development of the wearable sensor which permitted mobility through wireless. However, the research did not address the significance of coordinated interactions from a network sensor configuration and reconfiguration. The ability of applied WSN onto military applications are amplified by the possibility to provide intelligent cohesive network reconfiguration. In this research, the coordinated wireless sensor was not based on individual or pair human tracking system but is enhanced by the ability to focus on optimization based on multiple network configurations. Large networks of wireless sensors and actuators pose a number of problems that are not present in smaller networks of wired devices. Although current generation devices, such as the Mica motes, have limited processors (motes have an 8-bit, 7 MHz processor) and memory (motes have 4 KB of RAM and 512 KB of Flash), it is expected that in a few years these limitations will be much less severe. In distinguishing our research, test application encompassing human tracking in correlation to Game Analysis is proposed. The game constitutes of equipment control which is highly dependent on the human movement. This is distinctly different from those in deployment (Michael, 2005). The major findings were made in Real-time game analysis systems. The researcher developed the Football Interaction and Process Model (FIPM) and a software system that can acquire, interpret, and analyze this model. The FIPM system acquires models of player skills, infer action-selection criteria, and determine player and team strengths and weaknesses. However, the research has several evident limitations. Firstly, the research has confined correlation between the sensor networks to a specific problem domain involving mobility of nodes with a ratio of 1 device: n nodes. the utilization of equipment based nodes where a highly interdependency exist between : (i) equipment and node and (ii) node - to - node is clearly not addressed. Thus, requiring newly developed software which is able to provide a high distinction between the indicidual tracking to the real-time analysis of sensor data from human tracking with dependency of multiple sensory components (i.e. field hockey-sensor on player, stick and ball). The potential of hybrid systems encompassing communication technologies (i.e. WSN and adhoc) and human tracking remains immense. This research proposes the cohesive development of WSN field hockey strategy system and a Discrete Event Simulator. The focus is based on utilizing an Indoor Sensor System to correlate with the field hockey strategy board. The remainder of the Chapter is organized as follows. Section 2 reviews the existing physical magnetic board which provides static positioning. Section 3 discusses the Cricket Indoor Location system utilized to acquire the location of the mobile nodes. Section 4 discusses the developed Wireless Sensor based Field Hockey Strategy System. Section 5 deliberates the detail of the Grid formation both physically and in simulation. Section 6, discusses the results acquired from the experiments. Section 7 provides the conclusion and some pertinent discussion on the future research.

2. Magnetic board static positioning

The magnetic board for visualizing the multiple options of a strategy is generally used to illustrate the various strategies. The magnetic board for field hockey comprises of a magnetic board and several bi-colored magnets used to represent the players and the opponents. Figure 1 show the magnetic board being used for a discussion session with players. The movement explanation is of relation to certain set-pieces (i.e. pre-determined strategies). Figure 2 illustrates a practice drill which is conducted. The lines denote the expected movement of the players and the ball movement. The strategy board is also utilized in addition to video analysis such as the SportsCode (Sebastian et al, 2006) to capture and relate to the players the required movements. These pre-dominant software can be complemented for the purpose of strategy configuration and capitalizing group dynamics. Field hockey coaches utilize these magnetic boards during team video analysis sessions and even during half-time of matches. In view of the ability of the magnetic board to be enhanced to an intelligent board, the integration of sensor were used in our research. The magnetic strategy board allows single dimensional movement. In addition the board is unable to provide real-time computation on the deviation of the intended pre-determined movement as opposed to the multiple options which relate to a movement.

The objective of this research is to materialize a dynamic strategic board whereby movements of magnetic node will be able to provide the location of the opponent and the respective restricted or obstacle zones of the area. This paper contains the details of the location detection hardware (i.e. Cricket Indoor Location System) and the Virtual dynamic magnetic board. At present the integration of the system is being rapidly researched.

Fig. 1. Magnetic Board Utilized for Strategic Movement

Fig. 2. Pre-determined Set-Pieces conducted during training sessions.

3. Cricket indoor location system

The location detection system which was used for this project is the Crossbow Cricket Indoor Location System. The main motivation of utilizing the Cricket Indoor Location System is the scalabilty and the independence from pre-defined coordinate pre-requisite. Thus, the Mica2 sensors (i.e. Beacons) can be positioned on any field hockey Grid. The specifications of the system used is shown in Table 1.

Items and Descriptions
8 Cricket Mote Processors Radio Boards with Ultrasound (433 MHz)
1 MIB510CA Programming and Serial Interface Board

Table 1. Specifications of the Cricket Indoor Location System used in the research.

The project was able to be done using an Indoor location system as opposed to the Outdoor location system due to the fact that the developed system is intended to be strategy software for the team management to utilize either prior or during training. The sensors are attached as representation of the magnetic nodes and the area defined in the application varies in the terms of the set-piece intended. The beacons were attached to mobile stands to enable flexibility of movements. Figure 3 shows the attached sensors (i.e. beacons) on the experiment set-up.

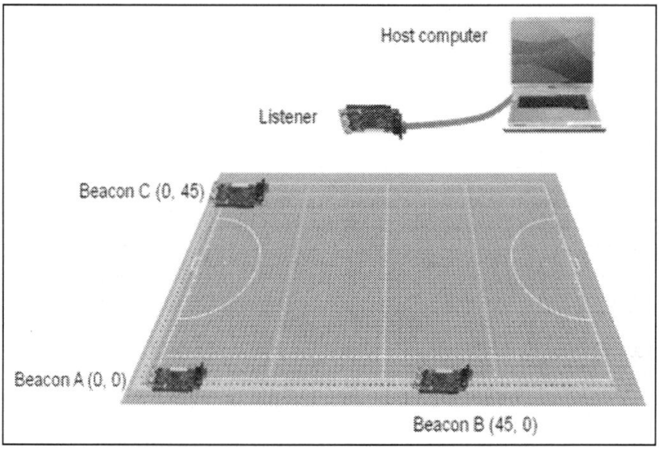

Fig. 3. Wireless Sensors (Beacons) attached Field Hockey Grid.

4. Wireless sensor based field Hockey strategy system (WiHoc Ver 1.0)

Concurrently to the deployment of the Cricket Indoor location system, the development of the application for the simulation of the field hockey was developed. The application is intended to visualize the movements and intended team coordination. The system enables the user to input the data movement using the simulation. In response the data movement is produced for the coach to analyze. The simulator enables the coach to input basic benchmarks, which subsequently is displayed on the screen.

5. Grid and DES development

The WiHoc Ver.1.0 was developed using the Cricket/Mica2 mote (Shamala et al, 2008). An important feature of the Cricket system is the ability to be independent of any pre-defined coordinate systems. Thus, advocating the importance of the beacon positions with the stipulated area of research. In this research, a Grid was formulated specifically for the field

hockey pitch specification. The formulation of the Grid must precede the subsequent algorithms due to the localization requirements. The magnetic board for visualizing the multiple options of a strategy is used to illustrate the various strategies and set-piece movements. The magnetic board for field hockey comprises of a magnetic board and several bi-colored magnets used to represent the players and the opponents.
Figure 5, illustrates the attributes and respective measurement metrics of a field hockey pitch. The measurements represent the actual physical measurements of the field of play scaled on a per meter to centimeter.

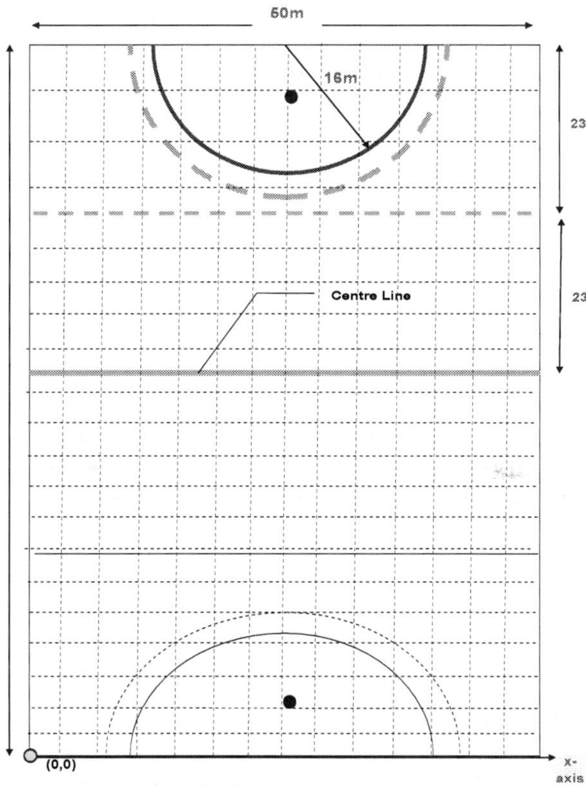

Fig. 5. Grid (x,y) formulation for field hockey

In this project, the magnetic components have been replaced with Mica2 sensors. Thus, enabling real-time data to be computed as opposed to passive and static visualization of the conventional strategy board. Each point represents an x and y coordinate respectively. The Mica2 beacon position were placed at the coordinates of (0,0), (45,0) and (0,45). The listener adopts mobility based on the user's discretion. For the purpose of performance analysis of the developed system, a Zig-Zag mobility movement was utilized on the physical Grid.
The WiHoc mobility benchmark utilized is shown in Figure 6. The listener is connected to the main software to compute the distances generated by the beacons Radio Frequency (RF)

and Ultrasound (US) data collection. The computed coordinates are subsequently visualized by the software. In the WiHoc Ver. 1.0, the data is computed and further analyzed utilizing a spreadsheet software. The main analysis was the mapping of the field hockey strategy board to the Cricket/Mica2 system catering it's respective perquisites.

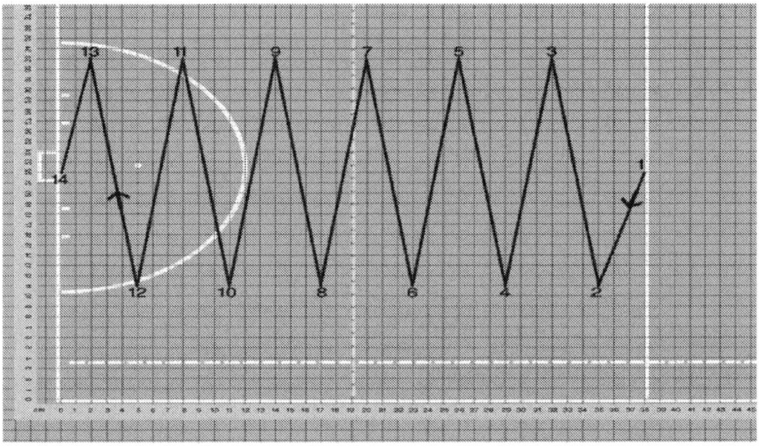

Fig. 6. WiHoc Ver.1.0 Model Development - Mobility Benchmark

Parallel to the deployment of the WiHoc Ver.1.0 testbed, a complementary performance analysis tool using simulation as the underlying platform was developed. The Discrete Event Simulator (DES) developed the following:

i. Event Definition - each event was derived based on the occurrences which causes statistical changes to the system. Four main events have been identified for this project as follows:
   a. Beacon Transmit RF
      Event to generate RF for the beacon
   b. Beacon Transmit US
      Event to generate US for the beacon
   c. Listener Receive RF
      Event to process receiving of RF by the listener
   d. Listener Receive US
      Event to process receiving of US by the listener
ii. Scheduler - the scheduling of the events. The main controller of the simulation is the scheduler and no direct control of the function deployment by the user
iii. The computation of the location utilizing the Geometrical formulation
iv. The performance measurement utilizing accuracy metrics and generation of graphs

The developed DES was derived based on the model in Figure 6. The simulation was developed using Microsoft Visual C++. The performance analysis used three beacons and one listener. The computation of the location was achieved using the signals transmitted by each beacon. Each beacon transmits a RF and an US signal simultaneously. RF carries location data, while US is a narrow pulse. The listener measures the time gap between the receipt of the RF and US signals. A time gap of x ms corresponds to a distance of x distance

from beacon. The simulation used fixed location coordinates of beacons and US rate at 344 ms and RF at 3x 10^8 ms. The computational requirements are deliberated in Table 2.
The Cricket units were set up in a grid coordinate, with beacons 1-3 at positions (0,0), (45, 0), (0, 45). An algorithm was deployed and tested for precision and accuracy. This algorithm solves the equations of 3 distances values received by the listener from 3 beacons. The distance between current position and target were derived using the following Equation (1) which was adopted from (Nissanka, 2005). The performance metrics used to validate the developed simulator and the ability to simulate the WiHoc Ver.1.0 is distance. Each beacon is directly involved in estimating the listener position. The information consists of space id, preset coordination (x,y) of the respective beacon.

$$\text{Distance} = \text{velocity} \times \text{time} \quad (1)$$

Where velocity is the speed of the sound and time is the difference between the time of arrival for the RF and US signals with the following adopted:

a. Y-axis – the y coordinates of the listener in the cricket field grid. The cricket field grid is 100m x 50m. The y value ranges from 0 to 50 m.
b. X-axis – the x coordinates of the listener in the cricket field grid. The cricket field grid is 100m x 50m. The x value ranges from 0 to 92 m.

Hardware	Specification
Processor	Intel Core(TM)2 Duo T300@2.00GHz
Memory	1 GB
Hard Disk	160 GB HDD with 40 GB for Linux partition
Display	Intel Graphic Media Accelerator 900
Monitor	14.1" WXGA Crystal Bright LCD
Operating System	Microsoft Office XP
Programming Language	Visual C++ version 6

Table 2. Computation Requirements of the developed DES

The DES functional operations encompasses of :

a. Initialization - function to provide starting values for control parameters, performance metrics and simulation paraemeters
b. Scheduler - the events are activated based on chronological activation for each of the events
c. The simulation was repeated for 42 cycles to acquire the coordinates
d. Generation of results via performance metrics of distance and coordinate generation

Extensive experiments were conducted to validate the developed simulator and it's ability to replicate the WiHoc Ver.1.0 system.

6. Results and discussions

A scenario of Zigzag movement was utilized to represent the listener's movements in the test-bed. The movement correlates to the gradual movement of two players moving a ball towards the goal scoring area. The reading from the Cricket 2.0 software for 14 positions while moving was captured. Table 3 displays the utilized movement of the listener, the first column (x, y) value is the initial coordinate of the listener and the subsequent movements. These reading were recorded on the actual physical strategy board.

Movement ID	Listener position	Movement ID	Listener position
1	(38.00, 22.00)	8	(17.00, 11.00)
2	(35.00, 11.00)	9	(14.00, 33.00)
3	(32.00, 33.00)	10	(11.00, 11.00)
4	(29.00, 11.00)	11	(8.00, 33.00)
5	(26.00, 33.00)	12	(5.00, 11.00)
6	(23.00, 11.00)	13	(2.00, 33.00)
7	(20.00, 33.00)	14	(0.00, 22.00)

Table 3. Listener Movement

The results obtained from the Cricket System are shown in Figure 7. The analysis of the results displays deviations between the physical readings and the Cricket software. This is due to the interference and the accuracy of the RF and US data collection. In order to validate the acquired results, the deviation and it's respective impact of the field hockey strategy was analyzed. The maximum x-axis deviation was 0.86 while the minimum was 0.18. For the y-axis deviation, the maximum was 2.62 and the minimum was 0.2. Mapping these deviations to the physical Grid, enabled a distinct observation on the results. The acquired results were indeed acceptable for the purpose of game analysis as the locations on the grid scaled to per unit factor of the physical location have a neglible effect and is displayed in Table 4.

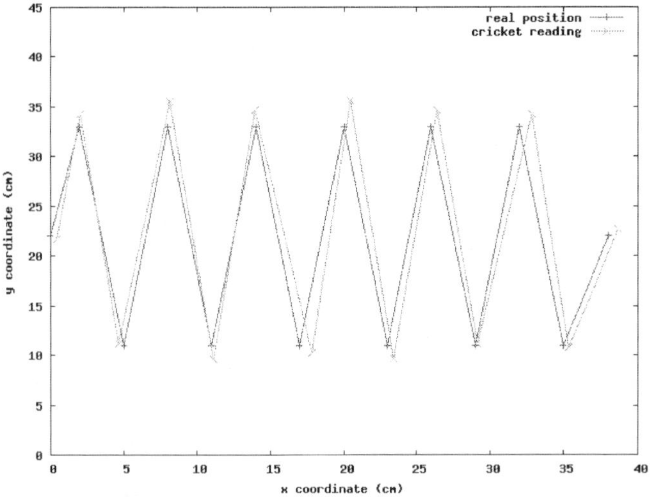

Fig. 7. True positioning error, comparing distance measured to distance expected

# of motion	Actual position	WiHoc Correlation	# of motion	Actual position	WiHoc Correlation
1	(38.00, 22.00)	(38.65, 22.69)	8	(17.00, 11.00)	(17.86, 10.26)
2	(35.00, 11.00)	(35.36, 10.80)	9	(14.00, 33.00)	(13.98, 34.63)
3	(32.00, 33.00)	(32.84, 34.29)	10	(11.00, 11.00)	(11.09, 9.58)
4	(29.00, 11.00)	(29.18, 11.17)	11	(8.00, 33.00)	(8.13, 35.53)
5	(26.00, 33.00)	(26.41, 34.67)	12	(5.00, 11.00)	(4.64, 11.13)
6	(23.00, 11.00)	(23.46, 9.74)	13	(2.00, 33.00)	(2.03, 34.22)
7	(20.00, 33.00)	(20.48, 35.62)	14	(0.00, 22.00)	(0.46, 21.71)

Table 4. Test-bed results, listener position reading from Cricket software

To validate the developed DES, the results in Figure 8 were generated and analyzed. The results validate the developed Simulator and it's respective ability to serve as a performance analysis tool complementary to the real physical experiemental testbed. The deviations acquired were between 5-8% difference. Many factors attributed towards the neglible difference including room temperature.

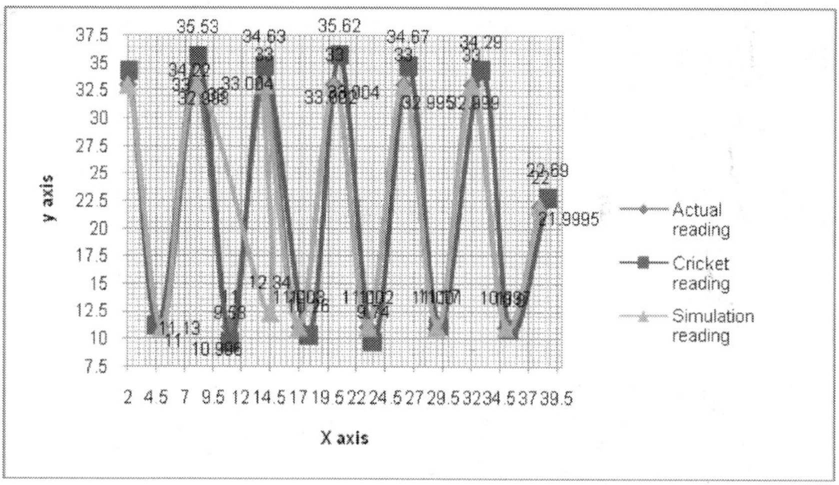

Fig. 8. True positioning error, comparing distance measured to distance expected of the developed DES

7. Conclusions and future work

This project has enabled the wireless sensor indoor location system to embark into an enhanced platform of sports in general and field hockey in particular. The Cricket Indoor Location System developed by Crossbow and MIT has the ability to detect the movement of players but at a scale most applicable to a strategy board. This project is in the process of rapid development to integrate the location detected by the sensors with an application enabling a layman to utilize it to its highest potential. The project is in the process of incorporating an application which translates the Cricket location coordinates into an application and integrating obstacle zonal computation intended to provide a wide spectrum of strategies for the use of the team management. In addition, this research has developed a Grid enhancement to the Wireless Hockey Strategy System to acquire the computation ability for Game Analysis. The derived coordinates, will enable the team personnel of field hockey to analyze the multitudes of analysis from even a singular movement. However, in the testbed further analysis such as localization algorithms and power consumptions are literally impossible to be done. Thus, a discrete event simulator was developed specifically to replicate the WiHoc Ver.1.0. The simulator was able to utilize the distance factor of the Cricket /Mica2 motes acquired from the physics formula of distance being equivalent to velocity multiplied by time. The simulator has indeed enabled a wide spectrum of experiments and analysis to enhance the performance of the development WiHoc Ver.1.0. The research is ongoing to produce WiHoc Ver.2.0 with a GUI based software to integrate Artificial Intelligence and expand the developed DES for a various mobility models and modules for power consumption.

8. Acknowledgment

This project is funded by the ScienceFund of the Ministry of Science, Technology and Innovation of Malaysia under the grant number 01-01-04-SF0224 and by University Putra Malaysia.

9. References

Lu. W.L. (2007). Tracking and Recognizing Actions of Multiple Hockey Players using the Boosted Particle Filter, *Master's Thesis*, The University of British Columbia.

Wang. Y. (2005). Human Movement tracking using a wearable sensor network, *Thesis*. IOWA State University.

Shamala.S, Soon.L, Tareq, R, Canda. R, Maher,A and Yahya.A. (2008). Wireless Sensor Based Field Hockey Strategy System, *In Proc. International Conference on Convergence and Hybrid Information Technology* (ICCIT'08), Busan, Korea.

Nissanka B.P. (2005). The Cricket Indoor Location System, *PhD Thesis*. Massachusetts Institute of Technology.

Michael B., Bernhard K. and Martin L. (2005). Computerized Real-Time Analysis of Football Games, *IEEE Pervasive Computing*, vol. 4, no. 3, pp. 33-39, July-Sept. 2005, doi:10.1109/MPRV.2005.53

24

Application of Game Theory to Wireless Networks

S. Mehta and K. S. Kwak
Inha University
Korea

1. Introduction

The modern information society will continue to emerge, and demand for wireless communication services will grow. Future generation wireless networks are considered necessary for the support of emerging services with their increasing requirements. Future generation wireless networks are characterized by a distributed, dynamic, self-organizing architecture (I. F. Akyildiz et al., 2006). These wireless networks are broadly categorized into different wireless networks according to their specific characteristics. Typical examples include Ad-Hoc/Mesh Networks, Sensor Networks, Cognitive Radio Networks, etc as shown in figure 1. These wireless networks could then constitute the infrastructure of numerous applications such as emergency and health-care systems, military, gaming, advertisements, customer-to-customer applications, etc. Not only their importance in military applications is growing, but also their impact on business is increasing. The emergence of these wireless networks created many open issues in network design too. More and more researchers are putting their efforts in designing the future generation wireless networks.

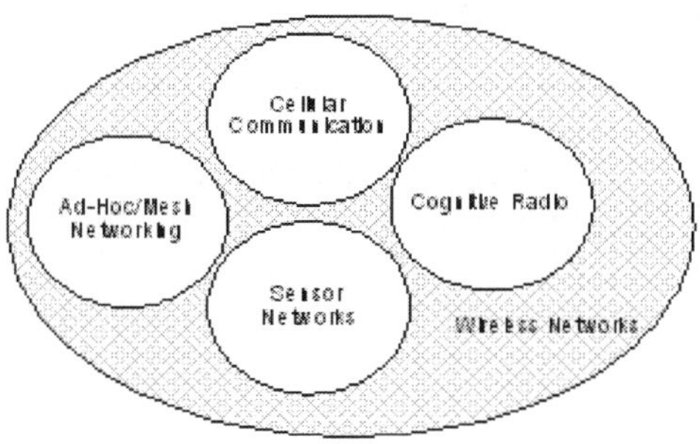

Fig. 1. Different kinds of wireless networks

Every node in the future wireless network is capable of changing its operation independently or in a small group of nodes according to the current dynamics of the network as all the nodes are distributed and self-organizing in nature. So every node in the network has conflicting situation with other nodes, and hence it is very hard to analytically model such network and to evaluate its performance.

2. Game Theory

Game Theory is a collection of mathematical tools to study the interactive decision problems between the rational players[1] (here it is wireless nodes). Furthermore it also helps to predict the possible outcome of the interactive decision problem. The most possible outcome for any decision process is "Nash Equilibrium." A Nash equilibrium is an out come of a game where no node (player) has any extra benefit for just changing its strategy one-sidedly. From the last three decades game theory has not just applied to economics but has also found application in sociology and psychology, political science, evolution and biology. Additionally, it has drawn lots of attention from computer scientist in recent because of its use in artificial intelligence, cybernetics, and networks. Specifically, Game theory allows us to model scenarios in which there is no centralized entity with full/partial information network conditions. Because of that from last few years game theory has gained a notable amount of popularity in solving communication and networking issues. These issues include congestion control, routing, power control and other issues in wired and wireless communications systems, to name a few. Figure 2 shows the applications of game theory, especially in computer science while figure 3 shows few key research areas in wireless networking (M. Felegyhazi et al., 2006).

As we mentioned earlier game theory is a branch of applied mathematics which helps players to analyze decision making in conflict situations. Such situations arise when two or more players, who have different aims act on the system or share the same resources. A game could be two player or multi-player. In a given game, game theory provides mathematical process for selecting an optimum response to player to face his/her opponent who also has a strategy of his/her own.

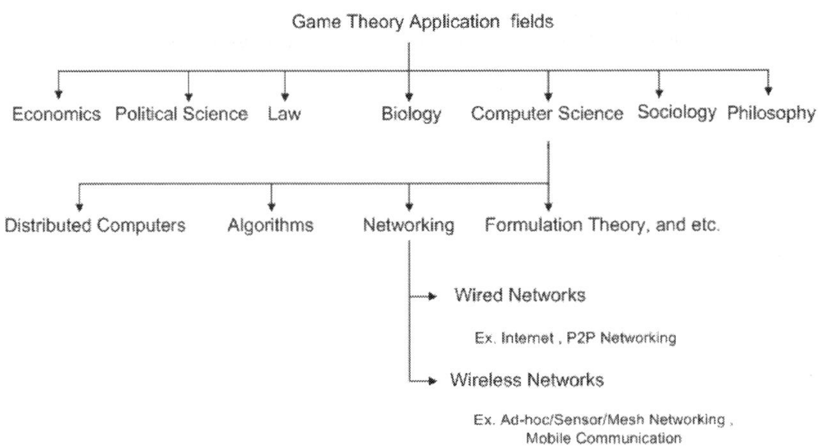

Fig. 2. Applications of game theory

[1] In rest of the paper we keep using terms 'node' and 'player' interchangeably.

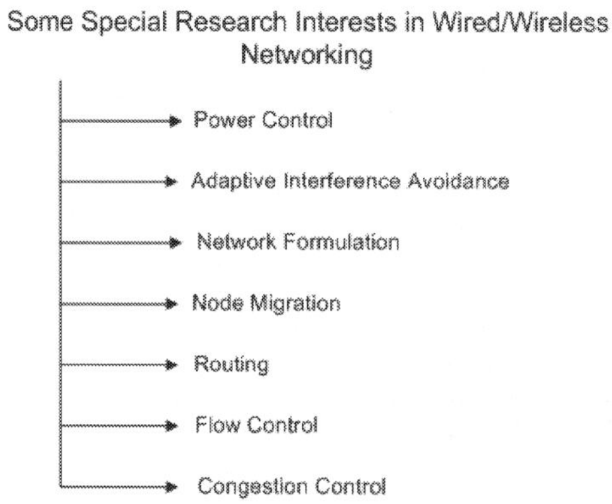

Fig. 3. Few key research areas in networking

2.1 Game theory: assumptions, challenges, advantages, and classification

In game theory (generally non-cooperative game theory) players usually make the following assumptions

- Each player has two or more well-specified moves/strategies.
- Every player has possible combinations of moves/strategy that leads to an optimum response (End-state like win, loss or draw) in a given game.
- Each player has a specified payoff for each optimum response.
- All players are rational; that is, each player, given the two moves/strategies, will choose that one that gives him/her the better payoff.

The use of game theory to analyze the performance of wireless networks is not without its challenges. We point out few challenges as follows:

- Assumption of rationality
- Realistic scenarios require complex model
- Choice of utility functions
- Mechanism design
- Mapping variables in the game

We will learn more about these challenges in subsequent sections of this chapter. Even with these challenges we have certain advantages in using game theory for analyzing wireless networks

- **Analysis tool for distributed systems:** As we mentioned earlier game theory is a natural choice to study the distributed systems as both deal with independent decision makers. With game theory we can investigate the steady state of such systems and also make the out come of an individual node both in the interest of the system and its own.
- **Cross layer designing and optimization:** In wireless networking, a node often needs to take its action based on some other layers to optimize its own performance but this could hurt the performances of that particular layers. In this situation game theoretic approach can provide a proper insight as well as mathematical back ground to optimize the overall protocol stack's performance.
- **Incentive Scheme:** As we mentioned above the selfishness of nodes is the biggest threat to the performance of the network and it's necessary to remove or discourage the selfish

behavior of nodes. Game theory tools such as mechanism design can assists the network designer to develop some networks rules that can discourage the nodes form selfish behavior and in some case provide some incentives for actively participation in network. Hence, we can get the desired outcome of the nodes from a network point of view.

Games can be classified formally at many level of detail, here; we in-general tried to classify the games for better understanding. As shown in the figure 4 games are broadly classified as co-operative and non-cooperative games. In non-cooperative games the player can not make commitments to coordinate their strategies. A non-cooperative game investigates answer for selecting an optimum strategy to player to face his/her opponent who also has a strategy of his/her own. Co-operative game can, and often does, arise in non-cooperative games, when players find it in their own best interests.

Conversely, a co-operative game is a game where groups of player may enforce to work together to maximize their returns (payoffs).Hence, a co-operative game is a competition between coalitions of players, rather than between individual players. There are lots of fundamental things need to be discussed about co-operative games which are simply out of the scope of this chapter. Furthermore, according to the players' moves, simultaneously or one by one, games can be further divided into two categories: static and dynamic games. In static game, players move their strategy simultaneously without any knowledge of what other players are going to play. In the dynamic game, players move their strategy in predetermined order and they also know what other players have played before them. So according to the knowledge of players on all aspects of game, the non-cooperative/co-operative game further classified into two categories: complete and incomplete information games. In the complete information game, each player has all the knowledge about others' characteristics, strategy spaces, payoff functions, etc., but all these information are not necessarily available in incomplete information game (M. Felegyhazi et al., 2006, M.J. Osborne & A Rubinstein , 1994, V. Srivastava et. al , 2005).

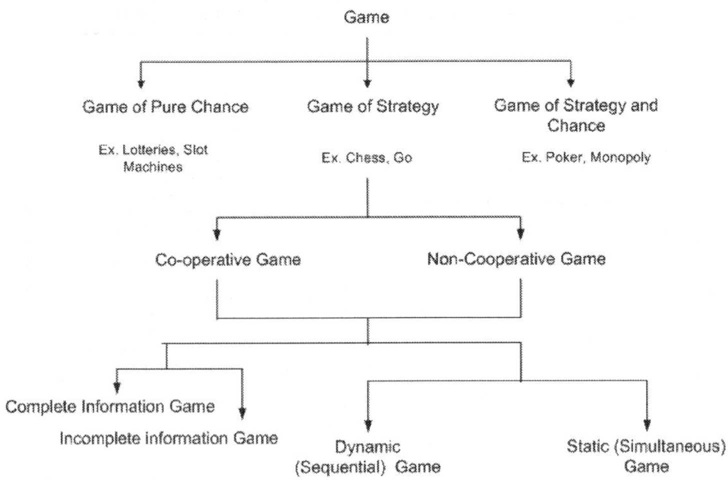

Fig. 4. Classification of games

A game is set of there fundamental components: A set of players, a set of actions, and a set of preferences. Players or nodes are the decision takers in the game. The actions (strategies) are the different choices available to nodes. In a wireless system, action may include the available options like coding scheme, power control, transmitting, listening, etc., factors that are under the control of the node. When each player selects its own strategy, the resulting strategy profile decides the outcome of the game. Finally, a utility function (preferences) decides the all possible outcomes for each player. Table 1 shows typical componets of a wireless networking game.

Components of a game	Elements of a wireless network
Players	Nodes in the wireless network
A set of actions	A modulation scheme, Coding rate, transmit power level, etc.
A set of preferences	Performance metrics (e.g. Throughput, Delay, SNR, etc.)

Table 1. Components of a wireless networking game

It is important to note that game theory models are only appropriate for the scenarios where decision of a node could impact the outcome of other nodes. Hence, a clear distinction should be drawn between a multiple decision making problem and an optimization problem where a single decision making entity is involved. Furthermore, appropriate modelling of preferences is one of the most challenging aspects of the application of game theory, so optimizing network's performance with game theory needs careful considerations (V. Srivastava et. al, 2005).

2.2 Game theory: networks games

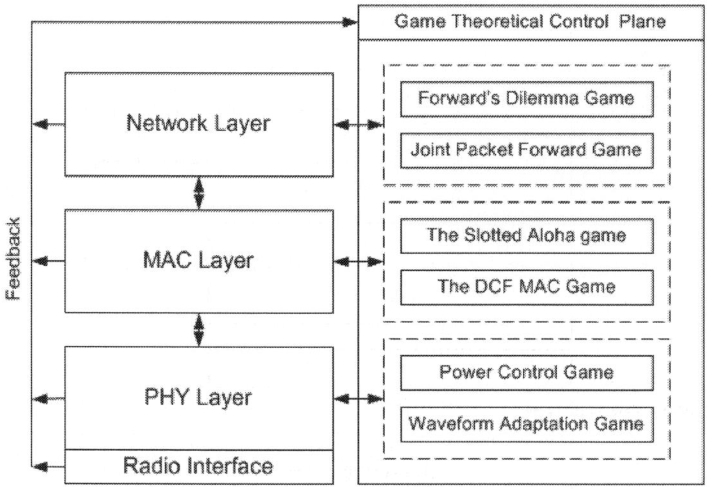

Fig. 5. Networks games at different levels of protocol stack

As shown in the figure 5 game theory can be applied to the modeling of a wireless network at the physical layer, link layer, and network layer. Applications at the transport layer and above exist also, but we restrict our discussion up to network layer. At all the mentioned levels we can formulate a game to optimize the performance of a network. The main objective of these games is to remove the selfish behavior of the nodes. Generally, selfish behavior is very serious problem for overall network performance. For example a node always refuse to forward data packets from other node can create unnecessary partition in the network, and hence limit the connectivity of the network.Here, we briefly describe a few games at different levels of protocol stack (M. Felegyhazi et al., 2006).

Physical Layer Games:

- **Power Control and waveform Adaptation games:** These games are representing very basic problems of improving performance at physical layer. At physical layer performance is generally measure in terms of signal to interference plus noise ratio at the nodes. When the nodes in a network respond to changes in perceived SINR by adapting their signal, a physical layer interactive decision making process occurs. This signal adaptation can occur in the transmit power level and the signaling waveform In power control game signals of other terminals can be modeled as interfering noise signals, the major goal of this game is to achieve a certain signal to interference (SIR) ratio regardless of the channel conditions while minimizing the interference due to terminal transmit power level. Waveform adaptation in wireless networks involves the selection of a waveform by a node such that the interference at its receiver is reduced. The interference at the receiver is a function of the correlation of a user's waveform with the waveforms of the other users in the network. Also, in general, the individual nodes involved in transmission have no or very little information about the receiver's interference environment. Hence to minimize the adaptation overhead, distributed waveform adaptation algorithms that require a minimal amount of feedback between receivers and transmitters need to be developed for these networks.

MAC Layer games:

- **Medium Access Games-The slotted aloha and DCF Games:** In these medium access control games, selfish users seek to maximize their utility by obtaining an unfair share of access to the channel. This action, though, decreases the ability of other users to access the channel. In slotted Aloha game, in a given slot, each user has two possible actions: the user can transmit or wait. If exactly one user chooses to transmit in a given slot, then that user's transmission is successful. If multiple users transmit in a slot, then all of their transmissions are unsuccessful. We assume that the payoff associated with a successful transmission is 1, while the cost of transmission (whether successful or unsuccessful) is c, where $0 < c < 1$. A user who waits will receive a payoff of 0; a user who transmits will receive a payoff of either $1 - c$ (if the transmission is successful) or $-c$ (if the transmission is unsuccessful).In this game main aim is to maximize the payoff (in terms of less cost) with fair access to the Medium. Similar to slotted aloha game, when a node has data to transmit, it autonomously decides when to transmit in IEEE 802.11 DCF based networks. Because the wireless channel is a shared channel, the transmission of a node often interferes with those of other nodes. For example, if there are two neighboring nodes transmitting their data frames simultaneously, both transmissions will fail. Therefore, one node must compete with its neighboring nodes so that it can transmit as many packets as possible. Authors in (M. Felegyhazi et al., 2006) model the IEEE 802.11 DCF with game theory and name the model the DCF game. In the DCF game, each player (node) has two strategies: Transmit or Not transmit (i.e., wait) and here again aim is the same as slotted aloha game.

Network Layers Games:

The main functionalities of network layer are establishing and updating routes and forwarding the packets along those routes. The presence of selfish nodes in those routes can degrade the overall network performance as well as the life time.

- **Forward's dilemma and Joint packet forward games:** In forwards dilemma game, as shown in figure 6 (a) the p1 intends to send a packet to node r1 through p2, while player p2 intends to send a packet to r2 through p1. The cost of transmitting a packet equals c, where c << 1 and reflects the energy spent by a node in forwarding a packet. If a packet is successfully received by the receiver then the sender gets a reward of 1. Each player has two possible actions: forward the packet (F) or drop the packet (D) of the other player. Similar to this game , in the joint packet forwarding game as shown in figure 6 (b) nodes intend to send a packet to node r through two intermediate nodes p1 and p2. If the packet successfully reaches r then each of the forwarding nodes gets a reward of one, otherwise none of the intermediate nodes gets any reward. The cost of forwarding a packet is c and has the same meaning as that in the forward's dilemma game. The players may take two actions: forward the packet (F) or drop the packet (D). The aim of both these game is to maintain the routing path as long as possible and hence a network connectivity (M. Felegyhazi et al., 20062).

p1 \ p2	F	D
F	(1-c, 1-c)	(-c,1)
D	(1, -c)	(0, 0)

Fig. 6. (a) Forward's Dilemma problem and its game form presentation

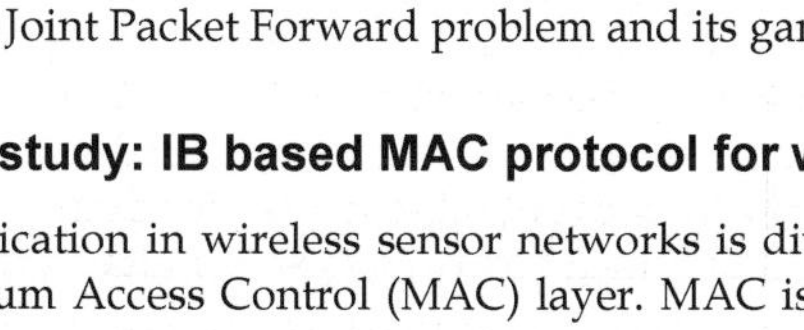

p1 \ p2	F	D
F	(1-c, 1-c)	(-c,0)
D	(0, 0)	(0, 0)

Fig. 6. (b) Joint Packet Forward problem and its game form presentation

3. Case study: IB based MAC protocol for wireless sensor networks

Communication in wireless sensor networks is divided into several layers. One of those is the Medium Access Control (MAC) layer. MAC is an important technique that enables the successful operation of the network. MAC protocol tries to avoid collisions so that two interfering nodes do not transmit at the same time. The main design goal of a typical MAC protocols is to provide high throughput and QoS. However, a good amount of energy gets wasted in traditional MAC layer protocols due to idle listening, collision, protocol overhead, and over-hearing (W. Ye et al , 2002).

There are some MAC protocols that have been especially developed for wireless sensor networks. Typical examples include S-MAC, T-MAC, and H-MAC (W. Ye et al , 2002, T.V. Dam et. al , 2003, S.Mehta et al, 2007). To maximize the battery lifetime, sensor networks MAC protocols implement the variation of active/sleep mechanism. S-MAC and T-MAC protocols trades networks QoS for energy savings, while H-MAC protocol reduces the comparable amount of energy consumption along with maintaining good network QoS. However, their backoff algorithm is similar to that of the IEEE 802.11 Distributed Coordinated Function (DCF), which is based on Carrier Sense Multiple Access with Collision Avoidance (CSMA/CA) Mechanism. The energy consumption using CSMA/CA is high when nodes are in backoff procedure and in idle mode. Moreover, a node that successfully transmits resets it Contention Window (CW) to a small, fixed minimum value of CW. Therefore, the node has to rediscover the correct CW, wasting channel capacity and increase the access delay as well. It is necessary to estimate the number of nodes in network to optimize the CSMA/CA operation.

In nutshell, during the CSMA/CA mechanism, backoff window size and the number of active nodes are the major factors to have impact on the energy-efficiency as well as the QoS performance of WSNs. As presented in (L. Zhao et. al, 2008) the concept of incomplete cooperative game theory that can improve energy efficiency as well as the QoS performance of MAC protocol in WSNs. Based on game theoretic model presented in (L. Zhao et. al, 2008) we use a fixed-size contention window, but a non-uniform, geometrically-increasing probability distribution for picking a transmission slot in the contention window interval to improve the energy efficiency of MAC protocol.

3.1 Incomplete cooperative game

As we mentioned earlier energy efficiency of MAC protocol in WSN is very sensitive to number of nodes competing for the access channel. It will be very difficult for a MAC protocol to accurately estimate the different parameters like collision probability, transmission probability, etc., by detecting channel. Because dynamics of WSN keep on changing due to various reasons like mobility of nodes, joining of some new nodes, and dying out of some exhausted nodes. Also, estimating about the other neighboring nodes information is too complex, as every node takes a distributed approach to estimate the current state of networks. For all these reasons an incomplete cooperative game could be a perfect candidate to optimize the performance of MAC protocol in sensor networks.

In this case study, we considered a MAC protocol with active/sleep duty cycle[2] to minimize the energy consumption of a node. In this MAC protocol time is divided into super-frames, and every super frame into two basic parts: active part and sleep part. During the active part a node tries to contend the channel if there is any data in buffer and turn down its radio during the sleeping part to save energy.

[2] We can easily relate the "Considered MAC Protocol" with available MAC protocols and standards for wireless sensor networks, as most of the popular MAC protocols are based on the active/sleep cycle mechanism.

In incomplete cooperative game, the considered MAC protocol can be modeled as stochastic game, which starts when there is a data packet in the node's transmission buffer and ends when the data packet is transmitted successfully or discarded. This game consists of many time slots and each time slot represents a game slot. As every node can try to transmit an unsuccessful data packet for some predetermined limit (Maximum retry limit), the game is finitely repeated rather than an infinitely repeated one. In each time slot, when the node is in active part, the node just not only tries to contend for the medium but also estimates the current game state based on history. After estimating the game state, the node adjusts its own equilibrium condition by adjusting its available parameters under the given strategies (here it is contention parameters like transmitting probability, collision probability, etc.). Then all the nodes act simultaneously with their best evaluated strategies. In this game we considered mainly three strategies available to nodes: Transmitting, Listening, and Sleeping. And contention window size as the parameter to adjust its equilibrium strategy.
In this stochastic game our main goal is to find an optimal equilibrium to maximize the network performance with minimum energy consumption. In general, with control theory we could achieve the best performance for an individual node rather than a whole network, and for this reason our game theoretic approach to the problem is justified.
Based on the game model presented in (L. Zhao et. al, 2008), the utility function of the node (node i) is represented by $\mu_i = \mu_i(s_i, \overline{s}_i)$ and the utility function of its opponents as $\overline{\mu}_i = \overline{\mu}_i(\overline{s}_i, s_i)$. Here, $s_i = (s_1, s_2, \ldots, s_{i-1}, \ldots, s_n)$ represents the strategy profile of a node and $\overline{s}_i$ of its opponent nodes, respectively. From the aforementioned discussion we can represent the above game as in table 2.

		Player 2 (all other n nodes)		
		Transmitting	Listening	Sleeping
Player 1 (Node i)	Transmitting	$(P_f, \overline{P}_f)$	$(P_s, \overline{P}_i)$	$(P_f, \overline{P}_w)$
	Listening	$(P_i, \overline{P}_s)$	$(P_i, \overline{P}_i)$	$(P_i, \overline{P}_w)$
	Sleeping	$(P_w, \overline{P}_f)$	$(P_w, \overline{P}_i)$	$(P_w, \overline{P}_w)$

Table 2. Strategy table

As presented in (L. Zhao et. al, 2008), we define P_i and $\overline{P}_i$ as the payoff for player 1 and 2 when they are listening, P_s and $\overline{P}_s$ when they are transmitting a data packet successfully, P_f and $\overline{P}_f$ when they are failed to transmit successfully, and P_w and $\overline{P}_w$ when they are in sleep mode, respectively. Whatever will be the payoff values, their self evident relationship is given by

$$P_f < P_i < P_w < P_S \qquad (1)$$

and similar relationship goes for player 2. As per our goal we are looking for the strategy that can lead us to an optimum equilibrium of the network. As in (L. Zhao et. al, 2008) we can define it formally as

$$\begin{cases} s_i^* = \arg\max\limits_{s_i} \overline{\mu}_i(\overline{s}_i, s_i) \mid (e_i < e_i^*) \\ \overline{s}_i^* = \arg\max\limits_{\overline{s}_i} \mu_i(s_i, \overline{s}_i) \mid (\overline{e}_i < \overline{e}_i^*) \end{cases} \qquad (2)$$

where $e_i, e_i^*, \overline{e}_i$ and $\overline{e}_i^*$ are the real energy consumption and energy limit of the player 1 and 2, respectively. Now to realize these conditions in practical approach we redefine them as follows

$$\begin{cases} s_i^* = \underset{(w_i,\tau_i)}{\arg\max} \begin{matrix} [(1-\overline{\tau}_i)(1-\overline{p}_i)(1-\overline{w}_i)(1-w_i)\tau_i\overline{P}_s + (1-\overline{\tau}_i)(1-\overline{w}_i)(1-w_i)\tau_i\overline{P}_i \\ +(1-\overline{p}_i)(1-\overline{w}_i)(1-w_i)\tau_i\overline{\tau}_i\overline{P}_f + \overline{\tau}_i\overline{p}_i(1-w_i)\overline{P}_f + w_i(1-\overline{w}_i)\overline{P}_w] \mid (e_i < e_i^*) \end{matrix} \\ \overline{s}_i^* = \underset{(w_i,\tau_i)}{\arg\max} \begin{matrix} [(1-\overline{\tau}_i)(1-\overline{w}_i)(1-w_i)\tau_i P_s + (1-\tau_i)(1-\overline{w}_i)(1-w_i)P_i \\ +\tau_i\overline{\tau}_i P_f + \overline{w}_i(1-w_i)P_w] \mid (\overline{e}_i < \overline{e}_i^*) \end{matrix} \end{cases} \quad (3)$$

Here, we define τ_i and $\overline{\tau}_i$ as the transmission probability of the player 1 and player 2, respectively. Similarly, w_i and $\overline{w}_i$ represents the sleeping probability of player 1 and player 2 while $\overline{p}_i$ is the conditional collision probability of player 2. Here we could not go into many details about these equations due to space limitation, so readers are referred to (S.Mehta et al., 2009) for more details on the same.

From the strategy table and equation (3) we can see that every node has to play its strategies with some probabilities as here the optimum equilibrium is in mixed strategy form. In addition, we can observe from the above equations that players can achieve their optimal response by helping each other to achieve their optimal utility. So the nodes have to play a cooperative game under the given constrained of energy.

As we mentioned earlier every node change its strategies by adjusting contention window size (i.e. properly estimating the number of competing nodes). There are some methods, especially (G. Bianchi et al., 2003, T. Vercauteren et al, 2007), to name a few, to accurately predict the number of competing nodes in the networks , however they are too complex and heavy to implement in wireless sensor networks. Also, we cannot expect to find an algorithm that can give the theoretical optimum solution, as the above mentioned problem has been proven to be NP-hard (M. S. Garey et al., 1979). So in this case study we present a sub optimal and a simple solution to achieve the optimum performance of a network.

3.2 Improved backoff

In this section we briefly introduce the improved backoff (IB), for more details on the same readers are refereed to (S.Mehta et al., 2009). This is very simple scheme to integrate with any energy efficient MAC protocols for WSNs. This method doesn't require any complex or hard method to estimate the number of nodes. Furthermore, IB can easily accommodate the changing dynamics of WSNs.

IB Mechanism:

In contrast to traditional backoff scheme, IB scheme uses a small and fixed CW. In IB scheme, nodes choose non-uniform geometrically increasing probability distribution (P) for picking a transmission slot in the contention window. Nodes which are executing IB scheme pick a slot in the range of (1, CW) with the probability distribution P. Here, CW is contention window and its value is fixed. More information on CW we will be presented in the later sections of this paper. Figure 8 shows the probability distribution P. The higher slot numbers have higher probability to get selected by nodes compared to lower slot numbers. In physical meaning we can explain this as: at the start node select a higher slot number for its CW by estimating large population of active nodes (n) and keep sensing the channel status. If no nodes transmits in the first or starting slots then each node adjust its estimation of competing nodes by multiplicatively increasing its transmission probability for the next slot selection cycle. Every node keeps repeating the process of estimation of active nodes in every slot selection cycle and allows the competition to happen at geometrically-decreasing values of n all within the fixed contention window (CW). In contrast to the probability distribution P, in uniform distribution, as shown in fig. 8 , all the contending nodes have the same probability of transmitting in a randomly chosen time slot. Here, it is worth to note that IB scheme doesn't use timer suspension like in IEEE 802.11 to save energy and reduce latency in case of a collision. The only problem with the IB is fairness, however, for WSNs, fairness is not a problem due to two main reasons. First, overall network performance is more important rather than an individual node. Second, all nodes don't have data to send all the time (i.e. unsaturated traffic condition). Using IB may give us the optimum network performance as it reduces the collision to minimum.

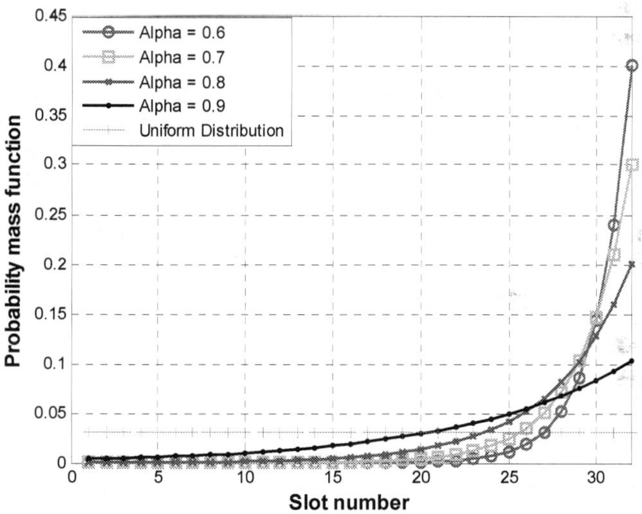

Fig. 8. Difference between uniform and truncated geometric distributions

3.3 Performance evaluation

In this subsection we present the performance comparison of incomplete cooperative game, ie. Incomplete Game, our "considered" or "normal" MAC protocol, and IB based MAC protocol in terms of channel efficiency, medium access delay and energy-efficiency . Latter two protocols are same in nature except for their backoff procedure. For the performance analysis we carried out simulation in Matlab. The main parameters for our simulation are listed in table 3. For calculating the energy consumption in nodes we choose ratio of idle: listen: transmit as 1:1:1.5, as measured in (M. Stemm et al., 1997). For the "normal" MAC protocol maximum retry limit is set to 3 (m=3), minimum contention window is set to 16 (also for the IB Based MAC), and traffic model is set to non-saturation.

As we have described in previous section channel efficiency is mostly depends on number of active nodes and contention window size. As shown in figure 9, at first "Normal MAC" (NM) gives high channel throughput at lower number of nodes. The reason is very obvious, less collision and low waiting time in backoff procedure, and as number of contenders increases channel throughput start decreasing. In contrast to NM, "IB based MAC" (IBM) maintains high channel efficiency due to its unique quality of collision avoidance among the competing nodes. In IBM most of the nodes choose higher contention slots while very few nodes selects lower contention slots, hence less or no collision and low waiting time in backoff procedure. For "Incomplete Game" channel efficiency almost keep constant after 30 nodes, as each node can adapt to the variable game state and choose corresponding equilibrium strategy. At start it shows lower channel efficiency because contention window is still too big for given number of nodes.

Parameters	Values
CW_{min}	16
Packet size	1024 Bytes
Nodes	5~100
Data Rate	1 Mbps
Transmitting Energy	50x10-6 J/Bit
Idle/listening Energy	75x10-6 J/Bit

Table 3. Simulation Parameters

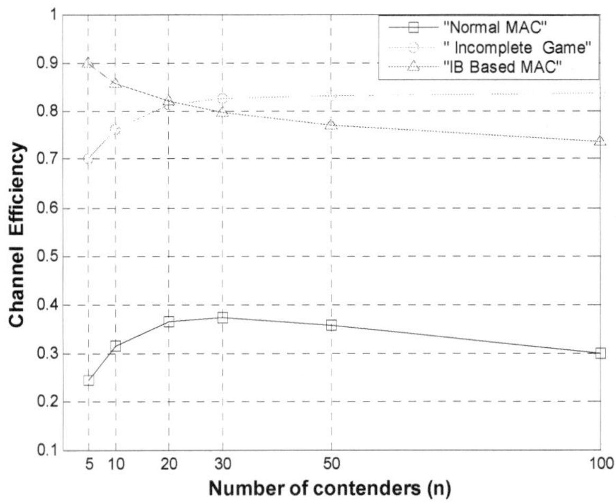

Fig. 9. shows the channel efficiency of "Normal MAC", "Incomplete Game" and "IB Based MAC".

Figure 10 shows the average medium access delay performances of NM, Incomplete Game and IBM. Here, medium access delay is defined as the time elapsed between the generation of a request packet and its successful reception. In NM scheme, as a large number of stations attempt to access the medium, more collision occurs, the number of retransmissions increases and nodes suffer longer delays. In IBM, as we expected access delay is very low compared to NM. This is because of low or no collision and less idle waiting time in backoff procedure. In "Incomplete Game", access delay performance is far more better than "NM",

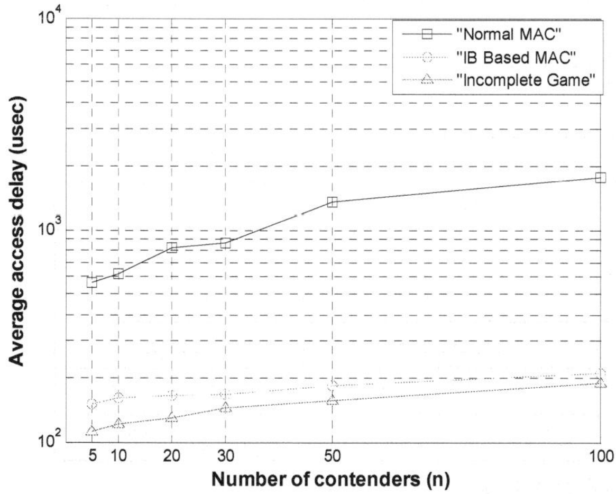

Fig. 10. Average access delay vs. number of nodes

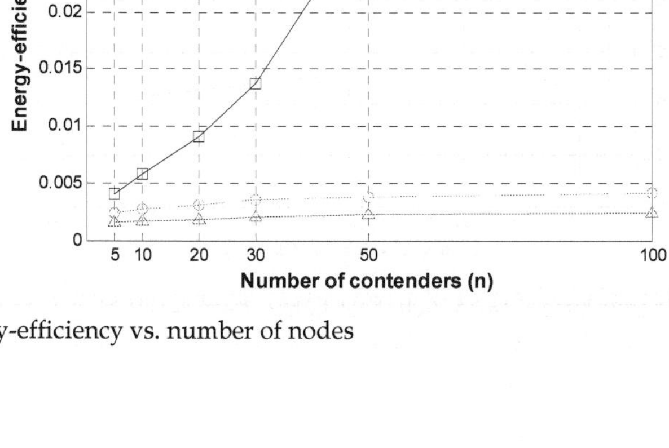

Fig. 11. Energy-efficiency vs. number of nodes

and comparable with "IBM", as it take some time to adjust its contention window according to number of nodes. Figure 11 illustrates the impact of CW on energy efficiency of NM, incomplete game, and IBM schemes.

From figure 11 we can see that as number of nodes increases NM scheme waste more energy due to increase in collision and retransmission attempts. In contrast IBM wastes very less energy due to its unique characteristics of collision avoidance. Similarly, "Incomplete Game" can also give the comparative performance to IBM, as it also reduces collision by adjusting its equilibrium strategy. From all aforementioned results we can see the superiority of IBM over NM. Accepting IBM as backoff scheme can increase the overall performance of an energy efficient MAC protocol to a large extends and we can also get the sub optimal solution for an incomplete cooperative game.

4. Related works

Along with the aforementioned examples and a case study there are notable amount of work presented in the area of game theory and wireless networks. We summarize some of the important current related works/trends as shown in the table 4. As describe in the above mentioned games selfish behavior by nodes in a wireless network may lead to a suboptimal equilibrium where nodes, through their actions, reach an undesirable steady state from a network point of view. Hence, incentive mechanisms are needed to steer nodes towards constructive behavior (i.e., towards a desirable equilibrium). Even though the bulk of work done in the past few years to answer above mentioned games still they are at a nascent stage.

Subject	The Proposed work/solution	References
Ad-hoc Networks	Cooperation with and without incentives -Currency & reputation -Virtual money and Cost -Reducing Selfish behaviour	(S.Mehta and K.S Kwak, 2007/8, and references in there.)
Sensor Networks	Cooperative Packet forwarding, Mac Protocol, non-cooperative Solutions, etc.	
Cognitive radio	Major works in resource allocation and IEEE 802.22 Working Group	
Cellular and Wi-Fi Networks (WWANs and WLANs)	Resource Allocation, Selfish behaviour, and reputation based networks	

Table 4. Summery of related works

5. Conclusions

In this chapter, we present the introduction of Game theory and show its application to wireless networks. Game theory can model the various interactions in wireless networks as games at different levels of protocol stack. With these games we can analysis the existing Routing/MAC protocols and resource management schemes, as well as the design of equilibrium-inducing mechanisms that provide incentives for individual nodes to behave inline with the network goals. We also present a case study on IB based MAC protocol as a concrete example of applicability of game theory to wireless networks. In short, this chapter paper serves three main objectives; first, to model some of the fundamental questions on wireless networks as interactive games between the nodes. Second object is to gain our understanding on inter-discipline research issues and third to motivate students and researchers to peep at this fascinating analytical tool, and encourage them in modeling problems of wireless networks.

6. References

Garey, S.M., & Johnson, D. S. (1979). Computers and Intractability: Guide to the Theory of NP-Completeness. W. H. Freeman, New York.

Osborne, M.J. & A Rubinstein.(1994).A course in game Theory. Cambridge, MA : The MIT Press.

Stemm, M., & Katz, R.H. (1997). Measuring and reducing energy consumption of network interfaces in hand-held devices. *IEICE Transactions on Communications E80-B (8),* pp.1125–1131.

Bianchi, G. (2000) Performance Analysis of the IEEE 802.11 Distributed Coordination Function. *IEEE Jour. SAC, 18 (3),* pp. 535-547.

Ye, W. & Heidemann, J. & Estrin D. (2002) . An Energy- Efficient MAC Protocol for wireless Sensor Networks. *In proceeding of IEEE INFOCOM 2002,* New York,pp.1567-1576.

Dam, T. V. & Langendone, K. (2003). An Adaptive Energy-Efficient MAC Protocol for Wireless Sensor Networks. *In proceeding of SenSys'03,* Los Angeles, pp.171-180.

Bianchi, G. & Tinnirello I. (2003). Kalman Filter Estimation of the Number of Competing Terminals in an IEEE 802.11 Network. *In proceeding of INFOCOM'03.*

Tay, Y. C., Jamieson, K. & Balakrishnan, H. (2004). Collision-Minimizing CSMA and Its Applications to Wireless Sensor Networks. *IEEE JSAC, Vol.22, No.6,* pp.1048-1057.

Srivastava, V. ; Neel, J. ; Mackenzie, A. B. ; Menon, R.; Dasilva, L. A. ; Hicks, J. E.; Reed, J. H., & Gilles, R. P. (2005). Using Game Theory to Analyze Wireless Ad-hoc Networks. *IEEE communications and survey, Fourth Quarter,* 2005.

Felegyhazi, M. & Hubaux, J.-P. (2006). Game Theory in Wireless Networks: A Tutorial. *In EPFL technical report,* LCA-REPORT-2006-002.

Akyildiz, I. F.; Lee, W. Y.; Vuran, M.C.; & Mohanty, S. (2006) NeXt generation/dynamic spectrum access/cognitive radio wireless networks: A survey. *Computer Networks 50 (2006),* pp.2127–2159.

Vercauteren, T., Toledo, A.L., & Wang, X. (2007). Batch and Sequential Bayesian Estimators of the Number of Active Terminals in an IEEE 802.11 Network. *In IEEE Trans. on Signal Processing,* vol. 55, no. 2, pp. 437-450.

Zaho, L., Zhang, H. & Zhang, J. (2008).Using In complete Cooperative Game Thory in wirless Sensor networks. *In proceeding of IEEE WCNC 2008.*pp . 1483-1488.

Mehta, S. & Kwak, K.S. (2007/8). Game Theoretic approach to Cognitive Radio based Tactical Maneuvering Networks. *Project Proposal,* UWB Research Center, Inha University.

Mehta, S. & Kwak, K.S. (2009). A GCSMA Based Contention Scheme for Wireless Sensor Networks. *Technical Report-6,* UWB Research Center, Inha University.

25

Comparison of *DP* Effects in *MANET AAPs* with Link Error

Sang-Chul Kim
School of Computer Science, Kookmin University,
861-1, Chongnung-dong, Songbuk-gu, Seoul, 136-702
Korea

1. Introduction

A *MANET* consists of a set of mobile nodes where mobile nodes have routing capabilities to forward packets. Each mobile host becomes a member of a self-organizing wireless network, where one another communicate over multi-hop wireless links, without relying on a fixed communication infrastructure, such as a base station or an access point. It is essential that all nodes are able to perform the operations required for the configuration of unique addresses to execute proper routing of data packets in a *MANET.*

Address auto-configuration is an important issue, since address pre-configuration is not always possible in MANETs. MANETs currently depend on checking the IP addresses of nodes to decide if the connection and identification of nodes participating in a *MANET* are established. In conventional networks, address auto-configuration is categorized as either a stateless or a stateful protocol. When a network is not especially required to control the exact IP address assignments if the addresses are unique and routable, the stateless approach is used.

In contrast, the stateful approach is used when a network demands exact IP address assignments. Dynamic host configuration protocol (*DHCP*) is an example of a stateful protocol, where a *DHCP* server assigns unique addresses to unconfigured nodes and keeps state address information in an address allocation table. However, in stateless protocols, a node can select an address and verify its uniqueness in a distributed manner using *DAD* algorithms. Using *DAD* algorithms, a node in a *MANET,* which lacks an IP address in the *MANET,* can determine if a candidate address it selects is available. A node already equipped with an IP address also depends on *DAD* to protect its IP address from being accidentally used by another node in the *MANET.*

Based on the conventional method [1], *DAD* can be classified as Strong *DAD* and Weak *DAD.* Strong *DAD* uses an address discovery mechanism, where a node randomly selects an address and requests the address within a *MANET,* checking if the address is being used in the *MANET.* Based on a reply to the claimed request, which needs to arrive at the node within a finite bounded time interval, the node can detect address duplication in the *MANET.*

Weak *DAD* is proposed, where ad hoc routing protocols are used to detect address duplication by modification of the routing protocol packet format. *MANET* routing protocols can be classified as proactive and on-demand. Proactive routing protocols, using periodic neighbor discovery messages and topology update messages, give route information to each node, before a node sends data packets to a destination. On-demand routing protocols issue route discovery mechanism messages, only when a node needs to send data to a destination node.

Since these protocols do not use a periodical message exchange, such as the neighbor discovery message used in proactive routing protocols, they do not hold route information at each node before a node sends data towards a destination node. Therefore, they need route request (*RQ*) and route reply (*RR*) messages to find and maintain a route when it is needed. Based on the above observation, the advantages and disadvantages of the proactive and on-demand routing protocols can be summarized as follow.

The main advantage of proactive routing protocols is that whenever a node sends a data packet, it obtains the route information to a destination searching its route table. Therefore, the route is already known and can be used immediately. In addition, there is no delay time in determining the route in the source node. However, a portion of the network resources in MANETs should be allocated to handle the periodic neighbor discovery and topology update messages, and this increases network traffic load.

The main advantage of on demand routing protocols is the reduction of network traffic overhead, as no messages are exchanged before the start of data communication. However, the delay caused by the route discovery mechanism to find a route to a destination could be a significant factor when considering *MANET*'s routing performance. As the node population and mobility increase, the routing control overhead in the *MANET* area also increases. This is a dominant factor to be considered in limited wireless bandwidth. The scalability issues in *MANET*'s proactive and on-demand routing protocols have been studied.

2. Related work

In regards to the mobility factor in MANETs, it is indicated in that the rate of link failure, due to node mobility, is the main concern of routing in ad hoc networks. *MANET* nodes move around according to their mobility scenarios, while they perform routing procedures simultaneously. Many papers deal with mobility patterns and mobility-based frameworks.

A broadcast request can be issued at any time by any host with a packet to be delivered to the entire network. A single transmission sent by each node will be received by all nodes within the node's transmission range. All other nodes need to cooperate to propagate the packet by rebroadcasting it. In [2], it is indicated that wireless ad hoc networks prefer localized algorithms and power-efficient network topologies, since a wireless ad hoc network has its own unavoidable limitations, where nodes have been powered by batteries and limited memory, in contrast to wired networks. The authors of [3] address the Lucent *WaveLAN* IEEE 802.11 wireless network interface consuming the power of 1,327 and 967 *mW* respectively when it transmits and receives at a transmission rate of 2 *Mbps*. [4] considers reduction of the number of broadcast messages, in which the authors focus on the concept of efficiency that is represented as the number of forward nodes, rather than reliability that is represented as the percentage of nodes receiving the broadcast packet [4].

One of possible methods to reduce broadcast redundancy is to perform the *AAP* and routing operations simultaneously. Passive Auto-configuration for Mobile Ad Hoc Networks (*PACMAN*) [5] uses routing protocol traffic to assign IP addresses. Since it uses routing messages to implement address configuration, it does not have control overhead to implement *PACMAN*. The author of [5] indicates that even though IPv6 has sufficient address space to provide a unique IP address, it needs the IPv6 stateless address auto-configuration (*SSA*), since there is no hardware ID (e.g., 48 bits IEEE medium address control (*MAC*) address) that is truly globally unique. The author of [6] analyzes various address auto-configuration protocols for *MANET* and introduces the necessary routing protocols to enable reliable detection of all conflicts.

Much recent research has been conducted to reduce broadcast redundancy, since blind flooding in a wireless ad hoc networks has high cost and excessive redundancy [7]. The authors address two research approaches, probabilistic and deterministic, to obtain an efficient broadcast [7]. The probabilistic approach uses no or limited neighbor information and requires high broadcasts to maintain an acceptable packet delivery ratio. However, the deterministic approach finds the list of forward nodes to guarantee full network coverage.

In [8], a node does not forward a broadcast packet if a self-pruning algorithm is satisfied based on neighborhood information. Even though only a set of nodes forward the broadcast packet, this process guarantees complete network delivery. Self-pruning-based broadcast protocols [8] collect neighborhood topology information based on the *Hello* message and form a connected dominating set via forward nodes. *DP* [9] also offers a promising approach to reduce redundant transmissions caused by blind flooding. It is considered as an approximation to the minimum flood tree problem. The self-pruning algorithm uses the information of one-hop neighboring nodes; however, the *DP* algorithm utilizes two-hop neighborhood information.

Due to the multitude of factors to be considered for a *MANET*, the reduction of the routing overhead is the main concern during the development of a *MANET* protocol. One essential measure of the quality of a *MANET* protocol is its scalability with regard to an increase in the number of *MANET* nodes. Message complexity is defined where the overhead of an algorithm is measured in terms of the number of messages needed to satisfy the algorithm's request. This chapter proposes a novel idea where the *AAPs* (Strong *DAD*, Weak *DAD* and MANETconf) are able to perform routing. Therefore, the proposed algorithm can perform the *AAP* operation and routing simultaneously. In addition, since it is not well known how much improvement can be achieved when the *DP* algorithm substitutes the conventional blind flooding in the *MANET AAPs*, the performance is investigated in reference to complexity and scalability.

Therefore, the next goal of this chapter is to obtain a quantitative ratio of percentage reduction when the *DP* algorithm is used in *MANET AAPs* for the broadcast operation. Research was conducted to provide a detailed simulation of a single node joining message complexity and extends the results to scalability and complexity analysis. This chapter adopts the analysis of the worst case scenario [10] to conduct a quantitative analysis of message complexity.

The remainder of this chapter is organized as follows: Section 3 describes a detailed explanation of the proposed algorithm, particularly the concept of *AAPs* routing capability to reduce redundant transmission. In addition, it describes the proposed architecture of *AAP* algorithms. Section 4 addresses the numerical experiments and results. Finally, Section 5 summarizes our work and concludes the chapter.

3. Proposed algorithm

The proposed algorithm can be described in three sections. The first section introduces the procedures to enable *AAPs* to have routing capability, by creating new messages. The second section illustrates how the *DP* algorithm substitutes blind flooding. The last section includes pseudocode to describe the detailed operation of the proposed *AAP* algorithms.

3.1 *AAP* with routing capability

In a standalone *MANET*, where a *MANET* has no connection to an external network, such as the Internet, the following two procedures are essential for each node in a *MANET* to be configured as a normal node in a conventional method. First, each node performs an *AAP* to obtain a unique IP address for proper routing of data packets in a *MANET*. Second, each node performs a *MANET* routing protocol to inform other nodes of the network topology and to send data packets towards a destination. This section addresses the procedure of a new *AAP* algorithm, where the routing capability has been implemented. Consequently, it is shown that the proposed algorithm reduces the complexity and solves scalability issues.

In the conventional approach where the *AAP* and routing are used separately, the messages can be classified into four categories. The message categories are: neighbor discovery (*Hello*), topology update (*TU*), address request (*AQ*) and address reply (*AR*). *Hello* and *TU* messages are designed for routing operation and *AQ* and *AR* messages are developed for *AAP* operation.

A new classification method, based on a forwarding method and a periodicity of message, can be proposed as follows. From the forwarding method, the message can be classified as broadcast, local broadcast, and unicast messages. From the periodicity, the message can be classified as periodical (implemented in the proactive *MANET* routing protocols) and non-periodical (implemented in the ondemand *MANET* routing protocols) messages.

Based on the above method, the *Hello* message is classified as a local broadcast message and a periodical message. *TU* message has the property of broadcast and periodical or non-periodical message, depending on routing protocols. *AQ* message is classified as broadcast and non-periodical message. *AR* message is unicast and non-periodical message. The summary of message property used in *MANET AAP* and *MANET* routing protocols are shown in Table 1.

Message	Forwarding Method	Periodicity	Used in	Prop. Algorithm
Hello	Local Broadcast	periodical	Routing	Yes
TU	Broadcast	non- or periodical	Routing	Yes
AQ	Broadcast	non-periodical	*AAP*	No
AR	Unicast	non-periodical	*AAP*	No

Table 1. Property of Messages

Two messages - *Hello* and *TU* - have been newly suggested in the proposed algorithm *MANET AAPs* to have the routing capability. As in the conventional use of the *Hello* message, the *Hello* message is designed only for neighbor discovery in the proposed algorithm. *TU* message has several different options, such as topology update, address request, and address reply. The following steps describe the process for the *TU* message to have routing capability and address auto-configuration. The topology update option gives mobile nodes the ability to implement routing capability.

In the *MANET* proactive routing protocols, *TU* message is generated periodically. In the *MANET* on-demand routing protocols, *TU* message is issued non-periodically, since on-demand message is randomly triggered, only when nodes find a route and respond by sending a route reply to the corresponding route request. The following procedure enables

the capability of address auto-configuration in the *TU* message. Whenever a node requires triggering an *AQ* message for a new joining node to be equipped with a unique IP address, it broadcasts *TU* message with the option of address request. In addition, it follows the periodic (when *TU* message is used in the proactive *MANET*) or non-periodic (when *TU* message is used in the on-demand *MANET*) property of *TU* message. That is, there might be some delay to generate *TU* message, until the next periodic (or non-periodic) time is issued.
When one of the nodes in a *MANET* detects a duplicated IP address, when the *TU* message with the option of address request is propagated into *MANET*, it responds by generating the *TU* message with the option of address reply. The *TU* message can broadcast, however, in the case of relaying the option of address reply, it unicasts the forwarding method where it follows the reverse path of the *TU* message with the option of the address request. A node waits until the next periodic (or non-periodic) time to generate and transmit the *TU* message with the option of route reply. Since non-periodicity does not guarantee triggering the *TU* message in a limited time, a node waits until a certain threshold time to generate or relay a non-periodic *TU* message. If a node does not have an event to trigger transmission of the *TU* message within the threshold time, the node autonomously generates a *TU* message.

3.2 *AAP* with *DP*

The detailed procedure of the proposed algorithm is described to implement the *DP* algorithm, to reduce the number of broadcast messages. The broadcast storm problem is a serious issue in a *MANET*. Hence, several algorithms are introduced to reduce the number of broadcast messages. The authors of [8] concluded that finding a minimum flood tree that gives the minimum number of forward nodes is proven to be *NP*-complete. They argued that even though a minimum flood tree is constructed, the maintenance cost of the tree in a mobile environment is too high to be useful in practice.
The *DP* algorithm [9] can reduce redundant transmission using 2-hop neighborhood information. Total dominant pruning (*TDP*) and partial dominant pruning (*PDP*) algorithms, introduced in [8], are proposed to overcome some deficiencies of the *DP* algorithm.
Since a source node knows the list of forward nodes, based on its neighboring nodes selected using the *DP*, *TDP* or *PDP* algorithm, all the neighboring nodes do not need to rebroadcast a packet issued by the source node. In contrast, all the neighboring nodes rebroadcast a packet issued by the source node in blind flooding. *DP*, *TDP* and *PDP* algorithms can reduce the total number of rebroadcasted packets and re-broadcast nodes compared to blind flooding. Adopting the *DP* algorithm can evaluate performance for the decision by nodes to rebroadcast packets in the proposed *AAP* algorithm that enables routing.
The following section describes the basic differences between blind flooding, self pruning and *DP* algorithms. Let us define $N(v)$ as the set of adjacent nodes of node v [8] [9]. $N(N(v))$ is defined as the set of nodes that is located within two-hops from node v [9] [10]. Due to the use of the periodic *Hello* message that informs the neighboring nodes of the presence of a node, self pruning and *DP* methods can collect the neighboring information periodically. Therefore, each node can construct its own neighboring list.
In self pruning, when a receiver node (r) receives a packet that piggybacks a neighboring list of a sender node (s), the receiver node r calculates if the set of $N(r)$ - $N(s)$ - r is empty. If the set is empty, the receiver node r does not rebroadcast the packet, since $N(r)$ is covered by the sender node s. Otherwise, the receiver node r rebroadcasts the packet.

In conventional blind flooding, the receiver node *r* always rebroadcasts the packet, even though the set of *N*(*r*) - *N*(*s*) - *r* is empty. This increases broadcast redundancy.

In *DP*, a sender node selects adjacent nodes in *B*(*s*, *r*) (that equals *N*(*r*) - *N*(*s*)) that rebroadcast the packet, so that all nodes in *U*=*N*(*N*(*r*)) - *N*(*s*) - *N*(*r*) receive the packet. The adjacent nodes also determine the forward list to complete flooding.

While self-pruning uses direct neighbor information only, *DP* uses neighborhood information up to two hops. The pruning methods require extra control overhead, since they use the periodic *Hello* messages for each node to get network topology information. Since nodes in a *MANET* use the periodic *Hello* messages in a normal (stable) status, the pruning methods can utilize the advantage of the periodic *Hello* messages.

Fig. 1 shows an example of the *DP* algorithm where node 2 is a source node. One-hop neighboring node set is represented as *x* and two hop neighboring node set is represented as *y*.

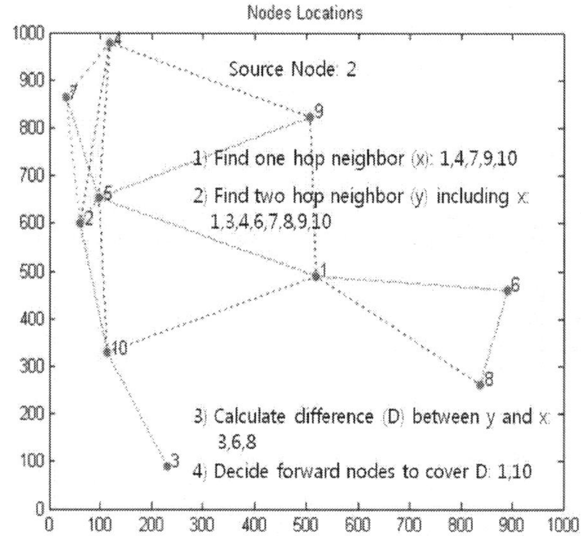

Fig. 1. An Example of Dominant Pruning

3.3 Proposed *AAP* algorithms

Strong *DAD* uses an address discovery mechanism, where a node randomly selects an address and requests the address within a *MANET*, checking if the address is being used in the *MANET*. Based on the reply to the claimed request, which needs to arrive at the node within a finite bounded time interval, the node can detect address duplication in the *MANET*. Weak *DAD* is used to detect address duplication by modification of the routing protocol packet format. MANETconf uses a mutual exclusion algorithm for a node to acquire a new IP address. Therefore, if a requester wants to acquire an IP address, the IP address should be approved by all nodes in a *MANET*.

Figs. 2, 3, and 4 show the pseudo code for Strong *DAD*, *WDP*, *WDO*, and MANETconf operations in the simulation respectively, where the newly proposed messages in this chapter are used with its option to implement the autoconfiguration process. In the conventional broadcast (and its simulation), the most common flooding method is used to broadcast a *TU* (*AQ*: Address Request option) message where every node retransmits a *TU* (*AQ* option) message to its entire one-hop neighbors whenever it receives the first copy of the a *TU* (*AQ* option).

```
Start
Step 01: A node selects a temporary address
         and configures it as its network interface address
Step 02: n=0; (Set retry count (n) =0)
Step 03: m=0; (Set DAD retry count (m) = 0)
Step 04: n++; (Increase the retry count (n) by 1)
Step 05: m++; (Increase the DAD retry count (m) by 1)
Step 06: The node randomly selects a source IP address
         and makes a TU (AQ) message for the IP address
Step 07: The node broadcasts the TU (AQ)
Step 08: if (all MANET nodes receive the TU (AQ) == TRUE)
Step 09:   if (a TU (AP) arrives to the node before timer expires
              == TRUE)
Step 10:     if ((retry count <= n ) == TRUE)
Step 11:      goto Step 4;
Step 12:     else
Step 13:      goto Step 21;
Step 14:   else
Step 15:     if ((DAD retry count <= m ) == TRUE)
Step 16:       The node replaces the source IP address with its IP address
            break;
Step 17:     else
Step 18:       goto Step 5;
Step 19: else
Step 20: goto Step 7;
Step 21: The node fails to get a source IP address
End
```

Fig. 2. Strong *DAD* Operations

However, in the proposed algorithm (and its simulation), the *DP* algorithm is used to replace the conventional flooding algorithm. *Dijkstra*'s shortest path algorithm at each node is used to calculate the number of hops in unicasting or relaying a unicast *TU* (*AP*: Address Reply option) from a destination node to a source node. In Strong *DAD*, the retry count limit (n) is five and for *DAD* the retry count limit (m) is three. In Weak *DAD* and MANETconf protocols, the retry count limit (n) is five and for *DAD* retry count limit (m) is one.

4. Numerical results

In the simulation, a single node joining case in the largest sub-network, among several partitioned sub-networks, is considered to perform the evaluation. The computer-based simulator was written to implement the proposed algorithm. In the simulator, the forward node list (F) implemented by the *DP* algorithm has been selected to rebroadcast messages. Since only the forward nodes in the neighboring list can broadcast the *TU* message, it is shown that the message complexities of the proposed *AAPs* are significantly reduced, compared to the blind flooding method.

```
Start
Step 01: A node selects a temporary address
           and configures it as its network interface address
Step 02: n=0; (Set retry count (n) =0)
Step 03: n++; (Increase the retry count (n) by 1)
Step 04: The node randomly selects a source IP address and picks a
           unique key value (e.g., MAC address) as the identification of the node;
Step 05: if (Proactive routing protocol is used == TRUE)
Step 06:   The node broadcasts a TU (LS) periodically
Step 07:     if (all MANET nodes receive the TU (LS)
               == TRUE)
Step 08:       if (the node receives a TU (AE) for the selected IP address
               == TRUE)
Step 09:         if (retry count <= n)
Step 10:           goto Step 3;
Step 11:         else
Step 12:           The node fails to get a source IP address, goto End
Step 13:       else
Step 14:         The node replaces the source IP address with
                   its IP address, goto End
Step 15:     else
Step 16:       goto Step 6;
Step 17: else
Step 18:   The node broadcasts a TU (RQ) whenever it needs to
Step 19:     if (all MANET nodes receive the TU (RQ))
Step 20:       if (the node is the destination of a TU (RQ))
Step 21:         The node unicasts a TU (RP).
Step 22:       else
Step 23:         goto Step 8
Step 24:     else
Step 25:       goto Step 18
End
```

Fig. 3. Weak *DAD* Operations

```
Start
Step 01: A requester (new joining node) selects an initiator and
           unicasts Hello (RR) to the initiator
Step 02: n=0; (Set retry count (n) =0)
Step 03: n++; (Increase the retry count (n) by 1)
Step 04: The initiator broadcasts a TU (IQ) to all the nodes of the MANET group
       with the address of the requestor
Step 05: if (all MANET nodes receive the TU (IQ) == TRUE)
Step 06:   Recipient nodes reply with an affirmative or
             a negative response (TU (IR)) to the initiator
Step 07: else
Step 08:   goto Step 4;
Step 09: if (the initiator receives affirmative TU (IR) messages
             from all nodes == TRUE)
Step 10:   The initiator assigns the IP address to the requestor
Step 11:   The initiator broadcasts a TU (AO) message to all
             recipient nodes of the MANET group, goto End
Step 12: else
Step 13:   The initiator selects another IP address
Step 14: if (retry count <= n)
Step 15:   The initiator sends a TU (AB) message to the requestor,
             goto End
Step 16: else
Step 17:   goto Step 3;
End
```

Fig. 4. *MANETconf* Operations

A system model that is used to analyze the proposed algorithm follows the system model introduced in [10]. For a given link error probability of P_e, the retransmission count limit value R can be defined based on the network manager's desired setting, some optimal criteria, and/or the mobile node's priority. For a given link error probability, the average number of transmissions (T_N) required for success ful reception is provided in (1). This can be used as a reference value for the retransmission count limit value R.

$$T_N = \frac{1}{1-P_e},\ for\ 0 \leq P_e < 1 \tag{1}$$

Since a link error can stop message propagations, a node that experiences link errors needs to rebroadcast the messages to its neighboring nodes. It is assumed that a node is able to learn of transmission failure using acknowledgments from the lower layers. Based on the detected link error probability, a network controller can set the retransmission count limit R to a desired value. A standalone *MANET* environment is needed to compare the message complexity between the conventional *AAPs* and the proposed *AAPs*, where the *MANET* nodes have no connection to an external network, such as the Internet.

A computer-based simulator was developed where nodes are randomly distributed with uniform density in a network area of $1km^2$. A discrete-event simulator was developed in *Matlab* to verify the various network topologies and to calculate message complexity. The random node generator and simulator performance were verified (number of nodes: 100, 125, 150, and 175) so that the average number of nodes per cluster as well as several of the specifications in the adaptive dynamic backbone (*ADB*) algorithm [10] matched the results in [10]. This was performed on *QualNet*, with less than a 1% difference in most cases. In our analysis, the conflict probability (P_c) is defined as the probability in which the IP address that a node requests to use is already in use in the *MANET* group. The conflict probability depends on the size of the address and the number of nodes in a *MANET* group.

The blind flooding used in the simulation, which is compared to the *DP* algorithm, is to have every node retransmit a message to all of its one-hop neighbors, whenever it receives the first copy of the message. In addition, the node transmission range is selected to be $150m$. The number of nodes is varied from 10 to 100.

In the computer simulation, the values of 0.25 and 0.5 are used for P_e; P_c of 0.5 is used in the following graphs. Corresponding to each of P_e values of 0.25, and 0.5, the retransmission count R has been set to 1.33 and 2 respectively, based on (1).

Figs. 5 and 6 show the simulation of message complexities between the conventional *AAP* algorithms and the proposed algorithm, when P_e values of 0.25 and 0.5 are used respectively. Even if the *DP* method reduces message complexity, it can be shown that message complexity linearly increases with increases in link error probability. The messages used in the conventional *AAP* and the proposed algorithm are different. It is assumed that the messages lengths are the same. For example, the conventional Strong *DAD* uses *AQ* and *AP* messages; however, the proposed Strong *DAD* uses the *TU* message with the option of address request and the *TU* message with the option of address reply.

In the graph, the x axis shows the number of nodes in a *MANET* and the y axis shows the message complexities of the conventional *AAP* and the proposed algorithm. It can be shown that at the conflict probability of 0.5, until the node number is 55, conventional Strong *DAD* has the largest message complexity, after the node number exceeds 55, conventional MANETconf has the largest message complexity and *WDP* with the proposed algorithm has the least message complexity.

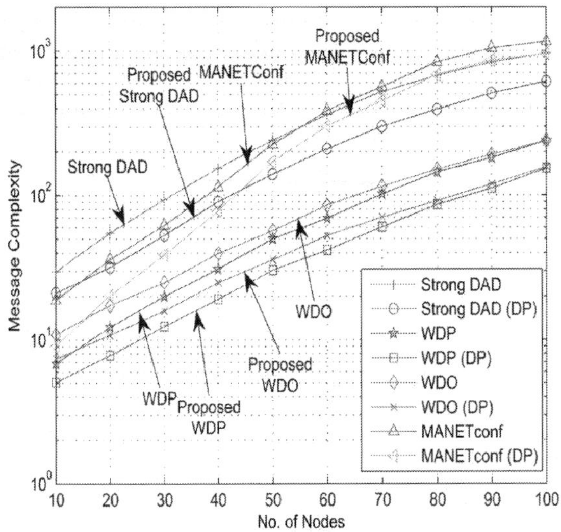

Fig. 5. Message Complexity (P_c=0.5, P_e=0.25)

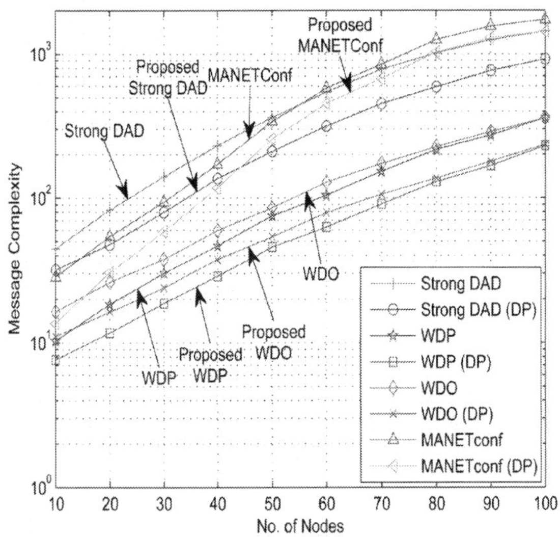

Fig. 6. Message Complexity (P_c=0.5, P_e=0.5)

As shown in Fig. 7, message complexity of 39.8%, 37.3%, 37.0% and 28.4% has been reduced respectively in comparison to the message complexity of the conventional Strong *DAD*, *WDP*, *WDO* and MANETconf when the Pe value equals zero. In the node range between 10 and 100, the reduced overhead percentage of the proposed algorithm is shown in Fig. 7.

It can be said that the reduction rate of Strong *DAD* is noticeably greater than the reduction rate of other *AAPs*, since Strong *DAD* uses more recursive broadcast mechanisms to resolve duplicated IP addresses or for routing than other *AAP*s. In MANETconf, it is shown that as node number increases, message complexity rapidly decreases. Since in MANETconf all nodes unicast as the main operation, as node number increases, message complexity affected by broadcasting is reduced. In contrast, the reduction rate of message complexity affected by all nodes unicasting increased.

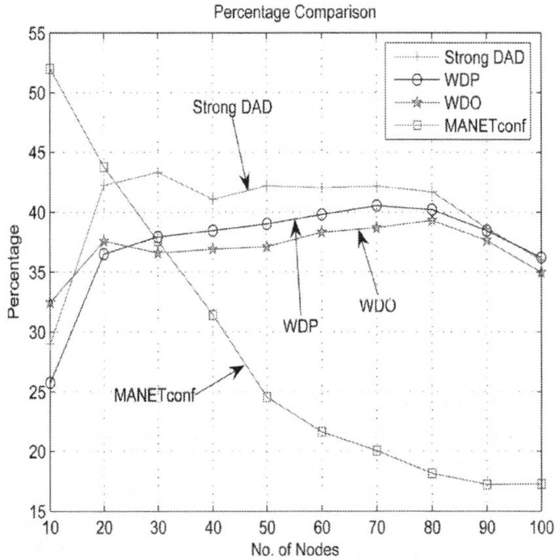

Fig. 7. Percentage Difference Comparison (P_c=0.5, P_e=0)

5. Conclusion

The wireless communication environment and the mobility of the nodes destabilize links. This results in link errors. Based on the link error probability, this chapter proposes two novel algorithms where the broadcasting redundancy was noticeably decreased using the *DP* algorithm and different messages used in *MANET AAP*s and routing algorithms are combined using *Hello* and *TU* messages.

The proposed algorithm can save the total number of control messages, compared to the conventional algorithm, due to the reduced number of *TU* messages generated in *AAP* and routing. The simulation shows the proposed algorithm saves 39.8%, 37.3%, 37.0% and 28.4% of message complexity compared to the conventional Strong *DAD, WDP, WDO* and MANETconf.

Several characteristics of *AAP*s are found. First, since Strong *DAD* uses more recursive broadcast mechanisms to resolve duplicated IP addresses compared to other *AAP*s, the reduction rate of Strong *DAD* is greater than the reduction rate of other *AAP*s. Second, it is shown in MANETconf that as node number increases, the reduction rate of message complexity rapidly decreases. Since in MANETconf in the main operation all nodes unicasts, as node number increases, the reduction rate of message complexity affected by broadcasting reduces, while the reduction rate of message complexity affected by unicasting by all nodes increases.

6. Acknowledgments

This work was supported by National Research Foundation of Korea Grant funded by the Korean Government (KRF-2009-007128) and the Seoul R&BD Program (No. 10848).

7. References

[1] N. H. Vaidya, "Weak duplicate address detection in mobile ad hoc networks," *Proc. ACM MobiHoc 2002*, pp. 206-216, June 2002, Lausanne, Switzerland.

[2] X.-Y. Li, Y. Wang, and W.-Z. Song, "Applications of k-local MST for topology control and broadcasting in wireless ad hoc networks," *IEEE Trans. on Parallel and Distributed Systems*, vol. 15, no. 12, pp. 1057-1069, Dec. 2004.

[3] C.-C. Shen, Z. Huang, and C. Jaikaeo, "Directional broadcast for mobile ad hoc networks with percolation theory," *IEEE Trans. Mobile Computing*, vol. 5, no. 4, pp. 317-332, Apr. 2006.

[4] J. Wu and F. Dai, "A Generic Distributed Broadcast Scheme in Ad Hoc Wireless Networks," *IEEE Trans. On Computers*, vol. 53, no. 10, pp. 1343-1354, Oct. 2004.

[5] K. Weniger, "PACMAN: passive autoconfiguration for mobile ad hoc networks," *IEEE J. Select. Areas Commun.*, vol. 23, no.3, pp.507-519, Mar. 2005.

[6] K. Weniger, and M. Zitterbart, "Mobile ad hoc networks - current approaches and future directions," *IEEE Network*, vol. 18, issue 4, pp.6-11, July-Aug. 2004.

[7] F. Dai and J. Wu, "Efficient broadcasting in ad hoc wireless networks using directional antennas," *IEEE Trans. on Parallel and Distributed Systems*, vol. 17, no. 4, pp. 335-347, Apr. 2006.

[8] W. Lou and J. Wu, "On reducing broadcast redundancy in Ad hoc wireless networks," *IEEE Trans. on Mobile Computing*, vol. 1, no. 2, pp. 111-122, Apr.-June, 2002.

[9] H. Lim and C. Kim, "Flooding in wireless ad hoc networks," *Computer Comm. J.*, vol. 24, no.3-4, pp. 353- 363, 2001.

[10] C-. C. Shen, C. Srisathapornphat, R. L. Z. Huang, C. Jaikaeo, and E. L. Lloyd, "CLTC: A cluseter-based topology control framework for ad hoc networks," *IEEE Trans. Mobile Computing*, vol. 3, no.1, pp. 18-32, Jan.- Mar. 2004.

[11] S.-C. Kim and J.-M. Chung,"Message Complexity Analysis of Mobile Ad Hoc Network Address Autoconfiguration Protocols," *IEEE Trans. Mobile Computing*, vol. 7, no. 3, pp. 358-371, Mar. 2008.

26

Design of Optimum Weighting Functions for LFM Signals

Anatoliy Kononov, Lars Ulander and Leif Eriksson
Department of Radio and Space Science
Chalmers University of Technology, Gothenburg
Sweden

1. Introduction

Linear frequency-modulated (LFM) pulse signals are probably the most common type of pulse compression waveforms for various radar systems (Barton, 2005; Cook&Bernfeld, 1967; Curlander & McDonough, 1991; Levanon & Mozeson, 2004; Richards, 2005; Skolnik, 2008). LFM signals are also often the waveform of choice for wideband systems, where the required bandwidth may be hundreds of megahertz. The ambiguity function of the LFM signal suffers from significant sidelobes, both in delay (range) and in Doppler. It is known, for example, that the first range sidelobe is approximately 13 dB below the main peak of the ambiguity function. Such sidelobes may be unacceptable in many applications due to system performance degradation caused by high sidelobes (Cook & Bernfeld, 1967; Levanon & Mozeson, 2004; Richards, 2005). To suppress the sidelobes some form of weighting can be applied to the matched filter response. The main drawbacks associated with conventional weighting functions (e.g., Hamming, Kaiser windows) are the broadening of the main lobe of the ambiguity function cut along the time axis and an inevitable attenuation in the peak response which decreases the signal-to-noise ratio.

The chapter provides theoretical justification for a new approach, which is being applied to the design of discrete weighting function, or in other words, digital mismatched receiving filters. This approach considers the design of weighting functions as a problem of finding such a digital mismatched filter that will maximize the proportion of the total response power that is concentrated in the specified time-frequency region.

Two applications of the proposed approach are theoretically addressed in sections 2 and 3. First, in section 2, we apply it to the problem of the optimum Doppler-tolerant pair signal-filter design when a given signal is specified to be an LFM signal. Section 3 addresses the specification of weighting functions in interferometric synthetic aperture radars with the purpose of improving the height measurement accuracy. Both of these sections are supplimented with numerical results, which demonstrate benefits that one can derive from using the proposed optimum weigthing functions as compared to conventional weighting functions. Conclusions are given in section 4.

2. Design of Doppler-tolerant weighting functions

In this section we develop a method for designing weighting functions or, in other words, mismatched filters for LFM signals in order to minimize the sidelobe level at the filter output with respect to that of the LFM ambiguity function and preserve its Doppler-tolerant behaviour as much as possible. First, we review the Doppler tolerance of LFM signals in terms of their analog and digital ambiguity functions, then we briefly discuss the concept of digital cross-ambiguity function and then proceed to the design of the optimum Doppler-tolerant weighting functions and numerical examples.

2.1 Doppler tolerance of LFM signals

The complex envelope $u(t)$ of a linear frequency modulated pulse (LFM pulse or signal) of duration T, bandwidth B and unity energy is given by

$$u(t) = \frac{1}{\sqrt{T}} \exp(j\pi\alpha t^2), \ \alpha = \pm\frac{B}{T} \tag{2-1}$$

where α is the frequency slope. The time - bandwidth product of the LFM signal is simply defined as BT. Hence, for the LFM pulse to be qualified as a pulse compression waveform, this product has to meet the condition $BT >> 1$.
The ambiguity function $\chi(\tau, \nu)$ of an LFM pulse can be analytically presented as

$$\chi(\tau,\ \nu) = \left| \left(1 - \frac{|\tau|}{T}\right) \frac{\sin\left[\pi T(\nu + \alpha\tau)(1 - |\tau|/T)\right]}{\left[\pi T(\nu + \alpha\tau)(1 - |\tau|/T)\right]} \right|, \quad |\tau| < T; \quad \text{zero otherwise} \tag{2-2}$$

where τ is the shift in time and ν is the Doppler shift of the received signal relative to the nominal values expected by the matched filter. From (2-2), the peak of this sinc-like function occurs when $\nu + \alpha\tau = 0$, i.e., at points lying on the straight line $\tau = \mp \nu T/B$. All the peaks occur along this line represent a so-called skewed "ridge" of the ambiguity function of LFM signals. Hence, when $\nu = \nu_s \neq 0$, which means that there is a Doppler mismatch between an LFM signal received from a moving point target and corresponding matched filter, the peak of (2-2) will not occur at $\tau = 0$ as it takes place when there is no Doppler mismatch ($\nu = 0$). Instead, the peak will be shifted with respect to the point $\tau = 0$ by an amount τ_s that is proportional to the Doppler shift ν_s

$$\tau = \mp \nu T / B \tag{2-3}$$

This phenomenon is termed "range-Doppler" coupling. An estimate of the target range is based on the position of this peak in time. Hence, any non-zero Doppler shift ν_s of an LFM signal results in a range measurement error proportional to the shift in time specified by equation (2-3). As also follows from (2-2), taking into account (2-3), the amplitude of the peak will be reduced by the factor

$$\delta = 1 - |\tau_s| / T = 1 - |\nu_s| / B\,. \tag{2-4}$$

Fig. 2-1 sketches out the ridge-like behaviour of the LFM ambiguity function along the straight line $\tau = -\nu T/B$ and the relationships (2-3) and (2-4).
Let the reduction factor δ be bounded below by a value of b; it is clear that $0 \le b \le \delta \le 1$. Using (2-4) yields the corresponding inequality for the acceptable Doppler shift

$$|\nu_s| \le B\left(1 - 10^{0.05b}\right) \tag{2-5}$$

and, from equation $|\nu_s| = 2|V_t|/\lambda$, for the radial target velocity V_t

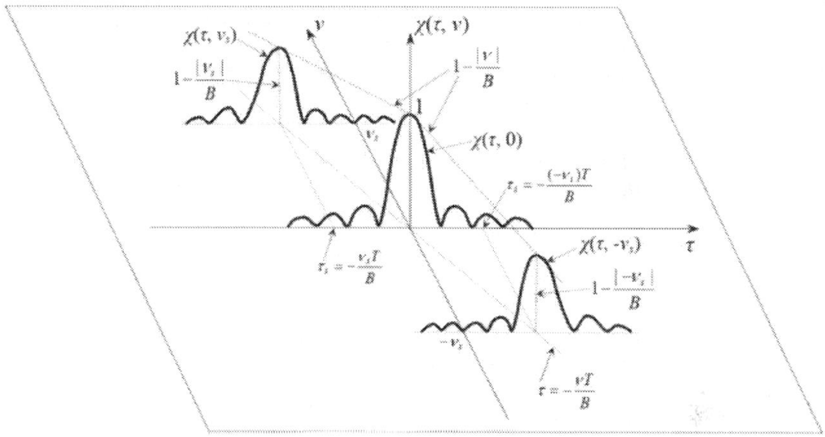

Fig. 2-1. Illusration of the ridge-like behaviour of the LFM ambiguity function

$$|V_t| \leq 0.5\lambda B\left(1-10^{0.05b}\right) \qquad (2\text{-}6)$$

where λ is the wavelength of the transmitted signal and b is specified in decibels.
Assuming B = 5 MHz, λ = 0.03m, and b = −0.1dB (this corresponds to b=0.9886≤δ ≤ 1) and using (2-5) and (2-6) yields $|v_s|/B \leq 0.0114$ and $|V_t| \leq 3090$ km/h, respectively. Hence, even for such a wide range of radial target velocity the reduction in amplitude at the output of the LFM matched filter does not exceed 0.1 dB (relative to the output peak for a zero-Doppler shift). Thus, one can conclude that Doppler tolerance is an intrinsic feature of the LFM signal, which reveals itself through the ridge of the LFM ambiguity function.
Athough the skewed ridge associated with the LFM ambiguity function causes errors in range and/or Doppler measurements it should be noted that the Doppler-tolerance of LFM signals can be an advantage in some applications. An example is in a search application since a preffered waveform to be used for target search should be Doppler-tolerant, so large Doppler shifts of targets whose velocity is not known does not prevent their detection due to a weak peak of the response at the matched filter output. This is also beneficial in terms of simplifying signal processor and detection hardware. If one were to use a biphase-coded signal in the same application one would need to have a bank of signal processors matched to a range of expected target Doppler shifts. This is because of the biphase-coded signal "thumbtack" ambiguity function, which features a single narrow central peak concentrated at the point $\tau = \nu = 0$, with the remaining energy spread uniformly all over the (τ, ν) plane (Levanon & Mozeson, 2004; Richards, 2005). Such features are useful for systems intended for high-resolution measurements in range and Doppler, or radar imaging.
Fig.2-2 compares the contours for the LFM ambiguity function and the ambiguity function of a biphase-coded signal. These contours correspond to a 3.92 dB level (Barton, 2005; Peebles, 1998) below maximum at (τ = 0, ν = 0). Both of the signals have equal pulse duration of T=MT_0 and bandwidth of $B \approx 1/T_0$, where M is the number of subpulses for the biphase-coded signal and T_0 is the duration of each subpulse.

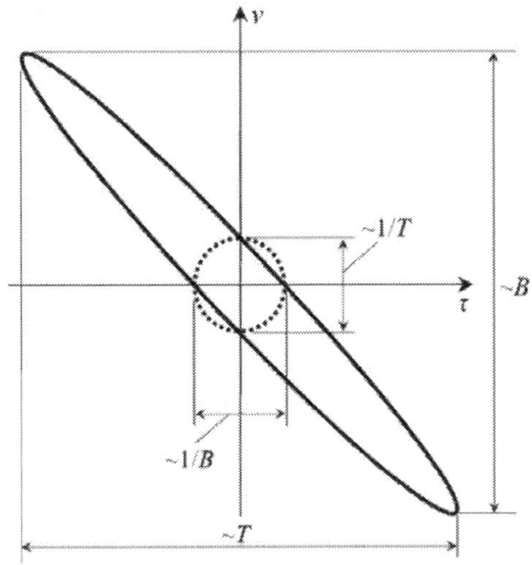

Fig. 2-2. Comparison of contours of ambiguity functions for LFM signal (solid line ellipse) and biphase-coded signal (dotted line circle) having the same pulse duration and badwidth

A disadvantage of the LFM ambiguity function is that it suffers from significant sidelobes, both in delay (range) and in Doppler. Consider, for example, a zero-Doppler cut of (2-2) $\chi(\tau\ ,\ 0)$, which is just the LFM matched filter output when there is no Doppler mismatch. Analyzing $\chi(\tau\ ,\ 0)$ under the condition $BT >> 1$, yelds that it exhibits the distinctly sinc-like main lobe and first few sidelobes (in magnitude). Due to this the first (and highest) range sidelobe in $\chi(\tau\ ,\ 0)$ is approximately equal to –13 dB and this value does not depend on the time-bandwidth product BT . Such a high sidelobe level is unacceptable in many applications since it may cause appreciable system performance degradation (Cook & Bernfeld, 1967; Levanon & Mozeson, 2004; Richards, 2005; Rosen et al., 2000).

2.2 Digital ambiguity function

The discussion in section 2.1 deals with analog LFM ambiguity function, i.e. it assumes that the LFM signal in radar receiver is processed by an ideal analog matched filter. Modern radar systems employ digital technologies so that it is instructive to discuss the features of a digital LFM ambiguity function that characterizes the response of a radar receiver when matched filtering is implemented by a digital signal processor.

First, we introduce a general relationship between the analog ambiguity function (analog matched filtering) and digital ambiguity function (digital implementation of the matched filter). In case of a point target the complex envelope of the received signal is given (ignoring amplitude coefficient) by $u(t-\tau)\exp[-j2\pi\nu(t-\tau)]$ where τ is the time delay and ν is the Doppler shift. Then, the complex envelope of a signal at the output of the analog filter matched to the transmitted signal $u(t)$ can be written as

$$\begin{aligned} A(t',\tau,\nu) &= \int_{-\infty}^{\infty} u(t-\tau)\exp[-j2\pi\nu(t-\tau)]\cdot u^*[-(t'-t)]dt \\ &= \exp[-j2\pi\nu(t'-\tau)]\cdot \int_{-\infty}^{\infty} u(t+t'-\tau)u^*(t)e^{-j2\pi\nu t}\,dt. \end{aligned} \tag{2-7}$$

Expression (2-7) is usually simplified by dropping the insignificant phase factor $\exp[-j2\pi v(t'-\tau)]$ and replacing $t' -\tau$ with τ . Thus, we arrive at the definition of the complex ambiguity function

$$A_a(\tau,v)=\int_{-\infty}^{\infty}u(t+\tau)u^*(t)e^{-j2\pi vt}\,dt \tag{2-8}$$

where subscript a stands for "analog". The analog ambiguity function is defined as the magnitude of (2-8)

$$\chi_a(\tau,v)=|A_a(\tau,v)|\cdot \tag{2-9}$$

In digital receivers, the sampled complex envelope of the received signal can be represented as $u(nT_s-\tau)\exp[-j2\pi v(nT_s-\tau)]$, where $n = ...,- 2,-1, 0, 1, 2, ...,$ and T_s is the sampling period that can be presented as $T_s= 1/(gB)$, where $g\geq 1$ is the oversampling factor.
Since the unit sample response of the digital version of the matched filter is given by $u^*(-nT_s)$ the complex digital ambiguity function can be easily shown to be

$$A_d(\tau,v)=\sum_{n=-\infty}^{\infty}u(nT_s+\tau)u^*(nT_s)e^{-j2\pi vnT_s}. \tag{2-10}$$

The definition for the digital ambiguity function is similar to (2-9)

$$\chi_d(\tau,v)=|A_d(\tau,v)|. \tag{2-11}$$

As has been shown (Blankenship & Hofstetter, 1975), there exists a simple relationship between the analog and digital ambiguity functions, which is given by

$$A_d(\tau,v)=\sum_{n=-\infty}^{\infty}A_a(\tau,\, v+nF_s) \tag{2-12}$$

where $F_s= 1/T_s$ is the sampling frequency. Thus, the complex digital ambiguity function is a sum of the replicas of the complex analog ambiguity function displaced to all frequencies nF_s. Inspecting (2-12) yields that it is similar to the well known relationship between the Fourier transforms of an analog signal and its sampled version. It is also clear that equation (2-12) allows to quickly draw contour plots (ambiguity diagrams) for the digital LFM ambiguity functions at different sampling frequencies by using contour plots for the analog LFM anbuguity finction. The contour plots provide insight into the gross behavior of the LFM digital ambiguity function. Thus, for the purpose of detailed analysis an exact mathematical expresson for this function is necessary. As has been shown (Blankenship & Hofstetter, 1975), the exact formula for the digital LFM ambiguity function is given by

$$\chi_d(\tau,v)=\left|\frac{\sin\left[\pi\frac{N}{M}\left(k+x-\frac{M}{N}y\right)\left(1-\frac{|k|}{M}\right)\right]}{\sin\left[\pi\frac{N}{M^2}\left(k+x-\frac{M}{N}y\right)\right]}\right|,\ |k|\leq M-1 \tag{2-13}$$

Where $N=BT$, $y=vT$, and $M=T/T_s$ is the integer number of the LFM signal samples taken over the total signal duration T. Formula (2-13) assumes $\tau=(k+x)T_s$, where k is an integer and $0\leq x<1$.

Blankenship and Hofstetter studied the digital LFM ambiguity function by using (2-13) and contour plots. In particular, they have shown that in the digital case even with Nyquist rate sampling, i.e. with $T_s = 1/B$, the sidelobes do not fall off uniformly with increasing $|\tau|$, but increase as $|\tau|$ nears the ends of the response interval ($\pm T$). The reason for this is that the aliased replicas of the analog ambiguity function produce increased sidelobe levels for large values of $|\tau|$. Hence, increasing the sampling rate should reduce this effect. Indeed, it has been shown that for sampling at twice the Nyquist rate, i.e., with $T_s = 1/(2B)$, the behavior of the digital LFM ambiguity functions is essentially indistinguishable from that of analog one. Here we supplement that study by illustrating the ridge (peak signal amplitude) for the digital LFM ambiguity function (Fig. 2-3) computed for $T_s = 1/B$ and $T_s = 1/(2B)$. Fig. 2-3 clearly demonstrates appreciable improvement in the Doppler tolerance for sampling at twice the Nyquist rate.

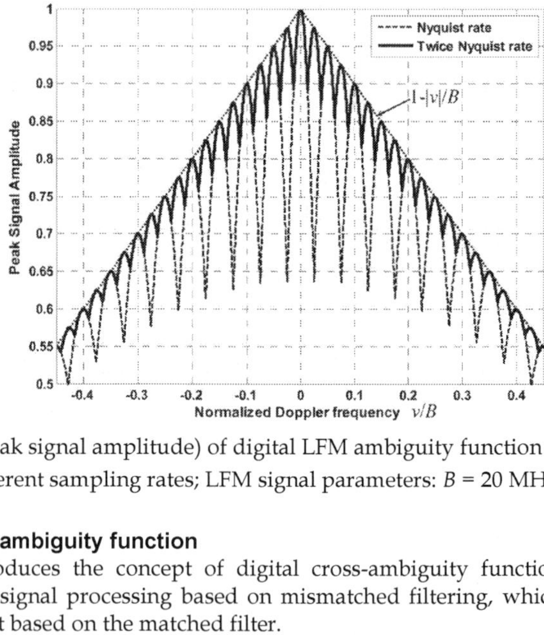

Fig. 2-3. Ridge (peak signal amplitude) of digital LFM ambiguity function versus Doppler frequency for different sampling rates; LFM signal parameters: B = 20 MHz, $T = 10^{-6}$ s

2.3 Digital cross-ambiguity function

This section introduces the concept of digital cross-ambiguity function that is directly related to digital signal processing based on mismatched filtering, which is more general structure than that based on the matched filter.

By analogy with (2-10) we have for the complex digital cross-ambiguity function

$$A_d^w(\tau,\nu) = \sum_{n=-\infty}^{\infty} u(nT_s + \tau) w^*(nT_s) e^{-j2\pi\nu nT_s} \tag{2-14}$$

where $w^*(nT_s)$ corresponds to the unit sample response of the digital mismatched filter.

By letting $\tau = (k+x)T_s$, where k is an integer and $0 \le x < 1$, one can represent the samples of the received signal $u(nT_s + \tau)e^{-j2\pi\nu nT_s}$ in (2-14) as the column vector

$$u^x(\nu) = [u_1^x(\nu)\ u_2^x(\nu)\ \dots\ u_N^x(\nu)]^T \tag{2-15}$$

where $u^x(\nu) = [u_1^x(\nu)\ u_2^x(\nu)\ \dots\ u_N^x(\nu)]^T$. The integer k is omitted since in computing the output of a digital filter the time shift kT_s is a shift of the train of N received samples [vector

$u^x(v)$] by k samples [to the left if $k < 0$ or to the right if $k \geq 0$ when we look at the filtering operation as a complex correlator] with respect to N samples of the reference sequence specified by the vector $u^0(0)$.
Next, define a receiving filter vector w of length $M \geq N$

$$w = [w_1 \; w_2 \; \dots \; w_M]^T \tag{2-16}$$

Since the filter length M can be equal to or greater than N we will use the extended signal vector $s^x(v) = [s_1^x(v)\; s_2^x(v) \dots s_M^x(v)]^T$, which is zero-padded vector $u^x(v)$, to match the length M of the vector w . We define this extended signal vector as

$$s^x(v) = \begin{cases} [\underbrace{0\;0 \dots 0}_{(M-N)/2\,\text{zeros}}\; u_1^x(v)\; u_2^x(v) \dots u_N^x(v)\; \underbrace{0\;0 \dots 0}_{(M-N)/2\,\text{zeros}}]^T, & \text{if } M-N \text{ is even} \\ [\underbrace{0\;0 \dots 0}_{(M-N-1)/2\,\text{zeros}}\; u_1^x(v)\; u_2^x(v) \dots u_N^x(v)\; \underbrace{0\;0 \dots 0}_{(M-N+1)/2\,\text{zeros}}]^T, & \text{if } M-N \text{ is odd} \end{cases} \tag{2-17}$$

Then the digital cross-ambiguity function (DCAF) is given by the cross-correlation function between the vectors $s^x(v)$ and w as

$$A_d^w[k,x,v] = \sum_{n=1}^{M} s_{n-k}^x(v) w_n^* \tag{2-18}$$

where $-(M-1) \leq k \leq M-1$, and $s_{n-k}^x(v)$ must be identically zero for $n-k < 1$ and $n-k > M$.
Next, consider the DCAF for integer delay k. As follows from (2-18), it is given by

$$A_d^w[k,v] = A_d^w[k,x,v]\Big|_{x=0} \tag{2-19}$$

where $A_d^w[0,0]$ is the main peak value of the DCAF. Defining the M-by-$(2M-1)$ matrix

$$S(v) = \begin{bmatrix} s_M^0(v) & \cdots & s_2^0(v) & s_1^0(v) & 0 & \cdots & 0 \\ 0 & s_M^0(v) & \cdots & s_2^0(v) & s_1^0(v) & \ddots & 0 \\ \vdots & \ddots & \ddots & \vdots & \ddots & \ddots & \vdots \\ 0 & \cdots & 0 & s_M^0(v) & \cdots & s_2^0(v) & s_1^0(v) \end{bmatrix} \tag{2-20}$$

permits to rewrite (2-18) in the matrix form as

$$r(v) = w^{\sim} S(v) \tag{2-21}$$

where the row vector $r(v) = [r_1(v), \cdots, r_{M-1}(v), r_M(v), r_{M+1}(v), \cdots, r_{2M-1}(v)]$ represents the DCAF (2-19) according to the relation

$$r_n(v) = A_d^w[n-M,v], \; n = 1,2,\dots,2M-1 \tag{2-22}$$

and the symbol "~" denotes a hermitian or conjugate transpose. From (2-19) and (2-22), one can observe that $r_M(0)$ corresponds to the peak value of the DCAF at the point $\tau = 0, v = 0$.

2.4 Optimum weighting functions

Following (Harris, 1978; Nuttal, 1981; Van Trees, 2002) one can choose among several different approaches to the design of optimum weighting functions. In view of our intention to minimize sidelobe level and preserve as much as possible the ridge-like behaviour of the mismatched filter response we shall follow an approach based on the physical meaning of the optimal discrete prolate sequences. For instance, in (Donald & James, 1970; Greene, 2007) the optimal discrete prolate sequence is interpreted as such a sequence that maximizes the proportion of its total power in a specified frequency interval or, referring to (Van Trees, 2002), as a weighting function that maximizes the percentage of the total power (radiated by an antenna) that is concentrated in a given angular region.

By analogy, the problem in question can be formulated as a problem of finding such a weighting function (mismatched filter) that will maximize the percentage of the total power that is concentrated in the specified mainlobe region of the DCAF. This percentage can be written as

$$\xi = \frac{\sum\limits_{n\in R_k}\sum\limits_{|v_k|\le v_{\max}} |r_n(v_k)|^2}{\sum\limits_{n=1}^{2M-1}\sum\limits_{|v_k|\le v_{\max}} |r_n(v_k)|^2}. \quad (2\text{-}23)$$

The numerator in (2-23) represents the power for a specified mainlobe region (Fig. 2-4), which is simply a sum of the squared samples of the DCAF $|r_n(v_k)|^2$, which belong to the set R_k that contains the points associated with the ridge for k th Doppler cut specified by the frequency $|v_k| \le v_{\max}$, where $k = 1,2,...,K = 2L+1$, $L = v_{\max}/\Delta v$, Δv is the step in Doppler frequency and $v_{\max}$ is the maximum Doppler shift of interest. The denominator represents the full power, which is the total sum of the squared samples of the DCAF taken over all points in range (n = 1, 2,..., $2M-1$) for each Doppler cut.

The integer parameter d_k represents the shift of the peak value of the DCAF for k th Doppler cut with respect to the point $\tau = 0$, $v = 0$ (this is the point $n = M$, $v_{L+1} = 0$ in Fig. 2- 4). To preserve the skew of the ridge it is reasonable to select the values of d_k to be equal to those of corresponding Doppler cuts from the digital LFM ambiguity function. The parameter m is a positive integer value that determines the width of the mainlobe region. For example, setting m=g (if the oversampling factor g is a positive integer) means that the mainlobe extent is equal to that of the standard sinc-function (at the first zero points $\tau = \pm 1/B$) that correspons to a signal having rectangular spectrum of width B or to that of a zero-Doppler cut of the LFM ambiguity function $\chi(\tau, 0)$ as can be seen from (2-2) provided $BT >> 1$. In general, the value of m can be varied depending on the Doppler cut. To formally specify the mainlobe region for kth Doppler cut of the DCAF we shall use a weighting vector V_{ML}^k of the length $2M$-1. As can be seen from Fig. 2-5, for a zero-Doppler cut this vector can be written as

$$V_{ML}^{L+1} = [\underbrace{\overset{1}{0}\,\overset{2}{0}\cdots\overset{M-m-1}{0}}_{\substack{M-m-1\text{ zeros}\\ \text{Sidelobe region}}}\;\underbrace{\overset{M-m}{1}\cdots\overset{M-1}{1}\;\overset{M}{1}\;\overset{M+1}{1}\cdots\overset{M+m}{1}}_{\substack{2m+1\text{ units}\\ \text{Mainlobe region}}}\;\underbrace{\overset{M+m+1}{0}\cdots\overset{2M-2}{0}\;\overset{2M-1}{0}}_{\substack{M-m-1\text{ zeros}\\ \text{Sidelobe region}}}]^{\mathrm{T}}. \quad (2\text{-}24)$$

For arbitrary k th Doppler cut this vector is given by

$$V_{ML}^{k} = [\underbrace{\overset{1}{0}\,\overset{2}{0}\cdots\overset{M-d_k-m-1}{0}}_{\substack{M-d_k-m-1\text{ zeros}\\ \text{Sidelobe region}}}\;\underbrace{\overset{M-d_k-m}{1}\cdots\overset{M-d_k-1}{1}\;\overset{M-d_k}{1}\;\overset{M-d_k+1}{1}\cdots\overset{M-d_k+m}{1}}_{\substack{2m+1\text{ units}\\ \text{Mainlobe region}}}\;\underbrace{\overset{M-d_k+m+1}{0}\cdots\overset{2M-2}{0}\;\overset{2M-1}{0}}_{\substack{M+d_k-m-1\text{ zeros}\\ \text{Sidelobe region}}}]^{\mathrm{T}}. \quad (2\text{-}25)$$

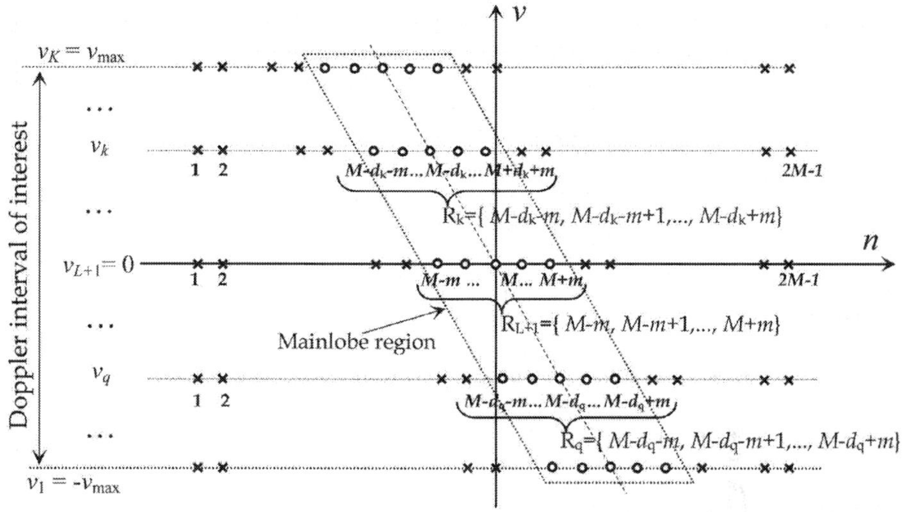

Fig. 2-4. Illustration of mainlobe region in the time-frequncy plane

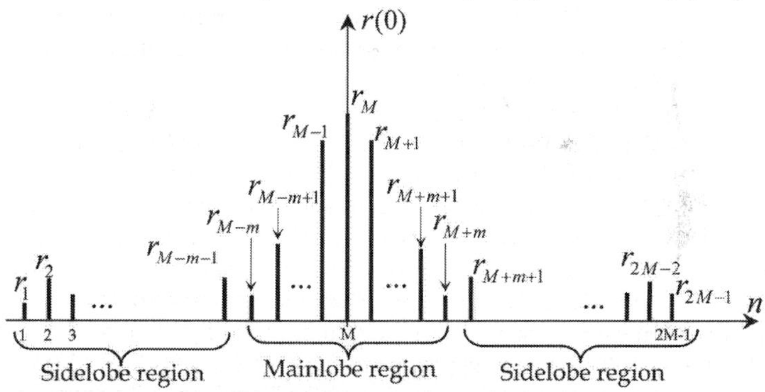

Fig. 2-5. Mainlobe and sidelobe regions for zero-Doppler cut

By using (2-25) the mainlobe power for the k th Doppler cut, which is a sum of $|r_n(v_k)|^2$ for $n \in R_k = \{M-d_k-m,\ M-d_k-m+1,\ldots,\ M-d_k+m\}$, can be written as

$$P_{ML}^{k} = \sum_{n\in R_k} |r_n(v_k)|^2 = r(v_k) Q_{ML}^{k} r^{\sim}(v_k) \tag{2-26}$$

where the matrix Q_{ML}^{k} is $(2M-1)$-by-$(2M-1)$ diagonal matrix: its diagonal is equal to the weighting vector V_{ML}^{k} and non-diagonal elements are zeros.

Substituting (2-21) into (2-26) yields the following real-valued quadratic form

$$P_{ML}^{k} = w^{\sim} B_{ML}^{k} w \tag{2-27}$$

where the M-by-M matrix B_{ML}^k is given by

$$B_{ML}^k = S(v_k) Q_{ML}^k S^{\sim}(v_k). \tag{2-28}$$

The total power in the mainlobe region is

$$P_{ML} = \sum_{k=1}^{K} P_{ML}^k = \sum_{k=1}^{K} w^{\sim} B_{ML}^k w = w^{\sim} B_{ML} w, \tag{2-29}$$

where the M-by-M matrix B_{ML} is given by

$$B_{ML} = \sum_{k=1}^{K} B_{ML}^k = \sum_{k=1}^{K} S(v_k) Q_{ML}^k S^{\sim}(v_k). \tag{2-30}$$

The total power in the k th Doppler cut is

$$P_{TL}^k = \sum_{n=1}^{2M-1} | r_n(v_k) |^2 = r(v_k) Q_{TL} r^{\sim}(v_k). \tag{2-31}$$

The matrix Q_{TL} in (2-31) is a $(2M-1)$-by-$(2M-1)$ unity matrix since (2-31) will present the total power only when the diagonal of Q_{TL} is equal to the weighting vector V_{TL} with all elements that are unity

$$V_{TL} = [\overset{1}{1}\ \overset{2}{1}\ \overset{3}{1}\ \cdots\ \overset{2M-2}{1}\ \ \overset{2M-1}{1}\ ]^{\mathrm{T}}. \tag{2-32}$$

Using (2-21) and (2-31) yields the total power for all Doppler cuts

$$P_{TL} = \sum_{k=1}^{K} P_{TL}^k = w^{\sim} B_{TL} w \tag{2-33}$$

where the M-by-M matrix B_{TL} is given by

$$B_{TL} = \sum_{k=1}^{K} B_{TL}^k = \sum_{k=1}^{K} S(v_k) Q_{TL} S^{\sim}(v_k). \tag{2-34}$$

Thus, the ratio (2-23), which is to be maximized with respect to w, can be written as

$$\xi = \frac{w^{\sim} B_{ML} w}{w^{\sim} B_{TL} w}. \tag{2-35}$$

The maximization of the ratio (2-35) is equivalent to the following minimization problem

$$\min_{w} w^{\sim} B_{TL} w \quad \text{subject to} \quad w^{\sim} B_{ML} w = 1. \tag{2-36}$$

The solution to (2-36) can be found by minimizing the function

$$f(w,\mu) = w^{\sim} B_{TL} w + \mu(1 - w^{\sim} B_{ML} w), \tag{2-37}$$

where μ is the Langrange multiplier. Taking the gradient of (2-37) with respect to w and equating it to zero, we find that the solution to (2-36) is given by the following generalized eigenvalue problem

$$B_{TL} w = \mu B_{ML} w, \tag{2-38}$$

where μ can be interpreted as a corresponding generalized eigenvalue. It should be noted that all generalized eigenvalue in (2-38) are positive real numbers. Indeed, multiplying both sides of (2-38) by $w^{\sim}$ yields $w^{\sim} B_{TL} w = \mu w^{\sim} B_{ML} w$. As follows from (2-26)-(2-29) and (2- 31)-(2-33) P_{TL} >0 and P_{ML} >0 because either of the sums in (2-29) and (2-33) contains at least one real positive term $|r_M(0)|^2$, hence, the matrices B_{TL} and B_{ML} are positive definite. This proves that μ is always real positive value.

Therefore, the solution to (2-37) is the generalized eigenvector corresponding to the minimum generalized eigenvalue of (2-38). Multiplying (2-38) by B_{TL}^{-1} yields

$$B_{TL}^{-1} B_{ML} w = \frac{1}{\mu} w = \zeta w \cdot \tag{2-39}$$

Since μ is always real and positive the minimum generalized eigenvalue $\mu_{\min}$ in (2-38) corresponds to the maximum eigenvalue $\zeta_{\max} = 1/\mu_{\min}$ in (2-39). By using this fact, the optimum weighting function (weighting coefficients of the optimum mismatched filter) can be represented as

$$w_{opt} = \mathbf{P}\{B_{TL}^{-1} B_{ML}\} \tag{2-40}$$

where $\mathbf{P}\{A\}$ is the operator, which returns the principal eigenvector of a matrix A, that is, the eigenvector corresponding to its maximum eigenvalue. As follows from (2-36), the optimum vector w_{opt} has to be normalized to satisfy the constraint in (2-36). Since any eigenvector can be normalized arbitrarily, is is clear that multiplying w_{opt} by an appropriate non-zero constant gives a vector w'_{opt}, which meets the requirement $(w'_{opt})^{\sim} B_{ML} w'_{opt} = 1$. On the other hand, it is clear from (2-35) that multiplying w_{opt} by any non-zero constant does not affect the ratio (2-35). Therefore, such normalization of w_{opt} is unimportant. In this chapter we use the vector of signal $u^x(s^x)$ and the weighting vectors w (both for the optimum and conventional weighting functions) that are normalized to be of unit norm vectors, that is, $\|u^x\| = \|s^x\| = 1$ and $\|w\| = 1$.

2.5 Numerical examples

In all numerical examples of this section, we assume an LFM signal of B = 20MHz, T = 1 μs, and the oversampling factor g = 2. Hence, N = 40 complex samples (vector of length N) are used to present the complex envelope of the LFM signal. The step in the normalized Doppler frequency $\Delta v/B$=0.005 is chosen in all calculations.

In our first example we consider the optimum weighting function of length M = N = 40 computed by using (2-40) with the parameter $m = g = 2$ for $v_{\max} / B$ =0, 0.05, 0.1, 0.2 and 0.4. The condition $m = g$ means that the mainlobe width of the DCAF is specified to be equal to that of a zero-Doppler cut of the LFM ambiguity function (2-2) measured at the first zeros. Table 2-1 compares the percentage of the mainlobe power (2-35) for the optimum weighting function (OF) with that for the matched filter (MF) and Kaiser window (KW). The parameter

β (Table 2-1) for the Kaiser window (in the time domain) is selected to provide the same mainlobe width as that for the optimum weighting function. The maximum sidelobe level, the loss L_w^0 in the signal-to-noise ratio (SNR) and 3 dB mainlobe broadening (all these parameters are measured in a zero-Doppler cut) for the optimum filter and Kaiser window are also included in Table 2-1.
One can easily show that the SNR loss due to weigthing is given by

$$L_w^x = \frac{|w^{\sim} s^x|^2}{w^{\sim} w \cdot s^{x\sim} s^x}, \quad 0 < L_w^x \leq 1. \tag{2-41}$$

The 3dB mainlobe broadening is defined as the ratio $b_{ML} = W_{WF}/W_{MF}$ where W_{WF} and W_{MF} are the mainlobe width at -3 dB level for a zero-Doppler cut of the DCAF in case of mismatched filtering (for conventional or optimum weighting functions) and digital LFM ambiguity function (matched filtering), respectively.

$\frac{v_{max}}{B}$	Percentage of the mainlobe power ξ, %			Maximum sidelobe, dB		SNR loss L_w^0, dB/ β		3dB mainlobe broadening, b_{ML}	
	MF	KW	OF	KW	OF	KW	OF	KW	OF
0	90.979	97.201	99.541	-20.6	-29.2	-0.483/2.7	-0.772	1.21	1.21
0.05	90.997	97.060	99.531	-20.2	-29.1	-0.442/2.6	-0.769	1.20	1.20
0.1	91.047	96.901	99.502	-19.8	-29.1	-0.402/2.5	-0.761	1.19	1.19
0.2	91.229	96.716	99.393	-19.5	-28.8	-0.363/2.4	-0.767	1.17	1.17
0.4	91.282	96.330	99.157	-18.7	-28.8	-0.289/2.2	-0.805	1.16	1.16

Table 2-1. Comparison of the matched filter (MF), Kaiser weighting (KW) and optimum filter (OF) in terms of the mainlobe power percentage, maximum sidelobe, SNR loss and mainlobe broadening for the optimum filter of length M= N = 40 designed for m = g=2

As can be seen from Table 2-1, the percentage of the mainlobe power (ξ) for the optimum weigthing exceeds those for the matched filter and Kaiser window by about 8.5% and 2.5%, respectively, for a wide range of the Doppler interval of interest ($|v_{max}|/B \leq 0.4$). Despite these relatively small gains in ξ the optimum weigthing provides appreciable reduction in sidelobes. As one can see, the maximum sidelobe level measured in a zero- Doppler cut is about -29 dB; this is by 15 dB below that for the matched filter and by about 9 dB below that for the KW (under the conditions the data in Table 2-1 are computed). The price paid for the sidelobe suppression is quite low. Indeed, the SNR loss for the OF is about -0.8 dB with respect to that of the MF and -(0.3 … 0.5) dB as compared to that for the KW. Second, the mainlobe broadening against the MF is also relatively small, it ranges from 1.21 to 1.16 for $|v_{max}|/B = 0, 0.05, 0.1, 0.2$ and 0.4, respectively.
Fig. 2-6 illustrates the sidelobe suppression for the optimum weighting by comparing a zero-Doppler cut of the digital cross-ambiguity function for the optimum filter (designed for $v_{max}/B = 0.1$) with corresponding zero-Doppler cuts for the Kaiser window and matched filter. To get more pictorial view for comparison all these cuts are normalized so that the magnitudes of their peak values are equal to unity (zero on the dB-scale). The Doppler tolerance of the optimum filter is illustrated in Fig. 2-7 that compares the ridge (peak signal amplitude) of the DCAF for the optimum filter ($v_{max}/B = 0.1$) with those for the

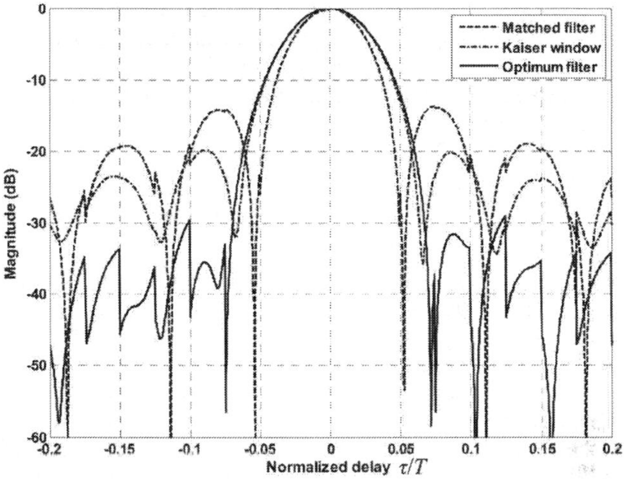

Fig. 2-6. Zero-Doppler cuts of digital cross-ambiguity functions for the optimum filter (M=N=40, m=g=2, $\nu_{max}/B = 0.1$) and Kaiser window and zero-Doppler cut of digital ambiguity function for the matched filter

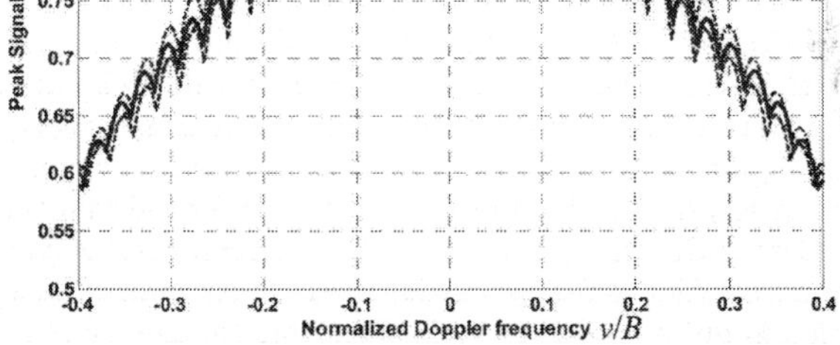

Fig. 2-7. Doppler tolerance of the optimum filter designed with M=N=40 and m=g=2 for $\nu_{max}/B = 0.1$

corresponding Kaiser window and matched filter. As one can see in Fig. 2-7, for $|\nu|/B \leq 0.1$ the ridge of the DCAF for the optimal filter goes slightly below that for the Kaiser window (due to the SNR loss of – 0.36 dB). This means that the optimum filter maximizes the ratio (2-35) chiefly through the sidelobe suppression.

In the second example we illustrate a new feature of the proposed optimum weighting that convetional weightings do not possess in principle. This feature can be realized when the parameter m, which determines the width of the mainlobe region in time delay, is less than the oversampling factor g. The condition $m<g$ means that the mainlobe width of the DCAF is specified to be less than that for a zero-Doppler cut of (2-2) measured at the first zeros. Since the optimum filter is designed under this condition the maximum percentage of the mainlobe power is concentrated within a narrower "strip" than for the matched filter. Hence, one should expect that there will be no mainlobe broadening and no range resolution degradation with respect to the matched filter.

Table 2-2 presents the percentage of the mainlobe power, maximum sidelobe level, the SNR loss L_w^0 and 3dB mainlobe broadening (in zero-Doppler cut) for the OF of length M=1.2N=48 designed under the condition $m = g - 1 = 1$. Since there is no simple formula that directly relates the SNR loss L_w^x to m and M for the OF, it was numerically found for $N \le M \le 1.5N$ that the SNR loss does not exceed 3 dB and the maximum sidelobe level is approximately minimized at M= 1.2N= 48 for all v_{max}/B given in Table 2-2.

$\frac{v_{max}}{B}$	Percentage of the mainlobe power ξ, % OF / MF	Maximum sidelobe, dB	SNR loss, dB	3dB mainlobe broadening, b_{ML}
0	99.351 / 90.730	-22.1	-1.426	0.97
0.05	99.302 / 90.651	-22.3	-1.459	0.96
0.1	99.172/ 90.429	-22.8	-1.571	0.95
0.2	98.725 / 89.556	-23.6	-2.120	0.92
0.4	98.275 / 88.631	-20.3	-2.775	0.89

Table 2-2. Percentage of the mainlobe power for optimum filter/matched filter (OF/MF), maximum sidelobe, SNR loss and mainlobe broadening for optimum filter of length M= 1.2N = 48 designed for $m = g$-1=1 at different v_{max}/B

As can be seen from Table 2-2, for the optimum weighting with M = 48, m = 1 the 3dB mainlobe broadening b_{ML} <1, as expected. Therefore, there is no degradation in the range resolution with respect to the matched filter. The price paid for this is relatively large SNR loss (from -1.5dB to -2.8dB depending on the Doppler extent v_{max}/B) and an increase in the maximum sidelobes (about 8 dB) with respect to the OF designed under the condition m=g (see Table 2-1). At the same time the maximum sidelobe level is somewhat lower (by about 1.5 dB) than that for the Kaiser window from Table 2-1.

The behaviour of the DCAF for the OF designed with M =48, m=1 for v_{max}/B=0.1 is illustrated by Figs. 2-8 - 2.10. Fig. 2-8 compares a zero-Doppler cut of the DCAF for the OF with that for the matched filter. The Doppler tolerance of this filter is illustrated in Fig. 2-9. The digital cross-ambigutiy functions (3-D presentations) and corresponding contour plots (at two levels of -3.92dB and -13.32dB) for the optimum filters with M = 40, m = 2 and M = 48, m = 1 (both are designed for v_{max}/B=0.1) are shown in Fig. 2-10 (a) and (b), respectively.

Analyzing the plots in Fig. 2-8 and Fig. 2-9 and the percentage of the mainlobe power for the OF and MF (Table 2-2) we again arrive at the conclusion that the optimum filter (2-40) chiefly maximizes the ratio (2-35) by supressing the sidelobes. Comparing Fig 2-10 (a) and (b) reveals increased sidelobes: additional contour lines at a level of -13.32 dB in the latter. This increase in sidelobe level is due to narrower mainlobe region for the OF with M =48, m =1 against that for the OF with M =40, m =2. The fundamental property of the cross-ambiguty function says that it is impossible to remove energy from one portion of the cross-ambiguity surface without placing it somewhere else on the (τ, v) plane.

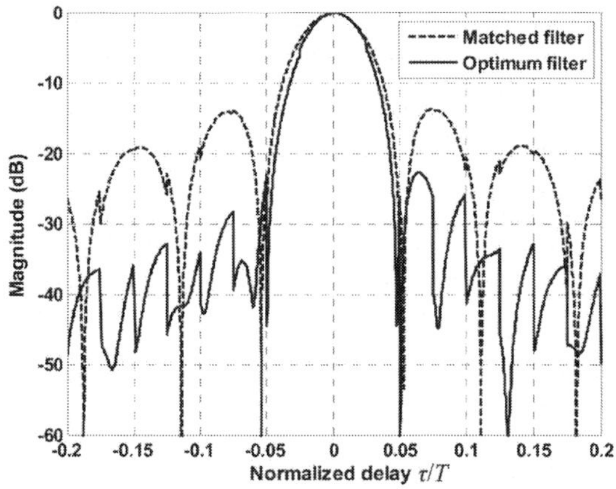

Fig. 2-8. Zero-Doppler cuts for the optimum (M= 48, m= 1) and matched filters

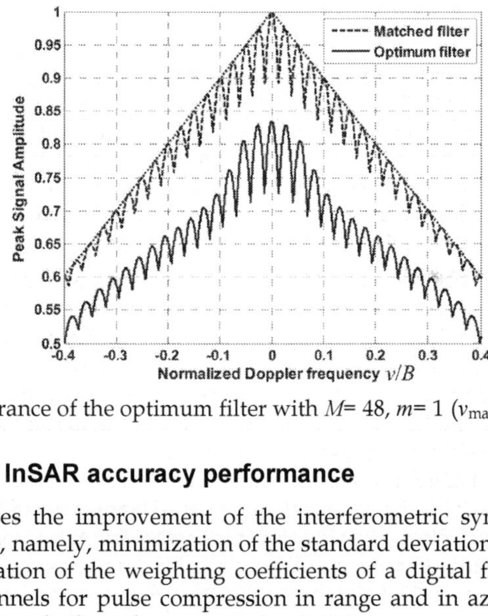

Fig. 2-9. Doppler tolerance of the optimum filter with M= 48, m= 1 ($\nu_{\max}/B$ = 0.1)

3. Optimization of InSAR accuracy performance

This section addresses the improvement of the interferometric synthetic aperture radar (InSAR) performance, namely, minimization of the standard deviation of the height estimate through the optimization of the weighting coefficients of a digital filter to be used in the InSAR receiving channels for pulse compression in range and in azimuth dimension. For simplicity we consider only the pulse compression in range.

The matched filter is an optimum filter under the criterion of maximum signal-to-noise ratio (SNR) in the presence of white noise. This section deals with such a filter that approximates to an optimum filter under a different criterion: the minimum of the height-standard deviation σ_h. As is well known, (e.g., Rosen et al., 2000) applying conventional weighting in the InSAR receiving channels allows decreasing σ_h against matched filtering although the SNR in the event of weighting is inevitably less than that in the event of matched filtering. Thus, strictly speaking, the optimum filter in terms of the minimum of the height-standard deviation σ_h belongs to a class of mismatched filters.

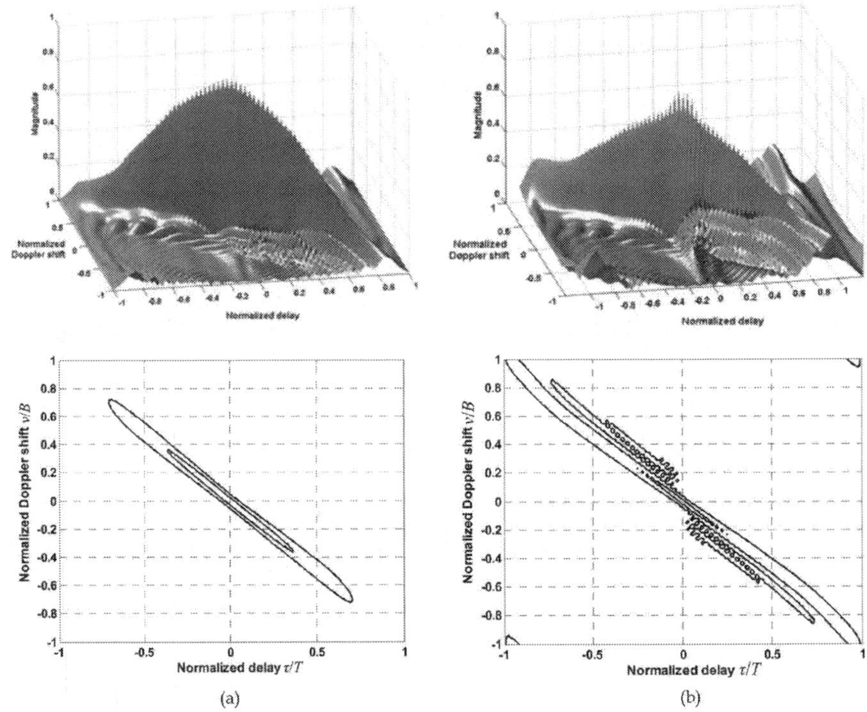

Fig. 2-10. Digital cross-ambiguity functions and corresponding contour plots (below) for optimum filters with (a) M= 40, m= 2 and (b) M= 48, m= 1 ($\nu_{\max}/B$ = 0.1)

3.1 Height estimation accuracy

The magnitude γ of the full correlation function between InSAR channels is given by $\gamma = \gamma_G \gamma_N \gamma_Z \gamma_T$ (Rosen et al., 2000), where γ_G is the geometric (baseline) correlation, γ_N is the correlation due to thermal noise in the interferometric channels, γ_Z is the correlation due to volume scattering, and γ_T represents the temporal correlation (in repeat-pass systems). From (Rodriguez & Martin, 1992; Rosen et al., 2000) it follows that increasing γ results in decreasing the standard deviation of inferred interferometric phase estimates and correspondingly derived height values.

As has been pointed out in (Baskakov&Ka, 2000; Rosen et al., 2000), modifying the system point target response (PTR) in range by applying different weighting functions in the InSAR receiving channels, one can change the shape of the geometric correlation γ_G to reduce the phase noise. It should be noted, that as has been shown (Gatteli et al., 1994) one can obtain γ_G = 1 (at least theoretically) by using a kind of band-pass filtering (Rosen et al., 2000) of signals from both channels so that they have slightly different center frequencies. The relationship between these frequencies depends on the look angle and surface slope, so that an adaptive iterative procedure is needed to implement this approach (Rosen et al., 2000). In this paper we will try deriving benefits from practically much simpler approach, which is based on using weighting.

The major implication of weighting in an InSAR is that it allows increasing the total correlation γ due to increasing the geometric correlation γ_G, and, consequently, reducing height estimation errors, other conditions being equal. Examples given in (Rosen, et al., 2000) for conventional weighting functions demonstrate improved shapes of geometric correlation with weightings against that for a standard sinc response with no weighting.

However, at least two significant problems associated with weighting have not been discussed in (Rosen et al., 2000). First, it is well-known, that applying weighting inevitably leads to the signal-to-noise (SNR) degradation in the interferometric channels, which, in turn, results in decreasing the correlation due to thermal noise γ_N. If this decrease in γ_N prevails over an increase in γ_G, then the full correlation γ will degrade that finally results in deterioration of the height estimation accuracy. Another problem associated with weighting is degradation of the InSAR resolution due to mainlobe broadening of the PTR in range.

The effect of conventional weighting on the InSAR performance was analyzed in (Baskakov & Ka, 2000) for Hamming and Gauss weightings. It has been claimed that conventional weighting gives an improvement in the height accuracy only for small relative baselines [the ratios of B(see Fig. 3-1) to the wavelength λ], while for large relative baselines weighting leads to significant deterioration in performance.

The maximum-likelihood (ML) estimator presented in (Rodriguez & Martin, 1992) can be used as an accurate estimator of the interferometric phase from homogeneous distributed targets. That ML estimator is unbiased modulo 2π, and its standard deviation can be easily obtained by using Monte-Carlo simulations. The Cramér-Rao lower bound (CRLB) on the standard deviation σ_Φ in unbiased estimation of the interferometric phase is given by

$$\sigma_\Phi = \frac{1}{\sqrt{(2N_L)}}\frac{\sqrt{1-\gamma^2}}{\gamma} \tag{3-1}$$

where N_L is the number of looks. It has been shown (Rodriguez & Martin, 1992) that the phase-standard deviation of the ML estimator approaches the limit given by (3-1) very rapidly with number of looks for the first four looks, especially if the correlation γ is high. Hence, formula (3-1) gives a reasonable approximation for the phase-standard deviation of the ML estimator when the inequality $N_L \geq 4$ holds true.

Using (3-1) one can relate the full correlation to height estimation errors as (Rodriguez & Martin, 1992; Ka & Kononov 2007)

$$\sigma_h = \frac{\lambda H \tan\theta}{2\pi B_n}\frac{1}{\sqrt{(2N_L)}}\frac{\sqrt{1-\gamma^2}}{\gamma} \tag{3-2}$$

where σ_h is the standard deviation of height errors, H is the height of a spacecraft, $B_n = B\cos(\alpha - \theta)$ is the projection of the baseline B (in section 2 B denoted the LFM signal bandwidth) onto the direction perpendicular to the look direction, and α and θ are the baseline tilt and look angles, respectively (Fig. 3-1). As was shown (Rodriguez & Martin, 1992) , σ_Φ is minimized, hence, σ_h is also minimized, by choosing $\alpha = \theta$.

In what follows we assume that the system operates in standard mode of data collection (Rosen et al., 2000) and its two interferometric channels have identical PTRs of the separable form $\chi_r(\rho)\cdot\chi_a(s)$, where $\chi_r(\rho)$ and $\chi_a(s)$ are the system PTR in range (ρ) and azimuth (s), respectively. For simplicity, we confine our analysis to the range dimension although the proposed technique can be also used in the azimuth dimension. To reveal the potential of

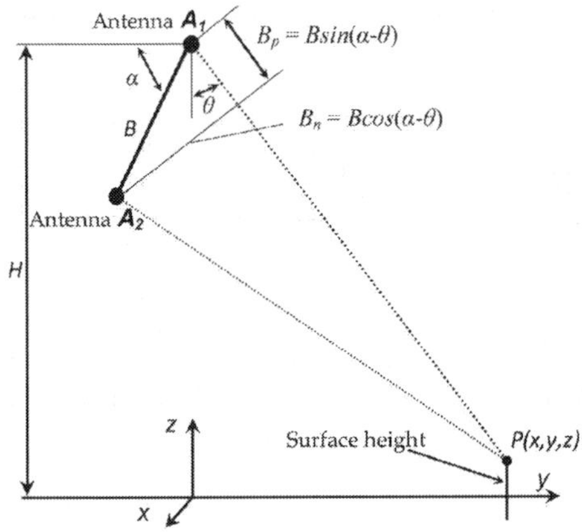

Fig. 3-1. Interferometric SAR looking geometry

the proposed technique we assume that the surface slope and coregistration errors can be neglected and the interferometric channels have equal center frequencies. Then, one can show that the general equation for γ_G (Rosen et al., 2000) reduces to

$$\gamma_G(\kappa_\rho) = \frac{\left|\int \left|\chi_r(\rho)\right|^2 \exp\left[-j\kappa_\rho \rho\right] d\rho\right|}{\int \left|\chi_r(\rho)\right|^2 d\rho} \tag{3-3}$$

where $\kappa_\rho = \kappa B_n / (r_o \tan\theta)$ is the interferometric fringe wavenumber in range ($\kappa = 2\pi/\lambda$ is the wavenumber) and r_o = H/cosθ is the slant range from the system to the middle point of a distributed resolution cell at the centre of the swath.

When the PTR in range is given by a standard sinc-function $\chi_r(\rho) = \sin(\pi\rho/R)/(\pi\rho/R)$, where $R = c/(2F_m)$ is the intrinsic range resolution (c is the speed of light and F_m is the system bandwidth), the geometric correlation was shown (Rodriguez & Martin, 1992; Ka & Kononov, 2007) to be given by

$$\gamma_G = 1 - \frac{R}{r_o \tan\theta}\frac{B_n}{\lambda}. \tag{3-4}$$

The second term γ_N is the correlation due to thermal noise alone. As was shown in (Rodriguez & Martin, 1992), assuming isotropic backscatter coefficient within the SAR resolution element, γ_N can be represented as

$$\gamma_N = \frac{1}{1+q^{-1}} \tag{3-5}$$

where q is the system signal-to-noise ratio (SNR), which is assumed to be equal in both channels.

The correlation term γ_Z is given by (Rodriguez & Martin, 1992; Ka & Kononov, 2007)

$$\gamma_Z = \exp\left[-2\pi^2\left(\frac{\sigma_s}{H\tan\theta}\frac{B_n}{\lambda}\right)^2\right] \tag{3-6}$$

where σ_s is the height standard deviation of specular points with respect to the mean topography.
The term γ_T is specific to repeat-pass systems (Rosen et al., 2000; Zebker & Villasenor, 1992) and represents a measure of decorrelation between two images (forming an interferogram) due to change in the surface itself over the temporal interval between the times when the images are acquired. In what follows we assume $\gamma_T = 1$.

3.2 Optimization of PTR

Examining (3-3) yields that its right-hand side has the form of a Fourier transform. From the Fourier transform properties, it follows that the narrower the PTR $\chi_r(\rho)$ in time (range) domain, the wider the baseline correlation function γ_G (3-3) and the better InSAR height estimation performance, other conditions being equal. For a given transmit signal, one of the possible ways to concentrate the PTR in range domain is designing such a receiving filter, which maximizes the percentage of the total power within a specified time interval around the PTR peak value point. To control the range resolution the length of this interval (mainlobe region) can be adjusted.
Noting that the module of PTR in range is a zero-Doppler cut (in case of ideal frequency stability of radar transmitter) of the cross-ambiguity function allows concluding that the method of section 2 can be directly used to optimize the PTR for the purpose of improving the accuracy of InSAR height measurements.
Then, as follows from equation (2-21), the digital PTR can be written as

$$r = r(0) = w^{\sim} S(0) \tag{3-7}$$

where the row vector $r = [r_1(0), \cdots, r_{M-1}(0), r_M(0), r_{M+1}(0), \cdots, r_{2M-1}(0)]$ represents the digital PTR $\chi_{dr}[\cdot]$, i.e., a zero-Doppler cut of the DCAF, according to the relation

$$r_n = r_n(0) = A_d^w[n-M, 0] = \chi_{dr}[n-M], \;\; n = 1, 2, ..., 2M-1 \tag{3-8}$$

Next, as can be seen from (2-23), for the problem in question the ratio to be maximized is

$$\xi = \frac{\sum_{n \in R_{L+1}} |\chi_{dr}[n-M]|^2}{\sum_{n=1}^{2M-1} |\chi_{dr}[n-M]|^2} = \frac{\sum_{n=M-m}^{M+m} |r_n|^2}{\sum_{n=1}^{2M-1} |r_n|^2} \tag{3-9}$$

where the set $R_{L+1} = \{\, M\text{-}m, ..., \; M\text{-}1, \; M, \; M+1, \; ..., M+m\}$ represents the specified mainlobe region around the PTR peak point.
Based on the derivation in section 2.4 one can write the solution for the optimum weighting function that maximally concentrates the PTR in range in terms of the ratio (3-9) as

$$w_{opt} = \mathbf{P}\{B_{TL}^{-1} B_{ML}\}\,. \tag{3-10}$$

The matrices B_{TL} and B_{ML} in (3-10) are given by

$$B_{TL} = S Q_{TL} S^{\sim} \text{ and } B_{ML} = S Q_{ML} S^{\sim} \tag{3-11}$$

respectively, where $S = S(0)$ [see formula (2-20)] and the matrix Q_{ML} is $(2M-1)$-by- $(2M-1)$ diagonal matrix: its diagonal is equal to the weighting vector V_{ML}^{L+1} [see (2-24)] and non-diagonal elements are zeros.

3.3 Numerical examples

Numerical examples illustrate the InSAR height accuracy and range resolution that can be achieved by using the optimum weighting function (3-10) for an LFM signal with T = 3 μs and B = 20 MHz. The oversampling factor g = 2 was chosen. Hence, the complex envelope of the LFM signal is given by a vector of length N = 120. To compute the baseline correlation function for digital interferometric channels the following digital counterpart of equation (3-3) was used

$$\gamma_G = \frac{\left|\sum_{i=-M+1}^{M-1} \left|\chi_{dr}[i,x]\right|^2 \exp\left[-j\kappa_p (i \cdot \Delta R_s)\right]\right|}{\sum_{i=-M+1}^{M-1} \left|\chi_{dr}[i,x]\right|^2}, \ \Delta R_s = cT_s/2. \tag{3-12}$$

where $\chi_{dr}[i,x] = A_d^w[i,x,0]$, see equation (2-18).

To quantify the change in the PTR mainlobe width due to weighting we use the 3dB mainlobe broadening parameter b_{ML} defined in subsection 2.5.

It can be shown, for a single SAR resolution element with isotropic backscatter coefficient, that in the event of mismatched filtering the SNR can be represented as

$$q = L_w^x q_{MF} \tag{3-13}$$

where q_{MF} is the SNR for the matched filter and L_w^x is the loss in SNR (due to weighting), which is given by equation (2-41).

Since there are no simple closed-form expressions that directly relate the coefficient of loss L_w^x to m and M for the optimum weighting filter given by (3-10), it was numerically found for $m=g-1$, g, $g+1$, i.e., for m = 1, 2, and 3 that the SNR loss is approximately minimized for $1.1N \le M \le 1.5N$. The parameters L_w^0 and b_{ML} for the optimum filter of length M =132 computed from (3-10) for m = 1, 2, 3 are summarized in Table 3-1. To estimate the mainlobe width, the digital PTRs were computed by using (2-18) at integer points $-(M-1) \le k \le M-1$ and between them for x = 0.01, 0.02,..., 0.99 . For comparison, the SNR loss and parameter β for the Kaiser window of length M = 132 are also given. The parameter β was selected to approximately provide the same value of b_{ML}, except for m = 1 (it is impossible for the Kaiser window to find such a parameter β, at which b_{ML} < 1). As can be seen from Table 3-1, for the optimum filter of length M = 132 at m = 2 the degradation in range resolution is quite appreciable (mainlobe broadening is 20%) and the SNR loss is relatively small (about -0.7 dB). The optimum filter with M =132, m = 1 gives a quite noticeable enhancement in the range resolution with respect to the matched filter. The price paid for this is relatively large SNR loss (about -3 dB) and an increase of 10% in the filter length. It will be shown that despite the relatively large SNR loss this optimum filter provides appreciable improvement

Parameter m	Optimum filter M = 132		Kaiser window N = 132	
	L_w^0, dB	b_{ML}	L_w^0, dB	β
1	-3.08	0.96	–	–
2	-0.72	1.20	-0.43	3.1
3	-1.07	1.36	-0.97	4.8

Table 3-1. SNR loss and PTR mainlobe broadening with weighting

in height accuracy. The range resolution enhancement for the optimum filter with M =132, m = 1 is evident from Fig. 3-2 that shows the magnitude of the digital PTR for the optimum filter in comparison with those for the Kaiser window (β = 3.1) and matched filter. To get more pictorial view, all the PTR's are normalized so that the magnitudes of their peak values are equal to unity (zero on the dB-scale).

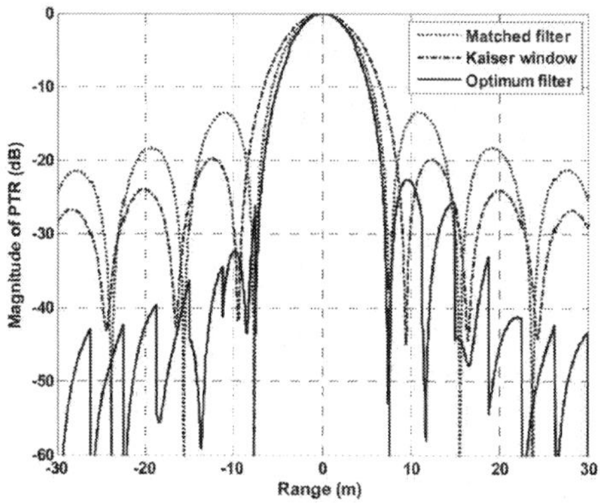

Fig. 3-2. Range resolution enhancement for the optimum filter

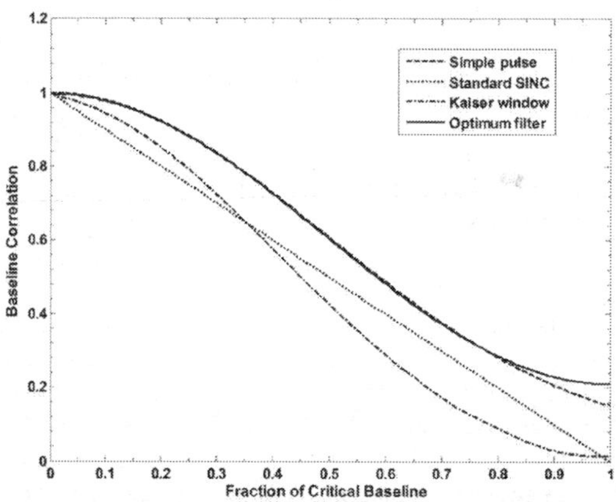

Fig. 3- 3. Baseline correlation functions for various point-target responses

Fig. 3-3 displays the baseline correlation functions corresponding to the digital PTR's for the optimal filter and Kaiser window shown in Fig. 3-2. For comparison, the baseline correlations for the standard sinc response and for the response of a filter matched to a simple rectangular pulse with pulsewidth $1/\ F_m$ are also plotted. A remarkable feature of the PTR for the simple rectangular pulse is that it has zero sidelobes outside of the mainlobe region for m=g. Therefore, the baseline correlation function for the simple rectangular pulse can be used as an example of ideal reference model for comparison. From the inspection of Fig. 3-3, one can conclude that narrowing the mainlobe region in designing an optimum filter allows a distinct improvement in the shape of the baseline correlation function in the sense of the phase (height) noise reduction. As can be seen, the baseline correlation curve for the optimal filter goes appreciably higher than those for the Kaiser window and standard sinc function and almost coincides with that corresponding to the simple rectangular pulse. As mentioned above, the SNR degradation due to weighting may result in a significant decrease in the correlation due to thermal noise γ_N and, finally, in performance deterioration. Thus, to draw a final conclusion concerning the effectiveness of the suggested approach one has to evaluate a potential improvement in the InSAR accuracy performances taking into account all the components of the full correlation. In Fig. 3-4 and Fig. 3-5 we plot for the optimal filter with M = 132 and m = 1, the height standard deviation σ_h calculated by using (3-2), (3-5), (3-6), (3-12) and (3-13) with inputs x = 0 , N_L = 9, $\theta = \alpha$ = 30°, H = 350 km, σ_s = 1 m, and γ_T = 1 versus SNR for B_n/λ = 1500 and versus the relative baseline B_n/λ for SNR=18dB, respectively. The calculations were also done at x = 0.5, which can be interpreted as a subpixel shift. The performance degradation for x = 0.5 (with respect to x = 0) did not exceed 15%. The performances for the matched filter, Kaiser window (β =3.1) and the simple pulse are also plotted (for x = 0).

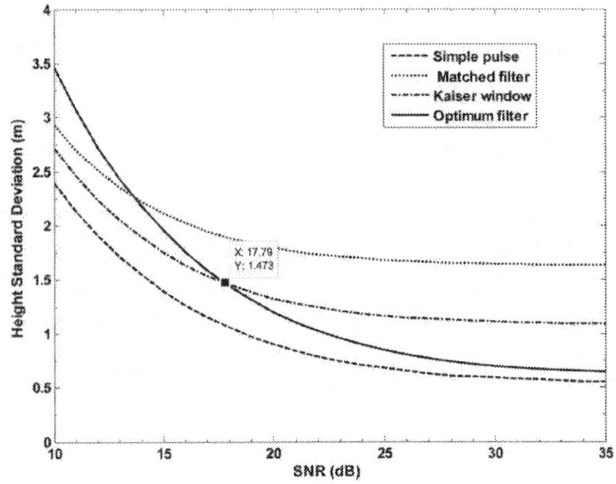

Fig. 3-4. Height-standard deviation σ_h versus signal-to-noise ratio (SNR) for B_n/λ = 1500

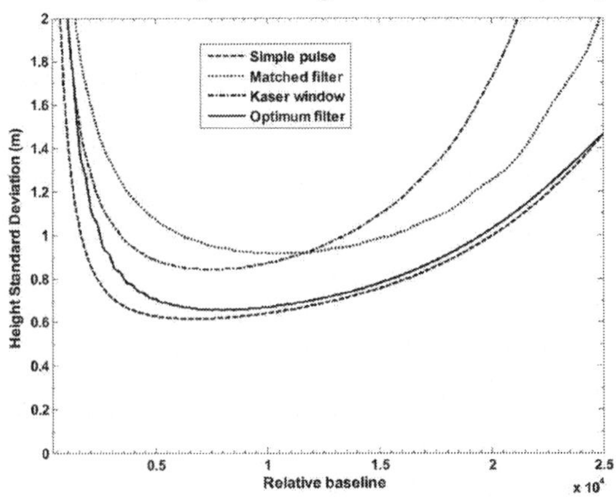

Fig. 3-5. Height-standard deviation σ_h versus relative baseline B_n/λ for SNR = 18 dB

It is clear from Fig. 3-4 that no performance improvement results for SNR<17.79 dB, but the improvement becomes noticeable when the SNR is on the order of 20 dB or larger. As can be seen from Fig. 3-5, despite the relatively large SNR loss this optimum filter provides appreciable improvement in height estimation accuracy against the matched filter and Kaiser window over a wide range of the relative baseline.

4. Conclusion

This chapter has introduced a new approach for the design of optimum weighting functions. By analogy with optimal discrete prolate sequences this approach considers the design of weighting functions as a problem of finding such a digital mismatched filter that will maximize the proportion of the total response power that is concentrated in the specified time-frequency region. A closed-form matrix equation to numerically design the optimum weigthing functions has been derived.

Two applications of the proposed approach have theoretically been addressed in the chapter. First, the problem of the optimum Doppler-tolerant pair signal-filter design when a given signal is specified to be an LFM signal and, second, the specification of weighting functions for interferometric synthetic aperture radars with the purpose of improving the accuracy of height measurements, have been considered.

There has been shown, for the first application, that the proposed optimum weighting functions (mismatched filters) provide significant sidelobe suppression with respect to conventional weighting functions at relatively low SNR loss. It has also been shown that they can provide appreciable improvement in the accuracy of height measurements, as compared to conventional weightings, for interferometric synthetic aperture radars.

A remarkable feature of the suggested optimum weightings is that improvement in the sidelobe suppression and height accuracy can be achieved without degradation in range resolution that is inevitable in the case of using traditional weighting functions.

5. References

Barton, D.K., (2005). *Radar System Analysis and Modeling*, Artech House, ISBN 1-58053-681-6, Norwood.

Baskakov, A.I. & Ka, M.-H., (2000). Analysis of the effect of phase noise on the accuracy characteristics of interferometric fixed-baseline SARs, *Earth Observations and Remote Sensing*, Vol. 16, 2000, pp. 247-256.

Blankenship, P., & Hofstetter, E., (1975). Digital Pulse Compression via Fast Convolution, *IEEE Trans. on Acoustic, Speech, and Signal Processing*, Vol. ASSP-23, No. 2, April 1975, pp. 189-201.

Cook, C. & Bernfeld, M. (1967). *Radar Signals: An Introduction to Theory and Application*, Academic Press, ISBN 0-89006-733-3, New York.

Curlander, J. & McDonough, R. (1991). *Synthetic Aperture Radar: Systems and Signal Processing*, Wiley, ISBN 0-471-85770-X, New Jersey.

Donald, T. & James, F. (1970). Designing Digital Low-Pass Filters - Comparison of Some Methods and Criteria, *IEEE Trans. on Audio and Electroacoustics*, Vol. AU-18, No. 4, December 1970, pp. 487-494.

Gatteli F. et al., (1994). The wavenumber shift in SAR interferometry, *IEEE Trans. Geoscience Remote Sensing*, Vol. 32, No. 4, July 1994, pp. 855-864.

Greene, M., (2007). The discrete prolate spheroidal sequences and a series expansion for seismic wavelets, *GEOPHYSICS,* Vol. 72, No. 6, November-December 2007, pp. V119-V132.

Harris, F. J. (1978). On the Use of Windows for Harmonic Analysis with the Discrete Fourier Transform, *Proceedings of the IEEE,* Vol. 68, No. 1, January 1978, pp. 51-83.

Ka, M.-H. & Kononov, A. (2007). Effect of look angle on the accuracy performance of fixed-baseline interferometric SAR, *IEEE Geoscience Remote Sensing Letters,* Vol. 4, No. 1, January 2007, pp. 65-69.

Levanon, N. & Mozeson, E. (2004). *Radar Signals,* Wiley, ISBN 0-471-47378-2, New Jersey.

Nuttal, A. (1981). Some windows with very good sidelobe behavior, *IEEE Trans. On Acoustics, Speech, and Signal Processing,* Vol. 29, No. 1, February 1981, pp. 84-91.

Peebles, P., JR., (1998). *Radar Principles,* Wiley, ISBN 0-471-25205-0, New York.

Richards, M. (2005). *Fundamentals of Radar Signal Processing,* McGraw-Hill, ISBN 0-07-144474-2, New York.

Rodriguez, E. & Martin, J. (1992). Theory and design of interferometric synthetic aperture radars, *Radar and Signal Processing, IEE Proceedings F,* Vol. 139, No. 2, April 1992, pp. 147-159, ISSN 1751-8784.

Rosen, P.A. et al., (2000). Synthetic aperture radar interferometry, *Proceedings IEEE,* Vol. 88, No. 3, March 2000, pp. 333-382.

Skolnik, M. (2008). *Radar Handbook,* 3rd ed., McGraw-Hill, ISBN 978-0-07-148547-0, New York.

Van Trees, H. L., (2002). *Detection, Estimation, and Modulation Theory, Part IV, Optimum Array Processing,* Wiley, ISBN 0-471-09390-4, New York.

Zebker H. A. & Villasenor, J., (1992). Decorrelation in interferometric radar echoes, *IEEE Trans. Geosci. Remote Sens.* Vol. 30, No. 5, September 1992, pp. 950-959.

27

Stress and EEG

Ssang-Hee Seo and Jung-Tae Lee
Department of Computer Science & Engineering, Pusan National University
30, Jangjeon-Dong, Geumjeong-Gu Busan,
Korea

1. Introduction

Many people suffer from stress in their everyday life. While there is a close relationship between stress and mental health, psychological stress (and associated emotions such as anger, anxiety, and depression), can also have effects on physical health. Indeed, chronic psychological stress can change the responsiveness of central-peripheral regulatory systems (Fuchs & Fluegee 1995; Fuchs, Uno, & Fluegge 1995), potentially rendering them less efficient or adaptive in terms of supporting health. Conditions such as chronic stress, depression, and anxiety have been found to be associated with abnormal autonomic nervous system (ANS) functioning (Cohen et al., 2000; Hughes & Stoney 2000). Accordingly, stress is one of the major factors contributing to chronic disorders (Decker et al., 1996; Lawrence & Kim 2000).

Stress also influences the desire to work, performance at work, and one's general attitude toward life (NIOSH, 1999). Within the industry sector, higher stress levels and stress-related disease lead to decrease in company performance and increase in medical expenses (Cooper, 1996; Manning, et al., 1996). In 2008 in Korea, there were 1,967 deaths associated with occupational cases. Almost half of these deaths (974, or 49.5%) could be ascribed to heart or brain blood vessel disease (Ministry of Labor, 2008). This is not surprising given that stress is implicated in 75% of all heart and brain blood vessel diseases (Belkic, et al., 2004). It is thus apparent that stress can increase social and economic losses and decrease a country's competitiveness (Driskell & Salas, 1996). Therefore, precautionary measures to reduce stress and adequate management of this condition are essential for both individual health and the welfare of society at a broader level.

This chapter reports on relationships among psychological stress, the EEG (Electroencephalogram), ECG, and salivary cortisol in people suffering from chronic stress. We hypothesized that chronic stress will have negative effects on the central-ANS and physiological responsiveness. There are many bio-signal channels by which stress can be potentially quantified, including ECG, EEG, and the skin conductance response (SCR) (Kohlish & Schaefer 1996; Gevins et al., 1998). Even so, determining the stress level of any given individual can be difficult. Related to this is debate concerning the extent to which the EEG can be used to reliably measure stress. However, this chapter presents data showing that there are significant correlations between EEG measures and other indices of stress, including the ECG and salivary cortisol. Also, it revealed relationships between high beta frequency EEG activity and each of HRV, measured as the standard deviation of all normal RR intervals (SDNN) and salivary cortisol during several different conditions. Our results suggest that inter-individual differences in stress can be reliably assessed by EEG.

2. The stress response

The human nervous system is very complex and contains two major divisions: central and peripheral. The peripheral nervous system includes the ANS, which has a particular association with negative psychological states such as stress, anxiety, and depression.

The ANS performs and regulates automatic bodily functions associated with breathing, heart rate, digestion, and the hormonal system. The ANS itself has two parts: sympathetic and parasympathetic. The sympathetic and parasympathetic nervous systems initiate the stress and relaxation response, respectively.

There is normally a balance maintained between the activities of the sympathetic and parasympathetic nervous systems. Chronic stress can disturb this balance and thereby cause stress-related health problems to arise.

When one is exposed to a physical or psychological stressor, the brain initiates a stress response, from which a series of chemical reactions ensue. The stress response is a healthy defense mechanism and involves the release of hormones that have numerous biochemical and physiological effects. However, the continued release of these hormones under conditions of chronic stress can have detrimental effects on health.

Indeed, the hormonal response associated with long-lasting stress increases the risk of many diseases, including heart disease, stroke, and angina. Stress hormones can weaken the immune system and thus promote vulnerability to infection. Stress hormones also trigger increases in blood pressure, heart rate, and respiration and raise the risk of stroke, heart attack, and kidney diseases (Noback et al., 1986).

Cognitive and physiological processes of the central nervous system (CNS) associated with stress are known to affect most organs of the human body.

The stress response involves activation of regulatory centers in the CNS that stimulate both the hypothalamic-pituitary-adrenal (HPA) axis and ANS.

The HPA axis is one of the major systems involved in the stress response. It facilitates adaptations to changes in the internal or external conditions of the body. The stress response involves central and peripheral changes that are coordinated by the CNS. The release of glucocorticoids (GCs) such as cortisol is controlled by the paraventricular nucleus of the hypothalamus, in which parvocellular neurons synthesize and release corticotrophin-releasing hormone (CRH) as a response to stress. These neurons also secrete other hormones, including arginine vasopressin. The combined actions of arginine vasopressin and CRH activate the HPA axis. The release of CRH into the pituitary portal system induces the pituitary to release adrenocorticotropic hormone (ACTH), which in turn induces the release of GCs from the adrenal cortex. GCs exert negative feedback on the hypothalamus and pituitary gland that serves to terminate the stress response when no longer required, thereby preventing excessive responses. GCs are involved in many aspects of the stress response; they facilitate adaptation of the body to changing conditions by regulating energy stores, inhibiting nonessential physiological activity, and promoting behavioral responses to stimuli perceived as stressful (Johnson et al., 1992; Bao et al., 2008).

3. Assessing levels of stress

3.1 Psychological assessment

The stress response can be measured and evaluated in terms of perceptual, behavioral, and physical responses. The evaluation of perceptual responses to a stressor involves subjective estimations and perceptions. Indeed, self-report questionnaires are one of the most common instruments used to measure an individual's level of stress (Cohen et al., 1997). Numerous questionnaires have been used in clinical practice and psychiatric research to evaluate stress, including the Perceived Stress Scale (PSS) (Cohen et al., 1983), the Life Events and Coping Inventory (LECI) (Lewis, 1988), and the Stress Response Inventory (SRI) (Koh et al., 2001). The PSS measures the degree to which situations are considered stressful, doing so by addressing events experienced in the preceding month. It was designed to quantify how unpredictable, uncontrollable, and overloaded adults find their lives. The LECI is composed of 125 questions that assess the extent to which children experience stress in association with life events. The SRI is designed for adults, but it differs from the PSS in assessing the mental and physical symptoms associated with psychological stress; it consists of 39 items and produces scores for seven factors: tension, aggression, somatization, anger, depression, fatigue, and frustration.

3.2 Physical assessment

The physical response to stress has two components: these are a physiological response indicative of central-autonomic activity and a biochemical response involving changes in the endocrine and immune systems (Cohen, Kessler & Gordon 1997).

3.2.1 Biochemical response

Stress induces changes in autonomic function and the secretion of hormones that include cortisol, corticosterone, and adrenal catecholamines (Van der Kar & Blair 1999).

The presence of stress hormones such as adrenaline, noradrenaline, and cortisol can be considered indicative of a stress response. Some studies have reported that repeated exposure to intense stress increases the secretion of cortisol (Schulz et al., 1998; Evans et al., 2001). Cortisol levels can be measured in numerous bodily fluids, including serum, urine, and saliva. There is a daily cycle in cortisol levels, which are normally high in the morning and low at night (Stone et al., 2001). However, repeated exposure to stress decreases the ability to regulate cortisol levels, leading to an elevated level that remains high at night. In such case, the levels may become abnormally low and show very little variation (Dallman, 1993; Pruessner et al., 1999). It has been shown that there are relationships between salivary cortisol levels and physiological variables used to assess stress, including HRV, skin temperature, blood pressure (BP), heart rate (HR), and galvanic skin response (GSR). Accordingly, salivary cortisol is routinely used as a biomarker of psychological stress and associated mental or physical diseases. Exposure to long-lasting stressors often results in elevated cortisol levels (Bigert, Bluhm, & Theorell 2005). Indeed, salivary cortisol is generally considered to be a reliable measure of HPA adaptation to stress (Park, & Kim 2007).

3.2.2 HRV (Heart rate variability)

Stress induces a change in autonomic functioning (Van der Kar & Blair 1999). Blood pressure and heart rate increase during stress, reflecting a predominance of sympathetic nervous system activity (Ritvanen et al., 2005). HRV is the beat-to-beat variation in heart rate, and it has recently been used as a biomarker of ANS activity associated with mental stress (Zhong et al. 2005). Time domain analysis of HRV involves quantifying the mean or standard deviation of RR intervals. Frequency domain analysis involves calculating the power of the respiratory-dependent high frequency and low frequency components of HRV. While high frequency power is mediated by vagal activity (Hayano et al., 1991), it has been suggested that low frequency power primarily reflects sympathetic modulation (Pomeranz et al., 1985; Malliani et al., 1991). Many studies have investigated abnormalities in ANS functioning associated with stress, with HRV as one of the measures shown to be affected (Salahuddin et al., 2007). Mental stress is reported to evoke a decrease in the high frequency component and an increase in the low frequency component of HRV (Bernardi et al., 2000). Job stress has been shown to induce excessive levels of sympathoadrenal activation, leading to increases in blood pressure and heart rate, the secretion of catecholamines, and the release of lipids and glucose into the bloodstream (Theorel et al. 1993). Abnormalities of ANS functioning (Horsten et al. 1999) that include decreased HRV are associated with mental stress in laboratory experiments (Myrtek et al. 1996; Sloan et al. 1994). Moreover, lower than normal HRV has been found in subjects with depression, high levels of hostility, and anxiety. Low HRV may reflect an inability to generate variable and complex physiological responses, rendering an individual physiologically rigid and vulnerable (Horsten et al. 1999). Sustained autonomic activation can result in arrhythmia or sudden heart attack because of an increase in sympathetic and decrease in parasympathetic activity.

3.2.3 EEG

In healthy people not experiencing stress, there is a balance between the sympathetic and parasympathetic arms of the ANS and flexibility in how these respond. Exposure to threatening situations induces a fight-or-flight response whereby emotional and vigilance systems are activated. Although most current day stress arises from psychosocial factors that are not life threatening, the fight-or-flight response may still be generated, for example, during tests or when called upon to give an impromptu speech (Johannes et al 2007). Studies into brain activity patterns under stressful conditions have focused on stress generated by words, examinations, noise, and mental tasks (Matsunami et al., 2001; Lewis et al., 2007; Tucker 1981; Davidson et al., 1979; Seo et al., 2008a; Seo et al., 2009).

A major aspect of neurophysiological research into emotion concerns hemispheric specialization. While the left hemisphere appears to be more involved in the processing of positive emotions and approach-related behaviors, the right hemisphere is more involved in the processing of negative emotions and withdrawal behaviors (Coan & Allen, 2004; Davidson, 2003). These differences are represented by a model of emotional processing in which the frontal cortex plays a key role. Evidence supporting this model has been obtained from studies concerning asymmetry in prefrontal EEG alpha activity. Positive moods or reactions have been shown to be associated with relatively greater left prefrontal activity (LFA) and negative moods or reactions with relatively greater right prefrontal activity (RFA) (Davidson, Jackson & Kalin, 2000).

The results of recent neuroimaging studies suggest that negative affect typically elicits activation in the right prefrontal cortex, amygdala, and insula, and the left prefrontal cortex is associated with positive emotions (Davidson; 1992). The right prefrontal cortex may be critically involved in the response to stress, since it is a fundamental component of both the emotional and vigilance networks. Some studies suggest that high levels of right-sided prefrontal activation are associated with a negative affective style and weakened immune system. For example, Davidson has reported that differences in prefrontal activity asymmetry reflect individual differences in affective styles (Bierhaus et al., 2003; Epel et al., 2004). Importantly, the prefrontal cortex may mediate the extent to which psychosocial stress affects mental and physical health (Segerstrom & Miller 2004; Cohen et al., 1993).

There appear to be differences in how activity of the left and right cortical hemispheres affects ANS functioning. Moreover, the extent of this asymmetry has been suggested to vary under conditions of chronic stress (Papousek, 2002). Related effects are reported for stress-related emotions, with preferential right hemispheric activation in the frontopolar region shown to be associated with electrodermal activity (EDA) in anxious subjects (Papousek & Schulter, 2001).

4. Neurofeedback

The side effects and inconvenience associated with long term use of medications has facilitated an interest in alternative therapies and self-regulation for maintaining health.

Alternative therapies such as yoga, meditation, and Ki Gong are widely used to manage stress. These therapies induce relaxation or decrease psychophysiological arousal by reducing the activities of the sympathetic nervous system. Another therapeutic approach involves biofeedback, in which ANS variables such as heart rate, blood pressure, skin tension, and temperature are regulated. Biofeedback has been applied to mental diseases such as anxiety and depression and to psychosomatic diseases such as migraine, tension headache, and hyperpiesia (Sadock B.J. & Sadock V.A. 2004). Neurofeedback is biofeedback using brain waves and has specific applications for brain diseases and associated symptoms (Ahn, 2006; Park, 2006). There have been many recent studies concerning the utility of neurofeedback within clinical medicine. Conditions for which neurofeedback has been most intensively used include alcoholism, epilepsy, ADHD, brain injury, and mood disorders (Peniston E.G., 1999; Mann C.A., 1992; Byers A.P., 1995; Baehr E., 2001). In a more general sense, neurofeedback has been demonstrated to improve concentration, memory, and musical performance (Gruzelier J, 2005).

Subjects undergoing neurofeedback training attempt to regulate their brain waves, wherein special signals are presented to the subject in a suitable form. Via operant conditioning, this feedback facilitates a subject's ability to adopt a desired brain wave state. Neurofeedback training focuses upon two components of the EEG spectrum: synchronized beta waves and alpha waves. Alpha waves reflect a calm, open, and balanced psychological state with a decrease in alpha wave activity during stress. Alpha wave training attempts to alleviate stress by inducing a state of relaxation. This involves removing or reducing habitual tendencies to respond to stressful situations with tension and anxiety.

Beta waves are associated with concentration, thought, and listening. Synchronized brain waves reflect attention or awareness or consciousness in the absence of motor activity. Synchronization at low frequencies (delta and theta) reflects awareness on an unconscious level. Conversely, synchronization of higher frequency alpha and beta waves reflects a state of conscious awareness. Beta training is reported to increase focus, concentration, energy levels, and mental clarity (Paul, 2008). Alpha and beta training supplement one another and can be used in combination to manage stress. Neurofeedback is a noninvasive technique potentially effective in reducing stress. However, there may be a particular benefit to be had in combining neurofeedback with medications that by themselves have a limited role in managing stress.

5. Experimental methods

5.1 Participants

The participants were 33 healthy, right-handed volunteers (9 females and 24 males) aged 30–40 years old. All participants had normal hearing, and none had a neurological disorder. Informed written consent was provided by all participants before completing questionnaires or undergoing psychophysiological assessment.

5.2 SRI(Stress Response Inventory) and SAM(Self Assessment Manikin)

Stress was assessed with the SRI, which participants completed prior to physiological measurements being obtained.
The SAM (Fig. 1) has been used widely to assess the emotional response of subjects to experimental stimuli. In being pictorial it can be used with people from a diverse range of backgrounds. The SAM quantifies pleasant and unpleasant emotions on a nine-point scale (Margaret et al. 1994).

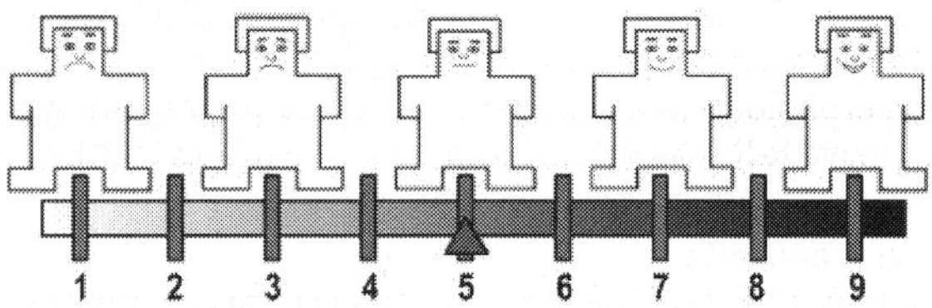

Fig. 1. SAM Valence (negative-positive)

5.3 Procedures

Visual stimuli from the International Affective Picture System (IAPS) were used to evoke emotional responses (Lang, Bradley & Cuthbert 1995). The stimuli were presented as a set of pleasant images and a set of unpleasant images. Each set lasted for 5 min, with individual images presented for 15 s. Participants made a rating with the SAM after each image set. Salivary cortisol was collected after the SRI had been completed, following which participants underwent the sequence of procedures shown in Figure 2: eyes-closed, eyes-open, pleasant images, SAM, rest, unpleasant images, and SAM. EEG and ECG recordings were obtained throughout the experiment. A 5-min portion of the ECG recording was used for short-term HRV analysis.

5.4 Cortisol

Cortisol levels quantify the endocrine response to stress. The collection of blood samples for measuring cortisol levels can be associated with greater inter-individual differences than when saliva samples are used (Park & Kim 2007). Saliva was obtained from our participants between noon and 3 pm. Cortisol levels were determined using a Solid-Phase Radioimmunoassay (RIA) Coat-A-Count Cortisol kit (Siemens, USA), as per the manufacturer's instructions, and a Gamma counter (Packard, USA).

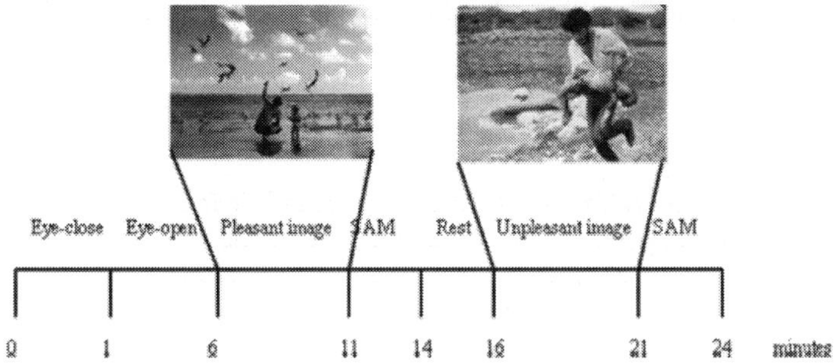

Fig. 2. Experimental sequence

5.5 ECG recording and analysis

The ECG was monitored continuously with a noninvasive system developed by us previously. Limb leads II and III were used, and the sampling rate was 512 Hz. HRV analysis requires accurate detection of the QRS complex. However, this can be difficult because ECG signals are easily corrupted by noise generated by muscular contraction or electrical power lines, and by a drift from baseline associated with respiration or motion artifacts. In addressing this issue, we used a novel QRS detection algorithm based on multi-scale mathematical morphology (3M). This was designed to specifically identify R waves, and with which successive R-R interval series could be reliably determined.

5.6 EEG recording and analysis

The EEG was recorded in each of the four conditions designed to induce different levels of stress: eyes-closed, eyes-open, pleasant images, and unpleasant images. Unpleasant and pleasant images were presented to evoke negative and positive emotions, respectively. Participants rested with their eyes closed for 1 min and with their eyes open for 5 min.

The EEG was recorded with Ag-AgCl disc electrodes from four Modified Combinatiorial Nomenclature (MCN) system sites: FC5, FC6, O1, and O2. These were specifically chosen to facilitate the detection of stress, anxiety, and dysphoria, as reflected by beta activity. The reference and ground sites were Cz and Iz, respectively. A QEEG-4 (LXE1104-RS232, LAXTHA Inc.) device obtained recordings at a sampling rate of 256 Hz. The resolution of the A/D converter was 12 bits, and electrode impedance was maintained as less than 5 kΩ.

EEG data was analyzed with Complexity v2.8 software (LAXTHA Inc.). Recordings were band-pass FFT filtered (4–30 Hz), to eliminate any influence of artifacts in the theta (4–8 Hz), alpha (8–13 Hz), and beta (13–30 Hz) ranges. Ocular artifacts were removed using a PCA-based procedure in Complexity v2.8.

5.7 Statistical analysis

Pearson's correlation was used to determine the strength of relationships among EEG, ECG (SDNN), salivary cortisol, and SRI data. Stress levels groupings of stress, non-stress and general were made with k-means cluster analysis of SDNN and cortisol data. Differences in SDNN and cortisol between these groups were examined with ANOVA. All statistical analyses were performed using SPSS v12.0, and considered to be significant at the level of $p < 0.05$.

6. Results

6.1 Relationships among EEG, ECG, salivary cortisol, and SRI data

Salivary cortisol was negatively correlated with SDNN (r = -0.498, p = 0.07). However, there was no significant relationship between SDNN and SRI, or between cortisol and SRI. In general, the high stress group showed decreased HRV features compared to the low stress group under chronic stress (Kim, Seo & Salahuddin 2008). Long lasting stress can produce elevated cortisol levels and restrict their typical overnight reduction (Bigert, Bluhm, Theorell 2005).

6.2 EEG and ECG

The relationship between SDNN and relative high beta power for each of the four EEG sites in the eyes-closed condition is shown in Table 1. There was a significant negative correlation between SDNN and relative high beta power at both the anterior temporal sites in this condition. Significant correlations were not found in any of the other conditions or at either of the occipital sites.

Recording site	r	p
FC5	-0.428	0.013
FC6	-0.346	0.049
O1	0.052	0.772
O2	0.070	0.697

Table 1. Relationships between SDNN and high beta activity in the eyes-closed condition

Table 2 shows the results of the k-means cluster analysis by which stress level groupings based on SDNN data were made.

	Cluster center			ANOVA	
	Stress (N = 13)	Non-Stress (N = 9)	General (N = 11)	F	p
SDNN	24.64	50.77	36.75	71.077	0.000

Table 2. K-means cluster analysis of SDNN data

The mean high beta power at the anterior temporal sites of each SDNN group is shown in Figure 3. There was a significant difference in high beta activity across the groups at FC5 (F = 4.271, p = 0.023) but not at FC6 (F = 2.262, p = 0.122). The stress group (with relatively low SDNN) had the highest level of beta activity.

6.3 Relationships between salivary cortisol and EEG data

The relationship between salivary cortisol level and relative high beta power at each of the four EEG sites in the eyes-closed condition is summarized in Table 4. In this condition, there was a significant positive correlation between the cortisol level and relative high beta power at both the anterior temporal sites, and a tendency toward a similar relationship at one of the occipital sites (O2). Significant relationships were not found in any of the other conditions.

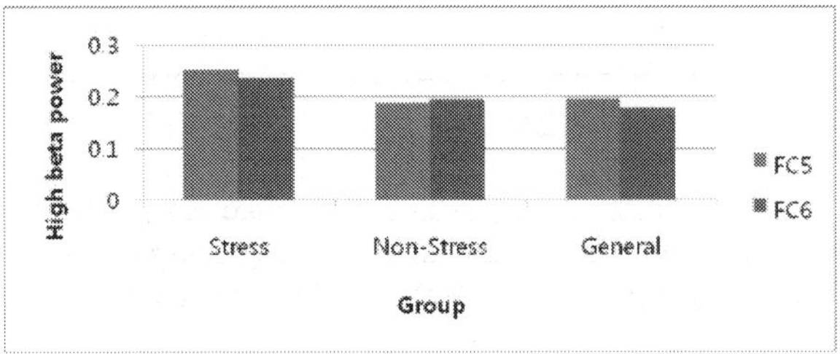

Fig. 3. Relative high beta power in each of the three SDNN-based stress level groups

Recording site	r	p
FC5	0.454	0.008
FC6	0.439	0.011
O1	0.247	0.165
O2	0.334	0.057

Table 3. Relationships between cortisol and high beta activity in the eyes-closed condition

Table 4 shows the results of the k-means cluster analysis by which stress level groupings based on cortisol data were made.

	Cluster center			**ANOVA**	
	Stress (N = 8)	**Non-Stress (N = 10)**	**General (N = 15)**	**F**	**p**
Cortisol (ug/dL)	0.32	0.11	0.21	71.378	0.000

Table 4. K-means cluster analysis of cortisol data

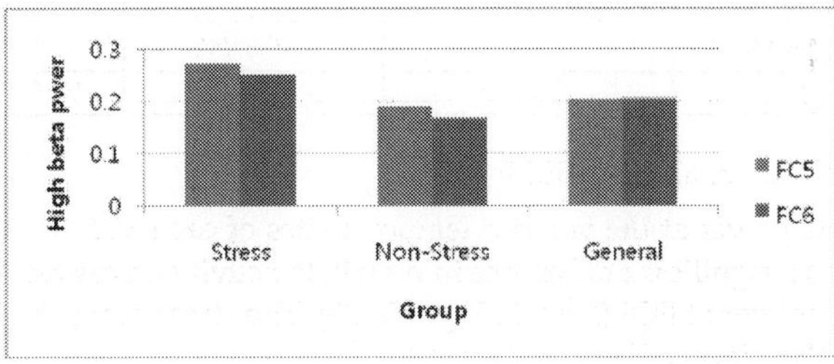

Fig. 4. Relative high beta power in each of the three cortisol-based stress level groups

The mean high beta power at the anterior temporal sites of each cortisol group is shown in Figure 4. There was a significant difference in high beta activity across the groups at both FC5 ($F = 5.556$, $p = 0.009$) and FC6 ($F = 3.635$, $p = 0.039$) sites. The stress group (with relatively high cortisol levels) had the highest level of beta activity.

The relationship between salivary cortisol level and relative high beta power at each of the four EEG sites in the eyes-closed condition is summarized in Table 4. In this condition, there was a significant positive correlation between the cortisol level and relative high beta power at both the anterior temporal sites, and a tendency toward a similar relationship at one of the occipital sites (O2). Significant relationships were not found in any of the other conditions.

7. Discussion

There are three major results to report from the present study. The first of these is a significant correlation between HRV and salivary cortisol (but not between HRV and SRI scores). Second, significant correlations exist between relative high beta EEG power at anterior temporal sites and each of HRV and salivary cortisol during an eyes-closed resting condition. The third finding is a difference in the relative high beta power across stress level groups determined on the basis of SDNN and cortisol data. In both instances, the stress group participants had the highest level of beta activity.

Chronic stress leads to increase in the variability of central-autonomic responses and decrease in physiological adaptability and immunity (Fuchs & Fluegee 1995; Fuchs, Uno & Fluegge 1995; Cohen et al., 2000; Hughes & Stoney 2000). There have been many studies using biosignals to quantify the stress associated with mental tasks or work load in healthy subjects (Jeon et al., 2002). These studies have established that biomarker profiles can distinguish between people experiencing chronic stress and those who are not, with sufferers of chronic stress typically having lower HRV and higher cortisol levels. The findings of the present study are thus consistent with those of previous research.

Although many researchers have reported EEG abnormalities as being associated with stress and negative emotions, the extent to which stress can be reliably evaluated from the EEG has been unclear. Recent EEG research on emotion has focused on relationships between dorsolateral prefrontal asymmetry and a dispositional tendency toward positive or negative affects (Davidson 2004). However, some researchers have suggested a need to pay more attention to frontopolar regions of the prefrontal cortex (Papousek & Schulter 2002). Thompson has indicated that the EEG of someone under stress displays decreases in both alpha (11-12 Hz) and sensorimotor rhythm (SMR, 12-15 Hz) activity, and increases in EEG amplitude in the 19-22 Hz and high beta (23-35 Hz) ranges at both Cz and FCz sites (Michael & Lynda 2007). Emotional intensity, particularly relating to anxiety, correlates with 19-22 Hz band activity, while activity within the 23-36 Hz band reflects an active brain state. Accortt has reported a relationship between premenstrual distress and frontal EEG alpha, an effect especially pronounced at the anterior temporal sites (Accortt & Allen 2006). It has also been found that beta rhythms are predominant under resting conditions in bilateral superior temporal and somato-motor regions of the cortex (Mantlnl et al., 2007), both of which are implicated in emotional processes (Hagemann et al., 1998; Davidson et al., 1990).

In the present study, we found a correlation between HRV and high beta activity at anterior temporal sites (FC5, FC6) during the eyes-closed condition. We also found a correlation between salivary cortisol and high beta activity in this condition. These results show that participants with relatively low HRV had relatively high levels of beta activity in premotor regions of the cortex. Participants with a higher level of salivary cortisol also had a higher level of beta activity. These results suggest that there are close relationships among EEG, ECG, and salivary cortisol indicative of chronic stress. Chronic stress was particularly associated with high levels of relative beta power at anterior temporal sites.

We assigned participants to stress level groups on the basis of SDNN and salivary cortisol data. Greater stress was associated with lower HRV (i.e., lower SDNN values) and a higher level of cortisol. The group with the highest stress level showed the highest level of beta activity during the eyes-closed condition. However, there were no significant correlations among EEG, ECG, and salivary cortisol data during any of the other conditions: eyes-open, pleasant images, and unpleasant images. These correlations need to be analyzed because of the difference in individual responses to stimuli. Participants experiencing chronic stress showed less HRV than those who were not. Range of variance of HRV features according to stimuli was little.

Finally, the present study demonstrated that there are consistent relationships among EEG, ECG, and salivary cortisol data associated with chronic stress. In addition to confirming the results of previous studies, our results suggest that chronic stress may be reliably assessed by relative high beta EEG power at anterior temporal sites. Indeed, this variable could even be seen as a diathesis for the dysphoria associated with chronic stress.

8. References

Accortt, Eynav Elgoavish and Allen, John J.B. 2006. Frontal EEG asymmetry and premenstrual dysphoric symptomatology. Journal of Abnormal Psychology. 115(1), 179-184.

Bao, A.M., Meynen, G., Swaab, D.F., 2008. The stress system in depression and neurodegeneration: focus on the human hypothalamus. Brain Res. Rev. 57, 531-553.

Barlow, J.H., Turner, A.P., and Wright, C.C. Br J Rheumatol, Comparison of clinical and self-reported diagnoses for participants on a community-based arthritis self-management programme , Vol. 37 , pp.985-987 , 1998

Belkic, K., Landsbergis, P., Schnall, P. and Baker D., Is job strain a major source of cardiovascular disease risk?, *Scandinavian Journal of Work Environment and Health*, 30(2), 85-128, 2004.

Bernardi, L., Wdowczyk-Szulc, J., Valenti, C., Castoldi, S., Passino, C., Spadacini, G., and Sleight, P. 2000. Effects of controlled breathing, mental activity, and mental stress with or without verbalization on heart rate variability. Journal of the American College of Cardiology. 35(6), 1462-1469.

Bierhaus, A., Wolf, J., Addrassy, M., Rohleder, N., Humpert, P.M., Petrov, D. et al., "A mechanism converting psychosocial stress into mononuclear cell activation", *Proc. Natl. Acad. Sci. USA.*, vol. 100, no. 4, pp. 1920-1925, 2003.

Bigert, C., Bluhm, G., and Theorell, T. 2005. Saliva cortisol - a new approach in noise research to study stress effects. International Journal of Hygiene and Environmental Health. 208, 227-230.

Cohen, H., Benjamin, J., Geva, A.B., Matar, M.A., Kaplan, Z., and Kotler, M. 2000. Autonomic dysregulation in panic disorder and in post-traumatic stress disorder: application of power spectrum analysis of heart rate variability at rest and in response to recollection of trauma or panic attacks. Psychiatry Research. 96, 1-13

Cohen, S., Kessler, R. and Gordon L. 1997. Measuring stress - A Guide for Health and Social Scientists, Oxford University Press.

Coan, J.A. and Allen, J.J.B., "Frontal EEG asymmetry as a moderator and mediator of emotion", *Biol. Psychol.*, vol. 67, no. 12, pp. 7-49, 2004.

Cohen, S. Tyrrell, D.A. and Smith, A.P. "Negative life events, perceived stress, negative affect, and susceptibility to the common cold", *J. Pers. Soc. Psychol.*, vol. 64, no. 1, pp. 131-140, 1993.

Cooper, C., Stress in the workplace, *British Journal of Hospital Medicine*, 55, 559-563, 1996.

Davidson, R.J., 2004. What does the prefrontal cortex "do" in affect: perspectives on frontal EEG asymmetry research. Biological Psychology. 67, 219-233.

Davidson, R.J. 1993. Cerebral asymmetry and emotion: Methodological conundrums. Cognition and Emotion, 7, 115-138

Davidson, R.J., Ekamn, P., Saron, C.D., Senalis, J.A., and Friesen, W.V. 1990. Approach-withdrawal and cerebral asymmetry: emotional expression and brain physiology I. Journal of Personality and Social Psychology. 58, 330-341.

Davidson, R.J., Jackson, D.C., and Kalin, N.H., "Emotion, plasticity, context and regulation: Perspectives from affective neuroscience", *Psychol. Bull.*, vol. 126, no. 6, pp. 890-906, 2000.

Davidson, R.J., Schwartz, G.E., Saron, C., Bennett, J. and Goldman, D.J., "Frontal versus parietal EEG asymmetry during positive and negative affect", *Psychophysiology.*, vol. 16, pp. 202-203, 1979.

Davidson, R.J., "Affective neuroscience and psychophysiology: Toward a synthesis", *Psychophysiology*, vol. 40, no. 5, pp. 655-665, 2003.

Davidson, R.J., "Anterior cerebral asymmetry and the nature of emotion", *Brain Cogn.*, vol. 20, no. 1, pp. 125-151, 1992.

Decker, D., Schondorf, M. Bidlingmaier, F., Himer, A., and von Ruecker, A.A. 1996. Surgical stress induces a shift in the type-1/type-2 T-helper cell balance, suggesting down-regulation of cell-mediated and up-regulation of antibody-mediated immunity commensurate to the trauma. Surgery. 119, 316-325.

Driskell, K. and Salas, E., *Stress and human performance*, Lawrence Erlbaum, 1996.

Epel, E.S., Blackburn, E.H., Lin, J., Dhabar, F., Adler, N., Morrow, J. and Cawthon, R. "Accelerated telomere shortening in response to life stress", *Proc. Natl. Acad. Sci. USA.*, vol. 101, no. 49, pp. 17312-17315, 2004.

Fuchs, E. and Fluegee, G. 1995. Modulation of binding sites for corticotrophin-releasing hormone by chronic psychosocial stress. Psychoneuroendocrinology. 20, 33-51.

Fuchs, E., Uno, H., and Fluegge, G. 1995. Chronic psychosocial stress induces morphological alterations in hippocampal pyramidal neurons of the tree shrew. Brain Research. 673, 275-282.

Gevins, A., Smith, M.E., Leong, H., McEvoy, L., Whitfield, S., Du, R. and Rush, G. 1998. Monitoring working memory load during computer-based tasks with EEG pattern recognition Methods. Human Factors. 40(1), 79-91.

Hayano J., Skakibara Y., Yamada A. et al. Accuracy of assessment of cardiac vagal tone by heart rate variability in normal subjects. Am J Cardiol 1991; 67; 199-204.

Hagemann, D., Naumann, E., Becker, G., Maire, S., and Bartussek, D. 1998. Frontal brain asymmetry and affective style: a conceptual replication. Psychophysiology. 35, 372-388.

Hilz, M.J., Dütsch, M., Perrine, K., Nelson, P.K., Rauhut, U., and Devinsky, O. 2001. Hemispheric influence on autonomic modulation and baroreflex sensitivity. Annals of Neurology. 49, 575-584.

Horsten M, Ericson M, Perski A, Wamala SP, Schenck-Gustaffson K, Orth-Gomér K ,1999, Psychosocial factors and heart rate variability in healthy women. Psychosom Med 61:49-57.

Hughes, J.W. and Stoney, C.M., 2000, Depressed mood is related to high-frequency heart rate variability during stressors. Psychosomatic Medicine. 62, 796-803.

Jeon, Y.J., Lee, N.B., Im, J. J., Kwan D.H., and Shin, G.S. 2002. A study for the extraction of stress index using physiological signal variations. Journal of the Ergonomics Society of Korea. 21(4), 1-13.

Johannes, K., Richard, W., and Ulrike, J. "The processing of word stress: EEG studies on task-related components", in *16th International Congress of Phonetic Sciences*, 2007, pp. 709-712.

Johnson, E.O., Kamilaris, T.C., Chrousos, G.P., Gold, P.W., 1992. Mechanisms of stress: a dynamic overview of hormonal and behavioral homeostasis. Neurosci. Biobehav. Rev. 16, 115-130.

Kim, D., Seo, Y., and Salahuddin L. 2008. Decreased Long Term Variations of Heart Rate Variability in Subjects with Higher Self Reporting Stress Scores. In Proceedings of the international conference on Pervasive Computing Technologies for Healthcare(The Tampere, The Finland Jan.30-Feb.1, 289-292, 2008).

Kim, J.Y, Park, M.Y. and Park, C.S. "Psychophysiological responses reflecting driver's emotional reaction to interior noise during simulated driving", Human Factors and Ergonomics Society Annual Meeting Proceedings, *Psychophysiology in Ergonomics*, vol. 3, pp. 196-199, 2000.

Koh, K., Park, J., Kim, C., and Cho, S. 2001. Development of the Stress Response Inventory and its application in clinical practive. Psychosomatic Medicine. 63, 668-678.

Kohlish, O. and Schaefer, F. 1996. Physiological changes during computer task: responses to mental load or to motor demands. Ergonomics. 39(2), 213-224.

Lawrence, D.A., and Kim, D. 2000. Central/Peripheral nervous system and immune responses. Toxicology. 142, 189-201.

Lang, P.J., Bradley, M.M., and Cuthbert, B.N. 1995. NIMH Center for the Study of Emotion and Attention, international Affective Picture System (IAPS). Technical Manual and Affective Ratings.

Lewis, R.S., Weekes, N.Y. and Wang, H.W. "The effect of a naturalistic stressor on frontal EEG asymmetry, stress, and health", *Biol. Psychol.*, vol. 75, no. 3, pp. 239-247, 2007.

Mantlnl, D., Perruccl, M.G., DelGratta, C., Romanl, G.L., and Corbetta, M. 2007. Electrophysiological signatures of resting state networks in the human brain. PANS. 104(32), 13170-13175.

Manning, M., Jackson, C. and Fusilier, M., Occupational stress, social support, and the costs of health care, *Academy of Management Journal*, 39, 738-750, 1996.

Malliani A., Pagani M., Lombardi F, Cerutti S. Cardiovascular neural regulation explored in the frequency domain. Circulation 1991; 84: 1482-92.

Margaret M. Bradley et, al. 1994. Measuring Emotion: The Self-Assessment Manikin and Semantic Differential. J. Behavther & Exp, Psychiat. 25(1), 49-59.

Matsunami, K., Homma, S., Han, X.Y. and Jiang, Y.F., "Generator sources of EEG Large Waves Elicited by mental stress of memory recall or mental calculation", *Jpn J Physiol.*, vol. 51, no. 5, pp. 621-624, 2001.

McEwen, B.S. *The End of Stress as We Know It*, Joseph Henry Press and Dana Press, 2002, pp. 17-54.

Michael Thompson and Lynda Thompson, 2007. Neurofeedback for Stress Management. Principles and Practice of Stress Management, Paul M. Lehrer, Robert L. Woolfolk, Wesley E. Sime Ed. Guilford Press, 249-287.

Ministry of Labor in South Korea, Present state of industrial disasters, 2008.

Myrtek M, Weber D, Brügner G, Müller W ,1996, Occupational stress and strain of female students: results of physiological, behavioural, and psychological monitoring. Biol Psychol 42:379-391.

NIOSH, *Stress at work*, NIOSH publication Number 99-101, 1999.

Noback C.R., Demarest R.J. ,1986, The Nervous System, Introduction and Review, McCraw Hill.

Park, S. and Kim, D. 2007. Relationship between Physiological Response and Salivary Cortisol Level to Life Stress. Journal of the Ergonomics Society of Korea. 26(1), 11-18.

Papousek, I. and Schulter, G. 2002. Covariations of EEG asymmetries and emotional states indicate that activity at frontpolar locations is particularly affected by state factors. Psychophysiology. 39(3), 350-60.

Patrick W. Corrigan, Kim T. Mueser, Gary R. Bond, Robert E. Drake, Phyllis Solomon, Principles and Practice of Psychiatric Rehabilitation, Guilford Press. 2008.

Paul G. Swingle., 2008, Biofeedback for the Brain: how neurotherapy effectively treats depression, ADHD, autism, and more, Rutgers university press.

Pomeranz B., Bacaulay R.J.B., Caudill M.A. et al. Assessment of autonomic function in humans by heart rate spectral analysis. Am J Physiol 1985; 248: H151-3

Ritvanen, T., Louhevaara, V., Helin, P., Vaisanen, S., and Hanninen, O. 2005. Responses of the autonomic nervous system during periods of perceived high and low work stress in younger and older female teachers. Applied Ergonomics 37, 311-318.

Rober L.Woolfolk, Wesley E. Sime, Paul M. Lehrer, Principles and practice of stress management, Gillford Press. 2007. Neurofeedback for stress management, Michael Thompson & Lynda Thompson p249-287

Schulter, G. and Papousek, I. 1998. Bilateral electrodermal activity: relationships to state and trait characteristics of hemisphere asymmetry. International Journal of Psychophysiology. 31, 1-12.

Segerstrom, S.C. and G.E. Miller, G.E. "Psychological stress and the human immune system: A meta-analytic study of 30 years of inquiry", *Psychol. Bull.,* vol. 130, no. 4, pp. 601-630, 2004.

Seo, S.H., Gil, Y.J., and Lee. J.T. 2008a. The effect of auditory stressor, with respect to affective style, on frontal EEG asymmetry and ERP analysis. In proceedings of the international conference on networked computing and advances in information management (Kyungju, The South Korea, 662-667, 2008)

Seo, S.H., Gil, Y.J., and Lee. J.T. 2008b. The relation between affective style of stressor on EEG asymmetry and stress scale during multimodal task. In proceedings of the international conference on convergence and hybrid information technology (Busan, The South Korea, 461-466, 2008)

Sloan RP, Shapiro PA, Bagiella E, Boni SM, Paik M, Bigger JT, Steinman RC, Gorman JM, 1994, Effect of mental stress throughout the day on cardiac autonomic control. Biol Psychol 37:89-99.

Theorell T, Ahlberg-Hulten G, Jodko M, Sigala F, de la Torre B ,1993, Influence of job strain and emotion on blood pressure in female hospital personnel during work hours. Scand J Work Environ Health 19: 313-318

Tucker, D.M. "Lateral brain function, emotion, and conceptualization", *Psychological Bulletin,* vol. 89, no. 1, pp. 19-46, 1981.

Turner Charles F, Ku Leighton, Rogers SusanM, Lindberg Laura D, Pleck Joseph H, Sonnenstein Freya L. Adolescent Sexual Behavior, Drug Use, and Violence: Increased Reporting with Computer Survey Technology. *Science.* 1998;280:867–73.

Van der Kar, L.D. and Blair, M.L. 1999. Forebrain pathways mediating stress induced hormone secretion. Frontiers in Neuroendocrinology. 20, 41-48.

Wittling, W. 1995. Brain asymmetry in the control of autonomic-physiological activity. In Brain Asymmetry, R.J. Davidson & K. Hugdahls, Ed. Cambridge: MIT press. 305-358.

Yoon, S.J., Kim, T.S., and Chae, J.H. 2005. Understanding Stress by Neuroscience. Journal Korean Acad. Fam. Med. 26, 439-450.

Zhong, X., Hilton, H.J., Gates, G.J., Jelic, S. Stern, Y, Bartels, M.N., DeMeersman, R.E., and Basner, R.C. 2005. Incresed sympathetic and decreased parasympathetic cardiovascular modulation in normal humans with acute sleep deprivation. J Appl Physiol. 98(6), 2024-2032.